HEART OF THE BLUE RIDGE
HIGHLANDS, NORTH CAROLINA

Aerial shot of Highlands and Whiteside Mountain. Photo by Dick Dillon, 1974.

HEART OF THE BLUE RIDGE
HIGHLANDS, NORTH CAROLINA

BY

RANDOLPH P. SHAFFNER

Randolph P. Shaffner

FARAWAY PUBLISHING
HIGHLANDS, NORTH CAROLINA
2001

Published by
FARAWAY PUBLISHING
P. O. Box 765
Highlands, N.C. 28741

Cover photograph by Cynthia Strain
Highlands from Sunset Rocks, October 31, 1999

Printed in the United States of America
by McNaughton & Gunn, Inc., 960 Woodland Drive, Saline, Michigan 48176-0010

10 9 8 7 6 5 4 3 2 1

FIRST EDITION

Library of Congress Control Number: 2001117092

ISBN: 0-9710130-0-4 (trade paperback)

∞ The paper used in this publication meets the minimum requirements of the American National Standard for Information Sciences–Permanence of Paper for Printed Library Materials, ANSI Z39 48-1992. Binding materials have been chosen for durability.

To the village and people of Highlands,
the inspiration for this book.
The Cherokee name for Highlands is *Onteeorah*:
Hills of the Sky.

To Be in Highlands

The freshness and the fragrance
Glint of a woodsy stream
Blue misty lift of the mountains
Green eternal dream

Bright wonder of the morning
After a sweet night rain:
It is not earth but Heaven—
The birds are making it plain

And the pines are reaffirming.
Where else would you go
But to Highlands, heart of the Blue Ridge
Above the world below!

—Bess Hines Harkins

Contents

Whiteside Mountain from Wildcat Cliffs. Photo by George Masa, 1929.

List of Illustrations

Acknowledgements

There is no one more sacred to me than my wife, Margaret, without whose sacrificial love and support this book would never have been written. It has also affected my sons Tom and Jack, who have spent half their lives growing familiar with stories about Highlands. I owe my entire family an enormous debt of gratitude for their enduring interest, loyalty, and patience.

It was my father and mother, Emil and Anna Shaffner, who introduced me to the mountains of Western North Carolina, and it was Chief C. Walton Johnson's Camp Sequoyah located in those mountains that inspired in me a love for their incomparable beauty that I've never lost. The miles of hikes that I've enjoyed, accompanied by friends and family, through these forested peaks and valleys over the years have only served to confirm the undying love that ancient mountains such as these can somehow create in the human heart. I owe to them, as much as to my family and friends, the decision to settle in Highlands.

Highlands is a village with a personality as unique as its setting in the land of the sky.[1] Of the many articles that I have found over the years purporting to give an accurate history of early Highlands, five are particularly reliable as detailed eye-witness reports.

E. E. Ewing, editor and owner of Highlands' first newspaper, the *Blue Ridge Enterprise*, published a "History of the Settlement of Highlands" on January 25, 1883, only eight years after the town's founding. He wrote an editorial "Eight Years old To-day" on March 29, 1883, which focused specifically on the first few days.

J. Walter Reese's unfinished, unpublished memoirs covered his life in Highlands from his arrival in 1885 at age four to 1957, with an update by his son Coleman Marshall "Peewee" Reese.

Elias D. White, son of Highlands' first postmaster, T. Baxter White, made a valuable contribution to the June 6, 1941, issue of the *Franklin Press and Highlands Maconian*, entitled "Early Highlands Days, An Historical Sketch," a well-organized account that described the first fifteen years in six chapters.

For details of the actual founding of Highlands from 1875 to 1882, the most reliable source was, of course, Samuel Kelsey's unpublished diary: "Record of Weather and Work." While devoted mostly to the weather, it nevertheless established first-hand facts through daily reporting by the town's founder.

The *Franklin Press* published a very helpful "Brief History of Highlands, Highest Town East of the Rockies" on July 5, 1928. And J. J. Moore, editor of the *Highlands Maconian*, penned a useful supplement in his two-part article of June 24 and July 29, 1931, entitled "Site of Highlands Was Carved From Mountain Wilderness." Mrs. H. G. Story's "Highlands Goes Forward in Ten Years of Progress" updated Moore's account in the *Franklin Press* to June 5, 1941.

Apart from other newspaper articles, diaries, letters, brochures, scrapbooks, organizational minutes, maps, references in books, individuals interviewed, etc., which are listed as sources in the Bibliography, I am extremely grateful to my son Ted Shaffner for his invaluable criticisms and suggestions regarding the structure and composition of the entire book. Likewise, Bob Zahner, Anne Sullivan Doggett, Edna Phillips Bryson, and my wife, Margaret, reviewed and critiqued it in its embryonic form. Their suggestions, support, and encouragement were essential to its birth. And finally I want to thank Rosemary Fleming for minding the store when I had to be absent for research.

I am indebted to Helen Wykle, Coordinator of the D. H. Ramsey Library Special Collections section of the University of North Carolina at Asheville for access to the R. Henry Scadin Photographic Collection and for her painstaking translations, aided extensively by history major Melissa Baldwin, of Scadin's diaries into digital format.

Beverly Cook Quinn provided the collection of photographs of Highlands that her father hired George Masa to take in 1929. Cynthia Strain gave permission to incorporate her unique photograph of Highlands from Sunset Rocks into the book's cover. And Martha Boone Macmillan lent her expertise to touching up a couple of otherwise unsalvageable old photos.

I owe particular thanks to librarians Henley Haslam and Mary Lou Worley for access to the indispensable archives of the Hudson Library in Highlands. Miss Haslam performed a vital service for the town when she organized, cataloged, and preserved the entire collection of records in the library. I want to thank librarian Karen Wallace for access to the extensive collection of newspapers on microfilm at Macon County Public Library in Franklin.

Extremely helpful were the general and special collections of the Hunter Library at Western Carolina University in Cullowhee, the Walter Davis Library and North Carolina Collection of the Louis Round Wilson Library at the University of North Carolina in Chapel Hill, the William R. Perkins Library at Duke University, the Robert W. Woodruff Library at Emory University in Atlanta, the Harold Washington Library in Chicago, and the Library of Congress in Washington, D.C.

Finally, my warmest thanks to the following individuals for information that they either volunteered or provided on request: Mary Alexander, Bob and Tonie Altstaetter Rhodes, Ann Baird, Mary Berry, Richard Betz, Dub Billingsley, Jane Billingsley, Dick and Elizabeth Bruce, Cason and Nancy

Callaway, Jack Calloway, Sky Campbell, Marna Cobb Chalker, Isabel Chambers, Tommy Chambers, Jan Chmar, Dave Clary, John and Wynn Cleaveland, Stan and Donna Cochran, Geri Crowe, Linda David, Ralph and Lynn deVille, Dennis DeWolf, Margaret Kies Dietterich, Maxie Duke, John Edwards, Louis and Elizabeth Edwards, Barbara Estes, Virginia Edwards Fleming, Rosemary Fleming, Katy and Paul and Robyn Fletcher, Ernest Franklin, Margaret Hall, Sue Hall, Henley Haslam, Clem Henry, Betty Holt, Bobby Houston, Frank James, Irene Picklesimer James, Alma Keener, Eloise Kelly, Judy Kight, Hazel Killebrew, Pearle Rogers Lambert, Alan and Jane Lewis, Frances Baumgarner Lombard, Tammy Lowe, Lydia Sargent Macauley, Dr. Richard Martorell, Patricia McAndrew, Mike and Debbie Dryman McCall, Charlie and Gladys McDowell, Anne McDonough, Louise Edwards Meisel, Richard Melvin, Ralph Morris, Alice Nelson, Edith Bolton Nix, Alisun Osteen, Button Parham, Collin Wilcox Paxton, Bud and Doris Potts, Steve Potts, Sue Potts, James Ramey, Joe and Lucille Reese, Marshall Reese, Wayne Reese, Louis Reynaud, Janet Reynolds, Janet Roberson, Hugh Sargent, George Schmitt, Esther Elliott Shay, Mary Ann Sloan, Victor Smith, Bernice Keener Talley, Ed Talley, Walter Taylor, Buck Trott, Harriet Zahner van Houten, Furman Vinson, John Watson, Polly Wax, Julie Weaver, Rebecca Welch, Larry Wheeler, Jeremy Wilcox, Everett Wilson, Louis and Frances Wilson, Wade Wilson, Loren and Sally Ann Wood, Vic and Betty Speed Wood, Jack Wotton, Harry Wright, Neil Wright, Robert Wyatt, Earle Young, and others whose names I may have failed unfortunately to dig from my files.

Obviously this book has depended for its existence on many, many people associated with the town of Highlands, and to all of them I am truly grateful for their help.

Satulah Mountain and Fodderstack. Photo by George Masa, 1929.

Introduction

In the big world things happen that are important;
in the little world, even more so.

It has taken me eight years to accept what my wife, Margaret, has been telling me for the last two, that I will *never* finish this book! There are so many fascinating facts and stories about Highlands and its history which I have not covered, that to publish a book now is an arbitrary act, for it will never be complete. Still, life is short, and this book is long enough! To its credit, I hope that it conveys some of the love that I and my wife, who has devoted much of her life to Highlands, have felt for the town and its people.

At the outset I should mention by way of disclaimer that some of my sources engage in mountain dialect. Readers who speak this language are asked not to take offense, while those who don't would be ill-advised to scorn it. Sometimes an idea cannot be better expressed in plain English with its current rules for correct spelling and grammar than in its unvarnished turn of phrase. There is a certain simplicity, irreplaceable humor, and courteous, self-effacing understatement that only mountain English can convey with a poetic dignity that speaks directly from the heart, like Chaucer or Shakespeare, when they wax colloquial.

In 1954 Weimar Jones, editor of the *Franklin Press*, was asked to speak to the North Carolina Press Association in Raleigh about the people in the western part of the state.[2] He spoke in the familiar mountain idiom more common a generation ago than today to show how mountain folks would respond in Elizabethan Mountain English to the president of Duke University if he were to invite them to dinner:

> *We got yore invite. We knowed you'd be a-lookin' fer us; so we come . . . several of us. It was a right smart piece fer some; had to start off soon in the mornin' to make it afore night.*

> *When we come round yander bend in the big road, we seed right off the latchstring was a-hangin' outside the door, but shucks! we hadn't hardly got in hollerin' distance till you'd th'rowed the door open and was a-standin' there, singin' out: "Light, strangers, an' come in!"*

> *We 'lowed as how we didn't keer if we did, and 'twarn't no time till we seed you'd put a big pot an' the little un.*

> *We're much obliged. Fact is, we're beholden to ye—plumb beholden.*

Now directly we'll have to take out foot in our hand and make it 'cross the ridge home. But afore we go, we aim to say one thing more—and we hain't sayin' it jist fer manners, hit's from the heart: You-uns come!

Without writing a dissertation to prove a point, I might at least note that some of Jones' terms are indeed Elizabethan English. We have Webster for our authority that *hit* is the Saxon for *it*; *haint* can mean *am not*, *are not*, or *have not*. We know grammatically that *come* is stronger than *came*; *knowed*, more regular than *knew*; *seed*, than *saw*; and *throwed*, than *threw*. When invited to come in, mountain folks, if they don't object, *don't care if we do*. They say *shucks* when they're a little surprised. They hardly ever use the *ing* in lookin', hangin', standin', etc. Indeed, *a-lookin'*, *a-hangin'*, and *a-standin'* reproduce exactly the initial inflections in Chaucer's Middle English: y-looken, y-hangen, and y-standen, all without the *g*.

Where mistakes are made in pronunciation, such as *gardeen* for guardian, *po'lice* for police, and *pint* for point, if not justifiable as accent—it's a small-minded orthographist who would pass judgment on them. Andrew Jackson claimed that it was a "mighty po' excuse for a full grown man" who could only think of one way to spell a word. Shakespeare spelled his own name five different ways before Dr. Samuel Johnson straight-jacketed the English language with his dictatorial dictionary.

Finally there's a cordial and generous charm to saying *you'uns* instead of the more indefinite *you*, which can't distinguish singular from plural. And *y'uns* is much less hackneyed than *y'all*.

Regarding historical facts in this book, the French Nobel prize author Anatole France once said: "When a history book contains no lies, it's always boring." The English philosopher David Hume believed, "The first quality of a historian is to be true and impartial; the next is to be interesting." Truth is a hard nut to crack. It leaves the professed historian doubly vulnerable. As Voltaire warned, "The man who tries to write a true and accurate history must expect to be attacked both for everything he says and everything he does not say."

Four problems stand out in my mind as formidable obstacles to writing a true and accurate history of Highlands. I class them as problems of name, place, time, and relationship. In the category of names, Gert McIntosh, who published her *Highlands, North Carolina . . . a walk into the past* in 1983, wrote a follow-up article five years later for the *Highlander* on the history of Horse Cove. Several times in the article she mentioned Walking Stick Road.

Not surprisingly she received a complaint from someone who had grown up in Horse Cove and fiercely protested applying the name *Walking Stick* to *that* road. "Walking Stick Road was *never ever* that!" her critic wrote. "It was Thompson's Lane,—all my long life; I've been here every summer of my life. Bishop Thompson of New Orleans had a beautiful summer home on that road, so it was known as Thompson's Lane. My mother was born in his summer home, so it has always been and always will be 'Thompson's Lane' to me. There are a few other errors (in the article) that I don't mind, but I *do* mind about my mother's birthplace!"

This is the problem of names. Gert's article doesn't mention Thompson's Lane, which might otherwise have softened the blow. Nor does it note that over the years Thompson's Lane has been known as Hawkins Road, Big Creek Road, Pin Mill Road (when Horse Cove itself was known as Victoria), and—yes—Walking Stick Road, presumably after a Cherokee Indian chief and his sycamore stick.[3] That road *was* indeed Thompson's Lane, but it has been and *is* today—as broadcast by its official sign—Walking Stick Road.

The issue is further complicated by the fact that two prominent Thompsons lived in Horse Cove, both on that road. Bishop or Major Hugh Miller Thompson owned 22,000 acres on which he had a summer cottage, which accommodated guests but which burned in 1900. His brother, postmaster John R. Thompson, had built on that road his frame houses accommodating up to thirty boarders, one of whom was Woodrow Wilson when he came to Horse Cove in 1879.

According to both Wilson and the minutes of the supervisors who began improving the road in that year, it was known as Jno. R. Thompson's Lane after the postmaster.[4] Whether the road was really named for the Bishop Thompson or postmaster Thompson or both only further illustrates the problem of names. Indeed, for three years from 1894 to 1897 the cove itself was called, *Saquilla*, *Sau-gwil-lah* being Cherokee for *horse*.[5]

The problem of place is easily exemplified by the property of James Soper. Arriving from Pennsylvania, Soper was the first Yankee farmer to settle the Highlands plateau. On February 29, 1875, he purchased 100 acres northwest of town on which he built one of the first four houses of the new settlement. Yet where exactly was James Soper's home? Presumably near Aunt Polly Norton's home in Shortoff, so perhaps the deed would help.

The deed reads, "Beginning at a chestnut, near the thunder struck pine, East 185 poles to a stake, thence S 45° W 175 poles to a black oak, thence N 70° W 80 poles to a chestnut, thence 10° E 100 poles to the beginning, containing 100 acres." Some deeds in those early days were even more enigmatic. One began at "a small pine on top of a ridge near a pile of rocks." Another started and ended, not at a growing tree at all but a dead locust stump. It would have been just as helpful to begin and end at a cow in Isaac Rice's cornfield!

Of all the problems involved in compiling a history, the one requiring the deepest digging often relates to time. As Jefferson observed, "Of all the faculties of the human mind, that of memory is the first which suffers decay from age." People usually remember *what* happened in their lives, but exactly *when* it happened, they're not so sure. Or what's worse, they *are* sure!

When I ask the old-timers of Highlands if they remember the altitude oak on Main Street, invariably they all do. But when was it cut down? During the thirties! No, the forties! It was the fifties! The issue is important because trees in Highlands, whether generally or specifically, have meant much to its residents. They are a vital part of the town's lovely natural setting. Indeed, they're what many folks come here to enjoy.

One of our greatest losses on the Highlands plateau was the primeval forest between Bear Pen and Whiteside mountains. This forest took a millennium to grow but disappeared in just a handful of years. Sold in 1943 for the war effort, it was decimated by 1948. It represented a huge loss for those who knew and loved it.

On a less grand scale but equally controversial was the cutting of one tree: the altitude oak on Main Street, which is described later in Chapter Twenty. The fact that this ancient oak *was* cut was not a problem for this history so much as determining *when* it was cut. Marion Day Arnold guessed it was 1936 when she was a senior at Highlands School. Her classmate June Thompson Medlin agreed. It's hard to dispute the memory of what happened during one's last year of high school, since most of us remember this if we remember nothing else. Indeed, the traumas that crash into adolescent life are indelibly unforgettable.

There are others, like Marian and June, who agree that the altitude oak was cut during the late thirties. But there are also those who insist on the forties, Joe Reese being a case in point. When confronted with the fact that two high school graduates remembered the date distinctly as 1936, Joe emphatically denied it. They were flat-out wrong, he countered, and he was sure of it. What made him so sure was the irrefutable fact, in his own words, that "I was the one who cut it!"

"It was 1947!" he said. "People wanted the street paved. The state said they'd pave it, but the trees had to be moved. I was on the street committee, and we had to take down all three."[6] People cried, he admitted, and his wife Lucille added, "I've bawled him out a number of times. I haven't given him any rest since."

If Joe Reese was mistaken, then perhaps he was referring to the large maples that he felled in Christopher Whittle's park to make way for the new home of Highlands Art Gallery in 1947, an act that provoked nearly as many tears and as much agony on account of the townspeople's love of that particular park's beauty and blessed shade. Or perhaps Marian and June were wrong in that their poems of 1936 were directed at something hopefully preventable instead of an accomplished fact, something that would wait a decade before it actually happened.

In the end, the truth would lie at the bottom of the barrel in a single line from the minutes of the town council that officially authorized cutting the altitude oak. That line established the year definitively as 1938, two years after Marian and June composed their poems to try to stop it and nine years before Joe supposedly cut it down.

And yet, no sooner is the problem definitely resolved than it's irreparably reopened. Even officially authorizing a tree's cutting is not the same as actually cutting it. If Sidney McCarty is right in his claim some forty years after the fact, that he was on the town board when the altitude oak was cut, then his election to that board, like Reese's, in May, 1947, leaves the question once again up in the air. In sympathy with Reese, McCarty voiced similar feelings about the matter in admitting, "Trouble is the price of progress."[7]

The fourth and thorniest problem of Highlands history involves relationships. A good old mountain custom in a community where families are close involves calling a familiar soul *aunt* or *uncle* regardless of whether he or she actually is or isn't. Highlanders unrelated to Rev. William T. Potts called him Uncle Billy the same as all his relatives, for ultimately he was related to almost everybody in town. Uncle Charlie Potts at the post office was too. So was Aunt Tudie Rice, and Aunt Mett Picklesimer Brooks, artist, dancer, part owner of a gas station, grocery store, and bowling alley, and avid coon hunter who died in the year 2000 at ninety-seven.

In the case of Aunt Mett, it's particularly revealing to ask who she really was related to? The Picklesimers, Jameses, Taylors, Gordons, and Crowes could legitimately call her aunt. But one truth I've learned during research into Highlands genealogies is that anybody related to anybody is probably related to everybody. Aunt Mett's father, for example, was a Picklesimer; her mother, a Rogers; her grandmother, a Keener. Right there we have three of the biggest families in Highlands, reaching back through 150 years of ancestors.

If we skip the Picklesimers and Keeners and look only at her Rogers relatives, Bob Rogers, who married a Holland, lived in the 1880s at Dog Mountain on the Dillard Road. His house was the oldest on the Highlands plateau until Tommy Chambers recently dismantled it. It was home to nine Rogers children. In 1927 the house of Bob's son Josh was moved to join it. It was home to sixteen occupants, all Rogers. In 1960 Uncle Billy McCoy's house in Goldmine was moved to join the former two. Billy McCoy, who married a Holland, was Bob Rogers' nephew through his sister Sarah Ann

Rogers McCoy. His house was home to twenty-two occupants, all Rogers including fourteen McCoy children.

All together forty-six descendants of Grandpa David and Margaret Young Rogers of Buck Creek had lived within the confines of these several walls before they were finally joined. Moreover, the descendants of anyone who married into this vast Rogers family were all Rogers-related.

Grandpa David himself had had ten Rogers children, three of whom married Holland sisters, making them all Rogers too. Grandpa David's father, Hugh Rogers, who married a Thornton, had had twelve Rogers sons!

Of course, none of these Rogers included the David Rogers who married Polly Berry and had nine Rogers children, one of whom was another David; nor the David Rogers who married Charity Franks. It does include the David Rogers who married a Mincey, the Robert David Rogers who married a Higdon and a Crunkleton and an Elliott, and the David Rogers who married Nora Rogers. This led, of course, to having to distinguish Big David Rogers from Little David Rogers in the same way that Nora Rogers' brother was Big Ed Rogers, Highlands' policeman also known as "Bennie," not to be confused with her son Little Ed Rogers, the town's electrician and fire chief.

In addition to her Rogers relatives, it appears that Aunt Mett was related by blood or by marriage at minimum to all the following families, listed alphabetically: Ammons, Bryson, Calloway, Corbin, Crisp, Crunkleton, Edwards, Gibson, Hedden, Holland, Houston, Jenkins, Keener, McCall, McCoy, Miller, Picklesimer, Potts, Rogers, Stiwinter, Talley, Webb, Wilson, and Zachary.

Mel Keener told a little story that demonstrates how this goes. In olden days when Billy and Lucretia Gibson "Creasy" Webb came to Highlands from Tennessee with a family of twelve, the McCall girls snatched up three of their eight boys: Mary Ann got Jim; Ruth, Ben; and Cindy, William.

The next generation saw the situation reversed. As soon as Jim and Mary Webb's five girls were of age, four of them married Jenkins boys. Jennie got Butler; Sarah got Allen; Creasy, John; and Betsy, Thomas.

As Mel put it, "Butler Jenkins' daddy come from Tennessee and married one of Jim Webb's bunch of girls. Allen from Tennessee married one of them, John come and married one of them, Thomas come, and he married one of them. Old man Jim said one day, 'Them damn Jenkins come in droves over here!'"[8] What Mel omitted, of course, was that Butler Jenkins' daddy's mother, Rhoda, was also a Webb.

The problem of the Highlands historian in sorting through all these droves of families is to discover who's who and who's really related to whom. An interesting consequence of the Webb genealogy, for instance, is that one of Billy and Granny Creasy Webb's descendants is alleged to be

Loretta Webb Lynn. If this proves true, then the Queen of Country is kin to half of Highlands.

L to R: Butler Jenkins, Sr., (m. Jennie Webb) holding Butler, Jr., and Eva; Allen Jenkins holding Myrtle with daughter Ethel (blurred) standing in front and wife Sara Webb to the right behind daughter Rittie. Back row: George Vinson with adopted sister and John Jenkins (m. Creasy Webb). Photo courtesy of Audrey Webb Derreberry.

The reward, of course, for all this sorting of facts relating to names, places, dates, and relationships has been the joy of discovering the multifaceted charm of Highlands. I trust the reader will pardon any errors, vital omissions, or indiscretions that I may have committed, all of which I've tried my best to avoid. In fact, I've added pages at the end of this book for readers to note errors found or just to take notes. If this book is popular enough to warrant a second edition, I welcome corrections or comments from Highlanders whom I did not meet or interview this time around, so that the next edition might prove relatively error free, if that's ever possible. This for me has been an eight-year love affair with the homeland of my heart.

Lucretia Gibson "Granny Creasy" Webb, alleged ancestor of Country Gospel singer Loretta Webb Lynn, seated by the chimney of the old Webb farmhouse on Brushy Face. Barney Wilson's family lived here at the time. Only the chimney remains today. Photo courtesy of Louis and Frances Wilson.

1. In the Beginning

When the Great Buzzard, the father of all the buzzards we now see, reached the Cherokee country, he was very tired, and his wings began to flap and strike the ground, and wherever they struck the earth there was a valley, and where they turned up again there was a mountain. When the animals above saw this, they were afraid that the whole world would be mountains, so they called him back, but the Cherokee country remains full of mountains to this day.

—James Mooney, *Myths of the Cherokee*

Geology's grand theory of plate tectonics tells us that Highlands, North Carolina, was born between 300 and 400 million years ago. When Laurentia (now North America) crunched into Baltica and Avalonia (northern Europe, Britain, and New England) and then into Gondwana (Africa and South America), the resulting collision pushed up the world's oldest mountains, the Caledonian and Appalachian ranges, in one great landmass, Pangaea, stretching from pole to pole.[9] When the continents separated again into three parts around 200 million years ago, the northern portion of the Appalachians broke off above today's state of Maine to become the Caledonian Mountains of Scotland. The southern portion, below the state of Georgia, would become the Atlas Range in North Africa.

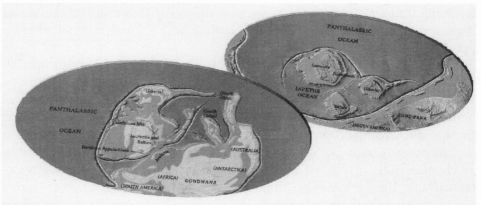

The creation of the Caledonian and Appalachian Mountains 300–400 million years ago

If the earth, as we are told, is nearly four billion years old, then the Highlands plateau is quite young, yet considerably older than the really young peaks of the European Alps and the Rockies.

It was on the great super continent Pangaea that the dinosaurs were born. They still roamed the land when Pangaea re-divided into three parts, indeed until that fateful day, we are told, when an asteroid crashed into their world and rendered them finally extinct. Then about 50 million years ago some sections of Pangaea reunited: Africa striking Europe to form the Alps, and India ramming into Asia to push up the Himalayas. Covered with subtropical forests as far as the Arctic, Pangaea became a greenhouse paradise when warming peaked, but global cooling brought the onset of permanent ice to Antarctica.

Dozens of glaciations followed, and for the final two and a half million years of the Pleistocene era, tons of ice covered much of the earth. Fortunately for the southern Appalachians, the Blue Ridge Highlands provided a place of refuge for many species of plants that were crushed by the great glaciers farther north. The Appalachians, thrust up by those earliest continental collisions and held aloft with no geological break, escaped the glacial advance, while to the immediate north 2,000 feet of relentless ice ground out the Great Lakes and pressed the Mississippi and Missouri river valleys into the North American landscape, virtually exterminating all plant life beneath.

The primeval forests of the Blue Ridge Highlands survived. Their trees ranged from a typical upper Piedmont type of yellow pine, gum, poplar, white and other oaks to a typical northern hardwood forest of white pine, cherry, walnut, poplar, basswood, locust, beech, sugar maple, soft maple, birch, buckeye, hemlock, and all species of oak.

Only one other region on the surface of the globe is said to have offered refuge for a similar diversity of plants. It stretched from the peaks of northern India through China to the mountains of Japan. This Oriental region and the southern Appalachians, both on or below the 35th Parallel, weathered the periods of glaciation.

One of the special survivors of the glaciers in the Appalachians was the yellow poplar or Tulip Tree (*Liriodendron tulipifera*), a pre-glacial species. After the last retreat of ice, it was able to repopulate the mountains as we know it today. Only fossils of the other species of this genus remain in Europe and Greenland, but a similar species survived in China.[10]

The more modest but no less significant *Shortia galacifolia*, also known as Oconee Bells or Little Colt's Foot, is another legacy of that ancient botanical age. Barely missing extinction worldwide, its mass of glossy green leaves greeted the French botanist André Michaux as a great surprise. Like trailing arbutus, or Mayflower, it remains almost identical to several species found only in Japan and China.

Other relics of the southern Appalachians and parts of East Asia, which can't be found in Europe or elsewhere in North America, are ginseng (*Panax quinquefolium*), Carolina or Yellow Jasmine (*Gelsemium jussieu*), the well-known Jack-in-the-pulpit (*Arisaema triphyllum*), Virginia Creeper

(*Parthenocissus quinquefolia*), and Witch-hazel (the *Harmamelis virginiana* of America, *H. japonica* of Japan, and *H. mollis* of China).

Margaret Morley, in her tribute to *The Carolina Mountains*, marveled that the resplendent wild azaleas—which burned on all sides of the mountains with flames that did not destroy and which the natives called yellow honeysuckles—thrived only in the mountains of Carolina. A similar species of this genus with fire in its veins also adorned the slopes of the Himalayans and "gave to the gardens of Europe their choicest azaleas long before these of the New World were known."[11]

It may be a quirk of geography that the last forms of life to populate the Highlands plateau were human beings, native Americans and then the Europeans, including their plants and animals. When the Europeans arrived, they came in large numbers, but only during the nineteenth century. A glance at a map in raised relief will show that Western North Carolina is shaped like a huge bow, laid from the northeast to the southwest, thirty to fifty miles in width and about 150 miles long. The Blue Ridge forms the arc, while the Unaka or White Range along the Tennessee boundary marks the string. Between the bow and the string, high transverse ridges are laid like massive arrows obstructing movement to the north or south.

Settlers migrating down the Ohio and Tennessee valleys or through the North Carolina Piedmont did well to steer clear of this intimidating bow, for anyone who crossed the Stone, Beech, Roan, and Yellow ranges on foot or horseback to reach the fir-crowned crest of the Black Mountains must certainly have despaired at what still lay ahead to the southwest.

Lovely but daunting, an inner sea of wave on wave of long, narrow, high ranges rose above profoundly deep valleys, all of which must be crossed to reach the flatlands. Beginning with the Newfound range, then Pisgah, the balmy Balsams, the wild Cowees, the bold Nantahalas, and finally the Valley River mountains, each cresting in an ocean of unapproachable glory stretching as far as the eye could see and beyond to the horizon, before abruptly sinking into the low country of South Carolina and Georgia.

To reach the Highlands plateau from any direction within this mighty bow meant climbing one side of a mountain and descending the other, only to climb and descend another just as high, and another, and another, without apparent end. More than a hundred and fifty summits between the bow and string reached altitudes of over 5,000 feet, fifteen of these in the Balsams alone towering above 6,000. Hundreds of creeks and thousands of brooks foamed and dashed over precipices, some hundreds of feet high, on their tortuous courses through dark gorges and deep ravines into the rivers Toe, French Broad, Pigeon, Little Tennessee, and Hiwassee, as they cut their way into the great Tennessee which flowed into the Ohio and emptied into the Mississippi.

Only natural mountaineers would have relished the thought of crossing a landscape so radically broken in contour. For the thousand or more years preceding the arrival of the Europeans on the Highlands plateau, Cherokees and pre-Cherokees or Mississippians, freely roamed these rugged mountains. The Cherokees built their towns upon the headwaters of the Savannah, Hiwassee, and Tuckasegee and all along the Little Tennessee River. Their ancient trails, crossing the heights above the valleys, were the worthy ancestors of many of today's torturous mountain roads.

A'yûñ'inĭ (Swimmer): shaman and chief storyteller of the Cherokee. Photo by James Mooney, 1887–88.

Anthropologists tell us that the ancestors of the Indians, immigrants from Siberia, arrived on the North American continent during the last one or two of the great ice ages. Spanning one period from 10,000 to 28,000 years ago, and another from 40,000 to 50,000, enough of the world's water was locked into frozen immobility to lower the sea level 300 to 500 feet.[12] This exposed not only the continental shelves but also, for a few thousand years, a land bridge of tundra as much as a thousand miles wide from Asia to the Americas. Archaeologists have set the migration of the first Americans across the Bering land bridge at over 12,000 years ago, but more probably 40,000.[13]

Exactly when the descendants of these earliest immigrants began to settle the Southern Appalachians is still uncertain. There is evidence of Paleo-Indians who followed herds of big game before 8,000 B. C., for they killed their prey with stone-tipped spears. There is also evidence of polished banner stones, with which Archaic hunters during the next 5,000 years weighted their spears for added force when hurled by atlatls (spear throwers). Unearthed remains of pottery in the South have been dated as far back as 2,500 B. C.

A highly organized farming culture appeared about the time of the mound builders around 1,000 B. C. These were the Woodland people, who created agriculture and for the first time no longer migrated with the herds but settled down in more permanent homes. When they hunted, they used bows and arrows, having abandoned the more bulky atlatls and spears. By 800 A. D. they were cultivating corn. As agriculture intensified, the native populations naturally increased. Corn farmers didn't reach the Appalachian highlands, however, until about 1,100 A. D.

In the spring of 1540 Hernando de Soto arrived in the land of the chilokkita, a Muskogean term for "people of a different language," which he Hispanicized as *Chelaque* but was later anglicized to *Cherokee*.[14] Some 30,000 natives occupied 70,000 square miles of territory centered in western North Carolina and eastern Tennessee but stretching to parts of five other present-day states, namely Georgia, South Carolina, Virginia, Kentucky, and West Virginia. They farmed along the rivers and hunted the forested mountains and fertile valleys. Among themselves they were known as *Tsalagi*, or "principle people," since the term *Cherokee* had no meaning in their own language.[15]

Whether de Soto actually passed through the Highlands plateau has been disputed in recent years as hotly as it has been affirmed. One claimant states that he and a considerable entourage camped at the Salt Rock in today's Wright Square on May 22, 1540.[16] The Smithsonian-sponsored historic marker, installed in Highlands on Main Street in 1975, claims that de Soto did indeed come our way, although the wording admits only "near here."[17]

The most recent scholarship, however, shows de Soto's route through present-day North Carolina began near Charlotte. Based on modern technology, archeological digs, and anthropological studies, revisionist Charles Hudson of the University of Georgia traces his journey up the Catawba

River, past Hickory, and along the French Broad through Asheville as far north as Spruce Pine.[18]

Although Hudson admits that de Soto might have taken a more easterly route along the North Toe River, it's nonetheless certain that he crossed the border into Tennessee. From there he followed the Tennessee River and its Little Tennessee Fork back into North Carolina, turning south at Tellico toward Belltown and Prospect, crossing the Hiwassee River, and arriving finally in the vicinity of present-day Carters, Georgia.

Determining de Soto's true route depends, of course, on where such ancient chiefdoms as Guaquili, Xuala (Joara), Chiaha, Coste, Tali, Tasqui, and Coosa actually existed half a millennium ago. Since none of today's maps show the Cherokee towns that de Soto described, scholars were reduced to educated guesswork. If de Soto's route, as proposed by Hudson, eventually replaces the Smithsonian proposal, then de Soto's expedition must be said to have followed the several rivers that completely encircle the high Blue Ridge Mountains of Western North Carolina.

And that being the case, his nearest approach to Highlands would have been, as some have reasonably contended—nowhere *near* the Highlands plateau, but *west* of Franklin. Whether he and his entourage of 650 armored soldiers, 220 armored horses, armored war dogs, slaves, workmen, and a herd of hogs could have—or even would have—fought their way up and over the densely thicketed heights of the Highlands plateau on their way to the Mississippi appears, at the least, impractical.

If de Soto didn't pass over the Highlands plateau, then the famous question of who carved the Spanish inscription "T. T." / UN LUEGO SANTA / A LA MEMORIA atop Devil's Courthouse needs explaining. This inscription appears on the dome-shaped rock at the north end of Whiteside Mountain, which the Cherokees called *Inda-culla*.[19] The white man often named this type of inaccessible rock after the extreme difficulty involved in penetrating thickets and scaling boulders to reach the top. From these dizzying heights the Devil might very well have hurled the hapless victims of his heartless judgments into the great abyss.

It's hard to believe that this particular inscription on Devil's Courthouse could have been chiseled into the granite by any member of de Soto's party and withstood 450 years of erosion. It is barely discernible today, even less so than when I photographed it only ten years ago. Who carved it and what it means have long been subjects of curiosity and debate on the Highlands plateau.

In 1965 Judge Felix Alley's nephew, Rev. Herman Alley, a Baptist preacher in Highlands during the early forties, is reported to have confessed to his own nephew, Howard, that he carved it in his youth around 1920. Howard reported the confession in a letter to the *Asheville Citizen-Times* on

Nov. 6, 1965. He said his Uncle Herman intended it as a sacred dedication to the profound beauty of a place which had restored his soul during a time of great sorrow in his life. He had gone there for much needed peace and solitude and had found it. T. W. Reynolds endorsed this explanation of the mysterious inscription in the first volume of his *Southern Appalachian Region* in 1966.[20]

Indacula, the Devil's Courthouse. Photo by the author, 2001.

Naturalist and life-long resident Henry Wright, however, disputed it. He remembered seeing the carving himself as a small boy about the time that Herman, the self-confessed carver, would have just been born, hardly able to speak English much less carve Spanish in stone.[21] Bob Zahner, in his recent *Mountain at the End of the Trail*, also discounts the Alley confession as well as other more recent explanations. In the end he agrees with Bob Padgett that "those who enjoy this Spanish mystery on the great mountain do not really want it solved. And apparently neither did the inscriber," Padgett reasoned, "else he would have left more clues to explain his noble venture."[22]

Be that as it may, the general agreement is that de Soto was not the inscriber. What the inscription meant, however, was another issue. The popular translation, "In memory of a future saint," left unresolved the puzzling initials, "T. T." The most plausible rendering that took into account the initials as well was offered in 1997 by the New Mexican scholar Eloy Gallegos, whose fluency in Spanish gives him a decided edge in any mean-

8

ingful interpretation.[23] Without questioning the contention that a Spaniard could have carved it, Gallegos translated the phrase, beginning with the double Ts, to mean: "Testimony! An ordinary walk for the record." In his estimation it was carved by a person passing through the area who merely wished to leave proof of his having *Pase por aqui*.

Spanish inscription at Devil's Courthouse, photographed by the author, 1991

Irrespective of a Spanish presence on the Highlands plateau, what remains irrefutable is the fact that the Cherokees crossed this rugged area quite frequently for centuries *en route* to their valley towns. Long before de Soto's expedition, Cherokee trails cut through the highlands from the Cullasaja and Little Tennessee river valleys to the west and the Chattooga and Tuckasegee valleys to the east. Cherokees found hidden in the forests and streams plenty of game and fish, to which the abundance of arrowheads, campsites, and graves discovered long after their departure will attest.

Many of the Indian relics that William Cleaveland collected and his son Will donated in 1927 to help establish the Highlands Museum were uncovered on the Highlands plateau. The collection consisted of over 2,500 artifacts, including beautifully carved arrow heads, pottery etched with Cherokee history, primitive tomahawks, and peace pipes—many pieces dating from the Archaic and Woodland periods.[24] Buck Horn Gap (also known as Sloan's Gap) on Satulah, which was named for its location where white-tail deer passed through, was a popular quarry for early Highlanders seeking artifacts from the ancient hunt.

On Whiteside Mountain, where eagles once flew out in great numbers and laid their clutches of three or four eggs, were frequent signs of long established Cherokee handiwork. Huge trunks of trees, their main branches cut off or bent to form steps, stood as ancient witnesses to a time long past. Once known as "Indian ladders," they are now recognized as "trail trees," sign posts that guided the Cherokees along their trails.[25] An old Whiteside camping ground bore evidence of Cherokee ceremonies in former days. A Cherokee burial ground on land owned in the 1880s by John Ledford was found to contain stone mounds covering some 700 battle casualties.[26]

Whiteside Mountain from Col. John Alley's home. Photo by R. Henry Scadin, 1899, courtesy of Hudson Library archives.

Until the treaty of 1819 with the United States, when the Cherokees sold to the federal government all their homeland north and east of the Nantahala mountains, together with the rich Tuckasegee River area, the Highlands plateau was definitely used for food gathering and hunting by the Cherokees.

The infamous New Eschota Treaty of 1835 virtually extinguished Cherokee occupation of all lands in the two Carolinas, Tennessee, Georgia, and Alabama with the cruel stipulation that the tribe would have to abandon its homeland and move west of the Mississippi. When they balked at leaving, President Andrew Jackson ordered the notorious forced march to Oklahoma in 1838 during which 4,000 Cherokees perished along the Trail of Tears.

UNAKA KANOOS.

Whiteside Mountain ca. 1877, as pictured by Zeigler and Grosscup[27]

Long before their departure, however, American colonists had settled along their rivers and in their coves and were well received. One welcomed friend of the Cherokees, a Virginian who had walked into Whiteside Cove from the Pickens District of South Carolina during the early 1820s, was Barak Norton.[28] In 1827 he became the first white settler in the cove. He moved his wife, Mary Nicholson, and seven children—Mira, Roderick, Elias, Jemima, William, Edward, and Martha— into a house under the brow of Whiteside Mountain, known to the Cherokee as *Unaka kanoos* (White Mountain).

According to Silas McDowell in 1877, the mighty mountain above Norton's home was named for its face of concave rock, as white as snow. In scientific terms, the granite of this ancient mountain contained more quartz, feldspar, and mica than pure granite due to hundreds of millions of years of erosion. Indeed, at this late stage in its evolution, it had retained less feldspar than mica, the source of its reflecting whiteness.

Named after this mountain, Barak's eighth child, Sarah Whiteside Norton, became on August 8, 1828, the first white child to be born in the cove. Her family would live for ten more years in this land of the Cherokee before her father was ordered to help round them up for the grueling exodus to Oklahoma. One of the soldiers who escorted them was Colonel John Alley of Rutherford County, N.C., who was returning from his assignment during the early 1840s when he first arrived in Whiteside Cove.[29] In short time he met and married Sarah, and they built a home at the base of Whiteside, now known as Lombard's Lodge.

Their son Felix Alley, who became a well-known judge of the N.C. Superior Court, would write *Random Thoughts and Musings of a Mountaineer*, a widely acclaimed source of much of this area's history, legends, and lore. Their daughter Mary would marry Grundy "Buck" Hill of Horse Cove, whose family played a large role in the founding of Highlands. It was Grundy's father, Stanhope Hill, who would establish Hill's Inn in Horse Cove as early as 1847 and later become the first elected mayor of Highlands.[30] Grundy's younger brother, Frank Hill, would build homes that still stand in both Highlands and the Cove.

Col. Alley lived in the cove only a short while before he was drafted into the war with Mexico and spent two years fighting to regain Texas for the Americans. He returned lame from his wounds in 1848, which is why he didn't participate a dozen years later in the Civil War. Serving in the Home Guard in the cove, however, didn't prevent his almost losing his life toward the end of that war when the infamous George W. Kirk and his Raiders invaded Cashiers Valley, Whiteside Cove, and Horse Cove.

Kirk's renegade band of robbers and murderers found Col. Alley at home in 1864. It is said that he escaped death only because one of Kirk's soldiers recognized him as having saved the soldier's life during the Mexican War. For his role in saving Alley's life, this soldier was subsequently murdered by Kirk's marauding bushwhackers. They even killed the youngest of his wife's brothers, Ned Norton, in the presence of Ned's wife and children.[31] A detestable lot, they plundered and terrorized the Western North Carolina populace.

The first white family to settle Horse Cove, according to historian John Arthur—was that of the Barnes, George and William.[32] Billy "Dismal" Barnes lived in a small log cabin where he cared for the livestock of American Revolutionary General Andrew Pickens. Indeed, it was this grazing land that Pickens' horses ranged for wild vetch and other pasturage that gave Horse Cove its name. Other early settlers of Horse Cove included the Hills, who are discussed later in Chapter Two, and Mark Burrell and Evan Talley.

The horse played an interesting role in the choice of names for the communities surrounding Highlands. James McKinney, who is said to have been the first or second white man to settle Cashiers (pronounced cash´-ers) Valley in the 1830s, was also said to own a particularly fine horse. The McKinney family claims he named it "Cash," in part because it was such a valuable animal but also for the large sums of money it won in racing. This horse preferred spending the winters grazing on the valley grass to being herded with the remaining horses to a milder climate in South Carolina.

This account is one of many that have sought to explain the name: Cash's Valley.[33] Another account derives the name from one of Wade Hampton's two prize bulls—Brutus and Cassius—that got caught in a mountain thicket in the valley and broke its neck. A third story tells of an Indian trader, named Cashiers, who Bobby McCall knew as the first real white settler of the valley but who moved west when the Indians left the region by treaty. Judge Felix Alley, who knew Bobby McCall, claimed the settlement was known from the start as Cashiers Valley, all other versions of its naming being mere legends.

Whatever the reason for the naming of Cashiers Valley, that name was shortened to Cashiers on September 14, 1881.[34] "Sheep Cliff," standing stark and stiff above the valley, was where James McKinney grazed his sheep high above and apart from his horses in the river bottom lands around the "Horsepasture River."

Incidentally, it was in the home of James and Sally McKinney, now the site of High Hampton Inn, that the legendary meeting between the governors of North and South Carolina took place to determine the route of today's Highway 107 after it reached Cashiers Valley. Generally known as the Winding Stairs Turnpike Road from Tamassee, S.C., this road across the Blue Ridge was built shortly after 1857 but before the Civil War by two men: Col. William M. Sloan, who took charge of the South Carolina section; and William H. "Will" Thomas, who supervised its North Carolina extension.[35]

As roadwork approached Cashiers Valley, a great debate arose as to whether the road should turn east toward Sapphire and Rosman or continue north through McKinney Gap, over Cullowhee Mountain (which it bypasses today), and down the Tuckasegee River on its course to Webster. As a state senator and first white chief of the Eastern Band of Cherokees, Will Thomas was a strong advocate of road improvement in western North Carolina.[36] Furthermore, living on the Tuckasegee River, he was quite familiar with the area through which he hoped the road would pass.

According to the story as passed down by the McKinneys, the volatile issue was resolved at a meeting of two governors over a keg of white lightning and a barrel of brandy. John Alley confirmed that he was at this meeting where the final route was decided. The guests of the McKinneys had just dined on generous servings of Aunt Sally's "yaller-legged" chickens, fried brown in golden melted butter, snow-white smothered cabbage, Irish potatoes, and buckwheat cakes covered with mountain honey and were deep into Mr. Mac's mountain dew before their conversation turned to the road.

The story goes that the governor of North Carolina wanted the road to follow the Tuckasegee River so as to link with Thomas' Oconalufty Turnpike over the Smokies into Tennessee, but the governor of South Carolina felt that trade with his state would greatly increase if the road veered east toward Brevard and the French Broad valley.

When the North Carolina governor got the best of the argument, his opponent, feeling insulted, turned his face to the wall, a gesture properly interpreted as a challenge to a duel. The pressure mounted until the North Carolina governor observed, "It's a helluva long time between drinks!" and in a burst of unrestrained laughter, the tension abruptly dissolved. Legend has it that this was the origin of the famous saying, "What did the governor of North Carolina say to the governor of South Carolina?"[37]

It may be that James McKinney was not the first white settler of Cashiers Valley, for both Baxter White and Jeremiah Pierson of Highlands always claimed a man named Millsaps settled the upper end of the valley about 1818 when it was still a part of Haywood County.[38] Millsaps built a fourteen-room, two-story log house for lodgers, which is where Wade Hampton, John C. Calhoun, and Henry Clay stayed when they came to hunt and fish in the valley. The land and lodge were later purchased by McKinney.

Regardless of whether the first settler was an Indian trader named Cashiers or a man named Millsaps or James McKinney, the family that arrived close on McKinney's heels was that of Col. John and Sarah Roberts Zachary with thirteen of their fourteen children from Surry County in North

Carolina.[39] During the mid 1830s they brought with them the artisan trades: brick mason, hatter, carpenter, etc. They bought land where High Hampton Inn now stands and built the first sawmill in Cashiers Valley.

In the early 1840s the McKinneys and the Zacharies were followed by James Wright, a gold prospector from Tennessee who came to farm and mine Whiteside Cove about the same time as Col. Alley.[40] America's first major gold rush had sprung from the discovery during the late 1820s of the precious metal in central North Carolina and north Georgia, long before the famous California rush of the late 1840s.

Prospectors in North Carolina and Georgia washed the metal from creek beds in pans and rockers and opened surface mines in the weathered out-croppings of gold-bearing quartz veins. Georgia's Dave Sloan, Sr., father of the explorer who would later write *Fogy Days and Now; or, The World Has Changed* about the area, worked gold mines in North Carolina while living on the Seneca River in South Carolina. Like his colleagues, he coined his gold dust at the U.S. Mint in Dahlonega, Georgia.

Shortoff Mountain, 1897. Photo from R. H. Scadin Collection, UNC-A.

As fate would have it, James Wright arrived in the cove toward the end of the rush when most of the creek beds and near-surface deposits of gold had been depleted and the attention had shifted to California. He married Barak Norton's daughter Jemima in 1844 and settled in the cove.

Their first son Marion, a master carpenter, would later construct many of the early buildings in Highlands, and their second son Barak, a first-rate surveyor, would lay out many of the roads connecting Highlands to the outside world.[41] Their daughter Mary Ellen would marry Julius "Jule" Phillips, a prolific builder in early Highlands.

In 1868, just short of twenty years after his settling in Whiteside Cove, James Wright moved his family to Short Off, nearer to today's Highlands. He bought a log cabin, built in 1865 by Pryor Talley within a stone's throw of Short Off Mountain. Although it no longer exists, the Wright farmhouse was at the time one of only two boarding houses on the Highlands plateau. It soon became a popular stopover for the few travelers who were bold enough to penetrate these forested heights.

Like the Wright home, the only other boarding house in the Short Off area was the home of another settler from Whiteside Cove, Polly Holden Norton. Granddaughter of Barak and Mary Nicholson Norton, Polly moved to Short Off soon after the marriage of her daughter Elizabeth "Vinetta" to Isaac "Peter" Rice, himself an immigrant to the cove from Charleston, South Carolina, during the late 1850s.[42]

Elias and Polly Norton. Photos courtesy of Tammy Lowe.

Polly's husband, Elias, according to their grandson Frank Norton, had been killed while living in the cove, so for many years Polly had had to rely on her own inner strength to provide for the family.[43] Not long after her arrival in Short Off, during August of 1865, while helping to clear the wilderness for their new home, she had to fight off wolves that roamed Cowee and Short Off mountains and pen the sheep up for their protection.[44] Frank remembered that Polly had a hog in a pen with a bear about to get it, and "she run that bear off." She had to walk to Billy Webb's, way out at Flat Mountain, to have him bring his dogs to kill it.

Aunt Polly's home, built in 1865, known today as the old Rice house on Chaney Lane

Polly set up her home as a boarding house, which Vinetta eventually inherited, calling it *Idlease Manor*. Vinetta supplied her guests from her own garden of fresh vegetables. It was after the birth of her eleventh child in 1881, however, that her husband, Peter, suddenly took a notion to head west and seek his fortune. He never returned, leaving Vinetta to raise all eleven children on her own at *Idlease*, which, by necessity, she continued to manage for income until her death in 1928. It was later reported that Peter died in 1914 somewhere in Texas.

Vinetta's daughter Darthula "Sula" Rice continued to run *Idlease* until her own death in 1945. Like her mother before her, Sula raised everything, had her own cows, churned her own butter. Bernice Rice Lowe remembers how she would go down to the creek to catch fresh trout to serve at breakfast to her seven guests who came every summer. Cub Rice recalled how she'd put her guests in a surrey and take them to the View to see the sunrise before breakfast, then feed them hot biscuits, eggs, bacon, and mush (stewed prunes)—all for $7 a week, room and board.

Known today as the old Rice home place in memory of Vinetta and Sula, though originally identified as Aunt Polly's home, the house still exists at the corner of Buck Creek Road and Chaney Lane.

Vinetta with nine of her eleven Rice children. Darthula "Sula" and Susan "Tudie" at the rear, Luther "Luke" on the right. Photo courtesy of Tammy Lowe.

Apart from these few individuals at Short Off, there were others farther down Buck Creek—like David and Margaret Young Rogers, James and Phoebe Peek Holland, and John and Mary Moss Stewart—who lived during the mid 1800s in almost total isolation but with large families to assure their survival under extremely trying conditions. Although the mountains and valleys, which had once been home to the Cherokee Nation, found a number of buyers of cheap state-sponsored land grants, very few of these speculators became homesteaders.

In 1869 Macon Land Company purchased 30,000 acres between the Cowee and Fishhawk Mountains and the Chattooga River, which amounted to a significant portion of the Highlands plateau. But the rest of the land would have to wait until 1875 before anyone would even conceive of founding a town on it, much less expect to fill the town with pioneers brave and hardy enough to live in such a remote godforsaken wilderness.

A Highlands forest in winter. Photo from R. H. Scadin Collection, UNC-A.

2. Where the Lines Cross

If you take a map of the United States and draw a line from Savannah to Chicago and another line from New York to New Orleans, where the lines cross is Highlands.

—Legend of the Founding of Highlands, N.C.

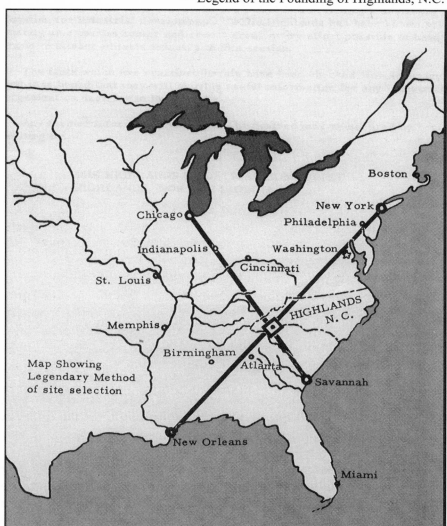

Map of the founding of Highlands. Drawing from Highlands, N.C.: Facts and Figures for Industry, *1956.*

Perched on the highest crest of the western Carolina plateau is the small town of Highlands. It was born on a plateau of the Southern Appalachians

Mountains near the tricorner of North Carolina, South Carolina, and Georgia on the 6th day of March, 1875. A well-known legend of the founding of the town claims that two developers living at the time in Kansas took a map in hand and drew a line from New York to New Orleans. Then they passed another line between Chicago and Savannah. These lines, they predicted, would be the great trade routes of the future, and where they crossed would someday be a great population center.

Whether or not this legend is true, the lines on a map do cross almost at Highlands. What is certain, however, is that these two developers were drawn to this mountainous region by Silas McDowell, a native South Carolinian who spent most of his life in Macon County.[45] McDowell lived southeast of Franklin in a house which he built for his mother in 1820 over the ruins of Sugartown.[46] This was one of thirty-six Cherokee towns that had fallen to the torch during the American Revolution, when Gen. Griffith Rutherford carried out his cruel raids against Indians suspected of siding with the British in 1776. In view of Rutherford's burning of towns, devastation of fertile cornfields, and merciless killings of men and women, the author and historian Wilma Dykeman called his crusade "a scorched earth policy such as even General Sherman of Civil War fame could not equal almost a hundred years later."[47] Rutherford's campaign was the beginning of the end of Cherokee stewardship over the land they had farmed, fished, and hunted for centuries. The very next year witnessed the first of the eight treaties that surrendered it all to the various states.[48]

Sugartown (today's Cullasaja Community at the junction of the Cullasaja River and Ellijay Creek where McDowell established his home) once sat on the bank of the Sugartown River, which we know today as the Cullasaja.[49] Derived from the Cherokee *Kŭlsetsi'yĭ* (abbreviated *Kŭlse'tsi*), Cullasaja meant literally *honey-locust place*, the place or town where the Cherokees grew their *kulsetsi* trees (*Gleditsia triacanthos*), but the nearest English equivalent to Cherokee *honey-locust* was sugar, hence sugartown. So the Europeans called the more properly named Cullasaja River the Sugartown River instead. The Cherokees pronounced the name "Cul-set-see-yuy-eh," which the English corrupted to "Cull'-uh-say'-jah."

In 1844 Joseph Dobson bought his first land grant (today's Highlands) near the headwaters of this Sugartown River far above McDowell's home at Sugartown. Ten years later the river was being called the Sugar Fork of the Little Tennessee River.

McDowell was a self-educated student of geology, mineralogy, zoology, and botany, who worked expertly as a tailor, farmer, court clerk, botanical explorer and guide, as well as writer, historian, and master storyteller. His fascinating, well-told tales served as the basis for Robert Strange's *Eoneguski*, the "first North Carolina novel." His stocky robust build, noble head, stern yet gentle face, and modest manners bore a remarkable resemblance to Sir Walter Scott, another great storyteller, both being of Scotch-Irish blood. As biographer Theodore Davidson described McDowell, he was "endowed with a noble soul, a faithful and tender heart, and a splendid imagination."[50]

McDowell's articles in the Smithsonian Reports of 1856 and in various horticultural publications between 1858 and 1861 were the first to describe the now-famous Thermal Belt in the Southern Appalachians.[51] A genius in the cultivation of apples, he propagated and named about fifteen new varieties, among which were Cullasaja, Nickajack, Ellijay, Chestooah, and others. But beginning with the disastrous freeze of April 28, 1858, which destroyed his orchard of 600 apple trees in the Sugartown River valley and turned him to raising grapes, he noticed a strange phenomenon. Early frosts, such as the one he had just experienced, failed to affect the mountainsides above three hundred and fifty feet. It was as though "a vast green ribbon" of warm dry air stretched above a perfectly horizontal frost line through the entire length of the mountains, a phenomenon of temperature inversion that he identified in western North Carolina as a "verdant zone" or "thermal belt."

This thermal belt or no frost zone was easy to identify in late fall and early spring, for its trees were the first to show green foliage and the last to lose their emerald tint entirely. Fruit within the borders of this zone was generally a sure crop, particularly the apple, grape, melon, pear, peach, and quince. Likewise, cattle and sheep found fair browsing through most of the winter on comparatively level areas within the belt.

McDowell was so moved by his discovery of this frostfree belt that he composed a poem to help people understand the paradox of why the top of a mountain is actually warmer than its base:

The reason why a thing is so,
Is some times very hard to know,
When all the long established laws,
By which we trace effect to cause,
Are wide at fault: and all the rules
That we've been taught by books and schools,
Are some times proved to be a lie,
Where Nature proves an alibi.
A case in point—In April last
When the frost killed all our fruit & mast
As well as our good ladies beans
And scarcely left us polk for greens;
Yet, still the mountains top, & covers,
Preserved the verdure of their groves,
While Peach and Apple, Plumb & Pear
Remain unharmed, abounding there,

And yet the books have taught most clear
That as you reach the atmosphere
The cold's increased, by calculation neat
As is one degree to three hundred feet;
That these facts are so, our senses shocks,
and we'd have you explain the paradox,
And make plain, & clear, the perplexing case,
Why a mountains top is warmer than its base. [52]

For thirty years McDowell tried to promote what he called the Sugartown Highlands near his home, not solely as an agricultural haven, but particularly as a health and summer resort without equal in the South.[53] As early as 1839 he had led the well-known North Carolina botanist Dr. Moses Ashley Curtis on a botanical expedition up to High Falls (today's Dry Falls), Whiteside Rock, and Stooley Mountain. As Dr. Bob Zahner points out, it was on his Sugartown Highlands that McDowell discovered a new species of sunflower, which Curtis named *Helianthus dowellianus* in his honor. On Whiteside Mountain he found the rare Blue Ridge St. John's-wort, originally named in his honor, *Hypericum dowellianum*, but later renamed *buckleyi*. Although McDowell never met the most celebrated American botanist Asa Gray personally, Gray heard about McDowell and requested a number of live specimens of mountain plants, which McDowell shipped him.

Samuel T. Kelsey, himself a horticulturalist, and Clinton C. Hutchinson, a founder of towns, both living in far-off Kansas, took an interest in McDowell's promotion of the Sugartown Highlands and, leaving Kansas, arrived in North Carolina on February 18, 1875. They traveled some six hundred miles through the mountains of the Blue Ridge to assess what the region had to offer.[54] But it was the vision of McDowell, the "Sage of Cullasaja" that inspired them to promote his Sugartown Highlands as a summer resort. They envisioned its bringing together a whole community of fruit growers, farmers, stock raisers, and health seekers. The natural beauty and climate of the region would serve, they believed, as drawing cards for settlers, located as the town would be at the hub of a swiftly developing nation whose roads would naturally radiate from this center.

If McDowell had had the initial vision, Kelsey and Hutchinson had the means to make it reality, which pleased McDowell enormously in his old age. "For thirty years," he wrote, "I have been trying to call attention to these Highlands. I have described these bold surroundings as having no peer in the Southern States, to wit: Whiteside Rock, Short-off Rock, Black Rock, Fodderstack and Stooley Mountains. I have piped and piped, but could get no one to dance, until now! But now, and for all time after this, the Sugartown Highlands will be as a 'city on a hill,' and no longer hidden from the world."[55]

The largest portion of unsettled land at these headwaters of the Sugartown River, known today as the Upper Cullasaja or Mill and Munger Creeks, belonged to a sheep and cattle farmer, Joseph W. Dobson, who made his home southwest of Franklin in the valley of Cartoogechaye.[56] Soon after the last treaty with the Cherokees in 1835, Dobson had requested from the state two land grants on the Highlands plateau. In 1844 land sold for ten cents an acre, which he paid for two tracts totaling 1,280 acres or two square miles.[57] There he grazed his livestock through the mild winters, increasing his purchase by another 300 acres during the following decade. The salt rock, around which his cattle gathered during the summer months still exists in the southwest corner of today's Wright Square. Salt was used by herdsmen of the time to calm their stock, and the rock prevented the salt from soaking into the ground.

There were only five dwellings in the immediate area at the time of Kelsey's and Hutchinson's arrival in March of 1875. Dobson's caretakers, Hugh and Mary Ann Gibson, had a hundred acres, which Hugh had purchased as a state grant in 1848, but they lived in a log cabin on Dobson's purchase.[58]

To the west near Dobson's salt rock stood a vacated single-room log *Law House*, which Jim Webb claimed he and his father, Billy Webb, helped build, as did Frank Hill of Horse Cove. In this small cabin the county sheriff collected taxes, elections took place, and circuit riders preached the Gospel.

Jackson Johnston lived in a log cabin, built about 1850, at today's juncture of Cobb and North Cobb roads of the Highlands Country Club. Legend claims his home was an old Cherokee cabin originally, for the Cherokees never lived in teepees. The front door was assembled with wooden pegs, and the cabin was made of hand-hewn poplar logs. In 1877 Johnston sold his house to Jonathan and Margaret Rogers Ford. Ten years later Judson Cobb bought and enlarged it, calling it *Altadona* (fine lady). Today it belongs to Cason and Nancy Callaway, who have named it *Apple Hill*. The log walls, rock fireplace, and front door in the living room are the only remaining evidence of Johnston's original cabin.

At one time Johnston, like Joseph Dobson, owned a lot of land on the Highlands plateau. In fact, it was Johnston who owned Dobson's Highlands tract for most of 1869 when Dobson was either hard up for money or undecided whether to keep his purchase.[59] Although Dobson bought it back at the end of that year, his son William would turn around and sell it in six years to Hutchinson and Kelsey in 1875.

Jackson Johnston house, built ca. 1850. Photo by R. Henry Scadin, 1895, courtesy of Cason and Nancy Callaway.

Kilpatrick/Rogers home, built ca. 1860, between Dog Mountain and Lake Sequoyah. Photo courtesy of Highlands Historic Inventory.

Jim Russell had had a home since 1853 out today's Dillard Road at Broadway Gap.[60] And Felix Kilpatrick lived in his cabin between Dog Mountain and today's Lake Sequoyah, on land he bought in 1859.[61] This is where Bob Rogers, the father of Noah, Phoebe, Josh, and Nannie, would live after 1881 and the two Rogers homes, discussed earlier in the Introduction, would be joined to it. It is listed in the Highlands Inventory as the house of Noah's wife, Laura Rogers. Until it was dismantled by Tommy Chambers in 2000, it was the oldest unaltered house on the Highlands plateau.

The fifth dwelling in the immediate Highlands area was a bark-covered cabin, which no longer exists on the side of the mountain that still bears its name. It was home to Billy Webb of Tennessee, remembered today as Billy's Cabin.[62] According to Butler Jenkins, Billy was a large, stout Civil War veteran from Tennessee who had killed a man with his fist in a duel and fled across the border to the Highlands plateau. This was during the late 1860s.

Mary McCall Webb, Ruth McCall Webb, Lucinda McCall "Cindy" Webb and a younger sister, probably Jane McCall Smith. Photo by Mary Lapham, 1915, courtesy of Hudson Library archives.

As his family grew, Billy built and moved to a double cabin made of huge logs hewn flat with an axe. Located out the Flat Mountain Road, the two cabins were joined by a dog-trot. In the dog-trot, saddle bags hung on the wall, against which firewood was piled. Lucretia Webb kept her pots and pans hanging around a huge fireplace.

Billy's third and final home, only the chimney of which remains today, was his Indian Hills cabin, which he built in 1875 off Brushy Face Road near its junction with the Walhalla Road. His grave is on this old Webb farm in the family plot. It was here in 1883 that Billy's son Joe Webb (not the Joe Webb—Billy's grandson—that we know today as cabin builder) would be crushed to death by a lodged tree when he was cutting another one to let it down.[63] This cabin, Billy's third, would eventually be owned by Eléonore Raoul and rented to Barney Wilson and his family.

Benson Picklesimer, Old Highlands Hunter. Photo by R. Henry Scadin, 1899, courtesy of Irene James.

Way off to the south, as Highlands was being founded, Benson Picklesimer, the "Old Highlands Hunter" who migrated from Tuckasegee, lived near Clear Creek. Himself one of three Picklesimers who settled on the Tuckasegee River, he had moved to Brevard before leaving for Tennessee. His granddaughter, Irene Picklesimer James, says Benson's father, Abraham, came from Germany and made guns. Working on a gun one day, he saw a black bear down in the field. So "he run him a bullet—they had to make bullets too—and he went down there and killed the bear 'fore he got his gun good and finished." Many of Abraham's and Benson's descendants live in Highlands today.

Between Benson Picklesimer's home and Satulah Mountain, Henson Queen in 1860 bought the mountain that would one day bear his name. He would later sell it to Asbel Madison "Mack" Wilson, who also bought 640 acres surrounding today's Wilson Gap Road.

With the exception of these few homes, and even fewer fertile clearings set aside for grazing, the Highlands plateau on Kelsey's and Hutchinson's arrival lay beneath a heavy growth of forest.[64] Much of it where the town exists today was hidden in a dense laurel thicket, hardly penetrable by anything larger or less supple than a wild cat.

There was one road of sorts, which Silas McDowell had helped build, that passed by his home on the floodplain southeast of Franklin, crossed Buck Creek, climbed through the mountain forest to Short Off Community. Beyond Short Off it dropped into Whiteside Cove. It was known locally as the Franklin–Walhalla wagon road, but it didn't show on any map of the time. There was, of course, a Cherokee trail that only inhabitants of the area knew well enough to avoid being diverted or lost, which followed the longer route up the Sugartown River and then to Short Off.

This was the trail taken by Edward King, the well-known journalist and war correspondent from Massachusetts who was hired by *Scribner's Monthly* in 1872 to explore and report on the reconstructed South. In June, 1873, he traveled from Waynesville by way of Webster and Franklin up the Sugar Fork of the Little Tennessee River to Whiteside Mountain in the Blue Ridge Highlands, two years before the town of Highlands existed.[65]

His guide was the same Silas McDowell whose articles would later attract Kelsey and Hutchinson and who owned land in the highlands. Despite his seventy-eight years, McDowell was as accustomed to finding his way along ancient Cherokee paths as though he were a young Cherokee himself.

King described the trail along which McDowell led him and his companions around the side of Lamb Mountain. Broken by ledges, tangled vines, and underbrush, it was scarcely perceptible, then lost, as the party, walking Indian file, crawled over rocks and dropped into caves and dens which, King claimed, local lore warned abounded with rattlesnakes.

When he asked his seasoned guide for his opinion of the local stories, McDowell replied fiercely, "Sir, I have a contempt for snakes, sir. I kick them out of my way, sir. I kill them before they have a chance to bite me, sir."

Silas McDowell, 1795–1879. Compliments Macon County Historical Society.

Normally one took the wagon road *up* Brush Creek and around Flat Mountain to Short Off, which was the shortcut to the plateau, but McDowell led King's party instead along a lower branch in the trail and *down* Brush

Creek to show them the spectacular falls of Lower Sugar Fork, today's Lower Cullasaja Falls. This side trail met the river near today's Jackson Hole turnoff onto Brush Creek Road.[66] Even before they could catch a glimpse of the river through the dense laurel and trees, King relates that they could hear the distinct roar of the falls. The path descended the river gorge so steeply that, grabbing tree branches for support, they had to swing down to a pool at the base of a great ledge. There, standing knee-deep in the chilly water, they gazed up in awe at the white foam leaping over the jagged summit of the falls.

Lower Sugar Fork Fall in 1873. From Edward King's The Great South.[67]

King described the scene in almost lyric prose, how the river sprang into blinding clouds of spray, dousing the tall trees and living green foliage that clothed the canyon walls. These walls reached up hundreds of feet on either side. Not one, nor two, but several falls poured over a giant hundred-foot staircase that terminated in a final thirty-foot plunge not far below the travelers, bubbling and seething where the current was swiftest and strongest. From the base of the falls it wound in and out among great boulders that had fallen from the high overhanging cliffs and then disappeared into the valley beyond.

Lower Sugar Fork Fall, 1898. Photo by R. Henry Scadin, courtesy of Hudson Library archives. Barak Wright is standing left of center.

Climbing the falls and for several miles farther on, the trail kept the fierce river as its companion, forcing its travelers to ford half a dozen times. Ascending through aisles of grand forest over knolls that rose like whale's backs every few hundred yards, they stopped frequently to catch their breath while McDowell sought his mark on a tree. At one point they entered a pass in the range and found themselves perched precariously at the edge of a great abyss. Here the entire river flung itself in a passionate leap over a great escarpment of gray bare rocks. Tall pines and spruces seventy feet high, we are told, leaned back as though shuddering before the fearful plunge.

These grand upper falls of the Sugar Fork River were known in 1873, like today, as "Dry Falls." Their affect then, as it is now when the whole river thunders over the verge, was to impose a reverent silence over the entire party of travelers. But in 1873 its solitude was breathless. Taking their oil capes, King's party worked their way down a set of rugged steps cut into a cliff and passed under the falls along slippery rocks to emerge facing a monument of solid granite rising dozens of feet from the watery chaos.

The fresh cool air was filled with mist and spray that gleamed in the sunshine, and there were hollows in the stones, which the thundering water had chiseled over centuries to a considerable depth. The magnificence of this astonishing fall moved their souls in such measure, King marveled, that its dazzling luster would linger long after in their memories, like the unforgettable beauty of a priceless diamond.

| *Dry Falls in 1873.*[68] | *Dry Falls in 1876.*[69] |
| *From Edward King,* Great South. | *From Richard Davis, "By-paths of the Mtns."* |

On the other hand, he mused rather prophetically, "the feet of thousands of the curious" would one day wander to these falls and to their brother a few miles below, and the grand solitude would be gone. He basked in the fact that no quack had yet painted "his shameless sign" on the virgin rocks, and the precipices had not yet been "invaded by the mob of the grand tour," so that the solitary voice of Dry Falls in its height, glow, gloom, and glory at this stage in its lonely existence thoroughly shocked and awed his soul.

From Dry Falls to the Highlands plateau was only three more miles, the main trail forking into narrow paths obstructed only by swampy holes and gnarled tree roots. As shadows were just beginning to creep over the mountains, the party arrived at last to spend the night at James Wright's farmhouse beneath the brow of Short Off.

King made his memorable trip one and a half years before Kelsey and Hutchinson appeared on the scene. These two men would retrace the same path to found the little village of Highlands. Unlike King, however, their guide to these rarefied heights would not be McDowell, for by then he was eighty and suffering declining health. Their guide instead was a determined nineteen-year-old adventurer named Charles N. Jenks.

Charlie Jenks, although quite young, was certainly no stranger to the Highlands plateau.[70] Back in 1871, four years after Hiram Crisp, a local shoemaker and farmer, had plowed up the first gemstone-bearing corundum discovered in Macon County, Charlie and his father, Col. Charles W. Jenks of St. Louis, opened the world's first corundum mine down where the Sugartown Creek poured out into the valley, known today as Corundum Hill.[71] There they mined rubies, sapphires, emeralds, amethysts, and topazes to sell to Tiffany's, the British Museum, J. P. Morgan, and Amherst. The mine was a blessing to many men of Macon County, for it gave them much needed work twelve hours a day. Unfortunately for the whole company, however, the money panic of 1872–73 shut the operation down, forcing the frail 95-pound Charlie to search for life outside the mines. He turned to the fresh cool air of the highlands to restore his health.

For three years, on a plateau covered with unbroken primeval forest, he hunted deer and trapped bear from Satulah to Whiteside Mountain. Twice a week he took the shortcut up Brush Creek to Short Off, an invigorating climb from his lodgings at George and Mollie Jacobs' home near the corundum mine. He explored every nook and cranny of the Blue Ridge highlands, headquartering at the home of James Wright, which James' son Barak soon owned in the shadow of Short Off Mountain.

He fished Brush Creek, Buck Creek, and other trout streams and killed, by his own count, twenty-seven black bears, many deer, wild cats, wolves, and panthers. The upshot of all this fresh outdoor air, vigorous exercise, and diet of bear meat, venison, cornbread, potatoes, and cabbage was that he gained sixty pounds of what he called "flesh hard as nails" and an intimate knowledge of the plateau.

He even braved the cave on the perpendicular face of Whiteside, setting traps for bears twice a week during one whole winter. Whiteside, as Edward King described this monarch mountain, was like a "waterfall 2,000 feet high suddenly turned to stone."[72]

Silas McDowell once compared it to "the carcass of some great monster, upon whose head you climb, and along whose mammoth spine you wander, giddy with terror each time you gaze over the skeleton sides." He also likened it to "a huge hog with his snout thrust up to his eyes into a potato ridge." It was on the face of this great precipice not far from the south end, known today as Nose End, that Charlie Jenks and Dave Sloan, author of *Fogy Days and Now; or, The World Has Changed*, found the perilous ledge leading to the cave.

"Nose End" of Whiteside Mountain. Photo by the author, 2000

This cave, as McDowell described it, was high up in the mountain's overhanging face, "one thousand feet above its base, with a mere projecting fissure (at places not eighteen inches wide) for a foot way, leading to it, and nothing for a hand hold but a smooth wall of rock above and below! O, horror! The tree tops away so far below that they look blue and distant." Only a person of strong nerve would dare make the giddy pass and return, ever again to be haunted with "nightmare" dreams.

Whiteside cave in 1873.[73] *From Edward King,* The Great South.

Some sixty years later Charlie described the experience of stepping out upon the narrow two-foot path and turning a corner on eighteen inches with no support above or below. It became one of the most harrowing experiences of his lifetime, no matter how many times he traversed it:

It overlooked at one place a drop of 1,000 feet, and views were obtained that are impossible to be seen from any other point on the mountain. On a later trip one of the men with us fainted as we were returning, but we secured water from a spring at the cave to revive him and helped him to safety. I knew then of only two women who ever attempted and made the trip. They were Mrs. George and Mrs. Ad Jacobs, who dressed for the adventure and traveled the trail safely. Today I could not be induced with all the money in North Carolina to return to Whitesides cave, but youth often is possessed with more daredevilry than sense.[74]

A dark, damp cavity about fifteen feet in width, the cave itself extended far back into the mountain and ended in a narrow passage, which, miner though he was, he never explored. On his first visit, he claimed, he found the remains of an Indian ceremonial fire. He was familiar with Cherokee legends that referred to this cave as the abode of the Great Spirit, as well as the Evil One. If the Great Yellow Jacket of Cherokee mythology or the Devil himself didn't inhabit the cave, the terrible ogress Utlunta (Spear-finger) was reputed to feed here on human livers, as James Mooney would confirm some twenty years later in his *Myths of the Cherokee*.[75]

Perhaps Charlie listened not to the chatter of the deceptive titmouse but the whistle of the honest chickadee, who told him truly not to risk exploring the cave lest he encounter the long, stony spear finger of the ogress and return home without his liver. The legendary Spear-finger had tried to build a great rock bridge through the air from the Hiwassee River to Whiteside, but lightning had struck it, scattering huge fragmented boulders, four or more feet in height, which can still be seen along the base of the ridge. Indeed, some of the rocks from her bridge that fell along the jeep road at the base of Whiteside were as large as a house, towering thirty to forty feet into the air.[76] Forever since, Spear-finger has haunted these mountains, always looking for fresh victims to satisfy her insatiable hunger.

If Spear-finger didn't haunt Charlie after he left his home in Macon County, misfortune nevertheless did. In 1888, while living in Asheville, he helped to organize the Western North Carolina Mining and Improvement Company, which bought all the land now known as Sapphire Valley. But the Panic of 1893 plunged him into bankruptcy and drove him to Europe.

There he attempted to found a world corundum company, but the invention of Carborundum—an artificial corundum—totally thwarted his grandiose plan. Eventually he left in quest of bauxite in South America. This adventure led him ultimately into the jungles of British, Dutch, and French Guiana, fraught with the dangers of poisonous insects and snakes, tropical diseases, and desperate escapees from France's penal colony—far more real than any imagined danger that Spear-finger might have posed.

Rock from Spear-finger's bridge at Whiteside base. Photo by the author, 2000.

It was twenty years prior to Charlie's fiascos and eventual plunge into the jungle when he stood with Kelsey and Hutchinson on the summit of Satulah Mountain on March 6, 1875, and pointed out far below the best location for their dream of a town. Satulah, known locally as Stuley or Stooly, was unique among mountains in the area due to its deceptive appearance.[77] It sloped to the north so gently that anyone viewing it from the Highlands plateau would hardly suspect it had so stern a southern face, an almost vertical precipice of hard granite, glittering with millions of minute particles of soft mica.

Southern cliffs of Satulah Mountain. Photo by the author, 2001.

From the southern summit, above the sheer drop, stretched the receding levels of Georgia and a clear, calm view of Rabun Bald. The photographer Henry Scadin would know this vantage point much later as the Sea of Views. At Satulah's east shoulder stood Fodderstack, which the Cherokees called *Gâ·te·gwâ'hĭ* (great-swamp or great-thicket place), beneath which bears were said to perform their annual hibernation dance.[78] Then came Black Rock and to the northeast the lofty peak of Whiteside with its sheer and terrible chalk-like wall and gorilla-like visage facing the sharp cliffs of Chimney Top to the east. Beyond stretched countless ridges into the Balsam and Pisgah Ranges. To the west of Whiteside stood Bear Pen, so named after the bears that were once actually penned there. Behind Bear Pen stretched the bold form of Short Off, conspicuously shorted off at its northeastern end. And over Short Off's western shoulder peered Yellow Mountain, flanked by the Fish Hawks, themselves stamped against the lovely Nantahala Range crowning the western horizon.

Surrounded by these peaks as though cradled in the palm of a huge hand, one-and-a-half miles wide and reaching three miles from Satulah to Short Off, lay the plateau on which Kelsey and Hutchinson would soon build their Highlands. John Jay Smith, in his account of the town's founding, claimed that Kelsey "named Highlands from the fact that it was some four thousand feet above sea level."[79] Smith wouldn't have known that Silas McDowell had been calling the area "Highlands" and the "Sugartown Highlands" since the 1840s. In any event, perched as it was atop a table land amid the sunny slopes of its surrounding sentinels, it would one day be touted as the highest incorporated town in eastern America.

Waters from this high natural Blue Ridge Divide descended ultimately into the level plains of both the Atlantic and Gulf coasts. The headwaters of the river Chattooga[80] sprang fresh from the heart of Whiteside Mountain and, joined by the Tallulah, poured into the Savannah River on its eastern course to the Atlantic. The Little Tennessee River, with its principal tributaries, the Tuckasegee,[81] Cullasaja, and Nantahala,[82] flowed west into the Tennessee, Ohio, and Mississippi Rivers en route to the Gulf. With an average annual rainfall of eighty-eight inches, exceeded in the United States only by a small section of the northwest Pacific Coast, the drainage of the streams on either side of the Highlands plateau contributed to the water flow of eastern America.

As Kelsey, Hutchinson, and Jenks looked out over this forested paradise fed by pure, cold, soft-water springs, Charlie pulled a compass from his pocket, and the three men commenced to visualize a town. They reckoned an east–west line for Main Street from the eastern drop into Horse Cove to the Sugartown cascades in the west. A north-south road would bisect Main Street to connect Bear Pen with Satulah. And where the two roads crossed would be the center of town. Hutchinson picked a forty-acre parcel of land north of Main where he would one day build his home, leaving Kelsey forty acres to the south.

Charlie's compass, given to the Hudson Library in 1925 by Kelsey's son Dr. Harlan Kelsey, is still on display in its attractive case as a valued treasure of Highlands' early days. His survey in 1875 was the first applied to the area. Kelsey's purchase of the town from Hutchinson three years later would, of course, necessitate a more thorough survey, which Charles Slagle would help complete during one week in June, 1878.[83]

In the meantime, Kelsey and Hutchinson set about creating a town. In the following year, during the fall of 1876, the great journalist and novelist Richard Harding Davis, having arranged a tour of the southern mountains, decided to pay a visit to the new town of Highlands still in its embryonic stage.[84]

In writing for *Harper's New Monthly Magazine*, however, he bemoaned the tremendous difficulties of trying to follow the "wretched road" up the mountain. It was the same Cherokee path that Edward King, guided by McDowell, and Kelsey and Hutchinson, guided by Jenks, had scaled from the foot of the Blue Ridge to the headwaters of the Sugar Fork, a torturous climb indeed to the high plateau.

Richard Harding Davis.

Upon his arrival in the new town Davis met Mr. Kelsey but lodged with Dobson's caretakers, Huey and Ann Gibson, who lived in the single-room log cabin across the creek from Kelsey's home.[85] Neither Huey nor Ann could write, he reported, for they were simple folk, but what impressed him more were their rugged honesty and open friendliness. He admired how Ann kept her mountain home spotlessly clean. Her husband explained as how she "got shet of the fleas by scalding the floor" with hot water.[86]

Davis spent ten days in the Highlands area. It was four years before his article finally appeared in *Harper's New Monthly*, including a character sketch and lithograph of Huey and Ann seated by the fire, chairs tilted back, both drawing on corncob pipes. Included were lithographs of Cullasaja Falls (his name for Dry Falls) and Whitesides Mountain, as he called it.

Huey and Ann Gibson, Autumn, 1876. From By-Paths in the Mountains.[87]

Before taking his leave from his hosts in Highlands, Davis recalled how he gave the Gibsons something they'd never seen before: an alarm clock. He wound it up for them, set it, and placed it on the rock ledge over the fireplace. Then he departed. Sometime after the Gibsons retired, Ann awoke with a terrified start at an unearthly clamor ringing in her ears. Sitting bolt upright in bed, she shook her man, still dead to the world, and croaked, "Huey! Huey! Get up and git yer gun! Thar's a varmint in the house!" We aren't told if Huey, stumbling half-asleep in the dark, shot the clock, but we do know that the varmint, winding down, must have eventually departed on its own.

3. A Convenience Center

Insects are very scarce here, owing largely, as we suppose, to the great number and variety of our birds. Mosquitoes—that great pest of wooded countries generally, and low countries, everywhere—are never found on these highlands. There are few flies to harm man or beast. No grasshoppers to injure the crops. No Chinch bugs, potato bugs or canker worms. There are some of the round-headed borers in neglected orchards, but we have examined dozens of neglected orchards and failed to find the work of a single flat-headed borer.
　　　　—S. T. Kelsey, *Blue Ridge Highlands in Western N.C., 1876.*

It was Hutchinson, not Kelsey, who on March 6, 1875, put up the money and signed the deed of purchase for land on the Sugartown Highlands. He borrowed $1,678 to purchase 839 acres, about one-and-a-third square miles, from Joseph Dobson's son, William, who had inherited it. The tract contained parts of all five State Grants purchased earlier by Joseph.[88] In the final analysis, at $2 an acre it was a sound investment, for three years later, he would sell the whole town to Kelsey for $6,000, just over $7 an acre, two and a half times what he paid for it.

The only cleared area of the entire purchase was some fifteen acres stripped of brush where half a hundred apple trees, presumably Joseph or William Dobson's at some earlier time, stood abandoned to the ravages of moss and borers. Hutchinson and Kelsey spent the spring and summer planting about twenty acres of crops and fencing in another hundred for pasture.

By late winter, Kelsey was beginning to visualize the town he now called "Highlands."[89] Fully convinced that the climate of this Blue Ridge plateau was more healthful, and the soil better adapted to fruit growing, than any in the country, he began laying out Main Street in the spring of 1876. He dispatched to every state in the Union a pamphlet entitled, The *Blue Ridge Highlands of Western North Carolina*, which proclaimed the new settlement—elevation above 4,000 feet—as a curative for respiratory ailments and a gardener's paradise.

When Richard Harding Davis arrived in the fall, he marveled at the ill-fated future of the precarious venture. There was something pathetic as well as comic, he wrote, in the gravity with which Kelsey picked his way "through the dense woods, frightening the squirrels as he pointed out 'Main Street,' 'Laurel Avenue,' and the sites for the town hall and churches."[90]

A year later explorers Wilbur Zeigler and Ben Grosscup described Kelsey's ardor as "savoring of monomania" as he "laid out by means of stakes, streets of an incipient city, and talked as though the imaginary avenues of the forests were already lined with peaceful homes and shadowed by the walls and spires of churches."

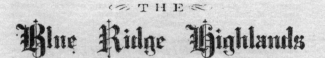

THE
Blue Ridge Highlands
— IN —
WESTERN NORTH CAROLINA.

Superior Fruit, Farming and Grazing Lands—
Grand and Beautiful Scenery—Pure
Air and Pure Water.

NO BETTER CLIMATE IN THE WORLD
— FOR —
HEALTH, COMFORT & ENJOYMENT,
— AND —
NO CLIMATE OR COUNTRY THAT BRINGS SURER RETURNS
— TO THE —
FARMER, FRUIT GROWER OR STOCK RAISER.

No Grasshoppers, Chinch Bugs, Canker Worms or Musquitoes
— TO —
DESTROY CROPS OR PERSONAL COMFORT.

GREENVILLE, S. C.
DAILY NEWS, PAMPHLET AND LAW PRESS.
1876.

Kelsey's 1876 pamphlet, "The Blue Ridge Highlands"

This paradisial settlement, however, as Kelsey viewed it, wasn't intended as "a commercial town."[91] In seeking to attract "good citizens," he billed it instead as "a convenience center," providing a post office, stores, shops, a schoolhouse, churches, hotels, etc. for its settlers. Occupying a central position on the highlands, from which good carriage roads could be built, it embraced all the grandest scenery of the surrounding country as an aid to the restoration of health and soul.

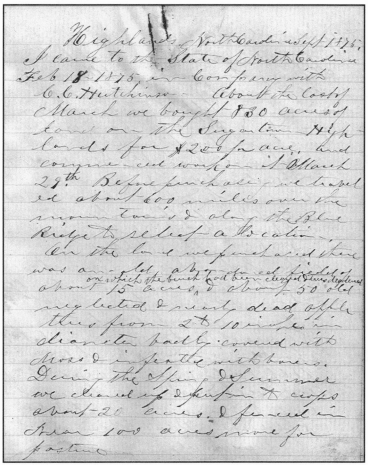

First page of Kelsey's diary about the founding of Highlands

No doubt Kelsey's intentions were honorable, for he was a horticulturist and forest conservationist but at the same time a consummate promoter. His ambitious plans for the town carried deep within them the seeds of conflict that have haunted Highlands from the day of its inception, even as they have divided many another small community throughout modern America as populations inevitably grow. Highlanders today still grapple with the unresolved question inherent in Kelsey's character: can the love of natural beauty and the desire for community development coexist? Or are they mutually exclusive?

A big tree in the primeval forest. Photo by George Masa, 1929.

Various observers of this on-going clash between ecologists and developers have recognized turning points in Highland's history, many of which have been feared as irreversible. Early on, it was the great botanists Bartram along with Michaux and Gray who appreciated the unspoiled beauty of these upper mountains. William Bartram, whose father, John, was a Philadelphia botanist and friend of Benjamin Franklin, was himself a friend of Thomas Jefferson and explored the southern Appalachians, passing through the Vale of Cowee, modern Macon County, in the spring of 1776. His account of his *Travels* was much admired by English Romantic writers, such as Coleridge, Wordsworth, Lamb, and Carlyle, who drew on his thoughts and observations.

The French botanist André Michaux made five journeys our way between 1787 and 1794; and Harvard Professor Asa Gray visited several times beginning as early as 1838, his last visit occurring in 1879. These men came to admire and observe ferns, fungi, orchids, white and pink rhododendron, and blazing azalea against every imaginable shade of green, but their coming and going had no perceptible effect on the natural environment.

So in a primary sense Kelsey, with Hutchinson's support, gave birth to the first significant turning point in the area's natural history with his founding of the town. Compass in hand, he and his companions surveyed and civilized 325 parcels of primeval forest. In time, even as streets were carved into the landscape, they were named after gigantic trees that had to be felled to accommodate them: Oak, Maple, Pine, Spruce, Laurel, Chestnut, Hickory, and Poplar.

The well-known North Carolina author Wilma Dykeman has clearly depicted this conflict in the human psyche as two opposing attitudes of place. The two most famous explorers of the area, she contends, were William Bartram and Hernando de Soto. What she regards as the Bartram attitude seeks to leave something of the beauty of a place for future generations to appreciate and enjoy. But the de Soto attitude, in its determination to conquer and rule, succeeds only in ruining the country sides, towns, and cities to the extent that years are required, often decades, to restore to a place the often irretrievable loss of its original and essential beauty. The difference lies in whether the encroaching explorer is exploiter or discoverer: the one, bent on active change; the other, on passive appreciation without thought of change.

In line with Mrs. Dykeman's concerns, it would be quite appropriate to replace the two current markers along Main Street honoring de Soto and Juan Carlos, who did not pass through Highlands, with historically accurate markers celebrating Bartram and Michaux, who did pass quite near Highlands but like proper Boy Scouts left no sign at all of their passage.

Regardless of which attitude one takes toward this issue, Kelsey appears to have incorporated within himself some of both perspectives: Bartram's and de Soto's. Born on November 14, 1832, in a small town about fifty miles northwest of New York City, named Florida—a name particularly ironic for Highlands—he was fifth in a family of thirteen children, who all moved to a farm in Cattaraugus County four hundred miles west of New York City and sixty miles south of Buffalo. The Kelseys were descendants of William Kelsey the Puritan, who immigrated to America from Chelmsford, Essex County, England as a founding settler of New Towne (now Cambridge), Massachusetts, in 1632 and New Towne (now Hartford), Connecticut, in 1636.[92]

During Little Sammy's early years and throughout his teens the Kelsey home was surrounded by virgin forests, wild woods where he and his brothers and sisters played and explored.[93] A crystal clear brook, the pride and glory of the valley, provided the family with an endless supply of speckled trout.

Of chief interest to Sammy, however, was an Early Harvest grafted apple tree that grew in his father's orchard.[94] The fruit of that tree tasted so good in contrast to the hard unsavory apples on all the other trees that he figured every farm should have apples like that in their orchards. And one day he would be the individual to grow and sell them. At age twelve he decided to make his fortune as a great nurseryman and benefactor to his country.

To this end, his father gave him a small piece of land, and he immediately set about collecting bright plump apple seeds, which he planted in well-prepared soil. With high hopes for his first nursery, he came home one day to find to his horror that it was plowed under with the rest of the farmland, utterly ruined. For young Sammy it was a crushing blow! So severe, in fact, that Sammy promptly gave up becoming a great nurseryman in the East, where no one seemed to care! He swore instead that, when he became twenty-one, he would go west to the Great American Desert, to the territory now known as Kansas which he'd read about in his school geography, and become a nurseryman there.

Meanwhile, as is often the case where natural beauty is suddenly valued as capital, commercialism discovered western New York, even as today it has invaded pristine areas across the United States and brought with it ruthless change on a grand scale. The railroad was slicing its way through the once-unconquerable wilderness of Southwestern New York. Lumberjacks leveled the big trees, alternately flooding and drying up Kelsey Creek and leaving behind slimy pools inhabited by bullfrogs, elfish snakes, and mosquitoes and enough silt to clog the family mill. Soon settlers swarmed in, clear cutting what remained of the understories for their homes and fields.

It was the irreparable devastation of his lovely homeland that ultimately drove the distraught young Kelsey into the study and practice of forestry. Salvaging all the remaining seedlings he could glean from the ruins of his homeland, he transplanted them to Bloomington, Illinois, where at twenty-one he began work for F. K. Phoenix Nursery, gathering healthy seedlings from eastern and northern forests and planting them on the barren Midwestern prairies. While in Bloomington he met an upstart young lawyer named Abraham Lincoln, befriended another named Daniel Webster, and married Katherine "Katy" E. Ricksecker.

During Kelsey's stay in Illinois, an incident occurred that would profoundly affect his decision, years later, to move to North Carolina. At a meeting of the American Pomological Society in Rochester, New York, he saw an exhibition of fruits—principally apples—grown by Westbrook and Mendenhall of Greensboro, N.C. In size, beauty, and flavor they proved far superior to any apples grown anywhere in the North. Fruit growers above the Mason-Dixon line, who never suspected that North Carolina could produce anything but tar, were astonished. In the back of his mind Kelsey began to entertain the notion that the high lands of North Carolina, with their mild winters and longer seasons, might be the ideal site for a profitable nursery business in apples.

In the meantime, however, he accepted a call in 1865 from the University at Ottawa, Kansas, to plant its 15,000 acres of prairie with forests, fruit orchards, and ornamental trees. Ottawa had just been founded by a Vermonter, a year younger than Kelsey, whom he met, named Clinton C. Hutchinson.

Able to plant elms, soft maples, and other shade trees that transformed Ottawa from a bleak and desolate treeless plain into the City Beautiful of the West, Kelsey was eager to take on a new project. He solicited the financial support of John H. Whetstone and bought 12,000 acres of land on which he planted 100 miles of Osage Orange hedgerows—as barbed wire had not yet been invented—and half a million plants. He then built himself a mill and a house so that he and Katy and their first child, Laura Olin (who would one day marry Augustus Barr and later Ansel Ogden), became the first citizens of Pomona, named from pomology, the science and practice of fruit growing.[95] Before the new town could thrive, however, the Country was plunged into a severe depression. People burned their corn for fuel. Kelsey sold three thousand bushels at eight cents each, but couldn't even give away his potatoes.

It was all he needed to drive him away from Kansas to North Carolina, but before he left, he hired on as a surveyor for the Atchison, Topeka, and Santa Fe Railway Company. This gave him not only much needed employment at $200 a month but also valuable experience in the establishment of experimental stations across the state, as well as some familiarity with railroads, an awareness that would prove very useful some thirty years hence in his connection with Highlands.

Throughout all these activities Kelsey's real interests lay in founding towns and organizations. He helped organize the Kansas State Horticultural Society in 1868, serving as its corresponding secretary. In 1871 he joined with Hutchinson to found the industrial town of Hutchinson, Kansas. It was three years later, February 10, 1875, that he and Hutchinson departed Kansas to establish another town, high in the forested mountains of western North Carolina, exploring the area around Rabun Gap in Georgia, then turning north to log six hundred miles over the Blue Ridge in search of the perfect site.[96] The site they eventually chose would become the first summer resort in the Blue Ridge, now known as Highlands.

Samuel Truman Kelsey 1832–1921. Photo courtesy of Sky Campbell.

The arrival in May, 1875, of his wife, daughter Laura, and three sons—Samuel Truman, Jr., the twins Harlan Page and Harry Estes, affectionately known as Bop and Harry—found him hard at work building his new home. While his family boarded with Stanhope Hill in Horse Cove, Kelsey constructed a house and barn on the south side of Main Street, across from today's Hudson Library, aided by Tom Keener and John Teague.

The house had a central hall, parlor, living room, and dining room downstairs, in back of which was a wing containing a butler's pantry, kitchen, and back porch. Upstairs housed three bedrooms with two large closets. Kelsey figured the cost of building the house at $350 plus $100 for the barn. His family moved to Highlands in mid June, and within two years he and

Katy had had their fifth child, Edith Browning (later Mrs. J. Clarence Hodges). Edith was born in their new home on May 23, 1878, the next child after Al McKinney to be born in the new town.

Sam Kelsey's home, built in 1875, burned in 1976. Photo from Bill Marett, Courage at Fool's Rock.

Kanonah Lodge—as this house would become known years later under Miss Minnie Warren's ownership—would have been the oldest house built in Highlands had it not burned to the ground in 1976.[97] Belonging at the time to Steve Potts and occupied by the *Good House*, a local entertainment and dining group, it caught fire in the early hours of October 22nd. Sparks from a newly installed wood stove drifted up the chimney to a second–floor flue, which had been boarded over for decoration, and destroyed the inside of the house before firemen, fighting freezing temperatures and high winds, could extinguish it. A sturdy stone chimney is all that remains today as sole testimony to the solid construction during those early days of Highlands. Originally built by Hanson McCall, who walked five miles each day to earn his dollar, the stones were laid with such consummate skill that the joints, like those in dry wall, show no mortar. It's the oldest chimney in Highlands.

Kelsey lived with his family in Highlands for fifteen years, during which time he worked long and hard on the roads, engaged in civic matters, traveled extensively to surrounding towns to promote Highlands abroad and to scout the possibility of bringing the railroad up the mountain.

Eight years into his stay in Highlands a lake was proposed below his and Squire Hill's properties that still exists today.[98] In late 1883 it was intended to cover approximately thirty acres of marshland overgrown with laurel, hemlocks, and other bramble, and it would reach a depth of seven to eight feet. Known today as Harris Lake, after Rebecca Harris who owned the land from the twenties through the forties, it was Harbison Lake when the Professor lived there and Kanonah Lake during Rebecca Harris' lifetime. It was rebuilt and named after her when the Potts brothers and Will Edwards bought it and the surrounding hundred acres in 1958.

Third page of Kelsey's diary about the building of his house

For Kelsey in the 1880s the lake provided much needed water for his nursery. He attended his trees daily with meticulous care, even washing them with lime soap and sulfur to keep the rabbits from gnawing them.[99] A specialty of his nursery, incidentally, was well-grown apple trees. No doubt reminded of the broken dream of his own childhood, he gave his thirteen-year-old son Harlan in 1885 a half-acre plot of land on which to found his own nursery. When Harlan issued a catalogue the next year, he was already considered "the youngest nurseryman" in America![100] The Kelsey–Highlands Nursery would eventually contain over six hundred species laid out in blocks across a hundred acres below the brow of Sunset Rocks (or Sunset Rock, as the outcrop is also often called).

The Kelsey–Highlands Nursery of Highlands 1885–1920.

It must have been a curious sight to the people of the surrounding mountains, who wondered at the notion of selling trees and shrubbery from a nursery. The idea that a business could be made from planting the very thing they'd had to fight all their lives with mattock, axe, and fire was certainly strange if not totally eccentric.

Why Kelsey left Highlands to found Linville, N.C., in 1890 is not certain. Perhaps he'd given up hope of convincing the railroad to come through Highlands. The last meeting of the Highlands Rail Road Company was in November, 1887. In 1890 Macon County was soliciting votes for a railroad bond that Highlanders felt would tax them without benefit since Franklin expected the railroad to come to them. Col. Boone was still pushing for a Highlands railroad as late as 1896, ten years before its actual extension to Franklin, but Kelsey was long gone by then.

This speculation about Kelsey's leaving Highlands assumes, of course, that the Ku Klux Klan had little or nothing to do with it, as might be otherwise inferred from the threat he received, as quoted below in another context. Whatever his reasons for abandoning Highlands in 1890, he and Harlan left their nursery in the care of Thomas F. Parker, Prioleau Ravenel's stepson, under whose supervision it continued to thrive until its closing in 1920.

Kelsey gave half interest in all his town property, apart from the nursery, to his son S. T. "Truman" Kelsey, Jr., who three years later sold out to H. M. Bascom. That was the year, 1893, that Kelsey resigned in absentia as town councilman and Prof. Thomas G. Harbison bought and occupied his home place.

Once he had made up his mind to found Linville, Kelsey poured into his new venture the same enthusiasm he had devoted to founding Highlands. He turned again to his friend Hutchinson for financial backing, just as he had in their acquisition of land on the Highlands plateau.[101] In this instance, however, Hutchinson was unable to provide the funds, so Kelsey turned to Highlands resident Henry Stewart, associate editor of the *New York Times* and owner of a considerable amount of property in and around the town, who agreed to finance the purchase. But when Stewart too broke with Kelsey, he approached Highlands summer resident Prioleau Ravenel.

In the end it was Ravenel who put up the necessary $500 to establish the Linville Improvement Company to purchase land and lay out a resort village. Principal stockholders were Ravenel, Kelsey, and Donald MacRae of Wilmington, N.C. Almost immediately the Linville Improvement Company began constructing one of the most beautiful roads in the state. Known as the Yonahlossie turnpike (N.C. 221), it skirted the southern slope of Grandfather Mountain from Linville to Blowing Rock. Twenty miles long and ten to fourteen feet wide, it cost about $10,000 to build. Kelsey, who supervised bush crews and log crews of 300 men from 1890 to 1891, intended for the new road to attract prospective residents to Linville from the east. Aware that the railroad would soon reach to within two miles of Linville in the west, he began promoting the new town far and wide, just as he had touted Highlands for its natural beauty and the healthfulness of its location and climate.

For a while, with the completion of a fine hotel at the site of today's Eseeola Lodge and a large dam for a lake, the project appeared destined to succeed, but serious disagreements broke out among the three directors over what Linville should become. MacRae's interest lay primarily in connecting the town with the railroad, Kelsey wanted to create an industrial center, and Ravenel wanted a health and pleasure resort, like his beloved summer home of Highlands. In time Kelsey sided with MacRae, and a legal dispute erupted that lasted over four long years. It ended when MacRae bought out Ravenel's interest, giving him a majority of the stock and the balance of power.

Alas! Too much time had elapsed, and the golden moment for Linville's glory had passed. Large numbers of people, arriving in response to the publicity and seeking prime lots on which to build cottages, found to their dismay that the land in Linville was tied up in litigation. So the boom shifted to neighboring Blowing Rock at the other end of the new turnpike where land was readily available a mere twenty miles to the east. By default the little hamlet of Blowing Rock suddenly blossomed into the fine health and pleasure resort that Linville had vaingloriously dreamed of becoming.

Actually it may be to Linville's benefit that it never achieved its original dream of becoming a population center. It remains today a small town, whose fame lies in the shadow of nearby Grandfather Mountain, where each July the internationally famous Highland Games are played out on MacRae Meadow, and for only a short while the overflow fills the town to capacity with kilted competitors and enthusiastic spectators in lieu of perpetual tourists, visitors, and home and health seekers.

The Kelsey–Highlands Nursery in Linville, built in 1892, now abandoned. Photo by the author, 2000.

Although Linville never developed into the industrial center that Kelsey had envisioned, the Kelsey–Highlands Nursery, which he and Harlan had founded in Highlands in 1885 and established in Linville in 1892 survived as the family's enduring legacy to both towns. Initially they had to endure in Linville the same confusion of the inhabitants surrounding that town as had confronted them in Highlands. An older citizen of Linville admonished Kelsey's son Harlan, "Kelsey, you look to me like a man of good sense. What in the world do you mean by coming up here in these mountains and planting shrubbery in a garden when there's worlds of it growing all around?" Undaunted, Harlan hired on a fourteen-year-old aid, Ed Robbins, confident as he was of his own auspicious beginnings in the nursery business at such a young and unprejudiced age.

In 1912 Harlan started a third Kelsey–Highlands Nursery on a ninety-acre farm he purchased in Boxford, Massachusetts. After the closing of the Highlands branch in 1920, he turned his attentions fulltime to his flourishing business in Massachusetts. Ed Robbins, who still worked the Linville nursery, bought it out, renaming it Gardens of the Blue Ridge, the name it bears today under the care of his granddaughter Katy and Paul Fletcher and their son Robyn.

By 1910 Sam Kelsey had retired to his son Harlan's Salem, Massachusetts home, where on Nov. 5, 1921, he died just short of his 89th birthday.[102] After his father's death, it was Harlan who carried the banner of his heritage into establishing himself as a national figure in horticulture, conservation, and landscape architecture.[103] His own legacy to America, in addition to his work as a nurseryman, was his contribution to plant nomenclature in the 1924 publication of *Standardized Plant Names*. Furthermore, he helped develope the Arnold Arboretum of Harvard University, particularly with his creation of Carolina Hemlock Hill. He was one of the founders of the Appalachian Mountain Club, which built the Appalachian Trail from Maine to Georgia. He became a driving force in acquiring land and establishing the Great Smoky Mountains National Park as well as the Shenandoah National Park, two heritages he considered "far too precious to turn over to the exploiter armed with ax and saw, to devastate and despoil." As a pioneer in city planning, he prepared city landscape plans for Columbia and Greenville, S.C., and Salem, Mass.

At the time of his death in 1958 Harlan had carried his father's interests in horticulture, including his talents as developer, to impressive heights of achievement. As landscape architect, conservationist, and developer of national, state, and municipal parks as well as plant nomenclature, the recognition that he acquired was as widespread as it was truly remarkable.

Equally remarkable were the achievements of Harlan's brother, Dr. Harry E. Kelsey, but the national recognition he received as a dentist for his pioneer work in odontology falls outside the restricted focus of this history of Highlands.

Clinton Carter "C. C." Hutchinson was the man who, on March 6, 1875, borrowed the money to buy the proposed town of Highlands. Himself the son of a map maker, he was forty-one when he made his purchase. He was born in Bernard, Vermont, on December 11, 1833. When he was twenty, he spent a couple of years in Chicago selling real estate. In his move to Topeka, Kansas, he met and married Martha Young, the beginning of a happiness that was doomed from the outset to be short-lived. Soon after the birth of their son Arthur Herbert in 1859, Martha died.

For the next two years Hutchinson served as the first pastor of the Topeka Baptist Church. Also engaged in real estate and immigration, he founded the town of Ottawa in 1966. In November, 1871, by making a deal with the Santa Fe Railroad to establish a community where the railroad was to cross the Arkansas River, he founded Hutchinson, Kansas, named in his honor. He bought one square mile of land at $15 an acre, which, lacking stones, had to be laid out with buffalo bones as markers.

Clinton Carter "Hutchinson, C. C." 1833–1909

To keep the town quiet rather than wild and wooly like its frontier sisters Wichita, Dodge City, and Abilene, he had a law passed in the legislature which prohibited cattle drives through Reno County. He also exercised his Baptist opposition to strong drink by stipulating in city deeds that if alcoholic beverages were sold or consumed on purchased property, the land would revert to him. Eventually the town of Hutchinson would become a railroad center for the Santa Fe, Rock Island, and Missouri Pacific lines, as well as an industrial center when it was discovered that Hutchinson had founded it on the world's largest deposit of salt.

The federal government appointed Hutchinson agent for the Sac, Fox, Chippewa, Munsee, and Ottawa Indians. With a grant of $50,000 in hand from the New York legislature, he and the Rev. Isaac Kalloch organized Roger Williams University. Then on 20,000 acres of Indian Reservation they built Ottawa University. With a subsidy from the Kansas Legislature, Hutchinson compiled and published *Hutchinson's Resources of Kansas, Fifteen Years Experience*, which led to his election in 1872 to the state legislature.

As an elected official, he supported improving the state's streets and highways with an experimental binder called "macadam." He promoted agriculture by organizing and leading the state's first Grange of Patrons of Husbandry. His prediction that plowing deeply and drilling seeds early would make Kansas the future winter wheat storehouse of America proved prophetic. What disturbed him most, however, was the persistent Eastern misconception that Kansas was still part of the Great American Desert.

All his accomplishments he achieved before 1873, for in that year Republican Representative Hutchinson married Gertrude Sherman. If Gertrude had any dreams of settling down, they were soon frustrated, for before long he was unfolding to her in glowing terms his personal dream, which he and his friend Sam Kelsey had formed, to build a town somewhere in the southeastern United States. Like Kelsey, Hutchinson's interest in Western N.C. was inspired by Silas McDowell's writings about the Thermal Belt.

It was not long after Hutchinson's purchase of the Highlands tract in March, 1875, that he returned to Kansas to retrieve Kelsey's family. During that first summer he helped Kelsey clear land before departing again for Kansas in October, giving his friend power of attorney over his holdings until Kelsey could afford to buy them all in July, 1878. During the fall he returned with his wife and son Reno and commenced building his home. By the spring of 1879, he had bought back half interest in the town.

In the manner that was to become a Highlands tradition, he gave his home a name: Corrymela.[104] He had the foundation built out of the giant oak trees on his property, which, when split down the middle lengthwise and dropped into eight-foot rock-lined trenches, would last till doomsday, as Dr. Frost used to tell his grandchildren.

If it wasn't clear by now that Hutchinson couldn't stay in one place for long, he left again with his family, which now included son Reno and daughter Gertrude (later Mrs. Ernest MacNaughton), in the spring of 1879 to settle unfinished business in Kansas and never returned. By the fall of 1880 his beautiful unfinished home had been sold to Dr. Charles Frost, just arriving from New York. It was Frost who would finish the house on Hutchinson's solid foundations. Constructed with massive hand-squared white pine logs placed upright as was done in old time stockades, its walls were then weather boarded on the inside and clap boarded on the outside to avoid the rough appearance of a stockade. Even in the strongest winds, it is said, this sturdy home never trembled. Now known as the old Farnsworth place, it is owned by Neal Allen and still stands on the north side of Main east of the Hudson Library.

Hutchinson home: Corrymela, begun in 1878, finished by Dr. Frost in 1880, here owned by T. T. Hall after 1890. Photo courtesy of Hudson Library archives.

Hutchinson sold half his interest in the town to his wife's brother Carlos Sherman and wife Clara, both of Rutland County, Vermont. By 1883, however, neither he nor the Shermans had any more interest in Highlands, for what remained unpurchased belonged wholly to Kelsey. All told, Hutchinson dwelt in Highlands little more than a year: the spring and summer of 1875 as he helped in the town's founding, and from the fall of 1878 to the spring of 1879, while he was building and living in his home.

After the Hutchinsons left Highlands, it wasn't long before they were on the move again from Kansas, this time to eastern Oregon. Still as enterprising as ever, Hutchinson built Oregon's first irrigation project with the aid of eastern capital and a federal grant. Throughout his long life he was involved in one way or another in creative projects. But for all he did to help create towns and improve living conditions among his fellows in the East as well as the West, it's a sad commentary that at 75, on May 10, 1909, he died penniless, recognized but broke, in Portland, Oregon.

Hutchinson's sojourns in Highlands amounted more to checking in and out of a health resort than to remaining long enough to leave any personal mark on the community or its inhabitants. His home remains his only enduring legacy. It was his friend Sam Kelsey, who played a more substantial role in the growth and welfare of the fledgling community during the fifteen years that he actively served Highlands.

It's to Kelsey's credit that he sought to bring the right kind of people to his Shangri-la. Himself a Yankee, he was well aware of the uncertainties that a Northerner might feel about coming South so soon after the uncivil war. Perhaps he'd met Uncle Billy McCoy, who lived at the time in the Gold Mine section near Highlands and had seen Sherman's Army when he visited Tennessee. Ask him what he thought about the Civil War, and he'd have said, "There weren't nothing civil about it!"

Years later his great niece Aunt Mett Picklesimer Brooks would tell you there were two groups in that war: the North and the South, but her granddad Benson Picklesimer didn't want to fight anybody, and Tennessee was a volunteer state where protesters could go and not have to fight. "Everybody was mean back then," Aunt Mett opined. "They'd kill each other."

Kelsey addressed the question of a Northerner's safety in his promotional pamphlet with the qualification that it depended entirely on the individual. What he came for and how he behaved after he got here would be the central deciding factor, because the South had acquired a deep distrust of political shysters from the North. Unscrupulous individuals who sought successfully to get office and steal themselves rich had inspired a righteous hatred among their victims in the South.

North or South, Europe, Asia, or Africa, Kelsey argued—it didn't really matter where one came from, what opinion he held, or what his previous condition so much as that he engaged himself in an honest, respectable pursuit, whether for pleasure or profit. If he behaved himself as any decent citizen should in any country, he'd be well received, kindly treated, and safe from harm. The countryside, he claimed, was sparsely settled by a "hardy, intelligent, kind and hospitable people," who stuck to their tasks of raising corn and vegetables for their families, some farming their small clearings, others tending fine orchards, raising hay and stock, or "making money."[105]

Apart from the warm reception that honest immigrants would receive on their arrival in Highlands, Kelsey praised the hospitable climate as well. Except in cloudy weather, there was no fog, the sky usually sunny—except during the summer season of daily showers—and never a drought sufficient to injure the crops. The temperature seldom rose above eighty in summer or dropped below ten in winter, and never above ninety or under zero.

A real draw for Highlands was the effect the climate produced on anyone seeking improved health. People suffering from pulmonary diseases were known to benefit greatly from the moderately cool and invigorating atmosphere of the high altitude as opposed to the hot, moist, debilitating climate of the southern lowlands or the extreme cold of the northern latitudes. Victims of that formidable disease, influenza, were invited to enjoy restored health in Highlands. Instances of bronchitis, pleurisy, pneumonia, and consumption were quickly cured in this environment, which served also as an escape from the yellow fevers and malarias of the low countries during the summer season.

Fruit farmers were invited to come grow apples unmatched in size, flavor, beauty, and preservative qualities and protected from late freezes by the thermal belt. Plums and cherries fared better here than peaches, pears, and grapes, which abounded at lower altitudes. Stock, sheep, and dairy farmers were offered almost year-round grazing on the plateau, and bees raised on white clover produced a large amount of honey of the best quality.

Although the Blue Ridge Railroad at the time reached only as far as Walhalla,[106] a German settlement founded in 1850 thirty miles to the south, its extension was already proposed to Knoxville, Tennessee, via Rabun Gap and Franklin, a scant fourteen miles from Highlands. In 1876 a passable road ran from Highlands to the railroad in Walhalla.

For the hunter there were deer and wild turkeys and an abundance of rabbits, squirrels, pheasants, and partridges, along with an occasional bear, a few wolves, and wild cats. Snakes were as scarce as insects, only the rattlesnake posing an occasional threat.

For people wishing to live economically, family costs for board in Highlands could be had at only $2.00 to $3.00 per week. Laborers expected a daily wage of fifty cents including board, or seventy-five cents without board. Carpenters and mechanics ran a bit higher, $1.50 a day, while good domestic help earned a dollar a week.

Building a log house was free for the cutting, but good hundred-board-foot lumber of white pine or poplar were available at $1.00 each from the mill. Unimproved land was priced at $1.50 to $3.00 an acre; pasture, orchard, and wood lots, from fifty cents to a dollar, while clearing an acre of its timber ranged from $6.00 to $12.00, or $1.50 to $3.00 just to grub the undergrowth.

The only buildings in Highlands in 1876, according to Kelsey's promotional pamphlet, were the post office and country store of T. Baxter White and two small saw and grist mills, belonging to William Dobson and Arthur House on Mill Creek. A hotel was in the offing and a first-class school already planned.

So a year after its founding, the little village of Highlands was hardly more than a crossroad, and a dirt one at that, with high hopes of attracting good citizens from all parts of the nation, though for the most part they hailed initially from the North, making Highlands a Southern town founded by Yankees.

4. North and South Delightfully Jumbled

At Highlands the birds were a mixed lot, Southerners and Northern -
ers delightfully jumbled: a few Carolina wrens, a single Bewick wren,
Carolina chickadees, Louisiana water thrushes and turkey buzzards,
and on the other side of the account, brown creepers, red -bellied nut-
hatches, black-throated blues, Canada warblers, snow-birds, and
olive-sided flycatchers.
—Bradford Torrey, *World of Green Hills*, 1896.

From its inception soon after the Civil War, Highlands has attracted a wide variety of unique individuals. T. W. Reynolds, in his book *High Lands*, called the community "a Southern Mountain Town Founded by Northerners." And it's true that so soon after our national tragedy where brother slaughtered brother, this mountain town evolved into a unique mingling of the Blue and the Gray. By 1883, what might otherwise have become a typically provincial Southern town was comprised instead of residents from twenty-seven states of the Union.[107]

1875

At the outset, however, growth in the little town proceeded at a rate that proved agonizingly slow. The first settler didn't arrive until a few months after Highlands' founding in 1875. T. Baxter White, a forty-one year old native of Marblehead, Massachusetts, was traveling west when he happened to pass through New York and heard about the new town from Henry Stewart, associate editor of the *New York Times*. So White, a former shoemaker and farmer, came to Highlands to check it out, liked it, and stayed.[108]

He built a white house "without doors and windows" on the south side of Main Street, which would serve as the town's first post office and country store. Years later this would be the site of Dr. Moreland's residence, now Town Square.[109] On July 10, 1875, he and his family moved in, and within a week were offering a few staple groceries for sale. For the next several years White's enterprise would be the entire business section of the town. He stocked groceries, dry goods, boots, shoes, galoshes, hats, notions, and stationery. He prided his canned goods as prepared by some of the best packers in the country, including lobsters, mackerel, oysters, peaches, corn, peas, pears, beef, beef tongue, and Boston baked beans. He touted the natural taste of his evaporated peaches and pears and the high quality of his teas and coffee.

Until the post office opened on January 1, 1876, citizens of the new town had to walk or ride horseback the four miles down into Horse Cove and back for their mail. But after White's appointment as postmaster and for the next thirteen years, he was seen daily on the trail between Highlands and Horse Cove, his large frame mounted on horseback, pockets bulging with the mail.

1876

McKinney Family Portrait. Photo courtesy of Doris Potts.
1ˢᵗ row: Margaret and Carl McKinney; 2ⁿᵈ row: Wendel McKinney holding Mary, Charlie holding Kenneth, John Palmer & Margaret Jane Gribble McKinney; 3ʳᵈ row: Helen McKinney Cleaveland, Emma Pierson McKinney, Jamie Cleaveland, Tom McKinney, Elzoria Evitt McKinney, Hiram Paul, Ada Taylor McKinney, Eula Belle McKinney Potts, Montie McKinney, Carrie McKinney Paul, Frank Potts, & Al McKinney

In those early days of Highlands there weren't many settlers to whom White could deliver mail. John Palmer "Dock" McKinney, grandson of James McKinney who settled Cashiers Valley, moved to Highlands soon after his marriage to Margaret Jane Gribble around Christmas, 1875.[110] They were one of the first three families to live in Highlands, and on Nov. 18,

1876, their son Allison "Al" D. McKinney was supposedly the first child to be born in the new town.[111] At first they lived on north 4th Street, but in 1898 they built a home on Chestnut Street where the Performing Arts Center stands today.

Another Southerner, George A. Jacobs, who lived near the Old Corundum mine where the Cullasaja River completed its plunge down the mountain from Highlands and where Charlie Jenks boarded when he worked the mine, bought land at the edge of Highlands west of the Salt Rock in January, 1876. He and his wife Mollie built and ran Highlands' first boarding house at the northwest corner of 1st and Main.

Jacobs would also work as business manager for Mrs. Annie Dimick's popular Cheap Cash Store near Main and 4th. He would serve as Highlands' first Justice of the Peace. And on March 5, 1879, an act of the N.C. General Assembly would establish him as the town's first appointed mayor, along with S. T. Kelsey, Stanhope "Squire" Hill, Baxter White, and John Norton as appointed commissioners. He would serve in this position until May 3, 1883, when a second act of incorporation reappointed him mayor, retained Squire Hill, but replaced Kelsey, White, and Norton with C. A. Boynton and M. I. Skinner.[112]

Jacobs' second term would last only four days, since Highlands' first ballot vote gave Squire Hill the honor of becoming the town's first elected mayor; H. M. Bascom, Charles B. Edwards, and Alfred Morgan, its first elected commissioners.

The first articles of incorporation that had installed Jacobs as mayor on March 5, 1879, also established the town's limits, beginning "at the Post Office known as Baxter White's store, running each way from there so as to make one square mile."[113] The second incorporation in 1883 would extend these limits another quarter mile in each direction from the intersection of Main and 4th streets so as to make two and a quarter square miles.

The town would remain this size for the next ninety-five years. Simultaneous with the second incorporation of the town, a petition to the legislature asked that the name of Blue Ridge township be changed to Highlands township, but the legislature referred the matter to the county commissioners for proper jurisdiction.[114]

At the end of 1876, James Soper from Pennsylvania became the first Yankee farmer to settle in Highlands. He set about improving a hundred acres of land to the northwest of town, presumably in Short Off, which, by the way, was spelled as two words until 1890, after which it was usually spelled as one: Shortoff.[115]

Almost two years passed after Kelsey's and Hutchinson's appearance on the plateau, yet the town consisted of very few occupied homes. There were

Kelsey's, McKinney's, White's, Jacobs', and Soper's, apart from the vacated log "Law House," which served as the schoolhouse.

Without alteration, the town's future loomed rather grim.[116] Money was running out, and there were few new prospects for sales. A number of people arriving in response to Kelsey's enthusiastic brochure grew disgusted with the newness of the place and the sorry condition of the roads and abruptly left.

The people of the surrounding towns and countryside considered the idea of a town way up in the wild woods of the Blue Ridge to be as unreasonable as it was impractical. Many were inclined to laugh at what they considered a sure failure. Some out of Christian kindness warned starry-eyed newcomers against the grim realities of life on the mountain, turning back potential settlers who were disillusioned even before setting eyes on the town.[117]

In 1883 Rev. David Keener from Baltimore stubbornly ploughed ahead only because he chose to ignore "the positive assertions" of those he met at Walhalla about the slim chance of ever reaching Highlands and the discomforts of the place. Even as late as the winter of 1886 two men on their way from Minnesota were told in Seneca that they'd find Highlands buried under six to eight feet of snow, whereupon they turned tail and headed home.

One of H. M. Bascom's earliest memories of his arrival from Illinois was hearing Kelsey scorned for believing that Highlands could ever exist. Bascom recalled that in 1881, when it was considered "little short of a crime to work on Saturday afternoon," he stood by "while John Houston, who had been working on Main street with his cattle, shook the silver dollars which had just been paid him and said, 'Mr. Kelsey, I wouldn't give you that for all the town you will ever have here.'" This was the year that James and Elizabeth Soper fled to Covington, Penn., selling their home and hundred acres in Shortoff to John McClearie.

Against all reasonable odds, Kelsey blindly persisted in laying out his town site. In the fall of 1876 he welcomed Arthur House from Hartford, Connecticut, and during the following year helped him raise Highlands' first sawmill on Mill Creek.[118] Built with timbers from Dobson's mill on the Cullasaja River, it stood just west of the 4th Street crossing at today's site of the Mill Creek Store. On the same tract of land House built his home, which remains today as the oldest existing house constructed after the founding of Highlands. Fortunately it has been preserved, as of 2000, as the home of the Highlands Historical Society, Inc.

Residing only a short while in town, House sold his mill in 1883 to Granville Willey, himself a six-month visitor, who in turn sold it to Will Trowbridge. By 1886 it belonged to John Jay Smith, whose stay in Highlands would eclipse even White's as a longstanding pioneer founder.

House/Wright/Prince home, built in 1877, oldest house in Highlands today. Photo by the author, 2001.

1877

Among the interesting arrivals from the North, West, and South during the first eight years of Highlands' existence, some, like House, would vanish with little to mark or preserve their having been in town; while others, like White, would stamp the town indelibly with their colorful personalities. The year 1877, for instance, saw John Morton and Ed Cunningham build their home and store at the corner of 3rd and Main where Reeves Hardware exists today. Subsequently nothing is heard from either man.

On the other hand during the same year, William Jesse "Will" Munger, having read Kelsey's promotional pamphlet, gave up his job as a school teacher in Utica, New York, and with his wife Emma Shipman moved permanently to Highlands. He bought a hundred-acre tract of land including today's second nine holes of Highlands Country Club and built a home near today's Country Club lake, where he farmed for a living. During the early 1900s Emma served Highlands as a much needed mid-wife. The Munger's son Robert H. "Rob," who became a carpenter and cabinet maker, would build his and Nancy's home which still stands beside Munger Creek off the Dillard Road.

As 1877 came to a close, new settlers were arriving but in numbers too meager for encouragement. In spite of the mail now being delivered weekly, the town was tottering like a reeling vessel between sinking and floating, its future poised in a precarious balance.

1878

Hill/Staub house at 6th and Main, built in 1878. Photo courtesy of Dr. Richard Martorell.

The year 1878 opened with a ray of optimism as Stanhope W. "Squire" and Celia Edwards Hill moved up from Horse Cove.[119] A native of Rutherford County, N.C., Stanhope had lived in Horse Cove for thirty-one years before his move to Highlands. During that time he was Horse Cove's first postmaster and magistrate. By his energy and thrift he amassed quite a fortune, becoming one of the largest land owners in the region.

Accompanied in his move by Charles B. Edwards, also of Horse Cove, he occupied a white Victorian frame house, which his son Frank built for him at the southeast corner of 6th and Main, known today as the Staub Cottage. His former slave Dan lived in the cabin to the rear and is buried in the family plot at the Little Church in the Wildwood in Horse Cove. The Hill house accommodated boarders, since many settlers who came to live in Highlands lived here initially. Its present owner, Dr. Richard Martorell, says one window bears the etching, "the first piece of glass brought to Highlands in 1883."

1883 would be the year that Squire Hill beat John Jay Smith by six votes to become Highlands' first "elected" mayor.[120] He would serve only two years, however, before returning to the Cove. Perhaps his greatest legacy to the town of Highlands as well as to Horse Cove was the Horse Cove Road, for it was his survey, which followed an old Indian trail, that determined today's grade and route.

Stanhope Walker Hill, Highlands' 1st Elected Mayor in 1883. Photo courtesy of Hudson Library archives.

Highlands' first resident practicing physician, Dr. George W. Kibbee, arrived the same year as Squire Hill, but his stay would prove even shorter. His untimely death, which was recounted previously in Chapter Fifteen, left his family and the town distraught, but there being no reason for his family to leave their new home, they devoted their own talents to serving the town.

The doctor's daughter Laura devoted her energies to teaching in Franklin and Highlands, including Shortoff School.[121] She would also become Highlands' first librarian. Affectionately known as "Kittie," she would enjoy considerable popularity as hostess to many public activities in her own home, where twice a month the Glee Club met. A variety of exciting performances included an amateur string band, a group of young men debating national issues, prose and poetry recitations, and Kittie Kibbee acting out amusing themes in pantomime.

Kittie would remain in Highlands until 1892 when her marriage to Franklin's Prof. Thomas C. Reese, a Baptist preacher, took her out west. She would teach in Idaho and Washington before eventually retiring in California. Her brother Horace, who owned a printing shop in early Highlands, would also spend his final days in California.[122]

As many Southerners as Northerners arrived in 1878, hoping to establish permanent year-round homes. The Nortons, John and David, moved from Whiteside Cove in 1878 and 1888, respectively. John purchased almost all the land on both sides of west Main Street, beginning with the south side and construction of the Central House but exchanging it in 1880 for Halleck's just completed Highlands House. David Norton, Barak Norton's grandson who started Norton Community, would buy Halleck's Central House upon his own arrival in 1888 and manage it until long after the turn of the century.

Wiley Smith migrated from Habersham, Georgia, and married Virgil Hedden's sister Parthenia, whose family Robert Reese claimed lived at Sunset Gap where the road turned down from the Ravenel gate toward Horse Cove. Smith's house stands today east of Hicks Road. The ruts of the old Hamburg–Cashiers Valley–Webster roadbed, replaced today by Hicks Road, can still be seen running just east of his home. From the late thirties through the fifties, Col. Fergus Kernan, the World War II military strategist who wrote *Defense Will Not Win the War*, would live in Smith's house. His anti-separatist book would argue in 1942 that the only way to win World War II was by thinking offensively, using the resources at America's disposal and directing an attack on land at the heart of the enemy's continental power, an uncanny prefiguring of the Normandy invasion of 1944. Smith's house would pass to Hudson Clary in the sixties and seventies and then Norman and Marie Sharp until Jack and Beth Henry purchased it at century's end. The Smiths' grandson Victor Smith lives in Highlands today.

Highlands' first justice of the peace and tax collector was a Northerner, Monroe Skinner, who came from Wyoming, New York. Arriving in November, 1878, he intended the move to give his wife Phebe relief from hereditary consumption. He built his home at 4th and South streets, later site of King's Inn, and set up Highland's first blacksmith shop, where Carl Zoellner would one day manage his garage at 4th and Pine.

By the time that Margaretta Ravenel bought Skinner's home in 1883 to create Islington House, later King's Inn, he had built a second home, which he called *Glencroft*, on a fifty-acre tract under Sunset Rock to provide Phebe with an even more tranquil environment for her condition.[123] It was definitely tranquil, for after Skinner died in 1891 and Professor Thomas Harbison bought it in 1901, Harbison's daughter Dolly remembered that their closest neighbor "was miles away at the Pierson Inn!" Harbison would double the size of Skinner's house, including an eighty-foot porch. In 1921, when he sold it to Leonard and Rebecca Harris, brother and sister from Havana, Cuba, they would change its name to *Trillium Lodge*, the name it bears today, and rent it as a summer residence to the Hepburn Many family and the Episcopal Bishop of Puerto Rico.

Another Skinner, Henry, was a furniture manufacturer, who came to Highlands from Boston, Massachusetts, in 1883. He built a house where Bank of America stands today at the northeast corner of 4th and Pine and a print shop on Main Street, known later as the Old Paul Store.[124] In 1890 he would buy a mill in Horse Cove, tear it down, and erect a new one.

Two Yankees from Geneva, New York, Henry Maxwell and John Anderson bought land at 5th and Pine streets in 1878.[125] This is where Alex Anderson (no relation to John) would build his stately mansion in 1906–09. It would be a lovely home that dominated the Highlands scene as an integral part of its landscape for almost seventy years.

By the end of 1878 nearly twenty new families had settled in Highlands, and income from land and lumber sales was beginning to pay off Hutchinson's speculative town-site loan.

1879

As 1879 commenced, mail was now being delivered daily. Only a few late responders to Kelsey's brochure were added to White's mail route, one of whom was Ebenezer "Eben" Selleck. Arriving during the summer with his wife Harriet from New York, however, Selleck barely had time to build his house and barn nestled in the Spring Street block between 3rd and 4th before he was summoned north again. James A. Garfield defeated Gen. Grant for the office of President in late 1880, and the following spring he appointed Eben Selleck to the office of collector of the Port of Philadelphia. It was a high and noteworthy distinction but unfortunately short-lived, for Garfield was assassinated by a mentally disturbed office-seeker in July and died in September. The change in administration left Selleck without a job.

In 1882 Selleck and Harriet returned to the joys of their little village farm. During the next twelve years he would serve two times as the town's mayor. A public-spirited individual, he would make a significant contribution of his own land to the building of today's Walhalla Road. When the Sellecks departed for Seattle, Washington, in 1905, they would sell their house to Mrs. C. Albert Hill of Washington, D.C. In the early thirties it would pass to Lilia Kennard McCall of New Orleans; and in the early sixties, to her sister-in-law Elizabeth Duffy Kennard and her daughter Elizabeth Kennard Neal.

Selleck/Hill/McCall house, "The Rabbit Hole," built in 1879. Photo courtesy Highlands Historic Inventory.

It was called the *Rabbit Hole* because it looked as if it were coming out of the ground so that entering it, like Alice in Wonderland, one went down the rabbit hole. On October 20, 2000, when fire originating at the furnace gutted the house, its destruction was a sad loss to the families associated with it during its last seventy years. Indeed, Lilia's granddaughter Chipsy Butler reacted, "It feels like a part of me died." But it would also be a great loss to many, many Highlanders who over the years had frequented this lovely home.

Joseph Halleck arrived in Highlands from Minnesota the same year as Selleck. Brother to Union General Henry W. Halleck of Civil War fame and himself a Major, he bought all the land south of South Street in a broad arc that included Muddy Hollow, today's Highlands School. His home, which in ten years would give way to Pierson Inn, sat on the corner of South and 4th. During the spring of 1880 Kelsey sold him three lots on Main Street for one dollar for the expressed purpose of the "building of a hotel."

Within five months he'd completed Highlands House, now on the National Register of Historic Places as Highlands Inn. No sooner had he finished the hotel, however, than he traded it for John Norton's Central House, already two years in operation across the street. He and his wife Vina would run Central House until their departure for Rock Creek near Blue Ridge, Georgia, in 1888.

John P. Arthur discovered Highlands as a young graduate of V. M. I. and the University of South Carolina Law School, arriving in the fall of 1879 from Columbia, South Carolina. He built his home of wide white vertically laid pine boards in the meadow east of Baxter White's post office, later site of Highlands Art Gallery, and fronted it with a white picket fence. There he lived with his mother Martha Ann and sister Fannie until his move to New York City in December, 1881, where he passed the New York state bar.

In 1887 he moved to Asheville and passed the N.C. state bar. An avid historian and meticulous researcher, he was urged by the Daughters of the American Revolution to write his monumental *Western North Carolina: A History: From 1730 to 1913*, which was ten years in the making and which they published for him in 1914.

As well-known and current as this history remains today, its publication didn't alleviate the financial difficulties that plagued him during his later years. Shortly before its appearance he had moved to Boone, N.C., and there published a publicly financed history of Watauga County. But it bought him only a year after his retirement from the practice of law. His last days saw his turning in desperation to earning fifty cents a day digging potatoes, gathering apples, and helping in a livery stable. Homeless, penniless, and heart-broken, he died in 1916.

It should be noted that Arthur's references to Highlands in his western N.C. history are authenticated by his having lived in the town and known its residents. His sister, Fannie, would sell their home after his and his mother's deaths to Christopher Whittle in 1925. The property is occupied today by all the shops from Town Square to the Cleaveland home.

Joseph A. McGuire, a Southerner who moved from Franklin in late 1879, built his cottage at today's entrance to the Recreation Park. His outstanding contributions to the town were building *Gray Cottage*, today's Wolfgangs On Main, for Miss Mary Chapin in 1883 and supervising construction of the Episcopal Church the year prior to its dedication in August, 1896.

For the most part, despite the arrivals of these few settlers in 1879, immigration to the town began to level off. President Hayes put an end to Reconstruction, which meant good news for the persecuted South but bad news for attracting settlers from the North, for the North was losing confidence in a recalcitrant South, even as early settlers in Highlands were losing their faith in Kelsey's folly and beginning to return home.

J. M. Abercrombie, for instance, gave up his newly built blacksmith shop on 4th street. Joseph Halleck bought Charles and Laura Allen's newly purchased Satulah farmhouse of 330 acres so that Allen could return to Maine. Others who departed on the heels of their arrival were Edward H. Baxter, the first principal of Highlands School, Vermonter Judson McQuivey, Alabaman Oscar Ricketson, and Thomas Dunn.

Even Macon County natives Robert Porter and the probate judge and tax collector William Allman shared the growing concern that Highlands had become a failure and chose to abandon the town. Whether it was the lack of conveniences, the poor roads, the difficulty of finding employment, or cabin fever during the winters, the pure and simple attractions of primitive living no longer held sway with these fleeing refugees, two years being the absolute limit of their love affair with rustic isolation.

1880

At the beginning of the second five years of early Highlands history, as the health and welfare of those who had remained more than just a few months or a year began to improve slightly, so also immigration began to pick up again. With an eye to a potential increase in the summer population, Joseph Halleck built his three-story Highlands House to attract boarders onto Main Street.

One intriguing yet ultimately tragic character to join the town in this year was a native of Ohio, William M. Partridge.[126] Partridge had moved first from Ohio to Wisconsin and then to Kansas before casting in his lot with Kelsey in the spring of 1880. For many years he was known as the Highlands miller, for he owned and operated a flour and corn mill downstream from Arthur House's sawmill, the turbine wheel and machinery for which he had bought and hauled up from Seneca City, S.C.[127] It was a fascinating sight at his mill to watch those enormous stone wheels revolving around and around, grinding out corn for meal and hominy grits.

In 1883 he and his wife Eliza built their home on Oak Ridge. It stands today just west of the former Phelps House, today's Main Street Inn. For almost twenty years Partridge ground the common grain for the people of Highlands. But by the end of the century he and Eliza, seeking some form of retirement in their old age, were enticed into joining a John Ruskin "commonwealth" near Waycross, Georgia.

According to Walter Reese, they were asked to sell their home and give up what money they had in exchange for security for the rest of their days. They said their farewells to Highlands in 1899, but not three years had passed before the money they'd paid for perpetual care gave out. By 1902 they were back in Highlands homeless, penniless, and totally at the mercy of the town.

Even before the Partridges had left Highlands on their ill-fated venture, Baxter White had speculated in his news column that it would fail. Acknowledging that only people of good character were permitted to join the commonwealth, he nonetheless doubted that there was any cohesive element in the venture. Like other experiments of this kind, time would surely dissolve it. "Human nature has not yet arrived at that state of perfection," White wrote, "which will admit of large numbers living together as one family, without disturbances, which will sooner or later end in dissolution."

William Partridge/Luke Rice home, Main Street, built 1883. Photo courtesy of Elizabeth R. Harbison via Tammy Lowe.

It was not long after their return that old Mr. Partridge, whose mind was failing fast, began wandering from home, and one cold January day in 1908 he didn't return. An intensive search failed to find any sign of him. Two or three years passed before a skull and bones were discovered, presumably his, near Dr. Hawkins' place in Glenwheer below Horse Cove about where Big Creek crossed Thompson's Lane, now Walking Stick Road. After his disappearance, his bereaved widow Eliza was cared for by the goodhearted people of Highlands until her death.

In the fall of 1880 Dr. Charles L. Frost from Hampstead, New York, arrived in Highlands at the ripe old age of fifty-nine and in very poor health.[128] He had received Kelsey's brochure promoting Highlands' moderate temperature and pure water as capable of restoring health, and in his state of nervous prostration, he was ready for a cure. Born of Quaker parents who felt he should be educated in the faith, he had resented their restraints so intensely that his anger alarmed his teachers and fellow students. He determined to become a doctor and at twenty-one graduated from Columbia University's School of Physicians and Surgeons.

Always restless and iron willed, he heard about the discovery of gold in California in 1848 and within a year had joined the rush. Traveling by ship, he led a mutiny to correct what he considered a gross injustice. The throng of gold seekers were being denied their food rations by the ship's officers. Docking in San Francisco, he barely avoided arrest by escaping to a mining camp. The miners were roughnecks, but then so was he, and they recognized in him someone not to be crossed.

On one occasion, a lawyer tried to swindle him out of his just payment for a claim, but discovering the scheme, he assigned a two o'clock deadline for the lawyer to reconsider his unjust action and give up the deed. Frost had to say it but once. When he returned to the lawyer's office at two, the deed was handed over without the slightest hesitation.

Frost bore a wound, which he'd received while fighting Indians out west. Actually he was in the act of stepping over a wounded warrior on the battlefield when the Indian thrust a poisoned arrow into his leg. For this perfidious act, the Indian lost his life, but Frost walked ever after with a limp. On his retirement to Highlands he brought with him Sarah, his daughter by his widow. They moved into the house just vacated by Hutchinson, which Frost commenced to finish.

His granddaughter Helen Hill Norris told of a mystery associated with his completing the house. It seems that it had a room that she never knew about in all the years she lived there as a child. Patrick Farnsworth discovered it years later when he was having the house repaired. Back of the dining room and completely sealed off was a secret empty room without windows or doors, neither entrance nor exit. "What on earth Grandfather Frost had that room built for," she exclaimed, "none of us will ever know. It has held the secret through all the years." Once opened and decorated by his nephew's wife Elizabeth Farnsworth, it became a beautiful and spacious part of their home.

Frost maintained a general medical practice in Highlands for twelve years. In 1888 he married David Norton's daughter, Meta, and two years later sold his original home to Tudor T. "T. T." Hall. He and Meta moved into a larger home that he had built with a pond to the rear of their property, which became known as *Meadow House*. Although Meta bore him no children, his daughter Sarah gave him many descendants through her marriage to Frank Hill of Horse Cove.

Until the very end Dr. Frost held to his strong sense of honor. Once when a man sought to collect a bill which Frost concluded he did not owe, the man launched into an offensive tirade, and the good doctor threw him out. "I will learn you better than to insult me in my own house," he fumed. In addition to his reputation as a man of honor, Frost was as compassionate as he was brave; and his Quaker upbringing notwithstanding, he regarded religion as a force that elevated and saved men.

Frost suffered a long lingering illness his last year, during which he inexplicably refused medical attention and shunned medicine. On the day he died in 1893, Baxter White tolled the church bell seventy-two times, which Walter Reese said was "the first time anyone at Highlands had heard a thing like that." Three years after his death, his widow Meta married the then-widowed T. T. Hall, and they set about converting *Meadow House* into Hall House, which would become a well-known summer hotel. Eventually, T. T. added tennis courts and a golf course, which was eventually expanded from three to nine holes.

One fellow Kansan whom Kelsey attracted to Highlands in 1880 by extolling the wonders of its pure air and water and mountain scenery was Jonathan Heacock (pronounced Hay-cock), a veteran of the Union Army who was originally from Pennsylvania but who came with his wife Annie from Minnesota in search of relief from malaria and pulmonary infection.[129] Although a photographer by trade, he also had a great interest in agriculture, and he bought farmland south of Highlands, known as Dobson's Buttermilk Tract, near Ahmihcahlahlagah Falls.

According to Sarah Summer, it was Heacock who renamed this succession of three large cascades, 400 feet in descent near his farmstead, each plunging almost sixty feet on the east fork of Overflow Creek. Fortunate for those of us with dyslexia, he renamed them Glen Falls, after one of the lovely waterfalls in his home state of Pennsylvania.[130] In 1886 an alternative way of pronouncing this onomatopoetic name for Overflow Falls on Overflow Creek was Omakaluka Falls. Heacock built a dam and sawmill near the headwaters of this creek in 1883.

For a few years Heacock and his family tried farming in Tallapoosa, Georgia, but returned to Highlands in the spring of 1891. Having lost their claim to their farm near Glen Falls, they moved into C. F. Diffenderfer's recently built house, the last one on the right on 5th Street, where Mrs. William H. Melvin lives today.

Heacock and Annie furthered their interest in agriculture by planting in their yard almost every tree indigenous to the area as well as some imports, such as Northern spy apples and buckeyes, in addition to flowers, fruits, and berries of all kinds: strawberries, blackberries, raspberries, blueberries, and the larger buckberries. A natural spring fed a fountain in the front yard.

The Heacock home was run for a number of years as a boarding house, where Heacock crafted furniture in his workshop and entertained his guests, including Mary Lapham, with one of the first radios in Highlands, his playing of the violin, and even a magic lantern.

Jonathan Heacock, 1842–1929.
Photo courtesy of Tammy Lowe.

Glen Falls, 1897–98. Photo from the
R. H. Scadin Collection, UNC-A.

Baxter White and John Jay Smith

Far more interesting than the physical growth of the town and the geographic origins of its population were the personalities of its strong-minded founders. Baxter White, for instance, served as Highlands' first postmaster but also as Justice of the Peace, town councilman, and trustee of the Hudson Library, for which he still holds the record as its longest-serving president, from 1889 to 1910.[131] During this same period, he wrote the Highlands column for the *Franklin Press*, in which he reported events of general interest about the little mountain town but also stated personal views on matters moral as well as politic.

For instance, as a leader of the temperance movement in the Highlands Methodist Church, he regarded strong drink as the mortal foe of the church and destroyer of young men. He complained strongly that the youth of Highlands were buying liquor at the Franklin dispensary. On the other hand, prohibition for him was not a viable solution to the problem. As early as 1902 he was arguing effectively that strong drink couldn't be regulated.

This didn't mean, of course, that its use could be justified, no, not even partially. A dispensary—known today as an ABC store—was in his opinion a sorry excuse for making money, and to justify its profits as increasing the school fund, as voters in Franklin were wont to argue, was not only short sighted, but a twisted product of deceptive reasoning. It was equivalent to saying, "Vote for the Devil and he will assist in the education of your children."

White quoted Shakespeare as calling intoxicants the "devil's broth." He praised Stonewall Jackson for announcing, "I never touch strong drink, I am more afraid of it than I am of Yankee bullets." Furthermore, if these authorities weren't proof enough of the evil of drink, he quoted the highest authority of all: "Woe unto him that giveth his neighbor drink, that puttest thy bottle to him, and makest him drunken also." A woe pronounced by God, White admonished, is a fearful thing to think of.

In matters of politics, Mr. White considered himself an honest Democrat, somewhere between the uneducated Populists and the evil Republicans who supported the policies of Reconstruction. He detested corruption in government with a passion. In 1895 he felt the welfare of the nation was in desperate need of leaders with strong moral character, clear heads, and brains free from the muddling influence of strong drink. Congress was being run by wire pulling politicians, more interested in the love of office and personal glory than in addressing national issues of economic stagnation and unemployment. The sorry result was that Grover Cleveland got no support for his plan to shift the national debt from abroad to home.

A great nation, like ours, White argued, should aim at absorbing its own debt instead of going to Europe with its bonds. But Congress couldn't stop making matters of economics and business, issues of party politics. Great statesmen and patriots, he concluded, must inevitably set fame aside in their love of liberty and devote all their unselfish efforts to making a free people happy and prosperous.

Mr. White's moral, political, and religious views influenced many Highlanders who attended the Christian Endeavor classes that he taught each

Sunday evening. They admired his ethics tempered by kindness, his intense love of education, and his faith. And he, in turn, loved Highlands. When old age forced him to leave in 1910 to join his son-in-law and daughter, Frank and Olive Sheldon in La Verne, California, he hated selling his house and business of thirty-five years. Even at seventy-five he was still selling fire insurance by horseback along Macon County roads and loving it.

Indeed, no sooner had he closed the sale on his home and business than, in a sudden change of heart, he tried to buy them back. He even turned back from the railroad station in Seneca, went to the foot of the mountain headed for Highlands, and sat down and cried over the intense pain of separation.[132] Twelve years after his move to California, he died in 1922 at age eighty-seven.

Eleanor C. and T. Baxter White. Photo ca. 1910, courtesy of the Bascom–Barratt Estate.

The White family of five children, though gone from Highlands after 1910 and remembered by few living here today, never forgot the town of their youth. One daughter, Jessie, had been the Hudson Library's 5th librarian. Olive, who married Frank Sheldon, the architect of Davis House, had assisted Professor Harbison as a teacher in the Highlands Academy.[133] Walter Reese especially remembered her black cat with seventeen names that rhymed like a piece of poetry, because in her search for an appropriate name, every person who came to her house gave one, with the result that she adopted them all.

White's son, Elias, kept Highlands' memory dearest in his heart. It was he, like his father before him, who kept the people of Highlands informed through the *Franklin Press* about their former citizens living in California, even as late as the forties, indeed until his sister Jessie died in 1956.[134] In 1949 it was Jessie who would donate the original map of Highlands to the Highlands Museum.

In some ways Baxter White was like a number of Highlanders who eventually left the town and moved out west. Land out west between 1900 and 1915 was free, which must have been the initial attraction, as had been the case almost a century earlier when cheap land grants attracted homesteaders to settle the former Cherokee territory of Western North Carolina and the Sugartown highlands. This migration of the 1900s saw Highlanders join homesteaders from Horse Cove, Whiteside Cove, and Cashiers Valley, all bent on seeking their fortunes.

If it wasn't LaVerne, California, where White retired, then it was Douglas, Wyoming, or somewhere in Oregon, where C. C. Hutchinson would finally settle. Oregon had a particular fascination for the young men of Highlands, who took Horace Greeley's call "Go West, young man" to heart. Joel Teague and Henry Smith left for Portland in 1895, and Bert Rideout, Ed Rice, and Quincy Pierson all departed either temporarily or permanently for Oregon in 1898. Antle Henry and Charles Miller moved there in 1901.

When Harley Smith left for Baker City, Oregon, in 1902, the *Franklin Press* remarked, "Macon County seems to be colonizing Baker City." But this was also the year that Sumner "Bud" Clark sold his farm in Oklahoma and returned to Highlands to resettle and run Cleaveland's grocery. His return led the *Franklin Press* to remark, "So the west turns to the south."[135]

Thomas Houston, however, was an entirely different story.[136] Son of John Houston, he left for Oregon in 1896 when still a boy. Eight years later he rode into town like a conquering hero bent on a single purpose. Seated on a pony and wielding a lariat and riding whip, he drove twenty-eight horses into Highlands, an impressive site indeed. Baxter White said he had a saddle unlike anything ever seen in this country, stirrups made of the finest leather, more like shoes or boots without the back or heel, and lined with felt to warm the feet in coldest weather.

The ladies of the town ran out to see this boy turned man bearing the ways and looks of a plainsman inured to hardships and in total control of his life. Alighting and greeting them with unaffected politeness, Houston sprang lightly into the saddle again and announced his intent, the sole reason for his month-long return to visit home: "I want to see my mother."

Baxter White was so impressed that he launched into a spontaneous ode to motherhood:

Ah, the love of a mother! Who can explain it? Distance instead of severing increases it. It is the talisman of safety and purity. As years of absence go by, it intensifies, and fills the heart with unutterable longing. Who can tell of the waiting and longing of this young man for his mother? What dreams and pictures of home, with mother in it, filled his heart, as upon the lonely plains, with nothing but the herd around him, and the silence of the night about, and the starry vault above. In those eight long years, the boy who never before had been away from home, by day, by night, he dreamed, he dreamed of his mother.

Reunions of this kind where young Highlanders returned from the West like homing pigeons weren't restricted to children seeking mom or dad, since adults also yearned for home. Fifteen years after Thomas Houston's return to his mountain origins, Luther Crow left Walhalla with his wife Cornelia and three children for Douglas, Wyoming.[137] When Cornelia died after a few months from pneumonia, he sent Alvin and Elsie back to live with their grandmother Sarah in Walhalla but kept Virginia, little "Virgie," for she was only a year old. One day while Luther was on a sheep drive, the Liningers, Virgie's caretakers, stole her away to Nebraska.

It wasn't until Virgie was eighteen that she discovered her true identity. The incident occurred when she married Verne Johnson whom Mrs. Lininger detested. In a moment of bitter rage Mrs. Lininger informed Virgie that she was not a Lininger but an adopted child, a Crow from Walhalla. Virgie and Verne began a search that ended with her deceased grandmother in Walhalla. There they were told that her family had moved to Highlands, so after nearly twenty years she was able to rejoin her long lost father, brother, and sister.

Despite the quick departure or eventual migration west of a number of disenchanted Highlanders, early pioneers like John Jay Smith of Warren County, Pennsylvania, who came to Highlands from Illinois in 1878, would remain in the town for the rest of their lives.[138] A builder and innovator, Smith caused quite a stir five years after his arrival when he delivered to Highlands from the Atlanta Exposition a steam saw-mill, a portable steam engine that rumbled down 4th Street hill past the Highlands House on its way to Bear Pen.

He employed it to saw the lumber for the new Presbyterian Church, which Marion Wright would build at 5th and Main. He then moved it to Mill Creek, nearer the center of town, where he erected the first sash and blind shop on the site occupied much later by Will Cleaveland's planing shop and office about where the Pizza Shop is today in Mountain Brook Shopping Center.

When his steam saw-mill burned to the ground in 1884, he built a new one that turned out 2,000 board feet a day. In 1886 he bought Will Trowbridge's water sawmill, which Arthur House had built slightly downstream from his own. Apart from William Partridge's grist mill, which existed even farther downstream, two sawmills were now under one ownership, giving Smith the advantage of furnishing most of the material used for houses in Highlands for the next thirty years. He enlisted the aid of Dock McKinney and Joe Henry to run the mill while he served on one occasion as postmaster and twice as mayor. In the mayoral race he had the unusual distinction in Highlands of receiving every vote cast.

John Jay Smith's Saw Mill, built by Arthur House, on Mill Creek. Photo probably by R. Henry Scadin, 1896, courtesy Gene Potts via Doris Potts.

In 1886 he married Mary Chapin, who had arrived three years earlier from Massachusetts. She brought to the marriage a most impressive dowry, for her Aunt Eliza Wheaton, founder of Wheaton Seminary (now Wheaton College) in Massachusetts, gave the newly weds the Highlands House, now on the National Register as Highlands Inn, as a wedding gift!

The next year the couple leased it to Mrs. Mary A. Davis, and John Jay began supervising the installation of a new kitchen, an enlarged dining room, casing for the windows and doors, papering and painting. The Smiths changed its name to Smith House, which is how it remained until 1925 when Mrs. A. J. Davis bought it and named it Highlands Inn.

John Jay's moonlighting as road surveyor ultimately led to his laying out the Dillard Road between 1904 and 1906, which for many years was known to older residents simply as Smith's Road, now Highway 106. Joe Reese recalled that Smith's favorite hobby was woodcarving. Initially he made vases, bowls, trays, lampshades, and furniture from native woods, but later he constructed framed three-dimensional pictures depicting the lakes and mountains around Highlands.

In 1929 he and Miss Jennie Burlingame were creating lovely landscapes from mosses, ferns, bark, colored paper, and delicately tinted bits of cotton that gave the impression of an actual scene in nature viewed through an open window, more natural in fact than oil paintings of the same scenes.

Until recently, one of these works of art, a beautifully crafted forest tableau, hung in Hildegard's Restaurant, Smith's former home, today's Wolfgangs On Main. According to Harriet Zahner van Houten, a larger scene depicting Dry Falls (sometimes called Cullasaja Falls) and made from the macerated wood pulp of a hornet's nest, was lost in a fire that consumed her father's house on Billy Cabin Ridge, where it had hung until the early 1970s. A picture of another waterfall—probably Bridal Veil, also made from a hornet's nest, bark, and moss—came into the possession of Charlie McDowell, who says he burned it before he knew who'd made it. "Twenty-twenty hindsight," he confessed with a chuckle. "I should have kept it!"

In actuality, John Jay Smith's many contributions to the welfare of Highlands consisted more in people's memories of the man than in what physical handiwork he bequeathed to the ravages of time. Marshall Reese remembers his resembling Teddy Roosevelt, for he was large and stout and wore brown leather leggings over his pant legs and shoes, and he shuffled when he walked. His calves were almost as large as his thighs. Marshall's father, Walter, considered him a number one carpenter but never much of a success in anything he started; his wife, Mary Chapin Smith, was better posted on city matters.[139] And from what we know of her through her lifelong service to the Hudson Library, this was doubtlessly true.

A native of Wethersfield, Illinois, who came to Highlands from Norton, Massachusetts, Mary Chapin built *Gray Cottage* in 1883, three years before she married John Jay. This home, after her death in the forties, would belong to Fred Edwards, then Jennie Burlingame, Brockway Enterprises in 1969, Hildegard's Bavarian Restaurant in 1980, and now Wolfgangs On Main.[140]

Mary Chapin poured much of her life in Highlands into the Hudson Library, which the *American Library Directory* lists today as the oldest public library in North Carolina. She served for all of her years in town as one of the Library's foremost trustees, indeed as acting librarian during the time of its move from a cozy room in the old Town Clock Schoolhouse to its first real home in an architectural gem built east of the Episcopal Church on Main Street. It was she who wrote a history of the Library's first fifty years.

Since childhood, she had loved music, art, and nature. A devoted student of botany, she created in the woodland setting of *Gray Cottage* a personal garden that emulated in its exceptional beauty the Anne Hathaway Garden in Stratford, England. Before her arrival in Highlands she had painted for the great botanist Asa Gray, and while in Highlands she published in 1910 a volume of verses she composed about nature in all its phases. *Earth Songs* is still held by the Hudson Library.[141]

Mary Chapin and John Jay Smith, ca. 1890. Courtesy of Earle Young.

Mrs. Smith was one of the organizers of the Highlands Improvement Society in 1905, for which she wrote a brief history. She was an active member of both the Floral and the Horticultural societies and served on the board of the Highlands Museum and Biological Laboratory.

At the time of her death in 1940, her husband's passing a year later, her civic contributions to the town during almost sixty years were valued as indispensable. Friends praised her for her keen interest in the civic welfare and beauty of the town to the extent that her passing was a tragic loss to the people of Highlands.[142]

These, then, were among the interesting arrivals from all across the North and the South during the first five years of the town's founding. According to the 1880 census, the population of the village stood at 82. Many of these were able to forge a living under very trying circumstances, and quite a few spent the rest of their lives content with managing the affairs of their favorite town.

If there was any animosity or hate among them, it didn't show up in the newspapers. On the contrary, Kelsey's advertisement for "good citizens" gathered around "a convenience center" appeared well on the way toward becoming a charming reality.

5. The Hermit Thrush

Of all the summer residents of Highlands, none has a more delightful song than the shy, elusive hermit thrush. It is rarely seen, and is only heard in quiet, shady woodlands. But it is numerous in Highlands. Frequently three or four can be heard at once in the coves and dells bordering the town, the liquid notes of their calls rising, falling, and dwelling on intricate trills. The song of no other summer resident of Highlands harmonizes so completely with the atmosphere of the forests and rugged mountains.

— Highlands Maconian, May 27, 1931

With the exception of immigrants from neighboring Southern communities who set up permanent homes in Highlands, such as those noted above, many families from the deep South resided in Highlands, like the hermit thrush, only during the summer. Residents of Georgia, Alabama, Louisiana, and South Carolina in particular favored Highlands as an escape from the stifling heat, mosquitoes, and epidemics of the flatland.

By 1931 among the hundred families that summered in Highlands were names like Bingham, Salinas, Warren, Jones, Eskrigge, Monroe, Sloan, Lyons, Perry, Lamb, Douglas, Elliott, Anderson, Foreman, Evins, Raoul, and Zahner most of them from the South.

One family that had a profound influence on the town and its inhabitants from the earliest days of their arrival as summer pioneers in 1879 were the Ravenels. S. Prioleau and Margaretta A. Ravenel hailed from Charleston. Prioleau Ravenel had visited the Highlands plateau much earlier, indeed entirely by accident around 1858.[143]

Still a bachelor and staying at the Ravenel plantation called *Seneca*, where the city by that name exists today, he was employed at the time by Col. William Sloan to help construct the ill-fated tunnel for the proposed Blue Ridge Railroad linking Charleston, S.C., with Knoxville, Tenn., and ultimately Cincinnati, Ohio. Boring through 5,863 feet of Stumphouse Mountain near Mountain Rest, work on the tunnel had begun in 1853 and progressed at a rate of approximately fifty feet a month.

During free time he would ride horseback into the higher elevations, where the wild, rugged landscape captured his heart. His jaunts through forests fragrant with hemlock and azalea, over cool, hurrying streams close by damp cliffs graced with moss and tiny yellow-eyed forget-me-nots, to the tablelands at the very summit of the Blue Ridge wove into his memory the fabric of a haunting dream. But as 1859 approached its end and the South

Carolina legislature refused to grant further funding, work on the tunnel, just 1,500 feet short of its goal, ground to a halt.

Interior of the unfinished Stumphouse Tunnel, constructed 1858–59. Photo from the pamphlet In the Heart of the Mountains.

In 1861 war broke out between the states, and Ravenel was conscripted into the Confederacy. It was sometime after the war ended in 1865 that Capt. Ravenel returned to his favorite sites on the Highlands plateau. He began to buy the land he had grown to love for his bride, the widow Margaretta Amelia Fleming Parker.

By the time of his death in 1902, she and their son Prioleau, Jr., had in their name some 30,000 acres, extending from Satulah to *Sagee* (meaning *protected* in Cherokee) and Whiteside mountains and extending to Cashiers Valley, including Devil's Courthouse, Wildcat Ridge, and most of the famed Primeval Forest between Bear Pen and Whiteside.[144]

In 1879–80 he and his wife Margaretta hired F. Poindexter to construct a home place. At an estimated cost of $3,503.50, it was planned for the northern end of Wolf Ridge, which commanded a magnificent view of the deep valley of Horse Cove and extending into an ocean of mountain peaks beyond.[145] On a clear day they could sit on the porch of their new home and actually set their clock by the train's arrival in Clemson, S.C. Margaretta could see her own home in Pendleton, S.C. This impressive showplace was the first summer residence in the new town of Highlands.

Wantoot, the first summer home in Highlands, built in 1879–80. The barn and Fodderstack Mountain to the right. Photo courtesy of Alice Monroe Nelson.

They named their home *Wantoot*, after the old Ravenel plantation near Charleston. It is now known as *Playmore*, the summer retreat of the J. Blanc Monroe family since 1914. Having withstood the storm of time, it still has its huge old-fashioned porch, large fire places in the parlor and dining room with flooring made of alternating strips of black walnut and oak, and grand stairway, the first in Highlands.

The Ravenel Family in 1897
1ˢᵗ row (L to R): Miss Marguerite Ravenel, Elise Ravenel Duane, Russell Duane
2ⁿᵈ row: S. Prioleau Ravenel, Sr., Margaretta A. Ravenel
3ʳᵈ row: Annie Francis Fisher Kane, Clarissa W. Ravenel, unknown (probably Clarissa Burt), S. Prioleau Ravenel, Jr.
Photo probably by R. Henry Scadin, courtesy of the History of First Presbyterian Church, Highlands, N.C.

During the early years of Highlands' founding, if anyone owned more land within and outside the town than Kelsey and Hutchinson or Henry Stewart, it was certainly the Ravenels, who also gave generously of what they had. In 1883 Margaretta bought the home of Justice of the Peace Monroe I. Skinner at South and 4th.[146] On this property she created Islington Inn, which would become one of Highlands' most gracious and popular lodgings and attract summer residents for the next thirty years. Renamed King's Inn in 1925, it would continue to thrive until the great fire of 1994 brought it to an ignominious end.[147]

In 1886 when the earthquake struck Charleston, it was a devoted and generous Capt. Ravenel who left Highlands to help his afflicted neighbors. Even Ravenel's servants, like himself, were dedicated to saving the lives of those they loved. In 1885 his black servant Tony Richardson, newly wedded to Emma Gray, succeeded in saving her from the flooding waters of the Chattooga River as they tried to ford it after a heavy rain but were dragged downstream by the relentless current. He lost his own life in the rescue.[148] For the Ravenels this loss was heart-rending, for Tony was as much loved as any member of the family.

Prioleau owned large portions of land around Highlands, while Margaretta owned a number of lots in town. Typical of her own generosity and preference for open spaces in town, she donated the vacant lot to the west of the Presbyterian Church to the church in 1885 with the stipulation that the parcel remain perpetually open. Then she and her sister, Clarissa Burt, pledged some $3,000 toward construction of the building itself, in memory of their deceased sister Mary Louisa Fleming.

In addition to town property, Margaretta purchased over 600 acres of wild land in the Hamburg Township, today's site of Lake Glenville and its environs. Today's town of Glenville was built after 1940–41 when the creation of Lake Glenville covered the town of Hamburg. Margaretta bought an additional 400 acres in the Cashiers Township. She acquired from Mrs. K. T. Bingham, a Naval officer's wife, her house on the Bowery Road, built in October, 1883, and named *Ka-la-lan-ta*, the Cherokee rendering for "high place" or "heaven," because it overlooked Horse Cove hundreds of feet below with a glorious backdrop of the South Carolina mountains.[149]

Over time it passed from the Ravenels to Relie Salinas of Augusta, Ga., during the twenties to the late forties and to Gene and Katherine "Katie" Howerdd until the early fifties. Unable to find land for a golf course in Highlands, Gene left in 1954 to build the Fairfield Sapphire Valley Country Club beyond Cashiers.[150] In the sixties and seventies *Kalalanta* belonged to Foy and Joanne Fleming of Fort Lauderdale.

During periods when it was deserted, *Kalalanta* was said to be haunted, mysterious things being heard or seen there. No child in Highlands dared venture anywhere near it after nightfall, and children gathering chestnuts during the day gave it an especially wide berth. On one occasion, however,

Bud and John Hall and a few other young friends led a group of girls staying at the Hall house to the Bowery Ridge, and draping themselves in sheets brought the ghosts of *Kalalanta* to life so effectively that one young lady fainted dead away and had to be revived.

Mrs. K. T. Bingham's Kalalanta, *built 1883. Photo by George Masa, 1929.*

The Ravenels built and improved many roads that gave access to the town. Among Capt. Ravenel's contributions to the area were a fine carriage road which he built in 1890 to the top of Satulah Mountain, owned at the time by Macon Land Company. He improved the Walhalla Road around Satulah in 1892 at his own expense and constructed a Locust Pin Factory on Thompson's Lane in Victoria (the official name for Horse Cove from 1897–1911) in 1901, the year that Queen Victoria died and that Bishop Thompson's cottage in Victoria burned to the ground.[151] His Pin Mill manufactured and threaded locust pins that attached insulators and wires to America's newest arrival on its landscape: telephone poles.

By May of 1901 he had a telephone line installed by a Walhalla company from Victoria to Highlands; another ran to Cashiers, where it met a line from Sapphire.[152] It was over this line that news was flashed in September of the attempted assassination of President McKinley by a Polish anarchist, which roused Baxter White to blame America's unrestricted emigration policies and to despair, "There may be danger in America's love of freedom, that she may become too free, if that is not already the case."[153]

In addition to his help in providing telephone service, Captain Ravenel supported Kelsey's campaign for railroad service to Highlands, becoming a major stock holder in the Highlands Railroad Company. And in the same generous way that he shared his wealth to assure that Highlands would survive as a town, he furnished the money in 1890 that Kelsey needed to help found Linville, N.C.[154] When he died in 1902, he was praised as strongly independent, good-natured and cultured, having sprung from Huguenot settlers of South Carolina. His friends considered him true as steel.[155]

Lakeside Road in Lindenwood Park, 1897–98. Photo from the R. H. Scadin Collection, UNC-A.

In the tradition of his father, it was the Captain's son, Prioleau Ravenel, Jr., who built the turnpike from Cashiers to Highlands. Completed in 1902, the year of his father's death, it's to his credit that the road of today essentially follows the same course from the Shortoff intersection near Highlands to the old tollgate, recently dismantled, near Cashiers. Ravenel, Jr., also opened to the Highlands public Lindenwood Park, which he inherited from his parents. It consisted of hundreds of acres of grand and varied scenery, winding paths, roads, a lake, boats and a boathouse.[156] Much of this park is home today to the Highlands Biological Station and Nature Center, including the lake.

Prioleau, Jr.'s first wife, Florence Leftwich, was a strong supporter of all he did for Highlands and contributed much herself to its social milieu.[157] The daughter of a Presbyterian minister, she was intellectually gifted, having graduated from Bryn Mawr with highest honors and subsequently studied on a European scholarship at both the Sorbonne in Paris and the University of Zurich in Switzerland before returning to Bryn Mawr for her Ph. D. She traveled extensively and was widely known as a writer for various magazines, one being the *N.C. Review*. Her many articles were gathered in book form as *Women of the French Tradition*. A lady of great social charm, she was quite lovable and sorely missed when she died in 1923.

Captain and Margaretta Ravenel's three daughters also lived in Highlands. They were Miss Marguerite and Miss Claire, who in 1916 had their summer residence *Wolf Ridge* built atop Sunset, and Elise, who became the wife of Russell Duane, Harvard professor of chemistry and direct descendent of Benjamin Franklin. He had helped Pierre Curie discover radium and worked with Marconi on the wireless.

After Captain Ravenel's death in 1902 and his wife's in 1912, their children took an interest in protecting the land that their parents had purchased over the years. In 1913 Prioleau Ravenel, Jr., sold significant portions of his parents' acreage north and east of Highlands at inexpensive prices to the government for preservation as National Forest land.[158] Two years earlier, the Weeks Law had authorized the U.S. government to purchase forests in the East and the South. Particularly vulnerable to wanton timber waste, burning, and soil erosion were the headwaters of the Tennessee and Savannah rivers, two of the most important eastern waterways.

In 1914 the Ravenel children chose to donate Sunset Rock (known also as Sunset Rocks) to the town in loving memory of their parents. By 1920, aided substantially on the Highlands plateau by inexpensive land purchases from the Ravenels and Macon County Land Company, the Nantahala National Forest was created throughout the region by presidential proclamation. By 1924 a million and a half dollars had funded the purchase of a quarter million acres, ranging from $2 to $12, averaging $7 an acre.

The View from Sunset Rocks. Postcard by R. Henry Scadin, 1907.

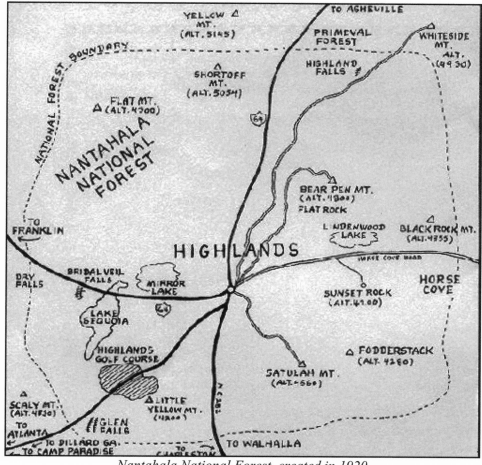

Nantahala National Forest, created in 1920

Margaret Morley, in her book on *The Carolina Mountains*, credits the Ravenel family with creating beautiful summer homes for themselves but, more importantly, with leaving behind a lasting legacy of good roads, a lovely church, a widely acclaimed inn, public parks, and many civic improvements through their altruistic interests in the people of Highlands.[159]

The Ravenels' influence extended beyond contacts with emigrants from the North and South to the native people themselves. In Morley's estimation, they gave "inspiration and hope to many a longing heart." Walter Reese, who moved to Highlands when his father was hired by the Ravenels to paint the Presbyterian Church, remembered them as "the poor man's best friend" for what they contributed to the people of Highlands.

In many ways the Ravenels gave far more to the town's development than either Kelsey or Hutchinson, for though Kelsey gave generously of his time and talents to the town's birth, he and Hutchinson were gone after fifteen years, whereas the Ravenels stayed on to assure the town's survival and sustain its growth, including recent efforts of descendants Clare and Wiley Ellis to help save Fodderstack from development. Their contributions to the community over many years guaranteed its continued existence as a cultural attraction as well as a summer resort.

6. Plum Like a City

An old gentleman, who was in town the other day bartering some chickens for tobacco and calico, was heard to remark: "I'll be dog-ged! If Highlands don't begin to look plum like a city."
—Albert Clark, ed., *Blue Ridge Enterprise*, Sept. 11, 1884

Two years after Kelsey's arrival on the Blue Ridge plateau we know from his diary that he began "working on a map of the Highlands town-site" on March 21, 1877. He ran a survey with Charles Slagle from Cartoogechaye and John Jay Smith in June of the following year but didn't actually make "a map of the town site" until January 1, 1881.[160]

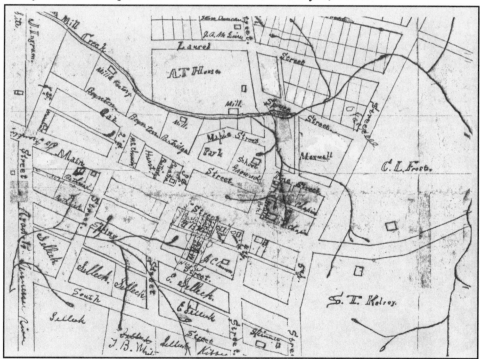

Kelsey's original map of Highlands, January 1, 1881. Copied by the author.

This original map was in the possession of Harry Wright before he died in 1999, but it disappeared from among the items of his estate so that only the copy that I made from it, as reproduced above, exists today. We wouldn't have had the original map but for Jessie White, Baxter White's daughter, who in 1949 mailed it to the Highlands Museum in care of the Hudson Library, with a note saying that her brother Elias considered it the original, drawn on durable paper with linen-like texture. The map bore no date, but Elias guessed it was made sometime between 1881 and 1885. Actually, the buildings that appear on the map, excluding later structures, which do not appear, confirm it as Kelsey's original of 1881. The words "Map of Highlands, Macon County, N.C. 1881" on the original that I copied were obviously inked in after its delivery to Highlands, for they appear in a different script from that employed throughout the rest of the map.

Title of Kelsey's 1881 map

A week after Kelsey made his map, Hutchinson's son Arthur had it printed in New York, copies of which still exist in Highlands.

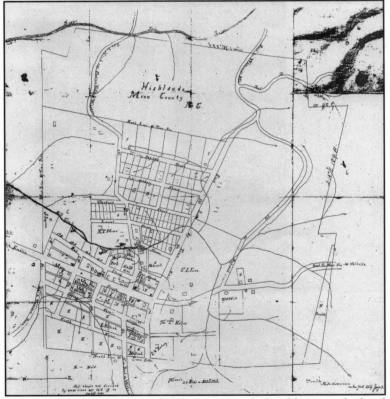

Arthur Hutchinson's tracing of Kelsey's map, with additions inked in later

The Hutchinson copy of Kelsey's map, printed on the same linen-like paper in New York, carries in the lower right hand corner the words: "A. H. Hutchinson, New York City Jany 7, 1881." Inked onto this copy—or at least the two I have seen—are boxes and partial boxes representing houses that were added or under proposal up to nine or ten years after the map's creation. This map is useful for determining what developed in Highlands between 1881 and 1891.

In 1895 the town plat was retraced and corrected on good paper, and this is the enlarged version, three by four feet in size with hundreds of lots laid out and numbered and bearing the words, "from the original by S. T. Kelsey, founder," appended in the lower right hand corner.[161]

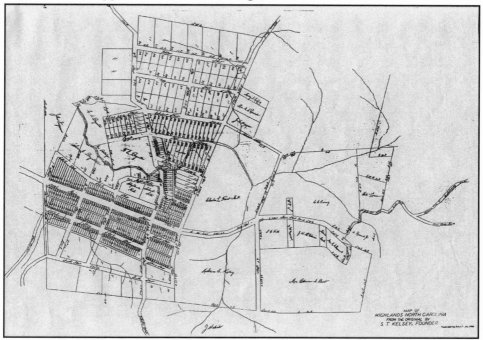

The 1895 map, enlarged and expanded from Kelsey's 1881 original

The town would have to wait until 1931 for Thomas Greville to furnish a good topographical map of Highlands, including main motor roads, secondary roads, roads passable by auto, poor roads or unopened streets, trails, contour lines, elevations, forest boundaries, mountain summits, viewpoints, and waterfalls with an enlarged map of the town inserted in one corner.[162]

For anyone interested in large scale maps covering a thirty mile radius from Highlands, including as many as six counties at a glance and identifying historical and natural landmarks, T. W. Reynolds would publish his carefully detailed mountain area maps in January, 1966, which served as the bases for his books: *High Lands*, *Born of the Mountains*, and the two volumes of *The Southern Appalachian Region*.[163] They were meticulously drawn and make a fascinating study, but for Highlanders living at the time of the 1881 map of the town, there was little in the way of roads or history that Kelsey might apply to the simple village that his map depicted.

From 1881 to 1883 year-round residents were arriving from all over the northeast: H. M. Bascom from Illinois, William B. Cleaveland from Connecticut, Sumner Clark and John Durgin from Massachusetts, Antle Henry from Wisconsin, and Charles A. Boynton and Henry Stewart from New Jersey. One immigrant, Louis Zoellner, was a native-born German, arriving with his new bride by way of Ohio.

These hardy families from so many different areas of the Country were the pioneer settlers of Highlands during its first eight years of its existence. By 1883, according to Albert Clark who had just taken over as editor of its first newspaper, the little community had established itself as a real town: a daily mail, a good school, several churches and societies, roads running in every direction, a number of businesses, and a population that had more than tripled in the previous three years, amounting to 300 residents from twenty-seven states extending from Florida to Oregon and from Maine to Texas. Moreover, plans were being formulated for the proposed Highlands Railroad.[164]

From a village population in 1880 of eighty-two to 300 in 1883, the outlook for the eight-year-old child was certainly less forbidding than when Richard and Rebecca Davis had visited it as a premature infant during its first year. Of course, population counts can be deceptive in a summer resort, for when the population hit 300 in 1883, the number of boarders at the Highlands House peaked at 409. By century's end the permanent population would drop somewhat to 250.

1881

One of Highlands' most distinguished pioneers was the Yankee who became its second mayor, H. M. Bascom.[165] A native-born New Yorker and son of a Presbyterian minister and missionary, he came to Highlands a widower at age twenty-eight from Rock Island, Illinois, in May of 1881 with $300 in his pocket and a death sentence on his brow. Burdened with a single lung, for which all insurance companies had turned him down as a bad risk, he spent sixty-one years regaining his health in the life-giving climate of Highlands, dying at the revered age of eighty-eight in 1942.

In the year of his arrival he built a home east of Squire Hill's house at Main and 6th. Today it belongs to Dr. Richard Martorell. In 1883 he built a fine two-story business with a tin roof, one of the first general merchandise stores in town. Known as H. M. Bascom's, it stood at the northeast corner of 4th and Main where the Texaco pumps stand today.

H. M. Bascom's Store ca. 1915. Photos courtesy of Hudson Library archives.

Initially established as a tin shop, it also carried drugs, hardware, sheet metal, and plumbing. A glass-covered showcase held gumdrops, one-cent stick candy, five-cent Baby Ruths, rock candy, and chewing gum, and in the back hung milk buckets, horse collars, and plow lines. Much later, as Herman Wilson remembered, meat was offered and kept in a barrel: "They'd take it out and cut you off a slab of it and put it on the scales and weigh.

Then they had coffee in a barrel." Everything was either in barrels or in hundred-pound bags, ready to scoop out.

During the first month of operation, Will Duncan moved his boot and shoe repair shop into one corner, and James Knight opened his barber shop in another. Mr. Bascom took pride in the fact that no one could ask for anything that he didn't carry. He even had the town scales placed just outside the entrance.

He rented out the upper story for an armory, but it was used so infrequently that when Mary Amanda Davis came from Indiana in search of her health, he offered her the second story. Mrs. Davis lived there with her niece, Amanda Florence Coffin, whom she had adopted after the death of her own sister, the wife of a North Carolina orchardist in Greensboro and first graduate of Guilford College.[166]

In the end Bascom's generosity was to be amply rewarded, for in 1887 he married Florence. Two years later he commissioned the building of the fabulous Davis House for Mrs. Davis to manage, for at the time she was running Highlands Inn. Davis house soon became one of the finest inns in the South, indeed one of the finest in the world, having achieved a listing in European guides as a "white star" hotel. Over its lifetime it was variously known as the Martin House, Tricemont Terrace, the Bascom–Louise, King's Inn II, and Lee's Inn before its tragic end in flames in 1982. The Kelsey and Hutchinson Lodge occupies the site today.

Bascom built a large livery stable on Main Street, where the post office would stand from the forties through the sixties and where Wit's End exists today. It served to transport people to Highlands and deliver provisions to Bascom's store. When Bascom wasn't having buildings built or selling hardware, he bought and sold real estate. Most of his purchases he made in town. In 1893, after Kelsey had left the area for good, he bought all the town lots not yet sold—seventy-two of them—from Kelsey's son, S. T. Kelsey, Jr., so that he essentially owned what remained of Highlands.

Around 1892 he built *Chetolah*, his home on a spur of Satulah Mountain, owned today by Tom and Linda Clark. Using his skill as a metal worker, he built a wood-burning furnace for central heating, something of a rarity at that time. This house would sell in 1981 for an impressive $350,100, a large part of which went toward the creation of the current Bascom–Louise Gallery as part of the Hudson Library.

For a total of seventeen or more years off and on, Bascom officiated as mayor of Highlands. He was a road commissioner, member of the police force, and Highlands' first Notary Public, a gubernatorial appointment.

Ever since age eleven, Henry Bascom had worked to support his two younger sisters and brother. Apprenticed to a tinsmith, he missed the opportunity for formal schooling, but he read voraciously. He was quite capable of quoting large sections of Shakespeare and the Bible from memory, and throughout his long life he devoured at least one—often two—books a day.

H. M. Bascom, 1853–1942. Photo by Janvie, 1920.

A friend once pointed out the romantic combination of business acumen, charming manner, and square dealing in H. M. Bascom's character. He always dressed as a gentleman in a coat, vest, and tie. In his friend's estimation, had he lived in New York City instead of this remote village where he chose to make his unpretentious home, he would have been a second J. Pierpont Morgan. Instead he became what the *New York Tribune* called, "Town Builder and Merchant Prince of Highlands."[167] Yet he always took time to read the comic strips with young Craig Cranston when his copy of the *Tribune* arrived.

If there were any faults in H. M. Bascom's character, they didn't go unnoticed by the home folks, but Walter Reese, who considered him one of his best friends, claims that it was because he was a shrewd dealer and the home people were unable to sucker him like they wanted to. "Just because he was able to make about a hundred thousand dollars in the time he was here, they called him Old Bascom," Reese explained.

One story from his early life that his daughter, Louise Bascom Barratt, often related was how, as a lad of twelve, he rode horseback through the state of Illinois to spread the news of President Lincoln's assassination. Unlike Paul Revere's famous ride, however, Henry Bascom's jaunt was cut short when he tried to cross a bridge over a swollen river and tumbled in. The whitewater had spooked his horse, and horse and rider together found themselves in the maelstrom with no option but to swim ashore.

William B. Cleaveland's grocery store. Photo ca. 1997–98, courtesy of Hudson Library archives..

Next to Bascom's hardware store on Main Street was the grocery store of William B. Cleaveland, who arrived from Bridgeport, Connecticut, in 1881.[168] His store would be the future site, from the twenties through the forties, of Fred Edwards' store, now Ann Jacob's gallery, and Tudor Hall's Real Estate beginning in the mid-forties, now Cyrano's Bookshop.

Like Mr. Bascom, Mr. Cleaveland came to Highlands to cure his lungs, but unlike Bascom he died within twelve years of his arrival, succumbing in 1892 to pneumonia. He and his wife, Ida Estelle "Stell" Bailey, lived at first in Joseph McGuire's house at 4th and Laurel, but buying Annie Dimick's store lots at auction, he built his final home in 1888 where it still stands to-day. When he died, he left behind a widow and seven children and an insurance policy on his life worth $2,000, which at the time was quite generous.

William B. Cleaveland Home, built in 1888. Photo ca. 1915, courtesy of Hudson Library archives.

An expert in mineralogy, he also left his rock collection valued at $5,000. It featured Indian relics that he had acquired over many years. He often accepted relics in exchange for goods at his store. Considered at the time to be one of the most complete collections in Western N.C., it was well known to collectors and ethnologists from many parts of the nation. Indeed, its value was fully recognized when, at his son Will Cleaveland's death in 1932, it was donated toward the founding of the Highlands Museum, subsequently the Highlands Museum and Biological Station. It was finally cataloged by Dan and Phyllis Morse in 1999.

Cleaveland's son Will, Highlands contractor and lumber manufacturer, built many homes and public buildings in Highlands, including the Maple Street calaboose in 1918, Highlands' first bank on 4th Street hill in 1923 (now Highlands Gem Shop), Anderson's Drug Store also on the hill in 1925 (now Mirror Lake Antiques), and the 1925 additions to Central House.[169]

It was neither William the father nor Will the son, however, whom Walter Reese credited among the Cleaveland family with having had the greatest affect on his young life. The family member whom Walter claimed converted him to Christianity, even inspired him to become a deacon in the Baptist Church, was William's widow, Stell, who lived in the Cleaveland home as it stands today, set back from the Stone Lantern behind the Loafer's Bench.

J. Walter and Anna Cabe Reese with son Joe, 1909. Photo courtesy of Allen Reese

Walter used to swing on the double gate of Mrs. Cleaveland's white picket fence and entice her boys to gamble with him. So he wasn't prepared for the transformation that she set out to produce in him when she invited him to take Thanksgiving dinner with her family. At the table she had him choose a passage from the Bible to read. Then saying grace, she posed a question that Walter has never forgotten.

"Walter?" she asked. "Why do you think and how is it that this fine turkey represents our savior on this Thanksgiving day?" Too bewildered to answer, Walter sat in reverent silence. She pointed to the turkey and asked, "Can't you see that this turkey was no good till it was killed?" She then launched into a mini-sermon about how our Lord and Master had to die before we as his children could be redeemed. And from that very day till his own dying day, Walter considered her a number one Christian.[170]

1882

In 1882 two builders arrived in Highlands who would contribute significantly to construction both private and public. R. Julius "Jule" Phillips, married to James Wright's daughter Mary Ellen, came from Franklin.[171] He bought 141 acres on Big Creek near the west end of Short Off Mountain for a total of $17.62½. He helped build the Presbyterian Church and renovate Islington House in 1886 and constructed the Masonic Hall for $297.85 in 1892–3. His son Roy would also become a builder of many homes on the Highlands plateau.

Millwright and machinist Capt. Charles A. Boynton came to Highlands from New Jersey. Down in the valley behind today's Baptist Church, he built a huge lumber mill and factory, which would later become the Wright Mill on the south bank of Mill Creek. Capt. Boynton was the architect and builder of the first church to be completed in Highlands, the Methodist, which would eventually become the Baptist Church on the same site. He built his home at the corner of Main and 3rd, currently Main Street Inn.

Boynton's two sons Frank E. and Charles L. "Charlie" (known as the Boynton brothers) worked as carpenters, builders, and contractors from the sawmill. Charlie became an expert ornithologist, whose specimens and notes established the breeding of many birds in Highlands. But it was Frank who made history in the wide world of botany. He helped rediscover *Shortia galacifolia*, long famous as the extremely rare galax-leaved plant of the *Diapensiaceae* family that was "lost" in the Highlands area for nearly a century.

Oconee bells (Shortia galacifolia)

In the summer of 1787 the French botanist André Michaux, having been sent by the French government to collect seeds, shrubs, and trees for the royal gardens, had discovered this plant without flowers in Jocassee Valley and sent a dried specimen to the herbarium in the Jardin des Plantes in Paris. There in 1839 Asa Gray, Harvard professor of Botany, had seen it with the identifying notation that it came from the "haute montagnes de Carolinie" (high mountains of Carolina), the only clue as to its location.

Twice before the Civil War, in 1841 and 1843, Gray tried in vain to locate Michaux's little plant. From a specimen of the same genus which he received from Japan, he predicted its blooms and named the American species after his friend Dr. Charles Wilkins Short, a botanist at Transylvania

University in Kentucky. In 1877 a young North Carolina teacher George W. Hymans found an outlying colony of *Shortia* growing on the banks of the Catawba River beyond the mountains near Marion, N.C. This stand Asa Gray and Prof. Charles Sprague Sargent, head of Harvard's Arnold Arboretum, visited two years later.

But it wasn't until September, 1885, that Prof. Sargent and Frank Boynton discovered the plant on the southern slopes of the Blue Ridge in Bear Camp Creek. Botanists were far more impressed with this event because it was nearer the area where André Michaux had gathered and dried his specimen to send back to Paris almost a hundred years earlier.

In November, 1886, they found an even greater stand farther downstream in Bear Camp Creek several miles south of Sapphire, N.C.[172] It's to their credit that they might never have found this patch growing in such profusion had they not braved extremely rugged and steep trails to reach it. In 1889 Prof. Harbison again found enough of the herb in Jocassee Valley to distribute it in wagon loads to many areas, including Highlands, where it is still growing. Many years later Ralph Sargent and Rufus Morgan would locate the plant along the Horsepasture River near the South Carolina border.

Thanks to botanists such as these we have today a strong appreciation of this lingering survivor of an earlier botanical age. Popularly known as Oconee Bells, it blooms in its native habitat along streams in deep shaded woods, its evergreen leaves and small cream-colored flower featuring a yellow center quite astonishing in its breathtaking beauty.

In the winter of 1882, soon after the Boyntons' arrival, Sumner and Ann Clark, immigrants from Massachusetts, bought property on the 4th Street hill and built their home. It soon passed to Margaretta Ravenel's sister, Clarissa Burt, and eventually to Susan "Tudie" Rice, behind today's Highlands Gem Shop.[173] Clark also bought the log "Law House" and the whole block of land surrounding it on which Wright Square and Helen's Barn stand today. Here in 1883 he built a dry-goods and grocery store, which in 1890 he converted to a Farmers' Alliance.

Clark's forte was education. When Thomas Harbison arrived in 1886 he was examined for competency by Clark, who at the time was Superintendent of Public Instruction. Five years later Clark served on the first elected school board in Highlands. He was one of the early masters of the Masonic Lodge. His family's love of the South appears to have been so strong that after he left Highlands to begin farming in Oklahoma, his son, Bud, returned in 1902 to settle in Macon County. Sumner's wife Ann, who died in 1908, was buried in the Highlands Cemetery.

Jeremiah Pierson with wife Emma Adams Pierson, daughter Lake, and sons Porter and Quincy, 1899. Photo taken on the Pierson Inn porch, courtesy of Dan Reese and Martha Reese Lamb.

Jeremiah Pierson, great-grandson of Barak Norton, became Highlands' second insurance agent in competition with Baxter White when he migrated with his wife Emma Adams and three children from the Norton Community in 1882.[174] He worked at first as caretaker of the Ravenel summer home. His wife's claim of descent from Presidents John Adams and John Quincy Adams led to their naming their first son, John Quincy, after his ancestors. Their oldest child Lake would marry W. S. Davis, building contractor and owner of the Rock Store which he bought from Lake's younger brother Porter.

Aside from selling insurance, Jerry developed a real estate agency that the family still controls today. In 1890 he purchased part of Dr. Frost's property bordering 5th Street, and in 1899 he purchased Joseph Halleck's old home on forty acres southeast of South and 4th streets. Dismantling it, he built the 35-room Pierson Inn, which he and Emma operated as a very popular boarding house. It featured the second golf links in Highlands, a nine-hole course that included a lake and boat for retrieving the balls that fell short of the green.

Jerry's oldest son John Quincy inherited the insurance and real estate agency, which he passed on to his son William. His daughter Lucile Pierson Reese became the Highlands School Librarian. According to Tom Crumpler, his son Porter married rather late in life because his intended, Miss Marjorie Marden, would not allow her duties as governess—first for the children of the Eskrigge family and then for the Monroe family—to be neglected until the children were old enough to fend for themselves.

One of the sights of Highlands, Crumpler reports, was Porter Pierson in sartorial elegance awaiting the bedtime of the Monroe children to pay his respects to Miss Marjorie. When at last the time arrived for marriage, Porter built a large farm on Kettle Rock Mountain for his English bride, which the Henley family of Birmingham would later own. Porter's and Marjorie's children were Col. Val and Kendall Pierson, the latter of whom would run the Inn during its final days in the late 1950s.

One of the most colorful immigrants to favor Highlands in 1882 was general merchandiser and postmaster James Rideout, a native of Maine and veteran of the Union Forces.[175] He arrived nursing a recurrence of malaria contracted during his war experiences in the South. He and his wife Margaret brought with them four children, and they built a house early the following year on 5th Street between Hickory and Chestnut, which they ran as Satulah House for boarding. This is where Bob Munger and W. T. Potts would live before it sold to the Whittles, who own it today.

In 1885, after three years had passed, the Rideouts made a temporary move to Judge Hunt's cottage on Oak Ridge, known today as the Aaron Esty place next to the Baptist Church. They were awaiting completion of a new and larger 21-room Satulah house under construction near the corner of 5th and Pine. Completed near today's site of the Catholic Church in September, 1886, this new Satulah House, as described later in Chapter Sixteen, soon rivaled Highlands House and Central House for comfort and popularity.

Rideout/Munger/Potts/Whittle house, 1st Satulah House. Photo by the author, 2001.

Rideout's first store, Rideout & Company, was located at the corner of 4th and Main next to Highlands House, where Dr. O'Farrell would later set up his drug store. Characteristic of his brand of humor, Rideout erected one or more signs at the edge of town that read:

> *Ride in to Rideout's,*
> *Buy your dry goods, and*
> *Ride out of town.*

He ran startling ads in the *Blue Ridge Enterprise*, such as "You Are a Liar! Rideout & Co. Have Failed to keep as fine a stock of groceries and general merchandise as they have on hand this winter," and clever ones, where a large blank space contained the single line: "This Space Belongs to Rideout."

By 1889 he was successful enough in his business to build a new general store across the street. At his request the town council granted him sixty days to move his store into Main Street so long as he left room for public travel. The long, low store that he built on the corner by Central House differed from all the other wooden buildings in town, for it was made of rock. He christened it the "Granite Store" in 1889, but it soon went by the more familiar name "Rock Store."

In 1890 he improved his property by building a fifty-foot-long plank culvert along the 4th Street side of his Rock Store, but by 1892 he was complaining to the town marshal about the boys playing football on the crossing of Main and 4th, for they sometimes broke out window glasses in the stores, including his own.

The long, low Rock Store, built in 1889, beside the Central House. Photo courtesy of Hudson Library archives.

Complaint, however, was rarely heard from this man of good humor. It was Rideout's sense of the ridiculous, fueled by an intense interest in science and astronomy, that sustained many early Highlanders during hard times.[176] Under the steps of Satulah House lived a huge toad, which he named *Bufo vulgaris* (*Bufo* being the genus of toads but *vulgaris* being Rideout's amendment). Every afternoon he would publicly summon Bufo vulgaris by name to enjoy bits of meat and a supply of fresh water.

Right up to the year before his death in 1907, Rideout exercised his seasoned wit. In that year he notified the Highlands Literary Society of his lifelong aversion to fleas—or *Pulex irritans*, as he called them. The flea, Rideout claimed in his lecture, was well named, for he was always "fleaing." When you put your finger where he was, he wasn't. If he were as large and agile as a fair-sized dog, he could pluck a man out of Highlands and with one leap land on Shortoff Mountain and pick his bones. His bite would kill a horse, and his hide would be impenetrable. A rifle ball would glance off without effect. Indeed, if he continued in his vicious and industrious ways, he'd depopulate the whole country "unless poisoned, trapped, shot by artillery, or dynamited." Rideout held Noah accountable for failing to extricate the flea from the ark so that it continued to punish mankind long after God had forgiven us.

Capt. James E. Rideout, Sr., 1838–1907.[177] *Photo courtesy of Ralph L. Rideout, Jr.*

Sporting a full beard, Rideout was ever the droll storyteller. In 1892 when he and T. D. Walden, Jonathan Heacock, and Hiram Paul attended a

G. A. R. (Grand Army of the Republic) reunion in Washington, D.C., he reported that Comrade Walden was up a lamppost playing a French harp while Comrade Paul was dancing on the pavement below. Mr. Walden, of course, was known in Highlands as the sedate master of Blue Ridge Lodge, Mr. Paul being an equally proper gray beard. Conspicuously missing from the report was, of course, Mr. Rideout's role in the revelry.

In 1896 when a Boston school teacher took a wrong turn home from Sunset Rocks to Stuly House and a search party found her lost and exhausted on Fodderstack, Rideout quipped the following morning that the next time she went on a coon hunt, she might better take along some matches.

When James Rideout wasn't engaged in repartee, he was entertaining students with his interest in astronomy, for he was said to have "much of astronomy at his tongue's end" when looking at the moon or Venus through his 12-inch lens.[178] Indeed, he even built a small observatory for his hobby, and as many adults as young folks came to share his interest in the stars. Walter Reese claimed his telescope was twelve feet long and two feet in diameter and stood in its tower sixteen feet off the ground. Once when a meteor shower was forecast at midnight in July, Walter couldn't see it with his naked eye, but he saw thousands of stars falling in the telescope. The photographer Henry Scadin got his first close-up view of the moon through Rideout's instrument.[179]

Perhaps it was Rideout's determination to see the stars up close that gave him his prophetic ability to read in them the future of Highlands. Walter Reese remembered how in 1898, the year that the United States fought a war with Spain over Cuba, Puerto Rico, and the Philippines, Rideout predicted uncannily what Highlands would be like in fifty years.

Addressing himself to either the Improvement Society or the Debating Society—we aren't told which—Rideout foresaw that Highlands would never have a railroad, but there would be autos and paved roads, possibly more than one. The autos would be powerful enough to climb to the top of Satulah Mountain, and there'd be aeroplanes flying over Highlands with mail from Asheville to Atlanta. He also prophesied that when these things came true, the "old town of Highlands would be a transient town." People from the North and South "would just pass through and maybe not spend the night." He foresaw that the pleasure of seeing the leaves change and gathering chestnuts on the sides of the mountains would then be over.

Walter marveled in 1947 that in one more year Rideout's fifty years would be up and already there had been autos driven up Satulah as well as Whiteside and Camp Parry-dise. Almost all that Rideout predicted had come true.

The owners of one of the earliest stores in Highlands, built in 1878 not long after Baxter White's country store but before Rideout's, were Frank L. and Anna G. Dimick.[180] Their Cheap Cash Store, managed by George Jacobs, stood on the site of today's Stone Lantern near the southwest corner of 4th and Main. They carried an assortment of boots, shoes, hats, dry goods, notions, hardware, glassware, Queensware, drugs, and general merchandise, including household sewing machines, "in fact Anything but Credit," as their ad announced. Everything was subject to barter in exchange for anything from a coon skin to a fat beef, and George Jacobs would receive you "with a kind word and a broad grin." Their specialty was a sack of good Rio coffee "strong enough to hold up an iron wedge."

In 1883, the year after Frank Dimick died at the young age of thirty-nine, his young widow Annie was still selling hardware. It was her inventory that H. M. Bascom bought to set up his own hardware store across the street in 1883. But she stayed in business until late the next year when Baxter Wilson bought the rest of her stock of goods— groceries, medicine, blind bridles, saddle blankets, etc.—and moved into his new store across from White's post office.

Unfortunately, like her husband, Annie Dimick died at the very young age of thirty-nine in 1886, so that her stay in Highlands wasn't long enough to establish a lasting legacy. She thrived just long enough for James Rideout to regard her as his chief competitor. In August of 1883 he ran the following ad: "I rise to explain, that I am not selling goods at cost—hope you do not think so. I ask as high prices as my conscience will permit—and take all I can get, and so they do at the Cheap Cash Stores. Try me."

Although Annie entered both the social and business spheres of Highlands life, she was quiet and unobtrusive in her manner, kind and gentle in her courtesies, and blessed with a warm and generous heart, the same organ that precipitated her premature death. She left to the town's care three orphaned children.

1883

One of Highlands' pioneer settlers who abandoned his reckless past with the expectation that he would die in the peaceful mountains was John H. "Papa" Durgin.[181] He came from West Roxbury, Massachusetts, in 1883 in search of his health. His wife was advised by his doctor that he was so sick a trip to Highlands would only extend his life a few weeks; she'd have to bring him back in a box. Typical of his lifestyle, however, he survived for fifty-six more years to the ripe old age of 95.

In his younger days he had served as a scout and Indian fighter, and for five years in the late 1860s he rode with General Custer. He took part in some of the hardest-fought campaigns directed by that daring and head-strong leader. Indeed, he could ride a horse at a mad gait one day and be champing at the bit for a repeat performance the next, which had earned him the post of Custer's personal courier. That he miraculously survived so many dispatches without a scratch, though plenty of nearlys, won him the nickname "Reckless Jack." In the words of his fellows: "Reckless Jack always comes back."

It's interesting to speculate whether Custer's infamous defeat at Little Big Horn might never have occurred if Reckless Jack had not received his discharge from the army five years earlier. This clever man could slip through the skirmish line as though it were the rear guard and, digging spurs into his mount, fly over the country like no other messenger to gather reinforcements, and he always saved the day.

In Highlands this reckless man was known more intimately as "Papa" Durgin, whose unselfish character and quiet, unobtrusive manner endeared him to many friends. But when he and Jonathan Heacock, both of whom were partially deaf, got together to discuss their Indian fighting days, all the neighbors could hear the raucous tales of these two old gray beards without even having to leave the comforts of home! Jane Emerson recalls how Papa Durgin would sit in his wheel chair by the bay window, his lap robe draped over his legs and she sitting at his feet, and scare the bejesus out of her with his blood thirsty tales.

Highlands' second major physician, after Dr. Frost, was Dr. William H. "Will" Anderson of Holmes County, Ohio.[182] He came in the fall of 1883 with his Quaker wife Susanna "Sudie" Brown. A veteran of the Civil War, he had enlisted at the first call in 1860 and served till the bitter end in 1865, after which he studied medicine at Keokuk Medical College in Birmingham, Iowa. He bought the twenty-acre Webb orchard on the Satulah Road half a mile south of town, where apples, peaches, cherries, quinces, and plums grew in profusion.

He set up his office in Joseph Halleck's Central House across from Highlands House, where he practiced medicine until his retirement in 1911, the year before he died. His daughter Christina married Luther "Luke" Rice, the town butcher, and wrote poetry celebrating the same beloved mountains that had inspired her father to come to Highlands and remain.

In the year of his arrival, Dr. Anderson was so completely captivated by the pure air and water and the wild and picturesque beauty of the area that he considered Highlands "the most healthful climate in the world." He described it as "too distressingly healthy" for the benefit of his medical profession. He was reduced to delivering annual contributions to the census and attending minor ills of the flesh. Just short of calling Highlands heaven, he wrote that this was the land where *they have to kill a man in order to start a grave yard or where people never die but live on and on till they finally dry up and blow away, but is certainly the nearest place to it [heaven] that I know of on this mundane sphere. There are people living in this county whose births date back to "the times that tried men's souls." A young man tells me about an old lady of 82 years who can turn "a double summerset," and then jump up and crack her heels together twice.*

Dr. William H. Anderson   Sudie Brown Anderson
Photos from Elizabeth Rice Harbison, courtesy of Tammy Lowe.

It was in response to one of his glowing tributes to Highlands that Dr. Anderson received a unique letter of inquiry from a man in Ohio, who is here quoted verbatim:

I want to no if thar is any gaim in them mountings and what kind, all so I want to no if thar is eny nice widders thar between 35 and 40. I am a widderwer myself. I have menes enuff to toat dubbel, and as soon as I locate thar I want to hitch onto a good pardner. If the widders want eny refferens as to my standin in this neck o woods they kin jist rite to eny offser in this county. I am now dun and I hope that you will take no offense at what I hev sed or dun, fur it is from my on-est hart.

Whether the man ever came to Highlands or found a good partner are matters of speculation, but it is certain that Dr. Anderson took no offense at the honest wishes of his heart.

1884

Since the year 1884 was when Satulah Mountain was supposed to have blown its top, a short digression from the discussion of pioneers who came to Highlands in this year might serve to set this published rumor to rest. There are Highlanders today who make the claim that Satulah on occasion has rumbled with the sound not of an earthquake but of a volcano. James Mooney during the late 1890s reported that "Satoolah Mountain, near Highlands, in Macon County, has crevices from which smoke is said to issue at intervals."[183] T. W. Reynolds quoted Cora Rogers Picklesimer of Clear Creek as having seen smoke and light issue from Satulah in 1897 when she was twenty-eight. Reynolds himself speculated on the possibility that the name *Satoolah*, meaning Six Killer, came from an ancient Cherokee myth.

The most definite statement of Satulah's volcanic nature came from Soyrieta Law quoting Dolph Picklesimer, who was hog hunting on December 10, 1884, a year and a half before the Charleston earthquake, and "was nearly scared to death on the crest of Satulah by sulphur fumes and rumblings from within the mountain as loud as a freight train. He felt the intense heat through his heavy cleated logging boots and fled down the mountain in terror as hot rocks and sulphur fumes spewed into the air." Mrs. Law claims the Cherokees reported disturbances as early as 1730 and wouldn't go near Satulah, which they called Big Grumbler Mountain.

Who is to doubt that Satulah has grumbled at times in the past, even within the last hundred years or so? But an eruption of hot rocks and sulphur fumes, such as Dolph described, would surely have made its way into the *Blue Ridge Enterprise*, Highlands' local newspaper, which appeared the next day and each week thereafter, but regrettably no notice was taken.

Helen Hill Norris relates a milder account of Dolph's experience. She says he told her grandfather, Stanhope Hill, that, short of an eruption, the mountain was definitely rumbling, and up near the cliff called the toadstool was where the rocks were hot enough to heat his shoe soles. Stanhope Hill accompanied Dolph home, but could confirm only "a faint, far off roaring which seemed to be coming from a few cracks in the mountain, but seemed to hold no menace."

Irene James, Dolph Picklesimer's niece, says she doesn't remember these stories in her family, but she does remember an incident when she was in her teens and she and her sister Mett and Irene Kinsland were walking the trail to brother Lyman's house in the gap between Satulah and Fodderstack, and a light followed them all the way up through the woods. "That was the nearest I ever came to seeing a ghost," she says. "I figured there must be some mineral going along with our bodies."

In the early history of Highlands one of the major landowners was Henry Stewart, Sr. from Hackensack, N.J., who was agricultural editor for the *Montreal Star* and *New York Times* and contributor to the *American Agriculturalist*.[184] Intending originally to become a physician, he studied medicine in Paris, but was driven out in 1852 when Louis Napoleon declared himself Emperor Napoleon III.

In 1884 Stewart purchased Capt. William Dobson's 450-acre farm just west of Highlands when Dobson left to farm in Franklin. In 1899 Stewart moved into the Henry Downing home on Seminary Hill at the corner of 4th and Hickory, known today as Stewart House. By 1903 he owned extensive property as far north as the Highlands Cemetery, and eventually he would own what later became the Powell-Murray tract, which the U.S. Forest Service bought in 1913 for protection as national forest land.

Main Street, Highlands, 1884. H. M. Bascom's store and Highlands House barely visible on the left. On the right: Baxter White's P. O., John Arthur's home and picket fence, T. D. Walden's Drugstore, and Joseph Halleck's Central House picket fence distantly visible. Arthur and Hallet built their picket fences in the fall of 1884. Photo probably by John Bundy, courtesy of the Hudson Library archives.

Stewart's *New York Times* columns on farming issues were well known and respected nationally. Indeed, by the time he was appointed Western North Carolina agent for the U.S. Fish Commission, he was already regarded as one of the most prolific agricultural writers in America. His practical knowledge was all-inclusive, for he gave Walter Reese some of the best advice in his profession of carpentry that he was able to find anywhere, such as the trick of driving chestnut stakes in the ground with the top end down since it reversed the pores of the wood and allowed the stake to last a third longer.

Emigration to Highlands in 1884 extended also from as far away as overseas. The leader of the first chamber music group in Highlands, Louis Zoellner, a former professor at a German university and himself a violinist of considerable talent, had played for Kaiser Wilhelm II's coronation.[185] After a short stay in Ohio where he and Margaretta Schafer were married, they moved to Highlands, setting up home near Glen Falls, where he raised bees on a small-scale farm. He also taught German and violin in the Highlands Academy. Many of his descendants still dwell in Highlands today.

1885

Highlands' first druggist arrived from Metamora, Illinois, in 1885. Theron D. Walden set up a drug store and the first Highlands Bank in the Martin building at 4th and Main, later home to Bill's Soda Shop.[186] He built his home in 1886 on eleven acres west of the Poplar Street intersection with 4th, later Joseph Richert's *Blackberry Hill*, today Toby West Antiques. In April, 1890, he organized Highlands' first Free Mason lodge in the Baxter Wilson building. He served on the school board and then as mayor in 1892, the year after his druggist successor, Dr. Henry T. O'Farrell, moved to Highlands from Horse Cove.

Walden was primarily a florist who loved flowers, especially the cactus. He had gathered 350 varieties of cacti, the most extensive collection anywhere in the South, valued at $600, a considerable sum in the early 1890s. Some individual specimens topped fifty dollars, and one in particular, *Cereus gigantus*, was a Mexican-grown plant from which native Mexicans distilled an intoxicating drink. Whether this had medicinal value in his drug store we are not told.

Walden's son Frank worked in his drug store as a watchmaker and jeweler. Years later Frank would be the one whom the hotel keepers trusted to keep correct or sun time, from which the post office clock was regulated, so that the town would have *one* time instead of many, as was the confusing case before he took charge.[187]

7. The Second Wave

There are more Potts than Pans in Highlands!
—Ben Bullard

By 1886, eleven years after its founding and the year that its altitude was corrected from 3,700 to 3,850, forty families from about thirty different states constituted the town of Highlands, its individual population numbering at the time about 300.[188] Quite a contrast to Atlanta's population in the same year of 50,000, Charlotte's 10,000, and Asheville's 6,000. The Baltimore *Sun* in September was praising Highlands as a little village, composed mostly of northern people and containing two churches [Methodist and Presbyterian], a schoolhouse, a circulating library, and no saloons.[189]

Actually the little village contained a bit more than reported. Fourteen commercial enterprises were advertising in *The Highlander*:

(1) Highlands House, a three-story hotel offering pure invigorating air, pure cold spring water, grand scenery, and good fare for low terms,

(2) H. M. Bascom's store for the purchase of hardware, stoves, tin ware, paints, oils, glass, etc.;

(3) Cleaveland's store for a full stock of groceries;

(4) T. Baxter White's for food products, coffees, teas, flour, staple hardware, hats, boots, shoes, pocket cutlery, family medicines, clothing, and insurance;

(5) Rideout & Company for groceries, boots, shoes, hats, clothing, and wool;

(6) John Jay Smith's sawmill and door and sash factory;

(7) the Boynton Brothers & Company lumber mill for building, contracting, and carpentry;

(8) J. H. Durgin, who also engaged in carpentry and building,

(9) William Partridge's water-powered Grist Mill for wheat, buckwheat, and rye flour;

(10) W. W. Cobb's Tannery;

(11) S. T. Kelsey's Land Agency for real estate,

(12) a stationery supply and job printing office at the *Highlander*,

(13) T. D. Walden's Highlands Bank, and

(14) James M. Zachary, surgeon dentist.[190]

Considering the early founders of Highlands, it should be evident by now that the demographic mixture of the village was remarkably unique. It amounted to a melting-pot of hardy pioneers from all over the Country, sober industrious tradesmen from the North, Scotch-Irish laborers and craftsmen from the surrounding mountains and valleys, and wealthy aristocratic planters and professionals from the South.

Indeed, with all their inherited differences, it's rather astonishing that their descendents still occupy the same mountaintop, and yet the very existence of these differences underlies the special qualities that have come to define Highlands. It is too cosmopolitan to be provincial, too broadly based to be singular in attitude and perspective, too enamored of its natural surroundings to be totally indifferent to them, and just isolated enough and small enough to be anxious about the benefits and setbacks of growth and development.

The old Rogers home as it is today at Buck Creek. Photo by Burt Talbott.

Of course, one characteristic of Highlands that tends to bind many of its inhabitants together is the fact, discussed in this book's introduction, that among those who have migrated from neighboring communities in the South, almost everyone who is related to anyone is related to everyone. Local genealogist Lawrence Wood called practically everybody he wrote about either Aunt or Uncle—not because it was customary among mountain folk to do so, which, of course, it was—but because he *was* related to almost everyone he wrote about.

As noted earlier in the Introduction, Grandpa David Rogers, who lived with his wife Margaret and their ten Rogers children in a Buck Creek house built during the mid 1820s, had eleven Rogers brothers, making just about everybody in and around Buck Creek related by blood or marriage to a Rogers, including Lawrence Wood. David's house stands today as the "old Rogers home," where Burton Talbott would live over a century later near the base of the steep road from Shookville up to Buck Gap.

1886-89

Apart from the native sons who multiplied on the land, the second wave of immigrants to come to Highlands, not as founders of the town so much as builders on an established foundation, began arriving in 1886. During the next forty years the town's population wouldn't change appreciably. It fluctuated from 300 down to 250 but back to 300 as the town consolidated, preparing for its second stage of growth, beginning around 1925.

One of the earliest and most vital of these early contributors to the town's identity was Professor Thomas G. Harbison. Born a botanist at heart and receiving one of Kelsey's promotionals, he actually walked with his close friend Elmer Magee from Pennsylvania in the spring of 1886, fully expecting his botanizing test to last only a year.[191] Instead, as will be seen later in Chapter Eleven, he took charge of the town's school and remained essentially for the rest of his life. In 1893 he spent a year's sabbatical in Europe studying schools and forestry. On his return to America he was engaged by George Vanderbilt as botanical collector for the Biltmore Herbarium, which was later presented by Mrs. Vanderbilt to the National Herbarium in Washington.

Harvard University hired Harbison as southern field botanist for the Arnold Arboretum, which position he held for eighteen years, traveling over the southern states researching shrubs and trees. He also collected material for Charles Sargent's *Manual of the Trees of North America*, discovering new or little known species in the southeast. One was a species of willow that took his name, *Salix harbisonii*. Another was the Harbison Hawthorn (*Crataegus harbisonii*); and a third, the beautiful Linden tree now known as *Tilia monticola*.

He found two hybrids growing within the corporate limits of Highlands, one being the chestnut and chinquapin; the other, the white oak and chestnut oak. But his insatiable drive to identify all the flora of the Highlands plateau never impinged on his determination to protect his finds from thoughtless explorers who didn't value them. "I believe," he would say, with a twinkle in his eye, "in keeping hogs from the woods."

Harbison's legacy to Highlands was considerable, for his marriage to Jessie Cobb produced worthy descendants, among whom were the two spinsters who ran the Hudson Library for fifty years and a son who built and landscaped many of the town's homes, public buildings, and roads, as will be seen below.

Dr. Henry O'Farrell was another immigrant of the second wave, a kind-hearted, garrulous Irish fellow who came to town with his wife Abigail from Colorado in 1886. They lived at first in Horse Cove, but by the end of the year they had moved to Squire Hill's boarding house in Highlands. Broken in health, he had sought unsuccessfully to find in the West a cure for his consumption. He replaced Thoren Walden as druggist when he set up his Highlands Drugs in James Rideout's building, catercornered from Walden's Drugs and next to Highlands House. Here he dispensed castor oil, paregoric, horse liniment, and worm medicine and made pills according to the needs of his clientele.

Dr. O'Farrell's pharmacy captured the interest and curiosity of many Highlanders when R. J. Reynolds came to town and personally sold finely cut tobacco in little white sacks.[192] He showed the men how to wrap it inside a thin sheet of paper and lick the roll closed, calling it a cigarette, or "little cigar."

In 1890 O'Farrell moved in with Bascom, taking over Bascom's pharmacy and turning his own drug business over to W. E. Capers. The ad that Dr. O'Farrell ran in 1891 couldn't have appeared today, for it announced, "No Drugs or Medicine in Highlands can equal Nature's great Panacea: Ozone." It went on to say, "I have a few choice Remedies, Drugs, Medicines, etc., just suited to your case until the Ozone has time to take effect." He cautioned his reader not to leave his wallet at home, "for my Drugs have no effect, even on a well man until they are paid for." His ad concluded, "I forgot to mention that I kept Good Cigars. But I would advise you not to smoke."[193]

Dr. O'Farrell drew up Highlands' first fire ordinance in 1894 and served as mayor of the town on three separate occasions spanning a total of eight years. His avocation was music, which he loved teaching, especially choral singing honed to the proper pitch of the tuning fork and accompanied by his wife on the piano. Each practice would end with Abigail's serving her delicious New England doughnuts and coffee.

Henry was a founding trustee of Harbison's Highlands Academy and of the Episcopal Church. He was elected first president of the Southern Blue Ridge Horticultural Society as well as the Highlands Advertising and Improvement Association. The Episcopal circuit rider, Rev. Archibald Deal, described Dr. O'Farrell as never seen without his immaculate and painfully stiff white waistcoat; his wife, with her corkscrew curls, looking as if she might have stepped from a daguerreotype.

If it weren't for Antle Henry, who came to town from Iouther, Wisconsin, in 1886, the youth of Highlands might never have known the joy of a strictly northern tradition that he introduced into the South in December soon after his arrival. This was the year of the two-foot snow, which didn't affect how the townspeople cooked, heated their homes, or traveled—as it would a century later during the blizzard of 1993—because the people in 1886 weren't reliant on electricity or automobiles for convenience or transportation. Nevertheless, the town lay silently beneath its white mantle, and all that moved was Antle Henry's team of four horses that he'd hitched up at his livery stable to break paths to the churches. He improvised a box-sleigh and gave everybody who wished, a sleigh ride on that Tuesday and Wednesday, culminating with a moonlight ride for the young people Wednesday night. With temperatures hovering at two below zero and a brilliant moon shining in a crystal clear sky, it was a thrillingly romantic experience the young folks would not easily forget.

In 1891 Antle Henry moved into Ellen Ellis' house across 2nd Street from the Methodist Church, west of today's Baptist Church. His home was later used as the church's manse, before it was moved in 1984 to 4th Street across from the Ball Park to make way for Mountain High Motel. In 1895 at Henry's request 2nd Street was closed so that he could farm the land with the proviso that he remove the stumps. It remained closed until 1946 when the Baptist Church agreed to share the cost of opening it with the town.

As liveryman, Henry hired out hacks, buggies, and carriages, according to his advertisement, furnishing pleasure parties with "fine Saddle Beasts" and invalids with "easy carriages and careful drivers." But his stay was only fifteen years, for he left Highlands in 1901 to join his sons in Oregon.

Not long after Harbison's arrival in Highlands, the girl that he would marry one day arrived with her family from Beloit, Wisconsin.[194] Vermont natives Judson M. and Lucy Cobb, with their daughters Gertrude and Jessie, stood one fall evening at dusk in 1887 at Buck Horn Gap on Satulah surveying the lay of the land where they would live. Gertrude, seeing only a very few lights flickering on the plateau between Satulah and Bear Pen, stood for a moment pensive and speechless and then piped up, "What kind of place have you brought us to?" For this young teenager brimming with life, Highlands seemed really remote! Yet she and Jessie, who ten years later would marry Prof. Harbison, spent the rest of their contented lives in this "kind of place." Some of their descendents still dwell in Highlands today.

Highlands from Satulah. Photo by R. Henry Scadin, 1898. Courtesy of Gene Potts via Doris Potts.

The Cobbs bought a log cabin from Tom Ford, which Tom's father Jonathan had built around 1860. Tom Ford had played a major role in the Moccasin War two years earlier, as will be seen later in Chapter Ten. Cobb set about expanding his house, for when he first moved in, the snow would sift through the cracks in the roof onto the beds upstairs, which had to be reached by an outside stairway from the porch. His addition to the back of the house allowed access to the upstairs from within. He and Lucy named their house *Altadona*, the name it still bears at the Highlands Country Club as the former home of James and Liz White, currently Cason and Nancy Callaway, facing the 5th green.

Having already established himself in Wisconsin as America's first manufacturer of building paper, a sort of felt that underlay rugs, Judson Cobb came to Highlands to raise Jersey cattle which he brought with him. On the land outside his home he grazed the first registered Jersey breeds in Highlands. It was a well-known fact among the cattle raisers in the area that thoroughbred cows yielded more milk and butter than two or three of a scrub stock, so Judson Cobb's fine Jersey bull was at a premium, as were the Ayrshire bulls of L. O. White, Benson Wells, and Benson Neely, along with Ravenel's Devon bull and Bascom's Holstein.

Before Judson and Lucy died in 1905 and 1934, respectively, they had produced several thoroughbreds of their own. These were the Harbison sisters of Hudson Library fame and the Holt brothers who ran the soda shop and café at Main and 4th for almost the same fifty years. Their granddaughter Helen Holt Hopper was editor of the *Highlander* newspaper.

The end of the 1880s saw other immigrants arrive in Highlands, as discussed later in Chapter Sixteen, such as David and Mattie Norton and T. T. Hall, for they too would remain for the rest of their lives, making significant contributions to the life and culture of the town.

The Last Decade

The year 1891 put Silas McDowell's theory of the thermal belt to its most serious test in Highlands. A frost in early May killed the town's entire fruit crop, leading Baxter White to conclude that "Highlands should depend on grass and not put much land to fruit."[195] Despite this unfortunate turn of events, the flow of immigrants in response to Kelsey's brochure continued. Hiram and Francena Paul, Seventh Day Adventists of Craftsbury, Vermont, came from a potato farm in Limestone, Maine, in 1891.[196] Seeing the brochure, Hiram remembered how much he had liked the South when he fought for the Union in Virginia. He settled in the Buttermilk Level section of Highlands on what later became the Gus Holt and Clara Dove farms.

He worked for H. M. Bascom until he could open his own store on Main Street in Henry Skinner's building, the site of today's Kent, Ltd., and Juliana's. He had thought to open a starch factory, like the one he'd run in Maine if it would pay, but instead he turned to dry goods, which he sold until his departure from Highlands in 1905. In High Point, N.C., he entered the furniture business.

An accomplished carpenter, Hiram also had a steam sawmill, which would later belong to Rich Cobb. It was at this sawmill that he lost part of his left arm, for which he received an increase in his pension due to a previous Civil War disability. To validate the increase, he and two of his thirteen children had to swear that he was sober when the accident occurred and that it was not done intentionally or through any known carelessness. Even his surgeon had to declare him "a moral man with no vicious habits."

Hiram and Francena's son Guy Paul, who came to Highlands as a small boy, helped build the town in quite a literal way. As a blacksmith, brick mason, carpenter, logger, machinist, miller, and construction foreman, Guy helped construct several homes, Lake Sequoyah dam, the Highlands Estates clubhouse, the Franklin road through the gorge, and the Baptist Church, when it was rebuilt in 1940. His marriage to Ethel Mae Potts produced many descendants still living in Highlands.

Dr. Theodore Lamb became the first summer resident to live on Satulah. He arrived from Augusta, Georgia, during the fall of 1891 and bought part of Charles Allen's old farm from Joseph Halleck. Then he built *Chestnut Lodge*, a lovely cruciform house with cross gable roof, wraparound front porch, circling driveway, pond, and interior walls of clear chestnut paneling.

Dr. Lamb's first wife was Jessie Coffin Wotton, who kept the house after her husband's death in 1896. Her descendant, Jack Wotton, is current owner of the home.

Lamb/Wotton home, built in 1892. Photo courtesy of Jack Wotton.

Arriving from Rabun County, Ga., in 1893, Calvin "Cal" Speed, Jr., with his wife Alpha settled on a hundred acres of land in Shortoff. Calvin's granddaughter Betty Speed Wood recalls his self-sufficiency in trapping and tanning hides for buckskin shoes which he fastened to the soles with hand-carved, soft maple pegs. During one winter he handmade 104 pairs of these comfortable shoes. Betty particularly enjoyed riding on Little Jack, Calvin's celebrated mule, which Edna Bryson claims brayed every morning within hearing distance of the children at school.[197]

If there is any truth to Ben Bullard's claim that "there are more Potts than pans in Highlands," then it all began with the first Potts' arrival in 1896. William T. Potts, at age thirty-nine, moved with his wife and six children from Cullasaja, near Franklin, and set up a livery stable in direct competition with H. M. Bascom on Main Street.[198] Married to Joshua Ammons' granddaughter Martha Jane "Mattie" Ammons, he had been a dealer in dry goods, notions, shoes, hats, and general merchandise. Eleven years earlier he had bought a lot near the corner of Main and 3rd, occupied now by Reeves stockyard, and by 1894 he was running a livery business out of Franklin and delivering mail to Highlands.

At first the family lived in the home that Arthur House had built, across from Spruce Street's intersection with 4th, owned today by the Highlands

Historical Society. In 1905 they bought the Central House from David Norton and in 1907 moved into a little house adjoining the Methodist Church South on Spruce Street, behind today's Funeral Home. When they sold the Central House to Grover and Minnie Edwards in 1914, they moved to a farm near Mirror Lake. By now it had become apparent that Mr. Potts tired easily of living in any one place for too long, for he moved his family again to a house on Main Street near today's Scudder's Galleries, then to the current Whittle house at 5th and Chestnut, back to his second home on Spruce, and once again to Mirror Lake.

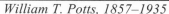

William T. Potts, 1857–1935   *Mattie Ammons Potts, 1862–1929*

Uncle Billy solidified Potts livery service in 1902 by building a new mammoth stable on the later site of Potts Market. It soon gained a reputation for fast horses and fast service. With Charles N. Wright as foreman, the Potts brothers all helped drive the wagons, buggies, and stagecoaches. Six Kentucky-bred fast-steppers pulled the stage between Walhalla and Seneca, outrunning the train across nine miles in thirty minutes, so that folks preferred the stage to the train.

When the Tallulah Falls Railroad extended its lines to Dillard, Georgia, in 1907, Potts Livery made the run to Highlands in only five hours, half the time and half the distance from Walhalla. Passengers rode in buggies, two- and three-seated surreys, and three- and four-seated hacks, all sporting fringed tops and curtains that pulled up and down. Besides the mail, all the groceries and hardware, including silver for the merchants and the bank, came by their livery service until Hiram Dillard purchased the operation in 1910 and ran a livery and freight service between Highlands and Dillard. Frank and Roy Potts built their Potts Brothers grocery here in 1926.

Three individuals who moved to Highlands in 1897 built homes that still exist today. Dr. Mary Lapham purchased a cabin, which she expanded into her home, *Faraway*. John and Mary Crosby of San Mateo, Florida bought John Manley's block at the corner of 5th and Spruce and built their three-story home, which still belongs to the Crosby family. And Thomas B. "Tom" Crunkleton moved with his parents and family from Ellijay near Franklin, becoming the first family to settle the section known at the time as Laurel Heights, now Webbmont.[199] The death of his father, Joseph W. Crunkleton, in 1900 left Tom with the responsibility for the Crunkleton clan, which included his mother, his wife Octa Rogers, and all their children at a time when painter cats still roamed the Highlands plateau, indeed entered the house if the door was left ajar.

In 1909 Tom bought a house owned by Prof. Harbison off the Dillard Road, which still exists across from today's Arnold Road turnoff, and moved his family there. Tom's uncle Isaac "Ike" Crunkleton owned a farmstead in the Cliffside Lake Recreation Area, which back contained no lake, just Skitty Creek.

One of the most important figures in the world of mining came to Highlands at the very end of the century, settling in the old Dobson home which Henry Stewart had just vacated at the corner of Main and 1st, today's site of Furniture South.[200] Born of German immigrants living in Charleston, he was C. Gustavus Memminger. An analytical chemist, he developed the Florida phosphate industry as a leading producer in the United States. His persuasion of the Seaboard Air Line Railroad to extend its lines into Florida, particularly Tampa, led to that city's development as a major port.

In line with his progressive business principles he reformed the whole mining industry by replacing the traditionally rough and turbulent neighborhoods with model villages, containing homes equipped with modern conveniences and beautiful landscaping to attract workers. Paying wages at the highest possible level, he pioneered the idea of workers profit sharing in the plant's earnings.

He took a personal interest in every member of his organization and in their families, and their dedication to him reflected his devotion to them. On one occasion when a watchman died at one of his plants, he canceled the remaining balance of the watchman's mortgage and issued the deed for his home to his widow. Memminger kept his home for thirteen years in Highlands. He spent the last eighteen years of his life, after leaving Highlands in 1912, as a leading citizen of Asheville.

1900–25

Highlands from Corinne Froneberger's school above Chestnut Street, ca. 1908.
Photo by R. Henry Scadin, courtesy of Gene Potts via Doris Potts.
Note H. M. Bascom's home on Satulah ridge (upper right), Davis Inn water tower,
Presbyterian Church (left) and Highlands House (right), Will Cleaveland's planing
mill (below Highlands House), Methodist Church South (left forward), Crosby
house (below Presbyterian Church).

Between 1900 and 1925 a number of immigrants who settled permanently in Highlands chose to live on Satulah Mountain. They too were part of the second wave rather than Old Guard pioneers. Hampton Perry, for instance, arrived in 1900 from Charleston. He and his wife Florence built *Highfield*, a three-story house on a promontory of the lower slope of Satulah, the second home after Dr. Lamb's built specifically as a summer residence on the mountain.

It took its name from Florence's family home in England, and its semi-circular living room and wraparound verandah embraced a splendid view of Whiteside and Bearpen, including a gaunt, craggy Lonesome Pine, which stood directly in the glow of the setting sun. The house was reached by a rustic gate on the Walhalla Road, which opened into a rhododendron tunnel winding its way along a flag-stoned path up to the piazza.

During the 1950s *Highfield* belonged to the Perrys' daughter Florence, known affectionately as "Flo," who married George Saussy, a native of Savannah.[201] George's hobby was wood sculpture, and his creations lent dignity and beauty to the town's churches, especially the Episcopal and Presbyterian, as well as his own home. In 1965 his son Hampton donated to the

Episcopal Church in his memory a set of twelve shields, emblematic of the twelve apostles.

Flo possessed an altruistic character as attuned to the interests and needs of the original settlers of Highlands as it was to the summer folk. Sarah Hicks Hines remembered her equally at home with her Milton and sterling table settings as with the muddy jeans of her grandson, Skip Foley, and his friend, Eddie Potts, when they brought her freshly caught trout for breakfast. She was undeniably a lady of thoughtful aristocratic breeding, but when occasion demanded truth, she could definitely "lay it on the line" with considerable but acrid wit. Anyone seeking flattery or the obscuring of facts need not ask for her opinion, for her response was always as straightforward as it was unequivocal.

Others, like the Perrys, who came to settle in Highlands during the first quarter of the new century also built on or near Satulah, such as Dr. Hugh Elliott from Savannah, who arrived only slightly after the Perrys and erected his mansion farther up the mountain; Charles Albert Hill of Washington, D.C., who bought Selleck's home just north of Satulah's base; and Robert Brockbank Eskrigge from New Orleans, who began building *World's End* near the very top.

Robert Eskrigge was an English-born emigrant to Australia who became one of the South's foremost cotton buyers for English firms in New Orleans. His wife, Virginia Logan, was sister to Blanc Monroe's wife, May, owner of *Playmore*, the original Ravenel home. The Eskrigge home, designed by Sam Labouisse, was built of clear chestnut and birch with oak floors and native gray stone, quarried from the property and laid in the English style by skilled Italian masons.

These foreign workers experienced considerable difficulty deciphering the English language as well as the non-metric units on the architectural plans. Consequently what was intended on the drawing to be a card room emerged as an alcove in the living room, and Eskrigge found to his consternation on one visit that the rockwork had progressed to a height of six feet with no window openings. The two-story plan evolved into a three-story house because the masons couldn't figure how to attach a roof, so they just kept building upward. Apart from gas lamps, the house was wired for electricity long before Highlands had electrical power. A furnace in the cellar burned six-foot logs for central heating.

The year after Eskrigge began building *World's End*, Miss Minnie D. Warren arrived from Scarsdale, New York. At first she lived in Kelsey's former home, which she bought from Prof. Harbison. But in 1918 she built her own home, *The Hedges*, on Satulah at the end of the road that still bears her name. Two terraces extended behind the house, which had a widow's walk over the side porch and double French doors, brown shingles, and a cream-pink trim. Miss Minnie served tea on her terrace and employed Claude Talley as her chauffeur. She had a small house built down below on the Old Walhalla Road for her servant Miss Maude Crain, who lived there from age sixteen until her death in 1977. It is currently the home of Ruth Layton.

Henry Worrell Sloan, a Philadelphian, arrived as a cotton broker from New Orleans in 1900 and built his lovely *Cheeononda* estate at Buck Horn Gap on Satulah. By 1915 his sister, Alice Lyons, had become his neighbor. Five years later Marie Huger from Savannah built across from the Elliotts, and in 1924 Judge Jim Hines of Faison, N.C., who had lived since 1912 in Sula Rice's *White Oak House* on East Main, moved into *Chestnut Burr Cottage*, the old Kibbee home, at Satulah's base.

A world-famous summer resident of Highlands, who built his mansion on 5th Street some distance north of Satulah in 1906–09, was Dr. Alexander P. "Alex" Anderson. Dr. Anderson was the Minnesota-born Clemson professor who in 1901 discovered the method of exploding or puffing starch granules of wheat and rice in sealed tubes placed in a copper oven, which brought him world renown for the commercial production of the popular breakfast cereals, Quaker Puffed Wheat and Quaker Puffed Rice. This was not, however, his only claim to fame, for during thirty-five years of research he completed records of 15,000 experiments, but the world knows him mainly for his one outstanding success.

Extremely well educated with degrees in botany from the University of Minnesota and the University of Munich in Germany, Dr. Anderson credited the old *McGuffey Readers*[202] of his childhood—six schoolbooks in a graded series—for having taught him not only how to read but how to pursue a specific career in science, where he soon found fame and fortune. Indeed, he so much appreciated what these six readers had taught him about what constitutes a rich and full life, that for fifty years he wrote short sketches, stories, and poems about life in the frontier days of Minnesota where he and other students had read the *McGuffey Readers* in lonely country schools.

He gathered illustrations until he had accumulated 625 pages of a *Seventh Reader*, which he published in 1941 and dedicated to his wife Lydia, "The Sweetheart of the Valley: My Only One." Dr. Anderson's daughter, Louise Anderson, grew up in Highlands, also raised on the *McGuffey Readers*, and married Dr. Ralph Sargent. They lived between the Billstein house and the corner of 6th and Main, their house still extant today.

The family that moved into C. C. Hutchinson's original home, which they purchased from the heirs of Dr. Frost, was that of Patrick T. and Dorothy McPherson Farnsworth, who arrived in Highlands around 1905. Patrick, a native of Memphis, Tennessee, was a journalist for Kentucky's leading newspapers, and Dorothy, from Athens, Georgia, contributed poems and songs to various magazines, but usually pseudonymously, rarely under her own name. After Patrick died, the family of his nephew, Sidney W. Farnsworth, lived in the house. Part of their property was sold to the Hudson Library for its new building in 1985.

W. S. Davis, ca. 1920. Photo courtesy of Edith Nix

William S. Davis came to Highlands in 1914 from Hampton, Georgia, widowed the prior year in his marriage to Carrie Wood and seeking with his daughter Lois a cure from tuberculosis.[203] At age fifty, hoping to postpone his death, he and Lois lived initially at the sanatorium, but businessman that he was, he grew impatient with the prescribed cure of only rest, without medication. According to his granddaughter Edith Nix, he questioned the effectiveness of staying in such expensive quarters just for the air which he was told was healing.

He decided to get out and find some less-expensive fresh air. He rented rooms from Mat Gottwals, married Jeremiah Pierson's daughter Rebecca Lake, and ran a grocery in Jeremiah's Rock Store. His shop smelled of brown sugar, shoe leather, and cheese, and he'd always give children a lump of brown sugar from a barrel. He liked children, as the Hines kids knew when they stopped by his store to buy a sack of chocolate drops, for he'd drop the candy into a small paper poke, as he called it, with his withered hand, victim of an accidental gunshot wound. They always noticed he kept his hand encased in a dark blue home-knit mitten.

Edith Nix confirmed that he loved children, so much in fact that he told his own children when they married, he'd give them each a lot from property he owned around Mirror Lake on which to build a home. And to keep them in Highlands, he told them when they accepted the offer, "It's yours if you don't sell it. But if you do sell it, you'll have to pay me for the lot."

Bess Hines considered the dexterity with which he used this hand to wrap packages or retrieve goods from the shelves as typical of the story of his life, as he strove to overcome insurmountable obstacles and achieve, regardless of circumstances. Joseph J. "Joe" Moore, the editor of the *Highlands Maconian*, called him a hustler, not in the conventional sense, but in his drive to succeed. He walked fast, but was never in too much of a hurry to stop and talk or tell a joke, or even to rest prone on a store counter when business was slow. He loved telling salesmen that there were so many drummers calling on him that he was afraid to cut a tree for fear it would fall on one of them. W. S. Davis lived in Highlands over forty years, reaching the mature age of ninety and serving two terms as mayor of the town.

Augustus C. "Gus" Holt came to Highlands in 1905 from Franklin. He set up his shop in 1913 at the corner of 4th and Main. His sons Bill, Harry, and Lawrence operated it from 1927 until 1939, when Bill took it over as Bill's Soda Shop and Harry established Harry's Café next door. Bill continued his very popular soda shop until 1972, and Harry, who dealt in electrical appliances and furniture, ran his café and taxi service until 1945. Lawrence set up a mirror shop at 1st and Spruce.

Levi B. Crane moved to Highlands in the early 1900s from Pine Mountain, Georgia. He arrived with his second wife, Janie Morgan, in 1906 but returned to Pine Mountain before settling permanently in Highlands around 1911. In 1926 he built a house that still exists on Oak Street, and he and his son Phil ran a freight line hauling produce and building materials between Dillard and Highlands.

In 1932 on the knoll near their home, Levi and his son Frank, a policeman who ran a home patrol service for twenty-five years, built Crane's Riding Stables, which moved across Oak Street in 1960 but continued to operate in Highlands until 2000. Two other barns were built, one on Chestnut Street for rides up the Kelsey Trail and the other where the Highlands Country Club caddy shack exists on the Dillard Road for rides to Glen Falls and into Blue Valley. For the equestrians of Highlands, Crane's Stables were indispensable.

Fred A. Edwards, a young man of twenty and son of Alec and Alpha Speed Edwards of Horse Cove, arrived in Highlands in 1916 and, by the time of his death in 1954, had become a legend in town. The nephew of Will Edwards, who in the thirties would own and manage Edwards Inn, Fred set up a grocery business in Charlie Wright's building next to Bascom's on Main Street, and for over thirty years Fred Edwards' store rivaled Potts Brothers next door. Even in winter the big potbellied stove glowed for old-timers who stood with their backs to it, warming themselves while they passed the time of day, two or three hound dogs asleep at their feet. Fred and his wife, Canty, offered friendly and gracious service from behind the counter, and children felt welcome and understood.

In the same year that Fred Edwards came to Highlands, 1916, the Raoul family arrived from Atlanta because Rosine Raoul needed the sanatorium cure for tuberculosis. She bought the old Dobson house from Gustavus Memminger at Main and 1st, currently part of Furniture South, and named it *Rosemary* after herself and her mother. She died in 1918, the year that the sanatorium burned, but left *Rosemary* to her sister Eléonore.

Eléonore was one of the South's earliest advocates of women's rights. As early as 1915 this spirited golden-haired green-eyed rebel rode a white stallion down Peachtree Street in Georgia's first suffrage parade. When she entered the all-male law school at Emory University, Chancellor Candler told her that women weren't allowed, but she typically responded, "Bishop, I have learned enough law to know I can sue you for breach of promise if you do not allow me to stay," for she had already been accepted. She went on in 1920 to become the school's first female graduate.

Her concern for anyone in need was not confined to those of her own sex or outside Highlands. In the twenties just after the Highlands Bank opened, Walter Reese had to borrow $1,800 to pay for his lumber, but come time to pay it off, he couldn't. His son Marshall recalls that the Bank arrived to auction off lots from Walter's land. They set up a table near today's site of

Dusty's Superette on the Dillard Road, ready to take bids. Eléonore happened to pass by and, learning from Walter what was going on, gave him a check for $1,800 so he could keep his land. During her life Eléonore endeared herself so much to the people of Highlands that a town street still bears the Raoul name.

Dobson/Stewart/Memminger/Raoul/Altstaetter home, built 1879. Photo by George Masa, 1929.

In 1926 Eléonore sold *Rosemary* to her sister Rebecca Raoul Altstaetter and bought Brushy Face Mountain for her summer home. It was Rebecca Altstaetter who ran *Rosemary* and the adjacent *Laurel Lodge* during the Depression as an Inn and Tea Room. Having herself served as president of the Savannah League of Women Voters, she hosted lively political discussions for friends and guests who loved to tackle the issues of the times. Many summer residents of Highlands began their interest in the area with a stay at *Laurel Lodge* or *Rosemary*.

Charles J. Anderson, who ran a drug store and then variety store for over thirty years, came to Highlands from Anderson, S.C., in 1921. In 1925 George W. Marett, from Fairplay, S.C., bought Bascom's hardware store and added his grocery, which he operated for fifteen years until his move to Sarasota, Florida, in 1940. He was one of the founders of Highlands Bank, where his brother S. T. Marett served as director.

The Marett brothers pronounced their last names differently. S. T. accented the first syllable: *Mar'-ett*. George, the second: *Ma-rett'*. According to George's wife, the rules of spelling, with only one *r*, put the accent on the second! The personalities of the two brothers were also different. S. T. was more reserved, more businesslike than George, according to Bill Holt, who says that when as a young man he would bring a dollar or two to deposit in his savings account at Highlands Bank, Mr. S. T. Marett would always say, "It isn't what you make that counts, Richard, it's what you save."

George Marett's Store, bought and expanded in 1925

After 1925

If there was a third wave of immigration to wash over Highlands at a time when the little town stood on the threshold of renewed growth, it probably occurred after 1925. First among the newcomers were the couple Joseph E. and Annie Root. They built a home in 1926 at the corner of Main and 3rd.

A native of Lincoln, Nebraska, Joseph was hired to install waterworks for the town as well as engineer the newly proposed Highlands Estate golf course. Annie set up and operated in her home a very popular gift shop and tea room, which thrived for thirty years from 1931 until her death in 1961. Their house in 1967 was the scene of the first practice burn for the Highlands Volunteer Fire Department, making room for today's Reeves Hardware.

Col. John Stephen Sewell, a fifty-seven-year-old long-retired U.S. Army engineer known to most Highlanders as "General Sewell," came to Highlands from Birmingham, Alabama, in 1926 and built a summer home.[204] He had had an illustrious career in the army. Having graduated second in his class at West Point, he worked in the Engineers' Corps, designing some of the most notable public buildings in the nation's capital, among which were the Government Printing Office, the Army War College and Engineers' School, and new buildings for the Department of Agriculture and the U.S. Soldiers' Home.

The year before his retirement in 1907 the American Society of Civil Engineers awarded him the Norman medal for his revolutionary paper on the "Design of Reinforced Concrete for Fire-Resisting Structures." Upon his retirement he joined the Alabama Marble Company in Birmingham, becoming its president in 1919 until his death in 1940.

Called back into service during the first World War, he commanded the 17th Railway Construction Regiment at Saint Nazaire, France, which amounted to supervising 39,000 men, in-going and out-going troops, and millions of tons of material. In 1933–34, while living in Highlands, he employed his engineering skills to serve as head of foreign exhibits at the Chicago World's Fair, whose theme was "Century of Progress." What distinguished this fair from previous world fairs was its notable exhibit of important scientific and industrial developments of the nineteenth century, particularly its focus on Sewell's specialty: modern architecture.

When Col. Sewell died at age seventy-two in 1940, his life had come full circle. His being born in a log cabin in Jackson County, Tennessee, and having risen to such a high position in modern design, it proved particularly ironic that he should die in a similar log cabin in Highlands. Between his birth and his death in simplicity stood a life of complex and elegant design.

Wilton H. Cobb came to Highlands from Walhalla, S.C., in 1927. He arrived as a hardware merchant who served a total of thirteen turbulent years as the town's mayor. In 1929 Ernest H. Brown came from Dillard to set up his clothing store next to the alley on West Main Street. For a while he had a store at Scaly. He ran his Highlands store until it was torn down in 1950.

Harvey S. Talley, a native of Macon County, came to Highlands in 1935. He and John D. Burnett of Scaly set up Talley and Burnett Grocery where the Royal Scott is today. In 1950 they built on East Main. When Burnette sold out four years later, Talley ran the grocery alone until 1967, when the Little Cheese Shop moved in and stayed until replaced by Paoletti's in 1984. Both Burnett and Talley served the town as commissioners.

When Jack H. Wilcox arrived in 1936 to summer in Highlands with his wife Virginia "Ted" Randall, they immediately set about developing Billy Cabin Farm. A native of Halifax, Nova Scotia, Jack served as town clerk during the years that the town was reducing its indebtedness. From 1948 to 1960 he taught economics at the University of Tennessee.

138

The farm house that Jack built on Billy Cabin served to all intents and purposes as a school for folks in the town, for he and Ted would entertain their many friends with intensely passionate discussions of all the political and social issues that seethed and fermented from the patriotic forties through the rebellious sixties. No one escaped their lively and stimulating suppers without an opinion expressed and challenged.

Talley and Burnett Grocery on East Main. Later the Little Cheese Shop, Paoletti's today.

In 1944 a new summer resident, Robert L. Conlon, began to write a poetry column for the *Galax News*. Since 1926 his real estate activities had established him as a pioneer developer of the winter resort of Hollywood, Florida. He had a house just over the rock quarry on Little Bear Pen. If he meant to escape the hustle and bustle of the booming city of Hollywood by summering in the peaceful village of Highlands, he was soon to discover much to his consternation that life above a quarry was quite a blast, as will be discussed later in Chapter Eight.

From the thirties to the sixties Miss Sara Gilder, a native of Mount Meigs near Birmingham, Alabama, lived on Satulah Road and ran a store in Highlands.[205] In 1930 she opened a grocery store in the Cobb Hardware building on 4th Street hill. She moved to the Holt building behind Bill's Soda Shop in the mid thirties and finally settled in the Rice Building, later home of the

Paintin' Place, now Buck's Coffee Cup as of 2001. Sara loved things "old fashioned." She filled her windows with potted azaleas, geraniums, gardenias, and fuchsia for the ladies and hired only very pretty girls for her male clientele.

There was no health department in those days to prohibit Felix, her black cat, from stalking and purring about the store as if he owned it. Indeed, he was featured one Christmas in her prize-winning window display, lying on a red cushion in front of a make-believe fireplace of red tissue paper and black andirons. For thirty-five years Sara Gilder's was where people gathered and gossiped, by the front window in the summer and around the wood stove at the rear in the winter. She was always interested in others, especially parents of a first child whom she'd advise, so she made friends with many a young mother.

A number of Highlanders who contributed to the town's history after 1925 weren't so much newcomers as pioneers' descendants, who made their lasting mark on their own merits rather than on the coattails of their illustrious ancestors. By the time Rev. Billy Potts had entered the Baptist ministry in 1908 he and Mattie had had ten children, seven of whom survived to become prominent citizens of Highlands.

Ed Potts served as town clerk for sixteen years. Frank established Potts' Market in 1909, which he ran with his brother Roy, better known as "Nick," and with Ed until his own retirement in 1956.[206] Ethel Mae, who married Guy Paul, was the scholar of the family. Charlie and Gene both served as postmaster (Charlie for sixteen years) and mayor. Arthur "Shine" Potts, so called because he used to shine shoes as a kid—nickel a pair—at the hotels in town, had a marvelous sense of humor and acted as the family storyteller.

These seven children of Rev. Potts produced thirty-eight children, all but two of whom grew up in Highlands. They too have produced more Potts. Indeed, Gene Potts' son Bud, himself postmaster for twenty-one years in Highlands, credits Ben Bullard with the saying, "There are more Potts than Pans in Highlands!"

The Rices too produced descendants who in their own right contributed to Highlands. Darthula "Sula" Rice, daughter of Isaac and Vinetta, ran the old Rice home place as a popular boarding house out at Short Off after her mother's passing in 1928 until her own death in 1945. Another daughter Susan, affectionately known as "Tudie," taught school at Shortoff, Flat Mountain, and Clear Creek in North Carolina, but also in Georgia, South Carolina, and central North Carolina.

She was in Smithfield when she taught the actress Ava Gardner. For a while she worked as secretary to the eminent Asheville novelist Thomas Wolfe, earning such high respect for her services that when he died, he left her his bed, dresser, and wash basin, owned now by the Jellens of Highlands.[207] She lived in the house behind Archie and Hazel Jellen's Gem Shop on 4th Street Hill.

Isaac and Vinetta's son Luther "Luke" Rice married Dr. Will Anderson's daughter Christina.[208] He served for a total of thirty-four years on the town council and was town clerk when the water and electric systems were established during the late twenties. In the early thirties he and Ed Potts represented Macon County in Washington in support of the establishment of a Great Smoky Mountains National Park to protect and preserve a national treasure. Nelson Rockefeller had just donated $5 million toward its realization. Luke attended Franklin Roosevelt's dedication of the Park at Newfound Gap in 1940.

In Highlands Luke operated the only meat market in town in the back of W. S. Davis' Rock Store until he had his own building in 1928 west of Potts Brothers, today's Wit's End and Buck's Coffee Café. In his screened room at the back with sawdust strewn over the floor, he sold native beef and lamb. His well-trained black and white shepherd dogs, Bill and Jack, when they weren't sunning themselves in front of his meat market, herded sheep, cattle, and hogs over long distances, long before the age of trucks. Luke's son "Little Luke" operated the Tar Heel Restaurant.[209]

Other descendants of early founders who left their personal imprint on the Highlands scene were T. T. Hall's son, Tudor N. Hall, whose real estate and insurance business thrived on Main Street from the fifties through the seventies where Cyrano's Bookshop exists today. It passed within the family to the Chambers Agency, located now in the Hall house on 5th Street.

Another realtor and insurance agent, the son of summer resident W. Hampton Perry, was John H. C. Perry. He came to Highlands in 1946 to establish his agency, which continued under Jack Taylor in its new building west of Reeves Hardware in 1979.

Dr. Jessie Moreland came to Highlands in 1936, bringing her dentist practice with her from Raleigh, but she was originally from Jackson County, the daughter of Highlands' first dentist James Zachary, returning home.

A descendant of the early Piersons served as a paratrooper in Italy during World War II, was captured, and escaped by jumping from a moving train and walking to safety. He was Lt. Col. Val Pierson. His wife, Norma T. "Boots" Pierson, before her premature death in 1987, contributed significantly to the Highlands community as a member or officer of the early planning and zoning boards, the library, the hospital, the Biological Foundation, the Macon County Program for Progress, and the Southwestern Regional Planning and Development Commission. She wrote the original study that enabled the town to establish the recreation park.

A grandson of W. T. Potts, who became one of the town's best-loved humanitarians and public servants, was Steve Potts, recipient in 1996 of the

Robert DuPree Award for his distinguished contributions to the community. He served for more than twenty-six years as town commissioner and two terms as mayor. With Bob DuPree he created the Highlander Café and Restaurant in 1948 and established Steve's Country Store in 1952, which he ran as a popular business. He was helped by his daughter Sherri Potts Kremser until his death in 1999. His sisters, Jessie and Nancy, described his indefatigable energy and tireless work habits as being so boundless that "if Steve would hire two or three to stand around watching him, he could do the labor of all of them."

A grandson of Charlie Wright, who died the same year as Steve Potts, was Harry Wright, a retired regional forester who served three terms as mayor from 1975 to 1981 and headed the 1975 Commission which celebrated Highlands' hundredth anniversary. He was particularly instrumental in setting up the Highlands Historical Preservation Society in 1979, which after a long period of inactivity was reactivated in 1999 as the Highlands Historical Society, Inc. The new Society appropriately bought for its home the oldest house still standing in Highlands, which Arthur T. House had built near his mill 122 years earlier, in 1877.

For the most part, aside from the descendants of local pioneers, new arrivals to Highlands during the first three decades of the twentieth century became known as the Atlanta invasion, followed after mid-century by the Florida invasion. Floridians swelled Highlands during the summers until the mid eighties, when Atlantans suddenly rediscovered the town as a convenient refuge from the summer heat but also as a weekend retreat even during the winter. John Cleaveland claims that almost 80% of his sales in real estate since the 1980s have been to Atlantans, and he foresees no slowdown with the population of Atlanta projected to reach six million by 2005.

Famous Visitors and Residents

In addition to both the permanent and summer residents of Highlands, many national and international celebrities have chosen to visit or settle in the little town over the years, in part because of its legendary charm but also because they had friends living in the area.

In 1906 the poet Vachel Lindsay visited Prof. Harbison while on a walk from Florida to Asheville. Golf ace Bobby Jones, baseball star Ty Cobb, and golfer Mary Rogers all played exhibition games in Highlands, and Jones built a summer home at the Highlands Country Club. Arnold Palmer designed the 18-hole championship golf course for the Cullasaja Club. Clark Howell, editor of the *Atlanta Constitution*, and his sister Rosalie, private secretary to Franklin D. Roosevelt, both had summer homes, as did Col. John Sewell, as discussed above. Rosalie's home on Cobb Road was modeled after a Japanese temple.

Highlands has held a particular fascination for scientists, such as Dr. Michael Hoke of the Roosevelt Foundation and Dr. Mary Lapham, whose fame sprang from her pioneer work in the area in the treatment of TB. The heads of Vanderbilt's Department of Biology, Dr. Edwin E. Reinke, and the University of North Carolina's Department of Botany, Dr. William C. Coker, as well as the Director of the Birmingham Museum, Dr. H. E. Wheeler, all served as Executive Director of the Highlands Biological Station.

The list includes distinguished literary artists, like the poet, short-story writer, and novelist Stephen Vincent Benét, author of the famous Pulitzer Prize winning Civil War narrative, *John Brown's Body*; Dorothy Ogburn, whose mystery *Death on the Mountain* had Highlands as its setting; the author of *Col. Effingham's Raid*, Berry Fleming; Alex Haley, acclaimed author of *Roots*; and historical novelist Herbert Ravenel Sass (third cousin to Prioleau Ravenel's granddaughter Margaretta Ravenel Duane Wood), whose *War Drums* in 1928 took place at Whiteside Mountain when the Cherokees still inhabited Western North Carolina. Pat Conroy spent the summer of 1985 in Highlands writing his best-seller *Prince of Tides*.

There were visits from artists Norman Rockwell and George B. Matthews, whose historic paintings graced the Nation's Capitol building; cartoonist Frank Willard of "Moon Mullins"; Dorothy Dix, Mrs. Henrietta Dull of *Southern Cooking* fame; and Dr. Robert F. Griggs of *National Geographic's Valley of the 10,000 Smokes*.

In the political and corporate realms the governors of N.C., Ga., Ala., and Tenn. all visited Highlands. Governors Lawton Chiles of Florida and Peter Dupont of Delaware were Highlands seasonal homeowners, as were Coca-Cola director and philanthropist, George W. Woodruff, and vice-president Charles Veazey Rainwater.

The visitor list includes the governor of the Federal Reserve Board, Eugene Black; Federal Court of Appeals Judge E. K. Campbell; Assist. Sec. of the U.S. Treasury L. W. Roberts; Major Gen. David Shanks; Assist. Director of the Metropolitan Museum of Fine Arts in New York, William Ivins; and president of the University of North Carolina, Frank Graham.

In June, 1947, years before he became president, Gerald R. Ford, Jr., spent two nights as a modest, affable, young wedding guest of the Westervelt Terhunes of New Orleans and attended the marriage of their daughter Elise "Sooky," which Rev. Rufus Morgan officiated at the Episcopal Church. Alfred W. Hudson, son of the Library's namesake Ella Hudson, visited Highlands in 1939 when he was president of Chase Manhattan Bank in New York City. Bishop John E. Hines, a native of Seneca, S.C., and presiding bishop of the Protestant Episcopal Church of the U.S. in 1964, lived with his wife, Helen, in the Lyons house on Satulah until his retirement.

During the thirties and forties a very colorful character from Anderson, S.C., summered in Highlands: retired Rear Admiral Newton A. McCully. Admiral McCully had served during World War I as commander of U.S. naval forces in Russia. Fluent in the Russian language, he was a close friend of Tsar Nicholas II at the birth of the Russian Revolution, which toppled three hundred years of Romanov rule and introduced the world to communism. Witnessing the disintegration of the tsarist empire was particularly painful for McCully on account of his deep affection for the Russian people.

As a humanitarian concerned for the welfare of Russian refugees, he had brought seven Russian children—two boys and five girls ages three to twelve—to the States in 1921 to raise and educate at his own expense. Despite his attempts to shun publicity, the *New York Times* applauded him for his "rescue" of the "Russian waifs," catapulting him into the national news.

Settling in his family home in Anderson, S.C., the competent bachelor proved himself a natural parent. Charles Weeks reported in his biography, *An American Naval Diplomat in Revolutionary Russia*, that McCully was as playful as he was stern.[210] Regimenting the children in a daily routine based on the U.S. Navy's *Mueller's Manual*, he never administered corporal punishment but treated disobedience with more meaningful consequences, like reduction of allowance to promote proper respect for personal responsibility within the family.

In his late seventies he moved to St. Augustine and summered in Highlands, where he quickly became well known and highly respected. He could be seen walking his seven miles per day, often with his children; playing tennis; and enthusiastically enjoying square dancing at Helen's Barn. In 1938, seven years after his retirement from the Navy, despite his advanced age at seventy-one, he attempted to rescue two boys from drowning in Highlands' Lake Sequoyah, the account of which is told below.

Other nationally known figures lived in Highlands, such as Ken Keyes of Miami. He was chairman of the largest realty company in the South, president of the National Association of Real Estate Boards, and widely known for his witness as a Christian, his message being "In Partnership with God," which he had given as a lecture more than 675 times by 1966. He also directed the magazines *Christianity Today* and *Presbyterian Journal*.

Charles L. Allen of Atlanta led several revivals at the Methodist Church in Highlands during the 1960s and 1970s. He is especially well known for his book of consolation, *When You Lose a Loved One*, but also for *God's Psychiatry* and *Meet the Methodists: An Introduction to the United Methodist Church*.

Rev. J. Bruce Medaris, a summer resident of Highlands, set up the Mission of the Holy Cross to provide a place for Episcopalians to worship according to the 1928 *Book of Common Prayer* instead of the 1979 revision. As a retired Major General of the U.S. Army, he was known to his friends as the man who "dragged the United States, kicking and screaming, into the Space Age by launching the free world's first earth satellite."

Judge Alto Adams, Chief Justice of Florida's Supreme Court, and his wife Carra divided their time between Fort Pierce and their Satulah Mountain home. Dr. John Steelman, former chief of the White House staff under President Truman and the first person in White House history to be given the title "assistant to the President," had a home at Highlands Falls Country Club. And Dr. Ken Sorensen, a retired airline pilot who pursued an international career as an expert on Eastern Europe and the Middle East, still summers in Highlands, as does Fletcher Wolfe, director of the internationally celebrated Boys Choir of Atlanta, who chose Flat Mountain Road for his magnificent home.

John Harbert III, who also summered in Highlands, had started a construction business in Birmingham, Ala., with $6,000 that he won gambling as a GI during World War II. His firm went under three times before his gamble on a Kentucky coal mining operation paid off, and with the profits he was able to buy a controlling interest in Amoco during the energy crisis, which in itself raised him to Forbes–400 status as a billionaire and extraordinary philanthropist before his death of pancreatic cancer in 1995.

William A. "Bill" Emerson, another summer resident, rose within the ranks of Merrill Lynch to become senior vice president and national sales director for the southern half of the United States. Constance Bess headquartered her design, wholesale, and mail order companies in Highlands, from where she coordinated her potpourri and tea manufacture, cosmetic distribution, and commercial and residential interior design.

Permanent resident Anna Schiffli Herz created her Annawear in 1986, beginning with T-shirts and expanding through representatives to wholesale clothes markets in New York, Los Angeles, Dallas, and Chicago. Block printing the clothes herself, she found buyers at Saks Fifth Avenue, Nordstrom, and boutiques all over the country. Seasonal resident William H. "Bill" Flowers advanced his father's wholesale bakery in Thomasville, Ga., to the nation's leading producer and marketer of fresh and frozen baked foods with current sales approaching $4.5 billion.

Dr. George Sandor, a native Hungarian and internationally recognized mechanical engineer, was a Highlands summer resident for several years during the eighties and nineties.[211] His specialty was the design of automation machinery, a form of robotics that aimed at high quantity mass production. He designed the first color press for *Life Magazine* as well as a working prototype for an autonomous unmanned exploration vehicle that would one day be used on the planet Mars. Conversant in seven languages, he produced over 150 articles and twelve books used in colleges and graduate schools worldwide.

Jack Eckerd, founder of the national drug store chain by his name, divided his time between Florida and Highlands. A champion of the rights of prison inmates, he led Florida's prison industry system which helped provide inmates with trades they could use after their release. He also worked with Chuck Colson, whose involvement in the Watergate scandal led to his fall from special counsel to President Richard Nixon into serving time in prison. He experienced a much publicized conversion to Christianity and began setting up Prison Fellowship, an international outreach to prisoners, ex-prisoners, victims, and their families. A frequent visitor to Highlands, Colson founded Justice Fellowship in 1983 to promote reform in the criminal justice system and Neighbors Who Care in 1989 to help victims of crime.

B. Eliot Wigginton, editor of the popular *Foxfire Book*, Doubleday's all time best seller, was an occasional visitor to Highlands. He and his students at Rabun Gap-Nacoochee School wrote and produced this work about the life and culture of the Appalachian Mountains and began publishing it as a magazine in 1967. To date, it has expanded to eleven volumes.

Dr. Carlton Joyce, a Highlands resident who shares Wigginton's passion for research but on a more professional level, is a spectroscopist who joined other American scientists in Italy in 1988 to verify the authenticity of the sacred Shroud of Turin. He explored Egyptian catacombs in search of Cleopatra's tomb and researched more than 300 battles of Normandy for a series of books containing detailed maps and diagrams for guided tours. He also founded Spectrometrics, an Atlanta-based company that applies the same principles of forensic spectroscopy worldwide to track oil through engines in order to predict when and if they will fail.

During the 1980s Burt Reynolds and Lonnie Anderson lived on King Mountain and frequented Helen's Barn when the dance floor was so crowded that the caller couldn't really tell who was dancing and how. Burt in particular expressed great concern in 1981 about the overdevelopment and condo fever he feared would gobble up "one of the most beautiful and magical spots in the United States."[212]

Well-known authors who came to autograph at Cyrano's Bookshop, established in 1978, were Wilma Dykeman in 1984, Malcolm Forbes in 1988, James Michener in 1989, and Charles Frasier in 1997. The existentialist writer Walker Percy had a summer home on Mirror Lake. Speaker of the House Newt Gingrich and his wife Marianne were frequent visitors to Highlands during the politically turbulent nineties. The Smathers brothers had summer homes in town: Frank, a self-made millionaire, and George, the U.S. senator from Florida.

James Michener autographing The Caribbean *in Highlands, 1989*

In 1984 former first lady "Lady Bird" Johnson, hosted by Mr. and Mrs. J. B. Fuqua, visited the Highlands Biological Station, calling for the use of wildflowers in national beautification projects, a popular program that continues to grace major highways with fields of lovely flowers today. In 1987 actors Hume Cronyn, Jessica Tandy, and singer John Denver chose the Highlands area to film the Hallmark production of "Foxfire." On August 4, 2000, former President George H. W. Bush attended a GOP fundraising reception on the grounds of *Wolf Ridge* in Highlands. The event raised over $300,000 toward his son George W. Bush's bid for the presidency.

These then were some of the better-known residents and visitors who appreciated Highlands' sequestered charm, refined culture, and openhearted hospitality, despite its muddy roads. Some, like George Washington, might have passed this way but once—George Washington never slept in Highlands, while Gerald Ford spent two nights—but many of them resided part-time or permanently or returned on many occasions because the town had something special to offer them. If they still visit or choose to live in Highlands, it's because that something special has not yet been lost or squandered away.

8. From Mud to Macadam

A wretched mountain road creeps uncertainly through these heights, passing at their bases through dense forests of oak, poplar, and walnut, colored with snowy rhododendrons, pink masses of the Carolina rose, and the scarlet service berries, or climbing to the summits through gloomy aisles of gigantic pines.
— Richard and Rebecca Harding Davis, 1876

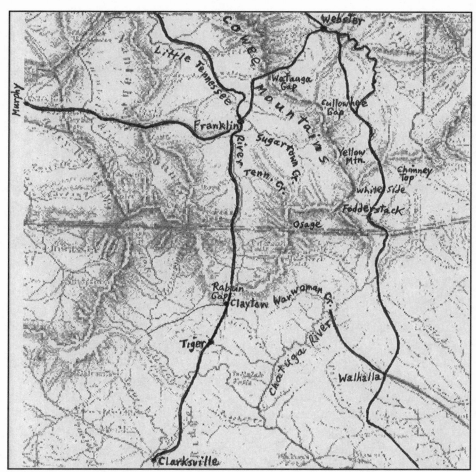

The Roads in Macon and Jackson Counties in 1865

Geography played a large role in the making of Highlands as it did of North Carolina itself, beginning at the seashore and ending in the mountains. From the earliest days of exploration, the Carolina coast developed the reputation of being a graveyard for sailors, and though the English made several attempts in the late sixteenth century to set up colonies along the eastern seaboard, the honor of the first permanent settlement went instead to Virginia. It was during the seventeenth century that Virginians began to spread into North Carolina's tributaries—farmers, hunters, immigrants seeking elbow room, even rogues fleeing Virginian law and soon followed by well-bred planters.

The central area of the state didn't attract settlers until the eighteenth century when leading Virginia families bought up cheap land for plantations. Accompanying them were Scotch-Irish and German farmers from Pennsylvania in search of independence and Highland Scotch fleeing political, economic, and religious woes in their homeland. The English brought along government; the Scotch, education; and the Germans, industry.

The mountains were the final section of the state to be settled. Until the early nineteenth century they were the last stand of the Cherokees. Unlike the piedmont and the coast, where rivers and roads afforded excellent travel, communication, and commerce, the mountains were relatively inaccessible. Which is why they became a natural refuge for political and religious dissenters, mainly Scotch-Irish and German but also French, who found their independence from tyrannical rules and centralized government with its burden of taxation.

Nathaniel Macon was one of these early nonconformists, after whom Macon County was named.[213] A states rights advocate who feared and mistrusted a strong central government, he fought against it for thirty-seven years in the U.S. House and Senate, determined to safeguard the rights and privileges of the people back home.

Just west of Macon's home, across the mountains, and some fifty years after his death, a similar assertion of independence erupted with the creation of the State of Franklin.[214] Named after Benjamin Franklin and now part of eastern Tennessee, the territory between the Blue Ridge and Cumberland Mountains declared itself a separate state in 1784. Although North Carolina tried to withdraw its permission before Congress could vote their approval, the new state wrote its own constitution and elected as its own governor, John Sevier, whom North Carolina declared a traitor. Without official currency, the people paid salaries in furs, whiskey, and tobacco for four years until North Carolina regained control in 1788, pardoned Franklin's leaders, and elected John Sevier to the N.C. Senate. When North Carolina again ceded the land beyond the mountains to the new state of Tennessee in 1796, Sevier became its first governor.

Freedom from government interference appealed instinctually to the mountaineers of western North Carolina, who purchased it at a high cost. They found themselves accordingly isolated from market facilities and state funding, either of which would allow them to survive. One-and-two-teacher schools in the mountains were poor because they were small, and communities had to rely entirely on their own resources because roads connecting them were either wretched or nonexistent.

It's no wonder that Highlands, as inaccessible as it was on top of the Blue Ridge escarpment, was so concerned even in its earliest days about building good roads to neighboring communities. Originally, at the end of the Civil War, there was no road to Highlands.

The Glade Mountain Road
From Walhalla

The nearest road of any consequence was the Walhalla Turnpike, which ran from Walhalla to Webster through Whiteside Cove and Cashiers Valley. It was a primitive wagon road that climbed the mountains north of Walhalla, forded the Chattooga River, continued around Glade Mountain, and ran past the home of Col. John and Sarah Alley (now Lombard's Lodge) in Whiteside Cove before arriving in Cashiers Valley.

The Road from Whiteside Cove to Franklin

At the time of the town's founding, indeed in the late 1860s and 1870s, a wagon road branched off the Walhalla Turnpike at the Alley homestead and ascended the south shoulder of Wildcat Cliffs. Climbing Norton Mill Creek past today's home of Jim Whitehearst, it emerged near the current home of Jim and Barbara Estes by the 15th hole of the Highlands Falls Country Club. Its passage through Wildcat Gap, the same route that Michaux took in 1787, is known today as Falcon Ridge Road. It continued to Short Off, where it followed the Flat Mountain and Brush Creek roads to Franklin. This is the route that Charlie Jenks took in reverse from Franklin to Short Off and Whiteside Mountain during the early 1870s.

The Whiteside Cove Road
to Highlands

Soon after the town's founding, a fork was created in the road up Wildcat Cliffs that led to today's Bowery and met the extension of East Main Street at Ravenel's Gate. On the Highlands map of 1881 this fork was known as the Whiteside Cove Road to Walhalla, today's Bowery Road. Indeed, in 1876, the year after the town's founding, it was the only way in or out of Highlands by horse-drawn hack, which is the reason Richard and Rebecca Harding Davis—like Kelsey and Hutchinson before them—were restricted to traveling either by horseback or on foot when they took the old Indian trail up the Sugartown or Cullasaja River. Their description in

Harper's Monthly of the Sugar Fork trail, which didn't appear on any map, gave an outsider's view of what the local folks had come to take for granted, and the Davises spared no words in depicting what they experienced:

> *A wretched mountain road creeps uncertainly through these heights, passing at their bases through dense forests of oak, poplar, and walnut, colored with snowy rhododendrons, pink masses of the Carolina rose, and the scarlet service berries, or climbing to the summits through gloomy aisles of gigantic pines. For many miles it has as its companion a beautiful river, the Sugar Fork. After our explorers had traveled forty or fifty miles through the chasms of these hills without meeting a human being, they began to regard the river as an old friend, especially after they had been forced to ford it half a dozen times, and had been nearly swept away by the fierce embrace of the current.*[215]

Whatever the setbacks of traveling the Sugar Fork trail from Franklin, the wagon road from Walhalla was certainly no turnpike by any modern standards. Though currently passable only by jeep, the Glades Road section posed a formidable challenge even in its own time. In 1877 Wilbur Zeigler and Ben Grosscup described it in their *Heart of the Alleghanies* as passing "through a wild and cheerless tract of uncultivated mountain country, where miserable farm-houses, and none others, but seldom show themselves, and where the unbroken solitude breeds blockade whisky stills, in its many dark ravines and pine forests. It would bother any officer, in penetrating this section, to definitely ascertain when his feet were on North Carolina, Georgia, or South Carolina soil."[216]

Woodrow Wilson traveled this road as early as 1879, when he summered at John R. Thompson's boarding house in Horse Cove and complained that the road was rough and ill-kept. He called it "simply terrible," endurable at best for himself, "but for delicate ladies and children it was trying in the extreme." He appropriately named the end of the road, "North Carolina's jumping off place."[217]

Despite its dreadful shortcomings, there was no alternative route for travelers from out-of-state wanting to reach Highlands. In his flyer seeking to attract settlers in 1876, Mr. Kelsey laid out directions to Highlands, as follows. A traveler from the northwest, west, or southwest regions of the United States would come first to the railroad station in Atlanta. From the east and northeast he would travel to Richmond. From either of these locations he could take the Atlanta & Richmond Air Line Railroad to Seneca, S.C.

Following an overnight stay, he would pay Mr. A. W. Thompson $8 or $10 for one or two passengers, $4 for each additional, to travel by carriage from Seneca to Walhalla. If he preferred to continue on the train to Walhalla, nine miles nearer Highlands, he could hire a carriage for a dollar or two less at W. A. Addington's livery stable.

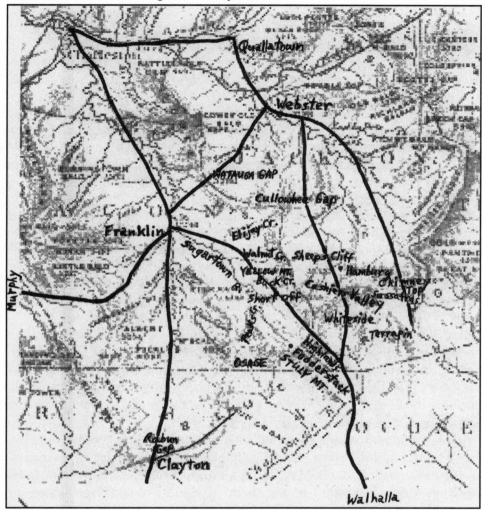

The Roads in Macon and Jackson Counties in 1882

Wisely enough, Kelsey failed to describe the road from Walhalla to Highlands in his promotional brochure. He wrote instead, "Most of the people who are locating here are from the North, but good citizens are welcomed from any part of the country."[218] Good citizens who made it as far as Walhalla would have had no forewarning of the long, arduous two-day trip still ahead to Highlands. Covering thirty-two miles, it would require another overnight stay at the old Russell House on the South Carolina bank of the Chattooga River.

The Russell House was built in 1867 by William Ganaway Russell from Franklin, N.C.[219] He intended it as a small home on land belonging to the family of his wife Jane Nicholson. He paid $1,200 for the property with gold he had mined in California and carried quilted into his vest for safe-keeping. Enlarged three times as its popularity increased over the next forty years, Russell House became the Half Way House for anyone traveling between Walhalla and Highlands. It was well known for the Southern hospitality it offered.

Among the fifteen rooms were a spacious hall, lovely old parlor, huge dining room that fed as many as eighty-three, sitting room, and old-time kitchen furnished with hand-made antique furniture and utensils. The bedrooms upstairs opened out onto the porch, and on the front porch was an upping block, used by the ladies to mount the horses they rode side saddle.

Mrs. Russell always kept a hot rock at the fire place for the mailman to place at his feet after she fed him his dinner and sent him on his way. Her granddaughter Elizabeth Russell Stelling remembers her as particularly attentive to her lodgers, for she would bring her sewing machine onto the front porch to talk with them while she made and repaired clothes for her fifteen children. Tragically the Russell House was burned to the ground, presumably the work of an arsonist, over a century later during the spring of 1988 so that only the great stone chimneys and huge shade trees remain.

By 1879 it was crystal clear to the residents of Highlands that roads were desperately needed to connect the town with the outside world. Kelsey confirmed this need when he described to John Jay Smith his dream of Highlands as the hub of a wheel: "People will eventually come through Highlands to reach every point in this part of North Carolina, in northwestern South Carolina, and points in North Georgia."[220]

Today's interstates and bypasses have watered down his prediction a bit, for they stick to the valleys, but early Highlanders were determined regardless to have good roads. In May, 1879, a board of supervisors was set up for the Blue Ridge Township. It was chaired by J. W. Wilson, with crews of men assigned to eleven districts, covering proposed roads in all four directions.[221] At the time, all able-bodied men were required to perform road duty, no excuse permitted. Indeed, it was not until 1891 that the men even had a choice.

The choice was to pay a tax of 15¢ per $100 valuation of your property and another tax of 45¢ with each poll for road construction, or to get out and work the roads yourself for a daily credit of 75¢ against your tax.[222] Work on the new roads required, at minimum, two tools: something with which to dig and scrape, and a small tin clock. "When a man works on the road," reported Bradford Torrey in 1896, "he needs a hoe to work with, and a time-piece to tell him when to begin and when to leave off."[223]

There was a major loophole in the law that gave each citizen a choice, and Albert Staub, Highlands professor from Switzerland, singled it out as the chief reason all roads, after ten years of roadwork, continued to be in such abominable condition.[224] He blamed the law that unjustly exempted all men over forty-five from either the road work or the tax. Boys of eighteen, with little interest in good roads and who regarded road repair as a kind of picnic, were making games of the work that stout, healthy, mature men over forty-five would better perform, he argued, and should perform!

Professor Staub vilified rich farmers and planters, who hauled their produce to market on roads they never repaired. Wealthy sawmill men, whose teams cut the roads to pieces, never paid a cent of road taxes because the law exempted them. His heart went out to the poor renter, widow's son, and day laborer who owned no team, wagon, or horse but had to tote the corn on his shoulders to the mill and still keep up the roads, ill equipped as he was to afford the tax.

Despite such pleas for better laws, all men under forty-five either worked the roads or paid the taxes. So for twenty-six years, from 1879 to 1905, road labor extended in every direction from Highlands as far as the boundaries of Georgia, Jackson County, and Sugarfork Township. Rocks and downed trees had to be manually removed or blasted from the roadbeds after many a stormy winter and spring, and bridges were in continuous need of repair. The best that could be hoped for, with frequent shortages of hands for the amount of work required, was roadbeds deemed only in fair-to-good or fairly good condition.

The Glades Road, by late nineteenth-century standards, was in fairly good condition. It took only two workers laboring under Charles D. Hill thirty days to repair its three-mile roadbed south along the shoulder of Glade Mountain and beneath the rock houses as far as the Georgia state line. The other roads, however, as Highlands struggled to connect itself to the outside world, would require far more workers and workdays just to meet the minimal standards of the Glades Road.

The Horse Cove Road and Thompson's Lane
to Walhalla

By 1879 the road from Highlands to Horse Cove had become a poor but passable alternative to the Whiteside Cove–Glades Road. It followed essentially the torturous switchbacks of an old Indian footpath that Stanhope "Squire" Hill surveyed from Highlands into the cove. Once it reached the valley, it followed the Bull Pen Road as far as Thompson's Lane, which paralleled the Glades Road into Georgia. Known today as Walking Stick Road, Thompson's Lane followed Big Creek down past Bishop Hugh Thompson's cottage, which served as a good-sized hotel, and his brother John Thompson's frame houses, which also accommodated boarders. Like the Glades, it joined today's Walhalla Road but at Satolah, Georgia.

Over the years Thompson's Lane has known many names: Hawkins Road for the well-known family that settled it, Big Creek Road for the creek it followed, and Pin Mill Road for the Ravenel pin factory that once stood on its shoulder. Younger than the Glades Road and not as well traveled, it stood in much greater need of repair. So from 1879 to 1880 it required as many as twelve men more than a hundred days to upgrade its five miles south to the Georgia border. It took thirteen more men another hundred days to create the thousand-foot four-mile climb from Thompson's Lane up out of Horse Cove to Baxter White's store in Highlands. By 1913 roadwork on the Horse Cove Road was still being carried out by Mack Edwards.

The Satulah Road

In 1879–80 the southern exit from Highlands (today's Walhalla Road) didn't bypass Satulah Mountain as it does today. Called the Stooly Road,[225] it existed as an extension of south 4th Street up the mountain as far as Buck Horn Gap, where Cherokees used to lie in wait for white-tail deer. Then it plunged across the rough west shoulder of Satulah, stair-stepping its way down to the Georgia line. There it more or less ended, because not until the late thirties could Georgia afford to greet it with a comparable road in passable condition. Even as late as the early 1890s the seven-mile section of the North Carolina road was still being cleared regularly of huge boulders as far as the Georgia state line.

In 1892 Prioleau Ravenel hired Barak Wright to build a much-needed detour around Satulah, which would replace the torturous climb up and across it.[226] It took four years to construct a 40-foot-wide swath through Hiram Paul's, Eben Selleck's, and Baxter White's properties that reached out around Satulah's west flank. This meant that South Street had to be closed off. Mr. White asked that he be compensated for his loss of property, but to Mr. Selleck's credit, he volunteered to donate the much needed corridor through his land. He even used the occasion to work off his road tax by helping to cut the road through. The result was what might be called Selleck's S-curve, where a 300-yard stretch of today's Walhalla road snakes from 3rd to 4th on its route from the Post Office to town.

In 1896, when the new Walhalla Road was completed, Highlanders abandoned with great relief and joy "the terrible climb up the Blue Ridge, over bowlders and rocks," which for twenty years had rested "like an incubus" on travelers—a thing now of the past![227] By 1913 improvements were still being made to the new Walhalla Road by Ed Picklesimer and Charlie and Will Wright.

The Old Walhalla Road five miles south of Highlands.
Satulah and Fodderstack lie ahead. Photo probably by R. Henry Scadin, 1913–15,
from the pamphlet In the Heart of the Mountains.

Nevertheless, travel along its deeply rutted course remained precarious. Claude Sullivan recalled how this road killed the Highlands Traction Company, organized by John Jay Smith and H. M. Bascom in 1913 to improve deliveries from Walhalla to Highlands. Stock had been sold in the company and a contraption created from an old steam engine which could pull three wagon loads of provisions instead of one. The trip down the mountain to Walhalla covered thirty-two miles, which took the tractor pulling three empty wagons three days to complete. On the return trip, however, bad weather set in as the tractor train left Walhalla loaded down with eighty-two sacks of cotton seed meal. Nothing was heard from the two attendants until three weeks later when they arrived in Highlands on foot, each carrying one sack of meal on his back. What happened to the tractor train on the Walhalla Road was never revealed.[228]

The Nat Ridge Road

If the Satulah route to Walhalla was particularly difficult, the Nat (Gnat) Ridge Road, which extended today's Glen Falls Road into Georgia, was outright dangerous. It plunged with the falls for seven miles to Blue Valley at the state line. In 1894 it was too expensive to improve, for it followed an extremely steep and rocky grade, quite treacherous around many curves, and was generally "in great need of amendments."[229] Two overseers and fourteen hands worked from Joseph Dobson's home on the Nat Ridge Road to W. P. Brown's near the state line. It took them over seventy days just to render it minimally safe and passable, yet only in the best of weather. By 1913 it was still being maintained by J. W. McCall, while today it effectively ends at the Glen Falls parking area.

The Flats or Tennessee River Road

There wasn't a road to Dillard in 1880. Four men worked on a road from 1st and Spring Street to J. W. Wilson's home near the town line. This route on the map of 1881 was named the road to the Tennessee River, but by 1883 it extended only as far as the Flats of Middle Creek at Scaly, about eight miles south of Highlands.[230] The line from Highlands to the Tennessee River wasn't even surveyed until June of 1883, and that for a distance of only 16.8 miles. An alternative route in 1881 was the Tessentee Road, which had been under construction for one year and ran from Broadway Gap up over Fork Mountain to Lickskillet and down into the Tessentee Creek valley.

Many years would pass before the idea of building a road all the way to Dillard would find its advocate in John Jay Smith.[231] In 1904, when the Tallulah Falls railway was extended from Georgia into North Carolina, Smith saw the advantage of a railroad point nearer than distant Walhalla to Highlands. He himself surveyed a scenic extension of the road through Saltrock Gap and over Scaly Mountain for a total of eighteen miles, which was completed in 1906.

By 1913 work on the Scaly Road was fully underway with payments and tax credits being given to Gus Holt, H. B. Talley, and Charlie and Will Wright. By 1919 it was being called the Dillard Road. Deliveries by this route, like the Walhalla Road, took several days, for as Wen McKinney recalled, there was a time when folks in Highlands were out of staples. Charlie Wright and Carl Dillard took a week to reach Dillard and return with supplies. With a good team of mules or a yoke of oxen carrying a thousand pounds of freight, they had to camp overnight at the campground above Mud Creek falls.

It's to Smith's credit as a competent surveyor that his route has held to-day in every respect except for the climb over Scaly Mountain, which was rerouted around the south flank to cut the distance to fifteen miles in 1937.

First mention of a connector between the Scaly and Franklin roads was made in 1891.[232] Known at the time and today as the Turtle Pond Road, it was maintained in 1913 by David McCall.

The Cowee Road
To Hamburg, Cashiers Valley, and Webster

In 1880 the northern route out of Highlands took its traveler to the Short Off Schoolhouse across from today's Shortoff Baptist Church. Known for this reason as the Short Off Road, it began at today's Franklin Road turnoff to Mirror Lake. Since no lake existed at the time, it had to ford the Cullasaja River. The 1881 map called it the road to Hamburg, Cashiers Valley, and Webster. It followed the west bank of the river east of today's Hick's Road. The old wagon ruts through the forest are still quite visible where it passed by Wiley Smith's home. Unlike today, no lake existed in front of Smith's home, for Col. Kernan wouldn't build it until half a century later. Instead the road skirted an apple orchard and a corn field before arriving at the Short Off Schoolhouse.

In the mid 1880s travel on this Short Off Road suffered a major disruption when Henry Stewart decided to create his mill pond, today's Mirror Lake.[233] Stewart's Pond flooded the Short Off Road with the waters of the Sugar Fork (Cullasaja) River, which meant that a bridge was desperately needed.

Not everyone approved of Stewart's damming up the river to form his pond. In the mid 1890s, while standing on the newly built White Oak Bridge over Stewart's Pond, m expressed his bitter regret at the cruel flooding of the forest floor. In *A World of Green Hills* he wrote, "The tall old trees and the ancient rhododendron bushes, which have been drowned by the brook they meant only to drink from, are too recently dead. Nature must have time to trim the ragged edges of man's work and fit it into her own plan. And she will do it, though it may take her longer than to absorb the man himself."

Beyond the Shortoff Schoolhouse, the Hamburg, Cashiers Valley, Webster Road ran past James Wright's home (at today's site of Wright Outdoors off Highway 64) as far as Cowee Gap at the Jackson County line. In 1880 Marion Wright oversaw six hands working a hundred or more days to improve these five miles to today's Whiteside Mountain overlook. In that same year Sam Kelsey surveyed an extension beyond Cowee Gap through the Norton community as far as Hamburg.[234] Hamburg at the time was a thriving town now covered by Lake Glenville and replaced by the town of Glenville. After the Civil War it was a village of only seven families, which had increased to twelve at the time of Highlands' founding, and by 1883 was boasting 115 families, a post office, two or three stores, several sawmills, and a bright future.

At Hamburg the road forked south to Cashiers Valley and north down the Tuckasegee River to Webster, which before 1913 was the Jackson County seat. In 1880, if you wished to make the trip to Cashiers as we do today, you would have had to wait twenty-two years for Prioleau Ravenel, Jr., to build his turnpike. In its youth this road was a masterpiece of construction. Broad and firmly built, with covered drains, it followed an easy grade "through virgin forests, leafy woods, with glimpses here and there of waterfalls, as they pour their silvery sheets over masses of rock on the mountain sides."[235]

In 1902 at a cost of about $5,000 Ravenel completed the seven miles of his turnpike to the outskirts of Cashiers, where he set up a toll booth to recoup the expense. Until recently this booth could be seen less than a mile short of the Cashiers crossroads. It stood in front of the old toll house, which still exists. Tolls on the "private road" were 15¢ for a man on a horse, 25¢ for a one-horse carriage, and 35¢ for a two-horse buggy, and averaged about $40 a year. When automobiles came along, the toll increased for them to 40¢ one way, 60¢ roundtrip.

Mel Keener recalled how Dora Bryson kept the gate locked and charged a dollar in 1925 just to get through. All proceeds went toward the maintenance and improvement of the road until the Macon and Jackson County Highway Departments bought it in 1931 and began to develop Highway 28 (now U.S. 64 East).

The Kelsey Trail and Whiteside Mountain Road

In 1883 a new road or bridal path was proposed to extend the north end of 5th Street to Whiteside Mountain, known today as the Kelsey Trail. It was completed by subscriptions from Highlands citizens and reached to within a quarter mile of the very top of the mountain.[236] Of the total number of work days required to complete it, most of them were volunteered by Kelsey himself, hence the name of the trail.

It wound up and over Bear Pen Gap and through a primeval forest of ancient trees including enormous hemlocks, which the locals called "giant sequoias," across four and a half miles to the beautiful cascade known as Highlands Falls (now the 16th green of the Highlands Falls Country Club) on the Cullasaja River.

A side trail led to the Falls, while the main trail continued by easy grades to Wildcat Cliffs with their impressive view of Whiteside Mountain, then skirted Garnet Rock strewn with gemstones, and crossed the crest of Wildcat Ridge to end at a Cherokee Indian campground.

Highlands Falls. Photo by R. Henry Scadin, 1898, courtesy of the Hudson Library archives.

Here a split in the trail led on the left directly to the top of one of the grandest mountains in the Blue Ridge range: Whiteside, altitude 4,930. The right fork climbed through Fat Man's Misery, also known as Squeeze Betty, to join the left fork again before the top. At the top stretched out almost 2,000 feet below was a grand view of the wrinkled valley of the Chattooga River, guarded by the surrounding mountains of Black Rock, Big and Little Terrapin; towering Chimney Top; Rocky, Toxaway, and Cold Mountains, and reaching across sharply defined blue and purple peaks for dim glimpses of South Carolina and Georgia. All the world below appeared dwarfed and insignificant.

Fat Man's Misery, aka Squeeze Betty. Photo by the author, 2001.

One of the most lyric descriptions of the reward at the end of this trail was penned by Herbert Ravenel Sass in his novel *War Drums*, published forty-five years after the trail's completion. Sass described the spectacle from the top of Whiteside as an outlook on the "Kingdom of the Cherokees," the Empire of Overhills, the vast grandeur of which took one's breath away. He depicted his central female character as standing on Sani'gilagi (*San-ta-ca-lougee* being the Cherokee name for White Sides, home of the Thunder God) just as the clouds were breaking up, except for a few drifting fragments that melted as she gazed.

Spread beneath her now she saw a blue hazy world of hills and valleys and mountains billowing to the horizon, while, directly in front, her gaze dropped down, down, down—down through space that seemed unfathomable to a deep wide valley which the long humped ridge of Sani'gilagi partly encircled like a wall. There was a clearing in this valley, she noticed; but except this one clearing, which resem-bled a tiny lake of vivid green, all the valley floor was clothed in for-est, while the great mountains looming beyond—mountains that seemed as huge as Sani'gilagi itself—were mantled with forest to their rounded summits, where wisps of white cloud still clung. Beyond these again rose other mountains, range upon range, as far as her eye could see, their dim outlines merging at last with the blue of the sky; and over all these also the forest lay, blue as the sea except where it darkened to purple beneath the shadow of some drifting cloud, un-ending, illimitable, continuous as the sea itself.[237]

Such was the splendid scene at the very end of the Kelsey Trail.

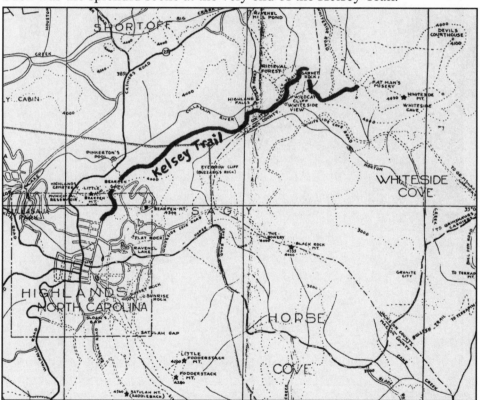

From Thomas Greville's map of Highlands and vicinity, Sept. 13, 1931

Although praised by its subscribers, the Kelsey Trail was not entirely without its critics. There were those who questioned its public benefit, claiming that it was of no use to the town, that it went nowhere and ended in nothing. Pen Holden argued that roads properly laid out and running in the

right direction were usually a good thing, but roads, like any other enterprise, could become "the greatest curse ever inflicted on a country."[238] He
was not in favor of roads per se, which included Kelsey's.

For the most part, however, the road was welcomed, and the first wagon
to travel the Kelsey Trail made its journey on July 11, 1883.

Wagon road to Whiteside, 1897. Photo from R. H. Scadin Collection, UNC-A.

In 1886 a newer and shorter road was built from Cowee Gap to Whiteside via Wild Cat Ridge.[239] This was the road that wagons and buggies
found easier to take to the top. It is essentially the Whiteside Mountain Road
of today. In 1891 4th Street was extended past the cemetery and over the

Cullasaja River to meet the Shortoff Road, as it does today. This was the year that both 4th and 5th streets ultimately led to the mountain, the former for wagons, the latter for hikers and riders on horseback. Not until 1949, however, did anyone have to pay a toll to travel the Cowee Gap wagon road to Whiteside Mountain. Protesting that toll by leaving his car behind, Bob Zahner carried his infant son to the top of the mountain on foot.

A Sunday ride up Whiteside Mountain Road ca. 1909. Courtesy of Tammy Lowe.

The Franklin Road

The first mention of a Franklin Road in the records of the Road Supervisors was on March 1, 1889.[240] James Keener was appointed overseer of the road that began at the end of West Main Street, followed the Shortoff Road across Stewart's Pond (Mirror Lake), climbed up over Billy Cabin Ridge, and descended to join Flat Mountain Road. Winding northwest it continued past Keener's house to cross Brush Creek and follow the Brush Creek Road to Emmaline Gap at Lamb Mountain. There it descended steeply to the Buck Creek crossing and emerged at today's entrance to Teague Estates on the Buck Creek Road.[241] In later years Herman Wilson remembered it in two parts: the Annaline Turns, which passed by Claude Keener's place and his uncle Albert Bryson's farm; and the Emmaline Turns, which continued to Buck Creek. He didn't know how they got their names; he just knew you always met yourself coming back. And when you got into the Sugar Fork community down there, "then you was on a better road, you know," which "wasn't paved."

After crossing Buck Creek the road continued up Moss Creek Branch to Walnut Creek Gap, where it promptly descended to Walnut Creek and eventually reached Franklin. For many years, according to Terry Bolick, the Moss Branch road was the mail route from Franklin to Alonzo, the post office at Buck Creek. This entire route was essentially an upgrade of the shortcut trail that Silas McDowell had used prior to 1850; and Charlie Jenks, from 1872 to 1874, before the founding of Highlands, when he hunted and fished the high plateau.

First Franklin–Highlands Road via Brush Creek. Taken by the author, 1999.

When in bad condition, this Franklin–Highlands road was especially hard to follow. In 1883, for instance, according to the *Blue Ridge Enterprise*, it was poorly maintained about Lamb Mountain, nothing marking its course but a notched stake driven into a bank. The only means one had of seeing the notches was to dismount and put a finger in each notch to count them.

In any case, this route adequately served the people of Highlands until 1896 when a new Franklin Road replaced it. No longer needing the Stewart's Pond turnoff, the new route extended West Main Street to a crossing through Big Creek. Since Lake Sequoyah didn't exist, the road forded Big

Creek at the site of today's bridge and veered up Laurel Heights, now Webbmont Road.[242] Paralleling today's more scenic route, it forded the stream *above* Bridal Veil Falls and, following Webbmont Road, turned northeast onto today's Hammond Road. It rose through Joe Webb's upper field to join the Flat Mountain Road, the "original" Franklin Road.

The ford at Big Creek. Photo from Tom Crumpler collection.

This second Franklin Road was completed about the same time as the new Walhalla Road around Satulah in 1896, as noted above. In 1903, to upgrade it, Macon County built a bridge over the Big Creek ford for $12.50.[243] Today this Franklin Road is no longer passable. It dead ends at "The Foxes' Den," the last of Jack Sparkes' "spec" houses on Hammond Road, no longer connecting to Flat Mountain Road.

There was a road in 1880 that ran in the direction of Buck Creek but stopped short of reaching it. Beginning at the Shortoff Schoolhouse, near James Soper's home, it led for three miles past the homes of Isaac Rice and John Houston to what was then called the Deep Gap (now Sugarfork) township line. This road stood in fairly good condition, for John Houston maintained it alone. But in 1883, when the Macon County commissioners approved a petition to build a new connecting road from Buck Creek to the Deep Gap line, their new route, called the Shookville Road, allowed passage from Highlands via Short Off all the way to the Shookville Community where the road joined the Moss Branch mail route to Franklin.[244]

It wasn't until the mid 1930s that the Civilian Conservation Corps (CCC), including Terry Bolick, blocked out the first passable extension of the Shookville Road from the Moss Branch turnoff to the Cullasaja River, today's lower entrance into the Buck Creek community. This entire road from the Cullasaja to Shortoff was viewed at the time by Bob Zahner, among others, as appropriately named because it "shook up" anyone driving it!

A third "new" Franklin Road in 1897 was the route via Short Creek. It began where today's Watkins Road turns off Webbmont Road. It followed the Homesite Trail for one and a half miles as far as Skitty Creek (which in 1939 would form Cliffside Lake) and, continuing well past today's dam, it veered up towards Miller Cemetery on land donated by Rev. David Miller of the Buck Creek Baptist Church. From there it followed Short Creek into the Cullasaja River at the Gold Mine crossing. Then, climbing the Gold Mine Branch up California Mountain, it passed over the Gap and descended Crow Creek to Peeks Creek and thence to Franklin.

By 1913 this third Franklin Road was being improved by Sam Calloway, Roy Phillips, Maiden and Ben Keener, Simon Speed, Frank Vinson, and the Webb brothers, George, William, and Joe. Butler Jenkins was left to maintain the old Franklin Road alone. In the late 1940s Irene James would walk the new Franklin Road every day from Gold Mine to Highlands School where she taught, a distance of seven and a half miles. When she had to go to Franklin, she would walk the fourteen miles over California Mountain. It seems that most anywhere Irene went, she walked—student or teacher, it didn't matter.

All Roads Lead to Highlands (1906)

During the nine years between 1876 and 1885, volunteer work on the roads around or leading to Highlands created a total of fifty miles of new roads at a cost of 3,150 workdays.[245] The Flats Road to Scaly consumed almost a thousand days; the Whiteside Mountain, Glade Mountain, and Satulah roads averaged 500; the Cowee Norton Gap and Whiteside Cove roads, 300; and the Buck Creek and Horse Cove roads together, 100. Kelsey himself put in 1,200 days of work, 40% of the total, not including considerable time spent scouting and surveying roadbeds. Appropriately, he devoted the most time, 300 days, to the road that would one day bear his name: the Kelsey Trail.

From 1876, when the only road to Highlands began at the train station in Seneca or Walhalla, until 1906, when Ravenel completed his toll road to Cashiers, thirty years passed before Highlands became fully accessible from all four directions of the compass.

As proud as the people of Highlands were of their completed highways to the outside world, their roads were still a far cry from ideal. To all intents and purposes they were passable, but passable in those days meant rocky, frequently muddy from heavy rains, always in need of repair, and some-times downright dangerous.

For anyone traveling to or from Highlands, including the use of town roads—the region being a rainforest—mud was a constant companion. As early as the very first issue of a Highlands newspaper, jokes were circulating about the deplorable condition of the town's streets. In early 1883 an editorial in the *Blue Ridge Enterprise* suggested that "a line of ferry boats should be established at some of our street crossings for the accommodation of the public. In some places the water and mud is too deep to ford during the rainy spells, and as we are not all swimmers, drowning accidents are liable to occur." By year's end the same newspaper was wailing, "Oh! This horrid mud!"

Nine months later the matter had grown so serious that a petition, signed by twenty-four citizens, asked the town council to sell the lumber intended for its new town hall and use the money to improve the streets of Highlands instead.[246] For this reason it was seventy years before Highlands had a town hall building of its own. The town council usually met in Bascom's or Ride-out's stores or the homes of White, Boynton, or Smith before the town rented the upstairs of Mr. Walden's Drug Store, where the House of Wong stands today, and eventually the lower floor of the Masonic Hall at its present location. The lot that Kelsey had deeded the town in 1883 for a town hall at 4th and Pine served instead to house the town's first calaboose in 1885.[247]

So, did the town's sacrifice of its town hall help to improve its roads? Ten years would pass with the *Franklin Press* still droning the same old dirge it always sang of Highlands: "The roads are muddy, especially the new ones. By February there has been so much freezing and thawing that the roads remain muddy and soft all winter."[248]

Mud was by far the most pressing obstacle to improving the town's streets. But other problems cropped up as well. The bridges were forever in need of repair: bridges where streams crossed Main Street near 1st, 5th, and 6th; bridges near Pine, Laurel, and Hickory on 5th; the Mill Creek bridge on 4th; the Shortoff Road bridge across Mirror Lake; and many more outside town.

In addition, the ordinance of 1890 had to address the increasing number of animals on town streets. It imposed a curfew on cattle, horses, mules or other animals, with or without bells, that were running at large so as to keep their activity to a minimum during the nights.

A particular thorn in the side of Highlanders who were fighting to improve their roads, especially connector roads to the outside world, was the outside world's apparent indifference to their urgent needs. Regardless of how significantly the road workers from Highlands improved their section of the Walhalla Road to the Georgia line, and South Carolina road workers the same, the road could never be considered adequate, or even passable during the winter so long as Georgia neglected its nine-mile link, a perilous stretch that rain continuously reduced to a sea of mud. Georgia wouldn't even consider addressing the problem until the early twenties, and it was the early thirties before they finally chose to act.

The problem wasn't peculiar to Georgia. It existed in North Carolina as well, involving the building of an iron bridge over the Chattooga River. In 1891 Highlands and Horse Cove desperately needed a bridge to carry the Bull Pen Road across the river as an alternative to the Glades Road south to Walhalla. The state of North Carolina expressed no interest, for the project would demand a considerable feat of engineering. James Rideout's response to this was as humorous as it was sardonic when he cut a personal check for the undertaking: "Given out of charity to a state not able to build its own bridges." The iron bridge, which is still used today as much for passage over the river as for picnics under it, was completed by John Jay Smith and T. Henry in 1893.[249]

While the roads in and out of Highlands often proved a traveler's nightmare, some streets within the town itself grew impossible to negotiate, such as the steep 2nd Street hill that ran between Antle Henry's home and the Methodist Church (today's Baptist Church), joining Main Street with Oak Street. In 1895 the town permitted Henry to fence in and farm the street provided he remove the stumps in it, and for the next fifty years it remained closed.

The topography of the town's streets in the early 1880s was considerably different from what it is today. In 1885 the town graded Main Street to an expanded width of fifty feet, which it deemed more practical than eighty, and installed a four-foot-wide hemlock boardwalk between Bascom's and Skinner's shops. A plank sidewalk was added in 1888, extending from White's post office to the 4th Street corner and from Bascom's corner to the school.

Even after the expansion, Main Street still climbed a steep hill from 4th to 3rd Street, dipping into a swag between Bascom's and Skinner's stores. According to Walter Reese, the swag was deep enough for a horse to pass under the boardwalk which rested on pilings between the two stores. The swag was not filled until 1895, and until handrails were installed, the boardwalk was especially dangerous for children.[250] In 1886 Dock McKinney's little daughter fell from Cleaveland's elevated section, breaking her arm and dislocating both wrists. The town council promptly installed 2x4 railings to prevent further accidents.

The current 4th Street hill actually rose seven feet higher than it does today. It was graded down in 1886 as too steep for braking horse-drawn carts that came barreling through the Main Street intersection. Herman Wilson remembered "a big cut, big high cut" right in front of where First Union National Bank stands today. This was the year that the Main Street hill was also graded down and a new 4th Street bridge constructed and pond created near John Jay Smith's sawmill on Mill Creek.[251] This bridge replaced the first 4th Street bridge, which Kelsey and William Soper had built in 1877.

The Mill Creek Bridge, built in 1886 over the Smith mill dam. Photo probably by R. Henry Scadin, 1913–15, courtesy of Hudson Library archives.

Construction of the new bridge over the Smith mill dam was the scene of a story that Joel Teague says he never forgot.[252] Years after he left Highlands and moved to Oregon, he wrote to the *Franklin Press and Highlands Maconian* about the old-time Georgia tonic that had played such a crucial role in getting that bridge built back in '86. John Alley, Teague said, was the contractor. When Smith let the water off on Monday, he and Joel and Joe McGuire, Bob Reese, and Logan Ramsey got into the creek to put up the mudsills. Not an easy job in the cold spring water of Highlands! Mr. Alley was down on his back in that cold water and mud, and he could hardly get up but by raising himself with the aid of Mr. Poole's fence which was close by.

So the next Monday when Mr. Alley was down in Georgia at one of those large laboratories that made the finest of health or death tonics,

Teague claimed he brought back ten gallons of that tonic and hid it down in the Bathrick laurel (today's eastern part of Wright Square). Bob Reese went up town to get the eggs and sugar, which he could get whether they were for sale or not, as he could talk the girls at the hotels out of enough to make eggnogs.

The crew had a water pail and a dipper. The eggs, sugar, and tonic were put in the pail, and as it was being stirred, John Alley eased himself down to where the eggnog manufacturing was going on. He took a little, said it was so good that he took some more, and two hours later he had sampled enough that they could distinctly hear him smile all the way up at Bascom's Main Street store, a crowbar in his hand and down in the mud and water up over the waist of his pants. When the bridge was finally built, Teague concluded, all the tonic was gone. So the bridge was built in a wet place by a wet crowd and lasted a long time. Indeed, it lasted right up until that last day in August, 1940, when the Ravenel Lake dam broke and washed it out, as recounted later in Chapter Nineteen.

The Road That Never Was

From the day that Kelsey first set foot on the Highlands Plateau, he knew from personal experience that this isolated town would eventually need the services of a railroad. As early as 1876, while acknowledging the Blue Ridge terminus as the nearest railroad to Highlands thirty miles distant in Walhalla, he fully anticipated its completion in reasonable time via Rabun Gap and Franklin to Knoxville, Tennessee. This would put Highlands only ten to fourteen miles from a station on the main line with ready access to all points to the south and northwest. By 1882 the railroad from Mt. Airy was being extended toward Franklin.

So in that year the Highlands Railroad Company was formed. Its stated purpose was to construct a stockholders narrow gauge railroad on the James plan, with wood or iron rails or both, from Highlands to some point on the Rabun Gap Railroad in Georgia or the Blue Ridge Railroad in North Carolina. Kelsey was elected president, and without a moment's delay, he began taking levels for a Highlands Railroad south of Satulah.[253] Initially capital stock in the company, at fifty dollars a share, amounted to $75,000. Subscriptions were issued which individuals and their families could redeem, when the link was completed, at the rate of five hundred miles for every twenty dollars contributed in cash, labor, or material.

Besides Kelsey, the initial directors of the company were Joseph Dobson, E. E. Ewing, Stanhope Hill, Barak Wright, Charles Boynton, and H. A. Fulton, who were soon joined by many others from Highlands. Estimated costs for the shortest and cheapest railroad figured at $2,000 per graded and trestled mile.

At its annual stockholder meeting in 1885, three years after its founding, the Highlands Railroad Company was still awaiting the extension of the tracks to Rabun Gap, which had to precede any consideration of a further extension to Highlands. At the end of 1886 rumors were spreading that a proposed Asheville–Atlanta railroad would pass through Highlands. Kelsey devoted much of his time to traveling to meetings and lobbying for such a route. When completed, the Baltimore & Ohio Railroad would serve Highlands from the north. Charleston already had a railroad to Walhalla, and Savannah was building one in the same direction. Either or both might also approach Highlands from the south.

No progress developed, however, on any line toward Highlands. By the end of 1887 Highlanders had begun to lose heart. The last recorded meeting of the Highlands Railroad Company took place in November of that year. By 1890 the Coe brothers of the *Star* were vehemently opposing a 30-year $100,000 county railroad bond vote because the newly proposed railroad would run through Franklin instead of Highlands.[254] This was the year that Kelsey abandoned Highlands to found Linville, having been hired by a group of land speculators to survey a projected scenic railroad through the Blue Ridge Mountains into Virginia. His interests had shifted to the towering grandeur of Grandfather Mountain.

So in 1906 that's how it ended. The main line of the Southern Railroad was extended to Franklin. Highlands connected with this line but by Smith's new wagon road, not by rail, to Clayton. The Highlands Railroad had become, in short shrift, the road that never was.

What Kelsey saw as a failure, however, would be viewed in the 1930s as an asset, when the Highlands Country Club published their flyer praising the town for having "No Railroads." It singled out as one of Highlands' best features the fact that it was twenty miles from a railroad: "No smoke, no railroad dirt and noise, and no week-end excursion crowds."

One railroad that summer residents often used to approach Highlands from the South was the Tallulah Falls, better known in Highlands as the "Total Failure," which it ultimately became. Sara Alice Darby, as a child, came to Highlands during the thirties via the Total Failure, overnighting at Bynum House in Clayton.

From Buggies to Motorcars

The first motorcar to brave the roads of Highlands appeared in 1913. Richard "Bill" Holt remembers a Sunday afternoon surrey ride with his mother and four siblings out the Dillard Road to Broadway Gap where, just past the old Russell Place, they met a motorcar coming from Franklin via Dillard and couldn't believe their eyes. Dolly Harbison remembered going down the path from her home, where the Kelsey's once lived, to the creek and hearing such a commotion. She turned and saw something she'd never seen before and cried out, "Is the gate shut"?

According to Mel Keener, the first car was driven by John Jay Smith, for Smith had bought a brand new Model T Ford for $400. Aunt Mett claimed it was her husband's uncle Will Brooks. Keener claimed the second Highlander to own a motorcar was Arthur Dillard.

Soon Bascom had at his store a fifty-five gallon drum of gasoline, which Mel would haul up for him from Mountain Rest, and a siphon for pumping it. Another early owner of a car was Henry Sloan, but his first wife Katherine refused to ride in it, so he had to keep the horse-drawn carriage and a coachman for her.

T-Model on Muddy Road. Photo probably by R. Henry Scadin, 1913–15, courtesy of Hudson Library archives.

The fact that the Model T Ford was about to replace the horse-drawn carriage didn't in any way lessen the difficulties encountered on the rocky, muddy, rutted roads from all four directions into Highlands. From 1914 until 1942 almost thirty years would pass still muddled in mud. Olin Dryman remembered as a child how he'd go up to Highlands when "there wasn't nothing but a board sidewalk, just old clay mud." He pitched horseshoes on the street on the 4th of July.

"Grandpa'd always tell us, 'Boys, get the corn laid by, and we'll go to Highlands for the fourth.' We'd either go to Highlands, or we'd go to the Cove and pick cherries, so we'd always want to go to Highlands. Right in front of that big high bank was where we pitched horseshoes. Old clay mud, pushing wagons through there. Main Street was just a big mud hole. If it was arainin', it was really a mud hole, I'm telling you." The speed limit for automobiles in Highlands in 1915 was eight miles an hour, with a five-dollar fine for each violation.

By 1920 Georgia finally agreed to improve its segment of the Walhalla Road, otherwise known as the Three-States Road from Walhalla to Highlands.[255] It covered twenty-eight miles over five ranges of the Blue Ridge Mountains: the Stump House and Callas mountains in South Carolina, Pine Mountain in Georgia, and Queen and Satulah mountains in North Carolina.

The land was a strong loam, so the road was extremely treacherous. Little more than an ordinary rain could render it in summer impassable, and in winter impossible by car except after a long dry spell. A horse-drawn wagon was the only vehicle capable of negotiating the seas of mud through thick forests. In the early twenties the trip during the summer months lasted one and a half hours. Much improved over the two days required before the turn of the century, nonetheless a very rough one and a half hours.

By 1923 Oconee County had spent $300,000 in federal aid for the link between Mountain Rest and Seneca just to obtain a satisfactory grade but needed $85,000 more to give it a hard surface. The timing of the road's completion was set to coincide with that of the Atlanta-Franklin-Asheville Highway during the summer. Yet, despite all the hype promoting the Three-States Road as a gorgeous detour through some of the most magnificent scenery in the U.S., in reality nothing changed.

With improvement of the roads to the south of Highlands forever uncertain, the focus shifted in 1926 to the northern routes. The road from Cashiers and Toxaway was dirt, paved only near Brevard. The road from Franklin was only improved to the base of the Cowees, so to reach Highlands via Walhalla from Franklin by car meant taking the motor road into Georgia and back into North Carolina three times.[256] The circuitous distance was thirty-five miles.

In the end, a grand plan was proposed to build a spectacular new road "under a thundering waterfall 150 feet high in the Cullasaja river." In the opinion of the district highway commissioner, this road would be one of the most beautiful and certainly the most unusual scenic attractions on any highway in eastern America.[257] It would cut fifteen miles off the northwest Georgia route, reducing the trip to ten.

Construction began on Highway 28 in the spring of 1927. The N.C. Highway Department hired W. F. Taylor to oversee the massive project, which entailed blasting a narrow ledge along the solid granite north wall of Cullasaja Gorge ten miles from Franklin and 200 feet above the river. J. E. McDowell, Charlie McDowell's father, was hired on as foreman.

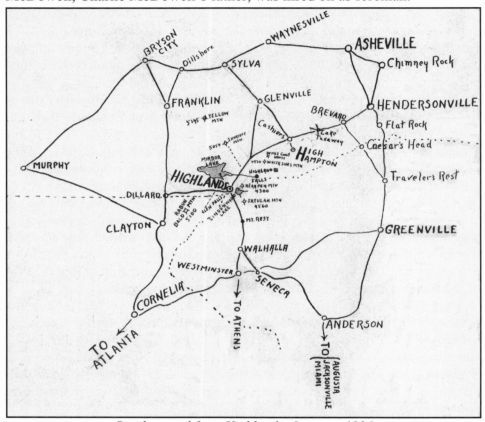

Roads to and from Highlands, January, 1926

At the time the accomplishment was an amazing feat of engineering. As many as sixty workers were employed by the summer of 1927. Explosives hurled blocks of granite weighing several tons into the river far below, while the men who handled the dynamite hung from ropes fastened to iron pins, which had been driven into holes drilled into the top of the mountain. Directly opposite arose a solid rock cliff more than 500 feet in height. One slip meant certain death from such dizzying heights.

These were the days before air compressors and jack hammers when holes were drilled into the rock by hand. Driving steel usually required three men, two drivers and a chucker, who turned the steel every time a driver struck it with his limber-handled eight-pound hammer. As Herman Wilson described it, the handle was made of high-grade white hickory wood thinned at the center until it bent like raw hide.

The granite cliffs of Highway 28. Photo by George Masa, 1929.

"The hammer that I used would flop over my right shoulder, but then I would bring it down on the top of the steel with dead accuracy," Herman claimed. He would never miss the steel, for a miss would break the chucker's hands. After the holes were drilled, three to five sticks of dyna-mite were inserted and tamped down; and a blasting cap, attached to the end of the fuse.

Then the cry, "Fire in the hole," three times before the blast would blow rocks high into the sky and the men would seek shelter under the trees.

Construction of the Gorge Road at the Quarry. Photos by George Masa, 1929

The *Franklin Press* called the new Highway 28 "probably the greatest scenic highway in all of the state." From the foot to the top of the Cowees it followed the entire length of the Cullasaja gorge, rising with the river almost 2,000 feet in only seven or eight miles.

It was unique in that it didn't follow the bank at the bottom of the gorge as did most other roads but wound its way along the side of the wall, clinging like some tiny creeper to cliffs of age-old granite, while far below, so far that one wondered how long it must have taken the river, roaring down among the tons and tons of rock shot out of the cliff, to cut its deep gash through stone so solid it gave the powder men on the construction work plenty to think about.[258]

Highway 28, blasted through solid granite, clings to the north wall of Cullasaja Gorge, 200 feet above the river. Photo from brochure Highlands: Roof Garden of the Southeast.

After crossing Brush Creek, the road ran past Raven's Cliff and the great flat rock, which itinerant preachers often used as a pulpit. It climbed to Kelly Falls and the Narrows, known today as Bust Your Butt Falls or the swimming hole, where rock was quarried for construction of the roadbed. Here the river rushed through an opening not more than six feet wide.

A mile or two farther up the road passed the thundering torrent of Dry Falls and, nearing its end, swerved into the gaping maw of Bridal Veil Falls, the only road in the state to pass under a river. Emerging, it reached at last the Highlands plateau.

Two years after construction had begun, the gorge section of the Franklin to Highlands road was completed in 1929. In the same year the town of Highlands took over maintenance of its town roads from the county, levying a street tax on all males residing in the town between the ages of twenty-one and forty-five in order to pay for it.[259] In 1923 it had contracted with Helen Heacock Edwards to quarry rock from her property adjoining Bear Pen at $25 a year for ten years, but in 1927 it bought the four or five acres as a permanent quarry from which it began to supply hard surfacing.

Road under Bridal Veil Falls. Photo by George Masa, 1929.

Meanwhile 6th Street was opened from Main to Chestnut, and the Highlands Improvement Society, feeling Main Street needed a face lift, requested and received a permit to build a twelve-foot circular fountain—actually a reservoir—in the center of 4th street intersection.[260]

Installed in the summer of 1928, it was a beautiful but short-lived idea. The board of commissioners in 1930 created parking down the center of

Main Street.[261] In 1931 they decided to surface each side of the street with crushed rock from the town quarry mixed with asphalt oil as binder and to pack rock screening in the center for parking. Consequently, Main Street had to be lowered near the Masonic Hall, the excess dirt used for fills on 4th Street, and the fountain had to be dismantled and carted away.

There were many who mourned the loss of the fountain. Bordered by large granite slab stones and chain-linked hitching posts and stocked with trout and goldfish, it had stood for three years at the center of Highlands. Horses brought into town were watered there. Kids balanced themselves along the top of the wall. Adults warned, "You'll fall in!" recalls Marion Day Arnold, "but we never did."

The fountain at the intersection of 4th and Main, 1928–31

In 1931, with the creation of the N.C. State Highway Department, the Works Progress Administration (WPA) crews began improving the roads leading out of Highlands. Gus Baty led a crew including Harry Wright and Terry Bolick to change the Horse Cove Road to an eight percent grade but left it dirt. The Dillard road too was graded but not paved, which left its sharp, steep curves up and over Scaly Mountain especially muddy during or after a rain. Lamira Sullivan remembers how her mother, Lamira Henley, would stop the car at those dangerous curves, some of which approached right angles, and instruct the children to get out and walk the inside edge to the straightaway. She didn't want them in the car, for fear it might slide off the slippery ledge and down the mountain.

Indeed, Bess Hines Harkins remembered riding this rugged, rarin' Dillard road with her family in an open buggy, before the advent of the Ford, and the mountain driver telling her mother about a summer visitor he'd brought this way once.[262] "She was awful skeered," he said. "When we reached this here place, she looked over and kinda squeaked, 'Whar would I go if the buggy was to slip off into thar?'"

"It'ud depend on how you'd been livin', lady." He reckoned that made her kind of mad, for he grinned dryly and added, "She didn't have no more to say after that."

A Model T approaches Highlands through Mortar Gap at Bear Pen Ridge, today's road to Cashiers. Photo by George Masa, 1929.

By 1932, with Georgia forever promising to pave its nine-mile link on the Three-States Walhalla Road, the only asphalt-surfaced road into and out of Highlands was Highway 28 from Franklin to Cashiers (At that time Highway 28 turned north from Highlands, today's 64, and Highway 282 ran south to Walhalla). As a result of public outcry the one mile road up Whiteside, which in winter was scarcely passable and never a pleasant drive, was rocked as an offshoot of the new highway project.

While the people of Highlands were celebrating their newly paved Highway 28, the people of Franklin were embroiled in a heated controversy over a proposed rerouting of that same highway through their town. Instead of following Main Street as it always had, the town council proposed that it leave Main Street at the eastern foot of the town hill and follow Palmer Street to the Georgian road intersection, cross a meadow, and cut through a gap in the mountain around which the old Highlands road still runs today. The proposal was so controversial that it split the Franklin town council, actually leading one councilman to resign.[263]

By 1934 the infamous "missing link" of the Tri-State Walhalla Road was being vilified as "a thorn in the flesh for Highlands, because it has been an almost constant mud hole."[264] It had been and still was a main artery of travel into Highlands from the South. During each of the next two years the Georgia Highway Commission approved plans—even arranging for Georgia to pay half the costs and the U.S. Forest Service the other half—and announced that work had finally begun. But nothing changed.

Meanwhile, thanks to the CCC camps, like Company 455, which was built in 1934 in Horse Cove near Alec Edwards' home, much needed roadwork was provided for the next three years.[265] All the main roads in and out of Highlands, except for the Horse Cove Road, were paved by 1937. The Dillard Road, which John Jay Smith had routed some thirty years earlier over Scaly Mountain, was shortened from eighteen to fifteen miles to detour around the mountain rather than climb over it and was surfaced with eight inches of crushed stone.[266]

At Rebecca Harris' request a new road along Harris Lake was created in 1937 and named after her brother Leonard, in exchange for closing off 6th Street south of Smallwood Avenue (Smallwood being Rebecca's maiden name). At the same time the North Carolina section of the Walhalla Road was paved, but only to the Georgia state line. Georgia made its annual promise in 1937 and again in 1938 to pave its notorious eight miles, but all in vain. Perhaps it was in desperation that in 1935 the town supported construction of an airport on the Cashiers road within sight of Shortoff.[267]

By 1942 the town was hard-surfacing the last of its major roads. Crushed stone was laid from the Highlands Inn to the Presbyterian Church, essentially completing Main Street from 3rd to 5th and Fourth Street from Chestnut to Faraway Drive up Satulah.[268] Mud, that ubiquitous enemy of all travelers to and from the town, was at long last a nightmare of the past.

All that remained then for the fifties would be the paving of side roads and the improvement and beautification of main ones, including the inevitable problems that accompany progress. The decade began with a toll road up Whiteside Mountain, but more significant were parking problems in town. Since 1930, parking on Main Street had been arbitrary. People left their cars wherever they pleased. With solid surfacing, however, the police and street committee in 1952 could mark off center lines and parking spaces on East Main and did the same for West Main in 1955.[269]

In 1957 the commissioners introduced a debate that would fester and rage for the next forty three years before it would finally be resolved. A proposal was made to impose one-hour parking limits or else install parking meters to solve a mounting dilemma in town.[270] While solutions to the problem were bantered about, the Highlands Garden Club took the initiative to beautify the street in question by planting five trees on each side between 3rd and 4th. The town considered but rejected trees for the center of Main as replacements of those lost in 1938. This idea would have to wait another twenty-eight years before it found acceptance and the four red maples that live on Main Street today were established.

For the roads outside town, the Flat Mountain section of the original road to Franklin was finally paved under Tom Harbison's supervision in 1955.[271] In 1958 the Wilson Gap road, which twice crossed an old narrow Indian trail winding through virgin forests, was built to connect the Walhalla and Horse Cove roads.[272]

With all the paving that took place during the thirties and forties, the rock quarry on Poplar Street fell under considerable demand.[273] After its purchase by the town, residents in the neighborhood began voicing growing concerns over the constant blasting that caused their windows to crack, dishes to fall from shelves, and walls to shake. By 1951 the issue had reached such a critical stage that the town agreed to close the quarry, dismissing all the street crew except Joe and Spear Henry and Fred Green.

Later that same year, however, the town leased the quarry to John Miller, and the blasting resumed. At the end of five more years, angry residents petitioned the town not to renew Miller's lease. The following January a motion to permanently close the quarry passed by only one vote when Mayor Bill McCall broke the tie.

A month later the town reversed itself and extended the lease another five years, provoking the unmitigated ire of Robert Conlon and Hal Copeland, who lived above the quarry on Little Bear Pen. Then on July 28, 1961, despite all the forewarnings, the unthinkable occurred! A dynamite blast at the quarry propelled a large rock 400 to 500 feet into the air, and it crashed through the roof of Copeland's home. It cut clean through the shingles and boarding, sending his wife to Dr. Goodwin for sedation from shock.

Copeland notified the *Highlander* that he was taking his wife "away from cool Highlands to Hampton, Virginia, where the temperatures have been 90 degrees for thirteen consecutive days. If this doesn't prove what a great hazard the quarry is, I don't know what will!" There were other reports, besides his, of stoves rising two inches from the floor every time a blast occurred.

The newspaper depicted the rocks falling over Bear Pen as putting its citizens behind shutters "in shudders," compelling them to arrange their social hours so as not to interfere with "blast-off time," which was between noon and 6:00 p.m. everyday but Sunday. Needless to say, the lease was not renewed a second time, and the blasting stopped. In 1963 the town constructed a 2,100 square foot warehouse and vehicle shed on the former blasting site, today's town maintenance shed.

Bridal Veil Falls before the 1958 bypass. Photo courtesy of Tammy Lowe.

During the early fifties a tragedy occurred which led to a dramatic change in the Franklin Road. Since 1928 its fame had derived in part from its passage under scenic Bridal Veil Falls. But one July day in 1954 Harold Hunnicutt, a twenty-nine-year-old from Seneca, drove off the Bridal Veil curve and plunged seventy-five feet down the mountain side to his death.[274] The dangers of driving under these falls were severe enough during the winter, when ice often piled as high as a car on the outside of the curve and layered up on the road itself. But an accident in mid-summer couldn't be blamed on the weather.

In 1958 the town board approved constructing a by-pass on the outside of the falls. Nostalgia over preserving a unique thing of beauty from Highlands' past, however, led the board to require that the road under the falls not be abandoned entirely but maintained, even as it is today.[275]

While the town struggled with the construction of a Bridal Veil bypass, a chronic problem re-emerged in its own back yard. The ever-growing number of cars were decimating the available parking, so the town turned to the grassed yard in front of the Presbyterian Church, which sloped so gently into the south side of Main. It was decided to slice the bank to street level and build the rock retaining wall that stands today.[276] Dogwood and maple trees planted along the curb line compensated somewhat for the beauty lost in breaking the natural grade of the Presbyterian hill.

From the fifties until today parking has recurred as a constant problem in a town as small as Highlands, which nonetheless hosts 15,000 to 20,000 tourists in season. While many solutions have been proposed—from marking tires and installing parking meters to prohibiting employers and employees from Main Street parking and creating new spaces along side streets with each new commercial development—no solution emerged into law until 2000. In that year the town created two blocks of spaces on the north side of Spring Street but more importantly limited parking on much of Main to two hours, which may at last have helped ameliorate the problem.

At the beginning of the 1970s an age-old dispute resurfaced between North Carolina and Georgia, not, however, about the infamous Three-State link on the Walhalla road, which had at long last been rectified. No, this dispute focused on road signs where each state announced its boundaries. The fallout began when Georgia accused North Carolina and Tennessee of occupying part of its land.

As far back as the early 1800s, when boundaries were being established for western lands after the American Revolution and the Cherokee cession of their territory, Georgia had argued it owned land in North Carolina because of errors made in the original survey of their common boundary, which King George II in 1732 had decreed should follow the 35th parallel of latitude. Georgia hired the renowned surveyor Major Andrew Ellicott in 1811 to prove its claim to land in North Carolina. But in locating the point where the 35th Parallel crossed the Chattooga River and marking it on the west bank with his now famous Ellicott's Rock, Ellicott failed to satisfy Georgia's wish. Actually, as would be later determined, he set his rock about 500 feet north of the 35th parallel, meaning North Carolina would have a counterclaim against Georgia.

When commissioners from North and South Carolina began meeting to establish permanently *their* common boundary, they were joined by commissioners from Georgia to determine again if the line west from Ellicott's Rock would confirm Georgia's claim. On September 25, 1819, surveyors Timothy Tyrrell of Georgia and Robert Love of North Carolina established Commissioners Rock, eleven miles west on the old forest road between Scaly and Rabun Bald. They also set a locust post sixteen miles farther west to mark the boundary on the Franklin–Dillard highway. In essence, they reconfirmed Ellicott's line, leaving unresolved Georgia's claim to an orphan triangle a third of a mile wide at the locust post.

A century passed before the dispute erupted again in 1905. In this year W. A. Curtis, editor of the *Franklin Press*, published the results of a twenty-four year study, during which he had examined some old records in the State Library in Raleigh, N.C., along with the latest topographical charts. He found discrepancies in the line west of Ellicott's Rock, which he claimed had never been correctly surveyed.[277] The result was that Neville Sloan of Franklin was hired in 1912 to retrace the line east from Commissioners Rock to Ellicott's Rock and west to the locust post on the old Franklin–Dillard highway. When the quarrel surfaced again in 1935, Sam Greenwood of Franklin was hired to survey it again.

The issue resurfacing yet again in 1971, North Carolina's governor Bob Scott shot off a message to Georgia's governor Jimmy Carter that he saw no need to reopen a question that had been debated ad nauseam since 1906, actually 1806. To which Carter naturally responded that Georgia claimed the 35th parallel as the true boundary between the two states. As Curtis had shown, the line on the map, instead of turning due west at Ellicott's Rock continued southwest about twenty miles almost to the top of the Ridge Pole, then turned west to parallel the 35th towards Alabama.

Included in Georgia's claim were portions of Jackson and Macon counties—just missing Highlands—up to a quarter mile north of Commissioners Rock and a third mile north of the locust post, including sections of Clay and Cherokee counties up to a mile but also Copper Hill and part of Chattanooga in Tennessee.

Presumably the only Georgian satisfied with leaving the line unchanged was Mal James, along with his wife, Claudia Mae, a Highlands native. Where the paved North Carolina section of Hale Ridge Road out of Scaly (sometimes called Hell Ridge Road or Moccasin) ended at Commissioners Rock and the graveled Georgia section began, he had located his cement block building a dozen yards on the Georgia side of the boundary with a hand lettered sign reading, "Only Beer To Go Sold." Most of what he earned from this vital location across the North Carolina line bought him considerable farmland, from which his descendants still earn their living today in the Flats.

It's conceivable that South Carolina had more right to question its boundary with North Carolina than Georgia, for no features on the map, much less any parallels of latitude, could support the erratic line from Tryon, N.C., to Indian Camp Mountain. It has been suggested, even if only facetiously, that the original surveyors maintained a straight line across the piedmont until they reached the mountains just west of Tryon. Then fighting to thread their way through entangling labyrinths of laurel and rhododendron, they cut an erratic zigzag from still to still, desperately intent on refreshing their tortured souls.

There was hardly an argument between North and South Carolina over the authenticity of their common line. Who would dare resurvey it? Indeed, this might explain why otherwise competent surveyors could miss the vital adjustment west at Ellicott's Rock, plunging as the line does instead for twenty more miles southwest, up to the Ridge Pole near the corner of Macon County before turning as an afterthought to parallel the 35th a mile south toward Alabama. As Herman Wilson used to say, that stuff would put you on Mary's back porch if you drank much of it.

In any event, the upshot of the dispute in 1971 was that nothing changed. In the words of surveyors Sloan and Greenwood, whose measurements essentially agreed: "They'll never change that line. It would create the biggest mess you ever saw. It's been here too long to change now."[278] Highlands steered clear of this raging debate, focusing instead on installing new bright red Christmas lanterns with evergreen decoration, which have adorned downtown light poles every Christmas season since.

With increased traffic on the roads entering and leaving Highlands during the 1990s, concern for safety became a priority, particularly on the gorge road to Franklin, but also on the road to Cashiers. Both roads skirted the edges of steep drops down the mountainsides where drivers could be catapulted to their doom in the river beds or valleys two hundred or more feet below. In 1996 three heavily laden tractor-trailer rigs collided with oncoming cars above the gorge within a period of three weeks, leading the state Department of Transportation at long last to divert all through-trucks away from Highlands entirely, rerouting them from Franklin and Hendersonville through Asheville instead. State engineers cited as the cause of the problem certain dispatchers who set the route for their truckers without realizing the hazards of U.S. 64 simply from looking at a map. Indeed, the enticement to send a rookie up or down the gorge as a rite of passage must have been a great temptation for roguish dispatchers. Although signs banning further use of the gorge road didn't stop uninformed truckers from using it illegally, the potential for accidents was reduced considerably.

In 1998 rust-colored guard rails were installed along the riverside of the Franklin Road from Lower Cullasaja Falls to Highlands and on U.S. 64 East from the Whiteside Mountain overlook to Cashiers. Though road problems would continue to spring up in a resort town as popular as Highlands had become, there was at last and without fail a built-in guarantee that these roads would never revert to the muddy nightmares that had plagued travelers to and from the high plateau before the "miracle of pavement." So in this sense Kelsey's dream of "good roads to all points on the Highlands," almost seventy years in the making, was at last fully realized.

9. Fireballs, Butchers, and Hogs

That any hogs found at large in the town of Highlands on or after the first day of January, 1884, shall be taken up by the Constable, or his Deputy, and a fine of twenty-five cents be levied on each hog and ten cents additional for each day they remain unclaimed.
—Ordinances for the town of Highlands, N.C., May 31, 1883.

In 1883 Highlands enacted its first set of town ordinances. It elected a police force of seven men to enforce these ordinances in 1885, namely William Duncan, Wilbur Trowbridge, H. M. Bascom, John Jay Smith, Charles A. Boynton, Frank Sheldon, and William Cleaveland.

Included among the earliest laws were the customary regulations. The town levied a 25¢ tax on each $100 of real and personal property to cover the expense of government and threatened anyone who refused or neglected payment with a 20% penalty. The purchase of a license and payment of $10 in tax were required for each billiard or pool table or bowling alley, and a permit fee of $5 to $50 applied to putting on a show or circus.

No one could fight, riot, or get drunk in the streets without punishment at the discretion of the mayor. This law was still on the books in 1892 when Dr. Frost's workman, Stub Nicholson, tied one on after church one Sunday and behaved so "boysterose" on Main Street in front of Bascom's and Cleaveland's stores that the constable had to haul him off to the calaboose. He broke out about 3:00 in the afternoon with the help of Hut Jastin, but his father went to Mr. Bascom with the promise that Stub would stand trial the next day, would plead guilty, and would pay the fine and costs.[279] So there were those in town who respected the ordinance enough to abide by it even if it meant enforcing it against their own kin.

But there were also those who considered all ordinances an invasion of their privacy. Helen Hill Norris tells of two locals who had "run afoul of the law" and found themselves overnight in the town's calaboose.[280] The next morning, during Helen's geography lesson at the school across the street, the wives of the culprits appeared "wearing wide calico skirts, sunbonnets, and all armed, one with a double-bitted axe across her shoulder, the other with a double-barreled shot gun." Warning their husbands to stand clear, the one with the shot gun blasted the hinges off the door, and the other finished the job with her axe. As they marched past Mayor O'Farrell's drugstore, he tried to inform them that "the law had been violated." All he got was a sharp retort from one of the women, "You'uns can just leave our men folks alone. We women up here tend to our men ourselves."

One law typical of the times forbade tethering a horse to a shade tree or leading him onto the wooden sidewalks, which clunked under foot and blocked free passage for the ladies. There was the usual prohibition against fireballs, guns, pistols, and sling shots. More controversial, however, was the law requiring livery owners and butchers to purchase a license. Not the livery's so much as the butcher's license was the contested issue, for the butcher's law, first passed in 1883, was repealed a year later, reinstated in three years, repealed again the following year, enacted a third time in 1889, and finally dropped altogether in 1890 as "an obstacle to the free development of the town."[281]

The butchers in Highlands, particularly one of them, caused the town more grief than the license was worth. Not long after the law was finally ditched, the town's butchers were ordered to "remove all remnants of their slaughter business and keep these places clear, or they would have to move their slaughter pens outside the corporation." The smell in the neighborhood adjacent to their pens was remarkably offensive, and the townspeople, rightly so, complained bitterly. A new ordinance of 1892 specifically forbade the slaughter of any cattle, hogs, or sheep within town limits because offal from butchered stock was routinely chucked on the ground and left rotting in the streets during the day.

In 1896 the town council reinstated the license law, demanding that Irvin Rice buy a butcher's license inside of three days or pay the dollar fine for every sale he made without it. Furthermore, it warned James Rideout, owner of the slaughter yard, to discontinue its use as such at once or suffer equally dire consequences. Butchery was an unavoidable necessity in early Highlands. Unfortunately its abuses were subject to olfactory detection more readily than those of other trades that might violate the law less obviously.

Marshall Reese remembers the slaughter house that Irvin's brother Luke had where Oak and 1st streets intersect. The steep hill behind it was where all the slaughter was thrown and left to rot, producing a stinking mess. A related problem forced the town council to decree that all privies and outhouses must be cleaned out and disinfected with lime inside of ten days.

The ordinance of 1883 and all subsequent ordinances forbade the sale or distribution of whiskey and other intoxicating drinks. But in 1890 it was expunged from the books as impossible to enforce.[282] During the seven years that prohibition was the law, an informer stood worthy of taking home half the fine for every moonshiner he might dare to squeal on, but after 1890 the only culprit punishable by local law was the unfortunate inebriate who, unable to hold his liquor, stirred up any ruckus in the streets. Respected citizens like John Norton, Charles Edwards, and Joe McGuire found that even they were not above this law, for their fines ranged from $3 to $8 depending on how quarrelsome or riotous they had managed to become.

In 1885 James Rideout was arrested, not for imbibing but for selling moonshine whiskey when the blockade runners law was still in effect. Fortunate for him the witnesses at the hearing in Franklin lacked corroborating evidence, case dismissed.

One method the revenuers employed to find out who was operating a still was to check Cleaveland's store in town to see who'd bought a hundred pounds of sugar. Bub Zachary explained, "Most of us wouldn't have that much money to buy a hundred pounds of sugar."

The ordinance that replaced the liquor law in 1890 was more enforceable. It forbade shooting birds within the streets and enclosures of the town. Contrary to the town's protection of its birds, however, was its strict prohibition against unidentified dogs that were becoming a public nuisance. A new ordinance slapped a $1 tax on every male dog, $3 on a bitch, with the warning that any dog running at large after June 1, 1890, and not listed by its owner for taxation would be "taken up and shot by the constable."[283]

Of far more consequence to early Highlanders than the dog law, however, was the hog law.[284] No ordinance enacted between 1883 and 1890 hogged the town council's agenda more regularly than this one. Animals were vying with people for total control of the town's streets and sidewalks. Early in 1883 the topic of debate at the Literary Society was "The Highlands hog, and what shall be done with him." The newspaper compared the town council and its failure to do anything about the hog with "Prairie," the cowardly red setter: "When set on the 'Highlands hog' he barks furiously till the hog faces about, when he thinks it prudent to retire, and the hog remains in possession of the field—or the street, which is his favorite stamping ground."

As the year progressed, the *Enterprise* expressed the public's growing concern: "The Highlands hog still has undisputed possession of our streets and sidewalks." With the subsequent passage of the ordinance of 1883, warnings were issued that any hogs found at large in the town of Highlands on or after January 1, 1884, would be taken up by the constable and a fine of 25¢ levied on its owner, including an additional 10¢ for each day that the animal remained unclaimed. From day one it would be advertised for sale and on the fifth day sold at public outcry to the highest bidder. So vital was the new law to the people of Highlands that, just before its passage, the editor of the *Blue Ridge Enterprise* implored "our city fathers" to have "the backbone to put this law in force." He went on to warn, "The result of next Spring's elections will rest largely on this one point. We hope the voters in Highlands will make it an issue."

The law took effect on January 1st, but proved unenforceable, until the council voted in 1885 to construct a hog pound in conjunction with Highlands' first calaboose at the northeast corner of 4th and Pine in front of today's Bank of America. In the ordinance of 1886 the town fathers deemed it necessary to add a section that would outlaw "injuring or destroying the [hog] pound or calaboose." This codicil proved prophetic, because three years later the hog pound was torn down "by parties unknown" and had to be rebuilt by the constable. The town sued Frank Hill and John Allen for the damage but never prosecuted.

Only once during a severe drought in the fall of 1885 did the council ever consider suspending the hog law to let the varmints have a chance at the mast in the streets. But the law was never actually suspended, for the matter was tabled indefinitely. By 1890 the town marshal was under severe criticism for not performing his duty regarding the razor backs. They were annoying well-nigh every citizen of the town. In his own defense the marshal argued he had to work for a living and couldn't afford to sacrifice more time than he already did chasing down pigs.

By century's end the town council was empowering the marshal to hire a boy to run the hogs out of town for an amount not to exceed $3.00 per month. The issue by then had spread to areas well outside the corporate limits with sometimes frightening results. On a Thursday evening the Walhalla mail boy's mule was spooked by hogs along the roadside.[285] The mule bolted up the mountain, and in its wild run the saddle girth broke, throwing its young rider to the ground. The mule continued its headlong run, lost its footing on loose rocks, and plunged over a cliff to its death. The boy arrived on foot with the mail in tact but was himself considerably bruised and shaken by the mishap.

Keeping one's hogs within the confines of one's own property was only part of the solution to a complex problem. Dr. Will Anderson, the town's health officer, chastised John Jay Smith for not cleaning and disinfecting his hog pen near Pine Street.[286] Indeed, considering all the town's efforts to stem the havoc that hogs wreaked on its otherwise peaceful atmosphere, only one remedy seemed to fill the bill, that is, until 1886 when even this remedy met its untimely death as "one of the most respected members of the community." Poisoned by some misguided miscreant, this deadly enemy to the razor back received a glowing eulogy from the editor of the *Highlander*. He lamented the loss of the faithful, affectionate, and intelligent Pete Skinner, the town's favorite dog. With Pete gone, the town's streets became hog heaven again!

The year 1889 proved particularly offensive to the senses of Highlanders. Not only the health officer but also private parties complained that Davis Hotel and Islington House needed to carry off excrement and slops from their premises rather than bury them in the ground along 5th Street, as was the prevailing custom. Moreover, Mr. Bascom was asked to remove his manure pile between his stable and Main Street as soon as possible. The putrid odors were bombarding the fragile senses of the townsfolk. John Jay Smith was ordered to remove his privy out of sight of 4th Street and was no longer permitted to empty the kitchen offal and slops from the rooms of Highlands House within the public's view.

Penalties for breaking the town's laws varied according to the severity of the crime. Instead of paying an assessed fine, convicted individuals were given the option of working off their payments through street repair, at 75¢ a day.[287] If a man left his belled cow or mule wandering in the streets over-night, for instance, he might work off his penalty by clearing stone to build the culvert between Bascom's and Paul's store.

The alternative, of course, was the calaboose, which was suffering at the time from considerable abuse. As confirmed by town council minutes, it was forever in need of repair. During Christmas of 1889 the council had to assign a patrol to the jail because of evidence "a certain party" had tried to set the building on fire, and fearing the attempt might be repeated, the board voted to secure the door and window at once.

The second town jail, built in 1918. Courtesy of the Highlands Historic Inventory.

In 1909 Mayor Harbison sold the town's calaboose lot at auction to Alex Anderson, who had just completed his mansion in the same block. Plans were made to build a new jail elsewhere, but the old calaboose remained in use until, according to T. T. Hall, its inmates tried to celebrate Christmas in 1915 and burned it to the ground. It was those same inmates who were re-cruited to help build a new concrete jail on the Partridge lot on Maple Street, known locally as Tobacco Road. Lester Talley was reported to have been one of those who participated in both cases. Will Cleaveland super-vised the building's construction from 1917 to 1918.

Although newly built, this much abused object of many pranks, as re-corded in the town's annals of rascality, developed a history of its own comparable to that of the infamous calaboose it replaced. In 1931 Albert Chastain, then 20, decided he hadn't had enough fun one Saturday night when town marshal Bennie Rogers slapped him in the clinker for drunken-ness, so he set fire to the mattress and bed clothes in his cell. By the time a passerby noticed the smoke and summoned the marshal, poor Albert was near suffocation. Mayor Hines fined him ten dollars plus $14.75 to cover the burnt mattress.[288]

It wasn't uncommon on Saturday evenings for the calaboose to rock with good ol' mountain music. By Sunday morning, however, the noise would die down completely, often lapsing into "O, I wish I had the wings of an an-gel," or one of those mournful mountain ballads whose theme is always a tearstained grave or a lonely willow tree. Whenever Bennie arrived at the break of day to rouse the sleepers and release them, they were usually good boys for at least a Saturday or two afterwards.

Much of the law in early Highlands was public oriented. In 1909 notices were posted on the 4th Street bridge over Mill Creek asking the public "to walk their horses, mules and other stock when crossing said bridge." Addi-tionally, town marshal W. P. Wilson was given specific instructions to look after "shooting and swearing on the street."

In short time these ordinances were expanded to address more modern concerns of public health, safety, and even courtesy.[289] Section 8 under the ordinance of 1922, for instance, required that a house placed under quaran-tine by the public health officer must display a red flag conspicuously out-side the main entrance and a placard stating the name of the contagious disease and forbidding anyone to enter.

Section 30 declared anyone riding, racing, or driving faster than an ordi-nary trot or gallop on the streets to be a nuisance subject to a ten dollar fine. Section 33 set the speed limit for cars in town at 15 m.p.h. on straight streets and 8 m.p.h. at crossings and corners where horns must be sounded. Any driving after sunset or before sunrise had to be lit by white lights on the front of the car and colored lights on the rear.

Sections 38 and 39 focused on public decency. Anyone who willfully in-sulted a woman or girl by indecent speech, motion, or gestures would, upon conviction, be fined ten dollars, and the same for anyone voicing indecent or vulgar language or telling indecent or smutty jokes in the presence of a child under sixteen.

Section 45 prohibited children under seventeen from loitering on the public streets after the ten o'clock curfew; indeed, no one could loiter after eleven. The Blue Law in section 47 forbade opening any business on Sundays during Sunday School or Church hours or after seven in the evening. And Section 51 established the first requirement in Highlands for a building permit.

For a cumulative total of over thirty years, beginning in 1912 or 1913, Ed "Bennie" Rogers was the town's police force, empowered to uphold its laws. His wasn't continuous service because the town fired him in 1934 "for failure on several occasions to obey the orders of the mayor," but rehired him for lack of an alternative three years later. In the words of Olin Dryman, who was hired on to succeed him as chief in 1945,

> *He's a good ol' Bennie. He run me down, arrested me, with liquor one time. He throwed it in the lake. Old man Davis was mayor when Bennie Rogers got hired. And they didn't have no po'lice, and they decided they'd hire Ed Rogers, meanest man in Highlands at that time. And they said if we can't do nothing with him, we'll just make po'lice out of him. So old man Davis met him on the street next morning, and he said, "Well, Bennie, we've hired you po'lice in Highlands."*
>
> *Bennie said, "The hell you have."*
>
> *Yeah, and he just pinned the badge up on 'im and said, "Now you're our po'lice." Bennie would scrap you, boy, I'm telling you, he was a rough 'un.*

Bennie was big and husky. He was overbearing in a fight but not always victorious. Herman Wilson told how his brother Hubert, who weighed in at a skimpy 175, got in a fight with Bennie, who was bent on arresting him for getting drunk during a chestnut hunt out at Shortoff. "It was just a fist and skull battering," said Herman, "but Hube had him licked completely." It took seven men "to get Hube in that little calaboose down there, he's fighting mad." Herman told how Bennie took up with Hube later on and made him deputy sheriff, "cause he knowed Hubert'd stay with ye in a fight."

In 1945 Bennie had his leg taken off and had to quit the police force. Marshall Reese says he lost it from diabetes and eventually gangrene. A doctor at Angel Hospital cut off half his big toe, then the rest of the toe, and later was about to cut off his foot above the ankle. Bennie figured the doctor was trying to squeeze money out of him, so he went to an Asheville doctor who cut off his whole leg near the hip.

Ed "Bennie" Rogers, the law in Highlands from 1912 or 1913 to 1945. Photo courtesy of Pearle Rogers Lambert.

Bennie was a huge man, Marshall claims. His hand was as big as two of Marshall's. According to Jimbud Rogers, Benny's leg is buried in the field adjoining his former home, now Ralph deVille's, but no ghosts have been reported.

According to Pearle Rogers Lambert, Bennie was a favorite with all the town's children. He was also a favorite of Pearle's rooster, which would saunter over to his old red house on the Dillard Road and roost on his porch. Despite his working till 1:00 or 2:00 at night, that rooster would wake him at 5:30 in the morning. Bennie asked Pearle if she was ready for some chicken, for he meant to kill that bird which roosted right there by his head and crowed at the first break of every day.

When Bennie retired, Olin took over as chief, and it wasn't long before he was making good use of the old jail, as he described it, "down there in the swamp." He told of a fifty- or sixty-gallon still he captured around 1945 and took it to the jail. "It belonged to Rob Lamb (Bud Lamb's daddy) and Sam Cunningham. We caught it back over here on Middle Creek, took Rob up there and put him in the jail; Rob's the only one we caught." Bennie, who was turning his job over to Olin at that time, took Rob back to Highlands.

"Well," Olin complained,

Bennie got a half a gallon of liquor and left, and he's supposed to come back after me. There's forty-four barrels of mash there, and I's a busting the barrels, cutting the staves out of 'um. The still held ninety gallons. You could stand up in the pot, and your head wouldn't go out the cap on top.

Well, I sat there till 'bout midnight, and nobody come after me. And finally my brother come, Hugh come and got me. We loaded up the whiskey, sugar, copper, and the still and everything and brought it up there and put it in jail, that old jail down in the laurel thicket.

Luke Rice was on the town board at that time. Old man Luke. Him and two or three more. The jail had holes through the windows you could put a hose pipe through, and they ciphered all the whiskey out and got away with it. And then they took a funnel and pour about five or six hundred pounds of sugar out of there and got away with that too, most of it. Old man Luke did that. I just had the empty can sitting there in the still the next morning. Bennie was into it, I guess, helped get the stuff out.

For many Highlanders, including subsequent officers of the law, bootlegging was a way of life. It was income at a time when there was no money or jobs, but it often ended with marriage.[290] J. D. Head gave up the wild life of moonshining when he married Annie Dryman in 1930. Furman Vinson hauled pints of white lightin' under every seat of his car, including two 20-

gallon kegs in the rumble seat, until he married his Effie Irene McClure of Goldmine. "I quit all that stuff once I had me a family," he said as he gave up $8 to $10 a gallon for the pure stuff with a $5 special for the police.

Radford "Rad" Talley used to pride himself on the runs he made from Georgia to Highlands in a car he said "could outrun the Word of God!" And Carl "Bub" Zachary went from moonshine maker to working for the Highlands police department in the seventies and becoming one of Macon County's best-known deputy sheriffs. He produced as much sugar liquor as corn liquor, for corn was quite common, but sugar, he claimed, was the best there ever was.

"Every human being should know what it is to get drunk on sugar liquor," Bub declared. "And once they do, well then they're apt to think they just never know how good water can be." Like Zachary, Bennie Rogers and Olin Dryman had an inside track on the trade as policemen, having themselves practiced it in the wilder days of their youth.

A mountain family and still. Photo by George Masa, 1929.

Olin served Highlands off and on for thirty years, from 1945, about the time Truman replaced Roosevelt as president, to 1979 during Jimmy Carter's administration. Just like Bennie before him, he was fired in 1949 but hired back in 1956 because there wouldn't anybody serve.[291] Indeed, he was originally hired "on probation subject to acceptable service" at $150 a month. His rehiring in 1956, after being twice turned down, squeaked by only because Mayor Bill McCall broke the tie in his favor.

Olin had a fighting appearance but wasn't entirely devoid of sympathy. He'd lock up drunk drivers down there in the swamp jail which wouldn't hold but four, because that was the only place he had to lock 'um up till the current town hall was built in 1954. Many a time he claimed he sat up "with several of 'um down there to keep a fire all night to keep 'um from freezing to death."

Olin Dryman, the Highlands police force off and on for thirty years. Photo courtesy of the Highlander.

During Olin's first watch in Highlands in the late forties, there wasn't much to the town, he claimed.

I tell you there wasn't. Walked most of the time. I had to furnish my own car, a '41 Ford. I had different ones, but that was the main one. I paid for it all myself, out of the $150, that's what we had to live on, a month, and furnish my car, my gas, and tires and everything. I went to 'um one time and asked to buy a spring. I's going up on Satulah and broke a spring on the car, and asked the town to buy. And they said, "No, we can't afford it." Didn't cost but $7, *but they said, No, they couldn't afford it. When I first went to work up there, I've sat in Highlands many a night in the winter time and never seen a car go through, and I've sat there some days and you never seen nothing but the mail truck go through. People that run business there, they'd walk, like the Potts, but there wasn't many business places in Highlands then.*

Olin's brand of law was tough but also pragmatic. Vengeance wasn't always for the Lord or the law to handle if the situation called for mountain logic, like the time a man's tires were slashed out at Skyline Lodge in 1970 or 1971, just after the fire. Olin was called in and heard the victim tell how he knew who'd done it, but he hadn't seen it done himself and there weren't any witnesses to prove who'd done it, so Olin couldn't lock anyone up.

As Olin turned to leave, the man voiced real frustration. Olin paused, turned, scratched his head, and pondering a bit, said, "'Course if someone was to slash *his* tires, same as your'n, and he ain't seen who done it and there wasn't no witness to prove who done it, I guess there just ain't nothing I could do 'bout him too."

In a real sense Olin's law was the law of the West, or in his case, Western Carolina. When Wilton Cobb from South Carolina was mayor of Highlands, Olin claimed he was told he could lock up the boys from the Flats, Highlands, Cashiers, and Franklin, but "South Carolina boys, leave 'um alone." Olin complained he couldn't do business like that and get along with people. His notion of law was evenhanded, no exceptions. One night he and state patrolman Jack Lansford were at Helen's Barn, and there were four or five boys there from South Carolina, "some of Cobb's friends," as Olin put it.

We rode around through the dance hall in a patrol car, and they called Jack a son-of-a-bitch. And I told Jack, I said, "Ride around again."

He said, "I can't do nothing. This is off state."

I said, "Ride around again. Maybe they'll call me one."

Shore nuf, they did. Told 'um to meet us down at the big cut. Couldn't lock 'um up, Wilton told us not to. Took 'um down to the big cut, whupped the devil out of 'um, sent 'um back to South Carolina.

There were rare occasions when being whupped or arrested by Olin didn't mean you were locked up in the old jail. Wade Wilson tells of how police cars in the seventies weren't like they are now: just a light stuck on top, and the back doors had handles. Olin caught a Cashiers boy raising hell at Helen's Barn where there used to be a corn patch nearby. Olin put the boy in the car and said, "How do you like your eggs, son?" The boy bounced right out the other door and vanished in the corn patch, hollering, "I like mine at home!" Olin never caught him.

By 1986, seven years after his retirement from the Highlands police force, Olin had definite opinions about police brutality, prisoner's rights, and child rearing in the modern world. He thought prisoners had too many rights. "An officer ain't got a chance in the world no more. If you're going to sentence a man, put on what you intend for him to have to start with. This paroling him out, that just makes him worse. I think you ought to have the death penalty, and I think you ought to enforce it. If you're going to give 'um a life sentence, give 'um a life sentence, and if you're going to give 'um death, give 'um death, and go on and do it."

With very few qualms, Olin endorsed the notion of police brutality, for he felt the law protected the criminal quicker than the public. "I believe the way the law reads now on it," he said, "you've got to wait till they hit you. Well, they done got you then, if you have to wait that long. If you don't get in there first to start with, you're messed up. And the way the law is now, you can't shoot a man unless he shoots you or comes at you with a deadly weapon. Well, if you kill him in the yard, jerk him in the house just as dang quick as you can before you call us."

Much of the problem with kids getting into trouble in Highlands Olin chalked up as caused by their parents. "Parents," he argued, "should keep a ten or twelve year old kid at home overnight or be with 'im. Instead of that they send 'um to town, and then they go to a party. Hell, you can't expect much more out of the kids, can ya? A kid's gonna be a kid. A pup and a boy's the same thing. They're gonna get into trouble if you don't watch 'um."

When Olin retired in 1979, he and Bennie Rogers before him had been the entire police force in Highlands for a total of almost seventy years. For three quarters of the town's existence these two men were essentially all that the people could rely on to restore some semblance of order. It has to be understood that what a lawman faced in those middle years of Highlands' history was vastly different, for the most part, from what he faces today. Those were rough times in the mountains. A man would just as soon kill as be killed, which by itself helped preserve a kind of natural order, a mutual fear if not guarded respect.

Olin himself barely escaped several close encounters with death, like the time he stopped some boys from Cashiers. Police at the time wore straps across the belt, like suspenders, and one of the boys grabbed him from the car by the straps and started to drag him up the road. "I cut down with my flashlight and hit across the arm over the door before he turned loose," Olin remembered. Today's police chief Jerry Cook would certainly sympathize with Olin's dilemma since he too only recently barely escaped serious injury in an incident where the culprit slammed Cook's hand in the car door and tried to drive off, forcing the chief to reach through the open window and shut off the ignition or else lose life or limb.

It was not just the ruffians and miscreants that the law in early Highlands had to discipline or control. Occasionally prominent citizens were called to account for some minor infraction. In 1890 Joseph and Alvina Halleck were fined for disorderly conduct. We aren't told what they did, but in response to Joseph's request that their fines be reduced, the board agreed to reduce his wife's fine from five dollars to fifty cents plus costs, amounting to $2.90, but they left his fine in tact "as he was to blame for the whole disturbance."

A practice born of prejudice that the law had to confront in 1932 was that of "rocking" the black servants of summer residents.[292] The town offered a fifty dollar reward for the arrest and conviction of any offenders hurling stones. Other issues during the thirties that were religious as much as legal dealt with noise at the bowling alleys and curfews, which prohibited their operation after certain hours at night and on any Sunday or Sabbath day. Bert Rideout's alley, for instance, could stay open until midnight, provided it be conducted "in a business-like manner and that no disturbance to anyone be maintained." Music boxes were prohibited in public places between eleven at night and nine in the morning.

During the fifties the state inspector of correctional institutions ordered that the town jail be remodeled, and the town passed a law making it a misdemeanor to pass cigarettes, tobacco, matches, drinks, etc. to anyone serving time in the jail. The loop hole in the law was the codicil "except in the presence of the Police Chief," who at the time was Robert Chastain.

By 1959 the old jail was out of favor, for the town leased it to Western Carolina Telephone Co. for ten years at an annual rate of $600 with the understanding that if telephone rates went up, the rent would increase accordingly. The monthly telephone rates at the time were $8.50 for a business line and $4.75 for residential.[293]

There have been very few really serious crimes committed in Highlands. One, however, occurred in the early forties as a case of mistaken identity. Olin Dryman says Miles Owens' boy, Alton, was killed and kept by his slayers in Munger's barn before they got scared and threw him in the Country Club lake. By the time his body was discovered, his own father couldn't identify him, except by the watch that he'd swapped with a friend while caddying on the golf course. The friend identified him.

Olin suspected his killers were aiming for another boy who'd been stealing their liquor, and it happened that the Owens boy was walking the old road to where Larry Rogers lives now, and it was too dark to tell who he was. If they'd taken him to the doctor, Olin claimed, the doctor himself admitted he would have lived. Instead they just got rid of him. Wayne Reese remembered that Alton was returning from a movie in town and was on his way to get golf balls from the lake.

One other death that proved so tragic it still opens wounds even at the mention of it is the Keener incident. This misfortune divided families in the community not only one against another but within themselves. Terry Bolick, who only knew what he heard, as do many who weren't actual witnesses, says that Hyatt Keener was just out of World War I and had a stripped down T-Model. He and John Potts from Norton Community were out carrying on and having some fun, when Uncle Ike Crunkleton, the strict, by-the-law town marshal at the time, and Deputy Sheriff Guy Paul (Sr., not Jr.) stopped them on Main Street.

The *Franklin Press* reported in June, 1921, that when Uncle Ike and Guy Paul tried to arrest the boys for being under the influence, Keener "reached as if to draw a pistol, and his uncle Ike drew his revolver and fired at the same time as Guy Paul."[294]

Although some believed that Guy Paul's shot was the fatal one, for which Ike chose to take the rap, the coroner's report and verification by Dr. Samuel H. Lyle, the county physician, concluded that the .32 bullet fired by Ike did the killing. Potts was locked up over night, fined five dollars, and released the next morning. At the Coroner's inquest it was reported that Keener was carrying a loaded pistol on him which, however, he never drew. In truth many young men in and around Highlands carried pistols despite the law against concealed weapons.

The jury declared Crunkleton innocent by reason of self-defense, and he was released. It was brought out, however, that an old grudge existed between Hyatt and his uncle Ike, which may have played a role in the killing.

In late July both Crunkleton and Paul were tried in Superior Court, and this time the jury returned a verdict of manslaughter. Judge Harding suspended judgment, ordering both defendants to pay court costs.

Terry Bolick claimed that Keener was rolling a cigarette when Ike pointed the gun at him. When Hyatt knocked the gun up in the air, Guy Paul slipped around behind John Potts, and in all the confusion Crunkleton killed Keener. Crunkleton got off in court, Bolick admitted, but people were ready to lynch him. In February, six months after the Keener incident, the town voted to dispense with Mr. Crunkleton's services and appointed Joseph Richert to replace him. Within the year Uncle Ike died. Walter Taylor recalls that there were members of his own Crunkleton family so severely affected that they wouldn't even speak to him after the incident.

Herman Wilson says it all took place in town on the sidewalk going toward Franklin. His brother John Wilson was with both Potts and Keener half an hour earlier but had come home to feed the livestock. And John allowed as how Hyatt was riding kind of high, and when they undertook to take him in, he had reached for his pistol, "which we carried in shoulder holsters under the arm," and he'd just gotten the handle out of his coat when they shot him.

Whatever the interpretation of what happened on that fatal Sunday afternoon in the streets of Highlands, the results saw the Keeners, the Crunkletons, the Pauls, and anyone married into these three families torn apart by the pain of the affair and the human need to lay blame. For those who can talk about it today, there may be residual anger, and for those who can't, there's a welling of tears. In both cases, there's a genuine and regrettable sadness at the core.

The first drugs introduced into the Highlands scene appeared during the mid sixties when Joe Baty was chief and Olin Dryman still served on the force. A student with marijuana rolled up in cigarettes in a shoe box had given a joint to a fellow student's girl. The fellow student got mad, and they had a big fight over it, which brought in Olin. It was his first dealings with drugs in Highlands.

For all the serious problems that demanded a policeman's attention in Highlands, some calls taxed his ingenuity and sense of humor. On July 4th, 1968, Mrs. M. M. Hopper put in a call that her nanny goat had escaped from its stake in her back yard, and the chain became entangled around the front porch post. The nanny had become so frustrated and disgusted that she was charging anyone who tried to help.

So the police were summoned to lay down the law. Neither grabbing nor coaxing her with food availed. Indeed, everything worked in reverse to produce an enraged goat and a hoard of frightened people. The next day the *Galax News* reported that the problem was finally solved by tear gas in large amounts. The nanny was content to be tethered again to her stake in the back yard, having concluded that one taste of freedom and tear gas were quite enough.

If police work in Highlands had its light moments, it also had its moments of real hilarity, like the time a youth climbed up on the roof of the Presbyterian Church and was ringing the church bell at 1:00 in the morning. Olin said he "went out there to get him off the Church, and the fire department and all come to help get him off, you know, and get ladders up," and Olin hollered, 'God, don't put ladders up, turn that big ol' fire hose up there and wash him off." He had frozen on the church and couldn't come down. "He's just stuck up there, that's all," said Olin. They finally got him off with ladders. "A lot of people get so high," Olin remarked, "then they get to where they can't come down nor go up, either one. He's just setting there, holding that flue, and he couldn't go nowhere. He's just aholding on, boy!"

When Olin Dryman completed his last term as police chief in 1974, the town was unable to find a satisfactory replacement. From 1975 to 1981 thirty-four officers joined and left the force, and almost one police chief per year either resigned or was fired.[295] The only police chiefs to hold office longer than a single year or two were Henry Chastain during the late fifties, Joe Baty in the mid sixties, and John Fay in the mid eighties, who was the first after Olin to last more than two years. Jerry Cook, having weathered thirteen years, has served the longest uninterrupted term of any police chief in the history of Highlands without being fired and rehired, like Bennie and Olin.

Perhaps at last the law in Highlands has matured to a level of stability that is not threatened by belligerent hogs and offensive offal in the streets. Old fashioned stills have given way to new fangled ABC dispensaries, although drug busts have replaced liquor raids. Ron Elliott, the developer of Mill Creek Village condominiums in the early 1980s, was indicted along with eleven others for smuggling and distributing marijuana and cocaine and was sentenced to twenty years.[296]

The murder of Terry Chastain by mistake on March 17, 2000, was drug related, for which two convicted killers from Atlanta received life sentences, and one Highlands resident still faces charges for allegedly urging them to rob a Yellow Mountain resident of money and drugs.[297]

The most recent round of arrests, including all of Macon County in the largest drug bust in its history, indicted twenty-seven dealers on 113 felony charges in the distribution and sale of marijuana, cocaine, crack-cocaine, methamphetamine, LSD, and prescription drugs.

When Jerry Cook first joined the Highlands police force in 1983, he dealt with offenses involving only marijuana and alcohol, for cocaine and crack-cocaine were not as prevalent then as now. In fact, he claims, alcohol is less problematic than when he arrived, primarily because of public awareness. The idea of designated drivers, friends looking after friends, has kept Highlands small. "When you lose neighbors taking care of neighbors, you've lost the small town," he says, while admitting that Highlands is no longer as small as it was. He remembers when he knew all the kids in school, in both the lower and upper grades, as well as their parents, but that day is gone. The biggest change, from his perspective, is the number of year-round residents. During off-season in 1983, by 9:00 or 10:00 in the evenings he'd see nothing but stray cats or dogs on Main Street, whereas today it's busy with people till midnight.

Although break-ins, averaging thirty-seven a year in 1983, have dropped to around twelve inside the town with most of them solved, property crime has increased, the larceny of small items. But the police force has also increased from six men to a current roster of ten full-time officers, including

Willie Houston, Todd Ensley, Jimmy McCall, Cliff Ammons, R. L. Forrester, Gary Dalton, Tony Corbin, C. D. Jenkins, and David Head, plus three auxiliary officers: Tim Cook, David Tippet, and Curtis Dowdel.

If there is any problem with the large increase in the Hispanic population, it has been one only of communication, which the department is working to solve through the Crosby Center in explaining its job roles while trying on its own to learn, at the least, survival Spanish. Local churches have aided police monitoring of indigents in town through funds they have established for people suddenly out of work or money until they can get back on their feet.

Chief Cook considers Highlands still a small town with relatively little crime. Its isolation from the interstate highway system means a person really has to intend to come to Highlands since it's not on the way to somewhere else. He has real hope for a town where people willingly help each other and volunteers readily pitch in.

10. The Late Disturbance

Joseph Fritts' Bill, charging Ten Dollars for the board of guards du r-ing the late disturbance being brought before the Council by the Mayor, on motion of Com. Fogartie, the Treasurer was autho rized to pay the same by unanimous vote.
—Minutes of Highlands Board of Commissioners, April 14, 1885

No history of the town of Highlands would be complete without at least mention of the now-famous Moccasin War, which occurred in 1885. Judge Felix Alley says it happened when he was eight or ten years old, which would put it in the year 1881 or 1883, but the public record places it officially in the spring of 1885 when the bill for "the late disturbance" was actually paid by the Highlands town council to Joseph Fritts, owner of the Highlands House at the time.[298]

Fritts and his wife Phoebe had come to Highlands from Alachua, Florida, during the spring of 1882. They owned a hundred acres at Clear Creek, had run the hotel for just over a year, and would run it another year before departing for Texas.

In 1885 Highlands was so small that if you were the mayor, as was H. M. Bascom, you would have won the election by only one vote as he did, 16 to 15, over E. E. Ewing, editor of the *Blue Ridge Enterprise*, Highlands' first newspaper.[299] The town was dry, without saloons or open sale of whiskey, but the immediate neighborhood was rife with moonshiners, who manufactured and peddled their product where the states of North and South Carolina and Georgia cornered.

This afforded them the convenience of dodging from one state to another whenever a revenue officer approached too near. Judge Alley recounts how Highlanders of the time, being a very sober folk with their own temperance society, were strenuously opposed to blockaders riding up the mountain from the Moccasin Township just south of the Georgia border and selling moonshine to the young men of the town.

Stephen Vincent Benét, in his poem "The Mountain Whippoorwill," voiced the general opinion about the preferred quality of Georgia imports:

> *Oh, Georgia booze is mighty fine booze,*
> *The best yuh ever poured yuh,*
> *But it eats the soles right offen yore shoes,*
> *For Hell's broke loose in Georgia.*[300]

Now, one day a U.S. revenuer arrested two Moccasin bootleggers in Georgia, one named Avery Henson and a friend who tried to help him escape. The officer brought them to Highlands, but there being no jail yet built in town, he confined his prisoners in the Highlands House (now Highlands Inn) to await trial.

The Moccasin Township, getting wind of the arrest, issued a formal declaration of war on Highlands and dispatched an army of eighteen volunteers led by the Billingsley brothers and including the Anderson boys. The Moccasin Army marched on Highlands and bivouacked directly across the street behind Central House, from where they laid siege. Mayor Bascom recruited local guards from among the men of the town to defend Highlands House and declared a state of martial law. For three days and nights the two sides sniped at each other. Any head that dared peer from behind either building became an instant target, and in time a stalemate settled over Main Street.

Judge Alley credits native Highlander Tom Ford with procuring a ladder and climbing up onto the roof of Highlands House. From there he shot and killed a Moccasin youth named Ramey. Frank Hill claimed, as a participant in the affair, that it wasn't Tom Ford who killed the Georgian, but rather Cliff Morris, perched in the Altitude Oak in front of Highlands House. Frank took Judge Alley to task for being too young at the time to know.[301]

Highlands House. Photo probably by R. Henry Scadin, ca. 1897–98. Courtesy of Hudson Library archives.

In any case, the immediate result of the killing was that hostilities ceased. The Georgia contingent withdrew to Rabun County to bury their dead. But they left behind a letter declaring that once the proper rites had been performed for their fallen comrade, they'd be returning to wage battle to the bitter end.

Fearing the worst, Highlands sent out messengers to the surrounding country for reinforcements. They recruited anyone old enough to tote a rifle from as far away as Whiteside Cove, Cashiers Valley, and Hamburg (the town now covered by Lake Glenville). Judge Alley's father and four brothers from Whiteside Cove as well as Frank Hill from Horse Cove joined the men pledged to guard and defend Highlands.

Several days passed, during which time the Moccasins reconsidered and sent a letter to announce that instead of risking their lives on North Carolina soil, they intended to shut off the only supply route from Walhalla to Highlands, which ran through their township. Any Highlander that dared venture onto Georgian soil would be killed.

In due time the larders of Highlands grew empty since no one ventured to test the Moccasins' resolve. But one brave soul allowed as how he was not afraid to face them. Joel Lovin, a Confederate veteran, grabbed his rifle, hitched up his team, and set out, fate willing, to make the run or do battle.

No sooner had he rounded Pine Mountain than he spied four Billingsley brothers—Gus, Bob, Cann, and Juan [pronounced Jew-an]—marching up the road, each toting a Winchester rifle. They were fully convinced that, law or no law, they had the right to make and sell moonshine in or out of state, and they were equally intent, conscience clear, on avenging Ramey's death. Though usually hospitable, their present purpose was perfectly clear.

Mr. Lovin had always harbored personal doubts as to the efficacy of prayer, but under such adverse conditions, he found himself imploring with conviction, "Oh, Lord, if there is a Lord, save my soul, if I have a soul, from going to hell, if there is a hell!"

His prayer, however, didn't slow their advance. They kept a-coming. So, grasping his rifle, he prayed again, the only prayer he knew by heart: "Oh, Lord, for what we are about to receive, let us be truly thankful!"

Still the boys came on. His spirits rising, as they always had when he fought battles for the Confederacy, Uncle Lovin laid his rifle across his arm and prayed fervently, "Oh, Lord, if you won't help me, just don't help the Billingsleys!"

It's certain that the Billingsleys recognized old man Lovin, even out of uniform. He was widely known for his military prowess, and they must have reckoned that once his mind was made up, he wouldn't back down. He was a formidable threat. But their course too was irrevocably set.

For whatever reason, which to this day remains a mystery, the Billingsley boys silently passed in single file and disappeared into the woods. Uncle Joel wiped the perspiration from his forehead and rolled on.

208

It was as simple as that: the war between the Moccasin and Highlands townships was at its end. With the Billingsleys back at home, Uncle Lovin returned with supplies from Walhalla. For his part, he never knew what actually saved him: the prayers or the threat. Nevertheless, one thing's for sure. The war ended, but the moonshining didn't. In these remote backwoods it was sure to continue unabated as long as one Appalachian mountain remained to curve across the sky.

In later years Olin Dryman had heard a slightly different version of this story. He claimed that old man Newt Billingsley's brother, Bob, the friend who'd tried to help Henson escape, shot the revenue officer as he was coming up the Highlands House steps to get him. He fired down the steps and killed the officer. When it was all over, he and his three brothers cleared out and joined the California gold rush.

Bob came back in the 1960s when he was almost 80 and tried to give his ranch to his nephew Dub (short for W.) F. Billingsley if he'd move out there and take care of it. "Dub wouldn't go," Olin said. "The old man never was married. And he didn't live but two or three year. Dub could've had all that, for he'd went out there and made a fortune, like the Edwards did, they went out there and made a fortune." Dub admits today that he didn't accept Bob's offer, but he also argues that a lot has been said about what happened back then that might not be true, or it might; we really don't know. In any case, he's come to believe that dealing in whiskey was wrong, even back then.

Home of A. Baxter Wilson at right, Presbyterian Church and Kelsey's house in background. Photo ca. 1890, courtesy of Hudson Library archives.

Walter Reese, in his personal remembrance of what happened during the Highlands incident, recalled that the revenuer was killed on the upper porch and fell over the balusters to the street. Walter, his father, and his mother witnessed the action themselves from the old Baxter Wilson home across the street, where it stands enlarged today east of Central House.

When the fighting was over, Walter's father went downstairs, and Walter—some seventy years later—could still see and hear his mother wringing her hands and crying over the whole affair.[302] Like Olin Dryman and Frank Hill, Walter Reese considered Jonathan Ford's son Tom clear of all blame. He was there in the midst of the fray, Walter admitted, and many thought he shot the officer, but years later it leaked out that Andy Burrell from Pine Mountain, Georgia, fired the fatal shot. There is some confusion as to when and where this happened, for Dub was told that Andy was sitting on a mare at Pine Mountain when the gun was fired, and Reagel's Gap near the old Law Ground there is named after the officer who was ambushed there.

These then are several versions of the facts of the story, with others perhaps in the wings. One fact that stands for certain, however, is that the potential for such a disturbance as the Moccasin War was quite real. Perhaps what happened in Highlands in 1885 was little less than the fulfillment of a previously declared threat from across the Georgia border.

Mailed from Walhalla on March 26 of the previous year, 1884, and addressed to Samuel Kelsey, a letter was kept by Kelsey in his desk drawer and labeled in his own handwriting: "Important KKK letter." Without corrections for punctuation or spelling, but with ellipses added for omissions and spaces and paragraphing provided for clarity, it read essentially as follows:

Mr Kelsey

this is to inform you that we have been hering fer a long time that you damed yankeys has ben threating to fetch the revenew to stop us ga boys from fetching whiskey to highlands   and we her that you have got them to come at last and we are a wating fer them . . .

you dam yankeys has been tring to run over white folks evry sence you have been her   now if you think there is no hel gist have one man tuck from ga or NC . . .

you have made your brags that you whipped us   not us but our fathers   and that is a damd lie   fer tha got out of ration or tha wood of ben with you yet   now if you lot thinks there is no hel gis ceap on   if there is any body bothered through her   we as a clue cluck clan will put evry staer and mil and barn in Ashes at risk of hel

but gist tend to your one busness   and we will tend to ours   don't fer git this   fer we mean gist what we say   and if burning don't do we have got some powder and lead and we will use it on yanks and at a time when the law will not take no fiot . . .

*this ant gist to you   it is to every yank that medle wher he ant got
no busness   if this don't give you all a causion we will give you something that will*

*sence we will have to colose in hops that evry thing will go rite
fer we don't want to have this to do but we can be persuade to do gist
what we promes*

yours as ever , tc

A logical extension of such a resolute threat from tc (the clan) would
have been the now-famous Moccasin War on Highlands. Be it the KKK or
an independent group of Georgia moonshiners, in either case the intent to
ply a time-honored trade without government interference was unmistakably
clear!

11. The Honor and the Glory

A crowded one-room building with poor furniture was filled to over-flowing with pupils and students from six to twenty years of age, un-graded in subjects from the primary to algebra—nearly 100 of them. Mr. Kelsey gave me to understand that I might have the honor and the glory, but that I might likewise take the cussing.

—Professor Thomas G. Harbison

It was in the summer of 1875, after Mr. Kelsey and Mr. Hutchinson had laid out the town and erected homes for their families, that school was held for anyone within walking or riding distance of the old Billy Cabin Farm in Highlands.[303] John N. Arnold, a native of Macon County, served as Highlands' first schoolmaster, setting up his home south of town near today's Dillard Road.[304] An honored Confederate veteran at thirty-five, he had volunteered for service when he was twenty-one, the year the war began.

Consequently he brought to his teaching a profound awareness of life and death, for he had fought with the 1st N.C. Cavalry regiment in the seven days battle near Richmond, with General Lee when he first crossed the Potomac into Maryland, with General Jackson at Harper's Ferry, and with J. E. B. Stuart in his famous raid into Pennsylvania. He had spent the last year and a half of the war in prison camps, beginning with his capture in 1863 until his return to Macon County in 1865. As a man respected for strength of character, he came to Highlands at a time when the brand new town most needed him.

Two of his students came from Highlands itself: the children of T. Baxter and Eleanor White, thirteen-year-old Emma and ten-year-old Fremont.[305] The rest came from outlying mountain farms as children of farmers. Their particular needs Mr. Arnold fully understood, as evidenced by the fact that he wouldn't start school until after the corn was laid by and he declared a two-week vacation at fodder pulling time.

Soon after the close of school in the fall of its first year, Mr. Arnold lost one of his Highlands scholars. Little Fremont died on October 16, 1875, only five months after his family's arrival from Massachusetts.[306] His father rememberd years later that as his life was fast ebbing out, he said to him, "Is the Savior with you?" And with the faintest whisper, Fremont answered, "Yes," and was gone. The young fellow, Highlands' first real sorrow, was laid to rest in the forest that covered 4th Street hill. In late 1880, as plans were under consideration to build Davis House (later known as Lee's Inn) on that same hill, his body was moved to the new Mount Hope Cemetery on Bear Pen Ridge.

Mount Hope Cemetery Association had been formed in November by Sam Kelsey, Baxter White, and Stanhope Hill to caretake four acres of land donated by Kelsey just west of Mortar Gap.[307] It would become Highlands Cemetery in 1887 and Highlands Memorial Park in 1966. Fremont was re-buried in the first grave, marked by an inconspicuous stone at the lower southwest corner in the first shade of the setting sun. His teacher, Mr. Arnold, was to outlive him by many years; indeed when he passed away in 1936, he was a grand old man of ninety-six, well loved and revered by all who knew him.

When school reopened in 1876, classes were held in the single-room log Law House. In the year since the town's founding it had been improved with a fireplace at one end, a new rough floor, slab seats, a teacher's desk, a door, and a window. It served as schoolhouse, courthouse, church, and community center.

Classes were initially taught by the Rev. Robert E. Campbell, a young divinity student, fresh out of Lutheran College in Walhalla. Like any new teacher from the low country, he was sorely tested by the mountain young-uns, a few of whom one cold morning arrived before he did and locked him out of school.

In time he was replaced by Miss Anna S. Porcher of Charleston, who ruled the unruly roost quite precisely until the community had grown large enough that a new school was needed to accommodate all its young schol-ars. Franklin, as the county seat, agreed to contribute money, materials, and labor toward construction. And together the two towns raised $300.50 to build "a school and church house." The site chosen was an acre of land do-nated by Mr. Kelsey on 4th Street, where the town hall exists today. [308] A good frame building of white pine planks, a dressed panel door, and six large windows, it was completed in 1879 by Arthur House, builder and owner of Highlands' first saw mill, and served the town with pride for the next forty years.

Even in its incomplete state, it was being used as early as March of 1878 for religious services, since the old Law House had outgrown its usefulness. From 1880–82 the Law House became the private property of Servetus and Jennette Bathrick and ended its career thereafter rather ignominiously as Sumner Clark's tool shed.

The school's move into its unfinished quarters in April of 1878 saw a changing of the guard from Miss Porcher to several new teachers under Ed-ward Baxter. As principal of the school, Mr. Baxter was an effective educa-tor, an accomplished flutist, and an avid marksman. One of his hobbies, when he wasn't bringing up students with a ruler, was bringing down mag-nolia blossoms with a rifle from the treetops behind Eben Selleck's place on Spring Street. He didn't last long as principal, and neither did his successor,

Mr. Holway, who a week after he took charge was asked by the School Committee to resign, reason not given. A Rev. Mr. Lukens served out the year as interim principal until Miss Orpha E. Rose arrived from Chicago to take charge. A new 360-pound bell arrived as the crowning finish to the new school, ringing out order and respect for learning to young ears as far away as Shortoff and Horse Cove.

The 1ˢᵗ Highlands School, built in 1878. Photo courtesy of the Highlander.

For the next five years Miss Rose brought character and organization to her role as beloved teacher and esteemed principal, so much so that her resignation and departure in 1884 left a great void. Rev. James Fogartie, a minister awaiting completion of the Highlands Presbyterian Church, tried to fill the gap, as did Miss Mary E. Brown, until Sumner Clark, who owned the land on which the Law House stood, agreed to serve.

Clark was himself a former schoolmaster and proved so effective that the following year the county tapped him for Superintendent of Public Instruction. Two more principals, Mrs. S. C. Davis[309] from Murphy and Mr. H. S. Duncan, barely held the school of four grades together until fate stepped in to take control in the spring of 1886, the same year that the Statue of Liberty was dedicated.

From the day of the town's founding, it had been Mr. Kelsey's intent, as advertised in the brochure he distributed throughout the country, to build up a "first-class school, and have all the facilities for improvement, and social and religious privileges, that are found in the best neighborhoods of the North or South."[310] Early Highlanders were determined to find a school teacher "capable of telling B from bull's foot at sight" or he wouldn't be allowed to teach their children—a high standard indeed, which thus far in the young school's short history had been met only by Miss Rose. But a fierce young teacher with energy, courage, and faith far greater than anything Highlands could have ever hoped to bargain for, walked straight out of the forest one day and, changing his own life, changed that of Highlands as well, irrevocably.

Professor Thomas G. Harbison. Photo courtesy of Dolly Harbison.

Himself a botanist, scientist, and educator, he was traveling on a three-month trek by foot all the way from Pennsylvania, accompanied only by his friend Elmer Magee. He carried a woolen blanket, a rubber poncho, a tin bucket, and a copy of Wood's *Manual of Botany* to study the animal and plant life of the Southern Appalachians. Recollecting from his classical education that Caesar's soldiers in the Gallic wars ate crushed wheat prepared as a mush, he sustained both his health and his weight by supplementing this staple diet with brown sugar for sweetener and berries picked on the wayside.

This learned and frugal man's name was Thomas G. Harbison.[311] It was certainly not Professor Harbison's intent to stay in Highlands, for he was really only visiting. But Mr. Kelsey, recognizing the critical need of the town, approached him with an offer to take charge of the school at $160 for four summer months, May through August. To which Harbison retorted facetiously that he'd take the job at $600 for a more proper term of ten months. Not giving the offer a second thought, he left for Pennsylvania after a short two month's stay.

Not to be deterred, however, Mr. Kelsey met his bluff. Informing Mr. Harbison by mail that $480 had been raised through private subscription, he added that he was expecting the professor to report to school the first Monday in August. Professor Harbison's fate was sealed. He himself admitted, "This is how I happened to be initiated into the order of 'Hopeful Highlanders.'"[312]

Thus was born Highlands Normal College in 1886, which Harbison reorganized the following year as Highlands Academy. In its early stages it was a cesarean birth. "I arrived," Harbison reported, "and my troubles began." He described the daunting circumstances confronting him in these doleful terms:

A crowded one-room building with poor furniture was filled to over-flowing with pupils and students from six to twenty years of age, ungraded in subjects from the primary to algebra—nearly 100 of them. Mr. Kelsey gave me to understand that I might have the honor and the glory, but that I might likewise take the cussing.

Harbison served as principal of the new Highlands Academy for ten years under a board of twelve trustees elected in January, 1887, from among the best citizens of the town: Charles Boynton, Dr. Henry O'Farrell, James Rideout, Thoren Walden, Baxter White, Stanhope Hill, Antle Henry, Prioleau Ravenel, Barak Wright, Sam Kelsey, Will Duncan, and Sumner Clark.

Designed to fit students for college, business, or teaching, the Academy opened in one room on November 8, 1886, with 26 students (perhaps Harbison's "100 of them" was a permissible overstatement). Within a year, class sizes had grown to warrant an addition to the building, and Baxter White's daughter, Olive, became Harbison's assistant. Gertrude Cobb Holt recalled there were sixty-five or seventy pupils.[313] She was one of the older students—in the eighth grade—who were allowed to take their books out behind the school and study in the small park that Mr. Kelsey had given to the town.

The first year of the Academy was the year of the "deep snow," which fell during the first week of December and proved to be a financial boon to the crowded one-room school. One fall of snow, measuring between two and three feet, covered the ground for over a month. Blocks of ice were cut from the deeply frozen surface of what is now Harris Lake. They were layered with sawdust for insulation and tightly stored in an old barn. The following summer the town enjoyed its first ice cream, sold by the students to buy lumber for a much needed additional room. The next year the ice cream bought school furniture. Moreover, the school had its first board of trustees.[314]

What Harbison brought to education in Highlands was quality and inspiration. New books, new equipment, new methods, and new desks, which he himself supplied to replace the clumsy, handmade wooden desks of 1878.[315] New students came from far beyond town, and new books were donated by avid admirers of the new principal. The school's faculty consisted of ten professors and teachers offering courses in modern languages, vocal and instrumental music, drawing and sketching, in addition to the regular courses of reading, writing, and arithmetic, with French and German taught by foreign professors.

Tuition for this private school was charged only to those able to pay it; the rest were admitted free. Divided into three levels, it amounted to an annual $11 to $25 (depending on ability to pay) for the Elementary, $27 for the Normal, and $36 for the Collegiate. When in 1889 the Macon County Board of Education granted the Highlands board the right to collect taxes for support of a public graded school, another two years would pass, and Highlands had a free school, running for six, instead of four, months of each year from May through October.[316] By 1891 Highlands had its own school board, composed of Thoren Walden, Sumner Clark, and Albert Staub.

In addition to his academic duties at the school during the early nineties, Harbison also devoted time to serving the community as town commissioner, town clerk, and mayor. He founded, edited, and published the *Mountain Eagle*, a highly respected Highlands newspaper, was elected first president of the Highlands Scientific Society, and served as fourth librarian of the Hudson Library. He chaired the Highlands Building and Loan Association and was instrumental in helping to found the Highlands Biological Station. His two daughters, Gertrude and Dolly, would carry on after him as the Hudson Library's longest serving librarians; and his son Tom, as a master mason, contractor, landscape architect, and universally loved citizen of the town.

At the peak of the school's meteoric rise to a position of high esteem as one of the first public graded schools in North Carolina, Harbison took a year's sabbatical in 1893, purchased Kelsey's home, and traveled to Europe, where he studied the methods and results of schools in Norway, Sweden, Denmark, Germany, and Switzerland. Upon his return he spent another year lecturing in the U.S. on European schools and farming. In 1896, having re-sumed his role as principal of the Highlands public school, he married Judd Cobb's daughter, Jessie. Before his arrival in Highlands, Mr. Cobb had achieved fame as the first building-paper manufacturer in America, apart from his being descended from John Cobb, builder and operator of America's first iron factory.

Highlands School, Mae Henry's class, 1895
Front Row (L to R): Ab Edwards, Arthur Griffin, George Cleaveland,
Bessie Anderson, Nettie Reese, & the twins Helen McKinney & Belle McKinney
2nd Row: Charlie Anderson, Jim Cleaveland, Charlie McKinney, Walter Reese,
Will Cleaveland, Jim Munger, Ed Anderson, Georgia Edwards,
Tina Anderson, Pearl Brown, Frank Henry (teacher's brother),
Bessie Reese, & Mae Henry (Teacher). Photo courtesy of Hudson Library archives.

The year that Prof. Harbison married Miss Cobb was when his life-long friend and companion of his walking trip from Pennsylvania to Highlands, Elmer E. Magee, invited him to become principal of Waynesville High School. He was asked to convert it, with the same success that he'd achieved in Highlands, from a private institution to a public graded school. His retirement, therefore, in 1896 as principal of the Highlands School, dealt a painful blow to the little community that had begun to discover itself so completely through his intellectual talents and extensive influence.

Perhaps he felt that esteem and, with all modesty, appreciated the town's loss, for before he left, he donated the annex to the school building, which he had built at his own expense for his own library, to the newly formed Hudson Library. The space was more than adequate, since Harbison, being essentially a self-educated man, had amassed a considerable library. His collection of books had passed a thousand by the time he was twenty-one and by age thirty-one was being extolled outside Highlands as "the best school library in Western North Carolina."[317]

During his ten years at Highlands School, Harbison was highly regarded throughout the town as a no-nonsense teacher. Stern but cordial, with a Prussian's military posture and a Vandyke beard, he had a keen eye for observation and a remarkably retentive memory. He subjected his students at the Academy to a classical education. To the student who found the first flower of each species in each new season, he gave a penny, and five cents for rare finds, that is, if the child could tell him, not just the common name of the find, but the Latin name as well, and what the Latin name meant! "He was rough as hell," said Shine Potts, one of his later students. "He didn't take baloney from anybody. Nobody acted up."[318]

On the other hand, in the opinion of his nephew Bill Holt, he had a way of relating things that happened to him that made dull things sound interesting: "He was a great storyteller. He should have been a Zane Grey." Joe Reese recalled how he'd sit in the soda shop and listen spellbound to Professor Harbison and Gus talk about what they'd read or experienced. Gus was well read himself; in fact, he read all the time. They'd talk all night about such bizarre topics as the taste of wild game, like hawk or buzzard, but mostly about what they'd read.

Harbison's service to Waynesville School was followed by five years' employment as collector of plants for the newly established Herbarium of George Vanderbilt's Biltmore Estate. From 1905 to 1926, when he wasn't teaching, he traveled extensively throughout the Southeast collecting data for Dr. Charles Sargent, Director of the Arnold Arboretum at Harvard University and author of the *Manual of the Trees of North America*. Among his discoveries of more than a hundred new species of perennial herbs, the best known is perhaps the large red *Trillium vaseyi*.

He sold his Kelsey home to Miss Minnie Warren in 1909 and moved into Monroe Skinner's *Glencroft* beneath Sunset Rocks, where he stayed until 1921 when he built his own home on the south slope of Satulah on the Walhalla Road. He commissioned Will Cleaveland to build it on the foundation of the old Martha or "Mart" Teague house, which had stood since the War Between the States. Considering that Harbison's three daughters who would inhabit this house for the next sixty years—Margaret, Gertrude, and Dolly— were ladies, like himself, imminently proper and beyond reproach, it's particularly ironic that Mart, the location's former tenant, had a shady reputation as a woman of ill-repute. If Harbison knew this fact, we aren't told that he did, but considering his reputation for caustic, indeed scathing reproofs, he was presumably never asked.

Prof. Thomas and Jessie Cobb Harbison with daughters Gertrude and Margaret on front porch of their Kelsey home. Photo ca. 1905.

From his extensive orchard which he and his friend Elmer Magee created on a ten-acre lot across the Walhalla Road in 1901, Harbison ran a small plant business called "Highland Plant Exchange," from where he shipped on demand wild plants, including *Shortia galacifolia*, to many different states. He grew many varieties of apples, experimenting to identify which thrived best on the Highlands plateau. In the early thirties he worked summers as nature instructor at Camp Sequoyah for Boys in Weaverville, N.C., and at Camp Nakanwa for Girls at Mayland, Tenn.

In all, he traveled by foot the equivalent of three times around the world—75,000 miles by his own count—collecting from the swamp lands of Florida to the mountain slopes of Switzerland. A hardier man would be difficult to find. From 1933 until his death three years later he served as curator of the Herbarium at the University of North Carolina at Chapel Hill. Not all his time was spent, however, outside Highlands, for from 1909 until 1911 he was teaching at the Emmons Industrial School at Shortoff, which is why some of his students still remember him today.[319]

Upon Harbison's initial retirement from Highlands School in 1896, Miss Mollie Carpenter took over as principal.[320] At that time there were five schools in the vicinity of Highlands: Shortoff, Highlands, Horse Cove, Clear

Creek, and Broadway. The next year, however, Macon County simplified its school system by grouping its fifty-five small and widely scattered schools into eleven districts. All five schools within reach of Highlands became part of the Highlands District while remaining separate entities.[321] This is how it remained until the consolidation of Clear Creek and Horse Cove into Highlands School in 1931.

Miss Tibbet's Highlands School Class of 1907–08
1st Row (L to R): Sam Reese, Rose Wilson (Wilbanks), Henry Stewart Jr.,
Dewey Rogers, Claude Henry, Helen Zachary (Potts)
2nd Row: Teacher Miss Tessler Tibbet, Alice Reese (Potts), Carrie Wilson,
Lilly Chastain (Calloway), Eva Chastain, Roy "Little Nick" Potts
3rd Row: Dora Chastain (Zachary), Belle Wilson, Bessie Wilson, Mary Stewart,
Nellie Cleaveland (West Cook),
4th Row: Margaret Stewart, Edith Rogers (Norton), Sally Wilson (Montieth),
Meta Pierson (Potts Collins). Photo courtesy of Hudson Library archives.

For a while there were also private schools handling the growing number of students in Highlands. Corinne Froneberger, a German native from Charleston whose home on Hickory Street served as a school, taught Tudor and Caroline Hall, Ethel Calloway, Mary Paul, Bill and Eva Potts, Sarah and Bess Hines, the Zoellners, three Stewart children, among several others from 1911 until her death in the mid twenties. There was also the Satulah School, on the Dillard Road which was functioning in 1909.

Satulah School, May 11, 1909. Photo courtesy of Walter Taylor.
Front Row (L to R): Claude Calloway, Lillie Chastain, Pearl Crunkleton, 4 un-
knowns, Ellefair Crunkleton, Gertrude Harbison, Jack Munger
2ⁿᵈ Row: Henry Stewart, Jr., Eva Chastain, Belle Wilson, Anita Stewart, Margaret
Harbison, Unknown
3ʳᵈ Row: Unknown, Victoria Maroda (from Cuba), Unknown, Dora Chastain,
3 unknowns
Back Row: 3 unknowns, Mary Stewart

Just a block from Mrs. Froneberger's home was another private school at the home of Annie Whipp Pierson on the southeast corner of 4th and Chestnut, a vacant lot today. Mrs. Pierson was the teacher whom any student attending Highlands School between 1908 and 1950 would long remember as the Boston lady who taught math.[322] Initially Harry Wright took lessons from her. She began her teaching career at the new Emmons Industrial School in Shortoff. This school was built in 1906 on the hill above the old Shortoff Schoolhouse, which still exists across from the Shortoff Baptist

Church. The Emmons Industrial School was known as Highlands 1 to distinguish it from Highlands 2 in town.

After 1903, when Macon County passed the first compulsory attendance law in the state of North Carolina, all children in the area were required to attend school until age fourteen.[323] Those who didn't attend the school in Highlands went to school in Shortoff. When it first opened in a new two-story structure, as Louise Edwards Meisel recalls, the students were allowed to vote whether they wanted school upstairs or down. They voted up, for up meant a beautiful view and a stage with velvet curtains for recitations.

Miss Annie left Highlands 1 after only three years to teach at Highlands 2 until her retirement. Presumably she left teaching at Shortoff with great relief, for by her own admission the Wells place where she boarded was visited often by Highlands' most famous ghost.[324]

When Miss Annie chaperoned camping trips for the school kids, she would tell by the flickering light of the fire about the tall ghost in white with long flowing black hair, who on many occasions glided silently through the curtains at her door and, while Miss Annie cowered in her bed, went straight to the washstand, lifted the pitcher, and slowly and thoroughly washed her hands. When she had finished, she would float lazily out the window and down the hill. She always appeared on a moonless night when the air was still and the curtains hung expectant in the doorway.

Other phenomena at the Wells place had witnesses besides Miss Annie. There was the white ball of glowing flames that would appear at the top of the hill, roll down, and hover momentarily over the grave of a black-haired beauty who once lived with the Wells but had died under mysterious circumstances and was buried in an unmarked grave in the yard. When the ball of fire reached the grave, it would dissolve into the misty air. Attempts to identify it as phosphorescence, reflections off mineral deposits, or electrical impulses failed to explain its pause over the grave, and a number of old-timers reported seeing the ghostly lady sitting on the front porch brushing her long black hair.

Apart from Miss Annie's love of the mysterious, which she would relate as though in a trance, she was a dedicated and determined "school mistress," always insisting on proper English grammar, correct pronunciation, and the development of good reading habits. She influenced the lives of hundreds of students during the forty-two years of her teaching career.

Irene James remembers the school that her parents, Ed Pickelsimer and Cora Rogers, attended in nearby Clear Creek. In those days, she says, the Committeemen thought they owned the school. "They said no courtin' in the schools, so I reckon there was no courtin', but my parents got married. And here I am to prove it." By the time Irene was old enough to go to school herself, she went to Highlands instead of Clear Creek. She remembers getting up before daybreak each morning and walking the five-mile Satulah Mountain trail up over the gap between Satulah and Fodder-stack and on to town, carrying a lantern to light her way dimly along the dark road. When she reached Highlands, she hid the lantern in the woods so no one would know and picked it up on her return home in the afternoon.

By 1915 the students of Highlands School had outgrown their forty-year-old building. Despite attempts to repair it in 1910–11, the year that school was held in the ground floor of the Masonic Hall, there was no saving the ancient structure, which had outlived its valued time. The town voted $6,000 in bonds to build and equip a new schoolhouse. The following year, as soon as work was scheduled to begin, a voter petition asked the town to collect $200 in taxes in order to install a four-sided tower on its roof. It was built to contain the town clock, which the Highlands Improvement Society donated as a gift.[325]

Erected high up on the hill behind the original one-story schoolhouse, about where the ABC Store exists today, the new two-story school would dominate the town's skyline for thirty years as one of its most familiar features. Its bell, transferred to the tower from the old school, rang out the hours for anyone wishing to know the time of day. Louis "Bud" Potts remembers spending a large part of his life climbing this clock tower every week, sticking his head out the small door in each clock face to reset the hands to correct time—or at least so the four clocks would occasionally agree.

The 2ⁿᵈ Highlands School, built 1916–19. Courtesy of the Highlander.

The Town Clock School or the big red schoolhouse on Knowledge Hill, as the new edifice was called, wasn't completed until 1919, when the town borrowed $750 from Henry Sloan to match a grant from the County Super-intendent and the District Trustees.[326] The money went toward equipping the building with electric lights and an auditorium of 400 seats, a motion picture outfit, and a Pianola. As long as construction was underway, Joe Reese remembered, the students again studied in the Masonic Hall, beginning in 1915 when Miss Annie A. Vaughn was principal. Meanwhile, Roderick Pierson salvaged timbers from the first schoolhouse to build a house on Buttermilk Level Road, north of the Dillard Road, which in 1917 became Paul Henry's home.

On September 1, 1919, in order to pay off the schoolhouse debt, Miss Margaret McConnell and the Misses Billstein assisted in staging *17*, a benefit play. The new school boasted three large classrooms and the principal's office on the ground floor and an auditorium and soup kitchen upstairs. A piano and Pianola aided in the performance of operas like *Lohengrin* and *Aïda* as well as compositions of Chopin and Beethoven. The people of Highlands were rightfully proud of their modern school.

In 1922 Henry Sloan supervised construction of steps and a walkway from the 4th Street sidewalk up to the schoolhouse, and the following year the county bought land behind the school for a playground, a particular delight to the students. Not that all students needed a break from learning! Tearley Picklesimer, for instance, who walked to school from Clear Creek each day, claimed that school wasn't all that bad. Louise Meisel remembers Tearley's teacher's announcing that he wasn't learning anything, so why did he come to school at all. Tearley's response? He came to have fun!

Among the earliest sports played at the new Highlands School were basketball, organized in 1923, and wrestling, which the new school principal, T. L. Tolar of Latta, S.C., added in 1926.[327] A graduate of Wake Forest College, Tolar actively promoted sports, but he also constructed two new rooms to house a standard high school and added four more acres of land. By 1927 there were 49 students attending the high school and 130 in the grades, and the building was steam heated. Six teachers—Annie Pierson, Joe Hays, Elizabeth Rice, Beatrice Keener, and Verna Holbrook—taught all 179 students. Two of these were the first to graduate from the new Highlands High School in May: Frank Paul, valedictorian, and Eric Edwards, salutatorian. The following year six graduated: Alice Hudson, Edna Bumgarner, Taft Henry, Carolina Hall, Eloise Rice, and Margaret Gilbert (later Hall).

In 1928, the year that Herbert Hoover's sweep of the presidential election split the South, Tolar took up arms in the fight that would boost his record as an effective and articulate administrator. He entered a controversial fray, which he characterized as a "battle between ignorance and truth in

Macon County."[328] The hot issue was school consolidation, and the solution from Tolar's practical point of view was that "a dollar spent in a consolidated school is well worth many dollars spent in a one-teacher school."

He wrote two articles for the *Franklin Press* in which he contended that an eight-teacher school with adequate equipment, like the one in Highlands, was far better equipped to prepare a child to face the hard-boiled world. He blamed parents for permitting their children "to waste their golden hours attending a one-teacher school where only brave, courageous Joan of Arc nuns fight six long hours to teach each of the seven grades a smattering of everything and nothing."

In the end Tolar won the battle for Highlands School, or so it would seem. In June of 1928 the Highlands Township voted 137 to 76, out of 245 registered voters, in favor of consolidation. Four schools would be bused to Highlands. The victory, however, was neither total nor immediate, for the following February four citizens of the Highlands Township, whose children had to walk two or three miles to catch the school bus to town, were hauled into court and charged with violating the compulsory attendance law. Andy and R. B. Wilson, Evan Talley, and R. B. Long complained in court about the distance their children had to walk and argued they had no protection from the weather while awaiting the bus. Judge Rickman dismissed the charges against them on grounds the state had failed to prove its case.

Mel Keener considered consolidation a crime; he called it theft. In effect, it killed his Flat Mountain school at Webb field on the Flat Mountain Road, where six grades of students, mostly Wrights, Heddens, and Phillipses, sat on logs in one big room and learned from Tudie Rice who rode out on a horse to teach them. "They consolidated our schools," he lamented. "They took it away from us, to Highlands."

Similar feelings were voiced where Frances Baumgarner Lombard taught in Horse Cove, Miss Virginia Edwards in Clear Creek, Miss Margie Hughes at Broadway, and Miss Annie Hughes at Flat Mountain. By the end of the twenties Shortoff, Horse Cove, Clear Creek, Broadway, and Flat Mountain were fully consolidated into Highlands School, giving 275 students the benefit of eight teachers, three in high school and five in the elementary grades, all of whom, however, were new, except for Annie Pierson.

In 1928 an organization was created in Highlands that gave its youth practical experience in agriculture, wholly apart from school requirements. Two 4-H Clubs were formed with Prof. Harbison heading one for boys and Miss Bernie Durgin, another for girls.[329] The following year Prof. Summer and Prof. Clyde "Luke" Hentz organized the first Boy Scout Patrol in Highlands, which met in Gus Holt's building at Main and 4th. Mrs. Leonard Pearson of Chicago led the Girl Scouts, followed by Dolly Harbison during the thirties. At the end of the thirties the Boy Scouts were cutting logs donated by the Forest Service to build a cabin, as Bud Potts remembers it, at the back of Christopher Whittle's lot on Main Street, later site of Highlands Art Gallery. The town even agreed to furnish lights for the hut and to extend the water line free of charge if the scouts would dig the ditch and install the pipe.

By the early fifties the Boy Scouts had been moved to a new hut constructed at the Municipal Park with lumber from the old fire shed. Sponsored by the Jaycees, Richard Harrison served as scoutmaster of Troop 7, aided by Dewey Hopper and Willard Crisp. By the time the first Cub Scout Pack was created in 1958, all scouts were meeting in the old school building. The sixties saw Ellison Magruder, Col. Val Pierson, and Stephen Foster, respectively, leading Troop 207 as scoutmaster; Frank McCall and then Alvin Crowe, Jr., leading Cub Scout Pack 207. Mrs. Victoria Bailey led the Girl Scouts. Eventually Bob Wright and Jim Bryson took on the Boy Scouts, then James "Jimbud" Rogers, Tommy Chambers, and today Noel McJunkin. Jack Taylor and John Bauknight took the Cubs, followed by Judy Bryson and Gay Rogers.

Priscilla Dunning led Girl Scout Troop 180, replaced later by Charlotte Biedron and Joyce Sloan. Carol Fox, Jill Prosser, and Wynn Cleaveland guided Brownie Troop 179, succeeded by Margie Melvin and Gail Garland, then Vicki Heller, Jerri Talley, and Kim Chenoweth.

By the turn of the century, after more than seventy years, scouting was still thriving in Highlands. At least ten boy scouts had achieved the rank of Eagle: Michael and Billy Crowe; Eric, Ted, Joe, Tom, and Jack Shaffner; Spencer and Sam Chambers; Rick Rodenbeck, Kelly Barbato, and Allen Houston.

In 1932 Miss Ethel Calloway joined Annie Pierson and over time become another of the stalwarts of Highlands school. Miss Ethel was effective at both teaching and discipline, for she knew well the appeal of mischievous behavior. Louise Edwards Meisel remembers when Ethel was a student at the Shortoff School and started a rumor that the local water carried typhoid fever, with the result that all the kids carted bottled water to school. She was locked in the book closet as punishment, but anyone who knew Miss Ethel also knew that being locked in a book closet was nothing short of reward. Miss Ethel loved to read.

For thirty-one years until her retirement in 1970, she taught at various times grades four through ten, but mostly grade five, the grade when the kids "are the most real in the world," she claimed.[330] "Nobody, but nobody's going to tell you the truth like a ten-year-old boy. You know, a fifth grader hasn't started painful adolescence and they're still interested in things." She claimed she paddled or taught over half the leading citizens of Highlands, including Steve Potts, Neville Bryson, Jamie Keener, Earle

Young, Jack and Doyle Calloway, and John Cleaveland, and she left it to speculation as to who got which.

Ethel Calloway. Photo 1975, courtesy of the Highlander.

She never confined her teaching to books or lesson plans but sought instead to show her students a better way to face life. Many of them still recall the way she read to them in class *The Secret Garden*, *Little Women*, and *Tom Sawyer*. Her performance beat any movie showing at the school auditorium or the Galax Theatre. What Gladys McDowell loved was how Kipling's absent-minded beggar marched to the rhythm of Miss Ethel's "Boots—boots—boots—boots—movin' up and down again! There's no discharge in the war!" Rosemary Fleming thrived on her nature walks. Miss Ethel had a distinct knack for bringing literature to life and drawing her rapt listeners into an unforgettable experience of the printed word.

No student ever pulled one over on Miss Ethel. She'd already done as a child whatever mischief was planned and had it covered from every angle.

As a child she used to help the town librarian, Miss Gertrude Harbison, after school and noticed how she hid new books behind a green curtain if she considered them improper for young eyes. "Gertrude was a moralist," Ethel remarked with a twinkle in her eye. "She didn't want to contaminate the community. I used to ask Miss Gertrude if she would like to go get her mail while I kept the library for her. Then I'd grab a book from behind the curtain to take it home, read it, and bring it back. Gore Vidal was one of those who landed behind the curtain."

For someone as devoutly religious as Ethel, she had a personal hold on sin, and with all humility and a chuckle would readily admit it. Wasn't it she who sat with Hixy Hines in the Episcopal Church and sang self-composed versions of the sacred hymns? Hixy's sister Bess told how they would stick with the tunes but insert their own words, like "What was that funny little man I saw you with last night?" and "Shut your mouth, Ethel. He's cuter than your fat boyfriend." Ethel could keep a straight face, but Hixy fell into fits of giggles and disapproving glances from the elders. Ethel, from experience, knew her students inside and out, and they loved her for it. She was strict in discipline, for although she could kid with a poker face, when she meant it—as one student remarked—her eyes didn't laugh.

When Miss Ethel came to teach at Highlands School, the principal was Otto Summer, of Pomoria, S.C., who himself would eventually rank among Highlands' longest serving principals.[331] Prof. Summer served the school for a total of thirty-two years—twenty-three as principal—beginning with his arrival in 1927 and ending with his retirement in 1965. He took a two-year break in the early forties to serve as principal of the school at Bryson City and worked three years during the early fifties as manager of the Galax Theatre in Highlands. As principal, he was very strict. Ethel once said that if he had a hundred straight pins, he'd line them up so all the heads would point the same way. If he felt a student or teacher wasn't performing to capacity, he'd say so. He liked to see people learn and put a high value on education.

During the initial stage of his reign as principal, student enrollment increased dramatically from 200 in 1929 to 350 in 1937, and the number of teachers, from seven to eleven. The high school became accredited, and the building was enlarged by a wing and two more classrooms. This increased the number of potbellied stoves that Rosie Baty had to stoke regularly, for Edna Bryson claims he spent the whole day every day carrying scuttles full of coal, one in each hand, from the basement to every room in the building when the weather was cold.

In 1933 the state took over the entire school system in North Carolina, which made little difference to Highlands, since it was already functioning under an eight-month school year for every child. Like most principals at

Highlands School, Otto Summer taught classes in addition to his administrative duties. Math and science were his forte, and he taught eighth and ninth grade; his wife, piano. Louise Edwards Meisel credits him with teaching her geometry so she'd pass, for without him both he and she knew it was hopeless. The high school auditorium (later the Highlands Community Theatre building) owed its creation to Prof. Summer's petitioning the town board to buy the land and in 1934 build it with WPA (what Herbert "Cub" Rice called "We Poke Along") funding."[332]

Even after retiring from teaching in 1965, Prof. Summer still devoted himself to serving the town for two years as mayor. Through his publication of the *Galax News*, he established a very popular monthly school paper, which the high school students issued for general town information. He was a stern, no-nonsense man whom my wife Margaret remembers as one who almost never smiled. Mike McCall worked for him at the *Galax News*, delivering flyers that announced the movies, a job for which Summer paid him 50¢, less federal and state withholding, for a net salary of 47¢ a trip.

Summer's colleague, Prof. Newton, ran the sandwich shop, which adjoined the theatre and where, according to Debbie Dryman (now McCall), he almost lost his life. Debbie and Pearl Vinson always prepared the hamburgers. Arriving early one afternoon, they turned on the gas grill to cook the burgers, and when it wouldn't light, they forgot about it. Later, when Prof. Newton arrived and questioned why the hamburgers weren't ready, he struck a match to show them how it was done. Before he could approach the grill, there was a huge whoosh, which blew him thirty feet into the candy rack. Debbie says it was the only time she ever heard him curse.

In January, 1936, Highlands lost two of its best teachers, who died within three days of each other: Prof. Harbison on Jan. 12th and John Arnold, its first schoolmaster, on Jan. 15th. The following year influenza struck half the population of Highlands, incapacitating some two hundred and fifty people and closing the school in March with forty percent absenteeism.

Epidemics were not uncommon in Highlands, despite its solid reputation as a health resort. In 1891 and again in '93 the grippe and pneumonia descended on the mountain and put half or more of its people instantly to bed.[333] Measles and chicken pox epidemics struck in 1924, and quarantines against polio began in the forties during Prof. Summer's tenure as school principal and teacher.

Indeed, until the hospital came to Highlands, the schoolhouse served as the annual site for vaccinations against these scourges of the community. As early as 1922 the State Tonsil and Adenoid Clinic was performing extractions on Wednesdays, Thursdays, and Fridays at the schoolhouse, which amounted almost to an epidemic itself.

In 1938, the year that French replaced Latin in the curriculum, Cynthia Moretz, Mattie Wilkes, and Elizabeth Whiteside raised the number of teachers on the Highlands School faculty to eleven (three times what it had been in 1926); student enrollment reached 356 (again three times as many) but the average class size remained the same: twenty-eight.[334]

The end of the school year in 1951 was significant for Highlands School. Otto Summer oversaw the school's move to a brand new home at the foot of Satulah Mountain, an area known to Highlanders as Muddy Hollow, which later generations would sorely rue. A year after the move was completed, while the state was paving 5th Street from Main to the new schoolhouse, the town bought the old schoolhouse and property for $10,000 from the county board of education.[335]

The 3rd Highlands School, built in 1950–51. Photo by the author, 2000.

For the next ten years the old schoolhouse filled a wide variety of uses by the people of Highlands. The basement served as a warehouse for storing town materials. The town office was moved to the 1st grade corner room on the first floor. The playground and recreational rooms provided space for Recreational Director Bob DuPree to supervise summer activities, including plays and music programs in the auditorium. The High School Auditorium was rented by DuPree's Little Theatre Group as early as 1951, and in 1954 James Christian Pfohl of the Transylvania Music Camp Faculty Orchestra (today's Brevard Music Festival) directed the first annual Pops Concert to benefit the Highlands Community Hospital. The Chamber of Commerce took a room, which the Highlands Community Club used for socials during the winter. In 1956 the Boy Scouts were meeting in one room every Thursday. The second floor was ruled off limits due to fire hazards, a dire omen for the rest of the building which in time would face demolition.

By 1957 plans were already in the offing to strip the building to its foundation and reconstruct a one-story recreation center. Teen Canteen had already enjoyed a winter success, which inspired proposals of a bowling alley and pool table as a better year-round program than a miniature golf course. Discussions of this nature continued until 1959 when the Chamber of Commerce ran an ad in the *Highlander* offering the old school building for sale to the highest bidder, requesting only that it be dismantled and removed from the premises within ninety days.[336]

It was a sad day when the old schoolhouse finally came down in the winter of 1960. For just over thirty years it had stood as a recognized landmark on Knowledge Hill, and many a Highlands child had grown up accustomed to the clang of its resonating bell and the laughter and tears that comprise a school child's life. By 1961 the hill where the old school had stood was bare, leveled for the Community Theatre's parking. The crown of the town was gone.

The bell, which Ben and Polly Wax bought for twenty-five dollars for their Camp Highlander (today's Mountain Learning Center on the Dillard Road) departed from Highlands in 1975 when Camp Highlander moved to Mills River near Asheville. There the bell remained until 1999 when the Millennium Committee brought it back to rest in its old Highlands home: the current clock tower above town hall. It rang in the new millennium from almost exactly the same spot where a hundred and twenty-one years earlier it had announced the first Highlands School.

Highlands School's move in 1951 to its third new location under Satulah was not without major problems. Muddy Hollow had a high water table, so much so that not three years had passed before the P. T. A. was seeking ways to dry out the playground area behind the school with a dam and a ditch.[337] In 1976–78 Bill Reese and his crew poured $50,000 worth of improvements, despite serious obstacles, into building an underground sheltered play area accessed by tunnels for the children. In 1999, with the area still suffering from the muddy conditions that had given it its original name, Margaret Shaffner would spearhead a P. T. O. drive to attempt once again to drain, grade, and surface the grounds with enough piping to finally dry it out.

When Prof. Summer left his post in the early forties to take over the school in Bryson City, Prof. Walter C. "Doc" Newton, a graduate of Lenoir Rhyne College, became principal of Highlands School, a position that he would hold twice more during the fifties and sixties. When he wasn't teaching history, math, and tenth grade in the high school, he was running his sandwich shop through the window he'd cut in the wall of the Galax Theatre lobby so theatergoers could supplement Prof. Summer's popcorn with his hamburgers. Later he would own the Highlander Restaurant.

The year 1954 saw the creation of a Highlands School band, directed by Mr. Orr and funded by over sixteen hundred dollars for instruments.[338] During this decade of the fifties Highlands School went through five principals subsequent to Otto Summer: F. N. Shearouse, 30-year-old Joseph Bowles, Doc Newton for another term, Frank Watson, and Guy Sutton. Newton would serve again in the sixties before his retirement in 1969. He and Charles Hendrix, Stoney Hinkle, and Jim Shepherd carried the school up to the late seventies when Larry Brooks, a native of Franklin, took over and held the reigns quite effectively for a total of twenty-one years.

With a background in teaching, athletics, and administration, Brooks favored Highlands for the problems it didn't share with larger cities, especially discipline. Before his arrival in Highlands he had taken a break from teaching because he "was about to starve to death." He ran the City Restaurant in Franklin from 1968 to 1973, when he returned to education in Hendersonville. Looking back at teaching during the sixties, he remarked, "When I left, it was still 'yes sir—no sir,' when I came back . . . whoo boy!" On his arrival in Highlands in 1976, however, he found caring, hardworking, and conscientious teachers and excellent parental support. That's not to say that student misbehavior didn't flourish. Just handling a bus load of students who didn't always behave as the angels' parents thought they should was a typical lesson in universality. Brooks quipped, "A lion tamer used to impress me, 'till I met a school bus driver!"

During the decade of the sixties Highlands School graduated an average of nineteen students a year. The mid sixties also saw the establishment of a very successful Head Start project, which sought to give preschool-aged children from poor homes the basics needed for entering school.[339] Sponsored by the Macon Program for Progress, it began in 1965 at Highlands School but moved the following year to Dr. Edwin Reinke's former home on East Main, later the Highland Hiker, where a private kindergarten teacher at the Episcopal Church, Virginia Worley, directed it with the aid of Bonnie Bryson and Jessie Manley. Virginia turned it over to Doris Picklesimer who with the aid of Babs Weston held the reins until 2000. Head Start still educates preschoolers under Vicki Ellenberg in the Assembly of God building off East Main Street where it moved in 1983.

With the growing number of working women in need of child care, the Presbyterian Church in 1979 set up a Child Care Center, directed by Bitsy Calloway, to provide a baby sitting service. A year earlier the Catholic Church had established a pre-school, headed by Jonna Buffington, to provide pre-kindergarten instruction, and in 1983 Wilma Gordon established Highlands Preschool at the Methodist Church where children sang about head and shoulders, knees and toes; read; listened; and learned to share.

The seventies began at Highlands School with nineteen graduating seniors donating the sign: Highlands School—Home of the Highlanders. During the eighties Jamie Keener became the first Highlander to chair the Macon County School Board, and his efforts from 1981–87 on behalf of Highlands helped pass a $10 million school bond and county funding for teaching positions which had been cut by the state.

The Highlands School building was expanded into more classrooms, including a new high school wing in 1985–86, despite the fact that it sank several inches into the water table and had to be shored up to prevent cracking or listing. Delays in construction meant that classes had to be held in 1986–87 in the newly built Civic Center. Donnie Edwards replaced Jamie Keener on the school board in 1988, and in 1996 the cafeteria was expanded and a two-story middle school building and science laboratory were added.

In addition to the regular curriculum at school, an extracurricular program, which enjoyed as much popularity as when it was first founded in 1954, was the rejuvenation in 1989 of the full-scale school band. Kathy Teem began with a group of thirteen students in a trailer that grew in a decade to over two hundred performing musicians drawn from the middle and high school grades. One of the first beneficiaries of her band was the town itself, whose annual Christmas parade, inaugurated by the Highlands Merchants Association in 1986, burst almost overnight from funereal silence into rousing rhythm and refrain.

Every graduating senior today receives a Town of Highlands scholarship. The Permanent Endowment Fund that pays these scholarships was established in 1975 by a five-year pledge of $5,000 from Jack Taylor of the Perry Insurance Agency. It was enabled by special legislation in the N.C. General Assembly, making Highlands one of the few towns, if not the only town, in the state and possibly the nation with legislative authority to administer such a fund. Scholarships were awarded to every graduate of the Highlands High School who planned to attend a college, university, or vocational training school.

In 1987 Jack Brockway, Charlie McDowell, Jan Chmar, and Ran Shaffner joined Jack Taylor in establishing a permanent endowment for this fund to lighten the scholarship committee's burden of having to depend on annual donations. By the year 2000 this endowment had achieved its goal of accumulating half a million dollars, much of it raised by the annual Highlands Falls Country Club benefit golf tournament. Thirty-three graduating seniors and thirty-seven previous graduates still in college received a total of $33,150 from the proceeds.

Today Highlands School houses 402 students K through 12 and twenty-three teachers during nine months of the school year, a considerable advance over the handful of students who studied under John Arnold in Billy's cabin for four months in 1875. Were Kelsey still alive, he might be pleased to agree that Highlands had at last a "first-class school" with the all the facilities for improvement found in the best neighborhoods of the North or South.

12. Bright Professions of Faith

There is a fine valley at the head of the Tennessee River, a fine farm-ing country, thickly settled. The Baptists once held that country pretty generally. But they fell out among themselves, and jars, discord and strife crept in among them, and they excluded some, and some took letters and went to Clayton. And while they were at that, the devil and the Methodists came in and were about to take the country. Some of the brethren came to see me, to get me to go and help them out. So I went. I found the Baptists and the Methodists, each with an organiza-tion, worshiping in an old dilapidated meeting-house. I commenced preaching twice a day, and the spirit came upon the people in great power. Soon there were bright professions of faith in Christ, and a time of great rejoicing.

—Elder F. M. Jordan, 1884

Organized religion in Highlands has emerged mostly along the lines of Protestant Christianity, with Roman Catholicism appearing rather late on the scene. Insomuch as Protestantism, as the name implies, is not so much a church as a movement of churches, its expected development has reflected the healthy diversity of the town's populace.

Believing in the Word of God as spoken to each individual soul di-rectly—the Bible being the living Word—Unitarians, Methodists, Presbyte-rians, Episcopalians, Baptists, and other protestants have followed their hearts in establishing forms of the church different from their neighbors'. In time, what once amounted to a single meeting place for a small group of founders has diversified—indeed is still diversifying—into a wide variety of churches.

Religious life like schooling in Highlands began within the first year of the town's founding. As early as March 12, 1876, "good citizens" formed a Highlands Union Sunday School, located in the log Law House.[340] Three years later a group of Presbyterians were meeting in the new schoolhouse, but it would be another six years before any of the denominations in the new town would have a sanctuary strictly its own.

The Presbyterians

The First Presbyterian Church at the southwest corner of Main and 5th was the second church in Highlands, after the Methodist, to hold services in its own building.[341] Sam Kelsey donated the land, and Margaretta Ravenel and her sister, Clarissa Burt, funded construction at an initial cost of around

$3,000. The project was completed by Marion Wright and personally supervised by Prioleau Ravenel and his step-son Thomas Parker. Mr. Ravenel inspected each timber to assure it bore no imperfections. The bell, weighing 550 pounds, arrived in the fall of 1884. And on Sept. 13, 1885, the building was dedicated by Rev. James E. Fogartie from Charleston. In 1997, over a century later, this lovely one-story frame structure would be placed on the National Register of Historic Places.

Presbyterian Church, 1897–98. Photo from R. H. Scadin Collection, UNC-A.

Rev. Fogartie was actually the Church's second minister, for A. Melvin Cooper had arrived from Michigan in 1879 to hold services in the new schoolhouse on north 4th Street where he also taught classes. He served, however, for only two years. Unlike others including Fogartie, who came to Highlands to postpone dying and lived many years because of its invigorating climate, Rev. Cooper continued to decline in health and finally succumbed at the tragically young age of twenty-nine.

As his successor, Rev. Fogartie organized the Church in its new building. The man called at the invitation of Margaretta Ravenel to paint the new church in 1885 was Robert "Bob" W. Reese from Franklin, who loved the little village so much that he brought his family up to dwell for the rest of their lives.[342] His son Walter claimed to be the second Southern boy to land in this town settled mostly by Yankees. Bob Reese signed his handiwork in the Church's belfry beside the name of his son Walter, who during his own lifetime would construct many public buildings and Highlands homes, especially a number of mansions on Satulah.

When Rev. Fogartie left in 1886 to take pastorates in Walhalla, S.C., Chapel Hill, N.C., and Greenwood, S.C., and to teach at several Presbyterian colleges in the Southeast, the Ravenels recruited Rev. Joel T. and Jenny Wade to replace him. Rev. Wade lived in Frank Sheldon's house on Hickory Street (today's Shaffner residence) and served Highlands while also attending outposts in Franklin, Shortoff, and Horse Cove.

His book, *Our Life History*, recalls his stay in Highlands before he left in 1899 to minister to other churches in the Carolinas, Virginia, Tennessee, and Kentucky and eventually become the first president of Nacoochee Institute, today's Rabun Gap-Nacoochee School. With his departure from Highlands, the church, reduced to visiting ministers, soon grew inactive and by 1910 stood closed.

In 1929, at the urging of Elbert and Isabel Gilbert, Meta Hall, Anna Anderson, and Agnes and Martha Perry, the church was reorganized and placed in the capable hands of Rev. Raymond McCarty, brother of Sidney McCarty of Highlands. Under his leadership membership tripled from nineteen to sixty-three, but sadly McCarty, like Rev. Cooper, died at the untimely age of thirty-one.

Robert B. "Bob" DuPree. Photo courtesy of Highlands Community Theatre.

Bob DuPree and his wife Mary accepted the call to head a now-active congregation as well as teach at Highlands School. Their special contributions during two turns at leading the church, 1936–41 and 1948–51, were in organizing a music program, particularly a choir, and a basketball team known as the Christian Endeavor All-Stars. They alternated homes between Highlands and Tamassee, S.C., where Bob served as principal, chaplain, and teacher.

In 1948 for an initial outlay of $850 he and Steve Potts set up the original Highlander Restaurant in the building that would later house the Mountaineer Restaurant. During the sixties he and Mary spent their last years before retirement teaching in Highlands. It was Bob's religious, educational, and civic contributions to the Highlands community that inspired the town to create the Robert DuPree award, given initially to him in 1980 and subsequently to outstanding citizens whose public service matched or approached his own.

After Rev. DuPree's first term as pastor, his post was filled by Harold Bridgman of Illinois and South Carolina, who had served twenty years as missionary to China and returned to China after his departure from Highlands. It was at the beginning of Dan McCall's tenure that the Church built a new entrance and walkway to the sanctuary as well as a manse on 5th Street, followed closely by a new Christian educational building in 1965. At the beginning of Mike Wingard's pastorate in 1982 a brick annex was added to house, among other purposes, the Sunday School and Day Care center.

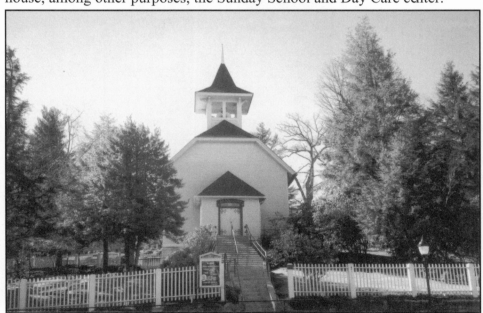

Highlands First Presbyterian Church. Photo by the author, 2001.

It was during this period that the Presbyterian Church experienced a major reorganization: a national reunion and a local split. Nationally the Presbyterian Church, which had divided at the beginning of the Civil War, reunited in 1983. Locally the Highlands Church became a member of the Presbyterian Church of the U.S.A., subject to its General Assembly. A number of the Assembly's decisions, however, didn't sit well with some Highlanders, who opted to separate and form their own churches rather than subscribe to policies they felt were too liberal.

The result, as Ron Botsford took over the First Presbyterian Church (USA), was the creation of a new Presbyterian Church of America (PCA) and a more evangelical Community Bible Church (EPC). The PCA of Highlands formed unofficially in 1981 when Andy and Anne McDonough couldn't sanction the National church's break with the Reformed Church's position that the Bible was the strict word of God and that women could not be ordained.

The next year a group of fellow sympathizers met in Cashiers, and soon eighteen to twenty summer residents were meeting at first in the town hall in Highlands and then in the Conference Center. In 1984 the group moved to Cashiers, where they built the Whiteside Presbyterian Church atop the hill at the town's entrance.

In the meantime, the EPC of Highlands remained with the main church until Easter, 1984. Then, calling themselves the Community Bible Church, twenty-one communicants met with Robert Bryan from Franklin at the home of Chet and Marge Schmidt. Soon John Cleaveland through his real estate office offered an unsold store on Carolina Way, but before they could even meet, as Wynn Cleaveland recalls, the store sold on the Saturday prior to their first service, so that members had to scramble the next day to set up chairs in the adjoining Sears building.

For a while they were facetiously called the Church of the Folding Chairs or the Church of St. Sears as they struggled to find a permanent home. During one summer they held their services in the Highlands School Cafeteria. In 1987 they at last constructed a sanctuary on the former site of Dock McKinney's home across from the 4½ Street intersection with Chestnut. Jerry Robinson from Clover, S.C., took the reins in 1989 as their second regular minister.

Ten years later they were building a cathedral-style sanctuary on a thirteen-acre tract across from the old Wright homestead on the Cashiers Road to accommodate their growing membership. They sold their Chestnut Street building as home to the newly created Performing Arts Center and held their first service in their new home on Easter, 2000, exactly sixteen years after the break with the mother church.

Despite the fact that schisms are not uncommon in protestant churches—indeed, the name *protestant* implies them—in the case of the Highlands Presbyterian Church the recent splits within it are less surprising than the fact that for almost a hundred years its close-knit congregation had remained essentially united in religious as well as sociological views. The result of the split is that both churches in Highlands appear content to remain separate today, each led by a very popular minister. Hunter Coleman has shepherded the First Presbyterian since 1997; and Steve Kerhoulas of Charlotte, N.C., the Community Bible Church since 1994.

Community Bible Church. Photo by the author, 2001.

The Methodists

The Methodists were the first denomination to construct their own sanctuary in Highlands.[343] Less than forty years after the initial North/South schism in the national Methodist Church over the issue of slavery—indeed, less than twenty years after the close of the great Civil War that intensified this division—the Northern and Southern branches of the Methodist Church each had their own devoted followers, but particularly among the Yankees who founded Highlands.

In 1882 under the pastorate of Rev. John H. Moore, the Highlands Methodist Episcopal Church (the church of the Northern Methodists) took out a mortgage of $500 and posted a $250 bond from the Board of Church Extension in Pennsylvania to be paid back in five years. Trustees Baxter White,

William Partridge, Daniel Rochester, and Jerry L. Potts proposed to build on land donated by Kelsey and Sherman north of Main and east of 2nd, where the Baptist Church stands today.

They wanted "a place of Divine Worship" to promote public morality and religion.[344] Within a year they had hired Capt. Charles Boynton, the architect who oversaw construction of the new building until summer's end, when Rev. Moore closed his pastorate in Highlands.

With Rev. Moore's departure, the Methodist Episcopal Church South (representing the Southern Methodists) offered to buy the property from the Northern Methodists for $540 and pay Capt. Boynton his $250 to finish the building.[345] Apparently their offer never materialized, for although Capt. Boynton did complete the building in August, 1884, it was not for the Southern Methodists. They would have to wait four years before they could afford to construct a building all their own.

Indeed, the Northern Methodists too had to wait a year for the arrival of their bell to call them to worship, so the first Highlands church building was not dedicated until July 5, 1885. Rev. E. O. Thayer, President and Professor of Mental and Moral Philosophy at Clark University in Atlanta, presided at the ceremony.

Prior to the dedication, Rev. J. D. Roberson preached to the Northern Methodists at the schoolhouse. The new sanctuary was shared by both Methodist groups and the Baptists. By 1886 Rev. J. H. Brendle preached to his Southern Methodists on the first Sunday of each month, Rev. S. H. Harrington to his Baptists on the second, and Rev. J. H. Gillespie to his Northern Methodists on the third. Rev. Fogartie preached every Sunday to the Presbyterians in their own newly completed building.[346]

In 1888 a group of Southern Methodists, under the trusteeship of Stanhope Hill, J. M. Brown, and John Norton, invited Kelsey to give them two lots on Spruce Street (the later homesite of Rev. Billy and his son Shine Potts). Here they finally erected their house of divine worship, a venture that almost failed, for no sooner had they completed the new sanctuary in 1890 than during one blustery March night the wind blew the structure plumb off its foundation, shifting it three feet to the east and damaging it to the amount of $50. It took the trustees two years to pay off repairs through benefits and a fair. The Southern Methodist Church would survive at this location for the next twenty years.[347]

In 1891, perhaps to rekindle interest in their branch of the church, the Northern Methodists organized a Christian Endeavor, led by Highlands school teacher Miss Olive White, daughter of postmaster Baxter White.[348] The original charter members included Allison McKinney; Charlie Wright; Mollie and Gertie Edwards; Charley, George, and Ike Henry; Olive's sister

Jessie White; Laura Bell Clark; Clift Hill; Bernie Durgin; and Rob Munger. Each member made the following solemn pledge:

Trusting in the Lord Jesus Christ for strength, I promise Him that I will strive to do whatever He would like to have me do; that I will make it the rule of my life to pray and to read the Bible every day, and to support my own church in every way, especially by attending all her regular Sunday and mid-week services, unless prevented by some reason which I can conscientiously give to my Saviour; and that just so far as I know how, throughout my whole life, I will endeavor to lead a Christian life.

Christian Endeavor was not so much denominational as universal. It sought particularly in the young to promote mutual respect and good will among different religious bodies. Indeed, it flourished so successfully that when Olive White married Frank Sheldon in 1896 and gave up the leader's role, her father took over and led it until his departure from Highlands in 1910.

At that time, deprived of his influence, interest in the group waned, and it disbanded. But in 1929 Raymond McCarty, the new minister of the Presbyterian Church, brought together old members of the original Christian Endeavor and many newly interested youths. The reorganized Christian Endeavor proved especially popular, meeting each Sunday at the Presbyterian school room, discussing interesting topics of Christian living, holding wiener roasts, leading hikes, arranging picnics, and forming teams for community sports.

Not until 1904 did the Northern and Southern Methodists fully reconcile their differences within the Highlands community and decide to unite, three decades before a similar union on the national level. In this year the Northern Methodists paid off their $500 mortgage and $250 bond and within a month had sold their building on Oak Ridge to the Baptists for $460.[349]

Four years later the Southern Methodists, represented by trustees Elias Norton, Nathan McKinney, Wiley Smith, Thomas Hawkins, and J. N. Bumgarner, tore down their old building on Spruce Street, and the two groups united to build a new sanctuary on the south side of Main. They paid $200 to Thomas and Harriet Parker for land next to the Masonic Hall and nearer the center of town.

Presumably Aunt Mat Gottwals paid the $200, and her husband John Z. Gottwals supervised construction of the new building in 1908. However, as in the past, the wind again played havoc with the Methodists. On two separate occasions violent gusts blew down the rafters of the new structure.

Still, the Methodists were not to be deterred: the completed sanctuary was dedicated on August 20, 1909. As the Southern and Northern Methodists united in their joint venture, the trustees Wiley Smith, Thomas Hawkins, and Wendell McKinney of the Methodist Church South gave the land of their old church on Spruce Street to the new Baptist minister, Rev. Billy Potts.

The new Highlands Methodist Church arose between the Masonic Hall and a corn field. It was heated by a large potbellied stove that stood in the center of the sanctuary. There was no basement, no chapel, no Sunday School rooms, and until the advent of electricity in Highlands during the late twenties, oil lamps furnished the only lighting.

New Methodist Church, built 1909   Highlands United Methodist Church, 1999
Photo courtesy of Tammy Lowe.   Photo courtesy of Methodist Church.

For a number of years the Methodist Church hosted Sunday afternoon religious services for the African–Americans serving families in the town. Beginning in 1948, with the arrival of pastors Bob Early and his successor Tom Houts, Jr., the African–Americans chose to repay the church that had welcomed them. For the next thirteen years at the end of each summer they performed a musical and divided the proceeds between the Highlands Community Hospital and the Methodist building fund.

By 1960, under the direction of Miss Carrie Smith and Mrs. Emma Mathis and accompanied by Mr. Pem Steele on the piano, they raised an impressive $625 for the Methodists and $524 for the hospital. Their program featured Southern spirituals, Spanish hymns, anthems, and gospel songs.[350]

It was partly through their help that the church renovated its sanctuary and expanded. In the early fifties Professor Harbison's son, Tom, rock veneered the outside walls. Rooms for Sunday School and child care were added along with a fellowship hall. In 1955 a 40-foot lighted steeple was erected, the top spire hoisted into place by the end of August. With the addition of a Smith-Tillett Memorial Chapel, the new building was dedicated on July 20, 1958.

The man who in 1950 had drafted the plans for the new church was Dr. Upton C. Ewing, a resident of Miami who from the forties to the sixties summered in Highlands.[351] The Church was quite fortunate to benefit, free of charge, from the services of this extraordinarily talented man. He may have been Highlands' one and only *uomo universale*, for he certainly commanded competence in almost all the arts and sciences. He was architect, sculptor, theologian, philosopher, religious author, musician, and humanitarian. He would draw the plans for the original hospital building (now the Crosby Center) in 1947; and in 1953–54, for the present town hall—all without charge.

Dr. Ewing was essentially a self-educated man. He left school in the fifth grade but supported himself as carpenter's helper, electrician, plumber, tile setter, cement pourer, and builder. In the end he became a Doctor of Metaphysics, Doctor of Divinity, and Doctor of Philosophy. Among his publications were *Thresholds of Existence*, a philosophical and metaphysical treatise on the theory of evolution, as well as books on the subject of Christian origins, such as *The Essene Christ, The Prophet of the Dead Sea Scrolls*, and *The Martyred Jew*.

The essence of his philosophy sprang from his belief that all life originated in one consciousness, that all men were sons of God and members of a great universal brotherhood, so all of life was sacred and should be held in the highest regard. A corollary asserted that an individual could become anything he wished so long as he cared enough to make the effort, which Ewing proved in his own life.

Ewing was a personal friend of Dr. Albert Schweitzer, whom he visited in 1955 in France and whose bust he sculpted in bronze, casts of which stand at Boston University and in Boston Symphony Hall. Schweitzer paid him the ultimate compliment when he said that Upton was the reincarnation of Leonardo da Vinci.

A renovation of the Methodist Church, more recent than that of the fifties, entailed its expansion in 1990–91 into an activities building. Moreover, the antique organ, which Aunt Tudie once pedaled with two feet and which tended in its old age to cough and wheeze, was replaced by the current mahogany Wicks eight-rank pipe organ with distinctly concert quality.

From Rev. John H. Moore in 1882 to Rev. Carl Linquist today the Highlands United Methodist Church has welcomed over sixty ministers, including those of the early Southern and Northern congregations. The current minister, Carl Linquist, a well-versed, insightful graduate of Duke Divinity School, has served the longest term—eight years to date—followed by the

Reverends Ben Bullard in the 1980s, Robert Early from the late forties to the early fifties, and Tom Steagald from the late eighties to the early nineties.

Presbyterian and Episcopal churches, 1910 and 1999. Above photo probably by R. Henry Scadin, courtesy of Gene Potts via Doris Potts. Photo below by the author.

The Episcopalians

The third church to build a home in Highlands was the Episcopal Church. As early as 1879 Episcopal services had been held in town by a circuit rider, John Archibald Deal.[352] Rev. Deal, a Confederate veteran who enlisted at sixteen as a drummer boy and was twice captured and exchanged, attended Trinity College in Connecticut after the war. He was called to serve at Cartoogechaye in North Carolina in 1877, where in four years he established St. John's, the first Episcopal Church in Macon County. From this base he walked or rode horseback to his missions in Murphy, Franklin, Highlands, and Cashiers Valley.

Rev. Archibald Deal with wife Cornelia Ann and oldest son. Photo from Tom Crumpler collection.

Considering the mileage and the rough dirt roads he had to maneuver through the mountains and the fact that he frequently arose at four in the morning to set out as soon as the bricks were warmed and wrapped in tow to keep his feet from freezing, his annual salary of $100 was only token at best. Traveling by buggy in the dead of winter, he recalled in his autobiographical *American Mountaineer*, "Sometimes the forest winds were bitter and cruel and it seemed as if they would whip my vehicle from the narrow, stony road past crag and frozen waterfall. Sometimes these roads were so uncertain and my progress so slow darkness had almost mantled the forest before I reached my destination."[353]

In Cashiers Valley he befriended General Wade Hampton summering at his father's home in ante-bellum splendor. In 1884 Deal laid the corner stone of the Church of the Good Shepherd financed there by the Hamptons. In Franklin he served for a time as chairman of the Macon County Board of Education. In Highlands he held periodic services in the Northern Methodist Church building while an Episcopal mission was being organized and plans made for their own structure.

Rev. Deal loved Highlands for its invigorating air, its clouds filled with the refreshing moisture of fog, and its many streams in every direction. He loved the surrounding mountains, their gigantic size as well as their delightful, suggestive names, like Devil's Courthouse, Whiteside, and Satulah, which he claimed meant "I wish" in Cherokee. He loved the squaw vine with its green leaves and red berries that sprang from Whiteside's granite heart with no foothold of earth, as well as the cool, rich beds of galax leaves suggestive of Yuletide evergreens.

His followers were particularly impressed by the beauty and dignity with which he preached the simple, practical gospel. In the opinion of Frank Siler, one of his protégés, "he was one of the truly great men who ministered in Western North Carolina at a time that meant much for her young life."[354]

For their new church in Highlands, trustees Dr. Henry O'Farrell, David Norton, Jeremiah Pierson, and T. T. Hall purchased land at the intersection of Main and 5th, catercornered from the Presbyterian Church, from James Rideout.[355] Presumably T. T. Hall donated the $100 for the purchase. By August, 1896, at a cost of just over $2,000, a building was begun by Will McGuire of Franklin. It was completed by Joe McGuire and named Church of the Transfiguration.

Surrounded by native rhododendron and laurel, its high-pitched roof and circular belfry crowned durable strength with beauty, for its sturdy mountain timbers withstood winds that buffeted other churches off their foundations. Heavy thirty-foot beams supported the high roof, and native chestnut and tulip poplar gave the inside finish and altar furnishings the benefit of native wood.

Miss Alicia Trapier, daughter of Bishop William Trapier of Charleston, S.C., had a bell inscribed for the belfry: "Ring it out among the hills, the Lord is King." Jerry Pierson donated the granite steps into the building, and much of the black walnut church furniture was made in the African–American shop of Rev. James T. Kennedy of Franklin.

T. T. Hall acquired two kerosene chandeliers of clustered brass lamps from Christ Church in Greenville, S.C. Though particularly beautiful, they required dexterity to light. Early church workers had to climb stepladders to replenish the kerosene, trim the wicks, polish the brass, and clean the chimneys of all twenty-six lamps. Eventually, attaching them to chains permitted their being lowered to the floor, dismissing the need for ladders. In 1936 Tudor Hall wired them, and the lamps gave way to bulbs.

It was in this little church that Miss Gertrude Cobb (later Mrs. Gus Holt) began her forty-year career as organist. She played a square piano as Rev. Deal led the singing from the Episcopal hymnbook. Soon the piano graduated into a pump organ, which Jerry Pierson's daughter Lake played throughout Rev. Deal's ministry. In contrast to the room in the schoolhouse, the new church had an altar instead of a blackboard, and real pews in lieu of desks.

Episcopal Church, 1897–98. Photo from R. H. Scadin Collection, UNC-A.

Surpassing Rev. Deal and John H. Griffith, who each served the Highlands Episcopal Church for eleven years, the longest serving priests were Rufus Morgan and Charlie Bryan. Born in 1885 in the shadows of the Nantahala Mountains and reared on Shakespeare, Dickens, Sir Walter Scott, and the Bible, Rufus Morgan worked his way from a simple log cabin home and a single-room schoolhouse up to the University of North Carolina at Chapel Hill, Theological Seminary, and Columbia University in New York City.[356] Highlands was only one of the many churches that he was serving when he replaced Frank Bloxham in 1940.

Almost instantaneously Dr. Morgan's charismatic personality attracted a good following, and the church grew exponentially. In 1947 it was modernized to include an electric organ installed at the back of the church and an oil furnace to replace the potbellied stove in the side aisle, despite Dr. Morgan's objection that the winter's weren't cold enough to warrant buying a furnace. An extremely thrifty man, he regarded as Christian fortitude the fact that his parishioners attended services carrying lap robes, muffs, and mittens.

A. Rufus Morgan, 1885–198?

In 1954 an annex to the church enlarged its seating capacity and provided a fellowship hall with a modern kitchen. In May, 1955, just before his first retirement at age seventy-two, Dr. Morgan founded the Highlands Interchurch Group to promote understanding and cooperation among the various denominations in the town. In a very real sense this sprang from his belief in Christian outreach, which expressed itself outside of Highlands in his organization of congregations for the blacks in North and South Carolina and the Indians in Cherokee.

In addition to his devotion to his circuit—twelve churches in Murphy, Hayesville, Franklin, Highlands, Cashiers, Cullowhee, Sylva, Cherokee, and Andrews—Dr. Morgan had extracurricular interests in botany, particularly ferns of the Southern Appalachians, as well as hiking. He established Boy Scout troops wherever he went, worked with them on the Appalachian Trail, and chaired the Red Cross. He grew famous for his stamina well into his nineties. In his 93rd year he climbed Mount LeConte for the 173rd time, no easy task at any age but especially as he was nearly blind and deaf. It was this climb that led Highlands poet, Jonathan Williams, to croon,

> *Rufus,*
>
> *you reckon*
> *there's anything*
> *in Heaven*
>
> *worth climbing*
> *173 times?*

When asked in his last years what he thought of the church and the world, he expressed the hope that the world was becoming more Christian but admitted that there were too many things that disproved it, such as "the great misuse of drugs, alcohol, and tobacco. We don't love ourselves enough to avoid those things that can destroy us."

Nevertheless, the great advance that Dr. Morgan saw in the church was in the area of ecumenical relations, especially the tolerance and cooperation, which he himself helped foster among the Catholic and Anglican churches and Protestant denominations.

In 1955 Dr. Morgan was succeeded by Rev. Dr. Herbert Koepp-Baker, a clinical psychologist whose specialty was speech and hearing disabilities. He helped reorganize the closed Highlands Community Hospital and with Jack Brockway founded the Ginger Brockway Hearing Clinic. Under his leadership the church became a self-sustaining parish within the Episcopal Diocese. Like Rufus Morgan, he was a charismatic teacher with spiritual depth and a worldly awareness that, joined with his disarming sense of humor, endeared him to parishioners and townspeople alike.

When Dr. Koepp, as he was affectionately called, took a professorship in 1960 at the University of Illinois, Gale D. "Pop" Webbe, a former chaplain of Christ School, took charge of a very active church. Under Fr. Webbe's guidance, services on Sundays increased to three, and in 1967 a rondette was installed behind the church for use as a Sunday School and meeting room.[357] The first of an annual event, the "Tour of Homes," was scheduled to give the public a view of several of the more interesting mansions in

Highlands, an event that the Hudson Library later adopted to supplement its fund-raising drive.

It was during Pop Webbe's watch that the Episcopal Church started a land purchase fund as the growth of the congregation made expansion necessary, and the search for land suitable for church purposes was begun. Toward the end of his tenure, Norma "Boots" Pierson and other women of the church established Mountain Findings in 1969 to recycle household goods and thereby help fund many charitable and service organizations.

Before coming to Highlands, Fr. Webbe authored two books for boys, under his pseudonym Stephen Cole: *The Pitcher and I* and *The Growing Season*. He wrote articles for *The Saturday Evening Post*, *Good Housekeeping*, *Esquire*, and *Redbook* and a book of twelve lectures called *The Hell of It*, a sort of devil's guide to tempting Americans, much like C. S. Lewis' *Screwtape Letters*.

His books for adults included *Sawdust and Incense: Worlds That Shape a Priest* and *Night and Nothing*, a manual of prayer which he wrote while in Highlands and which was hailed by Scott Peck and Gail Godwin, among others, as "a spiritual classic" on the meaning of Christian faith, again comparable to works by both C. S. Lewis and Thomas Merton. Father Webbe left Highlands in 1971 to become headmaster of Christ School in Asheville.

Episcopal Church of the Incarnation. Photo by the author, 1999.

During the fifteen years that Charlie Bryan steered the Church's course it experienced tremendous growth. Between 1979 and 1994 he reactivated the Highlands Interchurch Group, helped bring Hospice to town, sponsored the

Highlands Chamber Music performances, oversaw adding a Great Hall and rooms for Sunday School and a church library, and strove to integrate the summer residents with the year-round members of the congregation in such a way that when they arrived, they would feel they belonged.

His contribution to the stained glass windows of the church was that they now express not only symbols of the Christian faith but also themes of local history and the environment, such as Lake Glenville, the lost and found Oconee Bell (*Shortia*), and the native lady slipper and rainbow trout. Christ is depicted as holding the earth in his hand.

It was during Fr. Bryan's term that Margaret Rhodes (now Shaffner), raised funds to purchase the old Hudson Library building, which until the end of the 1990s was occupied by the charitable second-hand clothing store Fibber Magee's Closet and the Highlands Emergency Council.[358] Charlie's wife Jody lectured, wrote, and worked diligently for our fragile earth, which she considered our "island home."

Since 1995 R. Michael "Mike" Jones has served as rector of the Episcopal Church. His crusade has been to expand the church to accommodate its growing membership, the difficult choice being whether to enlarge the historic building on the corner of 5th and Main or to construct an additional church or mission.

Since 1998 overflows from the Episcopal churches in Highlands and Cashiers have been accommodated during the summers by the Summer Chapel in Whiteside Cove. Built in 1918 and operated until 1931 as Whiteside Cove School, which Tom Pickelsimer and Frances Baumgarner Lombard attended, it continued as a church and Sunday School as well as community center long before being adopted by the churches of Highlands and Cashiers as a summer chapel. Officiated by Jim Theus, a man of genuine wisdom and brotherly love from Alexandria, La., and Whiteside Mountain, its simple services are inspired with rousing bluegrass gospel hymns, which during recent summers have filled the church to overflowing with lively and joyful worshipers.

The Baptists

On July 13, 1884, Rev. S. H. Harrington, W. W. Wells, John P. Morgan, and F. M. Jordan organized a Baptist Church of Highlands, comprising twelve members without a church building of their own.[359] In his memoirs Elder Jordan remarked that the day and place were beautiful but the occasion had its hindrances and drawbacks.

"It would seem," he lamented, "that all the fleas from the four quarters of the globe had assembled here." Indeed, the infestation was so bad that the next morning when Dr. Miller baptized a baby, Jordan called it "a shame to palm off such an imposition upon a poor, little, innocent, helpless babe." He claimed the group did their level best for the next ten days to leave "all in the hand of God." Regarding the fleas, "God alone knows what became of them," Jordan marveled. "I can't see why fleas should want to get so many thousand feet above sea level."

As it turned out for the Baptists, fleas would be the least of their crosses to bear before owning their own place of worship. As noted earlier, they shared with the Methodists, but more frequently they met in private homes while holding baptismal services in ponds and lakes across the Highlands plateau, such as Mill Creek Pond, Lindenwood (now Ravenel) Lake, Harbison (now Harris) Lake, and in the Cullasaja River at Van Hook Glade.

From the start Rev. Harrington tried to collect funds to build a Baptist meeting house on land that in 1884 Kelsey proposed to donate. But six years passed before a hundred dollars could be raised to buy from Kelsey—who had left for Linville—the northeast corner of 2nd and Spring across from the original Methodist Church. Another forty-five dollars served to join it with the southeast corner of 2nd and Main in 1891. Yet despite the purchase of a complete land block, no church was ever built.

By 1904 Baptist trustees Sumner Clark, J. W. Houston, John Arnold, Thoren Walden, and Billy Potts had given up the idea of building a sanctuary all their own. On hearing that the Methodists wanted to build a new sanctuary, they bought the Methodist building and land for $460.[360] The property where they had planned to build their own church passed to Walter and Anna Reese for their home at the site of today's Highlands Suite Hotel.

For thirty-six years the Baptists worshiped in the old Methodist sanctuary. Marshall Reese remembers that it had real steep steps that climbed from Main Street straight up to the church: "steepest you ever saw." A pipe projected out the top of the church, attached to a huge stove. The sanctuary contained homemade pews.

He also remembers when Billy Potts was minister in the late twenties and early thirties, how he used to preach and often cry in the pulpit. Marshall, only nine or ten at the time, asked his mother why Rev. Potts cried, and his mother said it was probably when he got to thinking of all the bad things he used to do.

But Rev. Potts could laugh as heartily as he could cry. He was a great punster and told many anecdotes that spread his fame over the hundreds of miles he traveled as a circuit rider throughout Macon and Jackson counties as well as north Georgia.

Indeed, he could laugh one moment and cry the next in the spirit of a tender-hearted man full of compassion. Eva Potts Massey tells of how during one particularly drawn-out prayer at church, his words became so garbled that she feared he was having a stroke. She left her pew and crept up to see his problem, only to find that his dentures had come loose and, face as red as fire, he was struggling to continue his prayer against incredibly embarrassing odds. On looking up and seeing Eva, he closed his prayer abruptly.

Highlands Baptist Church, purchased in 1904. Photo courtesy of Helen Hopper.

In 1940–41 the Baptists rebuilt the sanctuary of their dilapidated half-century-old building farther back on the lot, adding $10,000 of stone veneer that graces it today. Guy Paul, Sr., took charge of the work and added a hot-air furnace and a dozen or so Sunday School rooms to accommodate a membership of 220, the largest church in Highlands at the time. Not until 1996, when a fire caused major smoke and water damage to the Sunday School classes and sanctuary, did the Baptists again renovate, at which time they also expanded.

From Rev. Harrington in the mid 1880s to Rev. Daniel Robinson today, the First Baptist Church has had twenty-nine pastors, among whom the longest serving was Rev. Lewis Gibson. From 1975–85 Rev. Gibson gave Highlands a decade of unpretentious, genuine wisdom and Christian devotion. A man of innate goodness, his sermons sparkled with human insight, optimism, and wonder, and his ability to apply the lessons of the Bible to daily life was especially appreciated by those who sought his advice.

First Baptist Church. Photo by the author, 2001.

If great things are done when men and mountains meet, then Rev. Gibson was the catalyst in the realization of dreams. His worldview—as expressed in his memoirs, *Meeting God in the Mountains*—reflected his belief that life has its mountains of opposition, which must never be held up as excuses for inaction but met as opportunities for victory.[361]

Yet his hope was realistic, for while acknowledging the realities of failure, corruption, and fear as products of negativism, he championed never quitting, even to the glorious end of life when one feels himself to be the last leaf on the tree. He was universally respected as much by those outside his church as within.

Like the Presbyterian Church, the First Baptist Church suffered a split around 1988, when forty of its members began meeting in the Community Building on Poplar Street. Tom Harris accepted the call as their minister in 1993, and they moved into the office space above the Sears Catalogue store in Carolina Square. By the time they were meeting at the First Presbyterian Church Community Room, they were known as the Westside Baptist Church, led since 1998 by interim minister John Cannon.

The Unitarian Church

In 1819 Dr. William Ellery Channing, a Congregational minister in Boston, became convinced that Calvinism was not for him and preached a sermon entitled "My Sympathy," which resulted in the establishment of Unitarianism. As the intellectual "Apostle of Unitarianism," he exercised wide influence through his sermons and writings on social and philanthropic issues of his time.

Since a number of early settlers of Highlands hailed from Massachusetts and Pennsylvania where the Unitarian Church was strong, they brought their liberal brand of practical Christianity with them. As early as 1880 it was Dr. Edward Everett Hale's Unitarian Lend-a-Hand Society in Boston, Massachusetts, that donated the beginnings of the Hudson Library as a memorial to Ella Emmons Hudson, one of their members who died only months after her arrival in Highlands to regain her health.

A graduate of Harvard, Dr. Hale was highly respected for his philanthropic projects to improve the human condition. He was author of the now-famous short story, "The Man Without a Country" and great-nephew of the famous revolutionary Nathan Hale, who had courageously claimed to have but one life to lose for his country. Dr. Hale's guiding principle was typically Unitarian in its trust in the power of one when multiplied by ten in the world of Christian service:

I am only one,
But still I am one.
I cannot do everything,
But still I can do something;
And because I cannot do everything
I will not refuse to do the something that I can do.

Ella Hudson's parents, who retired to Highlands to live with her sister Louise Emmons Wells at Shortoff, were also Unitarians. Rev. Henry Emmons was a Harvard graduate and once-popular Unitarian minister of the

Dr. Channing type who bore himself as a gentleman of the old school, and his wife Elizabeth was equally compassionate and always mindful of the needs of others.

Their death in 1899 was a double bereavement for the people of Shortoff and Highlands. Had it been just one or the other of this pair who had died on that overcast day in late November, the news would have been sad indeed, but not as remarkable as it turned out. Mrs. Emmons, age seventy-nine, died at seven in the morning; her devoted husband, age ninety-one, at four in the afternoon of the same day. Baxter White, as Highlands correspondent for the newspaper, remarked that "their departure within such a few hours of each other, was a singular coincidence. Beautiful in their lives, in death they were not divided."[362]

Bess Hines Harkins, also known as the earth child of Highlands, once depicted how much the complete life of such a mutually devoted and well-loved couple meant in a spiritual sense to those who remained behind:

Call Him God, or call Him what you will:
I only know there is a Power to fill
the receptive soul with all that's Great and Good:
That the Life Abundant is Truth understood. [363]

They were buried beside their daughter Ella in the family plot at the entrance to Highlands' Mount Hope Cemetery.

The Unitarian faith was by no means limited to communicants from the North. Barak Norton, the first settler in Whiteside Cove, was a Virginian migrating from South Carolina and a strong adherent to the Universalist belief until the day he died at the advanced age of 92. His wife Mary Nicholson Norton of Mountain Rest, S.C., who lived to 95, died also strong in the Unitarian faith.

By 1886 the Unitarian Society in Highlands was meeting every Sunday with Rev. Chaney of Atlanta.[364] Recognized as one of five societies in the South—the other four at Charleston, New Orleans, Atlanta, and Fort Worth, Texas—the Highlands gathering was receiving annual contributions of $100 from the American Unitarian Association, which was particularly impressed with the Highlands Academy for the children of the mountaineers, established by Prof. Harbison, himself a Unitarian.[365]

For a time the Highlands group met in the old Phelps House Annex at the corner of 3rd and Maple; and by 1896, in the Masonic Hall. Regarding themselves as free Christians, they shared with all Unitarian churches the same basic creed: "In the love of truth, and in the spirit of Jesus Christ, we unite for the worship of God and the service of man."

In 1975, fourteen years after the Unitarian and Universalist churches united on the national level, the Highlands Unitarians bought land on the Dillard Road, formerly Camp Parry-dise and Camp Highlander, and established a Unitarian camp and conference center, known as The Mountain. The official name it goes by today is the Mountain Retreat and Learning Center, where Elder Hostels are taught to registrants from all across the Country.

Other Denominations

From baptism to marriage to death, religion has played a significant role in the varied life of Highlands. Despite the predominance of Protestants, Roman Catholics held religious services in the town beginning in the 1930s. At one time four year-round residents—Bessie Crunkleton, Regina Schiffli, Miss Dyth Quinn, and Forest Ranger Don Peterson—were meeting at Miss Bessie's home, the school auditorium, and the Highlands Playhouse.

Presumably because of the strong Scotch-Irish contingency in the community, with its acquired suspicion of Catholics, they met clandestinely. Indeed, sometime before 1950, when the Bishop of Raleigh, the Most Rev. Vincent M. Waters, decided to purchase land for a church in Highlands, the proposed property was inspected after sundown, under cover of darkness. The Church decided to buy the old Satulah house on 5th Street and replaced the dilapidated structure with Our Lady of the Mountains Catholic Church.

Our Lady of the Mountains Catholic Church, built 1950. Photo by the author, 2001.

With only thirty-five year-round families and forty to fifty summer seasonal families, it has always been a mission church, variously served by

Waynesville, Brevard, Sapphire Valley, and Franklin. Rev. Charles J. O'Connor served the mission as its first pastor from 1950–54. In the mid sixties, during Charles Mulholland's tenure, the church expanded its sanctuary and hall, and in 1972 the Lechich sisters, Mary and Angela, funded the addition of a small apartment.

One of the longest serving and best loved priests was Father Mike Langell of St. Francis in Franklin, whose tenure covered eleven years from 1972–83. Henry Becker, a native Minnesotan, who had served the Highlands mission during the early sixties, returned in 1985 to become its first full-time priest in 1985, but this lasted only a year before he had to return to Franklin.

When Father John Hoover arrived in 1986 to divide his time between Highlands and St. Jude in Sapphire Valley, he established Elijah's Cave retreat ministry, where fifty to sixty "hermits" gravitated annually to experience the silence and solitude of listening to hear the still small voice just as the holy prophet had done when he fled to Mount Sinai in despair.

During his four years in Highlands, Father John saw the mission grow from a renovated building in 1987 to an added rectory the following year and two-story wing in 1989, doubling the sanctuary and providing a meeting hall. His spiritual focus rested on pre-dawn vigils, morning and evening body prayer, lively dialogues, and Mass only on Wednesdays, Fridays, and weekends or, on occasion, at Sunset Rocks. Meditation and spiritual direction were important ingredients of his monastic regimen. During his last year in Highlands, a bell and tower were erected above the church doors.

Rev. Frank Connolly of St. Francis in Franklin was aided for a short while in 1992 by Joe Ayathupadam of India and followed from 1994–98 by Richard McCue, whose aid was Ray Berg, before the current priest, Father Bill Evans, took over in 1998. During his tenure the parish membership has grown to more than 170 families during the summer months, who, unlike those four furtive exiles half a century earlier, wouldn't dream of having to meet in secret to celebrate their faith.

The Little Church in the Wildwood, though located at the base of the mountain in Horse Cove, has also served the people of Highlands of all religious denominations since 1946, when Mr. and Mrs. Leslie Misener began acting on Sunday nights as Master of Ceremonies and organist. The church was built by residents who had been gathering in one another's homes for the singing of hymns. It was constructed in part from the materials salvaged from the former CCC camp nearby. Weekly services are still held from June to September and attended by many Highlanders who drive down for the inspiration of an evening of hymns, prayer, and a stirring message.

The Little Church in the Wildwood. Photo by the author, 2001.

The Christian Science Reading Room, built 1955

The Christian Scientists rely on a book written in 1875—the year that Highlands was founded—by Mary Baker Eddy, who founded the Church of Christ in Lynn, Massachusetts, postmaster Baxter White's hometown. Her book, *Science and Health with Key to the Scriptures*, sought to teach how to practice Christian healing through an understanding of the Bible's spiritual meaning. Her book describes her own prayerful cure from forty-five years of illness and debilitation. While appreciating the compassionate humanity of doctors and nurses, Christian Science teaches how to rely progressively on prayer alone for the healing of sins and cure of physical sickness. There being no ordained clergy, lay readers, elected by the congregation for three-year terms, conduct weekly Lesson-Sermons from the Bible and *Science and Health*.

The first Christian Scientists in Highlands began meeting in 1940 in the home of Joseph and Annie Root. By 1944 they were holding services in the S. T. Marett building on Main Street, then in a room over the Main Street post office, and by the early fifties in the Masonic Hall. In 1955 they constructed their own one-room building at the corner of Spring and 3rd, which due to the growth of their congregation they had to enlarge in 1973. Regular services were held Sunday mornings and testimonies of healings heard every Wednesday.

Assembly of God, built 1974. Photo by the author, 2001.

The Assembly of God, more commonly known as the Pentecostal Church, was born in the United States on the first day of the twentieth century during a revival at Bethel Bible College in Topeka, Kansas. Topeka, incidentally, is where Highlands' founder C. C. Hutchinson and E. E. Ewing, editor of Highlands' first newspaper, lived before coming to Highlands. The founders of the Pentecostal faith experienced in 1901 what Paul described in Book 2 of Acts as a glorious "baptism in the Holy Spirit." The result was a miraculous speaking in unknown languages accompanied by prophesies of the future and healing of the sick. The Holy Spirit was received by the laying on of hands, according to the pattern set forth in the Book of Acts.

The Assemblies of God made no claim to be a new denomination or sect but structured their national organization as a cooperative fellowship that left each congregation self-governing and self-supporting. The Highlands Assembly of God had its first meeting on April 26, 1970, in the old Rogers house on the northwest corner of Main and 1st. The Revs. Claude and Barbara Head paid the first month's rent themselves, but soon attendance at the worship service reached thirty-five, and a building fund was begun with the proceeds from bake sales and community gospel sings.

In 1974 the congregation received a donation of land in the Sunset Hills development on 6th Street for its own building. The next year Dennis and Martha Preston, who had worked in the Church's youth ministry, took the reigns from the Heads, aided by Larry Bolick when needed. During the eighties Fred Sorrells, who had served the church in Franklin, took over in Highlands, followed by Ray Conner, Kenneth Howell for a short while, and Scott Holland in the nineties.

The Seventh-Day Adventists in Highlands held services in the community room of the First Presbyterian Church during the mid-eighties under the leadership of Lloyd B. Kidder, but for the most part they met in Franklin and still do. Around 1998 they met for a short while in Highlands at Marie Reese's home.

The Lutheran Church of the Holy Family was the latest of the denominations to form in Highlands. Beginning in 1993 Frank J. Meleschnig, a native of Hartford, Connecticut, held services without organ accompaniment but a beginning congregation of seven communicants. They met in the Professional Building at 5th and South streets until a church could be built on the Dillard Road, Highway 106, in 1998.

The following year Michael Weaver, a former reporter and bureau chief for the *Asheville Citizen-Times* and graduate of the Lutheran Theological Southern Seminary in Columbia, S.C., was installed as the new pastor. He was succeeded in 2000 by Pam Mitcham, a North Carolina native ministering in Sarasota, Florida.

Lutheran Church of the Holy Family. Photo by the author, 2001.

Over the years various churches in Highlands have occasionally been identified by particularly effective preachers or very significant members of their congregations. Wally Henry, a local churchgoer, once pointed out this fact to a visitor who stopped him on Main Street and asked, "Could you direct me to the Church of God?"

Wally considered the question a moment, scratched his head, and then said he knew the Methodist church, but it belonged to Mr. Davis; the Presbyterian church, he thought, belonged to the Ravenels; the Episcopal church belonged to the Halls; and the Baptist church belonged to the Potts. But for the life of him he didn't know any church in town that belonged to God.

Protestant diversity in Highlands today remains essentially as negligible as it did when the town was founded. Five organized denominations—Unitarian, Methodist, Presbyterian, Episcopal, and Baptist—quickly evolved from a handful of religious founders who met together in a single log Law House. To date, only three denominations—Christian Scientist, Pentecostal, and Lutheran—have been added along with Catholicism. Despite schisms within a few of the original five denominations that have given birth to two or three branches, Protestantism in Highlands is far from having evaporated into complete individualism.

On the contrary, for the most part Highlands protestants have held together as have their Catholic counterparts, and though they may differ only slightly or even dramatically concerning the nonessentials of their beliefs, they basically agree on the essentials.

Thomas Jefferson's observation to John Adams applies to Highlands as much as it did to the people of his own time, when he argued in 1813, "If thinking men would have the courage to think for themselves, and to speak what they think, it would be found they do not differ in religious opinions as much as is supposed."

There has been enough freedom of movement among the churches of Highlands over the past century and a quarter to support this claim, and the fact that almost every church in town today is outgrowing the confines of its original sanctuary is testimony to the fact that religion is still a vital part of the town's spiritual life.

13. Good Reading Material

Over the years the Hudson Library has grown to become what the American Library Directory *lists today as the oldest public library in North Carolina.*

When Ella Emmons Hudson, age 31, came to Highlands from Massachu-setts in June of 1880 to regain her health at the Short Off home of her sister, Louise Emmons Wells, her four-year-old son "Alferd" came with her. Con-tacting the office of Tillman Gaines in New York, she arranged for a train ticket south. Then she took leave of her many dear friends at the Lend-a-Hand Society, a philanthropic organization under the leadership of Dr. Ed-ward Everett Hale of Boston, and the Unitarian Church where she wor-shipped in Worcester. They wished her a quick recovery; indeed, they fully expected her safe return home.

Ella Emmons Hudson, 1849–80. Photo courtesy of Margaret Kies Dietterich.

Traveling to Richmond, Virginia, she and little Alferd boarded the At-lanta & Richmond Air–Line Railroad to Seneca City, South Carolina, where she spent the night. After breakfast she hired a hack for eight dollars at A. W. Thompson's livery stable and began the first leg of a two-day journey to Highlands.

It was an hour's ride to Walhalla, a village surrounded like an amphi-theater by towering mountains. While the horses watered, she lunched and climbed to the gallery of the hotel, from where she caught an enticing glimpse of the granite face of Whiteside, the vast back of Terrapin, the shaggy mantle of Stooley, and the bristling head of Rabun before they vanished behind clouds threatening rain. When the journey resumed, the horses strained against the abrupt climb through a tunnel of oaks, hemlocks, and chestnuts overshadowing a deeply rutted road. A light rain mixed with crystal spring water puddled in the scars, brimming and cascading down the steep shoulder of the mountain into the gorge. Below roared the torrent of a river.

Descending into a wooded glen, the carriage splashed through a rocky stream and began the long, steady climb over the summits of Stump House, Kadis, and Billings, up to eighteen hundred, two thousand, twenty-five hundred feet before leveling off at last just under the gray dome of the sky.

Arriving at the Russell House, the horses quenched their thirst in an ice-cold spring, while Ella enjoyed a good home-cooked meal and overnight lodging. The ride had been rough and, though breathtaking, exhausting! She was having second thoughts about the wisdom of undertaking such an arduous journey for the sake of her health. She fell asleep, however, in the instant that she closed her eyes to rest, oblivious of the night rain.

The next morning the storm had passed. The driver hitched up the horses and forded the Chattooga River. There were times when travelers stayed two or three days at the Russell House after a good rain, waiting for the swollen river to subside. However, Ella was fortunate in that the current was low enough to cross. Almost immediately the road arched into a steep climb, leveled, and fell into a creek crossing. Then began the torturous ascent up a thousand feet in two miles, the carriage twisting, turning, and pitching from side to side over slick boulders in the wet red clay, slimy from the night's downpour.

At one point near the Georgian turnoff into Thompson's Lane (today's Walking Stick Road) a fallen hemlock blocked the path, and the driver had to wield his ax to remove it. Fording Big Creek several times at the shallows between falls, the driver faltered only once as the buggy plunged down a steep, wet grade. Compelled to lock the hind wheels, he found he still needed the horses to hold back. Ella had never imagined travel this arduous.

At long last they reached the narrow pass between Chestnut and Rich mountains. Ella turned to see Big Creek at an altitude of 2,900 feet, breaking from its cradle in the first of many falls that plunged in frothy leaps down to a large pool two miles and four hundred feet below. The clamor of the water faded as the driver led the horses around the short turn ahead, arriving at dusk in the valley of the creek's birth: Horse Cove. Flanked by Sedgy and Fodderstack, Ella stared directly opposite into the dark looming face of Black Rock. Its massive shoulders held the gray clouds at bay a thousand feet above her. And in that moment she experienced the indescribable thrill and chill that such a scene impresses on the minds of newcomers and that time never obliterates.

The climb up the final thousand feet to the little village of Highlands concluded her two-day ordeal. Founded on the roof of the world, Highlands was being promoted by Kelsey as ideally suited to give "health and vigor" and to restore persons suffering from bronchitis, pleurisy, pneumonia, and consumption to a state of complete recovery.[366] Unfortunately for Ella, however, the long, rough ride over the rocks and potholes of the ill-kept mountain road proved too strenuous for her weakened lungs. She caught cold and, arriving at her sister's home at Short Off, was hustled off to bed.

It would never have even occurred to little Alferd at the time that within the year he would lose his dear mother, nor that sixty years later he would return to Highlands to see for himself the Hudson Library that grew from her friends' and relatives' despair over her death. During the final weeks before she died, Ella and her sister found some solace, even excitement, in a plan to provide "good reading material" for the little communities surrounding Highlands.[367] Before their dream could be realized, however, their worst fears became nightmare as Ella died. For Louise Wells the pain of her sister's swift demise was every bit as intense as that expressed almost a century later by Highlands poet Bess Hines Harkins:

> *If you know heart-break in these mountains*
> *You will never leave the past,*
> *Whether you go or stay*
> *The hills will hold it fast:*
>
> *It will float with the mist in the valleys,*
> *It will fall with the falling rain,*
> *It will cry with the birds in the twilight*
> *With the old undying pain.*
>
> *You will turn from the clouds of the sunset*
> *To brush the tears from your eyes—*
> *The evening star will pierce you,*
> *The frogs and the fireflies . . .*
>
> *If you know heart-break in these mountains*
> *You will never leave the past,*
> *For the Blue Ridge Hills will hold it*
> *As long as life shall last.*[368]

Ella was buried in Mount Hope Cemetery. Hers was the first adult grave near the entrance, her headstone still bathed each evening in the golden haze of the setting sun. Her friends in the North, members of Dr. Hale's Lend–a–Hand Society, in their heartfelt anguish donated in her loving memory a box of "mostly bound and new" books as a start toward fulfilling her final dream. Like everything else proposed by the Lend–a–Hand Society, these books were intended to put into practice its binding principle:

> *To look up and not down,*
> *To look forward and not back,*
> *To look out and not in, and*
> *To lend a hand.*[369]

Louise Wells gave the box of books to the town of Highlands, and over the years it has grown to become what the *American Library Directory* lists today as the oldest public library in North Carolina. It is certainly the oldest civic association in Highlands.

Its first librarian was Dr. George Kibbee's daughter, Kittie, who opened a corner cupboard of books in the schoolhouse twice a week. On June 13, 1884, the year that Grover Cleaveland was elected President of the U.S., these books were officially recognized as the Hudson Free Library Association, whose first trustee president was one of the founders of Highlands, Sam Kelsey.

So the first "official" librarian was Mary Sheldon, followed by Miss Ellison, and Prof. Thomas G. Harbison. Baxter White's daughter, Jessie, began her tenure during her father's term as the longest-serving president of the trustees. The library incorporated in 1895 and took on Miss Albertina Staub, as prim and precise a librarian as any miss who ever looked her name could be.

Miss Staub earned the munificent salary of $10 a year. She only worked two hours a week, but for the next seventeen years she and Book Committee Chairman Mary Chapin Smith, as guardians of the collection, assured its quality by culling out the "cheap trash" that people tried to dump on the library. They censored heavily, "sifting the books, rejecting the absolutely harmful and vulgar, and also freeing the shelves from much that was not only antiquated but valueless."[370]

Their stated goal was for the library to offer the best in science, nature study, literature, history, travel, fiction, etc., just as far as possible. They obviously operated under the high-minded notion that if books couldn't corrupt, then they couldn't improve anyone either, but since good books did in fact educate, then so did bad books miseducate, misinform, and misguide. Fortunately, since both ladies were quite well educated, precise and very particular, their aim was essentially achieved. For the next thirty to forty years Mary Chapin Smith and Albertina Staub had the run of what books were bought for the library. Yet Highlanders came every Friday and Saturday at the ring of the 360-pound school bell that could be heard under favorable conditions as far north as Shortoff and east into Horse Cove.

Mary Chapin Smith (1855–1940). Photo courtesy of the Hudson Library archives.

One of the most popular arrivals each month at the library was *St. Nicholas: An Illustrated Magazine for Young Folks*, which treated the children of Highlands to the latest literary installments by such popular and subsequently famous American authors as Louisa May Alcott, Mark Twain, Rudyard Kipling, Palmer Cox, Howard Pyle, Andrew Lang, and Joel Chandler

Harris. Many first editions of these authors are not books at all but install-ments in periodicals such as *St. Nicholas*. Mary Chapin Smith marveled that the children and young folks and even their parents read the magazine issues to pieces. Even the fragments were treasured and reread.[371]

Although Albertina Staub retired in 1912 as librarian, she remained on the scene for years to come. People today still remember her association with the library. "Everything was in such order when Miss Staub was around," recalls Louise Edwards Meisel. Twenty years after her retirement Miss Staub taught Louise the library's system of filing cards in metal boxes.

Unfailingly, Miss Staub's controlling influence extended beyond the li-brary, even in the late 1920s, for Louise also remembers the time when she wanted very much to sit next to Gene Murphy on a return motorcar trip from a party. She remembers Miss Staub's being there along with Mrs. John Durgin and a number of other older people. Miss Staub had never learned how to drive a motorcar and usually sat in the front with the chauffeur be-cause, as Joe Reese recalled, she said it "showed ownership." She generally wore a white skirt and spread a white napkin on the seat. Everyone else sat in the back. However, on this occasion when the party was over, Miss Staub deliberately stepped into the back and sat between Louise and her date. Louise admits her date "had TB," but "a healthy TB." Still, there was no countering Miss Staub.

The Hudson Library, built in 1915. Photo courtesy of Hudson Library archives.

By 1915 books had filled the little room of the library to overflowing with not a space for a wren's nest in an already overcrowded school. "We were like an old woman who lived in a shoe," said Mary Chapin Smith, "only we had so many books we didn't know what to do." So the library built a home of its own on East Main Street, on a lot practically donated by Margaret Rideout next to the Episcopal Church. Its architect was Huger (pronounced "U-gee") Elliott, whose family had a summer home on Satulah. Mr. Elliott was a director of the Museum of Fine Arts in Boston. A graduate of the Columbia University School of Architecture and with two years of study at the École des Beaux Arts in Paris, he had taught architectural design at the University of Pennsylvania and at Harvard before becoming a director initially of the Rhode Island School of Design and then of the Boston Museum. He would later hold directorial and teaching positions at the Philadelphia and New York Metropolitan Museums of Art.

Walter Reese won the bid over Will Cleaveland to construct the new library according to Elliott's plan at a cost of $553. The townspeople took two years to raise the money, but they wanted the library enough to stage every conceivable means of raising cash. Bug Hill, Dr. Mary Lapham's sanatorium on the hill, sponsored a benefit. There were loan exhibits, card and lawn parties, concerts, flower shows, travel lectures, and cash contributions, as well as donations of valuable material goods, like windows, doors, fixtures, an angle lamp and rugs, a large reading table, cement for the chimney (which Walter Reese volunteered to build without charge), rock for the foundation, mill work, and the loan of a machine for making cement bricks.

Fifteen hundred volumes were carted by hand from the little wing of the schoolhouse to the fine new building on Main Street. To celebrate the cooperative effort, the Hudson Free Library Association was dedicated on Independence Day, July 4, 1915, thirty-five years after its inception in a box of books and thirty-one years after its formal birth in a borrowed room.

Joe Reese, the builder's son, recalled that "you could carry all the books that there were in a pickup and not have a good load." Though its holdings were modest, the little library was certainly adequate for one of its most famous patrons: young Stephen Vincent Benét. Pulitzer Prize author of the great Civil War narrative poem *John Brown's Body* and of the delightful tale read by nearly every student today as a relatively painless assignment in school, *The Devil and Daniel Webster*, Stephen spent the summers of his teens before beginning his studies at Yale, in Highlands.

He was shy, chubby, wore thick-lense spectacles, and read Latin poetry for entertainment.[372] He frequented the library when it was still in the wing of the schoolhouse, and when it moved, he moved with it.

Stephen Vincent Benét, 1898–1943. Photo courtesy of Patricia McAndrew, Chairman of the Stephen Vincent Benét Centennial Committee.

Like young Jesus in the temple, he could be found lost in a corner of the room, slumped over a shabby copy of *St. Nicholas*, a collection of poetry, Gibbon's *Decline and Fall of the Roman Empire*, or a history of the Civil War. Through it all, he was never aware of the time, up to the very moment that Mary Chapin Smith, acting as interim librarian and "loth to interrupt such joys," pried him loose and drove him out at closing time.[373]

Since the great World War was raging during Stephen's vacations in Highlands, he kept a map of Europe on the wall in the post office. Relying on what he had gleaned from the newspaper before Mrs. Smith drove him out of the library, he would designate with colored pins on the map the current locations of the armies of the Central Powers and the Allies and would gladly update interested residents who gathered to hear details of the latest news.

Between 1913 and 1926 several interim librarians kept the library's standards high. Lucy and Charlotte Elliott, sisters of the new library's architect Huger, had been reared by a strong Savannah-bred mother, Lucy Huger, and a former Confederate army surgeon and Tulane University professor of philosophy and medicine, Dr. J. B. Elliott. The two sisters brought culture and intellect to the task of choosing books and advising library patrons. Lucy in particular was extraordinarily well read in the classics. A graduate of Sophie Newcomb College at Tulane University, she would joke that she was educated by decayed gentlewomen who taught her French and German, but the library benefited immensely from her erudition. Her daughter, Esther Elliott Shay, considered her "the best-read woman I've ever known, without being a professor."

Soon after Miss Lucy's marriage to Warren Cunningham, the reigns of the library passed to Rebecca Nall, a retired school teacher from Griffin, Ga., who held the position for a year until she became principal of Highlands School. Christina Anderson Rice took over in 1919 with her love of composing poetry, some of which is quoted later in Chapter Twenty-seven.

Christina steered children and adults alike not only to the best books on the shelves but to the books best suited for them. She introduced Margaret Gilbert (now Hall) to Dinah Craik's *Little Lame Prince*, which Margaret loved as much as Annie Fellows Johnston's *Little Colonel* series. At least they were far superior to those saccharine Elsie Dinsmore tales for Sunday-school girls, which Margaret hated, bound as they were in blue and red covers with a pansy imprinted on each. Elsie was such a cloyingly sweet goodie-goodie—refusing to play the piano on Sundays and fainting away like a little martyr to her faith—that Margaret wanted to give her a swift kick.[374]

Christina was the wife of the town butcher, Luke Rice, so she didn't seek compensation for her services to the library. But declining health forced her to retire in 1923, two years before her untimely death. Miss Lucy's sister, Miss Charlie (pronounced "Shar-lee," but also called "Darchie"), replaced her for a year, before returning the job to Rebecca Nall.

Miss Charlie was poured from a different side of the family mold than her more literary sister. She was a lady about town whom everyone knew as quite civic minded, yet she took her job at the library quite seriously. During one bitterly cold winter she considered opening the building so important that she trudged down from her home on Satulah Mountain despite subzero gusts of wind.[375] Louise Meisel remembers her beautiful fur coat, which she wouldn't wear and, when asked why, replied, "It's too ostentatious!"

Adults liked Miss Charlie, but children, such as Dolly Harbison in her teens, remembered her as rather stiff. Not that they feared her; on the contrary, they respected her. Esther Shay remembers her as a tall, stunningly handsome woman who had a sense of who she was. She never married, more from obedience to her father than by choice, though she had two serious interests—one a first cousin, the other a Catholic—both of whom her father rejected, and in keeping with the customs of her time she complied with his will while retaining her independence through a single-mindedness about her beliefs.

During the 1930s, for instance, the sign she attached to the hood of her beat-up Chevrolet when driving up to her home on Satulah read, "Up car has right of way," and she fully expected down cars to pull over to let her pass. Tudor Hall claimed that on her return, she reversed the sign to read, "Down car has right of way."

Miss Charlie had a singular personality. Her Model T, which Joe Reese had taught her to drive, she didn't trust with a mechanic. Louise Meisel remembers that if it didn't run properly, she'd take it to Hines and Zoellner's Garage on Church Street, put on a duster, and accompany the mechanic under the car to check out his work. Never mind that she lacked his skills! Her being there would assure he did the job right.

In 1923 Miss Charlie organized a meeting of seventeen women of the town to form a League of Woman Voters for a more powerful voice in town affairs. At the March meeting she was appointed president, Christina Rice, secretary, and Lilly Pierson, treasurer.[376] The organization soon expanded to become the Macon County League of Women Voters.

Miss Charlie's eccentricities grew to legendary proportions when, after the League was formed, with the right to vote in hand as a threat and a strong determination to support the newly proposed Equal Rights Amendment, she struck an unforgettable image when she demonstrated her opposition to the town's proposal to run water lines up Satulah. They would destroy its beautiful hemlock-lined road. Winnie Hertzberg remembered how she sported bloomers and middies; and flashing those gorgeous Huger-blue eyes, she challenged H. M. Bascom for the mayoralty of Highlands.

Though she lost the race for mayor, she won the respect of all who witnessed her self-assurance and brash chutzpah. Ironically, as it turned out, during the severe drought of 1925 when the springs on Satulah went dry, Satulah property owners had to beg the town to put in water lines. The town agreed, providing they pay for the installation themselves.

Between Rebecca Nall's second term as librarian and the onset of Gertrude Harbison's fifty-year rule, Leila Lewis Marett took up the reigns. Her husband, S. T. Marett, was a director of Highlands' first bank at today's Gem Shop. Leila was the first woman in Highlands to get a driver's license, says Edna Bryson, whose mother Octia Phillips was second.

Margaret Gilbert credits Mrs. Marett with having introduced her to the magic of Frances Burnett's *Secret Garden*, the warmth and humor of Louisa May Alcott's *Little Women*, and Lucy Montgomery's *Anne of Green Gables*. She read Hawthorne's *House of Seven Gables* and Poe's *Murders in the Rue Morgue* in preparation for Bram Stoker's *Dracula*. This scared her to death! Not the blood, but the notion that he had hair in the middle of his hands! One of her favorites was Alexandre Dumas' *Count of Monte Cristo*. For weeks she suffered through Edmond Dantès' unjust imprisonment and thrilled to the drama of his escape and conversion into a powerful and darkly mysterious avenger of all who had wronged him. For her, like so many other children in Highlands at the time, the library was the inexhaustible fount of their imagination.

Mrs. Marett directed much of their reading, but her real strength was not so much literary as it was organizational. Replacing the casual method of checking out and receiving books with a far more systematic and efficient system, she impressed the State Library Commission with professional reports of the library's circulation, its holdings, and the sources of its book additions during each year. She began to enforce more rigidly the regulations regarding the borrowing of books and the timely collection of fines on overdue returns. Upon her retirement in 1926 the library's holdings had attained within a decade roughly four thousand volumes, almost triple what had taken three decades of purchases and donations to accumulate prior to the move to its new home.

Primary among Leila Marett's contributions to the library, apart from inspiration and organization, was the training in library work that she gave her successors, two refined and accomplished daughters of Professor Harbison, whose names for the next half-century would be synonymous with that of the Hudson Library: Miss Gertrude and Miss Dolly Harbison.

Perhaps no two spinsters could have been better cast for library service. Jan Chmar remembered Miss Gertrude as stern and proper, a librarian first.

June Thompson considered her stoic, refined, and formidable. Miss Dolly, on the other hand, was a bit more affable. She was first and foremost a person, more folksy and everyday and, as Victor Smith recalls, smaller. Her being smaller, in his opinion, made her more "one of us." Both ladies were somewhat reserved, as Everett Wilson recalls. You knew them by the outer rim, but the second and third layer, you never got to know. They both had a habit of speaking quite fast, which reflected the speed of their thought, for there was no doubt that they were highly educated, yet at the same time, in Sarah Thompson McNamee's opinion, infinitely precious, sweet, and kind.

Librarian Gertrude Harbison, 1926–74, and Assistant Dolly, 1926–75. Photo courtesy of the Highlander.

Gertrude Harbison was Highlands' longest-serving librarian, almost fifty years. When she took over from Leila Marett in 1926, just out of her teens, Mary Chapin Smith's advice at the trustee meeting was "Take courage, brother. The Devil's dead."[377] Not that she wasn't quite capable, even then! She had a razor-sharp mind and a legendary memory, known to recall incidents from when she was three-years old. Lucile Pierson Reese said she never forgot anyone's birthday. Though she kept to herself more than her affable sister Dolly, both ladies educated the children of Highlands and many adults in ways that no school could ever match. The summer children, like Anne Altstaetter and Nancy Jussely, especially counted their lives as mostly lived in Highlands, the rest of the year spent in hibernation in their winter homes impatiently awaiting return to the wonderful views and cool mountain air of their summer homes.

One of the most popular authors, whose books the children checked out even before they reached the shelf, was Edward Stratemeyer. No child knew Stratemeyer's name, of course. They knew him instead as Carolyn Keene, author of the Nancy Drew mysteries, which Stratemeyer's daughter Harriet finished while taking on the Hardy boys as Franklin W. Dixon. Edward wrote the Tom Swift books, Harry Wright's favorites, under the name Victor Appleton, but the most popular of his mysteries, which Bill Holt and Cub Rice cherished, were the Rover boys by Arthur Winfield. Even the Bobbsey twins, presumably by Laura Lee Hope, sprang from Stratemeyer's prolific pen.

Gertrude and Dolly introduced to Highlands such new books as A. A. Milne's *Winnie the Pooh*, Ernest Hemingway's *Sun Also Rises*, and Highlands' own Stephen Vincent Benét's Pulitzer-Prize-Winning *John Brown's Body*, charging ten cents a day until the books paid for themselves, then shelving them with the regulars. The youngest set of children loved the puzzles, rhymes, and oatmeal-paper pictures to color in *John Martin's Book*. The older grades fought for *Child Life* with its more advanced selection of poetry, fiction, and puzzles. But the *Book of Knowledge* attracted children of all ages with its instructions on how to make things, such as a kite right there at the table to take home.

One frequenter of the Hudson Library would later repay the inspiration of his youth by becoming himself an author of books for children. When Robb White graduated from the Naval Academy, he penned sea adventure, screenplays, and thrillers from which movies were made, like the *House on Haunted Hill* and *Up Periscope*. Another teen, Allen Ordway, was home schooled on the armloads of books he took home each day on the advice of the Harbison sisters and his mother and faithfully returned when due.

The Misses Harbison, following the advice of Rabelais that a child is not a vase to be filled but a fire to be lit, inspired some seventy-five percent of the youth of Highlands long before there was any television to distract them. Sarah Thompson McNamee credits them with the balance of her education before leaving Highlands for college. Marion Day Arnold remembers that the library was all the young people had, especially in the winters, which were terrible, just "snow and ice, snow and ice."

Under the Harbison sisters the library survived the Great Depression through the good graces of golf-legend Bobby Jones. At a benefit game in 1931 he scored a record 64 on nine holes, which put nearly $600 in the library's coffers. Mary Chapin Smith remarked that "there was near being the spectacle of a whole society fainting away with joy and gratitude. Only being very modern women we thought we wouldn't faint. We went instead to spend the money."[378]

For three decades the library engaged in fund raisers, ranging from card parties and food sales to art shows and Silver Teas, and grew more like a mushroom than a tree, so fast that by the 1950s its books ate up the librarian's hours with mending, while the library's hours of operation increased from twelve to thirty a week during the summer seasons.

Like the town, the library thrived, not in the conventional sense of prosperity, but rather like the fragile butterfly that values its existence by the quality of its daily encounters. All Highlanders knew Miss Gertrude, who was seen every working day treading the two and a half miles between her home and the library—sun, rain, or snow—up and over Satulah Mountain. Miss Gertrude would call out, "Hello, Mary (or Sarah or Marion), have you done your reading?" She and Miss Dolly were the guiding lights of the town's children, who readily admitted, "Our lives would have been very bleak without the library."

The old Harbison house, built in 1920–21 just south of Satulah. Photo by the author, 1993.

It was the library that Marna Cobb (now Chalker) regarded as one of her four best friends during the early forties. Miss Gertrude and Miss Dolly put her onto the little collection *One Hundred and One Famous Poems* with its oval pictures of the authors and her favorite memories: "Hiawatha's Childhood," Joyce Kilmer's "Trees," Sandburg's description of the fog "that comes on little cat feet," and Tennyson's marvelous "Eagle":

He clasps the crag with crooked hands;
Close to the sun in lonely lands,
Ring'd with the azure world he stands.
The wrinkled sea beneath him crawls;
He watches from his mountain walls,
And like a thunderbolt he falls.

It was Miss Dolly who introduced her to Oscar Wilde's beautiful philosophy of life in his *Happy Prince*, where the little bird takes all the jewels and gives them to the poor without their ever knowing their benefactor. "Anonymous love," Marna calls it.[379] It was an accomplished fact that when Marna wasn't out with Sarah Hall, Mary Bascom Cook, or Anne Anderson, then she was spending time with her fourth friend, the library.

Gertrude and Dolly knew the library inside and out. Indeed, Marion Day Arnold recalls that when she volunteered to help introduce the Dewey Decimal System, none of these white-haired ladies were very keen on the idea. Why go to the trouble of classifying all these books with numbers and letters when one card for each borrower was enough? When someone wanted a book, Miss Gertrude or Miss Dolly noted it on a card, and when the book was returned, it was verified on the same card.

Both ladies knew where all the books were, every one of them. But for anyone who didn't, they were arranged alphabetically by author. Not by author within a section, mind you. No need for that! By author throughout the library from A to Z. All you had to know was who wrote the book, and if you didn't know that, you asked Miss Gertrude or Miss Dolly. As often as not, they let you take it without the hassle of a card. They knew you and knew you'd return it. It was as simple as that.

The death of Albertina Staub at age seventy-six in 1942 closed the book on fifty-five years of her association with Highlands.[380] Besides her role as Hudson librarian, during the sixteen years that she nursed it through the turn of the century, she had also contributed her exacting talents to the Highlands Museum and Biological Laboratory as one of its founders. She had assisted Jim Hines as postmaster when the Edwards building at Main and Fourth housed the old post office. After leaving the library, she eventually directed her business-like and commercially friendly manner to selling real estate and insurance for Quincy Pierson at one of Highlands' oldest insurance agencies, located initially in the Edwards building.

Her father, Professor Albert Staub, a Swiss immigrant, had taught with Professor Harbison in the Highlands Academy soon after her family's arrival from Atlanta in 1887. He came to America from the little village of Netstal in northeast Switzerland, nestled on the road between Lake Wallen and the 6,440-foot Alpine Klausen Pass. He arrived only with Albertina because his wife died of yellow fever on the trip over. They lived in Ohio, where

Albertina attended Urbana College, and then Savannah. Soon after their move to Atlanta, Professor Staub began searching for a mountainous area of the U.S. that might duplicate the beauty of his native Switzerland and be free of the mosquitoes that had killed his wife. He found it in Kelsey's brochure on Highlands.

Albertina spent the last years of her life very much like the first, steeped in nature in the heart of towering mountains. She was laid to rest without survivors in the Highlands Cemetery by the minister of the Presbyterian Church, where during her younger days she taught Sunday school. Her students still remember her in this capacity today. The list of her pallbearers read like a roster of Who Was Who in Highlands for the year 1942.

Albertina Staub, Librarian, on the porch of Staub House, 1895–1912

In 1973, the Hudson Library incorporated into the Fontana Regional Library system, which meant that all the books in the building—all 13,500 of them—which Miss Gertrude and Miss Dolly hadn't written down because they carried the titles in their heads, now needed to be catalogued. Lynn deVille chaired the committee whose tremendous job it was to cull out over five thousand worn-out and antiquated books and magazines stacked on the shelves, the floor, behind curtains, and badly in need of repair or rebinding. Many were discarded or put up for sale. A side benefit of the book sorting by Miss Dolly, Simone Kuehl (now Sorge), Estelle O'Brien, Harriet Brown, and Helen Chambers was that for the first time in its history the library stayed open throughout the winter.

When Gertrude Harbison retired in 1974, an old era passed into a new. The library had modernized with streamlined services and improved facilities. It was time to bid farewell to the dedicated woman who had weathered the two-and-a-half mile walk to and from the building every working day for fifty years of her life.[381] Even in winter's fury when she stoked the primitive stove with wood to keep warm, she was always there to tell the children what they would like better than they themselves, so that many of the summer children wrote notes of thanks to their Highlands librarian when they returned to their winter homes far away. Miss Gertrude's retirement brought a quiet age to a peaceful end, a time of considerable nostalgia.

After Miss Gertrude's departure, the library struggled under several interim librarians to maintain its character. Miss Dolly held the reigns for one year before they passed successively to Anne Ham, Melinda Russell, Martha Keener, and Gert McIntosh.

Miss Gert reading at story time. Photo 1981, courtesy of the Highlander..

In 1980 the library incorporated into the Macon County Library System. Miss Gert, with the professional advice and help of Betty Service of Sarasota, Florida, shepherded the institution through its transition from the one-story gray frame building with a low hip roof to the new half-million-dollar edifice which it occupies today on land purchased from Patrick Farnsworth's nephew Sidney. Built with the help of a most generous bequest by

H. M. Bascom's son-in-law Watson Barratt and an extraordinarily effective fundraiser by Robert Rhodes, the building was completed in 1985. Gert's staff and a small army of volunteers carted 14,000 books into their new home.

The new library's benefactor, Watson Barratt, was a Highlands resident and scenic designer and producer on Broadway, who died in 1962 with no issue other than the child of his own brain, the Bascom-Louise Gallery. This room he created in his will to become an endowed branch of the library. It was twenty years before his will was probated and the library informed of its good fortune, at which time the Bascom-Louise Gallery was named in honor of Watson's dear wife Louise and her esteemed father H. M. Bascom.

Watson's wife Louise was herself every bit as well-known outside the small circle of Highlands as within it. One of her many articles, mostly romantic and very popular, in *Harper's Weekly*, *Good Housekeeping*, and *Ladies' Home Journal* had attracted Watson to her in 1917 in much the same way that the celebrated poet Elizabeth Barrett some thirty years earlier had won the heart of Robert Browning. Watson illustrated much of her subsequent writing, which included instructional articles on how to compose popular stories without sacrificing quality, monthly guides for the New York tourist traveling by rail, several plays, and editorial pages for the *Sears Shopping Guide*. Louise's serials in *Housewife*, *Youth's Companion*, and *Woman's Home Companion* became a part of every woman's home.[382]

It was as much in honor of her good sense, good taste, and classic beauty as out of the high esteem in which he held her father that Watson created the Bascom-Louise Gallery. His own interest in the arts had led him into scenic design and theatrical production in New York. A student of the American impressionist James Whistler and the children's illustrator Howard Pyle, he designed a thousand plays on and off Broadway beginning in 1918 with a commission for *Sinbad* and including stage sets for Melville Ellis and Elizabeth Marbury, which drew public acclaim as some of the most beautiful ever seen in New York.

Watson was chief designer for the Ackerman studios, where he designed sets for the Winter Garden, Hippodrome, and high-class vaudeville. He was a pioneer in the use of the rotating stage, which permitted an almost instant change of scenery. As art director of the Metro–Rolfe Moving Picture company, he created the surroundings for Ethel Barrymore. In 1924 he designed Sigmund Romberg's *Student Prince*. He also worked for many years with J. J. and Lee Schubert and served as art director for the St. Louis Municipal Opera. Staging productions in London, Paris, and at the World's Fair in Brussels, he brought the curtain down on his long career with *Brigadoon* on his return to New York, where he passed away.[383]

Watson Barratt's will intended the gallery to become a wing of the library featuring local artists. But under the direction of Jackie Leebrick and some fifty volunteers it blossomed into a showroom for the arts and crafts. Its success continued under the direction of Ann Baird, with a popular schedule of art discussion groups, after-school workshops for children, craft and quilt exhibits, and classes in woodcarving, sculpture, photography, and needlepoint. In seeking to embrace the other arts, the Gallery cosponsored events with the Highlands Playhouse, Chamber Music Festival, and Audubon Society, held a film festival, and featured lectures in a Civil War Show. Its growth beyond the simple concept of a room featuring local art has offered a rich variety of educational programs for the community year round.

Hudson Library and Bascom–Louise Gallery, built in 1985. Photo by the author.

While the gallery flourished during the late eighties and early nineties, the library, under Karen Herchen and Carolyn Strader, replaced its increasingly cumbersome card catalogue with computer terminals. In 1999 the Gallery and Library agreed to become separate corporations under the same roof to permit each to raise funds and develop in its own unique way. Today the Gallery actively supports educational workshops, art exhibits, juried shows, and art auctions to supplement the acquisition of paintings by local artists, while the library, fully computerized and filled to capacity with 22,000 books, periodicals, and audio-visuals, enjoys an impressive circulation of over 42,000 and also sponsors cooking classes, lectures, and readings by well-known contemporary authors.

The library cannot return to the days of old when only a handful of yogis sat cross-legged in the aisles and read from the shelves or carried their books barefooted along the dusty road home. Nevertheless, librarian Henley Haslam and her successor Mary Lou Worley, with their small staffs were able to maintain the personal approach despite the profusion of new faces and urgent needs.

Indeed, from the perspective of Ralph Morris, the current editor of the *Highlander*, "Our library is one of the busiest places in town. There are book lovers coming and going in a steady stream. We're very fortunate to have the Hudson Library. It's a town treasure, a local institution, a Highlands landmark."

In the late 1990s Ella Hudson's granddaughter, Margaret Kies Dietterich of Solebury, Pennsylvania, updated the Hudson Library on the fate of Ella's son, "little Alferd," who at four in 1880 had accompanied his mother to Highlands. He went on at age twenty-eight to become president of First National Bank of Syracuse, New York, signing his first ten dollar bill in 1903.

$10 bill signed by Alfred W. Hudson, President, First National Bank of Syracuse, N.Y.

By the time he himself visited Highlands in 1939, he had advanced in the world of finance to become president of Chase Manhattan Bank in New York City and was often seen in Grand Central Park on his lunchtime "constitutional," the only real spot of natural beauty in the metropolis reminiscent of the bittersweet land of his mother's death.

In a very real sense the library is a monument to the lovely and courageous lady who was his mother, Ella Hudson, but also to her sister Louise Wells, who fulfilled Ella's last wish 117 years ago to provide good reading material for the people of the Highlands community. But it's also a tribute to the human spirit that thirsts for knowledge and pleasure between the covers of an old fashioned book. Despite the proliferation of books on tape, on microfilm, and on the computer screen, the joy of that private and cozy privilege is not yet diminished nor taken away.

14. Where the Eagle Builds Her Nest

Sweet waters of the Sugarfork
Lie just before my eyes;
'Tis there The Eagle builds her nest
And from those waters rise.
—Mr. Gee Page, *Highlands Maconian,* Oct. 15, 1930

Highlands' first newspaper, the *Blue Ridge Enterprise*, began publication in the Central House when the town was only eight years old. Beginning January 1, 1883, it appeared as a weekly every Thursday morning until it was discontinued early in 1885.[384] E. E. Ewing, former editor and publisher of a newspaper in Maryland and then of the *Topeka Daily Capital* and *Kansas Farmer*, was the only experienced newspaper man in the community, so the job of founding the town's first paper was wished on him. This proved much against his desires, of course, for he had sold his interest in the Kansas papers and moved to Highlands in late 1882 with the expressed intent of taking up bee keeping and other outdoor occupations to regain his impaired health.

Nevertheless, Ewing accepted his assignment with conscientious resolve and began publication of a model paper. He enlisted his own son Cecil; the youths Dode and Gus Kibbee, Warren Esty, and Ted Hill; and two of Albert Clark's boys to set the type. He then drafted Alfred Morgan and Mark Smith to compose each issue on an old Washington hand press in Franklin.

Determined that it be non-partisan in political matters, he targeted the tourist, capitalist, and immigrant who would not have known otherwise about the vast undeveloped wealth in agricultural land, minerals, and timber as well as unrivaled climate, pure water, and grand mountain scenery—all found, he claimed, on the Highlands plateau. His paper would feature a summary of world news including items of local interest in an effort to become a first-class local, country newspaper. A year's subscription was $1.50 payable in advance.

At the end of three months, however, he turned the project over to Albert Clark and headed again for the outdoors. By the end of 1884 he had left Highlands for Maryland. Clark built a new printing office on the south bank of Mill Creek near where Sweet Treats is today in Mountain Brook Shopping Center. And for the next two years he ran a four-page format, carefully edited, neatly printed, and including as much national news as local. When the *Blue Ridge Enterprise* ceased publication in Highlands on January 22, 1885, it moved to Webster as Jackson County's first newspaper but under a new name: *Webster Herald.*[385]

The first *Highlander*, established by Richard Goldie, appeared on August 7, 1885. In his opening editorial Goldie touted Southern newspapers in contrast to Northern as more civil, more respectable, and for the most part void of bad language.[386] Southern journalism, he felt, excelled that of the North, not because it was opposed to plain speaking and strong language where needed but because it shunned "dirt throwing, and everlasting dirt throwing, which some papers indulge in." A paper filled with offensive personalities, he argued, was not only detrimental to a place, it was also not respected. Though tolerant of it for a time, public opinion and the innate sense of propriety would ultimately tire of it.

Humor, Goldie added, was admissible in a newspaper as often containing the essence of wisdom, but mere frivolity was to be despised, for "when indulged in with the object of belittling estimable characters held in esteem or veneration by the community or by the world at large, or to make light of serious subjects, it is offensive and displeasing." He concluded that the Press of the South was committed to "a higher aim in life than dollars and cents." Its intent to reflect and promote sound public opinion grounded in logical thought had the aim of improving the sensible habits of society.

Goldie's reign over the mores of reporting Highlands lasted only a few months before he left for Iowa at the beginning of 1886, and Albert Clark's wife Minnie bought and published the paper under the auspices of the Highlander Publishing Company, a group of leading citizens of the town. She took over with an eight-page paper at a bargain: $1.00 for a year, payable in advance, with the following alternative: "Price for one year of the *Highlander* is six or eight chickens, or as many dozen eggs, two bushels of potatoes or apples, seventy bundles of fodder at the present price or two bushels of corn at fifty cents; any one of these will give you eight pages of good reading every week for a year, 416 pages in all."[387]

Although under new management, the paper continued Goldie's high-minded aim when among its efforts to bestow praise or lay blame, it condemned the act of white youths in Highlands who pelted a black boy with rotten eggs as "cowardly and contemptible."[388] It lauded Highlands as a "dry town," arguing that the absence of saloons contributed "enormously towards the quiet and order that prevails, and which is in strong contrast to the drunkenness and noise which so frequently annoy residents and visitors in some towns not very far away."

Like the *Blue Ridge Enterprise* before it, however, the *Highlander* too had to give up publication, its last issue appearing on February 25, 1887.[389] Minnie Clark bowed out with genuine regret, faulting the paper's demands on her time. She had served without compensation, in her own words, wholly for the love of Highlands. Unexpired subscriptions were repaid upon request, while the Clarks remained in Highlands for nine more years before moving to Westville, New Jersey.

For the next two years the town was without a newspaper of its own, though Baxter White's occasional "Highlands" column in the *Franklin Press* kept the world at large partly informed of local news.

On May 1, 1890, the Coe brothers, Charles and William, began publishing the *Star* in Henry Skinner's print shop on Main Street. A rather outspoken edition, it incensed a number of readers in both Franklin and Highlands and lasted only a year. It shut down on June 3, 1891, for lack of financial and popular support. A letter from the *Franklin Press* appeared in the September, 1890, special issue of the *Star* that took its editor Charlie Coe to task for trying to bulldoze Highlanders into voting down the Railroad bond as though he were their self-appointed mouthpiece.[390] Coe, according to his accuser, claimed to rule the roost in Highlands with the result that when he spoke, no other dog need bark or wag his tail. Indeed, the informant further assailed Coe's presumption to own and run the town that left his readers to decide if there was any "18-carot liar" abroad as brash as the editor of the *Star*.

Henry Stewart, Highlands' agent to the U.S. Fish Commission and agricultural editor for the *New York Times*, attacked Coe as well. And the editor of the *Franklin Press* came out in an editorial saying that there were three things on this earth that tempted him. One was a Mr. M. P. Long of Flats, whose letters to the editor never ceased, and the other two were the Highlands *Star* and the Devil. To the Coe brothers' credit, however, they published in 1890 a very attractive promotional pamphlet about Highlands including text and photographs, called *In the Heart of the Mountains*, revised copies of which were made in the 1920s and still exist today.[391]

On June 4, 1891, the day after the *Star* suspended publication, four issues of a paper called *Number Four*, published by No. 4 Publishing Company and claiming to be everybody's paper, appeared under a staff of four directors, a business manager, two foremen, three officers, and seven editors, the chief one being Professor Harbison. Baxter White's son Renwick served as chief compositor, Al McKinney inked the forms, and every paper went through the press four times.

The fifth newspaper, which McKinney called "the best paper ever published at Highlands," followed in September, 1891.[392] Edited by Professor Harbison, the *Mountain Eagle* kept the presses running in Henry Skinner's print shop for two years, was extremely popular, and inspired deep regret as much in Franklin as in Highlands when it ceased publication in 1893. The *Eagle* was partly owned by James Rideout's son, James, Jr. It published the poem by Mr. Gee Page that McKinney considered years later to be an appropriate epigraph for the paper:

> *Sweet waters of the Sugarfork*
> *Lie just before my eyes;*
> *'Tis there The Eagle builds her nest*
> *And from those waters rise.*

The *Eagle* was so astute that at times it appeared prophetic. In 1892 Cleveland and Harrison opposed each other for the presidential election. A week before the election Harbison concluded that Cleveland would carry the country, so he captioned the edition of the *Eagle* which would appear the morning following the election with the streamer, "Cleveland Sweeps Entire Country." The paper was printed a week before the election.

Harbison's brother in Pennsylvania received his copy on the afternoon of election day. In Highlands the *Eagle* broke the news shortly before the telephone calls from Walhalla reported the returns. Subscribers of the paper were highly pleased with the quick service they had been given. D. J. Moses, who helped Harbison print the *Eagle*, asked him what he would do if the election went instead to Harrison. "I'll write the hottest editorial you ever saw, cussing the Walhalla election officials for lying to us over the telephone," said the professor.[393]

When the *Eagle* ceased flying and for the next seventeen years, Highlanders were again without a newspaper of their own. Baxter White continued to submit occasional articles about Highlands to the *Franklin Press* until 1910, but for the researcher of Highlands history the great fire that swept the Franklin Press on December 20, 1922, resulted in a tragic loss. It destroyed all issues from 1903 to 1919. Only occasional columns from these years have survived, pasted into personal diaries and scrapbooks.

A Highlands column was still running in the Press in 1920 and continued until 1932 under various headings. During the twenties it was titled, "News of Week of Highlands: Brief Items of Interest from Macon's Pretty Mountain City as Told by Correspondent of The Press." From 1929–31 Sarah Hicks Hines wrote "Highlands Flings" under the heading, "Highlands—The Roof Garden of the Southeast." And for the next two years the column was called, "Social and Personal News from Highlands." The articles that bore Sarah's byline were rich with Highlands history by a genuinely capable raconteur. Some of these were recently published posthumously in her charming book, *Shaking Down the Chestnuts*.

Joe Moore, at age twenty-three, with his printer friend Jim Street, both of whom had worked for the *Franklin Press*, inaugurated Highlands' sixth newspaper, the *Highlands Maconian*, on Sept. 3, 1930. Operating from an office behind the Rock Store on 4th Street, it appeared weekly during the first two years of the Depression. Its introductory issue included a historical review of Highlands entitled "Stirring the Dust of 37 Years" and promised to follow a policy coined by Lincoln, who said, "I have never had a policy; I have simply tried to do what seemed best each day as each day came." Accordingly the paper promised (1) rigid political independence, (2) neutrality in religious differences, (3) interpretive editorials rather than antagonistic or over-zealous views on any issue, (4) belief in the economic future of Macon County and its towns, and (5) support to the agencies dedicated to the enlightenment of Macon's people.[394] For the most part the *Highlands Maconian* held to these fine principles. Bound copies are still owned and treasured by the Hudson Library and several individuals in Highlands. Unfortunately, on April 27, 1932, owing to insufficient local support and despite remarkable efforts for a town of 450 population to withstand the odds of hard times, arrangements were made to consolidate with the *Franklin Press*, which itself was in the throes of going under.

The fortunate result appeared as the *Franklin Press and Highlands Maconian*, which flourished from 1932–55 but focused predominantly on the news of Franklin. Highlands columns appeared under bylines of various individuals, such as Professor Harbison's daughter-in-law Elizabeth Rice Harbison; Rev. Frank Bloxham's wife; Stella Marett Burt; Pearl Story; James Blakley, Jan Burnette, and Geri James Crowe, respectively. Stella Burt wrote the most detailed reports of Highlands, including school news. For the two years after the designation *Highlands Maconian* was dropped from the paper's banner, beginning in 1956 no Highlands columns appeared any longer in the *Franklin Press*.

This posed no problem for Highlands, however, for it had already created its own alternative. In 1937, five years after the demise of the *Highlands Maconian*, the *Highlander* reappeared as the town's seventh weekly, edited by S. J. Fullwood. It ran for only five issues from August 6th to September 4th, but on November 24th the following year the Highlands School Theatre printed and distributed a very popular mimeographed paper known as *The Mountain Trail*, which for the next fifteen years was where Highlanders got their news. Managed by school principal Otto Summer and edited at various times by Pearl Story, Eugene Paul, Herbert Paul, Barbara Zoellner, Doris Hedden, and Lois Potts, this summer weekly was essentially student operated from the gathering of information to printing and distribution.

It flourished until 1952, when Summer's daughter, Mary, saw the continued need for a local publication to acquaint tourists and summer residents with Highlands and introduce them to year-round residents. Without any formal training in journalism, she created the *Galax News* and shifted its venue from the Highlands School Theatre to her father's recently opened Galax Theatre. Beginning with a tiny seven-page mimeographed issue, this paper grew in twenty years to thirty mimeographed legal sheets, covering each summer's activities until it ceased publication on September 2, 1971. It sold originally for five cents a copy, increasing to ten cents by the end.

Mary continued as editor while completing her degree at Western Carolina. She turned the position over to Jo Ann Keener and Tina Harbison in 1961, who were later assisted by Ella Cabe. Tina's sister, Jessie, assumed editorship in the mid-sixties, assisted by Frieda McCall. During the remainder of the sixties Betty Holt, Elizabeth Worley, Susan Whitmire, Dotty Dendy, and Sarah Summer ran the operation.

One very popular column, which began to appear in June of 1965, was Lawrence Wood's "Memories from the Hills." It had been featured in the *Highlander* since 1964 under the title it later took in book form, *Mountain Memories*. It offered a well-researched collection of stories about old-timers who helped create Lawrence's mountain heritage, most of whom he legitimately claimed as his kissing kin.

The fact that May 23, 1958, was the birth date of a new venture, the current *Highlander,* didn't draw readers away from their favorite *Galax News*, but it did provide a more professional format for general news as distinct from forthcoming movie attractions and items of strictly local interest. Founded by Jim and Martha Goode, it was Highlands' eighth or tenth newspaper—depending on whether the two mimeographed student-run papers are reckoned official.[395]

For the past forty-three years the *Highlander* has given continuous coverage once a week during the winter and twice weekly during the summer season. Less than a year after the paper was established, Jim died, leaving Martha, a Spartanburg native, to carry on alone, but with considerable courage and endurance in the face of extreme obstacles she met the challenge of operating a year-round newspaper in a town geared to a part-time economy. The paper operated out of her living room with a few part-time volunteers. Martha found herself driving to Walhalla, Cashiers, Clayton, and Franklin to solicit advertisers and trying to prepare copy, photos, and ads to deliver to the *Franklin Press*, which did the linotype and layout.

Helen Holt Hopper, who had grown up in Highlands as a member of the pioneer Cobb-Holt family, became the paper's first full-time employee when it moved into the old Baxter Wilson building, later site of the Bird Barn just east of Central House. Only four businesses in town advertised each week—Tudor Hall, John Perry Insurance, Wilson Electric, and Highlands Laundry—making the winters a losing effort.

In 1968, to give the *Highlander* a fighting chance of survival, Martha sold the publishing rights to the *Franklin Press*, a subsidiary of Community Newspapers, Inc. No longer the publisher, she nevertheless served two more years as editor and manager of "the only newspaper in this wide world devoted to the promotion of the Highlands area."

Martha Goode. Photo 1965, courtesy of Wynn Goode Cleaveland.

In 1970 she retired, taking a much-needed rest from twelve years of meeting deadlines on the first official Highlands newspaper—student mimeographs notwithstanding—to survive more than two or three years.

Having served as news editor since the paper began, Helen Holt Hopper now took the reins. In her usual self-deprecating way, she allowed as how she was just an old country girl but would do the best she could. "I was chief cook and bottle washer, you could say," she remarked. With her photographic memory, determination to get facts right, and the eventual assistance of Jim Fulton from Franklin, she developed a nine-column paper replete with pictures of newsworthy individuals and local scenes that grew each year from as few as four pages during the winter to as many as eighteen during the height of the summer season.

Helen Holt Hopper. Photo 1983, courtesy of Betty Holt.

Frederick "Skip" Taylor, an Ohioan from Franklin, replaced Jim Fulton as advertising manager and reporter in 1976, at which time the editorials increased considerably in length and content. When Helen Hopper stepped down to become office manager in the fall of 1979, Skip advanced to editor but served only a year before transferring to the *Asheville Citizen*. Howard Patterson, a recent graduate of the University of Georgia who had worked for the paper the summer before, assumed the editorship in April, 1981, aided by Wayne Hudgins, Judith Baty, and Helen Hopper. During Patterson's tenure, the *Highlander* earned first place in the editorial page awards from the N.C. Press Association.

When Helen decided to retire in 1983, she was sixty-eight and felt the time was right.[396] "Sometimes it was easy to write," she recalled, "sometimes it was just nerve wracking. At times I was tempted to jerk the phone loose from the wall." She had devoted twenty-three years to assuring that the paper would not only survive but thrive.

For years several columnists were regular contributors to each week's issue of the paper. Helen Hopper's "Highlands Piper," which Betty Holt would inherit, kept the readership informed of social news, illnesses, family visits, etc., which Jean Morris perpetuates today in her "This & That" column. Marie Chastain wrote "News from Clear Creek" which became "The Local People." Lee Copple, Agnes Scott professor of psychology, started his "One Man's Highlands" column in 1973 by focusing on colorful personalities and historic places of the area when he wasn't detailing topics from familial gatherings. His column ran for seventeen years, eventually appearing in book form, *One Man's Highlands,* before his death in 1990. Frances Baumgarner Lombard described Whiteside Cove in "The Hills of Home," which also evolved into a book by the same title. Frances-Elizabeth Signorelli, a Key West and Scaly resident, introduced her creative "Go Tell It On the Mountain" about Scaly and Highlands in 1980, which continues to date.

Returning to Highlands after a three-year absence, Skip Taylor took over again as editor for the five years from October, 1984, till June, 1989. The year after his return the *Highlander* began publishing twice weekly and assumed a decidedly more serious role in community affairs. The eighties were turbulent times in the town's rapid growth, and Skip's editorials took passionate positions on issues of local, regional, and national significance. Indeed, he was not averse occasionally to throwing himself into the midst of the fray, though his predominant plea was for the rule of reason and common sense.

Ralph Morris, a veteran Alabama and Georgia newspaperman, arrived from Perry, Georgia, to take over as editor and publisher in July, 1989. That was the year that Tom Wood, a seasonal resident of Highlands, and Dink NeSmith bought Community Newspapers, Inc. and introduced computer-generated type, full-color photos, and well-trained staffs. Twice-weekly publication continued from mid-May through mid-November with weekly issues covering the winter and spring.

At the time that Ralph Morris assumed the helm of the *Highlander*, the results of the community-wide survey had just been announced, and the town was on the threshold of determining the future extent and rate of its growth. His approach was even handed, laudatory, and low key, as it remains even today. In his own words he consciously avoided running "editorial beliefs" or advocating "goals to grow on," even while he strongly opposed the factioning of Highlands.[397] One of his staff writers won first-place in the N.C. Press Association's Contest for 1998 Feature Writing. The judges chose Kim Lewicki's social history of the 150-year-old Brooks–McCall cabin as it was being moved from Blue Valley to Walden Way.

On July 8, 1993, Highlands came of age with its own radio station. Chuck and Wanda Cooper of Augusta, Georgia, and Meridian, Mississippi, established WHLC FM 104.5 and began broadcasting "soft and easy music for the mountains," a middle ground between the classical music and jazz of public radio, the country music from Nashville, and the rock and roll out of Atlanta. Like cable TV, it provided an instant forum for public announcements in addition to advertising by local merchants.

In assessing the *Highlander* today, with a current staff of eleven, Ralph Morris' support is a far cry from the days when Martha Goode gave the paper its birth and had to shoulder the never-ending burden alone. For never-ending it was, as anyone who thrives in the newspaper business will acknowledge. According to a poem that Helen Hopper published the year after she took over as editor: once a newsman,

Always a Newsman
The editor leaned on a small pica case,
There were tears in his eyes and ink on his face;
He sighed as he gazed 'round the dirty old place:
"To Hell with the newspaper business.
It's tough to plug this way 'till a man dies,
I'll quit the damn business before the snow flies;
I'll catch some poor sucker who hasn't got wise
And start HIM in the newspaper business."
But suckers were shy, so he still plugged along
In the same dreary way, with the same woeful song
'Till Death one day rang the quitting-time gong
—He was out of the newspaper business.

His spirit soared up through the realms of the air
And he found himself climbing the Great Golden Stair.
But he sighed: "What's the use, I can't get in there
'Cause I've been in the newspaper business."
Then Saint Peter saw him and smilingly said:
"I don't wonder, poor fellow, you're glad that you're dead.
Come on inside, here's a crown for your head,
You've been in the newspaper business."
In the usual way this should end the sad tale
But a Medium saw him one day, through the veil;
He was hustling scoops for The Angel's Mail
—Still in the newspaper business![398]

15. Angels of the Mountain People

"They give him six weeks—three weeks, I believe maybe it was—to live. He come up and lived to be about ninety years old and made a fortune."

—Herman Wilson about W. S. Davis, 1989

Medical services began in Highlands with its first resident practicing physician Dr. George W. Kibbee, a native of Oregon, who arrived with his family from New Orleans in the spring of 1878. He was attracted to the climate, the people, and the small size of the town, so he built a home at the base of Satulah, known later as *Chestnut Burr Cottage*, the home of Judge Jim Hines with its distinctive turn-style gate, today's Nick's Restaurant.

Highly skilled as a physician, Kibbee's specialty was the treatment and control of specific types of fevers, especially yellow fever which he had treated in Knoxville by using rubber beds and cold water baths. So when yellow fever broke out in epidemic proportions so soon after his departure from New Orleans, he felt compelled to return to the aid of his stricken friends. Reports of his daily successes were encouraging until September 28th when his family and friends in Highlands were stunned at the news of his death. He was killed by the very pestilence he had fought so bravely to kill. In the truly Christian sense, he literally gave his life that others might live.[399]

Highlands would have to wait two years before it had another physician of Dr. Kibbee's caliber. Dr. Charles Frost, who was discussed previously in Chapter Four, arrived from New York in the fall of 1880. As Highlands' first long-term resident physician, he served the needs of Highlands for twelve years until his health failed him in 1892. What he prescribed for others in the way of medical care which cured them, he apparently would not allow for himself, and he died the following year.

Three interim physicians arrived in late 1882 and 1883, respectively, but stayed only a short while. Dr. Guy Wheeler from Swampscott, Massachusetts, practiced initially out of Baxter White's *White House* before building his own house on Cottage Ridge, but within three years he was gone. Dr. George Fritts came from Wisconsin, and Dr. William Fritts set up his practice as physician and surgeon in room four of Joseph Fritts' Highlands House. Perhaps the reason for their short stays, as the final issue of the first *Highlander* reported in early 1887, was that "almost every family in Highlands came hither in quest of health for one or more of its members, and yet a physician cannot make a living by his practice alone. Many who had been ailing for years, find themselves strong and well here."[400]

A long-term resident physician, "Doctor" Alfred Hawkins arrived from Hudson, Ohio, in the spring of 1883 but didn't live in the village.[401] Preferring the outback, he chose to settle quite remote from Highlands. Purchasing 1,000 acres south of Horse Cove and west of the Glade Mountain Road, he and his sons Huber and Barry spent the Spring building Rock House Farm, named after the rock house in which they lived during the long weeks of their labor. Actually there were three rows of rock houses that ascended Glade Mountain east of the road at today's junction with Rock House Road. The third level offered a 20-by-100 foot overhang for more than adequate protection from the elements beneath an enormous slab of granite.

Rock house, level one, on the Glade Mountain road. Photo by the author, 2001.

Rock houses were not uncommon in the mountains, for similar shelters from severe storms can still be found under Bridal Veil, Dry Falls, the Picklesimer Rock House in Blue Valley and in Granite City in Horse Cove, as well as Whiteside Mountain where deserters were known to hide during the Civil War.

Hawkins himself had fought for the union. He was a farmer by trade, but his interests as a self-made scholar had led him to study homeopathy under the German physician Hahnemann. Called upon by his new neighbors of the South to practice medicine as an unpaid avocation, he spent as much or more time walking on call than in farming. Professor Harbison recalled with admiration how "for years on end no night was too dark nor day too stormy to deter him from traveling, even to the most inaccessible of places, to alleviate the suffering of those in need." He would prescribe wild berries and poke sallet, wild raspberry tea during pregnancy, and yellowroot for soars. He also took time to teach school in Horse Cove and to work at John Jay Smith's sawmill in Highlands.

Dr. Hawkins won the affection of the whole community, but he had to earn it the hard way. His arrival as a Yankee in an isolated area known for blockading made him a ready target for those who suspected him a revenuer. They killed his cattle, burned his cabin and barn, and made attempts on his life. No less stubborn than they, he refused to give up his right to live wherever he chose. And in the end it was his Christian character that triumphed, for his death at eighty-three, from felling a chestnut near the rock houses, attracted mourners from miles around whose desperate souls he'd touched or bodies cured.

As distant as Dr. Hawkins was from Highlands, the village was blessed in the fall of 1883 to welcome William Anderson, who was previously introduced in Chapter Six. Like Hawkins, he hailed from Ohio and remained in the area the rest of his life. With a degree in medicine from Keokuk Medical College in Birmingham, Iowa, he rented for his office calls part of Joseph Halleck's Central House. With the onset of three cases of scarlet fever in Highlands in the fall of 1884, Dr. Anderson became the town's first health officer and closed school for a week to prevent the fever's spread. Other less serious but more noxious duties of the town's newly created health officer had to do with monitoring the disposal of the excrements, slops, kitchen offal, and manure piles improperly buried or left exposed to the eye and nose within the town limits. The prime offenders were the hotels, the stables, and private privies.

It was at his office in Central House that Dr. Anderson would train James Rideout's son, Herman, as a medical aid and inspire him to pursue a lifelong career in medicine. When Anderson had practiced in Highlands for twenty-eight years, young Herman, fresh out of Harvard, replaced him as Town Health Officer in 1911, the year prior to Anderson's death.

On his return to Highlands, Herman used his Harvard training to reconnect a boy's hand, which had almost been lost to an ax.[402] He also diagnosed an illness that doctors in Atlanta couldn't recognize and which only after extensive testing at Johns Hopkins was finally confirmed. Herman healed and saved lives when no one else could effect a recovery.

Highlands had its first Drug Store in 1884 when Thoren Walden took over the Martin Meat Market at 4th and Main, later Bill's Soda Shop, today's House of Wong. He dispensed prescriptions for three years until his successor, Dr. Henry O'Farrell from Colorado set up his own drug store adjacent to Highlands House.

The next few years were particularly trying ones. In 1888 the town had to be quarantined against all yellow fever refuges, especially from Jacksonville, Florida. Influenza, or the grippe as it was widely called, hit Highlands as an epidemic during the summer of 1891. It struck again in the winter of 1893, progressing in some cases to pneumonia. For a town founded as a health resort and especially noted for pulmonary cures, there was nowhere on earth to flee. All over town could be heard "bless you," the traditional prayer since A. D. 591 that wished health on anyone heard sneezing, the first sign of the disease.

Just before the second flu epidemic, Dr. Frost died, leaving Will Anderson as the only physician in town, except for the few years at the turn of the century when Dr. G. W. Hays practiced in town. Dr. Hays, a native of Knox County, Kentucky, arrived from Old Fort, N.C., and married William and Stell Cleaveland's daughter Mabel. In 1901, soon after his arrival, Prioleau Ravenel Jr.'s dog died of rabies. When a South Carolina dog ventured into town and bit John Norton's five-year-old son Logan, Dr. Hays had to post notice for nine dog owners to confine their animals.[403]

Two weeks after Logan left for Pasteur hospital in Baltimore, he sent word back to his mother that the doctor had pinched him, and that he didn't like the house because there were too many people in it. It wouldn't have taken many people at all for a kid from a village the size of Highlands to consider them far too many. Dr. Logan served the town only a few years, for he died in 1905 at age thirty-one, having sired two sons who would grow up in Highlands: Willie and Joe.

Essentially it was Dr. Anderson and Dr. Herman Rideout after him who prepared the town for the arrival of the most famous of its physicians, Dr. Mary E. Lapham. Daughter of a New England banker living in Michigan, she had worked successfully with her father in banking until her late thirties.[404] But on visiting Highlands in 1893, where she stayed at Davis House for two years and then at Heacock House on 5th Street for another two, she noticed the need for medical care by the small town, especially by the women. It was sufficient to inspire her to change careers. She bought a farm house on Satulah from the Ravenels on May 1, 1897, which she had Marion Wright enlarge into "Castle-far-away," abbreviated today as *Faraway*. Attending Women's Medical College of Philadelphia, she graduated in 1901 and turned to Vienna and Switzerland for advance study.

Her specialty became the Swiss therapy for tuberculosis, to which the conditions in Highlands were especially suited. Returning to Highlands to begin general practice, she moved into *Faraway* with her two friends, Mrs. Edith Bloomer Dougall from Winsor, Canada, and Miss Carolyn Barker from Flint, Michigan. These three ladies hosted many lavish and glittering social gatherings at their home and rode about town in a stylish carriage drawn by a matched team of horses with Love Henry as their liveried coachman. They loved music, and during their summer breaks from winter travels in Europe, they enjoyed playing a grand piano, a player piano, and Wagnerian operas on their Victrola. When Mrs. Dougall adopted Valerie Ashton, daughter of a recently deceased English mining engineer, the household became a merry one indeed.

Faraway, renovated from a farmhouse in 1897. Photo by George Masa, 1929.

Despite Mary Lapham's love of the good life, she harbored a genuine concern for the ill and the dying. In 1908 she bought the three-story home and surrounding property of Marietta Trowbridge, who had recently moved to San Francisco.[405] The intent was to establish a sanatorium. Located at the present site of the Highlands Recreation Park, it soon became known as *Bug Hill*, after the tuberculosis bacillus, or the *San*. Will and Jamie Cleaveland added two wings to the three-storied building which housed an infirmary, doctors' offices, medical equipment, kitchen, and a dining room.

Nationally recognized as a pioneer in the field of the artificial pneumothorax treatment of TB (involving the artificial collapse of one lung to give it rest), Dr. Lapham prescribed lots of fresh air for her patients. She had sixty open-air cottages, or "tents" as they were called, constructed with wooden floors and sides and canvas roofs. These cottages permitted tubercular patients to sleep exposed to the crisp, clear mountain air and sunshine. Among the workers at the San were Wen McKinney, Roy "Nick" Potts, and Charlie Potts. McKinney served as chief cook and had as one of his tasks the care of the pigeon loft, for the patients and the staff were quite fond of squab pie.

Since there was no light or water system in Highlands, the San relied on its own generating plant for electricity. Water was pumped from a spring nearby to a tank in the top story of the main building. The San had its own laundry operated by Mrs. Lycia Beal at the foot of the hill near Mill Creek. Patients came from as far away as Atlanta, Athens, Asheville, Savannah, and Charleston for treatment and cure, frequently requiring that Love Henry meet them at Lake Toxaway in Dr. Lapham's two-horse Babcock ambulance.

Tents at Bug Hill, 1910. Photo from R. H. Scadin Collection, UNC-A.

Herman Wilson remembered how people came to Highlands "on their last legs of life. There was no Highlanders ever caught TB that I know of." Mr. W. S. Davis arrived from Commerce, Ga., in critical condition on a stretcher, and nobody thought he'd make it. "They give him six weeks—three weeks, I believe maybe it was—to live. He come up and lived to be about ninety years old and made a fortune." Other patients who also came to die but stayed for the remainder of their days were H. M. Bascom, Jim Hines, Miss Sara "Sal" Gilder, and James Mell. Dr. Lapham "saved a lot of people," Herman concluded, "and she was a good doctor in a lot of ways."

In short time the San became a social center. Bridge dominated every night in the big living room, Christmas parties were extremely popular, and local poetess Laura Hawkins created for the patients challenging charades with answers embedded in rhymes. During the summer patients lounged in the long canvas deck chairs on the verandah, light "steamer rugs" thrown over their knees. The patients, doctor, nurses, and other helpers at the San were a little world unto themselves, not sterile and professional but jolly and individualistic.

Dr. Mary Lapham's Bug Hill, built in 1908 at current site of Recreation Park.
Photo probably by R. Henry Scadin, 1910, courtesy Hudson Library archives.

Here is where Jim Hines earned his title "The Judge" or "Judge Hines" for the way he settled gambling disputes among card players. For if anyone dared grumble over his ruling, he'd cut loose in his original and fancy way of cussing that made it worth the loser's while just to hear him carry on. It was Judge Hines' sense of humor as much as his skill at resolving arguments that got him elected mayor of Highlands years later, when he phrased his political ad to read: "If elected, and in the performance of my duty as mayor, any bouquets are thrown our way, they will be gracefully caught. Any brick bats will be received from in front."[406]

Dr. Lapham and her warm-hearted nurse Miss Bernie Durgin, John Durgin's daughter, regarded humor, even slapstick, as good a cure as a dry pill. At times the patients laughed so hard they fell into fits of coughing.

With the outbreak of the World War, Dr. Lapham chose to leave Highlands to head a Red Cross mission in war-torn Europe. She devoted herself to treating refugees and children in Czechoslovakia, where one of her close friends became its first president, Thomáš Masaryk. But her work with the unfortunate victims of the war undermined her health with the result that she finally had to abandon the work that had made her so famous.

Dr. Mary E. Lapham, 1861–1936. Photo courtesy of Tom Crumpler collection.

Meanwhile, at home in Highlands one fiercely cold night in February, 1918, Frank Fugate was called in to thaw the frozen pipes at the San but accidentally started a fire as the torch caught dry woodwork and consumed the main building in flames.[407] Fortunate for the patients, their living in tents saved their lives. They were bundled up and slid down the slippery hill to the laundry and then taken to Smith House, currently Highlands Inn The precious X-ray machine perished with the main building in the fire and was never replaced.

After the destruction of the San, only ten years after its establishment, Dr. Lapham decided not to rebuild. Nurse Bernie Durgin, however, had twenty-five of the cubicles moved across the road to the site of today's Highlands Trailer Park on Chestnut Street and continued to run a treatment center. One of these cubicles still stands at the back of the Park. Others, grouped into units of three, became cottages for Hall house. Even today one of these three-cottage units serves as the front office of Chandler Inn on north 4th Street.

The people of Highlands still remember Dr. Lapham's house calls at their homes. Often made in the middle of the night by horseback on "Old Molly" or the thoroughbred "Joe," she would travel up to ten miles. In wet weather she wore a black Macintosh with weatherproof hat. She was almost never followed by her pedigreed Boston bulldog, Louis d'Or. It was Dr. Lapham who in 1906 gave the Hudson Library a monthly subscription to *St. Nicholas Magazine*, the most sought-after item in the library's collection for years to come.

In 1915 she replaced Herman Rideout as the Town Health Officer. She carried the telephone and telegraph franchise for the town from 1910 until she left in 1919 when Highlands Telephone Company took over. Founded by J. L. Pierson and W. S. Davis of Highlands and W. H. Adkins of Atlanta, the telephone service was leased and operated by the Hall family.

It was a much-loved family physician who died in St. Augustine, Florida, her winter home, in 1936 at the age of 75, as much a world treasure as a local one. In addition to authoring many books and papers that made her the first to pioneer the Swiss therapy of pulmonary disease in the United States, she directed tuberculosis research work at Johns Hopkins University and at the University of Pennsylvania. She also served as the first woman president of the American Thoracic Society, a national medical group specializing in respiratory diseases.

Despite all her activities she kept a certain measure of sanity at her home in *Faraway*, where this lovely poem hung on the parlor wall:

> *They shut us round with misty rim*
> *Afar against the golden sky.*
> *Across their barrier, shadowy dim,*
> *The outer world can never pry.*
>
> *Here peace and calm unbroken stay,*

Nor strife nor passion here molest.
They guard us still from all unrest
The purple hills of Faraway.

Not long after Dr. Lapham's service with the Red Cross in Europe, the Red Cross sent Miss Margaret Harry, a trained nurse, to work among the mountain people. For eight years, from 1920 to 1928, she ran a five-bed health clinic in the Masonic Hall in Highlands.[408] She convinced Dr. Elbert Gilbert to come practice dentistry in the same quarters. Her character was such that she is still fondly remembered by older residents. As a compassionate midwife, if there was a baby to be delivered, Miss Harry was on the scene without fail. She delivered many a newborn in the outback where no doctor's foot ever trod.

Of slight build, weighing less than a hundred pounds, she rode in a rumbling wagon over rough roads for miles into the mountains, coves, and valleys. Often as a tribute to her tireless service, the new child became a namesake: the girl babies, Margaret; the boys, Harry. In many ways and for many years she was the Florence Nightingale of the Blue Ridge. The *Atlanta Constitution Magazine* called her "Angel of the Mountain People."

June Thompson Medlin remembers Miss Harry as quite spry, always full of fun and laughter. As fearless as she was in the face of most any kind of threat, however, she had a deathly fear of cows. Once when she had to cross a pasture on a nursing mission, she was chased by a curious cow. Climbing the nearest tree, she escaped to safety, but the cow spent the day under the tree with her in it. Having brought a sandwich for lunch, she was only able to return to Highlands when the cow wandered off late in the afternoon.

Practical jokes were Miss Harry's specialty. T. T. Hall remembered accompanying her on one of her calls. They found the skeleton of a horse on the Rhododendron Trail near Sam Evins' home. Intent on a practical joke, they rearranged the bones to look like a human skeleton near a fallen tree. Later Miss Harry brought some false teeth and pieces of male clothing, which she left with the bones. She summoned Dr. Thompson who concluded from a cursory glance, "That's somebody, all right." When word hit the town, the county coroner was notified. He, of course, exposed the gag but not without appreciating the fun.

When the town was still in its infancy, long before it had a dentist to call its own, if a Highlander had a dental emergency, he was obliged to travel a considerable distance to find relief. Kelsey noted in his diary in 1879 that he had to take his wife, Katy, to Hamburg (now Glenville) to have Dr. James M. Zachary pull a tooth. By 1883, however, Dr. Zachary was meeting patients on Saturdays in the Highlands House.

During the 1920s, at Miss Harry's urging, Dr. Gilbert began practicing dentistry during the summers in Cashiers and Highlands.[409] A winter resident of Westminster, S.C., and graduate of Atlanta Dental College, he set up a portable treadle-driven drill at High Hampton Inn in 1922. In 1924 he moved to the Masonic Hall in Highlands as its first resident dentist and in 1926 transferred his office to the second floor of Charlie Anderson's Drug Store on 4th Street. His daughter Margaret Gilbert Hall still lives in Highlands today.

Dr. Gilbert's successor in 1936 was Dr. Jessie Zachary Moreland, a native of Jackson County who gave up her practice in Raleigh, N.C., to move nearer to home in Highlands. The following year she bought Wilton Cobb's residence on Main Street and transferred her office into her new home. In 1962 she shifted her office to the recently built Town House Motel that stood in front of her home. Eventually she moved into a house beyond 1st Street on the Franklin Road.

Dr. H. P. P. "Percy" and Helen McKinney "Mama" Thompson. Photo courtesy of June Thompson Medlin.

At about the time that Miss Harry was filling the void left by Dr. Lapham's absence from attending medical emergencies, Dr. H. P. P. "Percy" Thompson, a valedictory graduate of Medical College of South Carolina at Charleston, arrived from Hancock, Maryland, himself a very sick man. He came in 1919 to regain his health and within a year had married the recently widowed Helen McKinney Cleaveland, mother of three surviving sons. He and Helen had three girls (Sarah, Peggy, and June) and two boys, the last of whom, Richard Byrd, was named after Dr. Thompson's friend and relative, the Antarctic explorer. They reared all eight children in their home near Mill Creek on the site occupied today by Bryant Funeral Home.

Dr. Thompson served Highlands for only a dozen years before he died during the Depression, but he made his mark on the town. As the only resident doctor in 1922, he supervised the state clinic on the stage of the schoolhouse, where children went to have their tonsils and adenoids extracted. He all too often took no pay for his services, especially as the Depression set in. So his death left his widow to support eight children with no money and unpaid doctor bills.

She achieved this, however, for the next thirty years by doing what she knew best: cooking. Not just for her family, but for the town. "Mama" ran the school lunchroom. Her recipes for the Highlander Restaurant were collected by her daughter June Thompson Medlin as *Mama's Recipes*, probably the only local cookbook that is genuinely Highlands with its homemade soups and bread, roast turkey or cheese soufflé, and buttermilk or black bottom pie.

After Dr. Thompson's death in 1931, Highlands was without a resident physician for the next sixteen years, relying, as it had in earlier days, on doctors in Franklin and Sylva or Dillard, Georgia, such as Dr. Neville. Life during this period was essentially unprotected. The flu epidemic that struck Highlands in 1937 temporarily robbed the school of forty percent of its students, forcing it to close, while half of Highlands, 250 residents, were laid up in misery for two weeks.[410]

At last in April, 1947, Dr. William Matthews, a native Georgian and radiologist fresh out medical school and the Army Medical Corps, moved to town and opened a year-round office on 4th Street hill in the little brick building just south of Anderson's dime store. He and his wife Beverly lived in the Episcopal Rectory behind the Presbyterian Church, for the Episcopal priest at the time resided in Franklin. One of Dr. Matthews' first concerns upon his arrival in Highlands was a polio epidemic, requiring a two-week quarantine of all children under sixteen brought into Highlands.

Dr. Matthews was not the first physician to feel the town needed a clinic or hospital, but he was the first to succeed in organizing one. Earlier in 1934 Dr. William C. Dabney had sought to construct one. He had even convinced the town to maintain South Street between 4th and 5th as an all-weather road to a proposed hospital and to provide lights and water for a charity ward, neither of which, however, materialized.[411]

Thirteen years would pass before his wish would become fact. A board of seven directors—including Dr. Matthews, Jessie Moreland Hedden, Harvey Talley, Robert Hager, Stacey Russell, Charlie Potts, and D. M. Robertson—was established to draw up plans and seek funding. Construction of their dream began in October, 1947.[412] Miss Eva Cleaveland, daughter of

William B. Cleaveland, donated land east of 5th at the South Street intersection. The town too became involved: South Street was finally graveled, lights and water and even crushed stone were furnished, and a sewer connection was supplied the following year.

The architect who drew the plans for the new hospital free of charge was Upton Ewing. Funds were raised from residents, visitors, and special events, such as a golf exhibition given by Bobby Jones in 1948, which, though his most popular, was unfortunately his last before his tragic end. Four years after its inception, the Highlands Community Hospital opened its doors at the former site of Joe Hays' home, today's Peggy Crosby Center, on June 25, 1951, with Dr. Matthews in charge.

Highlands Community Hospital, 1951. Photo courtesy of the Highlander.

For the next several years doctors arrived, served briefly, and departed. In January Dr. James Satterwhite took charge, succeeded within the year by Drs. C. T. Townsend and Sherman Pace, and the following year by Dr. Charles Bittle.

Beginning in 1953 support for the hospital flowed from a variety of sources. The Woman's Auxiliary began operating a shop known as the Woman's Exchange in the hospital's basement to provide year-round support. The following year James Christian Pfohl directed the Transylvania Music Camp Faculty Orchestra in its first annual Pops Concert as a benefit at the High School Auditorium. The African–American servants of Highlands donated half the proceeds of their annual music program, which for the previous six years had gone entirely to the Methodist Church. Contributions in 1954 accounted for half the hospital's budget, amounting to just under $26,000. The next year the town granted the Ladies of the Community permission to use the recreation hall for a hospital bazaar, a considerable source of income that has continued to this day

Despite such admirable efforts on the part of the community at large, the amounts raised soon fell short of what was needed to keep the hospital afloat. Doctors, such as W. S. Langford and Gene Morton, left as soon as they came, with the result that the hospital closed in 1957. Almost immediately the Episcopal Rev. Dr. Herbert Koepp-Baker lobbied successfully to have it reopened. And the string of doctors continued: Dr. Markham Berry, in 1958; Dr. Carl Strom from McCormick, S.C., the year after; Dr. Robert Johnston; Dr. Frank Goodwin; and in 1962, Dr. Doralea Harmon.

For ten years beginning in 1956 Ella Carter served as hospital administrator and director of nursing services as a new problem began to emerge under her supervision. Despite the addition of a new nursing home and a clinic to take care of the many patients from Cashiers, the once-large now-small eight-bed structure grew so crowded that a new wing was proposed as early as 1964. Annual fund drives to balance the peak demand of the summer months with the relative inactivity of the long winter months had been in place since 1959, but the hospital's needs were increasing exponentially.

On her arrival in 1962, Dr. Harmon focused on the children, whose emergencies sprang from prior deficiencies, such as malnutrition, bad teeth, poor eyesight, and untreated allergies. She created a free Children's Clinic on a monthly basis to dispel problems before they arose or at least treat them in their early curable stages.

By 1965, however, Dr. Harmon had become frustrated at being the only doctor in Highlands, which left her no time to hold the Cashiers Clinic in addition to her local obligations. She promptly resigned, blaming the hospital administrator and board, and then sued the hospital while setting up private practice in town, which a number of residents offered to fund.

When the hospital board hired Dr. George Rawlins of Franklin on a temporary basis and served a court order on Dr. Harmon to release patients' charts from her downtown office, the controversy intensified. Ella Carter resigned as administrator, a Citizen's Committee proposed a medical center instead of the hospital to be located in the Edwards Hotel, and the hospital threatened to sue the newspaper for biased reporting, which the newspaper vehemently denied, printing a blank editorial page featuring the single line: "Freedom of the Press?"

As if intended to cool tempers, the weather ushered in on January 29, 1966, the worst winter ever to hit Highlands, temperatures plunging to 20° below zero. The next issue of the paper called for all concerned to "work together for the good of the community," and the Methodist minister Vance Davis suggested Dr. Harmon might be saying too much, the hospital board too little, with the public making accusations too eagerly and spreading unproven rumors.[413] He advocated Christian charity toward an excellent doctor and an excellent hospital working together for a better community.

With an actual court summons served on the newspaper and with Ella Carter threatening legal action, negotiations in private began between the warring parties, and except for a number of letters supporting the paper's editor, the issue faded from center stage. Indeed the focus shifted early in the year to a new twenty-seven-bed wing, costing a third of a million dollars but with the fortunate backing of two Duke Endowment grants and federal funding.

Ella Carter returned as administrator, Dr. Harmon announced that she would leave Highlands to practice with Dr. Berry in Ellijay, Georgia, and the hospital announced contracts with two new year-round Georgian doctors: William Oglesby from Quitman and Eula Pate (Mrs. Tommy Norton in private life) from Fort Gaines. Both carried degrees from Medical College in Augusta. By August, 1965, under the administration of Alan Lewis, a new expanded Highlands–Cashiers Hospital opened its doors, debt free.[414] It was dedicated the following year with George W. Woodruff of Coca-Cola fame as its speaker.

As it turned out, the expansion was not enough. Conditions in the hospital remained crowded, so Dr. Oglesby chose to build his office in 1968 on Smallwood Avenue by Harris Lake, where Lakeside Restaurant exists today and where, unfortunately, he stayed but three years before returning to Georgia. Still, under his tenure as chief of the medical staff, the Gray Ladies were formed as volunteers to help at the crowded hospital. Not to slight the animals of the area, Dr. Frank Harris set up a veterinarian office in Scaly.

The seventies opened with the struggling Highlands–Cashiers Hospital's experiencing its first measure of permanency in the twenty years since its uncertain founding. With William Lees serving as hospital administrator, Dr. Carlyle "Mike" Mangum, Jr., a native Virginian and Harvard Medical School graduate from Eden, North Carolina, stepped into the role that Oglesby had just vacated as resident doctor and became the first physician in many years not to give up on Highlands, despite the fact that he felt most of the people in the hospital belonged in nursing homes.[415]

With over two decades of medical experience, Mangum had developed a reputation for bluntly saying exactly what he thought. As a diagnostician, his assessments of patients' ailments were unerring and often gruff if he felt only strong words would get through to the old codgers. Still he was as much loved as respected for his practice of the art of medicine, which he felt was being stamped out by specialization. He served Highlands from 1970 until his retirement in 1987. Arriving at the same time as Dr. Mangum, Jack Calloway replaced William Lees as the first long-term administrator of the hospital.

Dr. Mike Mangum, resident physician from 1970–1987. Photo courtesy of the Highlander.

Despite such auspicious growth during the early seventies, one last snag threatened to unravel the promise of a well-woven fabric. Dr. Pate left under somewhat of a cloud. She'd been given temporary office space in the hospital building itself, but the hospital board, with an eye to continued crowding, decided to recall it. She submitted her resignation, despite a petition signed by 250 townspeople asking her to reconsider. This time the *Highlander* stayed out of the fray, which only the *Galax News* reported.

With another potential crisis averted, the hospital nailed down its assurance of permanency with the recruitment in 1971 of Dr. John Baumrucker from Cincinnati, Ohio. His parents were Cashiers residents, his father having just built the Cashiers Plastic Plant. Sharing an office in the building with Dr. Mangum, Dr. Baumrucker is the only one of the early doctors who remains today as Highlands' longest-serving resident physician. His level-headed, compassionate approach to medical care has lent stability to an organization that once depended for its life on the dedication and inexhaustible energies of a single doctor, responsibilities now shared by many colleagues and a supportive staff. As an appropriate parallel, his leadership of the Methodist mission team to Bolivia over the past several years has resulted in an upgraded hospital and medical services, along with construction of a new orphanage and playground, for the people of Montero, a project that has involved quite a number of dedicated Highlanders.

Dr. John Baumrucker. Resident physician since 1971.

As if the constant burden on a small community to raise funds for the care of its own weren't enough, and despite the arrivals of its first really permanent doctors, the Highlands–Cashiers Hopsital in 1970 lost its Medicare support due to staffing problems. Fortunately, a concerned public sprang to the rescue. Ever generous since its first annual contribution of

$1,800 in 1959, the public suddenly showered its stricken medical facility with an astounding $160,000, setting a high benchmark for subsequent years. In 1971 the hospital received a bequest from the estate of Veazey Rainwater, Sr., whose mansion and property atop Little Yellow Mountain sold for $300 million, half of which went to the hospital.

With such openhanded support by the public at large, the hospital treated some 400 patients and over 1,400 emergencies in 1974, in addition to delivering twenty-nine babies. It had a full-time staff of thirty under Jack Calloway as administrator, plus four radiologists, four pathologists, a dietician, and a medical librarian on a consulting basis. And in 1976 Fred Rodenbeck of Asheville joined Dr. Willet Stubbs to meet the dental needs of the community.

In 1977, having met the required standards of quality care twenty-six years after its unsteady opening, the Highlands-Cashiers Hospital received notification from the Joint Commission of Accreditation of Hospitals that it was now officially approved.[416] The following year, ground was broken for a new medical-clinical building at 5th and South to provide space for Drs. Baumrucker, Mangum, and Rodenbeck. In 1981 Mark Heffington of Memphis, Tennessee, joined Baumrucker and Mangum as the hospital's third physician, though located in Cashiers.

Beginning in the eighties, Walter Wattles, a long time summer resident, started the Highlands Country Club Pro Am golf tournament to help raise funds for a Highlands–Cashiers Hospital Endowment. Despite the popular success of this annual event, federal changes in Medicare in 1983, while intended to stem skyrocketing medical costs nationally, served instead to hurt the Highlands–Cashiers Hospital, forcing it to charge patients less than the hospital's costs and eat the difference. Predetermined fees based on national averages made severe cases too expensive to treat, and the hospital lost $7,000 in the first two months of the new regulations. In 1985 it lost $42,000 on 170 Medicare patients who were admitted under one or more of 467 different diagnoses, amounting to what Jack Calloway characterized as "cookbook medicine." Fifteen years later, in the year 2000, uncollectible Medicare and Medicade charges reached $5 million.

Moreover, by 1992 the hospital was once again bursting at the seams. But this time expansion wouldn't suffice. A new home had to be located at Shortoff, about halfway between Highlands and Cashiers. A fund-raising blitz spearheaded by Robert "Bob" Rhodes raised an astonishing $6.5 million from local and summer residents of both towns to build the new facility. For his role in making the new home possible, Bob was awarded the Robert DuPree Award for outstanding citizenship.

The physical move took place during the initial stages of the great Blizzard of '93, which dumped almost a foot and a half of snow along the five miles that the move had to cover. Fortunately the relocation was hurried along on Friday, March 12th, a day earlier than originally planned, so that the hospital escaped by the skin of its teeth the four- to six-foot drifts that totally incapacitated the town the next morning.

Jack Eckerd, Highlands resident and founder of the national drugstore chain that bears his name, had contributed a half million dollars to the original fund drive to build the new hospital, and no sooner was the hospital finished than Jack launched another half-million-dollar challenge for a matching grant that led to the creation of the Fedelia Eckerd Nursing Center, named in honor of his mother, as an outright gift to the two towns.

In 1993, on a wooded forty-acre site next door to the hospital, Highlands first and only residential retirement community, Chestnut Hill, opened with the sale of its first ten units.[417] Today it comprises thirty-five cottages and a lodge of twenty apartments for independent living, with sixteen suites proposed for assisted living.

An organization seeking to parallel the hospital's role in promoting good health was the Carpe Diem Farms, founded off the Buck Creek Road in 1997 by Blair Foundation and intended eventually to become an international wellness center. Led by Sue Blair, it has served as a non-profit enrichment center surrounded by national forests and offering a variety of projects for skilled and unskilled volunteers of all ages, including construction, renovation, remodeling of its initial buildings and the planting and tending of its organic garden. It offers courses and programs in pastoral and private counseling, Feng Shui, Tai Chi, massage and muscle therapy and fitness training, and reflexology. Its focus, in other words, has been on alternative medicine.

By the beginning of the twenty-first century, the hospital had far exceeded its wildest dreams. What had begun almost fifty years earlier as an eight-bed infirmary staffed by Dr. Matthews had grown into a twenty-four bed medical center and eighty-bed long-term nursing home staffed by nine family physicians and nineteen specialists.

Sixteen of these doctors were associated full time with the hospital, including John Baumrucker, Mark Heffington, Patti and David Wheeler, Becky Brooks, and David Dennison as general practitioners and specialists Dan Richardson, Herbert Plauché, Carter Davis, Leila Martin, Robert Buchanan, David deHoll, Jr., Martin Teem, Jamie Recasens, Morris Minton, and Miles Hyman. Additional services comprised gynecological surgery; hand, foot, and ankle surgery; physical and respiratory therapy, therapeutic message; urologic, dermatologic, and cardiological care; mobile bone density scanning, stereotactic breast biopsy, diagnostic imaging, health and fitness programs, nutrition counseling, and lifeline home monitoring.

In 2000, faced with an exponential increase in patients and insufficient space, administrator Jim Graham announced a $5 million expansion of the hospital's surgical center, emergency facilities, radiology suite, pharmacy, and physical therapy department. A challenge campaign was initiated to raise $22 million in capital and endowment funds in hopes that this would guarantee the future of a community service that had experienced every high and low conceivable in its valiant half-century struggle to survive.

Highlands–Cashiers Hospital. Photo by the author, 2001.

16. Comfortable Rooms, Horses Well Cared For

Whoe'er has travell'd life's dull round,
Where'er his stages may have been,
May sigh to think he still has found
His warmest welcome at an inn.
—William Shenstone, 1714–63
Written on a window of an Inn at Henley

Central House, built in 1878. Photo probably by John Bundy, 1883, courtesy of Hudson Library archives. Halleck built his picket fence in front in 1884. [418]

In 1898 if you weren't deterred from traveling to Highlands by the steep muddy roads up the mountain, you were rewarded at the end of your tortuous journey by a summer's rest at your choice of five of the finest inns in the South.[419] Although the first boarding house in Highlands was established as early as 1876 by George Jacobs on his six-acre lot west of the Salt Rock, meaning where 1st and Main intersected, he sold it in May of the next year to John Ingram, so his inn was not one of the five favorite houses that end-of-the-century guests chose for their annual return: Central, Highlands, Satulah, Islington, or Davis.

Central House and Old Edwards Inn

Central House, now known jointly as Central House Restaurant and Old Edwards Inn, was Highlands' earliest boarding house, built on property purchased by John Norton in July of 1878. Norton paid $60 for four lots on the southeast corner of 4th and Main and the construction of a two-and-a-half story frame structure with a gabled roof and a two-tier front porch. In 1880 he exchanged Central House with Joseph Halleck for Halleck's just-completed Highlands House. Halleck ran Central House for eight years before selling it to James Rideout, who immediately traded it to David Norton of Norton Community for Satulah House, an inn that Rideout had just built on Norton's 5th Street property.[420]

David Norton family on Central House porch, 1900. Courtesy of Gene Potts.

For the next seventeen years, from May through October, David Norton and his wife Martha "Mattie" Adams, better known as Uncle Dave and Aunt Mat, managed Central House.[421] Beginning in 1890 they also ran a winter boarding house in Anderson, South Carolina. Their inn in Highlands became widely known for its hospitality, for the Nortons entertained generously and lavishly all who spent time in their home. Rev. Archibald Deal attributed to Aunt Mat a joyous spirit that warmed one like a sunbeam. Her beauty, he claimed, could tame the wildest beast. He used to thrill to the story of her experience with a panther that sprang upon her while she was riding horseback across Cowee Mountain. The ferocious beast became entangled in the shawl he tore from her shoulders, allowing the terrified horse and Mattie to speed to safety while he struggled to free himself. It was a classic case of beauty ensnaring the beast. Uncle Dave and Aunt Mattie were as good and honest as they were loyal to their friends, and their charity, usually given in secret, was known to be boundless.

Formerly a lieutenant in the Confederate army and then a teacher in the public schools, Dave Norton served as postmaster in Highlands during Grover Cleaveland's administration. In 1893 he established the post office in the Granite Store, also known as the Stone Store House, later the Rock Store.

In 1905 Norton sold both the Central House and his Stone Store House to Uncle Billy Potts and moved into Charles Boynton's home, known later as Phelps house, today's Main Street Inn. According to his descendant Isabel Chambers, he claimed to prefer the quiet outskirts out there at Main and 3rd to the bustle of town.

Uncle Billy Potts' wife Martha "Mattie" Ammons took in many boarders at Central House. Her son Shine remembered that there were eleven bedrooms and no plumbing or electricity. Water for the kitchen and the single tub on the second floor came from a half-mile pipe that ran down along 4th street from Lamb's Spring. Heat depended on wood stoves; kerosene lamps provided lighting. A four-hole outhouse, two for each sex, was located some thirty or forty feet to the east of the inn's back corner, and another small building housed the laundry and firewood. Cut from the lake, ice for the summer season was stored in the building behind.[422]

As a businessman, who ran a livery stable, but also a Baptist minister who traveled a great deal, Uncle Billy left the management of Central House up to Mattie. She supervised the help, which included emptying and cleaning the pitchers, bowls, and chamber pots provided for each room.

In 1911 Uncle Billy sold his Stone Store to Porter Pierson and in 1913, just before he took over as pastor of the Baptist Church, sold Central House to the town's police chief J. Grover "Diamond Joe" Edwards and his wife, Minnie Zoellner, daughter of Professor Louis Zoellner.[423] Minnie ran Central House for the next three dozen years. According to Pearl Potts, Minnie's job, working with her two sisters at Hall House, had prepared her to manage Central House according to certain routines that she trained her own help to follow. She also worked in the kitchen, helping her principal cook, Dolly McCall, prepare scrumptious meals of chicken, beef, or lamb and garden-fresh vegetables, including her own delicious specialties: turkey soup and snow pudding, a rich chocolate base generously topped with whipped cream. She was famous for her "big biscuits."

Minnie managed not only her help but the guests too when they struck her as unruly. One night the guests behaved unreasonably, causing the help considerable consternation, but by morning they acted like a whole new set of guests. When asked what she had done or said to them during the night, Minnie replied, "I made them over," meaning she'd decided not to put up with their shenanigans, and she meant it.

In 1920 Porter Pierson sold what had then become known as the Rock Store to his brother-in-law W. S. Davis of Hampton, Georgia. Having already managed it for the previous five years as a grocery store, Davis continued it as such for the next dozen or so.[424] When Grover Edwards died in 1925, Minnie hired Will Cleaveland, who at the time was building his own home on Foreman Road (today's Jim Sweeny house), to build a two-story addition to Central House and raise two dormers in the roof of the main building.[425] Four years had hardly passed before she married Grover's uncle Will Edwards on his return from twenty-five years living in Wyoming. Minnie's son Louis claimed this changed his life: "My mother married my father's uncle in '29 which made me my cousin and my mother my aunt."

In 1934 Will and Minnie hired Wilton Cobb, local builder and owner of the hardware store across the street, to construct today's Hotel Edwards. Raised on the site of the old Rock Store, it kept the store as its foundation and lobby.[426] The new three-story brick and rock hotel was designed by architect Linton H. Young, who as a child had lived only three blocks away at 5th and Spruce. A beautiful paradigm of the classical, traditional style, the hotel opened in 1935, the same year that Rev. Billy Potts passed away.

Minnie ran Hotel Edwards as well as Central House, and one of her best and most loyal helpers was Bernice Zachary Hedden. Bernice said that when she went to work at age fourteen, she helped feed 100 to 125 people every meal. Work began at 7:00 in the morning and ran until 9:00 or 10:00 at night, seven days a week. She lived in a room over the kitchen and made a dollar a day. If she worked especially hard, she got a secret bonus with her monthly pay.

There was no division of labor. Each day entailed setting up the dining room for meals, washing and drying dishes, making the beds and putting out fresh towels in the guest rooms, doing the laundry in the afternoon and separating the wash cloths, towels, pillow cases, and sheets to hang on the line, same for the table linens and napkins, and—when they were dry—ironing, stacking, and putting them away, each according to its own special place.

By 1950, the year of the Korean War, Minnie's health and eyesight were failing, so the Edwards leased the inn to Bob DuPree and Steve Potts. Dick and Marjorie Rawls managed it during the early sixties, but eventually Minnie's son Louis Edwards and his wife Elizabeth realized that neither they nor their lessees were really interested in running a hotel. They tried to remodel the space for shops, which proved, to the contrary, even less satisfactory. The inn closed in the mid sixties and remained so for eighteen years, until Rip and Pat Benton, who ran Blanche's Courtyard, an inn and restaurant at St. Simon's Island, Georgia, bought and remodeled it in 1982.[427] It's been said that the Bentons restored Central House and Edwards Inn to what they should have been originally. In 2001 Art and Andrea Williams of Atlanta bought the restaurant and inn, intending to continue the tradition of the past 123 years.

Central House and Hotel Edwards, built in 1935. Drawing by Walter Hunt, 1982.

Highlands House [Highlands Inn]

The first hotel built in Highlands was Highlands House. A large three-story frame structure with a gable roof and two-story front porch, it was constructed on the north side of 4th and Main, beginning in April of 1880. Its builder, Major Joseph Halleck, was brother to Union General and jurist Henry Halleck. When completed in September, Halleck exchanged it for John Norton's Central House across the street.[428] In 1882 James Rideout bought the vacant corner lot and put up his store, Rideout & Co. The next year Joseph Fritts bought Highlands House, which had already become a Mecca for summer lodgers. During the first year of his tenure as its owner, the number of guests at Highlands House exceeded the population of Highlands by a third. It jumped from 181 the previous year to 409, as compared with the town's population of only 300.[429] For Fritts, owning the hotel was not without its moments of excitement of historic proportions. In the spring of 1885 the now-famous Moccasin War, as discussed previously in Chapter Ten, stormed the ramparts of his Highlands House.

Whether because of that war or not, Fritts put his hotel on the market the next year and headed for Texas. Eliza Wheaton bought Highlands House as a wedding gift to the marriage of her niece Mary Chapin to John Jay Smith on July 20, 1886.[430] Even at the time, a wedding gift of such proportions was generous indeed. Frank Sheldon helped John Jay renovate the structure during the following winter. The old apology for a ramshackle kitchen was demolished and a new one installed. They enlarged the dining room with a double window to make it brighter and more cheerful, cased the windows and doors, and papered and painted.

Although retaining the official name Highlands House, the hotel became commonly known as Smith House, which accommodated about thirty guests. Mrs. Mary Davis, who had managed the Stanhope Hill House for boarders during the previous four years, rented Highlands House from the Smiths and ran it until her departure in 1890 to take over Mr. Bascom's Davis House. In 1898 rooms at Smith House rented for $7.00 per person per week, children under thirteen from four to six dollars a week, and transients $2.00 a day.

Highlands House. Photo probably by R. Henry Scadin, 1896, courtesy of Hudson Library archives. Dr. O'Farrell had his drugstore in Rideout's store to left.

Lodgers telling stories of their experiences during the day would occupy the evenings at Highlands House. In 1888, for instance, while Mrs. Davis was still running Highlands House, Miss Charlotte Crowinshield of Salem, Mass., paid a visit. She arrived when Prof. Harbison and Frank Boynton were lodgers, going on expeditions to collect flowers and plants.[431] She even accompanied them on one of their trips to Cashiers Valley where they gathered specimens of *Azalea vaseyi* and killed a rattlesnake. Prof. Harbison dumped the snake in his specimen can and that night announced his find to the guests at Highlands House: "We have some lovely specimens of *vaseyi azalea*." He caused quite a stir when the snake uncoiled from the can. He offered to dissect the head and demonstrated how its fangs worked. When boarders objected to Mrs. Davis' offer to cook the snake for breakfast, the men cooked it over a fire in the woods.

In addition to storytelling, playing cribbage passed the time, with guests at six or seven tables changing partners after each game and a cribbage board and pack of cards given to the ultimate winner. Before retiring, the guests would sing their favorite songs.

The Smiths sold their inn in 1925 when Frank Cook of Greenwood, S.C., visited Highlands and, taking a liking to it, returned to show the town to his friend A. J. Davis. All Cook had was a dream but no money with which to back it. Davis, on the other hand, had the wherewithal to buy Smith House and include his friend as co-owner. As incredulous as Cook was, he accepted Davis' offer of management of the inn. Davis' co-owner was F. M. Allen, also of Greenwood, S.C.

Cook changed the hotel's name to Highlands Inn. John Jay Smith was permitted to construct a one-story building with a front porch onto the east wing, which he set up as a store. It was a busy year for commercial construction in Highlands. Central House was undergoing expansion across the street, and the former Davis House, known as Martin House, was having its porches repaired. George Marett was constructing a two-story addition to the store he'd just bought from Bascom. So the corner of 4th and Main resounded in 1925 with the daily din of sawing and hammering as the whole town spruced up in preparation for the summer throng.

For a brief period Grover Edwards' widow, Minnie, managed both the Highlands Inn and Central House. But in 1934 Harvey and Angelyn Trice of Thomasville, Ga., took over management, buying the building in 1938 and giving Frank Cook and his wife Verna half interest and total management.[432] By 1952 Frank and Verna were sole owners of a thriving enterprise.

They sold it in 1969 to a lady with a reputation for serving excellent meals and arranging popular parties and receptions. A Canadian by birth, Miss Helen Major came from Athens and Decatur, Georgia. Herself a former officer in the Canadian Navy, she ran a tight ship for almost fourteen years. One of the specialties of her kitchen was her famous apple crisp dish, which she served daily.

Highlands Inn fronted by a row of rhododendrons. Photo by George Masa, 1929.

In 1983, the year before her death, she sold the inn to Glenn and Shan Arnette of Heathrow, Florida, who established a Cabaret in the wing that once housed Smith's store. An entertainment series that continues to this day, the Cabaret features local talent in the Highlands Inn Theatre Room during the summer season. Dinners during 2000 featured vocalist Carol Criminger and pianist Patty Campbell, professional actress Collin Wilcox-Paxton and actor Rex Reed, and community players Ralph Stevens and David Milford.

The year after Arnette's purchase of Highlands Inn, Wachovia Bank foreclosed on the sale, and Dr. Walter Hood of Atlanta assumed the mortgage.[433] Suddenly, for the first time in its history, the inn lost its attraction to summer lodgers. Over the next three years the building began to deteriorate to the extent that there was speculation it would have to be torn down. Once again in the throes of bankruptcy and threatened with foreclosure, it was only at the last minute in 1989 rescued from the auction block by Rip and Pat Benton, owners of Central House and Old Edwards Inn across the street. They mortgaged the latter to save their former competitor and immediately set about restoring it, just as they had revived Edwards Inn, to its former heyday of popularity and elegant charm.

When Rip and Pat left Highlands, they bequeathed to the town a generous legacy of hard work, graceful hospitality, and old-fashioned appeal. The Chamber of Commerce awarded Pat its cherished Robert DuPree Award for their sacrifices to the community. The year 2000 saw Billy Hawkins and wife Sabrina take the reigns of a 120-year tradition. Billy is the great-grandson of Dr. Alfred Hawkins who originally settled the wilderness south of Horse Cove.[434]

Satulah House, 1899. Photo from R. H. Scadin Collection, UNC-A.

Satulah House

Satulah House, otherwise known as Rideout House or Stuly House, was built in 1886 by James and Margaret Smith Rideout.[435] A 21-room boarding house, it stood about where the Catholic Church stands today and was the continuance of an institution that began in 1883 as the Rideout home at 5th and Chestnut. The success of Satulah House in rivaling Highlands House and Central House for comfort and popularity was due as much to Margaret's lively sense of humor as to her enjoyment of a good time. Both traits she had refined from growing up in a rather large family of brothers and teaching school. It was natural for her to care for and enjoy the summer visitors who came to stay at her boarding house. She became to her guests "Mother Rideout." She entertained with many parties, including dancing in the dining room. One especially memorable celebration at Satulah House was the marriage on August 11, 1898, of Miss Lydia Johnson to Dr. Alexander Anderson of puffed-wheat and puffed-rice fame. After the turn of the century Dr. Anderson would build his own mansion directly across the street from Satulah House.

Much has already been said previously in Chapter Six about James Rideout and the popularity of Satulah House. But by 1950, when the building gave way to Our Lady of the Mountains Catholic Church, it had become an abandoned but not yet haunted Mecca where kids would play. Charlie McDowell remembers how as a kid he played in the old Satulah house, cutting holes in the rotted floor boards to drop down and climb between levels, so the time had certainly come to replace it. It had been a Highlands fixture, especially for summer visitors, for over fifty years.

Islington House, 1897–98. Photo from R. H. Scadin Collection, UNC-A.

Islington House [King's Inn]

In 1883, when Highlands was still a very small community with only 300 residents and 45 houses, Margaretta Ravenel bought the home of Justice of the Peace Monroe Skinner at South and 4th streets, which he had built upon his arrival from Wyoming, N.Y., in 1878.[436] She set about immediately converting it into a large three-story frame hotel with a hip roof, rock interior chimney, and wrap-around first-level and second-story porches on the central front bay.

She named it Islington House, after an old section of Charleston, itself named for an eighteenth-century section of London. Annie Reese Richardson tells the story of two Islington brothers who lived in Highlands, one of whom won the heart of a mail order bride in England; but when the other brother went to pick her up, she married him instead. But this family doesn't appear to bear any relation to the naming of the inn.

In 1886 the Ravenels remodeled and enlarged the inn to more than three times its original size, adding a new kitchen constructed with lumber from Whiteside Cove and bricks from Franklin. They hired Jule Phillips for the renovations and Charles Edwards to paint the house, not the lower rooms ceiled in poplar (because oiling and hand finishing would better show the grain of their wood) but the upper rooms, which he painted in two shades of gray on the second floor and either pale pink or straw yellow on the third, all rooms accented by black walnut doors, mantels, and baseboards. The balusters and stair rails were honed from cherry by the Boynton brothers.

On August 31st of the year that Islington was being renovated and painted, the great Charleston earthquake shook the town of Highlands between nine and ten Tuesday night. Small bells were set to ringing and windows rattled loudly, lasting about one and a half minutes.[437] Houses trembled, and people rushed outside to discover the cause. An aftershock was felt Wednesday morning.

Mr. Ravenel, who was from Charleston, left with fellow Charlestonians, the Reverends W. T. Thompson and C. E. Chichester, to extend what help they could to the 40,000 homeless and bereaved. At the time of the quake in Charleston, which lifted the city and dropped it "as if on the crest of a billow" and sounded a frightful, half-smothered roar, quakes also occurred in Greece and Italy, where Vesuvius erupted twice. Aftershocks during the next week demolished the rest of Charleston and were felt as far away as Columbia, Augusta, Charlotte, Richmond, and Norfolk. They continued in Highlands until the end of October, when Islington House closed for the season.

In 1887 Mrs. L. J. Wiley, who had run a family house for more than ten years in Baltimore, Maryland, and in St. Augustine, Florida, rented Islington House from the Ravenels and managed it for four seasons. Then for the next three years it was called *Dixie House* after its manager Mary H. Dixie of Marblehead, Massachusetts, a unique innkeeper indeed.[438] She was the daughter of a sea captain; in fact, all the male members of her family were seafarers, she herself having spent much time at sea.

Once she came near losing her life aboard her brother's ship when a raging storm tossed the vessel like an eggshell in the troughs and crests of huge waves, and she spent a day and a night bound to the mast to keep from being tossed overboard, almost perishing from exposure and hunger. A large picture of that ship hung on the wall in the inn. Always cheerful and an entertaining conversationalist, having seen so much of the world, Mary was particularly sensitive to the needs of the poor and made many friends in Highlands.

Beginning with the summer of 1894 the inn was leased by Mrs. George Inglesby, wife of a Savannah cotton broker. Mrs. Margaretta Martin managed it from May 1st through October of each year before turning it over to Mrs. James McConnell, sister of Mrs. Robert Eskrigge and Mrs. Blanc Monroe. In 1913 Margaretta Ravenel put the inn up for either rent or sale, and Mrs. Martin left to run Bascom's Davis House, managing it under her own name as Martin House.[439]

King's Inn, originally Islington House, built in 1878, converted in 1883. Photo from King's Inn Cook Book.

Islington House was finally bought in 1925, its new owner R. R. "Bob" King of Anderson, S.C., who christened it King's Inn. He began remodeling it as a family-run inn, expanding the living room to three times its original size, doubling the size of the dining room, kitchen, and pantry, and adding nine new rooms for a total of thirty-nine. His wife furnished the food, calling it the best "eats" in western North Carolina; and the inn, "The Old Homey Place."

By the early forties King's Inn had become the honeymoon center of Highlands, twenty-nine couples having registered in 1939 and thirteen by midsummer 1940. Each bride was given a copy of the famous *King's Inn Cook Book*, compiled by Bob King's wife Mariana with scripture verses selected by Mrs. Pattie Morris Cole. The epigraph came from Shakespeare's *Pericles*: "To say you're welcome were superfluous." According to Frank James, who worked at the inn as a teenager during the fifties when Gene was cook, the most popular dish at King's Inn was Macaroni Moose served in a mushroom white sauce.

"KING'S INN SPECIAL"
Macaroni Mousse

1 cup macaroni broken in two-inch pieces	1 tablespoon chopped onion
1½ cups scalding milk	1½ cups Kraft American Cheese grated or Nukraft
1 cup soft bread crumbs	3/8 teaspoon salt
¼ cup melted butter	1/8 teaspoon pepper
1 pimiento, chopped	Dash of paprika
1 tablespoon chopped parsley	3 eggs

Cook the macaroni in boiling salted water, blanch in cold water and drain. Pour the scalding milk over the bread crumbs, add the butter, pimento, parsley, onion, grated cheese and seasonings. Then add the well-beaten eggs. Put the macaroni in a thickly buttered loaf pan and pour the milk and cheese mixture over it. Bake about 50 minutes in a slow oven, or until the loaf is firm and will hold its shape when turned out on a platter. Serve with mushroom sauce:

1½ cups milk	1 small can mushrooms
½ cup liquor drained from mushrooms	¼ teaspoon salt
1 tablespoon butter	1/8 teaspoon pepper
4 tablespoons flour	Dash of paprika

Make a sauce of the milk, mushroom liquor, butter, flour and seasonings, and when thick add mushrooms.

There is nothing better for a man, than that he should eat and drink, and that he should make his soul enjoy good in his labour. This also I saw, that it was from the hand of God.

—*Ecclesiastes* 2:24.

Like Tricemont Terrace next door, King's Inn had almost as many rooms—twenty-eight—and guest cottages surrounding the inn, each named for a wildflower in the area. To the six cottages already built, Balsam Cottage was added in 1940. During the fifties and sixties, Bob King's daughter, Betty Trowbridge, and her husband William managed the inn. In 1955 they bought the Bascom–Louise next door, intending it to be King's Inn II, but the plan lasted only two years.[440]

Meanwhile, Bob was busy adding a new dining hall to King's Inn I. Built to seat 150 at small and large tables, its walls were paneled in hemlock half way up to a wine-figured wallpaper in colonial style. The tie-backs and wine-figured ruffles of the white curtains blended with the wallpaper, and golden chandeliers featured five tiny lamps and golden shades. Paintings of large, exotic birds hung on the walls, and a hemlock-paneled half partition crowned with potted plants hid the kitchen doors. A Hammond Organ and record player provided dinner music. In addition to the beautiful new dining hall, King built the town's first swimming pool, heated, with a filter system and underwater lighting, while Tearley Picklesimer was busy just north of the King's Inn entrance establishing his Tastee-Freez and Sandwich Shop.

R. R. "Bob" King, Sr. Photo from King's Inn Cook Book.

In 1964, after Bob King's death, Betty bought King's Inn from the family. She sold it in 1967 to Gary Phelan and her husband John of Fort Lauderdale, Florida, who turned the food operations over to H. W. "Smitty" Smith. It was John Phelan's poem, "In These Hills," that appealed to so many devotees of Highlands and was his legacy to the community at the end of his six-year stay.[441] His tribute read as follows:

> *I sought seclusion in these hills,*
> *Away from the city's grinding mills,*
> *I awaken every silent morn*

With a great new feeling of being reborn.
Innocent naught as a new born child
But with exciting feelings here in the wild.
I love our mountains and their crests
And know that God has here done his best.
The lonely eagle soars serenely through
These hills and valleys all kissed with dew.
Old Fodderstack rises majestically above
Little Horse Cove which I fondly love.
This valley is our church
And Fodderstack our steeple
I love it here with these mountain people.

I ask my Lord and pray that I
Could stay in this valley beneath the sky.
To see the trees and hear each sound
The colors, the smells that here abound.
I love each mountain, I love each hill
The precious sound of each bird's trill.
I love this valley, I love each tree
And the constant humming of every bee;
If all could see this work of art
And know that someday he could become a part,
To every eye would bring a tear
For God has created his Masterpiece here.

During the early seventies Ken and Sarah Dunning of Miami, Florida, owned King's Inn.[442] When Hub Laws bought it in 1974, Nick Moschouris from Miami contributed his cooking skills as its new chef. Its last owner beginning in 1981 was a group of investors, who hired Claude and Judy Anderson of Maitland, Florida, to manage its daily affairs. During the Andersons' tenure the variety of guests ranged from politicians, both in and out of office, film stars associated with the production of *Foxfire* in Highlands, and prominent men of business, even an Arab sultan whose entourage monopolized nearly the entire inn.

Many seasonal residents returned annually to what they had come to regard as their second home, renewing long-standing friendships they had formed over the years, such that King's Inn was family to them. With enough beds to accommodate 150 people, each of the thirty-four old rooms—twenty-eight in the inn itself—had charm and character, every one different, unlike modern inns where all rooms are uniform. And the guests would sit in the front lobby before the log fireplace and talk of old times or lose themselves watching football in the TV room.

All this came to an abrupt and sad end when on February 20, 1994, twelve years after the town had lost Lee's Inn to fire, King's Inn too burst into flames just after midnight, and all that remained for town residents to see Sunday morning were two chimneys standing sentinel over the smoking rubble of a 116-year-old classic landmark. Strong winds kept seventy-five firefighters from Highlands and five neighboring communities battling the blaze for five hours, but they were unable to save the ill-fated inn and Chestnut Cottage, that stood too close by.[443] Faulty wiring was ruled out as a cause since the inn had no electric service during the winter. The losses of King's Inn and Lee's Inn were for the town of Highlands irretrievable and irreplaceable.

King's Inn fire, 1994. Photo by Tammy Lowe.

Davis House [Lee's Inn]

The Davis House was not the earliest of the five inns, but it was one of the most elegant. In 1889 H. M. Bascom hired architect and builder Frank Sheldon to design and construct a magnificent three-and-a-half story frame hotel on the 4th Street knoll behind the Presbyterian Church.[444] This was the knoll that once held the small body of Fremont White, the first person to die in Highlands, before he was moved to Mount Hope Cemetery.

Architect Sheldon, who had come to Highlands from Minnesota in 1884, lived in the home he had built for himself at the crest of Hickory Street hill.[445] For Davis House he designed and built a stately white frame mansion, surrounded on two levels by wide verandas, a rock interior chimney, and a gable roof. Bascom intended that the inn be named for Mary Davis, adopted mother of his recent bride, Florence Coffin Bascom. The stately structure was completed in 1890 when the third story was added and a 70-foot water tower erected in the yard.

Davis House, 1897–98. Photo from R. H. Scadin Collection, UNC-A.

Mrs. Davis, having already managed Hill House and Highlands House, took on Davis House in a manner so expertly that it soon enjoyed the distinction of being one of only three inns in the U.S. that rated three stars in the Baedeker guide. It boasted of thirty-five rooms and a 250-seat dining room. When Margaretta Ravenel put Islington House up for sale next door in 1913, Margaretta Martin shifted her managerial duties from there to Davis House. Ten years later she bought it, giving it her own name, *The Martin*.[446] Reselling it in 1930 to H. M. Bascom's daughter, Louise Bascom Barratt, she nevertheless continued to uphold its reputation as manager until the Trices, who also ran the Highlands Inn, took over in 1936, and for the next fourteen years it was widely known as *Tricemont Terrace*.

The untimely death of Louise Barratt left her husband, New York scenic designer and theatrical producer Watson Barratt, in charge of her family's former Davis House, now Tricemont Terrace. Utterly destitute, he retired from the glamour of New York and returned to the rustic life of Highlands to assume management of the inn, even as the Trices were retiring from their dual management of it and Highlands Inn. In 1951 Barratt renamed the inn *Bascom–Louise* in honor of his dearly departed wife and her esteemed father.[447]

The Bascom–Louise, 1951–55. Photo courtesy of Gene Potts via Doris Potts.

Barratt ran the Bascom–Louise in high style for five summer seasons before returning to the Broadway stage for the remainder of his life. At that time, 1955, Betty Trowbridge, who ran King's Inn next door, hired Dick and Jean Lee, managers of Hotel Wyoming in Orlando, Florida, who two years later became owners of the very popular *Lee's Inn*.[448] Within five years it had become so much in demand that the Lees built seven four-room cottages to accommodate the overflow. In 1969, after his divorce from Jean, Dick became sole owner and spent some $40,000 sprucing up the main building and its cottages and installing a swimming pool.

No sooner did the future look bright—for the inn was attracting 7,500 lodgers a season—than tragedy struck during the off-season in 1982. At 2:45 in the afternoon of December 8th, John Cleaveland spotted flames in the windows facing Church Street, and within the hour a spectacular blaze, sparked by a faulty fuse, had consumed one of the town's finest treasures.

Lined up like mourners at a funeral, the townspeople watched in anguished shock from safe distances along 4th Street as Rex Miller hosed down the roof of Dunfergot's, frantic to save his adjacent convenience store from the scorching heat. Forty firemen scrambled to keep the fire from spreading to a nearby propane tank and to the gas pumps at Dunfergot's, but even when extinguished, its coals and embers glowed a pulsating red and yellow throughout the night. When dawn broke, nothing remained but seven cottages circling a pile of smoldering ruins.[449]

Lee's Inn Fire, 1982. Photo by Mark McDowell.

Lee's Inn will never be restored, materials and labor costing what they do in today's market, but in 1998 Ralph Thomas, Gus Lard, Randy Baron, and the Jones brothers—Steve, Scott, and Stacey—from Baton Rouge bought the property and constructed their 35-room Kelsey and Hutchinson Lodge in a worthy attempt at replacement. Sandy Talley was hired to manage Highlands' newest inn.

Hall House

Built in 1888 by Dr. Charles Frost and his wife Meta Norton far back on the lot of their original Main Street Hutchinson home, this second home with its pond transferred after the doctor's death to Meta, who in 1896 married widower Tudor Tucker "T. T." Hall.[450] A veteran of the Civil War, Hall had worked for a cotton brokerage firm in Charleston before hearing about the healing climate of Highlands. He had brought his wife Harriet to High-lands for the sake of her health. Buying the Hutchinson house in 1890 from Dr. Frost, they had lived there for a time, but Harriet's health continued to decline, and she died in 1893, the same year as Dr. Frost. Three years passed before T. T. Hall married Frost's widow, Meta. They set about enlarging the house, and by 1900 had created a true country inn, in the style of a Dutch Colonial manor, which they named *Meadow House* but which their summer guests persisted in calling *Hall House*. The fireplace was set in beautiful Italian marble, and hand-beveled Venetian mirrors hung in the lobby.

Almost wholly self-sufficient, the Halls grazed their own cows which as-sured fresh meat on the table for guests, cut ice from their lake in the winter and stored it even through the summer months in their own ice house, and led their guests on short walks up Sunset Rocks or longer ones as far as Dry Falls, often joined by guests of the other hotels in town. Around 1905 they sold the Hutchinson house to Patrick Farnsworth of Memphis, Tennessee. They converted the pond near their boarding house into a lake and laid out the beginnings of what would eventually become a nine-hole golf course.

Hall House and lake, 1910. Photo from R. H. Scadin Collection, UNC-A.

When T. T. Hall died in 1918 and the main building of the Sanatorium burned to the ground, Meta adopted several of Bug Hill's cubicles, converting them into guest cottages. It was in one of these cabins with open rafters that a boy friend of widow Hattie Cole first experienced a practical joke for which the Halls were famous. One night James Howard and Jack Hall had raided the hen house and distributed several hens and a rooster along the rafters, so that when the friend retired late from playing several hands of bridge and dropped into bed in the dark, it was not long before he heard the shrill, raucous crowing of a rooster announcing the first crack of dawn, and all the hens took flight and landed on his bed.[451]

Meta ran Hall House, entertaining the guests and attending to their every need. She even looked after the help as though they were her own girls. When Effie Miller and her cousin Dena Ramey came to work at Hall House in 1922, Mrs. Hall informed them which boys in town were eligible to date, namely, Frank Crane and Jim Henry. And true to her instincts, within three years a double wedding, just across the Georgia border by the side of the road, had sealed her prediction. Meta also trained Minnie Zoellner, who benefited from her apprenticeship by later managing Central House.

Shortly before Meta's death in 1942, Hall House came under new management. During the summer of 1939 J. B. Lemon and W. C. Young of Miami Beach, Florida, renamed it Highlands Manor, managed by Gordon Otto.[452] It continued to serve as a boarding house for two more decades but in 1961 was torn down. The only evidence of it today is a grassy knoll near the center of Mill Creek Village, which Ron Elliott began building in 1981 near the intersection of 6th and Chestnut. The name "Highlands Manor" was reapplied in that year to the condominium village that exists today on the 5th Street side of the old golf course.

Three of the Halls' children married Highlands residents: Mattie married Charlie Anderson, who owned the variety store on 4th Street hill, Dorothy married Roy "Nick" Potts, co-owner of Potts Brothers grocery on Main Street, and Tudor N. married Margaret Gilbert, daughter of the town's only dentist. Many descendants of these families remain in Highlands today.

Pierson Inn

In 1879 Joseph Halleck bought forty acres south of South Street from the Kelseys for fifty dollars and built his home at the corner of 4th and South. Five years later he sold his home to McD. and Allie Adams and moved his family into the home he'd bought from Charles and Laura Allen, farther up Satulah. Dr. and Mrs. Theodore Lamb would build their home, *Chestnut Lodge*, on the lower part of Halleck's land after he moved his family to Rock Creek near Blue Ridge, Georgia, in 1891. Somewhat later, in 1899, the Adams family sold Halleck's first home on South Street to Jeremiah Pierson, husband of their daughter Emma, who tore it down and built the three-story 24-room Pierson Inn.[453] Jeremiah and Emma added two annex buildings, Piermont and Lakemont, for extra rooms. Piermont was also known as Hemlock Cottage, while Lakemont was so named because it overlooked the lake, around which the Piersons constructed golf links, designed by George Inglesby. The golf links are occupied today by Highlands School.

Pierson Inn, 1889–1993. Photo taken 1949–50, courtesy of Julie Weaver.

Hemlock Inn, 1950. Photo courtesy of Julie Weaver.

From its beginning in 1899 Jeremiah and Emma operated the inn as a summer lodge. Their daughter Lake, who married the town's mayor W. S. Davis in 1915, ran it until 1935, when Roberta Morton of Athens, Ga., took over, followed in 1943 by her daughter Mrs. Jack Sollenberger. Hugh and

Esteese Shearouse tried to run it in 1949–50, but a polio outbreak the following year turned away lodgers and left them insolvent. Reverting to Jeremiah Pierson's granddaughter Lucille Pierson Reese and her husband Joe, it was brought back into the family in 1954. Lucille's cousin Kendall Pierson rented the rooms to Community Theatre players until it closed down in 1958.

In 1993 the main building was in such a state of deterioration that it had to be demolished. A logging skidder knocked out its front posts and pushed it down from the rear. The property sold the following year to Julie Weaver of Monroe, Georgia. All that remains of the inn today are the two cottages: Piermont on South Street and Lakemont, which serves as a beauty shop, Mountain Magic Salon, on the road up Satulah. Julie is currently converting Piedmont into a five-room bed and breakfast.

Other Inns and Guest Houses

The Norton, Crisp, Potts, Paxton, Tate, Phelps house at the beginning of Oak Ridge, meaning the northwest corner of 3rd and Main, was built in 1881 by Capt. Charles A. Boynton for use as his residence. In 1905 Dave and Mat Norton made it their home when they left Central House. When Phoebe Rogers Crisp, accompanied by her brother Josh Rogers and sister Nannie, took over in 1924, she converted it into a boarding house accommodating fifty guests, which is how it would remain for the next forty years. Not only was Phoebe a superb cook, she also knew how to entertain graciously, and all three siblings loved people, so they had no trouble getting folks to stay at their home.

When Phoebe gave it up, it was still a paper mansion, with newspapers covering the walls. Helen Potts borrowed $75.00 and with the help of her mother, Mary Zachary, bought and upgraded the house in 1936, continuing its fine culinary tradition. They leased it to Walter Paxton for a few years during the early fifties until the Phil Tates bought it in 1957. As Tate House, its popularity derived in part from its country ham, red-eye gravy, fried chicken, and hot biscuits.

Evona Phelps in 1964 retained its use as a restaurant, managed by her elder sister, Milida Thurman, whose sumptuous meals became legendary. Her biscuits, which her mother had taught her to make when she was ten, contained just the right amount of flour as adjusted for Highlands' altitude. Although Mrs. Thurman never committed a single recipe to paper, she would taste what she made, and if it needed salt, she put some in. When she got it right, it suited everybody.

This is how the restaurant would remain even after Mrs. Thurman bought it in 1967, including the two years when she sold it to Eduardo's during the mid seventies but bought it back because she couldn't bear the separation. When she retired in 1986, Carol Williams, recently widowed and a weekend houseguest for years, along with her daughter and son-in-law purchased the house on a personal whim, preserving it as a restaurant.

The Boynton, Norton, Crisp, Potts, Paxton, Tate, Phelps house. Photo courtesy of Highlands Historic Inventory, 1981.

By the end of 1997, after over thirty years as a popular restaurant, it reverted to its earlier status as a boarding house or bed and breakfast, known today as Main Street Inn. In the lobby still stand the old clock, churns, and flat irons placed in front of the fire, which hearken back to a by-gone era of Highlands history.

In 1936 Natalie Hammond, daughter of former congressman Nathaniel Hammond from Atlanta and Highlands summer resident for almost thirty years, built the lovely *Apple Tree Cottage* behind today's Methodist Church, which the church bought in 1999 as a buffer for future expansion.[454] Natalie hosted friends that they might rest awhile, breathe the healing mountain air, and listen to her droll stories. She could regale and entertain for hours on end, often mimicking individuals whom everyone knew quite well.

During the few years that she lived, she wove over all who came a lovely spell. She died the year after she built the house, but her sister Laura kept the cottage open until 1969, even constructing a Fairy Pool in her departed sister's loving memory. Laura bought two lots from Susan "Tudie" Rice to the east, which became known as Laura's woods.

In the year that her sister died, Laura wrote this poem about the cottage, which she hung in the hallway for her guests to know its worth:

House Blessing

Bless the wee house on the mountain,
And be it always blest;
And bless the hearth aglow with light,
By which one may find rest;
And bless the door that opens wide
To welcome friends within;
And bless each shining window bright
Through which the sun comes in;
And bless each cozy room of charm,
Keeping one from earthly harm,
And bless the sheltering apple trees
Swaying in the summer breeze;
And bless the spring all sparkling clear,
Singing its song so near;
And may God's peace enfold each wall,
A Heavenly peace on all.

Guests came in June and left in September each year. The guest book read like a Who's Who of summer Highlanders: Henry and Daisy Sloan, Sara Gilder, Mrs. George Marett, S. T. and Stella Marett, Elise Terhune, Mrs. Arthur Bliss, Rebecca Raoul Altstaetter, George and Irene Woodruff, Veazey Rainwater, Edwin Reinke, Rob and Effie Foreman, Edith Eskrigge, Florence Bascom, the Dan Ravenels, Will Edwards, Tom Harbison, Dick and Molly Aeck, Margaret and TudorHall with Sarah, Isabel, and Bud, and Mrs. Clarence Bauknight.

Laura's diary, which itself read like poetry, told how they all took lovely walks in the woods, the sun so bright and warm, the air like wine. The mornings began cold, but the sun warmed them up during the day, and the evenings were cold again. There were bridge and tea parties at the Altstaetters', lunches with Miss Warren in her lovely garden, dinners with Mrs. Ravenel overlooking her glorious view, and rides to Dry Falls. The guests always hated to leave the little village when the days were bright and crisp, the mountains so lovely in all their autumn glory, and the evenings spent by the cozy fireside. It was so easy to drift along day to day among those lovely Blue Hills. One grew to love the peaceful quiet and the lovely beauty all about, as the other world seemed far away.

The Fairview Inn on 4½ Street was originally the home of Irvin Rice, who built it around 1910. When he sold it to Dr. Bennett of Hendersonville, N.C., he moved next door into Dana Hunt's house, which no longer exists, just east on Chestnut. In 1937 Ed and Ellie Pierson Potts bought his original home and for the next twenty years ran it as Fairview Inn. It served not only as a boarding house but also as a popular restaurant. During the seventies their heirs rented it to the Highlands Playhouse as lodging for their performers during the summer seasons.

Today it serves again as a boarding house, 4½ Street Inn, managed by Rick and Helene Siegel, despite reports that in the not-too-distant past Ellie Pierson Potts' ghost still moved furniture and broadcast the scent of her lilac perfume. She claimed as her own the rear room of the second floor over the kitchen. Emma Potts Pell discounts this report of her mother's ghost as dreamed up by a member of the Community Players when they summered in the house. This member noticed empty chairs rocking at odd times on the wrap-around porch and heard unmistakable movement upstairs, phenomena that Emma credits to wind and bats.

Mitchell's Motel, which opened in 1939 between the Dillard and Walhalla roads, was one of Highlands' earliest motels, as described later in Chapter 20. Doc Mitchell's grandson and his wife, Al and Renee Bolt, manage it today, having increased its capacity considerably in 2001 with twelve fully constructed modular units imported from Virginia.

Kalmia Court, also located off the Dillard Road, began under Dr. Jessie and Prioleau Hedden as a motor court in July, 1947, and still takes in lodgers.[455] It was named after *Kalmia latifolia* or mountain laurel, which populated the Highlands plateau with glorious white and pink flowers in May and June. Henry and Edna Whitmire, during their ownership between 1954 and 1980, increased its twelve rooms to fourteen and added six housekeeping cottages. Today, owned by John Lupoli, it is known as Old Creek Lodge.

Colonial Pines Inn on Hickory Street was built by Mack and Annie Pierson in 1937 as a two story home. Winifred Pierson Neely Parker had a beauty shop here. After Mack died, the home passed to George and Jessie Cleaveland in 1957, the year that 4½ Street opened between Chestnut and Hickory. Earl Coal of St. Petersburg, Florida, converted Cleaveland's home in 1962 into a guest house, which he named Colonial Pines. When his daughter Mrs. Fred Parr sold it to John and Florence Lupoli from Miami in 1972, it was known as Parrs Colonial Pines Guest House. Although currently owned by Chris and Donna Alley, it still functions as Colonial Pines Inn, nestled on a hill overlooking the town.

Skyline Lodge was originally the creation of Howard "Swede" Randall, inventor of a round, flat paper clip which he manufactured in Cincinnati and owner of hundreds of acres along Big Creek and Flat Mountain Road and on Billy Cabin Mountain. He intended the building in 1933 to be a hunting lodge and private men's club. Before he could finish it, however, the effects of the Depression led him to take his life. Pinky Falls, located across from the entrance on Flat Mountain Road, was named in honor of his red-haired wife, Louise Belle.

Randall's unfinished project stood abandoned for almost a third of a century until in 1965 English-born Derek Grumbar built upon its foundation walls and opened Skyline Lodge and Restaurant.[456] Retaining the original huge native stone chimneys, the new lodge added redwood paneling, hundreds of batts of insulation, a pebble-paved court, and a swimming pool, in addition to forty units and seating for two hundred. Derek came to Highlands from the Holiday Inn in Jesup, Georgia. The following year Jerome L. Myers, also of Holiday Inn, took over and ran it until 1967 when it burned to the ground. Oren and Marilou McClain had it rebuilt, after which it passed through several owners before Bob and Carrie Nass from Reinhods, Pennsylvania, purchased it in 1993 and renovated it to the status it enjoys today.

The 1980s and early 1990s saw the addition to Highlands of a plethora of new rooms for overnight lodgers. Mountain High Motel, a thirty-six unit project designed by Richard Worley at Oak and 2nd streets, once known as Pine Ridge, was built by Ron Allen in 1983–84. A second and third building containing twenty-two more units would follow. In 1986 Randy Power began converting the Burlap Bag shops at the intersection of 4th and Hickory into a sixteen-unit motel, Chandler Inn. Originally the home of Curt and Mildred Zachary Wilson with Wilson Electric at the rear, some of the cubicles comprising the front office of the inn were originally salvaged from Bug Hill.

Highlands Suite, Ed Spraker's twenty-eight unit inn, was designed, because of the lay of the land with parking underneath, by architects Bill Lindner and David Tichenor. It was completed in 1987 at Main and 2nd, on property intended a century earlier for a Baptist Church that was never built. Walter Reese built here instead, followed by Carl Zoellner, whose house was torn down when Highlands Pharmacy was constructed in 1979. Sabrina Hawkins of Highlands ran both Highlands Suite and Mountain High Motel simultaneously.

Hampton Inn, a fifty-two unit motel, was constructed in 1994 by Phil McNeill, Sr., of Memphis, Tennessee. Located at the Spring Street intersection with the Dillard Road, N.C. 106, it was the first appearance of this national franchise in Highlands. In 1997 Sabrina and Billy Hawkins purchased the inn, which Sabrina then ran while Billy maintained his tree-cutting trade.

Altogether during the eighties and early nineties more than 150 spaces were added for overnight lodgers visiting Highlands. For most of each year these new motels and inns, along with a number of bed and breakfast establishments that aren't even mentioned in this account, provided at the least a bed for the weary traveler arriving for a short stay on the Highlands plateau. About the only season that posted no vacancy was when the breath of autumn spread its russet mantle over the dying leaves of the mountains and flatlanders flocked to see their last full glory. There once was a time long ago, especially in the fall, when no Highlands home barred its door to any stranger in obvious need of a meal and a bed. But those days having passed, the weary wayfarer would still find his warmest welcome in most any season at a Highlands inn.

17. The Beauty and the Grandeur

From the first, people have been attracted to Highlands by the beauty and grandeur of the natural environment.
—Clark Foreman, founder of the Highlands Biological Station

The town of Highlands, situated at 35° 03' 24.6" N. latitude and 83° 11' 32.1" W. longitude and a specific altitude of 3834, is uniquely located at a Southern latitude but Northern altitude. For this reason flora and fauna of the North coexist with flora and fauna of the South to form a unique ecosystem of inestimable value to those interested in scientific research. Today's Highlands Biological Station owes its existence to its unrivaled location on the Highlands plateau.

The Station had two precursors in the town's early days. Thomas Harbison, as an extraordinarily erudite teacher and botanist, founded in 1886 the Highlands Scientific Society for the study of the natural sciences, which met regularly to discuss topics of general scientific interest. In accord with its stated purpose, it sought to educate the masses "to the point of observing intelligently the phenomena of nature as written in the soil, plant life, and rocks, thus making experts of the farmer and the merchant."[457]

A second forerunner of the Station was the Southern Blue Ridge Horticultural Society, which flourished from 1891 to 1895 under the successive leaderships of town physician Henry O'Farrell and millwright Charles Boynton. This Society aimed at promoting the science and art of horticulture, but in its broadest sense: trees, fruit, and flower culture, landscaping and street planting, vegetable gardening, and the industrial arts.[458]

The learned members of the Society read horticultural books and magazines and gave scientific reports to educate not only themselves but also the public. Town officials, for example, might not know, concerning shade trees, what to cut and what to leave as original forest trees. "We cannot have a beautiful town," Prof. Harbison argued, "without an educated public taste."

At one of its earliest meetings, the Horticultural Society discussed James B. Smith's article on "The Ideal Street Tree."[459] Smith dismissed the American Elm as favored by Northern writers but not appropriate for Highlands. He suggested what to consider in choosing the tree best suited to Highlands and then named the tree that met all these requirements.

The requirements included that the tree be easy to transplant, quick to grow but strong against storms, and accustomed to sprouting from the stump rather than sending up shoots from the roots. It should have a tall straight body with branches that don't droop too near the ground. Its canopy should reach a height and breadth which will give shade that is cool but not dense. It should be among the first to open its buds in the spring and the last to drop its leaves in the fall, and it must not carry its leaves through the winter, as Highlands needs sunshine for warmth and to dry up the mud.

It must have beautiful foliage that is free from noisome insects, for who would care to have the streets lined with trees

that are a breeding place for myriads of disgusting, loathsome ca ter-pillars that crawl all over the walks, fences, into the houses, upon our clothing, and suspend themselves from the branc hes by an almost in-visible thread and strike one in the face as he passes by? It is enough to make one wish to consign the trees to the fire and the planter with them, if we must endure this.

The ideal tree for Highlands must grow in all kinds of soils and in a cool moist climate yet be able to withstand the severest droughts. It must not pro-duce wind-borne seeds or give off an offensive odor or sticky gum. It shouldn't produce flowers to tempt passersby to break off the branches, nuts to tempt boys to climb it and shake them on the heads of people below, or prickly or gummy burrs that will litter the ground. But primarily it must be native American, free from either contracting or introducing disease.

Ted, Tom, Jack, and Joe Shaffner attempt to surround the Fodderstack or Bob Padgett tulip poplar. Photo by the author, 1990.

The candidate that fulfilled all these criteria, while attracting the greatest praise for its majestic size and lofty grandeur, was, in Smith's opinion, the

Liriodendron tulipifera, also known as Carolina or yellow poplar, the tulip tree of the mountains.

A prime example of how large the yellow poplar can grow exists today in Horse Cove, where the four-century-old Horse Cove or Fodderstack Poplar, known today as the "Bob Padgett Tulip Poplar," measuring twenty feet in girth and 127 feet tall with a crown spread of almost seventy-six feet, is the third largest of its kind in the U.S.[460] The tree was named after Bob Padgett because he saved it in 1966 when logger Tearley Picklesimer wanted to cut it for wood, offering $1,000.

Some of the horticulturists, floriculturists, and arboriculturists of these two early societies lived to see the incorporation in 1930 of the Highlands Museum and Biological Laboratory. The Museum was created in 1927 at the suggestion of Clark Foreman of Highlands and Atlanta, who served as its founder and first president. In his proposal to add a small room to the Hudson Library to be used as a museum of natural history, he argued, "I do not know of a town that can claim relatively so much intellectual history as that possessed by Highlands. From the first, people have been attracted to it by the beauty and grandeur of the natural environment."[461]

While acknowledging that early Highlands was almost isolated from the rest of civilization and needed to grow and change, Foreman warned that its standards were now in danger of being lowered:

It is with the idea of preserving as much as possible of the old intellectual spirit of Highlands that a few people have manifested an interest in a Highlands museum which will be a depository for what has already been collected and a stimulus for further research into the marvelous natural endowment of this section of the country. It is hoped that such a museum would not only be an educational factor for the people of Highlands, but that it would also attract to the town people of a kind that would appreciate the advantages which it would offer.

As its first exhibit, the Museum bought Will Cleaveland's life-long collection of 2,500 Indian artifacts inherited from his father. The Museum acquired additional items, such as plant and mineral specimens and mounted animals, and through a twist of irony an immense slab of hemlock, cut in 1928 for the new Highlands Estates Country Club, donated by its president Scott Hudson, and displaying 439 rings. This tree was a sapling of three years when Columbus set sail on his fateful voyage to America.

With the Museum established, the need grew for an experimental station, a Laboratory. This was the brainchild of three pioneers: Clark Foreman; Dr. William Coker, professor of botany at the University of North Carolina; and Dr. Edwin Reinke, professor of zoology at Vanderbilt, who became its first director.

Clark Foreman, Founder   Edwin Reinke, 1ˢᵗ Director William Coker, 2ⁿᵈ Director
Photos courtesy of the Highlands Biological Station.

Five acres of land around Lindenwood Lake, once owned by E. E. Ewing, were purchased from Frank Potts on which to construct the new Sam T. Weyman Laboratory, named after an early benefactor of the Station. Will Cleaveland, having built the Museum, was now asked to construct the laboratory as well. Designed by Oscar Stonorov, it stood as one of the best early examples of the International Style in America until the decision in 1958 to alter it with gable roof and asbestos siding. As beautiful as it was, flat roofs usually leak in Highlands, and water had become a problem.

At the dedication of the Laboratory, the name of the lake was changed from Lindenwood to Ravenel, in honor of Prioleau Ravenel's near relative, the distinguished southern botanist, Henry William Ravenel. His fondness for natural history had made him the leading nineteenth-century expert on American fungi.[462] Before the name change, this lake honored the beautiful *Tilia monticola*, or linden, growing naturally in Highlands.

Lindenwood Lake, 1907–08. Postcard by R. Henry Scadin, 1907.

Another Ravenel Lake, a private mill pond at the headwaters of the Cullasaja River on the grounds of today's Cullasaja Club on U.S. 64, had been named after Prioleau Jr., who built the dam that created it for private fishing in 1910. Before that time it bore the name *Osseroga*, which, for all we know, meant "This is the lake" in Cherokee. Translating Cherokee, as author and etymologist T. W. Reynolds has pointed out, can result in as many misunderstandings as clarifications.

"The white man," Reynolds explained, "asks the Indian to tell him what is the name of a place on the other side of some stream, and the Indian replies by giving him the Indian name for 'other side.' As for the name of the stream itself, he says 'That is a river,' or, too annoyed, says, 'Go to Hell,' all of which the white man sometimes faithfully recorded, and thus was born some place names of the Indian."[463]

Among the fifty founders of the combined Highlands Museum and Biological Laboratory were Kelsey's two sons: Harlan Kelsey, national park commissioner and prominent nurseryman of East Boxford, Mass.; and Dr. Harry Kelsey, nationally known odontologist of Baltimore. Also included were Gustavus Memminger, internationally known statesman who had moved to Asheville, and Dr. Alexander Anderson of puffed rice and puffed wheat fame.

Incorporated on July 5, 1930, the new organization published its first scientific document early the following year: a *Checklist of the Ligneous Flora of the Highlands Region* by Prof. Harbison, who knew the trees and shrubs of the area as no one else knew them. It listed 160 varieties at a time when their preservation was becoming as much a concern as their identification.

The mighty American chestnut, for instance, was already becoming a ghost tree, thanks to the grizzly work of a fungus, *Endothia parasitica*, presumably imported into the country on Asiatic chestnut seedlings.[464] Starting in New England and spreading through the Southern Appalachians during the 1920s and 1930s, it would destroy nine million acres of chestnut forest in less than fifty years.

Before the blight, chestnuts were gathered by the bushel in Highlands and sold. They could be baked, boiled, or just eaten when the wind blew them from the trees. Animals relished the nuts as keenly as people. Louis Edwards remembered having to get out early before the wild hogs and running from tree to tree to fill his feed sack.

Each chestnut tree grew hundreds of burrs—some four inches in diameter—and each burr contained three brown chestnuts. The burr would open the end of October or beginning of November. The tree itself, measuring in some stands up to thirteen feet across and 120 feet from forest floor to crown. It provided rot-resistant lumber for making fences, shingles, wall panels, and beautiful furniture. And its acid was ideal for tanning leather.

By 1923 the blight had spread southward to the east slope of the Blue Ridge in North Carolina, and by 1927 it had done much of its awful work so that dominance of the great chestnut tree, once comprising a third of the mountain forests, passed on to the oak and hickory.

Another threat, which evolved during this same period and was also Asiatic in origin, was the Japanese beetle.[465] It landed in New Jersey in 1912 and by 1932 had spread as far as Winston-Salem, Raleigh, and Durham in the piedmont, headed for the mountains. More troublesome than the boll weevil or the Mexican bean beetle, it would eventually announce its presence, just like the Balsam wooly aphid, which twenty-five years hence would itself begin destroying the majestic Fraser firs. In as little as seven years after its invasion of Mount Mitchell in 1957, the aphid would drain 275,000 trees of all life, leaving their skeletons to haunt the desecrated landscape.

A prime example of this magnificent tree is the Champion Fraser fir that Prof. Harbison planted in 1893 next to today's Crosby Center. Reaching ninety feet in height and twelve and a half feet in girth, it stands today as the largest known *Abies fraseri* in the world.[466] The Champion clammy locust (*Robinia viscisa*), reaching thirty-five feet in height, guards the Biological Station.

The new Biological Laboratory under Reinke's and Coker's direction from 1929–36 and 1936–44, respectively, would address many such environmental and ecological concerns of the Southern Appalachians. As its first director Dr. Reinke gave the Lab the nucleus of a decent library, to which his personal library would be added at his death. He was gifted in all three areas of scientific investigation: scientist, researcher, and teacher. His erudition was couched in a tolerant, courteous, kind, unpretentious, intensely sincere, and cooperative character. Under his supervision the Highlands Biological Laboratory and Museum first gained national recognition.

When Dr. Coker headed the Lab, he was quick to establish scholarships, allowing younger students to work alongside senior investigators throughout the summers, with the result that many new discoveries occurred. These included Prof. A. J. Sharp's finding of a new moss in Highlands, which he named *Bartramidula carolinae*; and a graduate student's discovery of a filmy fern, *Trichomanes boschianum*, which botanists in North Carolina had sought for over a century.

With scores of investigators and a steady stream of publications associating themselves with the Laboratory, the Museum might have fallen by the wayside if Dr. H. E. Wheeler hadn't assumed its directorship in 1935. During his four-year tenure, he increased the Museum's acquisitions, enlarged its classes for young people, and stepped up its lecture programs. He rallied so much local interest and support that the Museum outgrew its cramped Library annex.

Prof. Harbison's Fraser fir, the world's largest. Photo by the author, 2001.

An acre was purchased from Julius Berndt bordering Main Street and a new building constructed, mostly by the WPA. Louis Edwards of Highlands, a recent graduate of Clemson College, recruited and supervised the local labor. And Henry Wright, who had studied under Harbison and worked for the U.S. Forest Service, served as landscape architect. The structure, made of native granite, rough-hewn chestnut rafters, and one side of glass, was surrounded by plants native to Highlands.

The project cost almost $22,000 to complete and became known in 1941 as the "new" Highlands Museum, today's Nature Center. Its first director was Thomas Fitz Patrick, professor of architecture at Clemson, who broadened its appeal by introducing Southern handicrafts, local paintings, and benefit plays in the amphitheater by the Highlands Players.

Highlands Museum (Nature Center), built 1941. Note 439-year-old hemlock slab.
Photo courtesy of the Highlands Biological Station.

Over the years, several individuals have been prominently associated with either the Museum or the Laboratory. Ralph Sargent, professor of English at Haverford College and a botanist by avocation, was a Highlands summer resident and author of a history of the Station: *Biology in the Blue Ridge*. Miss "Doc" Thelma Howell, an energetic professor of biology at Wesleyan College in Georgia and an active political force in Highlands local government, published a *Check-List of the Birds of the Highlands Region* listing 119 species. She served the Station devotedly for twenty-seven years from 1945–72 as third director of the Laboratory, the first to be a full-time resident of Highlands.

Ralph M. Sargent   *"Doc" Thelma Howell*

Photo from Biology in the Blue Ridge. *Photo from Highlands Biological Station.*

Elsie Quarterman of Vanderbilt and Catherine Keever co-authored *A Summer Check-List of the Plants of the Highlands Region*, which at the time served as the manual for both amateur and professional botanists in Highlands.

Many other authors of standards in their fields did their investigative work at the Station. Albert Radford was leading author of the extraordinarily comprehensive *Manual of the Vascular Flora of the Carolinas*. Eugene Odum, from the University of Georgia, sought to bridge the gap between science and society through his studies of the basic ecology of birds and mammals of the Highlands region.

Howard Crum and Lewis Anderson produced the basic 2-volume set of *Mosses of Eastern North America*. Nelson Hairston, Sr., published a seminal study of *Community Ecology and Salamander Guilds*. And William Coker and Alma Beers compiled *The Boleti of North Carolina*. These books remain significant contributions to scientific knowledge in general, even as they relate in particular to the Highlands-Cashiers area.

In the 1950s and 1960s, an ecological crisis arose that begged for the Station's help. The richest and rarest flora and fauna along the North Carolina–South Carolina border near Highlands were in danger of being wiped out by Duke Power Company's proposed dams for a nuclear power plant. The Highlands Biological Station was awarded a series of National Science Foundation grants to coordinate a survey of 50,000 acres of biologically rich gorges, which it achieved before their treasures were destroyed.

During the same period and in the same spirit of preservation, Henry Wright, Ralph Sargent, and Miss Martina Wadewitz (later Haggard) began the meticulous task of creating a Botanical Garden behind the Museum. Under the chairmanship of Lindsay Olive, an internationally-known microbiologist and Highlands summer resident, this Garden would become a third part of the Station in addition to the Museum and the Laboratory and one of the finest gardens in the Appalachians featuring native plants.

Henry Wright   *Lindsay Olive*
Photos courtesy of the Highlands Biological Station.

Plants were gathered for the garden by such professional botanists as Dr. Lewis Anderson of Duke University and Drs. William Coker and Al Radford of the University of North Carolina at Chapel Hill, but often their guide was Henry Wright of Highlands, who had no doctorate and lacked the credentials of a professional but loved plants as a hobby.[467] A direct descendant of Barak Wright, he left Highlands to work for the Forest Service but returned home in 1924, eventually replacing Harbison, his former teacher, as an invaluable field man for the Biological Station.

Biologists from colleges in Tennessee, Florida, South Carolina, and Georgia sought out Henry Wright because he could show them where many different types of plants grew in the mountains and valleys around Highlands. Many a time he led a crew of experts to White Oak Bottoms, Walking Fern Cove down Buck Creek, or the backside of Chunky Gal to show them a new genus of moss, creeping phlox, trillium, or fringed gentian, including rare plants like the *Hexastylis ruthii* (Ruth's gingerroot) or a certain kind of grass of Parnassus, *Parnassia grandiflora*, underlain by olivine rock.

Henry knew the Highlands plateau like the back of his hand, but more importantly he possessed a sharp eye for noticing differences in plants. Ralph Sargent, who regarded Henry as one of nature's noblemen, marveled at how he would walk with the professional botanist and spot something that the professional would miss. He discovered, for instance, a new variety of club spur orchid down in Blue Valley, which didn't have the club spur on it and which Lindsey Olive named *Habenaria clavellata* of the variety *wrightii* in his honor.[468]

He also noticed differences that Al Radford missed in his authoritative *Manual of the Vascular Flora of the Carolinas*, such as the difference between *trillium erectum* and *trillium vaseyi*, which Radford lumped together as varieties of the same species. Henry didn't know that *vaseyi* was its name. He just knew that *vaseyi* was different, which is what made him a specialist. Sargent considered him a top field man.

There were times when Henry took a small class of students into the field to show them certain plants, but he learned fairly quickly to be wary of showing them ten or fifteen plants in a small area. They'd act "a little like a bunch of goats in a corn patch," he observed. They'd just pull them up, and when they finished, half the plants would be gone. "And I'd be careful 'bout taking 'um out," Henry said, "and real pretty places I didn't take 'em atall."

Henry claimed that the more flowers he found, the more interested he got. One day he was in his garden and found a new variety of Queen Anne's lace. "It was very pretty," he remarked. "I think I like it better than I did the other." His was a love affair with nature that lasted till the day he died. He once explained his need to investigate as like going to Highlands Inn, seeing somebody different, and knowing he was different. "And if I go someplace and I see a plant or flower and it's a stranger, I find out what it is. They all look different if you just look."

During the middle sixties the public enjoyed attending a wide variety of lectures at the Highlands Museum. The specialists included Malvina Trussell on bog plants, Ralph Sargent on wild flowers, William Justice on flowers, birds, and scenes of Western North Carolina, Lindsay Olive on fungi, James Hardin on poisonous plants of North Carolina, and Richard Bruce on salamanders of the Southern Blue Ridge.

By 1972 the Station had become a world center for salamander study. Since Highlands is one of the most favored regions for rare salamanders in the U.S., it was only natural that Richard Bruce, a herpetologist and professor of Biology at Western Carolina University, whose specialty in amphibians and reptiles focused particularly on salamanders, should become the Station's fourth director from 1972–99.

Under his leadership the Station hosted four international plethodontid salamander conferences. In 1976 it negotiated one of the most important changes in its history. It joined the University of North Carolina system. It agreed to give title of its buildings and facilities to the University in exchange for guaranteed financial support, freeing it partially from the uncertainty of local and regional fund raising.

A separate corporate Biological Foundation was set up to retain local control over endowments and special tracts of land while supporting and advising the Station. The paradoxical result of these changes was home rule in union with the state. The practical effect was that beginning in 1978 summer university-level courses were attracting undergraduates, graduate students, and professionals from across the country and around the world.

From its modest beginnings in a one-room annex to the library seventy-one years ago, the Station has grown today into an internationally recognized research center with a membership of thirty-four southern colleges and universities, all devoted to the study and preservation of the unsurpassed biological resources of the Highlands region. A variety of lectures and programs at the Museum, the flow of publications from work at the Laboratory, and the continual acquisition of native plants at the Garden have served to validate Dr. Reinke's prophecy as its first director: "With its natural wealth of vegetation and animal life the Highlands region will support indefinitely a varied program of research."[469]

To be sure, the Highlands Biological Station has opened in this small mountain town a unique window on the natural world, allowing local citizens and visiting scientists to appreciate and enjoy more fully and profoundly the loveliest of rare environments. Its future lies in the capable hands of its fifth director, Dr. Robert Wyatt of the University of Georgia, who took the reins in July, 1999.

While retaining the Station's emphasis on research, Dr. Wyatt has expanded the Nature Center's relationship with the public. A Native Plant Conference sparked wide-spread interest in the Botanical Garden and the uniqueness of the flora on the Highlands plateau. And in 2001, with the aid of grants from the state and the Highlands Biological Foundation, the Nature Center was winterized.

The overriding intent was to expand the very popular summer programs to accommodate year-round scheduling of classes, exhibits, and demonstrations for local education but also to reach out to the eight counties of Western North Carolina, two in northern South Carolina, and five in north Georgia with educational programs for the citizens and, in particular, the youth of the broader region. Teacher training workshops would further promote vital knowledge of the natural and environmental sciences.

The ultimate goal of such a year-round operation was primarily to impart a strong appreciation and understanding of the unique natural history of the southern Appalachian Mountains to its residents and visitors and to inspire them to protect and preserve their heritage not just for themselves but for future generations as well.

18. Fool's Rock

The very last bush on the edge had stopped him. Had he missed that bush or passed one foot on either side of it, he would have fallen fully 1,000 feet before ever touching a thing.

Rev. G. W. Belk, *Charlotte Observer*

Certainly the most famous tale of near-tragedy in Highlands history is Charlie Wright's incredible heroism at Whiteside Mountain. It occurred on a bright sunny May 14th in 1911 when a group of thirteen young picnickers piled into Will Dillard's surrey for a Sunday outing. The party was made up of Will and Maude Holden Dillard, Charlie and Helen Cabe Wright and her twin Frank Cabe, Gus Baty, Martha Heacock, Eliza Peck, Irene Edwards, Harley McCall, Sam Reese, Barney Wilson, and Gene Potts.

A Whiteside Mountain campground picnic, 1909. Photo courtesy of Tammy Lowe. Front row, L to R: Vinetta Rice, three Gottwals daughters and child, Mat and John Gottwals by the tree. Top left on rock: Harold Rideout and Bessie Anderson, boy unknown. The rest unknown.

Bill Marett's *Courage at Fool's Rock* offers the best and most comprehensive account of what happened that day to Gus Baty, who'd had a bit too much to drink and thought he'd show off and scare the girls by pretending to fall off Fool's Rock, a great tongue of granite that projected into space above Whiteside cliffs.[470] What happened when he actually fell is now Highlands legend.

Whiteside Mountain from the Cove. Photo by George Masa, 1929.

Several months after the event Rev. G. W. Belk, a Charlotte minister who preached during the summers at the Shortoff church in the old Emmons Industrial Schoolhouse, wrote an article for the *Charlotte Daily Observer* that helped Charlie Wright, age thirty-eight, earn the Carnegie gold medal for saving Gus' life.[471] In his plea to the Carnegie Foundation, Rev. Belk described how Gus Baty, age twenty-six, stood on the rock showing off in vain for Irene Edwards, how he tottered and fell off the rock, how he slipped under and shot like an arrow down an almost-vertical cliff. "Oh, Lord, he's killed, he's killed" was the cry that first alerted Charlie.

Charlie ran out on the rock, looked down, and saw Gus hanging over the edge of the precipice some sixty feet below. He was caught on a small rhododendron bush, two inches from the brink of a perpendicular rock eighteen hundred feet high.

When Charlie saw Gus move his hand, he knew for certain he was alive. But he also knew Whiteside mountain. He well knew the peril of trying to rescue Gus, who was hanging by the little bush, one arm and one leg dangling over the brink.

There were no lines or trace chains and no time to retrieve any. Turning to his companion, Will Dillard, he asked, "Can you go with me?" Will nodded, "I'll try."

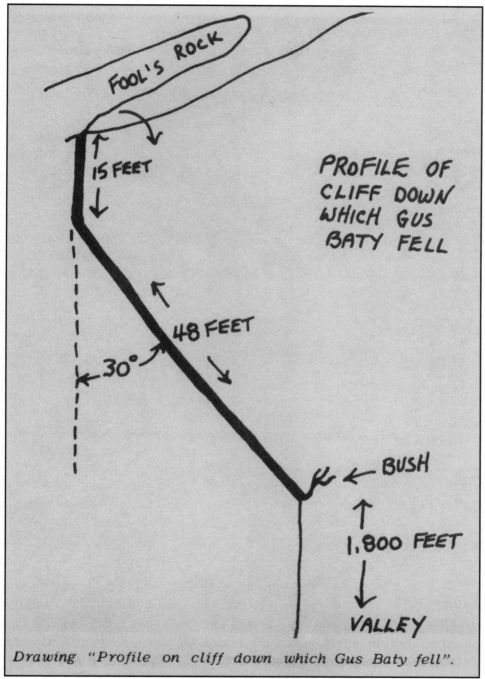

Drawing "Profile on cliff down which Gus Baty fell".

Drawing from Bill Marett's Courage at Fool's Rock

They located a ledge that Charlie remembered where some vegetation was growing northeast of Gus's fall and descended fifteen or twenty feet to the first slope of the cliff. Then crawling slowly, they crept and clung and inched their way down the bare rock, grasping for handholds and niches, at a full 30° grade. There was little vegetation, just patches of slippery moss. The only hand- or footholds were ridges and hollows not over an inch in height or depth.

Soon the rock became so steep that Will, who was following closely, said, "I can't cross that rock, Charlie," and stopped. Charlie too was nearly unnerved but saw some bushes growing from a crevice. Gripping his fingers in the crevice, he pulled himself to a bush just six feet above where Gus had fallen and, looking down, saw him wedged against the rhododendron on the very edge of the precipice.

Gus was lying partly on his left side, his left foot crossed under his knee, his right leg and arm hanging over the cliff. The very last bush on the edge had stopped him, a sharp branch having pierced his head behind his ear. "Had he missed that bush or passed one foot on either side of it," Rev. Belk remarked, "he would have fallen fully 1,000 feet before ever touching a thing."

"Be still, Gus, I'm coming to you. Don't move. It's Charlie."

Whiteside Cliffs: The sheerest rock face east of the Rockies

Charlie flattened himself against the steep rock. Then dangling his feet, he lowered himself inch by inch until he planted his feet on the tiny ledge two feet above the brink. Since there wasn't room to turn around, he reached behind him to pull the stick from the wound in Gus' head. Then he grasped the collar of Gus' coat and pulled him upright. Gus gave a sudden jerk, which frightened Charlie badly, but he kept his hold on Gus and threatened him to keep him quiet.

Gus was badly hurt; one knee was terribly bruised. Charlie said, "Now, Gus, you must not think of your pain; you must help yourself all you can. Be cool and do as I tell you."

Not daring to look down or up, Charlie grasped the trunk of the bush above, and jamming his toes into the cracks of the rock, he drew the wounded man up to where he could maneuver from below. With his shoulder he pushed Gus up the mountain until they reached a point where the rock was so sheer that help was needed.

They were now at the opposite edge of the incline which Will had refused to cross. Gus was in great pain, and it was apparent his strength would not last.

Charlie called grimly to Will for help. "If you can't do it, get Henry [Charlie's brother]. I must have help." Looking on from above, Charlie's wife, Helen, screamed, and Charlie's numbed, bleeding fingers almost lost their hold. Someone muffled Helen, pulling her back from sight.

Fully aware of the peril, Will reached out cautiously. "I'm coming, Charlie."

By now Gus was delirious. They dragged and shoved him, one on each side, up the nearly perpendicular rock until they reached the ledge near the top.

Lines and halters from the surrey were lowered, which they tied around Gus, and he was hoisted to the summit. Once on top, Gus fainted, and it took all of half an hour to revive him. Compared with the two and a half hours it had taken to perform the rescue, however, it was a blessed rest for Charlie and Will, who dropped from exhaustion.

At first the Carnegie Commission in Pittsburgh was hesitant to award the gold medal, since, of the 840 awards—including medals, watches, and cash conferred for all kinds of rescues since the fund's establishment in 1904—only fifteen had been gold, which were solely restricted to cases where every requirement was met. Charlie's gold medal would be the Carnegie Foundation's sixteenth.[472]

The final proof, however, that he deserved the medal was permanently impressed upon the skeptical investigator, who was led to the edge of Whiteside Mountain and down to Fool's Rock, from where he took one look and, "shaking like an aspen leaf," ended his report. Charlie had earned the gold!

Charlie Wright   *Helen Cabe Wright*   *Gus Baty at age 70*
Photos from Bill Marett's Courage at Fool's Rock

Charlie used the accompanying $2,000 cash award in 1914 to buy land on which he and Helen built their home. He could not have otherwise afforded the purchase on his income as a grocer. Helen's Barn and Wright Square are located on this property today. Will Dillard, who received the Silver Medal, spent his $2,000 on a farm near Dillard, Ga.

For one who had risked his own life to save his friend from plunging down a mountainside, Charlie Wright died a death he himself didn't deserve. In 1927, sixteen years after the rescue, while driving his Model T Ford one foggy night on the Lake Toxaway road, Charlie plunged 300 feet to his own death near the dam.[473] He was fifty-four at the time. Gus Baty lived on to carry out his carpenter trade until his death in 1969 at the ripe old age of eighty-two.

19. The Day the Dam Broke

If it rains on St. Switchin's Day (July 15ᵗʰ), it will rain for forty more days.
—An old legend

One of the prime reasons for founding Highlands was its weather. "No Better Climate in the World!" boasted Kelsey's flyer in 1876. Its atmosphere was light, clear, and pure. No fog except when accompanied by clouds. Bright sunlight. Regular showers during the summer. Occasional light snows in winter. The average temperature for the fourteen years from 1883 to 1897 was 50.5°.[474] Indeed, the temperature never climbed above ninety or sank below zero.

The flyer said nothing, of course, about the fall season when the greatest threat facing the earliest settlers was forest fires. For the first dozen or more years during dry periods the settlers had to burn off the ground around their homes to prevent what almost consumed Kelsey's home in the fall of 1875: a raging brush fire. During these burns Elias White reported that "the pungent odor of burning vegetation filled the atmosphere for days at a time. Eyes smarted and throats choked. Some days the sun rose and set a dull ball of fire; on other days it was invisible."[475] Even at night the surrounding mountains gave off a ruddy glow.

Kelsey claimed there were no droughts, but the drought of 1883 would greet newcomers with what the *Blue Ridge Enterprise* called the driest season in over 200 years, presumably by regional or national rather than strictly local standards.[476] In 1886 the *Highlander* was reporting exceptionally severe weather: 19° below zero, the lowest ever.[477] This was also the year of the deep snow. It opened with severe cold in January and closed with a two-foot snowfall in December.

Extreme weather, more than any political agenda, led Highlands in December, 1886, the year of the deep snow, to consider becoming the seat of a new county, comprising the inhabitants of south Jackson and south-east Macon.[478] The chief argument expressed in favor of forming a separate county was that the mountainous areas of Highlands and Cashiers Valley were far removed from their respective county seats, Franklin and Webster, making it extremely inconvenient to reach them when the weather and roads were bad.

The prospect of a new county to serve these two towns was not just a whim, for the citizens of upper Jackson County had already begun such efforts in 1884. Indeed, by 1887 legal notices were announcing in the *Highlander* that application had been made to the state legislature, but all pleas fell on deaf ears. The Legislators, meeting in the piedmont, couldn't imagine the problems faced in the mountains, especially as they related to weather and roads. The reply simply stated that the legislature was opposed to forming more counties.

Snow

If we are to trust today the standards of measurement employed over a century ago, then the "deep snow" of December 3rd–5th, 1886, was the most ever to cover Highlands in a single, continuous fall. As described by Highlands poet Mary Chapin Smith, who married John Jay Smith in the year of the deep snow,

> *The white-winged snow falls down most silently*
> *And softly in large flakes, like many small*
> *White birds that fly to earth; the snowbirds come*
> *With fluttering wings, alighting on the tree,*
> *The little tree that is their resting place,*
> *Their fluffy feathers white like heaps of snow*
> *Upon the limbs; they come in endless flight,*
> *Blown through the air and dropping down to earth,*
> *As swift and silent as the falling snow.*[479]

James Rideout, who was, of course, "famous for statements free of exaggeration," reported that he measured thirty-two inches at several locations on level ground.[480] Prof. Harbison observed that a single, continuous fall of snow covered the ground that winter to a depth of three feet. At variance with both of these estimates was the *Highlander*, which on December 10, 1886, concluded that only "two feet or perhaps nearly 25 inches" of snow fell in that three-day span. This was also the year of the coldest weather, as will be seen shortly, the cold coming at the beginning and the snow arriving at the end.

Not long after the deep snow of 1886, a thirteen-inch snow in 1893 followed by extended temperatures of eight degrees below zero left the Chattooga river frozen for the first time ever. It made delivering the mail up the mountain next to impossible for Mr. Teague, but in Highlands the people adjusted readily. William Munger, for instance, continued hauling logs with hardly a break by building a sled for them.

The deep snow in 1942 proved far more disruptive for Highlands than those of 1886 and 1893.[481] During the first three days of March, according to Gertrude Harbison's reckoning, snow piled up to thirteen inches; one and a half to two feet with no drifts, according to the local newspaper. The crux of the problem was that by 1942 many Highlanders had accustomed themselves to automobiles and electricity, without which they found themselves virtually snowbound and incapacitated.

Snow on Main Street. Photo probably by R. Henry Scadin, 1910, courtesy of Louis Edwards.

During the earlier deep snows all Highlanders had cords of wood customarily laid by for heat, and if they didn't ride horseback, they walked wherever they absolutely needed to go, especially the kids attending school. The snow of 1942 closed school all week long, releasing the students to duel one another, all in fun, with yard-long ice cycles and to ice skate on Lake Sequoyah, which, after a deep snow and extended cold, would often freeze to a depth of up to fifteen inches.

Like the snow of '42, an eleven-inch snow on February 18, 1979, similarly disrupted life in Highlands. But the Blizzard of '93, billed as the "storm of the century," threw the town into real turmoil, dumping sixteen and a half inches onto the landscape overnight Friday, March 12th, probably the record for a single twelve-hour period in Highlands.[482] People awoke Saturday morning to drifts of up to four and six feet. Power was restored to most homes and businesses within five days, but many were without electricity and water for an entire week. The up side was that the town pulled together to help those in real need, and family members reacquainted themselves with one another without the distractions of television, boom boxes, and computers.

With all the freezing and thawing that took place on the Highlands plateau during the winters, if it wasn't the occasional snow drifts covering the fences, fields, and woods, then it was the soft mud that rendered most of the roads, especially the new ones, often impassable. Baxter White described these conditions in 1895 when he quoted a gentleman complaining that he was going back North where the roads remained firm all winter and there was only one mud season when the frost left the ground in the spring.

The deep snow of 1942. Photos courtesy of Allen Reese.

Temperature

Cold wasn't the only extreme that Kelsey neglected to note in his promotional flyer of 1876. Though the temperature would never climb above 100°, it did reach into the nineties occasionally. The highest temperature ever recorded at the Government weather station three miles south of Highlands, which Gertrude Harbison attended for fifty long years, was 98° on July 12,

1930, and again in 1936, when on July 29th it climbed to 97°.[483] This was the year that December was the mildest on record, 61° on Christmas Day.

The 98° peak would remain the record throughout the rest of the twentieth century, the Highlands Biological Station confirming recently that the hottest day between 1950 and 2000 at its altitude was July 29, 1952, when the temperature reached 93°.[484]

The coldest day ever recorded in Highlands was an official 20° below zero F. on January 29, 1966.[485] The previous low had been −19° eighty years earlier on January 11, 1886, the year of the deep snow. The next time the thermometer registered −19° was on January 21, 1895.[486] On February 9, 1895, nineteen days later, a low of −17° was recorded by the Government thermometer on a Friday when the temperature fell thirty-five degrees in a twenty-hour period. At a point west of Highlands it was measured unofficially as low as −21°.

With wind blowing at gale force, Baxter White reported that a man returning to his home one mile from Highlands grew so numb that he sank helplessly into the snow. Fortunate for him, he was near enough home that his cries were heard, and his family rescued him. Not so fortunate, however, were many livestock. Indeed, one man, entering his stable for food, found partridges and owls in his loft so grateful for the shelter that his presence failed to frighten them away.

In 1930 there were three stations monitoring the weather in the Highlands township, according to Barry Hawkins, who ran the station south of Horse Cove.[487] His station, known as Rock-House, stood at an altitude of 3,100. Gertrude Harbison ran the Highlands station, altitude 3,350 and located on the south flank of Satulah. The third station was the newly founded Biological Laboratory, situated at 3,800 within the town itself.

Temperatures tended to vary from station to station depending on the altitude of the locality. For example, the January 29th, 1966, record low of −20° F. was recorded at the Biological Station.[488] Gertrude Harbison, two miles south of Highlands and 250 feet lower, recorded a warmer −14° on the same day. The difference proved to be an exception, for the general rule subtracted about two degrees from Rock-House temperature south of Horse Cove to arrive at the correct Highlands temperature—in other words, one degree decrease for each 300 feet increase in altitude.

For the most part the Highlands plateau has been spared late spring frosts and early fall freezes, just as Silas McDowell predicted in his theory of the thermal belt, but brutal exceptions, such as the frost that killed Highlands' entire fruit crop in May, 1891, have occurred. In the late forties and early fifties Clifford and Earl Dendy planted trees at Dendy Orchard, which their father Joe had started near Goldmine in 1909, only to encounter freezes during the last week of April that caught their young trees in full bloom. In 1949 and 1955 their crops of Rome Beauties, Jonathans, Staymans, McIntoshes, Grimes Goldens, Red Delicious, and Golden Delicious apples suffered total losses. At the other end of the season during good years, harvests were usually safe by October 20, but a subsequent cold snap would freeze the fruit on the trees.

Rainfall

While temperatures varied in the region surrounding Highlands depending on location, the total rainfall at either of the other two stations was usually comparable to that of Highlands in general. Centrally located in a rain belt, second only to the Pacific Northwest in highest annual precipitation, Highlands averages 87.9 inches of rain a year.[489] There have been exceptions to this average, some quite extreme even for Highlands.

In 1979, for instance, 115.6 inches of precipitation fell on the town, 114.5 inches in 1955, 112.5 inches in 1964, and 111 inches in 1915. The year 1916 saw thirty-five inches of rain in the month of July alone, which still stands as the record high for a single month. The total for the year, as recorded by Gertrude's father, Professor Harbison, was 120 inches, the wettest year in Highlands history. That was the year that Asheville suffered its greatest flood on the French Broad River, and the Toxaway Dam, built in 1902 to a height of sixty feet, broke with a roar heard for miles.

On occasion Highlands has suffered devastating downpours in as few as one or two days, which have significantly influenced its annual statistics. On June 15, 1876, a year after the town's founding, heavy rain over a twenty-four hour period filled small streams up to four and a half feet above their usual flow; large streams, higher than known for the previous sixty years. Mills and bridges on the Sugar Fork were totally destroyed.[490]

In the summer of 1928 during one day in mid-August a record eight inches of rain deluged the town.[491] Then came 1940, the year that decimated the record of 1928. On August 13 Miss Gertrude measured over nine inches. And, as if this weren't enough, 11.65 more inches fell from the morning of August 29th to the morning of the 30th.[492]

All told during the month, some twenty-five inches spilled on Highlands, marooning it like an island in the sea. Bridges and culverts washed out completely on every road. Whole trees slid down from the mountainsides to stand in the highways. Falling tree trunks and limbs severed all telephone and telegraph lines.

Pressure built-up in Ravenel Lake at the Biological Laboratory until it eventually broke the earthen dam, sending a wall of water down Mill Creek that washed out the bridge over Highway 64 and parts of the highway itself.

Many of the pillars that held up the Cleaveland Woodwork Plant near the bridge were swept downstream in the maelstrom.

4th Street bridge over Mill Creek after great flood of 1940. Photo courtesy of Tammy Lowe

Residents in the flood's path weren't caught entirely off guard, for some had taken precautions against the dreaded eventuality, despite Henry Baty's assurances that "those dams have been there for a long time. Besides who ever heard of a flood in the highest incorporated town east of the Rockies? No sweat."[493]

Thirteen-year-old Bud Thompson advised his mother that Mr. Baty worked for the Forest Service, so she didn't need to worry, but his mother replied that watching for floods wasn't Henry Baty's job, and when Mr. Baty began turning the gold band on his finger, even Bud knew that there was good cause for concern.

When the general alarm sounded, Shine and Pearl Potts rushed their pigs and cow from their barn to higher ground for safety. But Bud's family was less fortunate: Mama's chickens all drowned. She had the children up plucking them from the water so as not to waste a good meal.

The home of Henry's son, Ronald "Rosie" Baty, sat directly on the bank of Mill Creek, which gave an existential edge to his concern. Reckoning that the dam would go about midnight, he set his alarm clock for 11:30 in the evening, barely escaping before the flood hit. By the time he was scrambling out his window, the water was well nigh waist-high.

What saved Mirror Lake dam from breaking farther downstream was the steel bridge of Mirror Lake Road that caught the timbers barreling downstream, but the bridge itself was judged unsafe for traffic. Although damage was extensive, Highlands, compared with towns in the valleys, suffered far less devastation than Cullowhee, Sylva, and Dillsboro. Franklin fell victim to record flooding as the Cullasaja jumped its banks, cresting at twelve and a half feet. The raging current wiped out all but a two-foot stretch of the Franklin road at the quarry.

Franklin Road washout at quarry below the narrows. Photo courtesy Tammy Lowe.

In a rainforest, such as the Highlands plateau, flooding will always pose potential problems, perhaps less severely than down the mountain but problems nevertheless. When the Mirror Lake dam broke during a flood in August of 1962, the lake, but for a tiny trickle, vanished for a time.[494]

The effects of the great flood of September 28 to 30, 1964, were felt more generally. Rain began falling on a Monday evening and continued in torrents into Wednesday morning. Eight inches fell in the first fifteen hours, 11.87 inches or almost a foot on September 29th alone, the most in any twenty-four hour period of recorded Highlands history.[495]

Small creeks swelled into raging rivers that overflowed their banks, swept over bridges, and inundated streets. Shine Potts' son Jimbo awoke in the middle of the night to a foot and a half of water lapping at his bedside. He and his family were compelled to abandon their home.

The dam at the small lake near Helen Edwards' home to the north of town burst and flooded 5th Street. Between the creek and the road, Caroline Reeve found herself awakened in the night by the police and carted off to dry land.

Except for the deluge of '40, the only comparable flood occurred on October 4, 1898, when water rose two-thirds up the Nikwasi Indian Mound in Franklin, reducing it to a tiny island in a swirling maelstrom.

The great flood of 1898. Iron bridge over Little Tennessee at far left. Nikwasi Indian mound at center. Photo courtesy of Hudson Library archives.

Regardless of how heavy the rain might fall, it has always been counted an integral part of Highlands life—it's the price we pay for our beautiful green. In conjunction with the altitude, the rainfall actually cools the temperatures.

Change Over the Years

There has been some concern in Highlands recently that over the past several years temperatures have grown warmer. Whether attributable to more pavement and fewer trees, as some would have it, or a global change in climate, which environmentalists blame on excessive ozone and air pollution, the facts do appear to confirm slightly higher average temperatures, but not during the summers, as popularly conceived.

At first glance, when considering the records of the past eighty years, the contrary would appear true.[496] For instance, the U.S. Weather Bureau's figures, as recorded by Prof. Thomas Harbison and his daughter Gertrude in Highlands during the forty-year period 1915–55, showed highs in June averaging 74.9°; July, 76.4°; and August, 75.8°.

During a subsequent thirty-eight year period, from 1962 to 2000, the Highlands Biological Station reported average highs in June of 74.5°; July, 77.4°; and August, 76.9°. Ignoring other factors, these figures would appear to confirm the fact that average summer temperatures have increased in July and August by at least a full degree.

But the Biological Station's measurements were taken at a different altitude from the Harbison post. Furthermore, the Station's instruments themselves were moved in 1978 to a higher location. So the Harbison averages can't compare with the Station's. It's even possible that the Station's own pre-1978 data can't compare with its post-1978 data because of the move.

Still, some valid conclusions can be drawn for the twenty-two years from 1979 to 2000. Meteorologist Nathaniel "Pete" Winstead at the Johns Hopkins University Applied Physics Laboratory, aided by former Station director Richard Bruce and current secretary Rebecca Welch, analyzed the data collected since 1979. He concluded that the winters from January through March have warmed significantly by an average of 1.9° F. But this warming trend was offset by cooler springs, April through June, which decreased at an average of 1.5° F.

The surprising result is that the overall annual average temperature of 50.43° for the past twenty-two years has shown no significant change.[497] The warming trend has affected only the winters, as evidenced by less snow and ice than in former years when Mirror Lake and Lake Sequoyah abounded for weeks on end with ice skaters and an occasional Volkswagen.

Furthermore, as it turns out, this conclusion applies to the entire thirty-eight-year period from 1962 to 2000 as well, since the overall annual average temperature for that period amounted to 50.28°, just fifteen hundredths of a degree lower than the twenty-two-year average of 50.43°, which is not enough for the move of the Biological Station's instruments to have made any significant difference.

If it's true, then, that average summer temperatures in Highlands have not increased significantly over the past quarter or half century, it's also true that neither have daily highs. In a revealing letter that Quincy Pierson wrote to S. P. Ravenel, Jr., in 1913, he complained of the hottest July in twenty-six years. During one day, he reported, the Government thermometer registered a record-breaking 87 degrees![498]

How often in modern times has the temperature exceeded this 1913 record? With the exception of the two extremes of 98° and 97° in 1930 and 1936, as noted earlier in this chapter, relatively few days have topped 87°.

In 1952 during June and July daily highs on nine occasions ranged between 88° and 93°. On seven occasions between July and September in 1954 it surpassed 87 by only one or two degrees. During the late 1970s and early 1980s, fourteen days topped out between 88° and 91°. On the other hand, the 1990s saw only three days beat the 1913 record, again by no more than one or two degrees.

All told, highs during the forty years since 1948 have beat the 1913 record only forty-one times, or .2%. None have surpassed the 1952 high of 93° or even approached the earlier two extremes in the high 90s.

So the summers in Highlands, except for a few aberrations, have really not warmed significantly at all. The fact that there are fewer trees in town under which to find shade from the summer heat, however, may help explain the mistaken popular belief that mean temperatures have increased. Hot days are felt more in the open.

Shade trees on Main Street in 1910. Photo courtesy of Hudson Library archives.

Droughts

Droughts in Highlands have been as serious as flooding but also as rare. The early fifties, for instance, were difficult times for Highlanders, who found themselves facing a relentless drought, but it was not the first time Highlands had fallen short of water. As already noted, the great drought of '83, which the *Blue Ridge Enterprise* dubbed the driest in over 200 years, dried up springs and persisted into 1885.[499]

The driest year on record in Highlands was 1925, which saw scarcely fifty-three inches of precipitation. In other climes this would have seemed adequate, but in Highlands as a rainforest it amounted to only sixty percent of its average 87.43 inches annually.

In 1952 Highlands was hit by its real first multi-year drought. Water grew so scarce that wells were sunk on Chestnut Street, Fred Edward's corner at 4th and Main, and Dolly McCall's lot. Drilling to a depth of 500 feet, the town tapped no more than fourteen gallons a minute at the Chestnut Street well, far short of the fifty-gallon minimum they were seeking.

Two years later a 250-foot Pine Street well was extended to 500 feet without success, so it was capped. A pump was installed in the Chestnut Street well, and the well on the Walhalla Road was drilled from 500 to 800 feet before water was found. By 1955 the situation had grown so desperate that water dowser Jerry Smith was invited from Barstow, California, to locate a successful well site and to advise about shooting a second well on the Walhalla Road.[500] The results of his venture were never reported.

The drought of the mid fifties was severe, but dry conditions at the end of the twentieth century were vying to surpass it, as a growing Highlands population found its water table threatened. Wells were being sunk to 1,000 feet to tap what once flowed readily at half that depth or less. The source of these wells being unknown, the concern was that it might be ancient underground water, which, when pumped dry is gone, rather than new water, which, on land that is not solid rock, is replenished.

Hurricane

Highlands' one and only experience with a hurricane came the night of October 4, 1995, when Opal roared up from the Gulf of Mexico.[501] Downgraded to a tropical storm of 75–100 mile-per-hour winds, it ripped through Highlands, leaving widespread damage that resembled a war zone.

It felled hundreds of trees, snapped power lines and poles, and scattered branches and limbs, blocking all major roads into Highlands. It spawned in its path a number of tornados that twisted tree trunks and toppled hardwoods. Sarah Olson, surveying the damage on Holt Knob, quipped, "There sure isn't going to be a shortage of hardwood for fires this winter."

Lightning

One of the perils that often accompanies severe weather, particularly in the South but even more particularly in Highlands, is lightning. Anyone who has grown up in Highlands knows not to linger on Whiteside Mountain at the approach of a thunder cloud.

The most recent fatality due to lightning involved South Carolina visitors to Whiteside in August, 1999, but native Highlanders are no less vulnerable to its indiscriminate strike. As early as 1885 we have the account of Ab McCall, struck by lightning in his own home, his right boot torn off, face blackened, and feet burnt.[502]

A far more tragic bolt struck the former Emmons Industrial School building at Shortoff during a sprinkling rain one Sunday, July 20, 1913. Prince Calloway's daughter Lula, newly married to Walter Turner, was barely inside the building which served at the time as the Shortoff church. She was sitting with Barak Wright's daughter Ellie as it started to rain.

Mel Keener says the preacher warned them they needed to come down off the hill to Roy Phillips' place. Uncle Tom Calloway was also there when lightning hit the church. It killed both girls, burning them badly, and knocked Tom Calloway into the yard, scorching his leg.

Emmons Industrial School/Shortoff Church. Photo courtesy of Ed Talley.

Ellie's brother Henry Wright remembered how Professor Harbison, who was standing nearby, sustained a severe shock and had to be hauled home. Henry said Harbison never seemed the same afterwards, for he was hurt rather badly.

Henry's brother had a new pair of shoes, its being the first day he'd worn them. The bolt sheared the hair off his legs as if he'd shaved them. "It came down to his shoes and just busted them wide open," Henry recalled. "He probably sat with his feet on the drain."

Mel attributes Lula's and Ellie's deaths to the fact that both were wearing hats with pins so that the lightning caught the pins. "Lightning," wrote Edward King when he visited the Highlands plateau in 1873, "is an experience that gives one an enlarged idea of the powers of Heaven."[503] At a distance it appears spectacular, but up close its force is terrifying.

Weather Reporting in Highlands

Until the Highlands Biological Station commenced full time reporting of the weather of Highlands in the summer of 1961, Gertrude Harbison and her father before her were the town's sole source of data for the record. In 1978 the National Weather Board presented Miss Harbison with the highest honor it could bestow on a volunteer observer: the Thomas Jefferson Award.

In an article in the *Asheville Citizen*, entitled, "She Watched the Skies for More Than 50 Years," John Parris praised her "rare and unselfish dedication to public service." [504] She had faithfully continued her father's readings of the daily temperature, which he began as early as 1909 for the National Weather Service. The Biological Station carries the baton today, which includes reporting the precipitation.

Although these individuals and institutions report the weather, none of them make any attempt to predict it. That's left to the meteorological pundits on the radio and television, whose prognostications seldom apply to Highlands. Back when my sons attended school in Highlands, they would get accurate weather reports from Shannon Reese, whose grandfather never failed to correctly predict a snow.

Shannon's grandfather, like his own mother before him, would step outside, check the wind from the south or southeast blowing from Satulah, temperatures at 35° and falling, gray clouds moving in, and if he said it was going to snow, nine times out of ten it snowed, no matter what the U.S. Weather Bureau forecast.

When Shannon Reese left Highlands School, I lost my weather source until I finally identified his grandfather: Wayne Reese. Wayne considers studying the wooly bears, noting the size of the leaves on hickory trees, counting foggy mornings in August, and watching for rings around the moon a "bunch of bull" that the old-timers got started and the younger folks keep up. He admits that during the last thirty-five years the wind source has shifted from the south to the west, but his predictions still hold true. If he says it's time to get in a lot of wood, then there's a ninety percent chance that there's going to be a big snow in Highlands!

Highlands Weather Chart

Average annual temperature: 50.28° F.

Highest temperature: 98° F. on July 12, 1930

Lowest temperature: –20° F. on Jan. 29, 1966

Average annual rainfall: 87.9″

Highest annual rainfall: 120″ in 1916

Lowest annual rainfall: 53.44″ in 1925

Highest rainfall in a single day: 11.87″ on Sept. 29,1964
  [2nd highest: 11.65″ on Aug. 29, 1940]

Deepest continuous snow: 24″ on Dec. 3–5, 1886

Deepest snow in a single day: 16.5″ on March 12–13, 1993

20. Oldies But Goodies

Well, we fared better'n anybody in the whole country. I'll tell you why we did. We grew our meat, our vegetables, our corn and hogs and chickens, and we never went hungry.

—Herman Wilson on the Depression

Note: An illustrated aid to this chapter appears in Appendix 12 (pp. 626–39).

In a little over a hundred years, commercial life in Highlands grew from only five stores in 1884 to 222 businesses in 2000, an increase of just under 5,000 percent.[505] For the first three years of the town's existence Baxter White's combination post office and country store had been the only place to shop. But by 1884 Highlands was just beginning to pride itself on a hotel, five stores, two mills, a church, a school, and a library. Apart from Sumner's Clark's store near the old log Law House on West Main, the four shops belonging to Baxter White, H. M. Bascom, Thoren Walden, and James Rideout clustered mainly around the Main Street block between 3rd and 4th streets.

A few individuals worked out of their homes, such as Sam Kelsey in real estate, Joe McGuire as contractor, and Charles Edwards as house and sign painter. J. M. Abercrombie had a blacksmith shop in a building that Henry Skinner had constructed earlier for his smithy at 4th and Pine. And John Jay Smith sold sashes and blinds on north 4th Street near Mill Creek. In late 1885 W. W. "Tanner" Cobb moved from Franklin to set up Highlands' first tannery the following spring.[506]

By 1890 the editor of the New Haven *Palladium* was calling Highlands the "Gem of the Mountains," a sobriquet that would stay with the town for many years to come. Charlie Coe, editor of the *Star*, claimed in this year that, even with a population of 350 and 26 registered voters, Highlands still had only five stores.[507] With Walden and Clark out of the competition, the two newcomers were William Cleaveland and Henry Skinner. Cleaveland's gabled grocery stood to the west of Bascom's hardware on the 4th Street corner, followed by Bascom's large barn set way back from the street and fronted by Sinle Hood's plank shack, where he lived while he drove for Bascom. A vacant lot separated Hood's shack from Henry Skinner's double store where the ill-fated *Star* and very popular *Mountain Eagle* were both published on the printer at the rear.

The End of the 19th Century: The Rock Store

Very little changed in the commercial face of Main Street between 1884 and the end of the nineteenth century, despite changes affecting the street itself. As noted previously in Chapter Eight, the great dig between Bascom's and Skinner's stores was filled and railings applied to the sidewalks.

Main Street looking west, 1910 and 1999. Above photo probably by R. Henry Scadin, courtesy of Hudson Library archives. Photo below by the author.

Main Street West looking east, 1910, below 1999. Above photo by R. Henry Scadin, courtesy of Hudson Library archives. Photo below by the author.

Expenditures for such downtown projects were not exorbitant by today's standards. Indeed, the town's entire outlay for capital improvements in 1896 amounted to $1,178.36, comparable to Main Street improvements in 2000 costing $2.5 million.

4th Street bridge over Mill Creek looking south. Above photo probably by R. Henry Scadin, 1913–15, courtesy of Gene Potts. Buildings left: Will Cleaveland's planing mill and office and Anderson/Sullivan house. Photo below by the author, 1999.

The year 1897 was a bright one for the town of Highlands, for six tubular street lamps were installed, encouraging evening strolls down Main Street during the summer months. Oil for the lamps was regularly replenished by the town.

The only shop added before the last decade of the twentieth century was Rideout's Granite Store, into which he transferred his dry goods and groceries from Rideout and Company across Main Street in 1889. Hiram Paul bought Skinner's shop in 1897, converting it to dry goods, so that years later it was known as the old Paul store.

The Beginning of the 20th Century: Potts Livery Stable

Two years after the turn of the century William T. "Billy" Potts bought Cleaveland's grocery and the vacant lot next to it, where he built a mammoth 120-foot livery stable.[508] It showed off a distinctive, finished front, while inside, in addition to stock, were plenty of grain, hay, harnesses, and vehicles. Uncle Billy hired Sumner Clark's son—Sumner, Jr., known as Bud—to run his grocery as a general store; and Charlie Wright, to manage his stable. Everett Franks of Franklin bought the old Potts livery on 4th Street hill. This was the last change to affect the face of the town for the next eighteen years.

North side of Main Street West as seen first from east and then from west, 1910. Right photo, R to L after Highlands Inn: H. M. Bascom's hardware, W. B. Cleaveland's grocery, Potts Livery Stable, Sinle Hood's quarters fronting Bascom's barn, Hiram Paul's (originally Henry Skinner's) double store

In 1905 there began instead a general shifting of ownership. Uncle Billy moved his grocery to Rideout's Granite Store, which he ran until Porter Pierson converted it into a real estate office in 1911. During this period, as Shine Potts described the town, there were sixty-seven houses, four churches, and four stores including a meat market and drugstore within the town limits.[509] Hiram Dillard with his brother Zack and three sons—Arthur, Will, and Jim—bought Uncle Billy's stable to complete their livery service from Dillard, Georgia, to Highlands.

It was Hiram's son Will Dillard who would aid Charlie Wright in their famous rescue on Whiteside Mountain. And it was Hiram's son Arthur who would marry Fred Edwards' sister Carrie of Horse Cove and in 1917 establish the Dillard House, still famous down the mountain for its family style meals, Southern cooking, and genuine hospitality. In 1914 Charlie Wright bought Cleaveland's former grocery and managed it for the remainder of the decade.

The Early Twenties: The Beginnings of Change

During the early 1920s downtown Highlands experienced a significant metamorphosis. Old buildings came down, and new buildings went up. In 1920 Charlie Wright sold his general store to Fred Edwards, who tore it down to build a new one. And for the next thirty years the Fred Edwards' store would peddle its complete line of staple and fancy groceries, notions, and dry goods.

As if in anticipating of an upsurge in new construction, the town appointed Will Cleaveland and Quincy Pierson to draft Highlands' first building law.[510] Henry Sloan and W. S. Davis joined an ordinance committee, which posted the requirement for a building permit in 1922, just in time for an application the following year from Quincy Pierson, Will Cleaveland, George Marett, and Alec Edwards to construct Highlands' first bank on the 4th Street Hill. Before 1923 Highlanders had to take their banking to Franklin, Walhalla, or Westminster, S.C.

In 1924 Charlie and Knox Anderson from Westminster, S.C., built a Café on the 4th Street hill; followed the next year by Porter Pierson's and Albertina Staub's real estate office between the bank and the Café. The Café lasted only a short while before Charlie converted it into Highlands Rexall Drugs, which became the gathering place for many residents seeking entertainment. It was here during the early thirties, when Amos and Andy were cruising at their peak of radio fame, that a number of Highlanders formed a late afternoon Amos and Andy Club with Charlie Anderson as their "president." They met daily in his drug store to hoot and guffaw at their favorite comedians. On the second floor above all this revelry, Dr. Elbert Gilbert practiced the more serious profession of dentistry, succeeded in 1936 by Dr. Jessie Moreland.

Next door to the Drug Store, Anderson built his very popular Five and Ten Cent Store in 1925. It was filled with fascinating, affordable items displayed in wooden cubbies on counter tops and spinner racks. It offered everything from hairpins and nail polish to popguns and children's dress-up high heels. The dime store and drug store were connected internally by a doorway that gave free access between the two buildings.

4th Street on the Hill. Photo taken 1938, courtesy of Hudson Library archives.

The Late Twenties: Preparation for Growth

In 1925 Highlands sat poised on the crest of a wave of progress. Total real and personal property value had more than doubled between 1917 and 1925, exceeding $350,000. Indeed, during the final seven months of 1925, within a radius of twelve miles, real estate sales soared to over a million dollars. Spurred on in part by new roads, like the Atlanta–Franklin–Asheville Highway and the just-completed Three-States Road from Walhalla, including Georgia's renewed promise to improve its seven-mile stretch.[511] Many summer homes were built between 1900–25 which enhanced Highlands' reputation as a summer resort. A thirty-year period of real growth was about to begin.

With twenty-two businesses now in place and a population brimming around 500, twice what it had been in 1900 and swelling to 2,500 during the summer, the town let a contract in February, 1925, to Conrad Construction of Florence, S.C., for a municipal water supply system.[512] By a vote of ninety-seven to eleven from among 122 voters, the electorate approved $30,000 in water bonds to be paid off in forty years. The estimate jumped within the year to $45,000. In December, with the water system installed and producing ninety pounds pressure, a referendum to issue electric light and sewer bonds passed 107 to 1, adding another $75,000 to create a gross debt of $120,000.

In May, 1925, work began on clearing the dam site just above Kalakalaski Falls on the Cullasaja River about two miles below town. The intent was to impound the river to form a seventy acre lake, backing up the river as far as Naiad Falls. The following May the lake bed itself was being cleared of huge trees and thick undergrowth.

Kalakalaski and Naiad Falls, below and above today's Lake Sequoyah, 1898. Photos from R. H. Scadin Collection, UNC-A.

Clearing land for Lake Sequoyah, 1925–26. Courtesy Hudson Library archives.

Even as cost estimates rose, personnel problems threatened the project. The superintendent in charge of clearing the land, Mr. Shockley, who had been paid in advance, refused an audit of his accounts and time books, so he was fired and replaced by Roy Phillips.[513] A month later Shockley was reported to be building a house for Phoebe Crisp with the wood he'd scavenged from the lake basin, wood claimed by the town.

In February, 1927, as the water level at the dam reached the desired height, the town determined that the costs of the hydroelectric light system, under contract to Tucker & Laxton, Inc. of Charlotte, were well over estimates.[514] Since additional bonds would have to be sold at a large discount, Warren Booker, the consulting engineer, was requested to consult the board before he placed any more orders. Early on, Highway 28 had had to be relocated around the dam site above the hydroelectric plant.

Lake Sequoyah dam. Photo by George Masa, 1929.

The concrete arch dam itself was only twenty-five feet tall, but the vertical distance from its top to the power plant farther downstream was 220 feet, enough to give the town up to 900 horse power with only one 300-h.p. unit installed until more power might be needed. The power plant rose one and a half stories with a basement acting as a boat house on the river and cost more than $100,000 to construct. Indeed, the dam overran budget, for its builder had not anticipated having to haul sand by truck up the mountain from Seneca, a one-way distance of about forty miles and many, many loads of sand.

The power plant would serve the town admirably for forty productive years. In 1934 Nantahala Power and Light Company would offer to provide supplemental electricity, but the town was feeling self-sufficient enough to reject their proposal for a franchise. Indeed, when Nantahala tried to buy the Highlands Country Club electric light and power system in 1938, the town paid $3,000 to own it itself rather than lose a large number of customers. Only once, in early 1949, did the hydroelectric system verge on failure when the penstock to the power plant collapsed and the flume line had to be replaced.

Apart from these early threats to its existence, the power plant functioned efficiently until it shut down in 1969. By that time Duke Power had already installed lines to Highlands via Cowee Gap, Highlands Falls, and Bear Pen; and the Highlands plant, suffering a temporary mechanical breakdown, had become obsolete.[515] Several attempts to reactivate the plant, which would have generated 900 additional kilowatts of electricity, were made during the eighties and nineties, but they were all deemed cost ineffective and environmentally disruptive.

Initially, the water supply system lasted only a decade before a federal grant and bond election in 1938 financed a $50,000 extension and improvement. Ten years later a dam was built on the Houston Branch of Big Creek to take care of the increased demand. The watershed for this dam consisted of pristine old growth National Forest.

For all the toil, trouble, and expense that the original projects incurred, there was no sign of complaint on April 9, 1927, when the town of Highlands celebrated its first taste of water and electric power.[516] Kerosene lamps on the walls of homes, stores, and churches were replaced as soon as feasible with brand new electric bulbs, and Dolly Harbison fetched water from a faucet instead of toting a pail. Jack Hall was employed initially to operate the power plant. Eventually Frank Neely took over as manager and town electrician. When he died in 1932, Tudor Hall was elected to replace him.

The body of water formed by the dam was officially named "Lake Sequoyah" in 1928, in honor of Sikwâ′ya, "the half-breed Cherokee Indian Chief George Guess."[517] Sarah-Hicks Hines explained why Sequoyah won out over the many poetic and prosaic names submitted as possible candidates. It was chosen because "nothing but an Indian name, expressive more than anything else, of the towering mountains, tumbling torrents, and lonely crags, would be fitting; and because Sequoyah, the Indian, was as outstanding among his tribe as our beautiful lake is outstanding among other lakes."

At the same time that the brand new municipal water system, hydroelectric plant, and sewage system were being installed, businesses were springing up all along Main Street. George Marett bought Bascom's corner store in 1925 to operate as Highlands Hardware and hired Will Cleaveland to fill in the space between his and Fred Edwards' store to serve as a grocery. Cleaveland merely extended the painted siding of the Marett's structure with its built-up square front of porch and glass. In the upstairs above the grocery Agnes Medlock and Pearl Walker opened their popular Highlands Tea Room. Marett ran his hardware store in partnership with Dr. Gilbert. Despite its lasting only five years in the Marett building, it would continue many years at other locations, such as 4th Street on the hill and eventually east Main.

When Cleaveland wasn't improving Marett's store, he was busy constructing a two-story dormered addition to Central House and repairing the porches of Martin House (later Lee's Inn). John Jay Smith was expanding Highlands Inn to the east for his one-story store with a porch.

In 1926 Frank and Roy Potts bought their father's former livery stable from the Dillards and, tearing it down, put up a new brick structure, known for the next thirty years as Potts Brothers, to sell dry goods and groceries.[518]

Frank H. Potts, 1888–1960 *W. Roy "Nick" Potts, 1892–1964*
Photos from Jessie Potts Owens, Family of W. T. and Martha Ammons Potts.

Like Fred Edwards' store next door, Potts Brothers (later site of the Highlander Restaurant) became a popular source of delightful, appetizing foods that their ads claimed would contribute just the right tang to the home or picnic lunch, including a wide variety of fruits and vegetables. Potts Brothers was the second firm in western North Carolina to introduce Bird-seye Frozen Foods when the frozen food industry was still in its infancy. They also pioneered in Highlands the combination of a meat market and grocery. What the Hetzel children—Joyce in particular—remember even today about Potts Grocery was getting themselves weighed on the scales in the meat department and then riding home in the delivery truck.

Marett's double grocery and hardware store, Fred Edwards store, Potts Brothers, Rice's meat market, and Highlands Grille and barber shop on Main Street, 1930. Courtesy of Gene Potts via Doris Potts.

The year after Potts Brothers appeared on Main Street, Jim Hicks and Elinor Cleaveland established their barber shop and restaurant: The Cut In and the Highlands Grille. They were housed in a new one-story frame build-ing that Hicks constructed in 1927 in the open space between Potts Brothers and the old Paul store.[519]

It was here, Mary Paul Rice remembered, that Doyle Speed and Joe Hays ran the grill. They'd get an order for something they didn't know how to cook or couldn't, so they'd walk across the road and ask Mary's mother, Mrs. Paul, to cook it for them, which she did. Mary recalled one time when they brought her mother a dressed turtle, and she didn't know much about turtles herself, but she put it in the pot, and it wiggled the whole time it was cooking. That was the first restaurant Mary could remember. Years later the Highlander Restaurant, Tate's Restaurant, and the Mountaineer would thrive at this prime location on Main.

In 1928 between Potts Brothers and the Hicks building, Irvin Rice built his Meat Market and Grocery, today's Wit's End and Buck's Coffee

Café.[520] His brother Luke ran the butchery in the rear, boasting that his new up-to-date walk-in Frigidaire would insure plenty of good fresh meat for the summer. At the Meat Market, hamburger sold for ten cents a pound, liver cost the same, a round steak was a quarter, white bacon or salt pork, starting at three cents, quickly soared to five cents a pound. Eggs sold for twelve cents a dozen during the summer, but at Christmas you paid a dollar because, although everybody had chickens, they didn't lay as well in the winter.

Luther W. "Luke" Rice, Sr. (1879–1968) and George W. Marett (1873–1962) measuring water flow velocity at proposed town intake ca. 1925. Courtesy of Tammy Lowe.

Telephone service during the early twenties was operated by the Hall family.[521] Tudor and his brother Jack handled maintenance and repairs, frequently traveling the long-distance line from Highlands to Dillard to solder worn or broken connections. The Hall sisters, Dorothy and Caroline, serviced nearly fifty customers as daytime operators where the Holts would have their soda shop at 4th and Main. According to Margaret Hall, it was not considered an imposition to have someone call on the phone and ask Caroline or Dorothy, "Look down Main Street, and see if you see [Jim or Frank or whoever], and tell him I need to see him!"

The year 1929 saw Western Carolina Telephone installing an updated communication system for the whole town of Highlands with open toll lines to Cashiers. Highlanders could now order groceries at Davis' Rock Store merely by dialing 23 or Potts Brothers by calling 11. You dialed 14 to report Highlands news to Mrs. Tom Harbison for her column in the *Franklin Press*.

In the year that Wall Street's crashed, a new store arose at the site of Baxter Wilson's former dry goods and grocery shop just west of today's little alley on Main. Presumably the materials from Wilson's shop were recycled into Will and Minnie Edwards' new home on Wilson Drive, so that Ernest and Flora Brown could build their new clothing store on the Main Street site. For the next two decades Brown's store would carry lingerie, hosiery, sportswear, play clothes, shoes, and groceries until 1950 when it had seen its day and the town council ordered it torn down.

Throughout all the demolition and construction on 4th and Main streets during the twenties, beginning with Fred Edwards' store and ending with Brown's store, residents expressed their emerging concern that the town might be losing its restful charm. In 1922 the ladies of the Highlands Improvement Society dreamed up a project to install benches along Main Street. Once the project was approved, Will Cleaveland constructed six of them fronting the meadow between the Cleaveland house and Dr. Gilbert's home. The meadow itself was well shaded with large maple trees. Although only one "Loafer's Bench" exists today beneath the great maple in front of the Cleaveland house, the six benches of 1922 enjoyed considerable use as the ladies of the Improvement Society had imagined they would. Marshall Reese remembers one of these benches from the onset of World War II, when he was seated on it and first learned that England had declared war on Germany. His friend remarked at the time, "Looks like we'll be crossing the pond again."

In 1974, long after these benches were gone, Ralph deVille commissioned today's Loafer's Bench as a much desired replacement. It combined the architectural talents of Dennis DeWolf and Jeff Cox with the labor of Edgar and James McCall, Mike Thompson, and Jimbud Rogers, including lumber donated by Tudor Hall and cement by John Phelan.[522]

In stark contrast to the building frenzy that would begin during the twenties in Highlands, the community of Turtle Pond, which lay between the Franklin and Dillard roads a scant five miles west of town, remained as placid as its pond. Receiving weekly or biweekly reports from Highlands, the *Franklin Press* pled again and again for some bit of gossip or newsworthy item—anything!—from Turtle Pond, but to no avail. Then as if suddenly provoked, a report flashed in the *Press* under the heading, "Turtle Pond News," stating simply, "It's awfully hard to get anything to write about on Turtle Pond, as nobody ever dies or gets married, but just keeps plodding along in the same old way."[523] This was, and still is, the charm of Turtle Pond.

The Great Depression That Wasn't

If Highlands missed the Great Depression of the early thirties, it was because many residents were already accustomed to surviving hard times. It's not that Highlanders were unaware that a great depression was underway. On the contrary, in an article written for the *Franklin Press* in 1930, Prof. Harbison set out to explain the reasons for the current "hard times," which he called the third periodic depression of his lifetime.[524]

The first occurred during the early 1870s with the shutting down of furnaces, factories, and mines across the country. The second spread worldwide during the late 1880s. Harbison described the current depression as having commenced during the late teens and early twenties with the World War.

The oldsters, he remarked, who argued for thrift, economy, and retrenchment had known it was coming. But the youngsters who hadn't experienced the two earlier depressions "took the bit in their teeth and ran away. Now they are wondering what in the name of Hoover has hit them." At the end of one grand big spree, he summarized, the bills were now to pay.

Ordinarily the party in power was blamed by the ignorant for their hard times, and unscrupulous politicians took advantage of the chance to profit from their ignorance. But Harbison regarded Harrison, Cleaveland, Wilson, and Hoover as no more to blame than they should be for a drought. "To read history and political economy is to learn to work, save, and pay, which is nothing new to us oldsters, but the youngsters have been in for an awakening that they have more to learn than they think they now know."

"Meanwhile," Harbison concluded severely, "the most wicked, unreasonable, and asinine act of the whole tragedy was the crash on Wall Street! It was an insane performance."

To say that the relatively isolated town of Highlands escaped a national tragedy might appear naïve, but old-timers remembered it as no great change in their lives, rather just more of the same bare bones of existence.

"They law, do I remember it," quipped Herman Wilson, who described himself as quite lucky through the Depression. He recalled,

Well, we fared better'n anybody in the whole country. I'll tell you why we did. We grew our meat, our vegetables, our corn and hogs and chickens, and we never went hungry.

Herman Wilson on his banjo. Photo courtesy of Wade Wilson.

But you didn't have no money to buy you no clothes, and you didn't have no money to buy you no shoes, and you just couldn't get ahold of money. It's just something that stopped, that's all. Like it just vanished from the earth. I'd mend the children's shoes, and some of them was growing up back then, and kids, you know, they'd wear out their knees playing marbles, and my wife would put a big patch on there, and she kept them clean, neat and cleaned, and ironed and pressed, but shucks it was tough. I mean there's a lot of people went hungry, thousands of them went hungry. You see there wasn't no soup line in Highlands, and if there was in Franklin, I never did know anything about it.

Herman was acquainted with a lot of people and had a lot of friends, and the state gave him a job improving old dirt side roads, him and Lawrence Hicks, at a dollar and a half a day. "Yes," he admitted, "it's pretty rough, but we had enough to eat" and didn't need "no big fine clothing or anything like that."

Old-timers all over Highlands tell similar stories about the Depression. Cub Rice said he never went hungry, because people helped out, and the Rices had the meat market and a garden. Out on Buck Creek Road, Carl "Bub" Zachary recalled that it was rough, but his family lived on a farm where they grew their own potatoes, corn, beans, hogs, cows, milk, and butter. This meant they had the same fare every day, but they had plenty of what they had and never went hungry. Even after they gave up the farm, they still had gardens, so if a depression were to come years later, they'd still survive it, unlike the new Highlands Bank which fell by the wayside.

For folks who didn't have their own gardens, particularly stores, hotels, and restaurants, the Millers of Scaly Mountain provided essential needs. They made their living by growing cabbage, potatoes, beans, squash, and cucumbers. They had cows for milk and butter and chickens for eggs and meat, as well as hogs. Bessie and Ethel Miller would walk all the way to Highlands to sell these goods to the stores, hotels, and restaurants and even private homes. Albie Picklesimer McCall walked the eight miles from Clear Creek to deliver her choice vegetables and berries for special customers, including Potts Brothers and the Condiment Shop. Both of these ladies lived well into their nineties, Aunt Albie to 103.

Ironically the chestnut blight, which robbed the Highlands plateau of one of its most majestic trees, provided income for local men who cut the dead timber and sold it for "acid wood." With crosscut saws, horses, and mules, they salvaged many thousands of National Forest acres from the late twenties to the late thirties.

The only local people who fared poorly in Highlands during the Depression were those who ran stores dependent on weekend business, dealt in transportation, or managed motels, like Doc Mitchell, who claimed that Mitchell Cottages suffered a hard time. Yet even he acknowledged that the local people were happy with their gardens. "They had cows and pigs and got along just fine," he said. "Joe Reese had a cow. Mrs. Henry had a cow. That was in thirty-four. Had hogs back then too." One of the earliest casualties of the Depression was the auto dealership that Walter Bryson and Claude Smith of Seneca tried to establish in 1925 in Monroe Skinner's old blacksmith shop at 4th and Pine. Bryson–Volrath Chevrolet Company of Highlands lasted three years before going under with the Depression.

Self-sufficiency was the sterling quality that saved Highlands from the despair, bankruptcies, bread lines, and suicides of the early thirties in much the same way that it gave those early pioneers caught in the deep snow of 1886 their advantage over the more recent victims of power outages during the great blizzard of 1993. If what John Cleaveland argues is true, that Highlands was indeed entrenched in a depression from the very beginnings of the town and didn't emerge from hard times until the mid 1960s, it's equally true that strong character born of independence and self-reliance is what sustained year-round Highlanders through it all.

Growth in the Thirties

By 1930 Highlands was waist deep in the inevitable concerns that accompany growth, some of these reflected in the topics argued by the Kelsey Literary Society for boys. In October, 1930, Ed Picklesimer and Roy Potts argued, "Resolved, that chain stores are detrimental to our country." They won for the affirmative against Glen Shuler and Henry Cleaveland. Then in September, 1931, the topic switched to crime: "Resolved, that newspapers increase crime by publishing crime stories in their columns." Chester Wright and Wendell Cleaveland exonerated the news media, winning this debate for the negative against Cub Rice and Ed Potts, .

With increased traffic generated by better communication, improved roads, and new stores, parking in 1930 became for the first time a problem for Highlands. The town council passed a resolution permitting parking in the center of Main Street from Brown's clothing store to Smith's store east of Highlands Inn. Although no parking was allowed on any part of 4th Street within eighty feet of the fountain at the intersection, three trees on 3rd Street south of Main had to be removed. Indeed, as early as 1928, discussion about also felling the "ancient oak" in front of the Highlands Inn had been referred to the street committee for consideration, but nothing had been done in this regard, nor would be until the great tree controversy, as discussed later in this chapter.

The 1930 census listed 447 residents within the corporate limits of Highlands and a summer population of 2,500 to 3,000. In thirty years since the turn of the century, the town had grown exponentially at geometric rates of seven, seventeen, and forty-three percent, from 249 residents in 1900, to 268 in 1910, and 313 in 1920. So by 1930 its population of 447 was being projected over the next ten years to reach 930, that is, to double![525]

Unbeknownst at the time, of course, the actual count in 1940 would not even approach 600, much less 900. To be sure, it would continue to rise to 547 in 1940, but by 1950 it would drop back to 514. Surging again in 1960 to 592, it would fall back to 583 in 1970. Not until 1980 did it even pass 600—actual count 653—but by then the summer population had jumped significantly to an estimated 20,000.

Riders on Satulah. Photo by George Masa, 1929.

Although the population of the town held relatively steady during the half century from 1925 to 1975, physical growth exploded after 1927 when the new water and electric systems and new sewer lines were installed. In addition to the Highlands Country Club, which had its own electric light and power system, new stores and new homes began to appear, all contributing to the biggest boom in building since the founding of the town. In 1931, anticipating real growth, Highlands became a member of the North Carolina Municipal Association. The roads leading into the town by this date were almost all paved. Indeed, the prospect of a hard-surfaced Highway 28 passing through Highlands in the near future was what prompted the revival of the Chamber of Commerce in the spring of 1931.[526]

An earlier Chamber had been organized in September, 1923, with more than sixty members including both summer and permanent residents. But the time wasn't ripe for such an organization in the twenties, the town being too deeply involved in preparing the physical facilities necessary for the thirties, so the first Chamber plunged into inactivity. The bustling thirties, however, needed a chamber desperately, as James Mell became its first president. One of its first acts was to publish an eight-page booklet filled with information and photos showing the south side of Satulah, Glen Falls, Bridal Veil Falls, Wildcat cliffs on Whiteside, horseback riders on Satulah, and the Highlands Estates golf course.

Throughout the thirties businesses popped up everywhere in town. In 1930 Florence Thompson and Lilly Pierson fronted Rice's Meat Market and Grocery with a Tea Room and a Hat and Dress Shop, both of which thrived for about five years. Indeed, so long as Florence's Tea Room lasted, it was Highlands' second restaurant after Elinor Cleaveland's Grille.

Edwards and Hines Garage during the early 1920s. Courtesy of Tammy Lowe. Jim Hines is standing on the right.

If you had a car during the twenties you would have taken it for service to Jim Hines' and Grover Edwards' Texaco Station on Church Street. Hines, however, was soon joined by Carl Zoellner; and in 1931, by Sam Creswell from Troy, S.C., who would help for nine years before setting up his own garage. The ad for the garage directed the motorist to drive to the sign of the yellow disk for the powerful nonox ethyl gas. There he had his choice of Gulf Supreme, Quaker State, or Mobil A oil, along with Goodyear tires and a Firestone battery. Taxi Service was offered as a specialty. In order not to offend the refined guests next door at the Martin House, Judge Hines put up a hand-crafted sign that read, "Please don't cuss, not that we give a damn but it sounds like hell to the ladies on the hill."

Hines and Zoellner Garage during the early 1930s. Courtesy of Tammy Lowe.

In 1935, Zoellner parted company with Hines and set up his own Esso Station and Garage at the Pine Street intersection with 4th, current home of Cleaveland Real Estate and Harllee Gallery/CK Swan. Marshall Reese remembers buying his own car in 1937 when he was only seventeen, from Uncle Carl on 4th Street. Walter Bryson took over the Texaco station on the hill, converting it to Gulf and moving to 4th and Main, where he worked until his retirement in 1955.

In 1931 Charlie Anderson constructed on 4th Street hill a two-story house and garage next to his drug store which he converted after four years into another Texaco Service Station. This is where Dr. William Matthews, the physician responsible for the founding of the Highlands Community Hospital, had his first office and waiting room in the brick addition at the front. Over time this tiny structure would be home to a variety of stores and organizations: Highlands China and Crystal Shop, Desjardins TV, Tick Tock Gifts, the Chamber of Commerce, Western Union, Hallelujah Health Food Store, and today's Highlands Whole Life Supply.

In 1932 Levi and Frank Crane erected Crane's Riding Stables, which served the town until the end of the century, and Louis Edwards opened a new woodwork and souvenir shop around the core of the old Baxter Wilson home east of Central House, a later site of the Bird Barn.

In 1933 Frazier Redden built his store on the north side of west Main across from the Methodist Church. It soon housed the Jam Pot, which shoppers remember for its home-made preserves stored in beautiful glass jars and Western N.C. pottery, all bearing Highlands labels. Gift baskets were filled with shredded waxed tissue and miniature cars and canoes carrying jam pots. The ribbon-tied jars were adorned with tiny hemlock cones and acorns. This building housed Maynard's Colonial Shop during the sixties, Town and Country in the seventies, Brush Strokes in the eighties, and Nancy's Fancies since the nineties.

In 1935 the long, low, familiar stone structure of W. S. Davis' Rock Store grew two new stories to become Highlands' second skyscraper, Hotel Edwards, itself a town landmark to this day. Charlie Anderson built his and Mattie's home at 4th and Spring streets, where it too still stands. On Main Street, John Burnett of Scaly and Harvey Talley of Macon County erected their grocery (today's Royal Scot) next to the Jam Pot. In addition to groceries, they carried coal, and though Harvey didn't advertise it, he would often deliver a pail of coal in the dead of a winter night to someone in dire need of a little heat.

West of Talley and Burnett, W. S. Bearden of Clayton established his Sinclair Service Station on the corner, which Prioleau Hedden ran before relinquishing it to Shine and Jimbo Potts. Bert Rideout transformed Florence Thompson's Tea Room into the Satulah Café, the first business in Highlands to display a neon sign. In the last years before Wit's End moved in, Harold Rideout converted his Café into a drug store. At the same time Sara Gilder was transforming Lilly Pierson's Dress Shop into her enduring and quite popular grocery, which she moved from across the street.

During the late twenties and early thirties, contributing to the boom in commercial building in Highlands, new residential developments on the outskirts of town were also evolving: Lindenwood Lake development around the Biological Laboratory, Highlands Estates at the new country club, the William Sullivan development which opened on Mirror Lake in 1926, and Indian Hills on the Walhalla Road. Between 1925 and 1935 Joe Webb and his stepson Furman Vinson built some two dozen log homes in the area later known as Webbmont.

One interesting enterprise that developed in 1937 was a silver fox farm. Sid McCarty had been coming to Highlands since 1923.[527] He married Highlands native Betty Neely and built their stone home at the corner of the Bowery and Upper Lake Road. They started their farm with eight pairs of foxes and expanded in just a few years to 250 foxes. Until 1941 they sold pelts to Northern markets and offered them during the summers at Annie Root's Gift Shop and Tea Room.

By 1938 Highlands was growing so fast that Main Street parking became once again a critical issue. Indeed, it was during this fateful year that in order to help alleviate the problem, the town council at last cast a wary eye on

East Main Street. Having discussed the matter of "the ancient oak" since 1928, before there was any pavement at all in town, and with pavement now high on the agenda, the Council finally made the controversial decision to remove it. In the absence of mayor W. S. Davis, mayor pro-tem Wilton Cobb chaired the April meeting at which George Marett, D. W. Wiley, Grover "Bullfrog" Edwards, and Harvey Talley voted to cut down "the three trees on Main Street between fourth and fifth streets."[528]

The choice proved enormously unpopular. The altitude oak, also regarded as the "charter oak," had stood in front of Highlands House as a symbol of the town since before its founding. Enclosed initially by a square wooden frame and later a circular rock wall, the tree bore a plaque designating Highlands' average altitude of 4,118 feet.[529] Lucille Pierson Reese knew it simply as "the big old oak tree in the middle of the street." Regardless of what it was called, everyone knew it as indispensable to the town's identity, like a well-loved patriarch of a large family.

Altitude Oak and blacksmith M. V. Cheney astride his steer. Photo probably by R. Henry Scadin, 1897–98, courtesy Gene Potts via Doris Potts.

Trees in Highlands have always appealed to its residents. They constitute a vital part of the beauty of the area, and to a large extent they are what people come to the area to see. Old trees especially evoke feelings beyond the simple appreciation of their beauty when they inhabit people's lives for decades. And when one of these old, old trees is cut down, there is no disputing the considerable pain its devoted friends feel at its destruction. Stephen Vincent Benét described the emotion that such a tree evokes in a town like Highlands, where he himself summered during the 1910s, when he wrote:

The trees in the streets are old trees
used to living with people,
Family-trees that remember
your grandfather's name.[530]

The Altitude Oak in front of Highlands House. Photo probably by R. Henry Scadin,
1910, courtesy of Hudson Library archives.

Anyone over seventy today who grew up in Highlands will remember this honored altitude oak and its two red oak companions. As noted earlier in the Introduction, Marion Day Arnold recalls writing a poem in 1936 about the town's decision to cut it. The women in the old Satulah Club were terribly upset and wanted someone to write a protest, which she took upon herself to do, imitating Longfellow's "Village Blacksmith," and the news-paper published it. Since she no longer has the poem and unfortunately no issues of the *Franklin Press and Highlands Maconian* were ever micro-filmed for the year that it was published, its content can only be deduced, but presumably it went something like this:

Under the spreading altitude oak
The village of Highlands stands;
The tree, a mighty oak is he,
With large and sinewy hands;
And the muscles of his brawny arms
Are strong as iron bands.

June Thompson Medlin remembers the incident with just a twinge of jealousy, for she too wrote a poem about it, but hers wasn't published.

There were some individuals in town who were ready and willing to give their lives to prevent the tree's destruction. Elizabeth Edwards actually chained herself to the trunk, called the town employees sent to do the dastardly deed "old Arabs," and threatened to cleave them with her meat ax. Edna Bryson remembers how Steve Potts, who was only sixteen at the time, was so upset about it that he stood tall and brave, reciting the poem he'd learned in school:

> *Woodman, spare that tree,*
> *Touch not a single bough,*
> *In Youth it sheltered me,*
> *And I'll protect it now.*[531]

Despite the fervent protestations of these devoted rebels seeking to stave off progress, the fate of the venerated altitude oak in 1938, along with that of its two companions, was forever sealed. It fell heavily, and four years later pavement sealed its grave.

The four red maples that were planted in rock planters down the center of Main Street in 1985 were the townspeople's endeavor to replace those revered graybeards, victims of the progressive demands of macadam and asphalt. An unsuccessful attempt in 1970 was nixed by the State Highway Commission as posing traffic hazards.

In 1939—not long after Len Appley built *Hemlock Lawn*, the first motel in Highlands, indeed the first in Macon County—Doc Mitchell created just below it Mitchell Cottages. By this time the number of communities outside the town that were served by electric light lines and water was sufficient to consider extending the town limits. The last extension had occurred in 1883 when the one-mile square established in 1879 was expended to one and a half miles square. Nothing, however, came of the resolution to expand again in 1939. Indeed, subsequent attempts to extend the 1883 limits all failed as well. A bill introduced in the state legislature to triple the town's size to nine square miles in 1947 was killed as soon as it hit the floor.[532] It was reintroduced and killed again in 1949.

In 1977 the town board tried to annex the Highlands Country Club without necessarily providing a required level of services to the new area, such as water, sewer, garbage, police and fire protection. Led by George Woodruff and represented by Herbert Hyde, the Club sued the town and won its case. Not until July 1, 1980, did Highlands finally succeed in extending its town limits with the necessary services to include such areas as Bear Pen, Indian Hills, Highlands Country Club, Cullasaja Heights, Mt. Lori,

Webbmont, the Bowery, and Sagee—almost doubling the assessed value of land within the town.[533]

The Forties: Continued Growth

It was sometime during the forties that Joe Waller was caddying for a golfer who asked him, "Tell me, young fellow, just what in the world do you mountain people live off?" Without hesitating, Joe shot back, "Tourists in the summer and 'taters in the winter." His clever assessment became a sort of motto for the town's annual fluctuations between feast and famine. Highlands was growing, but its survival still depended heavily on the summer people for its economic base. Although patronized by year-round residents, each new structure catered substantially to the needs of second homers.

The culmination of all the building in the thirties was the construction in 1940 of a brand new two-story brick and tile post office on the north side of Main Street between the Hicks and Rice buildings, where Sinle Hood's plank shack had stood before and after the turn of the century. Fred Edwards had the building on this lot razed and gave the contract to Walter Reese, who had to shore up the building on pilings over a spring. For the next quarter century Highlanders flocked here for their mail, exchanged local gossip, and heard the latest news. The Red Cross set up its workroom on the second floor.

Certainly the biggest change to old Highlands in 1940 occurred on the corner of Main and 4th with the breakup of the Marett–Bascom building. This store combination had sold Highlanders groceries for over a decade and hardware since the town's founding. Charles Anderson bought the two-story building and had it moved to make room for a new Gulf Service Station. Edna Bryson says both sections, the Bascom original and the Marett addition, were rolled on logs to their new homes. The Bascom section, containing Bert Rideout's café, moved across 4th Street to sit beside Zoellner's Garage, which is where it still stands as Schmitt Building Contractors. The Marett section was rolled to the back of the lot to face 4th Street.

Farther down Main Street, where the Rideout brothers had had their café and drug store, a new store inaugurated a tradition that has endured for sixty years and continues to thrive. In 1940 next to Sara Gilder's grocery, Mrs. O. E. Young established Wit's End for residents and visitors seeking classic ladies apparel and children's clothing under the slogan: "Where ye come when ye are already at thy own wit's end and have found nobodie home."

By 1941 the business section of Highlands had changed enough in appearance to jeopardize its village charm. Harlan Kelsey, the founder's son, and his own son Seth came from Boxford, Massachusetts, for a visit and were very much impressed with the growth of the town. But Harlan, who by then was a nationally recognized landscape architect, horticulturalist, and conservationist, couldn't help suggesting that the town's charm would be best preserved by dispensing with the parking area in the center of Main Street and planting the space with native shrubbery instead.[534] This novel idea, though brought up a number of times since, has never been carried out.

A controversy was already brewing over Main Street since Wilton Cobb had made public his request that the Highlands Inn porch be lowered to street level to allow through passage to his new bowling alley, the site of to-day's Dry Sink. The dispute that erupted over this request in 1940 dragged on for thirteen years, eight years longer than the world at war in which America was engaged at the time.[535] The new owners of the Highlands Inn, Frank Cook and Harvey Trice, adamantly opposed tampering with the raised boardwalk and porch that had projected into Main Street throughout the sixty years of the Inn's existence, for they allowed residents to relax in rocking chairs and watch the happenings of the town.

When nothing changed, however, despite the town council's decree that the porches be dismantled and with Cobb himself on the town council, the matter advanced to Superior Court. Still nothing happened, so in 1944 with Cobb now mayor, the board passed a resolution requiring the porches be removed by January 1, 1945, and empowered town attorney Horner Stockton to proceed with legal action to that end.

In November, 1946, with no change in the offing, the board was forced to revise the deadline to January 1, 1947, else the porches would be removed summarily. When this date had passed, the town attorney was directed to prosecute the Inn. Two years later the board voted to buy enough steel fence posts and chain to fence off a sidewalk in front of the porch. But it wasn't until December, 1953, that Frank Cook, now sole owner, agreed in a consent judgment to remove only the lower porch and boardwalk, adding ten-by-ten wooden posts to support the upper porch and leaving flower pot holes in the paved sidewalk for vines and flowers to circle the posts.

By then, of course, the town was filled with more paved roads and side-walks than could have been imagined when the controversy first erupted in 1940. Indeed 1941 was the year that the WPA project for street improvement asphalted Chestnut Street as far as Bear Pen Road, Main Street from 4th to 5th in front of the Highlands Inn, Satulah Road to Faraway Drive, Foreman Road, and Laurel and South streets.

Ironically, during the same year, 1941, even while the Baptist Church was completely renovating its sanctuary on Oak Ridge with a beautiful new stone face, Albert Brown was erecting his pool room between his brother Ernest's clothing store and Frazier Redden's Jam Pot. Not much building occurred in Highlands during the war years from 1941 to 1945, but significant changes did affect business ownership. Clarence "Doc" Mitchell of Westminster, S.C., had come to Highlands in 1933 to work at Charlie Anderson's Drug Store but within two years had joined Jackson County Bank. Now in 1943, he took over the drug store, leaving Anderson to concentrate all his talents on his dime store. During the next thirty years Doc would succeed in making it one of the largest and most modern drug stores in Western North Carolina.

Wade Sutton, who had opened his Green Forest Electric Shop on East Main the year before America's involvement in the war, built a new brick building on 4th Street just north of Jackson County Bank (occupied today by Highlands Wine and Cheese), but two years would pass once its foundation had been poured before he could occupy it. An airline pilot with a winter home in West Palm Beach, he entertained the town with movies of Florida and his round-the-world plane flight when work on his building was finally finished.

In 1944 a store moved to Highlands from Clayton, Georgia, that would serve the town for the next sixty years. Lewis Reeves opened a branch of his hardware store to be managed by Norman Reese in the Marett building, the two-story grocery that had been moved to the back of its lot on Main Street, facing 4th. It sold hardware and building materials to individuals and the construction industry for a dozen years before constructing its own home on Main Street, occupied today by Scudder's Galleries. Since 1970 it has existed at its current location at the corner of 3rd and Main.

Until 1945 one lot, actually a half lot, between Fred Edwards' store and Potts Brothers remained vacant. For years and years it was where kids in town played and threw ball. It was during the spring of this year that Will and Fred Edwards filled the narrow space with a building that Tudor Hall rented for his Real Estate firm from the fifties until the seventies. After 1978 this would be the home of Cyrano's Bookshop.

Another business that emerged after the war and lasted from 1945 well into the eighties was a much needed enterprise founded almost entirely on a whim. Charlie Potts' sons, Ed and R. L., had just returned to town as veterans of the army and merchant marines, respectively. They suddenly found themselves at home without any definite plans for the future. So they set up Highlands Cleaners and Laundry where Carl Zoellner had had his garage and Esso Station. This was where year-round and summer residents took all their clothes and linen to be washed or dry cleaned. Eventually it was run by Ed's wife Hazel "Broadie" Potts. Broadie made full use of her environment and every bit of available space when she hung leather breeches to dry on long strings from the rafters.

4th Street South on the Hill, looking north. Photo taken ca. 1948. Dr. Bill Matthews had his office in the little building with the brick front on the left, then Anderson's Five and Ten, Highlands Rexall Pharmacy, Highlands Hardware, and Jackson County Bank. Doc Mitchell's '47 Pontiac and Wilton Cobb's Chrysler on the right. Photo below by the author, 2000

Children in Highlands found a number of stores that catered to them as much as adults. The Country Mouse Gift Shop opened in 1947 on Lake Sequoyah, and Mrs. W. E. McGuire from Clemson had surprise balls for the children. My wife Margaret fondly remembers them as decorated on the outside with a clown or a ballerina and strips of colored crepe paper, while the inside held toys that fell out to every child's intense delight, the best prize being a whistle in the very center.

For Margaret the alternative to the Country Mouse was Anderson's dime store on the 4th Street hill or Mrs. Root's gift shop and tea room on Main Street, where tall pines shaded the home, garden flowers bordered the pathway, and visitors always found themselves welcomed to relax in comfortable chairs or shop among rare and exquisite articles of Chinese art, the craft work of mountain schools, and Staffordshire ware from England; or just visit with their hostess. There was always the fresh smell of baking, and Mrs. Root gave each child a cookie. She stocked antiques selected with exquisite taste as well as dogwood jewelry.

Not long after the town appointed Louis Edwards building inspector in 1946, he decided to move his woodworking shop from just east of Central House on Main Street into W. C. Newton's shop on Spring Street. At about the same time Barak Wright applied for a permit to build a sawmill and planer nearby, provoking protests from Drs. Mitchell and Moreland and Harvey Talley against the potential noise. The town responded with an ordinance against any sawmill or planing mill within the town limits.

The new stoplight, including instructions, at 4th and Main, installed 1947

With traffic ever increasing on Main Street the town felt compelled at last to install its first stoplight. It chose the intersection of 4th and Main, where congestion in 1947 had become, in the town council's judgment, "very heavy and continuous."[536] A flashing caution light had been installed at this intersection back in 1935, but the time had now come for complete and timed stops to prevent a major accident. The concept was so new that the device had signs attached to it, explaining the three lights to the driving public: green for "Go," yellow for "Caution," and red for "Stop," with elaborate instructions regarding each.

Two years passed before a caution light, which was later removed, graced the intersection of Satulah and Walhalla roads. Right turns were soon permitted on a red light at town center. Indeed, there was so much opposition to a red light in Highlands that for years it reverted to blinking like the caution signal it had replaced. By 1959, however, it became by necessity a stop and go, because motorists were ignoring the caution.

Highlands became a two stoplight town when a signal went up in 1966 between the Episcopal and Presbyterian churches at 5th and Main. Eventually a third light appeared at the corner of 1st and Main, which by the end of the nineties had given way to eight lights on a single corner.

The year 1947 saw the beginning of a new tradition in town as Arthur Trock and Morris Stone opened their Highlands Art Gallery in the Sutton Electric building on 4th Street hill. Inaugurated in St. Petersburg, Florida, during 1927 and then in the Carolinas in 1931, it held public auctions in Highlands for merchandise gathered from all over the world. Diamonds, watches, silverware, dinner and crystal ware, linens, oriental rugs, and furniture whether for a cabin or a castle were offered twice daily except Sunday from 10:30 in the morning till 7:30 in the evening. By the sixties Trock was managing the Highlands branch, while his partner operated the gallery in Waynesville.

In exchange for permission to do business in Highlands, the gallery agreed to contribute one percent of its gross receipts to the town, amounting to $60,000 in 1949, $100,000 the following year. By 1954 it had proved itself popular enough to construct its own building between the Galax Theatre and the Cleaveland home on Main. Like Helen's Barn and the Galax, it provided evening entertainment in Highlands for many years. Although gone today, replaced by a series of shops between the Pizza Place and the Little Flower Shoppe, it attracted during its heyday a great following from the day it opened until its closing under William Daley in 1992.

Its counterpart, Scudder's Galleries, which Frank A. "Al" Scudder of Silver Springs, Florida, opened in 1976, still operates across Main Street today. When Al Scudder wasn't donating his time and talents as master of ceremonies at fundraising auctions for various service organizations and charities in town, he was entertaining patrons during the evenings with his auctions of antique and contemporary furniture, 500-carat diamonds, paintings, bronze statues, oriental rugs, and sterling and silver plated items from estate liquidations and consignments.

Occasionally items were sold from the estates of famous celebrities, like Arthur Godfrey or Joan Crawford. Al's strengths were his wit and knowledge gleaned from traveling among experts and artisans abroad. He'd readily explain where giant wood-carved Foo Dogs came from, which once stood guard over a Chinese palace.

About the same time that the first auction gallery appeared in Highlands, a new restaurant opened in the Hicks building, replacing Jim Hicks' barber shop and Elinor Cleaveland's Highlands Grille. Steve Potts and Bob DuPree began a tradition that would attract loyal customers for the next half century. They created in 1948 the Highlander Restaurant based in large part on the tried and true recipes that Helen "Mama" Thompson had tested with resounding success on her eight kids and all the children at Highlands School.

The venture lasted only four years in the Hicks building before Steve bought Fred Edwards store next to Marett's and moved into his Country Store. Phil Tate took over the facilities and continued the popular Highlander Restaurant which he eventually emblazoned under his own name: Tate's Restaurant. Harvey Trice and Tearley Picklesimer ran it during the late fifties and sixties so that when Marie Henry (now Reese) bought it in 1969, she inherited an established Mecca for hungry souls. She poured her own soul into the business, keeping late hours for her customers and rising especially early on mornings when the fire or rescue teams needed feeding after a hard night of saving lives or property. In many instances her cooking was as much a lifesaver as the lifesavers she was nourishing.

After nine years the restaurant passed to Buddy Taylor, but according to Marie, Phil made him change the name because he considered it headed downhill, which is why it became the Mountaineer. Despite Tate's reservations, the Mountaineer Restaurant under successive ownerships of Buddy and Betty Taylor, Morris and Cindy Reed, Rev. Joe Tuten, and Sara Lee attracted Highlanders from every class and profession for the next twenty-two years. Its loyal patrons relished its Southern fried chicken, homemade soups, catfish and flounder specials, and famous holdover from *Mama's Recipes*: homemade buttermilk pie. It was a sad day in December of 1999 when, with prices rising and labor hard to find, Sara Lee had to close the Mountaineer. One of the last really popular local restaurants, it offered inexpensive mountain cooking to staunchly loyal regulars.

Dave Clary, one of the Mountaineer's most loyal patrons who ate breakfast there every morning with John Schiffli, claims that John ate the same breakfast for ten years. Indeed, when a new waitress asked him one morning for his order, it had been so long since he'd had to give one, he couldn't remember what he usually got. He handed her his card and told her to slow that to the kitchen staff. They'd know what to serve him.

When the Mountaineer closed on December 20th, there was little doubt about the impact it had had on those who spent much of their eating lives at its booths and tables and came to bid it a tearstained and heartfelt farewell. Here is a eulogy written that night in its honor and called, "Biscuits in Sausage Gravy":

Homemade biscuits soaked in gravy.
Griddle cakes and country ham.
Sausage and eggs, any style,
With buttered toast and jam.

Where, oh where! in Highlands now
Is a cup of coffee always filled?
A hamburger sold for six ninety-five?
And chicken fried or grilled?

No vichyssoise, no crème brûlée,
On menus no one can spell.
Just grits and collards with buttermilk pie,
And rib eye medium well.

Much has changed in seventy years
Since Prioleau's recipe.
From Steve to Phil, Harvey and Tearley,
Marie and Buddy and Sara Lee.

It's not just the food that people loved,
Though the food was the cheapest around.
It's the people that the people loved,
Who came from all over town.

They took as much flack as a waitress could dish
From Bernice and Tine and Lil,
Who knew from the moment they walked in the door
Just what to put on the bill.

If a place where friends can gather
Is what life is all about,
Then the death of the Mountaineer,
Is reason enough to pout.

The loss of a spot where people meet
To talk and laugh and cry
Over BLTs with chips and a pie
Draws more than a tear and a sigh.

It cuts to the quick in the stomach;
In the heart, a painful hole;
There's something indefinably lost,
In a far-off part of the soul.

Restaurants come and restaurants go:
It's part of the new frontier.
But few remain long aft' their day
In the mind like the Mountaineer![537]

The same year that Steve Potts and Bob DuPree founded the Highlander Restaurant, the much welcomed Galax Theatre opened its doors across the street in 1948. In line with other improvements already underway, black topped sidewalks were installed from the new theatre to 4th Street and around the corner as far as the newly opened Church Street on the hill. Almost immediately speed limit and school zone signs popped up all around town, and in anticipation of increased development the town had R. E. Norton draw up a new street map, so Highlands could qualify for state aid under the Powell bill.[538]

Parking in the center of town had begun to wreak so much havoc that the police and street committee marked off center lines and spaces to regulate where to drive or park a car. The police were asked to advise all who worked in town during the day and didn't use a vehicle in their business "to park their cars off the main streets of the town."[539] In 1963 the town was still requesting that businessmen park off Main Street so as to free up spaces for their own customers. Indeed, it would be the year 2000 before this request was ever officially enforced, but no sooner was it made law than it was abruptly rescinded as most likely unenforceable.

The Fifties: Slowdown

The onset of the fifties saw blacktop radiate from the center of town. By 1952 it extended up Satulah as far as Buck Horn gap, down Spring Street to 1st, and along Oak Street parallel to Main. In 1957 more streets were opened under the Powell bill: Laurel, Spruce, 2nd, Oak extension, 4 ½ Street, Leonard, and Bruner Lane. A year later the south side of East Main Street was graded to street level; and the gradual slope from the Presbyterian Church, sliced back to the property line.

This left the church without a fence or front yard, just a huge drop-off necessitating a rock retaining wall. The town sought to compensate for the severe break in the landscape by planting dogwood and maple trees along the curb line, as proposed by the Highlands Garden Club two years earlier.

Actually the Club had asked to plant five Carolina hemlock trees in the center of Main Street, but the state had advised them to plant on each side of Main between 3rd and 4th, which plantings were now extended from 4th to 5th. By the end of the decade the town was opening 3rd Street as a proposed bypass for trucks, intending that 3rd and Maple connect the Walhalla Road with U.S. 64 East. So long as Maple Street—affectionately known as Tobacco Road—remained unimproved, however, it wouldn't become a bypass for any but local motorists.

Even as the streets were growing and changing, so was the face of the commercial district. In 1952 with Fred Edwards' health failing, Steve Potts replaced Edwards' shop with his own Country Store, destined to thrive for eight years at this location before its move to East Main. Two years later the town was celebrating the realization of a dream it had held but had had to postpone since 1883—over seventy years—when it first tried unsuccessfully to build its own town hall at the corner of 4th and Pine. In 1954 at the site of the first Highlands School on the corner of 4th and Oak, Dr. Upton Ewing designed a brick structure that would serve as a combination town hall, fire station, and police headquarters. Although the latter two have since relocated into their own buildings at the west end of the same block, on what originally comprised Highlands Park, the town hall remained where it lives today.

In 1956 at the south end of 4th Street on the hill, Jackson County Bank vacated its first home to occupy a new Roman brick building across the street. Six years later it would merge with First Union of Asheville, the bank that exists there today. Bill McCall, a South Carolina native, served as its first cashier; Miss Carolina Hall, his assistant. In the year 2001 this bank would merge with Wachovia.

In the building that the Jackson County Bank abandoned, Archie and Hazel Jellen from Miami set up the first gem store in Macon County: Highlands Gem Cutting and Mineral Shop. Archie had considerable experience in gemology, having helped open the mining section of Cowee Creek, a local source for many of his minerals and gems. He and Hazel carried some of the rarest and finest emeralds, rubies, and sapphires in the area. His own *Mineralogy Handbook* contained a brief history of Carolina minerals and gems and a map of the local mines to which he arranged guided field trips. At the Gem Shop a child could expect to receive a free sample to mix with any garnets he or she might have found along Highlands' rocky roads, and in those days they were inexhaustibly plentiful.

Another delight of kids of all ages was the grand opening at King's Inn corner of Margaret Picklesimer's Tastee-Freez and Sandwich Shop in 1950. Her daughters Ann and Sue helped run it until Edna Hawland bought and managed it from the late sixties into the seventies. Highlands School coach Bill Lanford ran it as Coach's Corner until 1991, and it still sells ice cream along with burgers and dogs as Joel Porter's and David Bee's Hill Top Grill.

Despite new stores and turnovers in managements and ownerships, there were some losses during the fifties, perhaps the greatest of which was Sara Gilder's grocery. Sara sold out to Phil Tate in 1956, the year that Miss Nellie Cleaveland moved the Marett building down Main Street to its current location between Marett's former home and the Masonic Hall on 3rd, and retired to the apartment above her shop. Sara's retirement marked the end of a thirty-year tradition on Main Street, and her services to the town were greatly missed.

And yet, even as one institution passed away, another was born. Across the street from Sara Gilder's, Prioleau and Dr. Jessie Zachary Moreland Hedden launched Highlands' newest motel. Built of crab orchard stone from Tennessee—the fad of the fifties—the Town House Motel would thrive for the next thirty years, until Town Square replaced its twenty units with nine shops in 1984.

The popular institution that relocated in 1957 was the Highlander Restaurant. Phil Tate had replaced the Highlander with his own Tate's Restaurant, so Prof. W. C. Newton bought the Potts Brothers building and moved the Highlander three lots east. Here for the next forty years, in competition with Tate's and the Mountaineer, was where Highlanders enjoyed more of the best food and atmosphere for miles around.

Mary Thompson and her son John Cleaveland would buy the restaurant in 1967 and treat their patrons to many of the old recipes from Mama Thompson's cookbook which had endowed the old Highlander Restaurant with so much of its original attraction. They would serve homemade buns, apple in a dish, and, of course, crumb and buttermilk pies. Upon their retirement in 1981 as Cleaveland turned his sights to real estate, the Highlander would lose much of its driving force, many of its patrons returning to the Mountaineer, former home of the original Highlander.

When the Highlander finally closed its doors in 1999, the same year as the Mountaineer, it would be missed but not with the same intense nostalgia that accompanied the death of the Mountaineer, for its day had passed. The building currently houses Highlands Fine Arts and Jewelry, Dutchman's Designs, and Apple Trout.

In 1958 a thirty-four-year-old building came down on the 4th Street hill to make way for Doc Mitchell's new Highlands Rx Drug Store and several other shops between Alan Lewis' Variety Store and the Gem Shop. Made of crab orchard stone, the new structure upgraded Doc's old drug store. Where Highlands Hardware and the bowling alley once thrived, Anisa now sold gowns and sportswear; and Yrene's, dresses.

This was a banner year for the town's financial solvency: it was able to pay off the last of its original issue electric, water, and sewer bonds a full ten years prior to their maturity date. The town celebrated being at last debt free! The feat was accomplished through a sinking fund into which the town had paid each year a third of its revenues from taxes along with $1,000 from water and $4,000 from light receipts.

The Holt Building, which housed Billy Potts' post office in 1917

Throughout all the changes of the fifties, one old standby could be counted on to dominate the future as much as it had the past. This was Bill's Soda Shop "on the Corner." With each new issue of the newspaper, Bill's ad invited moviegoers to drop in "for a rich, creamy milkshake or a bracing, three-dip ice cream soda," and his shop filled with lighthearted customers seeking a treat after every show.

Cub and Mary Paul Rice recalled how they used to run the shop when Gus Holt owned it during the thirties, for even at that time they had a popular soda fountain that served sandwiches, stocked magazines and souvenirs, and provided curb service with trays for personal delivery to cars parked outside. During that earlier era, however, they made carbonated water by hand, turning the crank to mix the soda and water.

Bill's Soda Shop and Harry's Café during the 1940s. Courtesy of Gene Potts via Doris Potts.

Bill's Soda Shop, with its old fashioned soda fountain tables with wooden tops framed in metal, and chairs with wooden seats and wire backs and legs, was a place for the locals to congregate, but the tourists also loved it for its picturesque atmosphere. At the rear of the shop were pinball machines where the guys hung out, and up front Bill sold cigarettes and candies where folks enjoyed cherry cokes and smashes and an occasional ammonia coke.

The Sixties: Consolidation

The sixties opened in Highlands with an astonishing number of stores already established for a village that eighty years earlier had boasted of only five. In the first year Yrene's, which the children loved to call "Why-rene's" and which sold lovely dresses and slack suits on the hill, moved to Steve's former Country Store on Main. Across the street Ralph and Richard deVille from Miami opened a new Oriental gift shop, known today as the Stone Lantern. Its specialty from 1978 until the end of the twentieth century would be its annual sponsorship of the Japanese Flower and Arts Festival, featuring workshops in Ikebana Japanese flower arranging taught by such Master Teachers as Martha Neese, Mutsuo Tomita, Kimiko Gunji, Ikka Nakashima, and Shuko Kobayashi of the Ohara, Ikenobo, and Sogetsu schools. De-Ville's shop joined a list of old and new stores that over the next thirty or forty years would earn the newspaper's praise as the "oldies but goodies" of Highlands.

Many of these had long since survived the annual attrition, such as Helen's Barn, the Hudson Library, the Highlands Museum and Biological Station and Botanical Garden, Highlands Variety Store and Rexall Pharmacy, Highlands Gem Shop, Highlands Furniture, and Wit's End.

The Condiment Shop still carried the best wild elderberry jelly; wild coon, fox, and possum grape jelly and jam; pomegranate and wild black raspberry jelly; pickled okra, dill tomatoes, watermelon rind, chow-chow, apple butter, and dilly beans—all put up by Elizabeth Edwards and her helpers. Having opened the Condiment Shop as a hobby in 1945 to take her mind off poor health and a tragic loss in her family, Elizabeth eventually reached the stage of canning as many as 900 pints of fresh fruits, berries, and vegetables in a single day, which would continue until its closing in 1999, the end of a fifty-four-year institution. Likewise, Bill's Soda Shop, already a favorite gathering place for over forty years, would live on for another dozen years before its demise.

Alice Inman Shop, owned by Angelyn Trice, was the oldest dress store in town. Located originally in Mrs. Root's shop, it would operate during the sixties in the Masonic Hall. Mr. and Mrs. Hank Laskey's Blue Moon would sell sparkling glass wear, basket goods, and cards at 4th and Church on the hill until replaced by Alice Inman's in the seventies. Dusty and Manila Reese Rhodes set up Rhodes Superette on the Dillard Road in 1959, which would continue to provide discriminating customers with fresh cut meat, fruit, and vegetables through the end of the century.

Stone and Trock still ran Highlands Art Gallery, and Elisabeth Cates Wall of Spartanburg opened to sell English and American antique furniture, porcelains, silver, and gifts at the Ark Antique Shop initially near Bill's Soda Shop on 4th Street hill, then in Bryson's garage on Church Street, until it had its own building in 1972, today's McCulley's. Kitty Byers ran her Style Center for ladies' and men's sportswear in the old post office on Main until her move at the end of the sixties to new quarters on 5th Street, home today of the *Highlander* newspaper office. Lee Roi's fine apparel and boutique would survive until Nicole's replaced it in 1971.

The Galax Theatre, the Highlands Community Theatre (HTC), Highlands Cleaners and Laundry, the Highlander Restaurant, and the Mountaineer Restaurant (assuming that name in 1978) would all prosper well into the eighties and nineties. The Little Red Hen would sell knitting supplies on the banks of the old mill stream; McNair's, yarn and crewel work; and the Pink Dogwood, arts and crafts beginning in 1968.

Reeves Hardware, which had moved in 1956 from 4th and Oak to build its own store (later Tate's Supermarket, today's Scudder's Galleries), would build in 1970 where it exists today. Roy and Steve Potts built their Supermarket and nursery at the corner of Main and 5th in 1962, the same year that Clarence Gast introduced his Little Cheese Shop. Henry and Edna Whitmire continued to attract lodgers at Kalmia Court on the Dillard Road, one of the first courts in Highlands, featuring twelve units and ten baths, since 1947. Highlands Court offered fifteen rooms with private baths as well as cottages with electric kitchenettes on the Franklin Road. And Ben and Georgette Williams, having operated their Highland Fling at the corner of 4th and Foreman Road since 1951, were still specializing in interiors, antiques, and decorative accessories.

The Arnold Rosses operated Mary Norton Shop, coordinator of the Miss Universe Fashion Show each year at the Fontainebleau Hotel in Miami Beach. And last but not least were the old standbys that, having existed for years and years, would continue to serve the town for years to come, like the Highlands Inn, Hotel Edwards, Lee's Inn, King's Inn, and the *Highlander* newspaper.

In addition to these popular favorites, there were the realtors and insurance agents: Tudor Hall, Wilton Cobb, Frank Cook and Norma Pierson, McGruder and O'Brien (Allison McGruder always greeted everybody loudly), Lydia Harcombe, little Luke Rice, and John H. C. Perry. There were the service stations: Neville Wilson's Hilltop Amoco, Neville Bryson's Gulf, Shine and Jimbo Potts' Sinclair, Miller's 66, and Chastain's Highway Service, which also carried groceries.

If you washed your own clothes, you went to Peggy Potts' Wash Pot, where washers often overflowed and sent waves of suds and water down the front steps and across the sidewalk into Main Street. If you wanted flowers, you bought them from Reese's on the Country Club Road. If you needed a general contractor, you called Jamie Keener or Alvin Crowe.

If you wished a coiffeur, you went to Esther's or Anne's Beauty Shop, Emma Potts Pell's Vogue Beauty Shop, or Martha Reese's Klip 'N Kurl. For just a plain haircut, Jimmy Crawford, Herbert Bryson, or Walter Wilson, who preached a good sermon at the Shortoff Baptist Church when he wasn't spinning fascinating yarns at his barber chair. Jimmy also sold real estate in the developments he laid out at Queen and King mountains and Pinecrest. One of his competitors jokingly complained, "No wonder he outsells us. He goes out and shows a piece of property, and then he offers the prospective buyer a free shave. When he's got the razor right over the man's Adam's apple, he says, 'You're going to buy, aren't you?'"

Building materials for a repair job were available at either Highlands Hardware or Reeves. You didn't always get what you requested, of course, especially if you weren't exactly sure what it was you wanted, but you were treated cordially nonetheless. Jack Calloway remembers a customer who entered Reeves during the sixties when it was located where Scudder's Galleries are today. Dusty Rogers happened to be buying supplies at the front counter, and a fellow came in, thought Dusty worked there, and asked for half a stove pipe. Dusty looked at him kinda funny, then retreated to the back office, for the store was quite deep. He hollered, "Hey, Joe! Some fool out front wants half a stove pipe!" Suddenly aware that the man had followed him into the back office, he turned and gestured toward him without skipping a beat: "And this fine gentleman wants the other half!"

Main Street West during the 1960s

In view of all these stores operating in Highlands, the town and the Chamber began advertising in TV films, *The State* magazine, and a new 1964 brochure.[540] At the same time, however, even as early as 1959, the town board began to address the need for controlled growth. In 1958 it had set up Highlands' first planning board, composed of Tom Harbison, Dusty Rhodes, and Bud Potts, but it was soon defunct. So the board decided to participate in a community planning program sponsored by the Western N.C. Regional Planning Commission. A survey in 1959, based on an economic study, a set of prepared maps, and a land use questionnaire, sought to produce a balanced plan for future growth, including a zoning ordinance, subdivision regulations, a thoroughfare plan, and a land use plan to protect its natural assets and take care of anticipated development.[541] The purported intent of the plan was to protect the area from uncontrolled development and potential destruction of its natural attractions.

By 1964, aided by a federal grant of $175,000 and financing, the town began installing new water and sewer lines reaching across Mirror Lake on Hicks Road and extending along Pine Street to the new Potts Super Market and Highlands School. It also built a new water filtering plant on Big Creek and a sewage disposal plant on Mill Creek, which Simon Pell would manage for the next twenty years. Total cost, just under half a million dollars.

The following year the post office, which had dominated Main Street for a quarter century, moved to the corner lot of 5th and Pine. Giving up the blacktop of Main Street, it opted for more space at the expense of mud on 5th Street, which had not yet been graveled or paved. For another quarter century it remained here, its latest move in 1994 to the Walhalla Road.

Concerned that a proliferation of buildings and roads were turning Highlands from a quaint village into a common town, the Highlands Garden Club concocted a plan, like the Improvement Society's benches during the twenties, to help the business district regain some of its original charming village atmosphere. Georgette Williams suggested that the club place flower boxes at the store fronts, around the motor courts, on the streets, and in all yards. Money raised at the annual garden tour would pay to fill the boxes with colorful impatiens, geraniums, begonias, and alyssums.

In the summer of 1970 the *Asheville Citizen* correspondent John Parris was so impressed with the results that he named Highlands "the flower box town." He called it "a unique mountain resort where flowers, instead of neon, provide the color. . . . There's nothing like it in all the mountains. The whole town is a symphony of beauty in bloom."[542]

Catching the spirit of keeping Highlands beautiful, Ginger Edwards Brockway opened her new accessory shop in *Gray Cottage* on East Main with benches on the lawn for anyone who might wish "to sit and talk, and wait for the mail."

But as much as Highlands residents strove to keep their village simple, the new body was outgrowing its old clothes. Before the sixties, if you wanted to phone Potts Brothers for groceries, you called 11; Davis' Rock Store, 23. If you missed the Rock Store by one number, you got the *Franklin Press* at 24. But the early sixties were requiring four-digit dialing: 4731 rang up Dusty at Rhodes Superette. With a 526 prefix added in 1966, you had to dial at minimum five numbers to make a connection. Continental

Telephone Company began to require all seven numbers in 1987. A second prefix, 787, would be activated in 1999.

One of the first book stores to operate in Highlands opened in 1967 in Harry Holt's Real Estate Office at Main and 4th. It was the Hudson Library's outlet for discarded and donated books, known as the Book Mart. It operated successfully Thursday through Saturday for two hours in the morning and again in the afternoon. All the proceeds went toward the purchase of new books for the library.

In 1997 another Hudson Library bookshop, created by Jean Sarjeant and run today by Leila Chapman, was the very popular Bookworm, which opened at the Peggy Crosby Center during the same days as the earlier store but for longer hours. It grossed almost overnight more than $10,000 from the sale of used books for the purchase of new books for the library.

While the library was raising much needed funds from its first book store in 1967, the volunteer firemen in town were sponsoring their first barbecue to raise $1,000 toward construction of a new station. The success of the event led to its move by the end of the year into new housing which it occupies today on Oak Street behind the Playhouse.

Only five new stores opened at the end of the sixties, the first three of which prospered into the nineties, the fourth no longer open, but the last one still strong today. Dave and Lee Todd opened Antiques by Lee between Bill's Soda Shop and the Stone Lantern in 1968 before moving to 4th Street hill, where Dave installed his famous "For Bored Husbands Only" bench to give wives unfettered shopping time. In the same year the Blue Ridge Pharmacy opened in the Cobb building where the bowling alley used to be.

Dee McCollum opened her Paintin' Place in the Rice–Thompson building on Main Street and sold paintings well into the nineties, while she herself wrote award-winning North Carolina poetry and books of humorous and insightful lyrics and limericks about women. Tom and Carol Turek replaced her paintings for a short time in 1995 with Kilwin's handmade ice cream, hand-paddled fudge, and fine chocolates before abandoning the building to Buck's Coffee Cup, today's occupant.

On Church Street beyond the Condiment Shop, Burton Talbott opened his Burdick Galleries to display his black-and-white and color photographs he'd taken of many well-known personalities of the Highlands plateau. But though First Union Bank for a time displayed collages of his photos on its walls, his gallery existed for only a short while.

To meet the mounting construction demands of a growing town, George Schmitt founded in 1969 Schmitt Building Contractors in the old transplanted Marett building across from town hall. This firm alone would survive well into the third millennium as building needs increased over the next forty years.

The Early Seventies: Taxation vs. Representation

By 1970 there were enough businesses in Highlands to fill an illuminated directory and bulletin board that hung next to Jim Fox's architectural office where the Little Flower Shop is today. But even after it was posted, new stores were being added. John and Bill Tate established their Supermarket in the Main Street building vacated by Reeves Hardware as it moved to the 3rd Street corner. Where Harry's Café had stood adjacent to Bill's Soda Shop, Betty Wong from Hong Kong opened her House of Wong, specializing in ladies apparel and oriental imports. On north 4th Street, where the Thompsons used to live, Harry Neal constructed Bryant Funeral Chapel, still extant today. Farther out 4th Street beyond the Buck Creek turnoff, Margaret Ann "Maggie" Grady of Vero Beach, Florida, wife of R. W. "Mac" Grady, opened her Wee Scottish Shoppe in 1975, which she sold in 1994 but which still thrives today.

These enterprises survived the fate of so many less fortunate stores in Highlands, which would open one year in anticipation of great success only to close the next in disillusionment or failure. The short summer seasons, busy as they were, didn't bring in enough income to offset the long winters. Names like Casual Modes, the Wee Do-Nut Shop, Tick Tock Gifts, or the Cracked Pot are hardly remembered today, for they only survived a year or two at most.

The early seventies was another time for change of ownership more than new construction. Jack Alexander, a native of Asheville, bought Mitchell's Drug Store on the hill. The following year a sixty-year Highlands tradition on Main Street died with the closing of Bill's Soda Shop in 1972. It became the real estate office of Tom Allen, then Harry Long, and finally John Cleaveland.

In 1974 a new issue surfaced that would plague Highlands residents for the rest of the twentieth century. A dispute erupted between the people of Highlands and Macon County over what Highlanders considered unjust taxation. More fundamentally, the problem entailed taxation without representation, similar to what two centuries earlier had led to the hurling of sacks of tea into Boston harbor at the start of an angry revolution. The ire of the people, however, was not directed solely at the county but at the town and the state as- well.

Highlands had outgrown its capacity to serve its taxpayers. Individual citizens were paying higher and higher taxes without receiving any additional services, so Professor Tom Crumpler organized the Highlands Township Taxpayers Association to represent all individuals in the township.[543] His grievances, like all who joined the association and elected him president, were that tax revenues, library services, and municipal services which the county and the town owed the people were woefully inadequate, as were road improvements by the State Department of Transportation. The problem with the town, as Professor Tom Fitz Patrick depicted it, was occasioned by the unique fact that so many people lived in the Highlands Township full-time but without establishing legal residence. Private funds would have to be sought where government funds were not available.

The problem with the county, however, was taken for correction to at its source. Crumpler presented Highlands' complaints to the county commissioners. He argued that whereas the Franklin township contained 44% of the county's taxpayers and paid 45% of the county's taxes, the Highlands township contained only 10% of the taxpayers who paid a disproportionate 27% of the taxes. Property evaluation for the whole county averaged $467 per acre; for Franklin it was $703; for Highlands, a whopping $1,910. Furthermore, the annual budget for Franklin was only $500,000 vs. Highlands' $700,000. Crumpler concluded that somebody was getting a free ride!

The Taxpayers Association presented a proposal in 1975 to create two new electoral districts, which would expand the county board of commissioners from three to five members, each living in and representing a different district but elected at large. The same plan would apply to the board of education. Despite cynical predictions that the proposed changes in representation would die at the polls, voters in 1976 approved the whole package two to one countywide. Highlands approved a Highlands district 16-to-1 in an 80% turnout of 900 registered voters.[544] So by 1978 Highlands had its own county representative. It also had its own seat, along with Nantahala, on the school board, also authorized by the state legislature. Jamie Keener served as Highlands' first representative on the expanded school board.

The upshot of this four-year campaign by the Taxpayers Association was that though the original argument over inequities in taxation would continue, representation on the county level after 1978 was no longer at issue. Highlands had full county representation. What remained to correct would be the recurring fact that several times during the past twenty years dramatic increases in property revaluations have forced Highlands individuals, faced with unbearable taxes, to sell off either piecemeal or entirely their family farms. At the end of the twentieth century, as eight-year revaluations were rescheduled for every four years, no relief appeared on the horizon.

When Tom Crumpler bought Faraway in 1971, he had found a letter in a dresser drawer that spoke to just such a hardship.[545] It might as well have been addressed to the County Tax Collector during the recent summer of

1999, when the Taxpayers' Association was reactivated to fight another instance of inflated property assessments despite county representation. It was addressed "From debtor to Creditor" and read,

Dear Sir—I got your letter about what I owe you. Now be pachunt. I aint forgot you. Plees wate. When some fools pay me, I pay you. If this wuz judgement Day and you wuz no more prepaired tomeet your maker as I am to meat your account, you shure would have to go to Hell. Trusting you will do this, I remain

Yours truly B

21. Buildings Grown Together

All the buildings have all grown together.
—Olive Crane, 1986

By the mid seventies great changes lay in store for Highlands. As the oil-producing nations boosted prices in 1974, leading to fuel shortages, long lines at the filling stations, and worldwide inflation, brush was being cleared and burned at the old Appley home tract on Walhalla Road to make way for Highlands' first Shopping Center.

Building from this point forward was no longer restricted to single stores, with the notable exception, of course, of Margaret Hoff's Happy Hiker, an outdoor equipment and clothing store which she established on Chestnut Street in 1975. Her store exists today as David and Carol Wilkes' Highland Hiker on Church Street.

The first business to occupy a space in the new Highlands Plaza in 1977 was Bryson's Food Store, a mainstay of today's grocery needs. In the same year the ABC Store was erected where the old two-story red schoolhouse had sat overlooking the town on Knowledge Hill. Quite a change from those early years of prohibition and temperance. The store won a controversial two-to-one approval by popular vote, and Steve Pierson had the dubious honor of making the first legal purchase of liquor in the history of Highlands.

At the outset of the eighties, according to a Chamber of Commerce census, there were sixty shops and sixty-eight other businesses in Highlands. Some of these enterprises began advertising on the new medium of Cable TV. Formed by Nin Bond, the Northland franchise began transmission on Channel 14 in July, 1982.[546]

Meanwhile, as if a precedent had been set by the creation of a shopping center south of town, a second shopping center arose beginning in 1982 to the north, extending the business district out 4th Street to Mill Creek. Larry Torrence of Mountain Investments set up a two-story complex of six shops and a restaurant, which he called Mallard Square, today's Mountain Brook Center. Two years later Harry Wright sold the Helen's Barn property to Ron Allen and Harold Bramer of A&B Properties, who in 1986 began extending the town to the west with another nine stores and nine apartments at Wright Square. Not until 2000 would Buddy and Sherri Kremser stretch the town to the east with a two-story twelve-store unit, including offices, known as The Falls on Main, across from the Hudson Library.

With the influx of shopping centers, new businesses began filling new spaces as soon as the dust of construction had settled. In 1982 twenty spaces became available for stores at Mallard Square, Highlands Hardware at the Highlands Plaza, two shops west of Scudder's Auction Gallery—today's Serendipity and Azure Rose—and six shops stretching back to Hildegard's Restaurant on Main Street. Nine shops and four office spaces were under construction as Carolina Mountain Shops, today's Carolina Square, east of Mallard Square.[547]

Ron Allen began construction of Mountain High Motel, a thirty-six unit complex on Pine Ridge, in 1983, the same year that John Cleaveland began his fourteen-year tenure as mayor, the second longest term after H. M. Bascom. Highlands' first chain store opened in 1985 as Majik Market and World Bazaar, one of 1,129 retail operations owned by Dillard Munford, replaced Bryson's Gulf Station at 4th and Main. Carolina Way, a new complex of shops at the site of the old Anderson/Sullivan mansion, opened in 1988.

In anticipation of the commercial needs of all these new enterprises, new banks had already begun to appear. Mountain Federal Savings and Loan, which was established under Ted Hoffman in 1974.[548] It merged in 1982 with Brevard Federal, which in 1993 joined today's Centura Bank.

West of 1st and Main, Carolina Mountain Bank was set up in 1979.[549] By 1990 it would grow into an $8 million purchase by North Carolina National Bank, which became Nations Bank when it merged with Citizens and Southern. The final merger in 1999 became today's Bank of America.

First Citizens Bank, intending originally to buy Carolina Mountain Bank in 1990, two years later built its own home at 4th and Laurel across from the Recreation Park. And Macon Savings Bank opened its Highlands branch in Carolina Way in 1995.

In the early stages of the shopping center craze, the town had authorized a land use survey in 1982 to help chart its own future, and the N.C. Division of Archives and History at the request of the Highlands Historical Preservation Society, Inc., conducted a Highlands Historical Inventory to determine what in town might be worth saving.

It identified 173 historic structures so diverse in architectural style that Carol Perrin Cobb, who wrote up the report, depicted two personalities of the town: "the stable, practical and provincial year-round personality and the playful, cosmopolitan summer personality" including a wide range of building styles and materials ranging from "a log cabin to an English manor house, from a Japanese pavilion to a Southern plantation house."[550]

The report recommended four districts and seven historical structures as worthy of local or national designation. The Satulah Mountain District and the Inn District in town would qualify on their own merit for the National

Register along with five buildings in the area: the Episcopal and Presbyterian churches, the Frank Hill house in Horse Cove, the Stanhope Hill–Albert Staub house at 6th Main, and the Prioleau Ravenel–Jules Blanc Monroe house at the crest of the Horse Cove Road.

The remaining two districts of historical significance were the Highlands Country Club and the Northern Residential District between Maple and Poplar streets. Two historical houses that would qualify were the Hutchinson–Frost–Hall–Farnsworth home and the Ravenel–Parker house known as *Wolf Ridge*.

Although the Highlands Inn and Old Edwards Inn, Episcopal and Presbyterian churches, and Satulah Mountain District were eventually given national recognition, the town failed to write any of its historic structures into a protective ordinance as growth in the commercial and residential districts continued.

In addition to the rise of shopping centers along the roads leading into and out of town, multi-store units began to appear within the central business district itself. In 1975 Jack and Robert McCulloch created Highlands Village Square near the Post Office on 5th Street.[551] It was a shopping and professional promenade of six office/stores, similar to the Pinebrook Condominiums project which they had just completed as Highlands' first year-round residential apartments at the corner of 5th and Spruce.

Soon after the Pinebrook development, Town Square arose on the south side of Main Street as a conversion of Town House Motel into nine new shops looking for owners. That same year, 1984, Mike Cannon proposed Oak Square, a half-million dollar mini-mall consisting of two two-story buildings connected by a covered plaza resembling a Spanish mission and containing ten stores and five apartments at the corner of Main and 3rd where the Fina and Sinclair service stations had stood since the mid thirties. In 1987 a hotel sprang up at the corner of Main and 2nd as Ed Spraker replaced Carl Zoellner's (originally Walter Reese's) house with twenty-eight rooms, known today as Highlands Suite.

Altogether, after the mid seventies the town of Highlands would experience more growth in its commercial district than in all one hundred years of its existence. Straying far afield from Kelsey's original concept of "a convenience center"—a post office, stores, shops, a schoolhouse, churches, hotels, etc. for its settlers—Highlands was fast succumbing to what Kelsey had specifically ruled out: "a commercial town." Furthermore, it was becoming a tourist attraction.

Kelsey had favored instead a summer resort, a second home for part-time residents seeking their health or pleasure in its restorative climate, rather than a passing attraction for day travelers or—as Sarah-Hicks Hines put it—Tin-Can Tourists.[552]

Sarah had applied her label during the early thirties to the day tourist whom she regarded as "so undesirable in every resort town" because he is "usually on his way to some large place and simply passing through smaller towns like Highlands; but those who come here usually have for their destination Highlands and no other place." In the early thirties, when the roads were still in their embryonic stages, the tin can tourist was just beginning to appear.

As if to restore a small part of what the town had lost in its headlong drive to commercialize, the Highlands Merchants Association was formed in 1984 as plans for Ron Allen's nine-shop Town Square and Mike Cannon's ten-shop Oak Square began to materialize and parking became a major concern.[553] Earle Young of Wit's End defined the association's role as seeking "to maintain the value of Highlands now and what it has always been," meaning unique and distinctive in character. Headed by Stan Cochran of Mirror Lake Antiques, it embarked on improvement projects around town.

One project involved a tree committee, which Ran Shaffner headed and which gained the town's approval in 1985 to plant four large red maple trees down the middle of Main Street. They would replace the altitude oak and its two red-oak companions that had fallen to the ax of progress in 1938. A number of big trees had also fallen recently on the Wright property in preparation for the shopping center to be built there.

Between October 4th and December 24th the public gave its unqualified support to the idea by contributing $6,400 to construct stone planters and purchase the trees to beautify them. Included in this donation were 8,000 pennies, the brainchild of Ted Shaffner who solicited contributions from the children of Highlands School to help restore to the town something of its original beauty. "The tall trees in Highlands are really what sets us apart from all these other places," remarked local surveyor Charlie McDowell at the planting.[554]

In the same year that the town's first subdivision ordinance was passed, 1978, the town had enacted a minimal tree ordinance setting up a tree board chaired by Ralph deVille to beautify the town's streets, highways, and public areas and to encourage the protection of its trees.

In 1987, still lamenting the sale of the Wright property surrounding Helen's Barn and the clear-cutting of the large trees on it that had graced the west end of the town for generations, the public was calling for a more comprehensive tree ordinance, which Ran Shaffner authored with the help of the tree board, the tree committee of the Merchants Association, and town officials. After many revisions that sought to balance individual property rights against the public's cry for protection from abuses during development, the town board approved it.

The new tree ordinance was amended in 1988 to allow for variances, but then suspended, leaving no controls in place over tree cutting on commercial property. After several moratoriums on tree cutting and repeated attempts at a workable replacement of the suspended ordinance, the town board chose instead to change the zoning ordinance.

It agreed to protect trees on commercially zoned land and encourage landscaping but scrapped the idea of a separate tree law and along with it the tree board. In the end, protection of very large trees, eighteen inches in diameter or greater, was also dropped.[555] Not until ten years had passed and Philip deVille had cut approximately twenty white pines and a scarlet oak at Main and 5th would the ordinance be amended again to protect trees over eight inches on commercial property.[556]

Meanwhile, in 1989, tree protection outside town was also becoming a hot issue. A hundred years earlier German emigrants to America had introduced clear-cutting as a method of land clearance, which in 1914 the newly formed U.S. Forest Service had rejected in favor of "selection."[557] But Forest Service practices had changed since then to include clear-cutting, which now faced public scrutiny.

This wasn't the first time the Highlands public had expressed disapproval of the policy. Back in 1971 a debate had raged over the use of clear-cutting vs. selective cutting on forty acres of Nantahala National Forest. At that time Dr. Malvina Trussell, former professor of science education at Florida State University and an outstanding naturalist, had led the opposition, citing a sixty-acre clear-cut from the forest in Horse Cove as a prime example of the wanton destructing of nature.[558] Now it was Bob Zahner and Bob Padgett who led the crusade to replace decades of timber exploitation under the aegis of the Forest Service with a multiple-use policy of responsible forest management.

In a 1989 letter to the *Highlander*, Zahner compared the timber industry's claim that "clear-cutting is necessary for a healthy forest" to the tobacco industry's claim that "smoking is not addictive."[559] Zahner and Padgett were joined by the Western North Carolina Alliance's "cut the clear-cutting" campaign in 1990. Five years later, when public opinion prevailed and an ecosystem approach was adopted by the Forest Service, the Alliance recognized Zahner with its coveted Esther C. Cunningham Award for his role in protecting the Big Creek and Chattooga River watersheds around Highlands. Zahner has often been cited as the "father of old-growth management" of the forests.

A Highlands Forest, 1897. Photo from R. H. Scadin Collection, UNC-A.

Throughout the eighties, mounting fears of overdevelopment in downtown Highlands fueled public opposition to almost any proposed project that might endanger the goose that laid the golden egg, as Highlands was now being dubbed. Like a virgin exposed to rape and plunder, the town's natural beauty—its major asset that over the years had attracted people to the area—was at risk, as was its quality of life. Gatlinburg, a once idyllic village in nearby Tennessee, became the catchword to warn against what Highlands might soon become if it too gave in to uncontrolled growth, strip development along its highways, and cheap commercialism.

As early as 1982, in the recurring interest of protecting the town's endangered charm, a beautification committee, chaired by Mrs. Robert L. Searle, had been set up to review architectural features in commercial construction, but it had lacked official jurisdiction. A sign ordinance, however, was written into law on January 1, 1984, and two years later all billboards were effectively banned within the town limits, their removal required within five years. In 1985, a week after the *Highlander* published architectural plans for Oak Square's two-story mini-mall at 3rd and Main, zoning board chairman Boots Pierson was calling for the creation of an official appearance commission.[560] Objecting to an alarming trend in what she called "obscene construction" in town, she described the board as needing some kind of architectural standards as guidelines for responsible decisions.

By 1987 five years had passed since the 1982 land use survey, during which time it was never formally adopted by the town. The time was accordingly ripe for another community-wide survey to update the earlier one. Inviting the North Carolina Department of Natural Resources and Community Development to carry out the project, the board voted to table several zoning changes in the works, such as size restrictions for new buildings along with minimum square footage per store.[561] It declared instead an interim ban on commercial construction until the new survey could be completed.

By August the following year, after Geoffrey Willett and his planning staff had poured over 2,000 hours into the survey's preparation with extensive input from local citizens as well as experts throughout the state and nation, the results were announced in the hope that at last the town would adopt a comprehensive plan. Of the 3,600 questionnaires that were mailed out, 1,315 useable responses or 37% had been received, which planner Geoffrey Willett regarded as terrific returns. The results showed an overwhelming majority of Highlanders wanted commercial development to slow down.[562]

Paramount among their concerns were downtown parking and traffic, recent commercial build-up, and the town's water system. There was almost unanimous opposition to mini-malls, and an overwhelming majority wanted no chain stores, especially fast food chains, and no more motels or overnight accommodations. There was strong support for a land use plan, better architectural standards, extraterritorial zoning, and more entertainment opportunities. "I've never seen a town that feels as strongly as this one," Willett remarked, noting the even greater consensus than in the previous survey.

The chief problem of downtown parking, which had plagued the town since the early fifties, had reached its climax at the time of the survey in the late eighties. A main reason for the creation of the Merchants Association in 1984 had been to address the question of parking, but struggle as it might to implement many an innovative solution, most of which had been proposed or tried many times before, it arrived at no satisfactory solution. The town board too wrestled with the problem, having itself waived the parking requirement for new shops in the main business district in 1982.

In 1987 construction in Highlands had approached $7 million.[563] With Town Square, Oak Square, and Wright Square planning to introduce a total of twenty-eight new shops onto Main Street, the issue reached a head in 1988 with Mike Cannon's proposal to convert the upstairs of Oak Square into eighteen motel units.[564] The zoning board's decision to require off-street parking for the project on a nearby adjacent lot, which Cannon owned, upset the Mayor and the town board, but within a month the board had issued a moratorium on motels, hotels, and eateries on Main Street, while the new land use survey was being distributed for public opinion of the overall quandary.

What evolved from the survey was the scrapping of the tabled zoning changes but a retention of the moratorium on all new commercial construction in order to provide a cooling off period in downtown development until the new land use plan could be implemented. Hearings on the already discussed tree ordinance usurped most of the town's energies until early 1989.

In June, despite recommendations from both the zoning and planning boards that a new law requiring shop owners to pave their driveways and parking lots be dropped, the town board voted to retain the requirement.[565] At issue was the contention that paving helped increase heat in the summer, caused more water runoff, was hard on nearby trees and greenery, and fostered a big-city atmosphere not in keeping with the village décor of Highlands, which the town board dismissed in favor of being able to mark off parking spaces in a paved lot.

When the new land use plan was finally unveiled on June 27, 1989, it recommended a complete overhaul of the zoning, subdivision, and sign ordinances, the enactment of architectural appearance and landscaping requirements, the establishment of a historical preservation commission, and extraterritorial zoning.[566] Its mission statement read, "to preserve, protect, and enhance those gifts of nature which make up the unique quality of our town and its environs."

More specifically the plan considered the natural environment to be of "immeasurable value" to the area, unusually fragile and not well suited to development. Particular attention had to be paid to soil erosion and sedimentation, protection of the water quality, the N.C. Ridge Law, preservation of trees and vegetation, and upgrading the classification of the area's lakes. In the residential areas the plan called for low-density development, extension of the sign ordinance to residential districts, incorporation of basic appearance standards into the ordinance including the protection of historic structures, the creation of a land trust to purchase and protect green areas, and provisions in the subdivision ordinance for green spaces and open areas.

For the commercial areas the plan aimed for a mixed atmosphere of businesses and aesthetic character. This would entail discouraging high-volume mini-malls with their concomitant parking problems, promoting the historic preservation of Main Street, acquainting prospective businesses with the market conditions peculiar to Highlands so as to reduce annual turnover, passing a stricter sign ordinance regarding size and quantity, reducing the area available for commercial development, and adopting appearance criteria for new and remodeled structures that would include landscaping requirements. All utilities would be placed underground, and a walking district of more sidewalks and paths would give pedestrians easier access to the downtown.

In the area of government the plan called for a joint appearance and historic preservation commission and the planning board's implementation and supervision of the overall plan. It recommended job descriptions for the town's staff and a program to recognize and appreciate the work of town employees.

Finally, concerning the parking dilemma, the plan recommended adopting a parking and traffic study previously prepared by the Department of Transportation engineers.[567] That study had concluded that the problem in Highlands was ineffective "parking management" rather than inadequate "parking supply." It recommended improving public access to what the town already had, rather than adding more spaces.

Access to spaces already available but not used on Oak Street (up to 150) and public parking behind town hall (up to 50) would be facilitated by the widening of Oak Street for sidewalks and more efficient angle parking. Paving Maple Street (Tobacco Road) would allow easier and safer passage to the public lot. Creating a walkway between Main and Oak streets would improve pedestrian access to these additional spaces, and construction of a left-turn lane at 3rd and Main would direct Franklin and Dillard through-traffic off Main Street. Paving the Church Street alleyway along the hill south of Main for use by service vehicles would divert them off Main Street, and posting one-hour and two-hour parking signs on Main and 4th would end the domination of spaces by visitors, residents, or employees who habitually parked there all day. These proposals, in DOT's view, were all that was really necessary to solve the parking problem that had been festering in Highlands for thirty years.

The 1989 land use plan's implementation, whether in part or in its entirety, Willett advised, would, of course, take time and involve adjustments along the way. Indeed, formal adoption of the plan by the town board would entail a schedule for updating the town's ordinances and policies over the next twenty years.

At its first opportunity to put one of the recommendations of the plan into effect, however, the town backed off, accepting a compromise instead. The planning board with input from the plan proposed amending the zoning ordinance to require that new or expanded businesses downtown provide one parking space for each 250 square feet of planned floor space. Implied but unstated in the proposal was the slowdown that such a requirement would place on commercial growth, reflecting the popular sentiment against further development.

At a public hearing, however, responding to opposition from several merchants who questioned the fairness of such a law, the board decided against the plan's recommendation. Instead it opted to limit new construction and expansions to one square foot per square foot of land, a provision that still exists in today's ordinance.

At the same time the board voted to install a sidewalk and angle parking on the Wright Square side of West Main. This decision provoked a petition opposing the project and ended with adult and young protesters—some perched in the branches of the last remaining dogwoods and the ancient arborvitae that fronted Helen's Barn—intent on preventing their removal. It was an act that harked back many years to a similar protest when the altitude oak was cut to allow paving at the east end of Main Street in 1938 and the large shade trees were extracted from the Main Street park to make room for the Art Gallery in 1947. Indeed, the issue helped cost two commissioners their seats on the town board in a near-record turnout for the November election.[568]

In a less controversial vein, a very popular program arose during the mid eighties that captured the attention of enthusiastic residents, even drawing praise in the land use survey. In 1986, an organization headed by Glenn

Magner and called "For A Clean Environment" or FACE, announced its intention to clean up Highlands and its surroundings through an effective project christened "Adopt-a-Road," involving periodic clean-up days by the whole community. The program caught on like wildfire, residents of all ages and from many service clubs toting trash bags and picking up litter along the town's streets and highways. By 1988 reports of the Highlands Adopt-a-Road project had spread to the state's capital, where it became a model for North Carolina's subsequent Adopt-a-Highway program.

In direct response to a need expressed in the survey, the town board proposed constructing a new sewage treatment plant. The expressed intent was to clean up the town's water supply by replacing septic tanks around Mirror Lake and Lake Sequoyah with sewer hookups. Opponents of the project argued that a limited sewage plant was one of the few remaining natural means of controlling growth.

But with a narrow voter approval and a permit granted for half a million gallons per day, plans were set in motion to close the existing sewage plant at Mill Creek and construct a new plant and outfall pipe below the Lake Sequoyah dam, putting the effluent into the Cullasaja River instead of the lake. Almost immediately the town found itself engaged in a lawsuit as funeral home operator Harry Neal sought $450,000 in compensation for the five acres of his land that the town condemned for the new plant. The town had to settle for $375,000, but more problems, waiting in the closet, would emerge during the nineties.

The Nineties: The New Plan

Despite the large quantity of new arrivals in the town's shopping area during the eighties, the usual turnover remained significantly high. For every two new businesses that opened in town, a previous business would fail, giving new shops a 37% chance of surviving for four years.[569] These failures weren't limited to small single shops. Indeed, they began on a grand scale with the Highlands Inn in 1989, which Rip and Pat Benton had to rescue from the auction block. Then, in 1990 Wachovia Bank foreclosed on Mallard Square, and Ron Allen took over, renaming it Mountain Brook Center, creating six motel suites on the second level, and recruiting new stores to fill the vacancies downstairs. That same year Dillard Munford's Majik Market chain filed for bankruptcy, closing its Highlands store at 4th and Main.

The nineties opened with the land use planning committee's proposal of a new zoning ordinance including provisions for a sign law, new zoning map, and extraterritorial zoning based on the community-wide survey. Almost immediately the recommendation for extraterritorial zoning was killed, primarily by those outside town who might be affected. They complained they wouldn't have a vote in town affairs.[570]

The intent of the new zone would have been to help protect the town's watershed but also to keep the business districts restricted to downtown, thus avoiding commercial strips sprawled along the highways. But the basic objection, expressed by Lonnie Manley and those who chose not to live within the town limits, was this: "We don't need anyone else telling us what to do with our land." So the new ordinance and zoning map with adjustments but excluding extraterritorial zoning were approved.

White Oak House, built 1883. Drawing by Walter Hunt, 1982.

In 1991 the town adopted land use recommendations for an appearance commission, made up of planning board members but acting in an advisory capacity.[571] It also passed a ban on drive-through windows at restaurants. The appearance commission, which had existed unofficially since 1982, was now chaired by Ruth Fox. It produced a thirty-seven page report of recommended architectural guidelines for buildings in both the business and residential areas of town.[572]

Favoring the traditional, historic design that predominately characterized Main Street, while opposing artificial facades and corny Indian, western, mountain, and alpine styles, the report designated salient models within the commercial district, such as Highlands Inn for its simple design and colors; Old Edwards Inn for its harmonious blend of wood, brick, and native stone; the Hudson Library for its traditional wood siding and inviting porch and rockers; White Oak Antiques (Judge Dana Hunt's second cottage or the Aaron Esty house) on West Main, and Hanover House Antiques (architect John Gottwals' creation) on the Cashiers Road across from the ball park. Architect Jim Fox's unorthodox *Highlander* newspaper building was deemed successful because it employed traditional materials of wood and native stone.

Native materials were also recommended in the residential areas, where good examples included the Corb Hankey residence on Cobb Road, Robert Morris' *Caretaker House* (designed by Fox) on Worley Road, the Henry Sloan–George Heery house on Satulah Mountain, *World's End* (the Eskrigge mansion) on Satulah, and the Shaffner residence (built by architect Frank Sheldon) on Hickory Street.

The report emphasized that these were only suggestions of the tasteful, simple, low-key design that gave Highlands its unique flavor. The wish, of course, was to preserve this flavor through careful management and quality growth.

The year 1990 saw the revitalization in Highlands of the Macon County League of Women Voters, which Charlotte Elliott had first formed in 1923.[573] Spearheaded by Eleanor Metzger, it attracted approximately fifty members, who were concerned about the future of the town and the county. They produced well-researched and informative profiles: *Know Your County*, *Know Your Public Schools*, and a handbook for citizens, *Government in Macon County*.

They held a public forum on watershed protection and carried out careful studies of community issues with the intent of supporting or opposing, not particular candidates, but vital issues affecting the town and its surroundings. In conjunction with the Western North Carolina Alliance, they published five articles about the future of Macon County, including methods of controlling sprawl while still encouraging growth in appropriate areas. Concluding that sprawl stoppers were essential to preserving the traditional character of a community and its quality of life, they argued,

We must reflect upon what type of commercial centers we want to see in our communities. In town after town, commercial strips are replacing village centers. As commercial strips and mini-malls extend down major roads, people cannot walk from store to store, traffic safety and tie-ups become more and more of a problem, and our communities lose their individuality and traditional character. One town begins to look just like the next.

These articles by the League sought to balance control with growth. They not only defined the problems inherent in both urban and rural development but also offered detailed and well-reasoned solutions to every problem considered.

As the town struggled to put more parts of its new plan into effect, it established staggered terms for town commissioners in 1994 and upgraded the position of town clerk, which Herb James had held for twenty-eight years, to town administrator, the position now held by Richard Betz.[574]

In the prior year the town had begun construction on the new sewage treatment plant. But in 1995, before Cullasaja Operating Services of Asheville could place the plant in operation, Margaret "Peg" Jones of Save Our Rivers, Inc., in Franklin expressed concern about the environmental impact the plant would have on the wild and scenic Cullasaja River. Since it would generate an additional flow of only a quarter million gallons per day, well below the half million required for an Environmental Assessment, no assessment had been required and was therefore never carried out. Save Our Rivers (SOR) expressed concern about micro invertebrates and fish in the river as well as the quality of the water for traditional baptisms and recreational use.

When the sewage plant permit expired in 1997, the Environmental Protection Agency withheld renewal until some of these issues were addressed. Attempts by SOR to have seven and a half miles of the river designated "natural and scenic" by the state legislature in 2000 failed, not because the designation would actually impose additional water quality standards on the town's plant, but because the town council, unable to secure guarantees from the attorney general, feared it might and asked the legislature to kill the bill, which it did.

As the twentieth century drew to a close, Highlands appeared poised uncertainly on the threshold of more growth, even with all the proper controls in place: a planning board, a zoning board, and an appearance commission. When Ken Adams proposed building a Burger King fast-food restaurant in

1995 at the intersection of Spring Street and the Dillard Road, he set off a furor of protests, for citizen opposition had previously scared off a proposed Hardee's franchise, which chose to locate in Cashiers instead.

The arguments against a fast-food enterprise in Highlands included references to the community-wide survey, concerns that the town would lose its unique character in the growing sameness of American towns and cities, and environmental worries about the accompanying trash. But some citizens favored the project for making available a more affordable alternative to tourist-priced restaurants. Approved by the planning board, the appearance commission, and the zoning board, it was successfully contested in Superior Court by Ralph Stevens and remanded to the zoning board for a rehearing. In the end Adams abandoned his plans to build the restaurant.

Although a hotel chain put up a Hampton Inn at the corner of 1st and Spring Street in 1994 and the Kelsey and Hutchinson Lodge replaced the former Lee's Inn in 1998, the long-serving Blue Ridge Pharmacy and the ever-popular Highlander and Mountaineer restaurants all closed. The town's first hotel, Highlands Inn, came under new management. Highlands Memorial Park shifted from private to public ownership as the town, under the supervision of public works director and town engineer Lamar Nix, accepted perpetual care.

Of the 222 businesses in town at the end of the twentieth century, twenty-eight had served the public on Main and 4th for twenty years or more and were still alive and well. On Main Street they were the Bird Barn, Central House Restaurant and Old Edwards Inn, Cyrano's Bookshop, the Dry Sink, Farmer's Market (formerly Red Carpet), Furniture South (formerly Haber Furniture), the Highland Hiker, Highlands Pharmacy, Highlands Inn, House of Wong, Juliana's, Mountain Fresh (formerly Tate's Supermarket and Potts Supermarket), Reeves Hardware, the Royal Scot, Scudder's Galleries, the Stone Lantern, Wit's End, and the Washpot. On 4th Street they were the Christmas Tree on the Hill, First Union National Bank, Highlands Decorating Center (formerly Paint and Mirror), Highlands Furniture, Highlands Gem Shop, Hill Top Grill (formerly Coach's Corner, Highlands Tasty Shoppe, Quick-N-Easy, and Tastee-Freeze), Le Pavillon Fashions, Mirror Lake Antiques, Nick's Restaurant, and Schmitt Building Contractors.

Main Street wore a new and expectant face as a 1999 town project, under Mayor Allen "Buck" Trott's administration, replaced sewer lines; laid electric, phone, and TV cables underground as proposed in the 1989 plan; and converted Main and 4th street sidewalks from concrete to red brick.

Despite the 1989 plan's discouragement of commercial development along the highways entering town, the year 2000 would see the onset of such growth as construction began on the Shoppes at Old Creek across from

Dusty's Superette on the Dillard Road. In 2001 the town installed new traffic-control stoplights activated by magnetic fields at 4th and 5th street intersections, and Maple Street was at long last widened from a dirt Tobacco Road to a paved bypass, as recommended by the Department of Transportation in 1987 and planning board in 1993, to facilitate parking in the town lot and decrease traffic on Main Street.[575]

In the doorway of the new millennium, the town of Highlands was no longer a village. Walter Taylor and John Cleaveland have expressed the two prevalent views of what they both consider the tremendous change. Walter feels that the town has lost its charm. "You used to look down on a corn field or a cabbage patch and hear cow bells or horses. Now when you climb Yellow Mountain in the winter, the ridges are covered with houses. The town has grown so that Highlands will never get its old charm back."

John attributes some of the problem to speculators. In the past, families bought a house and kept it for generations, but today more houses are bought as investments, the intent being to sell for profit. And as population grows and affluence increases, the market force changes, leaving John to conclude that the town will one day have to face the chain stores. "Progress is a strange word," he claims. "It has allowed the local people to make a living, which wasn't possible twenty to twenty-five years ago. They couldn't work twelves months a year. But people have to survive."

While John feels the town has done an admirable job in trying to keep growth from overcoming its residents, he admits, "We've all seen things we wish hadn't occurred." Still, he doesn't see Highlands falling back, for the one draw it will always have, barring the current concern over the drought, is its cool climate. Yet even more important than its climate is its people. "This is a slow, sleepy town," he says. "The people still make Highlands. They're friendly. They welcome people with open arms."

Perhaps the last word on the perceived change in the town between the end of the nineteenth century and the beginning of the twentieth was expressed by Olive Crane, who at ninety-five clearly remembered a whole different way of life in the old days.[576] The contrast is particularly striking considering how she grew up.

We went to the store every two weeks to get coffee, sugar, flour — couldn't grow it. Potts had a store. Luke Rice had a meat market.

Used to cut ice off Mirror Lake to keep things cold.

We traded what we growed on the farm for a pack of green coffee. It hadn't been parched. You parched it yourself and ground it.

We washed the flour sacks and used them to stuff quilts and made clothing from them. Made little girls' dresses out of cotton seed sacks, chicken feed sacks.

My dad would go coon hunting. He'd get in bed and go to sleep till one or two o'clock and then go hunting. He said, "That's when you get the fat ones."

We used to have squirrels and rabbits. Now you never see a rabbit, and we've got one squirrel that's been here a year or two.

When asked how she felt about the town of Highlands in 1986, Olive admitted she hardly recognized the place. There used to be spaces between the stores so that she could immediately identify which was which, but now "all the buildings have all grown together," she said. Highlands had really changed.

Whether it would ultimately fall victim to the overdevelopment and overpopulation that had tarnished other golden isles of paradise or be able to retain enough of the quaint charm and natural beauty that had attracted "good citizens" over the years to fight for its preservation as a place where people loved to live and visit, the two opposing forces of exploitation and preservation stood in the balance, each quite capable of making or breaking the town.

The town of Highlands, Main and 4ᵗʰ, in the year 2000. Photos by the author.

22. Just Like Home

A house is built of logs and stone,
Of tiles and posts and piers;
A home is built of loving deeds
That stand a thousand years.

—Victor Hugo

The earliest homes in Highlands, apart from those few that predated its founding, were constructed along Main Street, with a few scattered to the north and south. A quick tour of Kelsey's first map of the town, which he created on January 1, 1881, will serve to identify them all.[577]

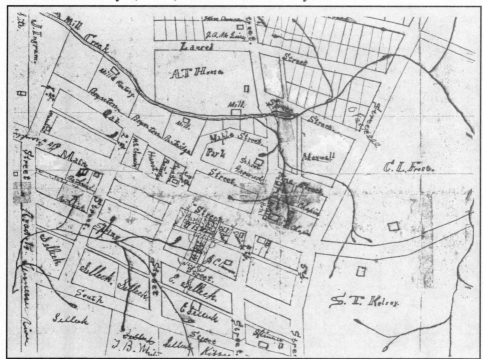

Buildings as they appeared on a section of Kelsey's original map of Highlands, penned on Jan. 1, 1881

Beginning at the western edge of town and progressing east along the entire length of Main Street, William B. Dobson's house stood just west of 1st Street's intersection with Main.[578] Original owner of all the land on which Hutchinson and Kelsey developed Highlands, Dobson built his home between 1877 and 1879. It became Henry Stewart's first home in 1885, C. G. Memminger's in 1899, and home to the Raoul family in 1916. Rebecca

Raoul Altstaetter ran it as *Rosemary*, a boarding house, beginning in 1926. It still exists, adjacent to its enormous brick addition of 1977, as today's Furniture South.

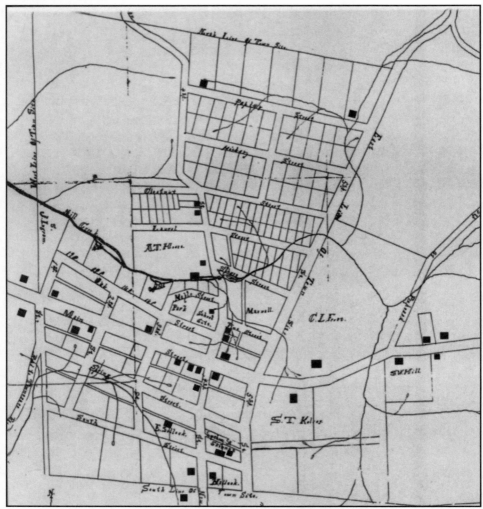

A clarified view of Kelsey's map of 1881

In the first block of Main Street, east of Dobson's home and site of today's Wright Square, stood the log Law House, which Servitus and Jennette Bathrick bought in 1880 and owned for two years before selling to Sumner Clark.[579] Near 2nd Street, they built their home, owning also two or three hundred acres to the south.

Only one house existed in the second block. It was the home and store of Ed Cunningham and John Morton, which they built in 1877 on the site later occupied by Annie Root, now Reeves Hardware.[580]

In the third block, the very middle of town, a clover field, now occupied by the Masonic Hall and Methodist Church, stretched as far as Baxter White's home, store, and post office. White's home rivaled Kelsey's as possibly the first built in the new town in 1875. At least, his ad in the paper made this claim.[581]

OLDEST HOUSE In Highlands.	T. BAXTER WHITE, HIGHLANDS, N. C.

White left Highlands in 1911, and within eight years his house was home to Guy and Ethel Mae Potts Paul. Their son Guy "Butchie" laid claim legitimately to being born in the "White House." The Pauls razed it around 1921 and built a new home on the same spot. There it stood until Town House Motel replaced it in 1956, the site of today's Town Square.

East of Baxter White's home and post office, still in the third block, John Arthur built his home in 1879, fronted with a white picket fence.[582] By the time Christopher Whittle bought it in 1925, it had reverted to a vacant meadow. It was here that the Highlands Art Gallery would locate in 1954, site of all the shops between Town Square and the Cleaveland home today.

William B. Cleaveland wouldn't build his home, where it stands today east of the Stone Lantern, until 1888, so it doesn't appear on the first map of the town. What does appear is Annie Dimick's Cheap Cash Store, constructed in 1878 as the only other store in Highlands apart from postmaster Baxter White's grocery.

East of Dimick's store, on the corner lot but not shown on the first map, Charles L. Martin would build his Central Meat Market in 1883.[583] It would offer fresh beef, pork, mutton, and poultry every day. But his endeavors were short lived, for within the same year he would return with his family to Columbus, Ohio, his market replaced by Theron Walden's Drug Store. From 1913–72, as most Highlanders will remember, this building housed the Holts' soda shop. This was where Herman Wilson said "you bought a Coke, and they'd mash a little liquid in a little glass, you know, five cents!" Half of the building in 1937 became Harry Holt's Café. Today both halves are occupied by the House of Wong.

In 1878 the fourth block began with Central House, for James Rideout's corner Granite Store, which doesn't appear on the early map, wasn't built until 1889. Highlands' first newspaper, the *Blue Ridge Enterprise*, would rent a room in Central House in 1883, as would Dr. Will Anderson for his first office.

Baxter Wilson would construct his home, also not on the map, in 1884 east of Central House, the core of which still exists today as the former longtime home of the Bird Barn.[584] The Presbyterian Church, another construction too late for the map, would appear at the 5th Street corner in 1885.

In the sixth block, Kelsey had built in 1875 what purported to be the first house in town.[585] It was certainly the oldest when it burned to the ground in October, 1976, leaving only the handsome chimney behind today's Falls on Main that marks its grave today.

The Kelsey/Harbison/Warren/Harris house when it burned in 1976. Photo courtesy of the Highlander.

There was no home in 1881 at the current corner of Leonard Street and Main, but this is where Orpha Rose would build her cottage in November, 1883, across from Dr. Frost's house.[586] She was one of the earliest principals and teachers of Highlands School. The site is currently occupied by I'm Precious Too, the house that Louis Edwards built for Mrs. C. K. Wall in 1936.

Stanhope Hill's home of 1878 exists today as the home of Dr. Richard Martorell, just east of 6th and Main.[587] East of it was Bascom's first residence, owned today by Ernest and Joyce Franklin. Then came John and Nettie McClearie's, later home to the Atlanta sisters Lucia Harville and Marie Harville Van Huss; and today, Atlanta's Ian and Debbie Dixon. Both of these homes were built in 1881 and appear on the original map. Bascom would relocate his home to Satulah in 1892, and John and Nettie McClearie would leave for San Diego, California, in the fall of 1887.

The first house east of today's Gibson Road, belonging to Melinda Cook from Volusa, Fla., wasn't built until the year after the map, 1882. Soon after Melinda departed in 1890, this house belonged to Margaretta Ravenel. The site was later home to the Akers; and today, Dr. John Nickerson.

Finally, beyond the east edge of town, was Prioleau Ravenel's summer home, built in 1879 as *Wantoot* and known today as *Playmore*.

Beginning on the north side of East Main across from McClearie's home stood the home of E. E. Ewing, editor of Highlands' first newspaper.[588] Built in 1881, it was later owned by Porter Pierson, then Dr. J. Manson Valentine, before it was given to the Highlands Biological Foundation. Today it is the Richard Bruce House just west of the Nature Center.

Between Ewing's home and 6th Street was the home of builder Frank Hill, which he constructed in 1880.[589] This is where Annie Dimick would live from 1882 to 1886 while she ran her Cheap Cash Store on Main Street. Nathan and Emma Billstein dwelt here in 1903. When it burned in 1931, they rebuilt the home that Don and Carole O'Neal own today.

Hutchinson's home, begun in 1878, sat on the forty acres between 6th and 5th.[590] Dr. Frost bought it in 1880, finished it, and sold it to T. T. Hall in 1890. It still stands as the old Farnsworth place on East Main just east of the Hudson Library and is owned today by Neal Allen.

There was no Episcopal Church in 1881, so the next home to appear on the map, moving west, was Mary Chapin's *Gray Cottage*, which she built near the 5th Street corner in 1883.[591] She and her husband John Jay Smith lived here until their deaths in 1940 and 41, after which it became the home of Fred Edwards, then Jennie Burlingame, and today, Wolfgangs On Main.

The only other building to occupy this block was Highlands House, constructed in 1880 as a wedding gift to John Jay and Mary Chapin Smith from Mary Chapin's Aunt Eliza Wheaton. The year after the map of 1881 James Rideout built his first store, Rideout & Company, as a corner attachment to Highlands House.[592] Dr. O'Farrell had his drug store here in the 1890s; H. M. Bascom, his real estate office in the 1930s, followed by Frank Cook; and today it's the home of Country Inn Antiques.

There were no homes in the block between 4th and 3rd. The map of 1881 shows no store either. The five buildings between 4th and 5th were added after the map. Bascom's store on the corner, for example, was completed in August, 1883; W. B. Cleaveland's store and Bascom's barn and livery stable, in 1885; and Henry Skinner's building, known much later as the old Paul store, in 1883. Baxter Wilson built his store across from White's post office in 1884.

Two homes crowned the beginning and end of the high ridge that arched from 3rd to 1st streets. Known as Oak Ridge, it ran from 3rd to 2nd, beginning with Capt. Charles Boynton's home, which he built in 1881.[593] In 1905 this was home to David Norton, but for forty years from 1924 to 1964 Phoebe Crisp, Helen Potts, Walter Paxton, and Phil Tate would run it as an inn, and for thirty-five more years Evona Phelps would operate it as a popular restaurant. Today it's known as Main Street Inn.

There was nothing west of Boynton's home on Oak Ridge in 1881, for it was 1883 before the miller William Partridge built his one-and-a-half story frame home next door.[594] In 1909 this would be Luke Rice's home. Today it's a shop: Executive Gifts.

Also in 1883 Judge Dana Hunt from Excelsior, Minnesota, would build the next house, a beautiful cottage with a wrap-around porch, belonging eventually to Aaron Esty and later Darthula Rice but known today as *White Oak House*.[595] This would be Hunt's second home adjacent to his first farther on, built a year earlier but no longer extant, having been replaced by the current Baptist parsonage in 1939. In 1886 Judge Hunt would build his third dwelling on Chestnut Street, which during the 1920s became the second home of Irvin Rice's.

Except for Boynton's home, none of these houses on Oak Ridge, including the first Methodist Church of 1883–84 (today's Baptist Church), existed on the map of 1881.

From 2nd to 1st streets, today's site of Mountain High Motel, stretched Pine Ridge, and the only house in this block was that of Robert Marchant at the far west corner of First Street.[596] By 1884 Thomas Parker, Prioleau Ravenel's step-son who had come from Greenville, S.C., the year earlier, lived here. Though the house burned in the 1920s, its foundations and chimney supported the structure where W. S. Davis would live for many years, followed by Claude "Pat" Patterson. Today it is being renovated by Gus and Jan Lard.

Two more homes would show up on Pine Ridge as later additions to the early map: Ellen Ellis built at the east end of Pine Ridge in 1882.[597] By 1891 this was the home of Antle Henry, who left for Oregon in 1901, leaving it to become the Baptist manse and later a private home. When the Mountain High Motel was built, it was moved in 1984 to where it exists today, remodeled by Mary Ann Williams from Atlanta, across from the ballpark on 4th Street and behind Hanover House Antiques.

William Blanchard from New Hampshire built the second home atop Pine Ridge. It was fronted by a fence in 1883, high up near the center of today's motel.[598]

Last but certainly not least on the earliest map was the home of George and Mollie Jacobs. Built in 1876 on the corner of 1st and Main, it served as Highlands' first boarding house.[599] In 1914 it was home to Jim Rogers.

These then were the nineteen homes on Main Street, which appeared on the earliest map of Highlands in 1881, almost five times the total number of buildings in the little village of 1876. Six more homes existed south of Main, five of them clustered around the intersection of South and 4th at the base of today's Satulah Road. Charles Allen built his farmhouse west of the climb up Satulah in the early spring of 1878, but he kept it only a year before selling it to Joseph Halleck.[600]

At the southwest corner of 4th and South, Dr. Kibbee built his home in 1878 just below Allen's farmhouse.[601] When Judge Jim Hines and his family purchased it in 1924, it became *Chestnut Burr Cottage*, known since 1976 as Nick's Restaurant. At the northeast corner of 4th and South, Monroe Skinner erected his home in 1878.[602] Five years later it became Islington House, eventually King's Inn. In 1879 at the southeast corner of 4th and South, Joseph Halleck built his home, which in twenty years would give way to Pierson Inn, neither of which exist today.[603] Within the same year, at the northwest corner of 4th and South, Eben Selleck's home and lot occupied all of the Spring Street block between 3rd and 4th, as it does today.[604] From the thirties to the sixties this was home to the McCalls. It is now the *Rabbit Hole*, summer home of Bernard and Betty Neal.

One more home south of Main was that of Sumner Clark which he built in 1882, at the southwest corner of 4th and today's Church Street on the hill.[605] It was later home to Clarissa Burt, who helped her sister Margaretta Ravenel fund the building of the Presbyterian Church, and eventually Aunt Tudie Rice. It belongs today to the Jellens, behind their Gem Shop.

North of Main in 1881 there were eight homes. In the block across from today's town hall at the current site of Schmitt Building Contractors, Oscar Ricketson of Blunt County, Alabama, built his home in the summer of 1878.[606] At the northwest corner of that block, occupied today by John Cleaveland Realty and Harllee Gallery/CK Swan, was Monroe Skinner's blacksmith shop, which he constructed upon his arrival in 1878. In 1883 J. M. Abercrombie would replace Skinner's enterprise with his own home and blacksmith shop, site of Carl Zoellner's garage during the late forties and early fifties and then Potts laundry.[607]

Farther north on 4th Street due of the Spruce Street intersection, Arthur House built his home in 1877 above his mill.[608] It is today the oldest house in the original town of Highlands. North of House's house and beyond today's entrance into the Recreation Park, which in 1880 was known as West Laurel Street, Joseph McGuire constructed his home.[609]

William "Will" Duncan, arriving from Seneca, S.C. in 1883, would build next to Joseph McGuire, across from today's Best of the Bunch Florist.[610] He set up his boot-and-shoe repair shop in a corner of H. M. Bascom's store on Main, but he also ran a planing mill. In appearance he had what Walter Reese described as dark red hair and chin whiskers three feet long. They were the most outstanding red that Walter had ever seen, for which Will was reported to have been offered money to display them on a road show. Will stayed only a year in Highlands and died not long after he left. Having sold his shoe business to L. O. White and moved to Clayton, he was planing a rough board when it caught in his planer, broke apart, and shot a long splinter through his body, killing him instantly.

The northeast corner of 4th and Chestnut is empty today, but it was here in 1877 that Walker Clingon of New Haven, Connecticut, erected his home, in which Annie Whipp Pierson would later live and hold home school.[611]

The only other house off 4th Street in 1878 stood at the north end of town. Benson and Louise Wells built their home in the spring of that year at the corner of 4th and Poplar.[612] The sister of Ella Emmons Hudson, Louise established the library with a single box of donated books in her sister's name. Mildred Wilson lives in a different house on the original Wells lot today.

At the east end of Poplar where it would have met 5th, had it been extended, Charles Edwards built his home and barn in 1878.[613] Though the original home is gone today, the Edwards family owns the second home he built to replace it in 1891. Sometime after finishing it, Charles left Highlands for Savannah in search of work and totally disappeared. His son Grover had to quit school to support the bereaved family. He married Jonathan Heacock's daughter Helen and had three children while he worked for Prioleau Ravenel, eventually becoming a painter and a small dairy farmer.

A few other homes still exist from early Highlands days. They appear as additions on Hutchinson's copy of the Kelsey map during the ten years after 1881. One of these was a unique and beautifully constructed home that still graces 4th Street opposite today's ballpark was not built until 1885. Known today as Hanover House Antiques, it was home to a consummate architect, John Z. Gottwals, a native of Pennsylvania who moved from Savannah.[614] He married Barak Wright's granddaughter Martha Norton, twenty-three years his junior.

He built his own home with timber cut in the sawmill he bought from the Boynton brothers on Mill Creek. He designed the outside walls to protrude from many different angles so as to withstand strong winds. Even the main rooms had unusual shapes, several with eight walls. The doorbell was a trigger atop an ornate doorknob. There was a third-floor turret room offering peace and quiet. He also supervised the construction of the current Methodist Church at its present site, aided by Martha who even put up some of the rafters.

Home of John Z. and Martha Norton Gottwals, built in 1885. Photo from High-lands Historic Inventory.

Across the street from Gottwals' residence was the home of Henry Downing of Yazoo, Michigan, built in 1890 on what was then called Seminary Hill.[615] Henry Stewart bought it as his second home nine years later, having sold his Dobson home at 1st and Main to the Memmingers. It became Frank Cook's home in 1969 and today serves as Bruce and Barbara Werder's bed and breakfast, known as Stewart House, on Hickory Street.

A second home, built at about the same time, 1890, was Downing's neighbor to the east, Sophie Smith of Charleston, S.C. This is where Corinne Froneberger would live and run her home school from 1913 until her death around 1925. It is where Bill and Henrietta Marett would live in 1975; Steve and Beth Ham, today.

On the other side of Hickory Street just before the plunge down Thrill or Monkey Hill is the home that Frank Sheldon, architect for Davis House (later Lee's Inn), built in October, 1886. It served at the turn of the century as home of the Presbyterian Church's second minister, Rev. Joel Wade. Claudian Northrop of Washington, D.C., lived here during the teens and twenties; R. K. Nimmons of Seneca, S.C., during the thirties; and Roy "Nick" Potts, from the forties to the sixties. The Shaffners own it today.

The only African–American family to actually own a home in Highlands was that of Mack and Mary McAfee, who in 1910 paid Henry Bascom $350 for a small one-and-a-half story wooden shingled frame house on Laurel

Street, later Henrietta Marett's Real Estate office, behind today's Stop & Shop convenience store on north 4th Street. The McAfees sold it back to Bascom in 1923 for $400. Their granddaughter Patricia, until recently, lived in Black Mountain, N.C.

Homes with a Name

Many homes in Highlands, like the people who built and inhabited them over the years, had colorful names, often reflecting the personalities of the homes if not their builders. Hutchinson's *Corrymela* in 1878 (which Patrick Farnsworth later changed to *Connemara*, his ancestral home in Scotland[616]) was one of the earliest to carry a name. S. P. and Margaretta Ravenel built *Wantoot*, the first summer home in Highlands in 1879 on the south side of Horse Cove Road. When Blanc Monroe of New Orleans bought it in 1914, he christened it *Playmore*, the name it bears today.

Mrs. K. T. Bingham called her home which she constructed on the south side of the Bowery Road in 1883 *Kalalanta*. Justice of the Peace M. I. Skinner's home, which he built under Sunset Rocks in 1883, was called *Glencroft*, later *Trillium Lodge*. *Gray Cottage*, today's Wolfgangs on Main, was also built in 1883 by Cynthia Loomis Chapin, mother of Mary Chapin Smith, who occupied it with her husband John Jay Smith. Judson Cobb built his *Altadona* in 1886 surrounding Jackson Johnston's and Jonathan Ford's old log cabin at the site of today's 5th hole at the Highlands Country Club, Cason and Nancy Callaway's home today.

Henry W. Sloan's house, built 1906–07. Photo courtesy of Tammy Lowe.

Many other summer homes followed the established tradition of having names. Dr. Mary Lapham bought a farmhouse on Satulah from Prioleau Ravenel in 1897 which she enlarged and occupied with her two friends, Mrs. Edith Dougall and Miss Carolyn Barker. She named it *Faraway*. Around 1906–07 Henry Sloan, who had lived as a young man in England and Italy, built his home as a Mediterranean showplace on Satulah. He christened it *Cheeononda*, meaning in Cherokee "little hills upon little hills," with its tremendous sloping lawn, flower-bordered walkways, and sunken garden.[617]

Henry Sloan's Cheeononda Gardens. Photo by George Masa, 1929.

His garden consisted of a series of terraces, filled with natural flora of the mountainside, including rhododendron and laurel as well as native trees but also Italian imports, and supported by dry walls of native stone, some crowned with carved balustrades, classical urns, and statuary. Henry, his first wife Katherine Depew, and his second wife Daisy Moody are all buried on one of the lower terraces of the garden. Since 1979 the home has belonged to George and Betty Heery of Atlanta.

Near Henry Sloan's house was *Wind Rush*, home of his sister Alice Lyons. Minnie Warren's *The Hedges* stood on the east side of the road that bears her name today overlooking the Highlands club property and golf links with a magnificent sweep of mountains in the background. At the end of this road was Edward Moore's *Pooh's Corner*. George Worley called his Satulah home *The Big House in the Wood*, and Margaret Young named her Joe Webb home *Lawhorn Shack*. Between the Sloan estate and Dr. Lapham's home, there was Professor Huger Elliott's *Ocoee*. And near the top of

Satulah, Robert Eskrigge built *World's End*, which Italian masons erected with native gray stone in the English style in 1908–11.

Alice Lyons' Wind Rush. Photo by George Masa, 1929.

Robert Eskrigge's World's End, built 1908–11 on Satulah

Wolf Ridge, the Ravenel/Parker house, looking east to Whiteside, Black Rock, and Horse Cove. Photos by George Masa, 1929.

Wolf Ridge, overlooking Horse Cove, was the large classic Craftsman home that Thomas Parker built for his half-sisters Marguerite and Claire Ravenel in 1915. Its panoramic view of Whiteside, Sagee, Horse Cove, Fodderstack, Satulah, Wayah Bald; the Fishhawks, Balsams, and Smokies; Yellow Mountain, even Clingman's Dome, and the village was one of the loveliest in the region.

Judge George Janvier tucked away his *No-Vue Atol* on the southwest slope of Satulah; and Hampton Perry, his *Highfield* on the north slope, the later home of George Saussy.

By 1935 homes in Highlands had names like *Idylease*, *The Waterwitch*, *Topside*, Robert Foreman's *Tanglewood* on Lindenwood (now Ravenel) Lake, *Poco No Mos*, *Kareska*, *Chetolah*, *Belle Vista*, *Shakmoore*, and *Midlinks*.

The mountains were covered with named homes from O. W. McConnell's *Eagle Nest* beyond Whiteside to Frank Wightman's *Above Blue Valley* on Brushy Face. Dr. Theodore Lamb's *Chestnut Lodge* with its distinctive turnstile gate was the first house built on Satulah Mountain in 1892. It is not to be confused with *Chestnut Burr Cottage* of Dr. George Kibbee, today's Nick's Restaurant just below it at the base of Satulah, or Stephanie Nathan's *Chestnut Perch* atop Little Bear Pen. Also on Little Bear Pen was William Crawford's *Ctzunayla*, meaning "Octagon," depicting its shape.

The Rainwater Estate, a thirty-six room mansion, was built over several years from 1937 to 1940 above Highlands Estates by Charles Veazey Rainwater, Sr., who directed the bottle design, basic sales technique, and standard operation practices of Coca Cola Bottling Company in Atlanta. It was appropriately called *VZTop* until it burned to the ground in 1980. *Ruffwood* was the Highlands Estates home of Coca Cola director, George W. Woodruff.

In the relatively flat area of town, besides Darthula Rice's *White Oak House* on west Main, stood Natalie Hammond's *Apple Tree Cottage* north of Spring Street, Irvin Rice's *Will o' the Wisp* on Chestnut Street, and Miss Rebecca Bridges' *The Waldorf* near 4th Street's intersection with Martha's Lane. Theron Walden's *Blackberry Hill* stood west of 4th and Poplar, today's Toby West Antiques.

There were also Harvey Talley's *Tally Ho*, James Floyd's *Brigadoon*, and Margaret Cannon Howell's *The Chalet* off the Dillard Road; Len Appley's *Hemlock Lawn* off the Walhalla Road; and W. E. "Monk" Godfrey's *Cabin Ben*, which he built along with Mrs. Lewis Doggett, Sr., and Miss Anne England in the Clemson Colony area bordering Mirror Lake. Porter Pierson (later John Henley) lived at *Kettle Rock*; Tearley Picklesimer, at *Se-*

rene Acres; Harry and Dean Hetzel, at *Rockledge Cottage* on Cullasaja Drive; Mrs. C. K. Wall, at *Bois Fleuri* (Flowering Woods); Samuel Evins, at his mansion just below *Kalalanta* which he dubbed *The Fling*; and Rebecca Raoul Altstaetter owned *Rosemary* and *Laurel Lodge*.

Occasionally a well-known home in Highlands would go unnamed for a while, like the Bascom home on Chestnut Ridge of Satulah. When Bascom's son-in-law Watson Barratt bought it during the 1950s, he christened it *Chetolah*, meaning "Place of Rest," the name it carried when it passed to Helen Augur.

H. M. Bascom's house, built 1892, later christened Chetolah. *Photo by George Masa, 1929.*

Many homes, however, were known only by their family names: the Robert Hughs and Al Maynard homes on Big Bear Pen, the Westervelt Terhune mountain farmhouse, John Harbert's home (the Raymond Kline house) at Highlands Country club, Bobby Jones' home overlooking Blue Valley on Little Yellow Mountain above the club, Henry Burns Jr.'s home over Wildcat Cliffs, Dr. William Matthews' dwelling on the back side of the mountain, and Arthur Bliss's home on Cowee Ridge above the Whiteside Mountain overlook, known as the Big View on Highway 64 East.

The Crosby "cottage" at Spruce and 5th, built by John Crosby from San Mateo, Florida, in 1897 and still existing, had three stories and heaven knows how many rooms but no name, though *Mirimichi* is the name posted on it today. Stanhope Hill's three-story "cottage" on the Horse Cove Road was known at first as *Squire Hill House* and then *Staub Cottage* when Albert and Albertina Staub occupied it. Robert Morris' home on Satulah, designed by architect Jim Fox in 1983 to cling to the mountain like a diamond, was named for its originally intended purpose, the *Caretaker House*.

Joe Webb Cabins

In 1922 Joe Webb, grandson of Billy Webb of Billy Cabin, began constructing his special brand of homes in Laurel Heights where the Franklin road used to ford Big Creek and either ascend to Flat Mountain or descend to Cliffside Lake.[618] After Margaretta Ravenel's death in 1913, Joe had purchased 135 acres of this area from Prioleau Ravenel, Jr. The only occupants at the time of his purchase had been Tom Crunkleton followed by Henry Talley. Joe had moved into Talley's house, currently Jack and Sara Mayer's at the end of the pavement on Webbmont Road. Tom would move in 1909 to the house that still exists beyond the Highlands Country Club on the Dillard Road. By 1931 Joe's development had taken on his name as Webbmont, and he was declared its mayor.

The first house that Joe Webb built in the Webbmont area was *Cullasaja Lodge*, a frame home in 1922 for H. P. Hunter, a native of New Hampshire from Anderson, S.C. At about the same time he built the first of his famous log cabins for David Watson, a Clemson College professor of architecture, on the road that bordered Lindenwood (now Ravenel) Lake. It eventually became the secluded home of Dr. William Coker, owned today by Sam and Florence Inman of Atlanta.

For five years beginning in 1930 Joe could be found building log cabins all over Highlands. He and his stepson Furman Vinson built and owned *The Dugout* on Lake Sequoyah, where they also raised the log houses of Kenyon Zahner and of Mr. Roberts across the lake, whose home was accessible only by boat. Joe fashioned the Fred Gould house at the Highlands Country Club and a summer home with multi-gable roof and rock chimney for L. M. Brown between Bascom's home and *Chestnut Lodge* on Satulah.

He built *Big Billy Cabin* for Howard Doane Randall on Billy Cabin Ridge, Rucker L. Ragland's cabin on Big Bear Pen, Dr. Edwin Reinke's house (today's Highland Hiker) on east Main, Dr. O. E. Reschke's home on Cherokee Drive, Aunt Sadie Moss' house at Indian Hills, the W. C. Stringer house on Dillard Road (now the log cabin restaurant behind Hampton Inn), and *Lawhorn Shack*, the later name for Margaret Young's home on Many

Road, as well as her second home on Kline Drive. Altogether, counting the near dozen homes he built in Webbmont, there were almost thirty Joe Webb houses on the Highlands plateau.

The first Margaret Young House, built ca. 1932 by Joe Webb. Photo courtesy of Highlands Historic Inventory.

In 1935 Joe moved to Flat Mountain and purchased Ben Keener's seventeen acres and small house for Furman Vinson. Not entirely adequate, Keener's house was soon replaced. Though Furman continued to build houses in Highlands and the surrounding area, Joe moved to Ellijay in 1945. He died five years later and is buried in Miller Cemetery.

1925–55: Colonies of Homes

As a direct result of Kelsey's pamphlet of 1876 advertising the virtues of living in Highlands, forty-five dwellings ranging from $300 to $3,000 in cost were distributed throughout the town by 1883. By 1928, almost fifty years later, there were a hundred summer homes in a town of 547 population, 2,500 during the summer.[619] But with the coming of serviceable roads at the beginning of the thirties, Highlands was about to participate in the biggest boom in building since its founding. Already the business section was developing, but the late twenties and early thirties also witnessed a burst of new homes, between forty and fifty in 1932 alone. Perhaps it was just coincidence that in that year Highlands recorded its highest temperature in forty years: 87°.[620]

Colonies of homes sprang up on the outskirts of town: Lindenwood Lake development near the Biological Laboratory, Highlands Estates at the new country club, the William Sullivan development along the north shore of Mirror Lake, the Clemson Colony of college professors along the south shore, and Indian Hills development west of the Walhalla Road.

By 1946 Flat Mountain was undergoing development by Frank Pitcock, whose 140-acre tract, belonging originally to Ravenel, provided new homes until his death in 1962. By then Mel Keener was developing his own Flat Mountain Estates.

The mid fifties saw developments opening north and south of town. C. A. Phinney established Broadview Acres at Little Horseshoe Mountain on the Dillard Road. Toward Cashiers a new subdivision opened at Rolling Acres, and farther on, Earle Young created Whiteside Estates. Meanwhile, in town Will Edwards with Frank, Roy, and Steve Potts bought Rebecca Harris' hundred-acre tract, subdivided it into "Sunset Hill," and rebuilt the lake. New homes sprang up here during the early sixties. By the late sixties Clyde and Charlotte Mehder at the John H. C. Perry Agency were advertising sixty-five new two-acre home sites at Sagee Mountain.

Getting a home built in Highlands, from the earliest days to the present, did not always proceed according to schedule, no matter how carefully one planned. Unforeseen interruptions plagued living in the mountains. During hunting season, for instance, workers were known to vanish into the forests for weeks at a time. Contractors who subcontracted particular jobs to specialists had the devil of a time coordinating who would show up when, if at all. And if a builder had a backlog of commitments, he'd just as soon add another as say no, knowing full well he might never get around to doing the work promised. It was often frustrating—and still is—to new arrivals wanting to build a first or second home in Highlands.

But equally frustrating, on the side of the builder, was the neglect or refusal of some homeowners to pay for work already done. A few clever locals developed ways of dealing with nonpayment without engaging in confrontations but rather exhibiting infinite patience. Dennis "Doc" Wilson tells of Frank Houston, a local mason, who had been subcontracted to build a stone fireplace for a new homeowner in Blue Valley. He worked slowly but deliberately, as did the other workers, who were all fired without pay by the irate homeowner.

They all left, but Houston stayed. He finished the chimney, for which the owner still gave him no pay. When the owner completed his house the following year, he built a roaring fire to celebrate his new home, only to find the room filling with acrid smoke. When Houston was called to fix the problem, he reminded the owner that he hadn't yet been paid. The fee now would have to be considerably more than the original estimate.

Not in a position to bargain, the owner reluctantly agreed, and Houston arrived, insisting this time that he be paid prior to the fix. Raising a ladder against the chimney, he climbed up and dropped a stone through the opening at the top. There was a loud crash of glass as it broke through the pane cemented halfway down the flue. Had the owner looked up when he first lit the fire, he would have only seen light gleaming from the chimney top. Houston returned to Highlands amply paid and fully satisfied.

Many of the homes and public buildings in Highlands were constructed under the supervision of a few prolific builders. Early homes were built by Frank Hill from Horse Cove; John Jay Smith, whose sawmill was capable of putting out 2,000 board feet of lumber a day; and the Boynton brothers, Frank and Charles. Later homes and shops were usually built by Walter Reese, Will Cleaveland, Roy Phillips, or Guy Paul. Many buildings in addition to the Edwards Inn, such as those of Mrs. Clark Howell and Bobby Jones, were designed by Linton Young of Rosman, Georgia, who also designed the Whiteside homes of Arthur Bliss and Charles Holcomb and some of the most beautiful homes in Atlanta.

Major Charles Clarkson was a pioneer developer of scenic property in the vicinity of Whiteside Mountain to the north of town and overlooking Blue Valley to the south. Rock work was often performed by Professor Harbison's son Tom, such as the first hospital, the Methodist Church, and the homes of Ralph Sargent and Richard Aeck. From the year of his father's death, 1936, until the tragedy that took his own life when a car that he was repairing pinned and killed him in 1959, Tom Harbison served the town as its arboriculturist and landscape advisor.

As noted earlier in Chapter Twenty regarding the increase in number of businesses, Highlands experienced a comparable growth in number of homes during the thirty years from 1925–55. Real and personal property values climbed steadily, broken only by a slight dip in the early thirties. From reports in 1916 and 1917 which valued Highlands real estate at around $150,000, real and personal values doubled by the mid twenties to almost $350,000, rose during the first three years of the Depression to $470,000, dropped again to $350,000 in 1933, but by 1936 had returned to $400,000. Values climbed from half a million dollars at the beginning of the forties to $600,000 at the end and by 1961 had surpassed the million mark.

With an eye to expanding Highlands' growth beyond its attraction as a tourist and resort center, a Highlands Industrial Committee was created by the Chamber of Commerce to attract suitable industry to the area.[621] It con-

458

ducted an extensive study of available resources in 1956, but due to lack of interest both inside and outside Highlands, no industry evolved.

One result of the thirty-years' growth before 1955 was the town's decision in 1959, as previously described in Chapter Twenty's treatment of the commercial districts in town, to formulate a balanced plan for future growth under the guidance of the Western N.C. Regional Planning Commission, which would include the residential sectors.

Two years later the Highlands Builders' Association was formed to promote a better understanding and stabilization of the building and related trades. In 1965 the town revived the defunct planning board and four years later printed its first zoning map.

In 1970 the citizens unanimously adopted Highlands' first zoning ordinance, designating three residential zones, ranging in lot size from 5,000 to 12,000 square feet and two business districts covering downtown and along the highways. A zoning board composed of Clarence Mitchell, Charlie McDowell, Wilton Cobb, and Roy Potts was established; and Toliver Crunkleton, appointed the first zoning administrator.

A Grievous Loss

Anderson/Whittle/Sullivan home, built 1906–9. Photo courtesy of Highlands Historic Inventory.

Even as all these guardians and laws stood imminent in the wings, intent on controlling the town's growth, a grievous loss captured center state at the beginning of the seventies. One of the most, if not *the* most, beautiful homes in Highlands was the landscaped mansion on north 5th Street above Pine which Roy Phillips had built for Dr. Alexander P. "Alex" Anderson in 1906–09.[622] In its heyday the Anderson house, built in the Scottish tradition for Alex's Scottish wife Lydia McDougall Johnson, had a barn, an ice house, sheds, and a clay tennis court. Unique for the times it relied on a windmill to pump water from a well to the kitchen and to lift water to the second floor bathrooms.

Alexander P. "Alex" Anderson at University of Munich, 1895–96. Photo from the biography, Alexander P. Anderson: 1862-1943.

It stood in the northeast corner of the property, near where Wild Thyme Gourmet exists today on Carolina Way. Except for its cypress doors, it was built entirely of native wood: maple, white pine, hemlock, oak, poplar, and cherry and was insulated with mineral wool, similar to today's rock wool. The pantry and closet shelves came from a 300-year-old tree four feet in diameter, seventy feet up to the first limb. Separating the dining and living rooms was an enormous fireplace radiating heat from openings on both sides, and upstairs six spacious bedrooms accommodated the family and guests, including what Anne Sullivan Doggett considered the largest feather-bed east of the Mississippi.

By today's standards the house was built at a bargain $13,770, including the pine grove improvements on the property. Alex Anderson had the four and a half acres of yard landscaped by Aylor Chastain, who brought on the job his two hound dogs, Biggun and Littlun, and hand-operated the machine that made the hundreds of small concrete blocks used in the chimneys and walls as well as the steps bordering the property. Chastain helped Prof. Thomas Harbison care for the native trees and shrubs. Some were imported from Minnesota, while some of the small early plants, like the vast bed of heather, came from Scotland. Chastain was the only caretaker at the house brave enough to climb the windmill to oil it. A white picket fence surrounded the home and arboretum.

At the same time that Anderson was landscaping his homestead with balsams and spruces, he ordered 14,000 pines in 1909 from Dr. C. A. Schenck at the Biltmore Estate in Asheville and forested the entire valley behind the current Baptist Church and Mountain High Motel. For these he paid $210, and almost a century later the forest still exists in all its natural glory. The pine lot was given to the town of Highlands during the 1940s.

In 1921 Christopher Whittle of Sarasota, Florida, bought the Anderson house. He lived there five years before moving to the original Rideout house at the corner of north 5th and Chestnut, where his family has lived ever since.

In 1926 William and Anne Sullivan purchased the Anderson house from Whittle and moved to Highlands, as much for William's health as for that of his large family of eight children, mostly grown.[623] A founder of Anderson College in Anderson, S.C., he also ran the family-established Sullivan Hardware Company and helped build the John C. Calhoun hotel. By the time his health finally failed him in 1937, he was executive head of the Sullivan Hardware Company of Anderson, Greenville, Spartanburg, Greer, and Belton in South Carolina and developer of the Cullasaja Heights subdivision north of Mirror Lake in Highlands.

The Sullivan family continued to summer at their Highlands home until 1962, the year before Anne's death, when it was sold to the Lechich sisters, Mary and Angela, from Miami, Florida. The sad result was that the lovely grounds were indiscriminately cleared and the house indifferently abandoned. When Walter Sheppard bought the property, he had the house dismantled in 1973.[624] All that was salvaged of the stately mansion was the dining room that Kevin Fitz Patrick now owns above his Media Divide, Inc., located behind the Funeral Home. Today, after thirty years, the property lies fallow except where Carolina Way has planted a few shops along its northern ridge.

Multiple Housing

Throughout all the early efforts to control growth in Highlands, residential building continued unabated. Indeed, the growth spurt that would originate during the late sixties and run through century's end would all but eclipse the slow, steady development that had preceded the fifties.

The town's first apartment house complex materialized in 1967 at the corner of 6th and East Main Street. Built by Mr. M. C. Minella, it exists today as Highlands Townsite Condominium Apartments.[625]

A second set, the first year-round residential apartments, was the inspiration of the McCulloch family—George and sons Bob and Jack—in 1973. Known as Pinebrook Condominiums, they replaced the Mary Howell Young house—which had existed at the corner of 5th and Spruce since the late 1910s until it burned—with sixteen residences in a two-storied design.[626] Each apartment had two bedrooms and two baths, a garden porch that opened to the sky, a fireplace in the living room, and a kitchen at a cost of $30,000 to $40,000. The project was meant to develop in two stages, twenty more apartments to follow the original sixteen, but the McCullochs created instead a complex of stores and offices known as Highlands Village Square on the alley between Main and Pine in town.

To refine its controls over commercial development, the town began requiring special use permits in 1977 to replace a controversial and increasingly vulnerable "discretionary" zoning system procedures less capricious and less arbitrary. Atlanta architect Pope Fuller was named zoning administrator to issue the new permits. And to regulate development in the residential districts, the town's first subdivision ordinance was enacted in 1978.

In 1980 a third cluster of nineteen apartments, known as Trillium Place, was constructed on the south side of Main directly across from Townsite Condominiums. And a fourth set of five proposed condominiums, named Highlands Manor after the final name of the old Hall House on the same general property, was begun off 5th Street in 1981, as was Mill Creek Village off 6th Street.

When, in the same year, a sixth project, known as Shelby Place off the Walhalla Road, proposed constructing 326 condo units on fifty-five acres and won zoning board approval in 1981 at the rate of twenty units per year, the public expressed alarm over the ballooning trend toward high-density development in residential zones by effectively killing the project on appeal.

Today, except for house trailers huddled together in two established parks zoned specifically for that purpose, single homes are still the norm in Highlands, many attractively designed by local architects Dennis DeWolf, Jim Fox, Peter Jefferson, and Jeff Cox.

The cry on the threshold of the new millennium, however, was for low-income housing for workers who would service the area but couldn't afford the high-ticket homes on the market. Houses on relatively small lots that sold for a third of a million dollars or more—indeed, for one to two-and-a-half million at the clubs—were not uncommon. Furthermore, high property appraisals were splitting up farmland that families had held for generations so that descendants, unable to afford substantial increases in taxes, were being forced to sell off. Realtor John Cleaveland says he doesn't see low income housing coming to Highlands so long as labor is supplied by surrounding communities. The market for houses is upscale, and construction is expensive on the mountain.

Cleaveland credits the Forest Service with keeping every hilltop from being covered up with homes. But as Highlands faced the third millennium, with land at a premium, density in the residential as in the business districts loomed as a growing concern. In Vermont there's a saying: close trees, distant people. Highlands too would have to maintain a fine balance between its trees and its people if it was to remain the natural attraction that Kelsey envisioned when he founded the town in the heart of the forested Appalachians.

23. Carriers of Knowledge

Neither snow nor rain nor heat nor gloom of night stays these co u-riers from the swift accomplishment of their appointed routes.
—Herodotus, *Histories, VI, ca. 430 B. C.*
"Well boys, the U.S. mail has to run. What're we gonna do?"
—Gene Mays, 1961

In 1875, if you lived in the new town of Highlands and wanted your mail, you had to walk or ride horseback the three miles to Horse Cove to pick it up. After New Year's Day, 1876, postmaster Baxter White made the trip instead, and you picked up your mail at his post office, home, and gro-cery store, all under one roof, and for the first fourteen years of Highlands' existence, the post office remained here.[627]

At first postal arrangements were such that four to six weeks would pass from the time you mailed a letter till you received a reply. Newspapers ar-rived no earlier than two or three weeks after their publication. In 1876 when Rutherford Hayes beat Samuel Tilden in a hotly contested election for the presidency, Highlanders learned of the dispute over twenty votes only after it had been resolved. News of Alexander Graham Bell's invention of the telephone arrived by rumor long before the *New York Tribune* reached Baxter White's post office. Even as late as 1885 mail deliveries down to Walhalla took ten hours; the return up hill, twelve hours. The trip down to Franklin took six and a half hours, seven for the return.

William Coe became postmaster in 1889 and moved the post office across Main Street to Skinner's printing office, where his brother, Charles, served as editor of Highlands' third newspaper. Four years later David Nor-ton would move to Baxter Wilson's home between Central House and the Presbyterian Church. It was the year after Gran Matney took command as postmaster in 1897 that the Walhalla mail boy's mule, as described previ-ously in Chapter Six, was spooked by wild hogs along the roadside, which cost the life of the mule and shook up the boy, for animals as much as bad roads were the hazards of the courier's route. Bears and "painters" also in-habited the forests through which the mail had to pass.

In this same year as the mail boy's mishap, 1898, Alex Anderson, who had come to Highlands to marry Lydia McDougall Johnson at the Hall House, paid a visit to the postmaster at Grimshawe's. Recognized as the world's smallest post office—six feet by five and a half feet—it stood in Whiteside Cove just below the high cliff of Whiteside Mountain and was run by the son of migrants from Cobourg, Ontario, Canada.[628]

Grimshawe's post office, 1899. Photo from R. H. Scadin Collection, UNC-A.

Thomas and Helena Grimshawe had established the office in 1878, four years after their arrival in the cove. Their son, Thomas, Jr., took over when his parents moved on. He and his wife Bessie lived a hard life on meager wages while he served as the only doctor in the area.

Indeed, one of the most poignant tragedies ever to afflict Whiteside Cove occurred during the winter of 1888, ten years into the existence of the tiny post office. For children to die very young in those times was not uncommon. But for a single family to lose four members in a single week was heartrending. Between October 31 and November 7, while Tom was away on call, his four daughters ages two to seven, came down with severe cases of diphtheria and died, one every two days until they were all gone. Upon his return, Tom learned that his distraught wife had built each casket out of rough wood, dug each grave herself, and—in the absence of a winter priest—read each burial service from the Prayer Book. They lie today in the Grimshawe Plot behind the Episcopal Church of the Good Shepherd in Cashiers, which in 1888 was just a summer chapel. Eleven years later, in October, 1899, as the Grimshawes' friend Henry Scadin would report, they lost still another child to the same dreaded affliction.[629]

Grimshawe's, world's smallest post office, 1878–1953. Photo by George Masa, 1929.

What astonished Alex Anderson most about this hardy couple, however, was not their will to outlive life's tragedies or even the small dimensions of their now-famous post office—a picture of which hangs today in the Smithsonian Institute in Washington—but rather the fact that in this isolated region the Grimshawes, Tom and Bessie, spoke the Elizabethan English of their ancestors. If Alex Alexander had known the region better as one who grew up in it, like Weimar Jones of Franklin who was not from Canada, he would have heard that sturdy, vivid Elizabethan English quite often in the backwoods of the Appalachians and not found it so surprising. Unfortunately, no so many folks today speak the same English as those early pioneers, although vestiges of it remain to color the spoken word.

Gran Matney served the Highlands post office until James Rideout moved it to his Stone Store in 1901, where for the next six years it remained, waiting for John Jay Smith to move it across the corner to today's House of Wong. Here it would stay until the year after Gus Holt set up his shop in 1913.

In 1914 the mail was being delivered to and picked up at Judge Jim Hines' garage on 4th Street hill where, except for the year that Billy Potts moved it back to Main Street, it remained until 1923. Getting the mail from Judge Hines was always a memorable experience. There was no escaping his cordial attention and his wit, to say nothing of his penchant for swearing. As refined and courtly as Jim Hines knew how to be, he was no hypocrite. His daughter Bess Hines said of him, "What he had to say, he'd say right now—and he'd as soon say it to a man's face as behind his back. And if anyone didn't like what he said, they could 'go to hell hoppin'." He had black hair, a handle-bar moustache, and dark-blue eyes that could shoot sparks one minute and twinkle the next.

No one could remain mad at Judge Hines because of his sincerity and sense of humor, which, by the way, he was wont to lavish on his wife as quick as anyone else. There was, for instance, the evening that Bessie swept into the living room, according to daughter Bess, "all rigged out in her no-foolishness tailored suit and a wide brimmed, severe looking hat, on her way to a meeting of the Macon County League of Women Voters." Drawing on her gloves, she noticed Papa peering over the top of his newspaper, a glint in his eye.

"Do you know what the two most useless things in the world are?" he asked rhetorically. And promptly answering his own question: "A man's teats and the Macon County League of Women Voters." He resumed reading his paper, while the rest of the family, including Mama, cracked up. Hobnobbing with Jim Hines, whether at home, his garage, or his post office, was always straight-forward. He showed the same unpretentious face to everyone he met, yet was full of surprises.

It was during Hines' watch that John Passmore delivered the mail between Highlands and Horse Cove. Indeed, Passmore was responsible for the footpath known as the "Passmore trail," which ran straight up the Highlands mountain and which, as Frances Lombard observes, "was steep as a horse's face."[630] Herman Wilson remembered his being hired by Passmore after he quit the seventh grade because Passmore needed a boy to carry the mail so he could run a sawmill. Herman walked across the mountain to apply for the job and met Mr. Passmore on his route from Cashiers to Highlands.

The work, as Passmore described it, involved riding a mule loaded with saddlebags full of mail under lock and key. The keys were retained in various post offices to keep the mail secure. A tall man in the Cashiers post office swore Herman in on a Monday morning. Herm remembered how he was "supposed to support and defend the United States mail and all that, you know." The mule that he was to ride "was pretty wild, and so was I," he admitted. Mr. Passmore wouldn't allow him to ride as far as Highlands. He had to stop at Olin Lombard's barn, put the mule up, feed him some corn, and then walk with the mailbags up the Passmore trail.

Its being a good piece to walk and the mail bags weighing ten to fifteen pounds, Herman did his job for a long while but grew discouraged when Mr. Passmore didn't pay him. "He'd give me half my pay, so I began to get out of heart with my job," he complained. Then Herman quit, still without his pay. He reported the matter to Judge Hines, who, instead of scolding him for being a quitter, replied, "Herman, you ain't the only boy or man that he's done this way. You're going to get your money." The Judge knew that Mr. Passmore's paycheck had to come through Highlands. So Herman got his money, and ever after, he had a high respect for Judge Hines.

The Highlands carrier on the mail route south to Walhalla was a rugged, burly man named Gene Mays, whose slow-gated easy manner and every-present cigar made him legendary during the fifty years that he delivered the mail. He never smoked that old cigar, according to Frances Wilson, but just chewed on it in the corner of his mouth. Mays took over from his father in 1916 at age twenty-eight.

At first he rode a bicycle, then graduated to a mule, followed by a buggy, and finally an old 1911 Model T Ford. In the Model T the lever on the right side of the steering wheel served as the accelerator, and the lever on the left side controlled the spark. Mays kept from freezing in his unheated car by wrapping a heated brick in a sack and placing it at his feet. It lasted one way only. He split the distance with another postman from Walhalla, exchanging mail bags at the half-way point. The entire trip in those early days of the bicycle and the mule took ten hours. The advent of cars reduced the time to five hours, but frequent stops were made to refill the radiator and patch the tires. By the sixties five hours had been reduced to two.

Helen Hill Norris told of the early buggy days when the narrow road was sometimes so muddy that two wagons couldn't pass, and on one such day Mays met a wagon train returning from the market.[631] Both Mays and the wagon came to a stop, and after an expectant pause, Mays leaned back and said, "Well boys, the U.S. mail has to run. What're we gonna do?" Without hesitating, the hefty wagoners climbed down from their seats, picked up Mr. Mays in his wagon, and set it alongside the road. They then drove through, stopped, repositioned his wagon on the road, and waved him on his merry way.

At a point along May's route, known as Regal's Gap just below the Georgia state line, there was an old law ground where court was held, because Clayton was just too far to travel by such awful roads. On the first Monday of every month, crowds gathered at the law ground to hear the proceedings. Women were not allowed. But on one Monday Mays drove up with Aunt Sallie seated in his wagon, dressed in a sunbonnet and full calico skirt. All calm and composed, she watched and waited. The men asked her why she was there.

Well known for speaking her mind, Aunt Sallie answered forthrightly, "They aim to try my man today, and I'm here to see that they clear him, because if he's done anything he ought not to have done, I'll tend to him myself." Mays must have swallowed a grin as he watched the proceedings, for in short order her husband was cleared!

Mays endeared himself to many who were fortunate enough to know his amiable, courteous manner and unfailing kindness. He died in the performance of his duty when in 1966 his truck wrecked on his return to Walhalla with the Highlands mail. His death at seventy-eight was attributed to a heart attack

Mays' tenure during his fifty years of faithful service spanned the terms of ten postmasters in Highlands. In 1923, the year that Calvin Coolidge suddenly became president, Jim Hines turned the office over to Nellie Cleaveland, who gave it an entirely new home behind the Rock Store on 4th Street. Apple-cheeked, bright-eyed, and always ready for a laugh, Nellie ran the office that many who live in Highlands today still remember.

The problem under Judge Hines' care had been that the roads in and around Highlands were in poor shape, so it was a matter of speculation when the mail would arrive. Residents felt frustrated when, coming to town, they had to sit and wait. One summer resident, in fact, felt so exasperated that she bought a bugle and paid a man to sound it after the mail was sorted each day. Taking the cue, the Highlands Improvement Society donated to the post office a large bell intended for the Library which unfortunately lacked a belfry. From 1923–35 it was Miss Nellie's duty to ring this bell, perched atop a high pole in front, every day when the mail was up.

From 1936–39 Gene Potts ran the office at its previous location on the corner of 4th and Main. His brother Charlie served for a while as postal clerk, where he got a taste of the irregularities that plagued postmasters in early Highlands. When a man sought to determine the weight of a package he wanted mailed, Charlie asked if it contained anything breakable. The answer was "Yes."

"What?" asked Charlie.

"A quart jar of white liquor," was the ingenuous reply.

"Liquor!" Charlie exclaimed. "You can't send liquor through the mail!"

"Been doin' it every week," said the man, unimpressed and not about to quit for some new feller on the scene.

Charlie advanced from postal clerk to postmaster in 1940, the year that Fred Edwards built a brand new post office mid-block on Main Street, just west of today's Wit's End. Marshall Reese recalls that Fred hired Marshall's father, Walter, to oversee the job and Fred's brother, John, to help lay the floor boards, one inch wide, tongue and groove. But when Walter sent Marshall to supervise the work, Marshall saw "the first board was laid so crooked that a black snake could hardly run it." He made them rip it up and nail it down straight, but they still busted boards with the nails. The Reeses, he affirmed, demanded perfection in any work they supervised.

It was in this fine new post office on Main Street that Charlie spent sixteen years performing his official duties so effectively that when time came for him to retire, he was asked to continue in office until a qualified replacement could be found. Uncle Charlie was totally unprepared for such popularity, for he was eagerly anticipating fox hunting season but was obliged to postpone his retirement.

Throughout his long tenure as postmaster, what had kept him attached to the job was often the out of the ordinary or the unexpected. On one occasion he received a letter of complaint from an irate woman on Bearpen Mountain, who wrote, "The post office must be run by a good-sized idiot!" He kept it as a trophy, along with an envelope addressed simply: "Uncle Charlie, give this to Bill," followed by "Highlands, N.C." The times were comfortably casual back then, far less complicated than they must, by necessity, be today.

When Uncle Charlie took over a third class post office in 1935, it had receipts of $4,000. In 1945 it became a second class office with receipts of $9,000. Even when he retired—or tried to—in 1956, it had attained only $19,000, far short of the $40,000 required of a first class office. For the five years after his retirement, the job settled on Carl Talley as acting postmaster until Gene Potts' son, Louis "Bud" Potts, restored it to the family. Bud Potts was a native Highlander, a graduate of UNC, and former sports writer for the Shelby *Star*. He became the longest-serving postmaster in Highlands history, following eight years as town clerk in 1961. He administered Highlands' transition to a five-digit ZIP code in 1963 and supervised the move into larger quarters at 5th and Pine in 1966, retiring in 1985.

It was during Bud Potts' tenure that Henry Cleaveland served as the rural mail carrier, not only along routes around Highlands but including Horse Cove, Whiteside Cove, Cashiers, and Norton. A son of Jamie and Helen McKinney Cleaveland, he delivered his daily load of newspapers, magazines, and letters no matter the condition of the roads. On snow days he would leave his car and walk to the door of old-timers awaiting their mail. Like many a mail carrier assigned to the outbacks, he would go out of his way to do anyone a personal service or favor, merely by the asking.

From the fifties through the seventies the star mail route from Dillard through Scaly Mountain to Highlands was the responsibility of Claude Penland, who could be seen in his red Bronco jeep stopping every day, but one, at Susan Head's post office in Scaly and the Village Superette for lunch.

With Bud Potts' retirement in 1982 as Highlands' postmaster, the U.S. Postal Service had to reach as far away as Hendersonville to find his replacement. For the next twelve years Keith Barnard negotiated every day the exhausting thirty-mile commute along winding mountain roads to serve the Highlands office. In 1994 our current postmaster, Elizabeth Kelley, took the reigns and directed the last move to the largest building yet, located at the shopping center on Walhalla Road.

By the end of the century the little post office that fifty years earlier had achieved second-class status with revenues in the $10,000s had reached level eighteen on the first-class ladder with total revenues topping $800,000.[632] Regarding delivery in the year 2000, the number of pieces ranged from 100,000 per week in the summer to 70,000 in the winter for an annual average of 80,000. Such a volume kept Ray Archer, David Keener, Joyce Sanders, Konda McCauley, and Mike Penland working full time to cover the rural routes while Beverly Vanhook, Marilyn Vinson Hughes, Dennis Hurst, and Belinda Byrd served the boxes and the front desk.

Certainly the inscription on the post office building in our nation's capital applied to Highlands as much as it did to the more urban of our cities and towns, for without the mail and its delivery by foot, horseback, carriage, and car, the town would never have survived, much less flourished, as it has in such splendid isolation from the world at large. Charles Eliot's words for the national inscription in 1905 constitute a fitting tribute:

Carrier of news and knowledge,
Instrument of trade and industry,
Promoter of mutual acquaintance,
Of peace and good-will
Among men and nations.

24. Acts of Kindness and of Love

I shall pass through this world but once. If, therefore, there be any kindness I can show, or any good thing I can do, let me do it now; let me not defer or neglect it, for I shall not pass this way again.
                                                    —Author Unknown[633]

If there is one salient trait that stands out in the character of Highlands as most representative of its people, it is volunteerism. Setting business and the profit motive aside—including those who would seek to plunder what a town has to offer and give nothing in return, taking their booty and departing—Highlands has enjoyed an extraordinary number of individuals whose gifts of time and talent have created organizations that run on air. If there has been any expense, it was not in wages for employees. Indeed, it was out of the pockets of volunteers that these civic and charitable institutions found their essential support.

Since the days of the town's founding, the number of Highlanders who have served long hours without pay as trustees and directors on corporate boards and service organizations is legion. Volunteers have run the Highlands Fire Department and the Emergency Council. They have served on boards that run the hospital, the Land Trust, the Hudson Library and Bascom-Louise Gallery, the Chamber of Commerce, the Highlands Playhouse and Chamber Music, in addition to the zoning and planning boards and appearance commission, and the Peggy Crosby Center, which in 1993 brought seventeen service organizations together under one roof, including Fibber Magee's Closet for recycled clothing and the Literacy Council for teaching reading, writing, and oral expression and essential math skills to adults and students of all ages free of charge. Within the past decade the Literacy Council has offered English as a second language to the growing number of Hispanics living in town and in migrant camps in Scaly, many of whom have entered the Highlands work force and school.

Perhaps the earliest service organization to be founded in Highlands was the Highlands Improvement Association sometime around 1883. Close on its heels came the Masonic Blue Ridge Lodge # 435. First organized by Thoren Walden on March 8, 1890, in the Wilson building on Main Street, the Masonic Lodge moved in 1893 into its own home, where it functions to-day.[634] Built by Jule Phillips for nearly $300, it stands on land donated by Prioleau Ravenel's step-son Thomas Parker. Its charter, dated January 14, 1891, listed eight founding members: Thoren Walden, Baxter White, Aaron Esty, Jeremiah Pierson, Sumner Clark, David Norton, Thomas Vinson, and

Mack Wilson. Walden was the organization's first Grand Master, which post is currently held by Harold Neely. Originally, the Masons met once a month on Friday "at or preceding every full moon," but it was later decided to hold meetings at 10:00 in the morning "railroad time."

The Freemasons are the largest secret fraternal organization in the world. Clem Henry, past Grand Master and current secretary of the Highlands Lodge, describes it as a fraternity based on religion through its recognition of a Supreme Being. Its goal is "to take good men and make better people out of them." This is done as Masons advance through three degrees of personal improvement, from Apprentice to Fellow Craft to Master Mason. The Highlands Lodge, made up of slightly over fifty members, has long sponsored two important causes: the Masonic Home for orphans at Oxford, N.C., and the Senior Citizens Home in Greensboro.

The Lodge Manual of the North Carolina masons gives a powerful description of their salient principals and goals:

"Freemasonry, a beautiful system of morality, veiled in allegory, and illustrated by symbols." The most ancient society in the world; its principals are based on pure morality, its ethics are the ethics of pure religion; its doctrines, the doctrines of brotherly love; and its sentiments, the sentiments of exalted benevolence. It encourages all that is good, kind, and charitable; and reproves all that is vicious, cruel, and oppressive.[635]

The Lions Club, the national institution devoted to helping the blind, made an aborted attempt at organizing a branch in Highlands in 1938.[636] Otto Summer was elected its first president; Wilton Cobb, Jack Wilcox, and Frank Cook, vice-presidents; Sidney McCarty, secretary; Thad Smith, lion tamer; and Rev. Bob DuPree, tail twister, with Willie Hays and Rev. Frank Bloxham serving on its board of directors. But the new organization failed to survive.

Sixteen years later, on November 18, 1954, it was reorganized under a new charter at the Highlands Methodist Church, where Neville Bryson was elected its president. It met in the Old Edwards Hotel. Under James Ramey, its current president, the Lions provide white canes, leader or hearing dogs, hearing aids, Braille literature and learning tapes—all free of charge to the handicapped in need. They supply eye glasses and eye surgery to needy residents and school children and support a summer camp for the visually handicapped or otherwise impaired. They raise money for research and the treatment of diabetes to reduce the chances of blindness. Local lions and their ladies incur no administrative costs, for all their labor is rendered free.

If the ideal of service is the basis of all worthy enterprise, then the Highlands Rotary Club, established on May 2, 1945, has over the last half century lived up to its chief principle.[637] Its first president was Stacey Russell; Otto Summer serving as vice-president; Rev. W. T. Medlin, Jr., secretary; and Wade Sutton, treasurer. True to the 1905 origin of its name, which derives from the notion of rotating its meetings from business to business, Rotary in Highlands had its first meeting in 1945 on Main Street at the Highlands Grille (later the Mountaineer, Kilwin's today).

Over the years the Highlands Rotary has sponsored the academic and athletic award banquets for Highlands School, as well as foreign exchange students, college scholarships, career education, the school Safety Patrol, and Interact Club. It has served the community through its support of the Art Walk, the Literacy Council, Scouting, Halloween night, and the Christmas parade as well as generous contributions to many civic and charitable organizations. It is regularly engaged in cleanup programs, recycling, wood cutting, and maintenance of the Red Cross Disaster Shelter, in addition to searching for affordable housing, park and recreation areas, and ways to protect the Highlands environment. By century's end the Highlands Rotary Club was honored twice as the best large club in Western North Carolina, once in 1999 and again in 2000, for its "service above self."

Closely associated with Rotary, beginning in 1983 was the Inner Wheel Club of wives, widows, daughters, and sisters of Rotarians, led initially by Betty Coffeen.[638] The Inner Wheel gave support to Rotary projects until 1993 when the two organizations merged. Five years later Dr. Mary "Mo" Wheeler was elected Highlands' first woman president.

The Highlands Chapter 284 of the Order of the Eastern Star (OES) was created April 29, 1949, at the Masonic Hall and chartered on June 14, 1950, by thirty-five founding members.[639] Established nationally a hundred years earlier by Dr. Rob Morris, the Eastern Star sought to share the benefits of freemasonry with the female relatives of masons. Their advancement proceeded along degrees represented by the five points of the Star. The Highlands chapter installed Jessie Zachary Moreland as its first worthy matron and Thomas C. Harbison as worthy patron. Today's worthy matron is Kathleen Wilson.

The Highlands Garden Club was founded on Sept. 25, 1953, when Dr. Jessie Zachary Hedden organized thirty-five women with the objective of making Highlands "the most beautiful town in the state."[640] They met at the home of Mrs. A. T. Carter, whom they elected its first president. To carry out their objective they planted flowers around the Kelsey memorial, the Chamber of Commerce, and the new town hall and fire station. They landscaped the grounds around the library with native rhododendron, laurel, and azalea in front; dogwoods and hemlocks at the sides; and set a wildflower garden off from the street with a low white picket fence. They did the same for the hospital and the school.

They had street lamps installed and, though the State Highway Department denied their proposal in 1957 to plant five Carolina Hemlock trees in the center of Main Street, they planted five trees on each side instead. They sponsored annual tours of especially beautiful homes and gardens in Highlands, Cashiers, and Sapphire Valley, held annual flower shows, Christmas decoration contests, and silver teas, and offered prizes for the best school essays on conservation and landscaping to involve the school children. By sponsoring annual fashion shows, they raised money for the scholarship fund. And to involve the public at large, they scheduled programs of talks and demonstrations.

Within the first eight years the club had doubled to sixty-five members. In 1965 they planted flower boxes in front of the town's businesses. The project so impressed John Parris that he wrote up Highlands in the *Asheville Citizen* as "the flower box town," there being nothing like it in all the mountains. Intrigued by the Club's success in Highlands, women from Cashiers expressed their interest in joining, and the Club expanded to include their town as well, renaming itself the Highlands-Cashiers Garden Club. By 1973 they had planted 115 dogwoods along the sides of Highlands' streets.

In 1999 the Highlands–Cashiers Garden Club disbanded, leaving the gardening concerns of the town to its sisters: the Mountain and Laurel garden clubs. The Mountain Garden Club, formed in 1979 from the overflow of gardeners interested in the Highlands–Cashiers Club, sponsored Arbor Day tree plantings, litter clean-ups, trashcan painting projects, the purchase of blight-resistant chestnut trees, home tours, flower shows, and landscape work at the town hall and Highlands School.

The Laurel Garden Club too was born by default on August 26, 1982. Its charter members, on the waiting list to join the Mountain Garden Club, decided instead to form their own club. They elected Eleanor Metzger president, and she, Betty Heery, and Judith Mackie, along with twenty-three subsequent members, are still active today.

The Macon County Humane Society sought funds as early as 1963 to erect a shelter for unwanted and stray animals, but did not achieve their goal until 1980.[641] By the end of the twentieth century the Society was receiving as many as 1,800 animals in a single year, which put it in desperate need of funding from the communities it served.

The year 1969 saw the beginnings of one of the most generous charities in Highlands history. Mountain Findings, the brainchild of Norma "Boots" Pierson and other women of Father Gale Webbe's Episcopal Church, began receiving donated household goods and reselling them to the public. Managed by Mrs. Peter Many, it was located in Helen Holt Hopper's building on the 4th Street hill between the soda shop and the former shooting gallery. This worthy organization, run entirely by volunteers, not only served as a valuable recycling center but also channeled all its proceeds into supporting many service organizations and charities in Highlands.

By the end of the century, under the leadership of John and Florence Lupoli, Sr., and aided by fifty volunteers, the list of donees would increase to twenty-one, including the library, school, hospital, Crosby Center, Day Care, regional fire departments, Head Start, Hospice, the Humane Society, the Land Trust, Playhouse, Town Scholarship Fund, Inter-Church Council, Girl Scouts, cemetery, and more. The amount raised and distributed exceeded $70,000. In effect, Mountain Findings, considering how many organizations it supported annually, had become the backbone of Highlands.

In 1973 the Highlands Woman's Club was organized to create among the women of Highlands an awareness of their civic responsibility and to promote education and social welfare in the community, including the giving of financial aid wherever it might be needed.[642] Today the club supports two dozen nonprofit and charitable organizations in the town and provides Highlands School students with substantial scholarships for postgraduate education.

Much of the money is raised through the club's thrift shop, Fibber Magee's Closet, which was established at Sue Reese's suggestion on March 25, 1978, in the alley behind the Cheese Shop.[643] For the quality and price—from twenty-five cents to three dollars—it was the best place in town to shop for recycled clothing, earning $2,500 in its first year of operation. It still functions today in the Crosby Center, having netted in the year 2000 over $40,000, three-fourths of which went into donations.

The Woman's Club also formed the Helping Hand, a project to aid the elderly, shut-ins, and needy, which later evolved into the Highlands Emergency Council. From 1979–87 the club compiled and published a Highlands Own Telephone Directory and in 1983 co-sponsored with the Recreation Department a Highlands Own Crafts Festival to give local people a commercial outlet for their crafts while allowing them to retain all the profits.

Each year for fundraising, the club raffled a specially made Highlands Quilt and sponsored the Fabulous Fibber's Fashion Show and Luncheon. It supported programs for the youth of the community, such as Save the Children, Concern for Kids, Just Say No drug education, Beware of Strangers, Latchkey Kids, Bicycle Safety, and Home Alone. Among its original charter members were Sue Hall, Sue Reese, and Sara Nell Wright.

The Highlands Jaycees were organized to promote personal growth through community development for young men between the ages of eighteen and thirty-five. Receiving their charter at the Phelps House on March 21, 1973, the new chapter elected Jack Taylor its first president.[644] The following year it awarded John Phil Tate, Jr., its first annual Jaycee of the Year Award.

The Jaycees were the first to actually accomplish what several organizations before them had proposed but failed to carry out. A Highlands Community Building for social activities and charities had been planned as early as 1931 on the Dillard Road. In 1958 the Chamber of Commerce proposed tearing down the old school building, which had served informally as a community center, and replacing it with an official Community Center. In 1969 the Highlands Rotary voted to support construction of a community building. In 1971 the new recreation park was planning a community center as a later phase in its own development.

But none of these dreams ever materialized until the Jaycees set out to build a new community building at the north end of the ball park on Poplar Street. Designed by Jim Fox to hold 120 people, construction was begun by the Jaycees themselves after they had raised the necessary funds. In 1973 they sponsored the first Monte Carlo as a charity benefit, followed by annual Jaycee golf tournaments, ox roast festivals, and mock slave auctions, until in 1979 the completed Highlands Community Center became a physical reality, bringing home for the Jaycees the following year the state's "best project" award. Included among their activities was sponsoring the Highlands Boy Scout troop.

In 1974, the year after the Jaycees were organized, a Jaycettes Club was formed on April 22nd by wives of the Jaycees who proposed to support and work with their husbands.[645] Led by Mrs. John "Anne" Tate, president, they raised funds through bake sales and a Hospital Bazaar booth. They also sponsored the house of horror at the Highlands School Fall Festival and produced a Highlands Jaycettes Cookbook.

In 1976 Dr. Mary "Mo" Wheeler was instrumental in establishing Macon County's first Red Cross Disaster Shelter at the Peggy Crosby Center in Highlands.[646] In 1982 Anne Chastain, in close cooperation with area churches, created an organization modeled after a food closet for those in need in Highlands. The closet evolved into the Highlands Emergency Council that provided food, clothing, firewood, and payments of power bills and rent to the elderly and disabled, needy families, victims of fires, and others requiring emergency assistance. For her role in coordinating the various activities and services, Anne was given the Robert Dupree Citizen of the Year Award in 1983.

In the fall of 1993 Ervin Baumrucker and Mary Ann Sloan proposed converting the former Highlands Community Hospital building into a community service center. Funded by a challenge grant from Peggy and Philip Crosby in addition to donations from Mrs. Louis Brandely, the Duke Endowment, and the Kate B. Reynolds Charitable Trust, the center brought together under one roof seventeen service organizations, which included counseling for educational and career opportunities, health care for children and the aging and their families, the literacy council, the land trust, the library's used book store or Bookworm, Fibber Magee's thrift shop, the Center for Life Enrichment, and a number of county offices.

Phil Crosby, after whose wife the new organization was named the Peggy Crosby Center, had helped found the movement that awakened American business to the importance of quality management. He authored a number of nationally recognized books that sought to base effective, common-sense leadership on finances, technology, employees, and customers. His own forty-year career had seen him rise from junior engineer to vice president of the ITT Corporation. Suzie deVille (now Schiffli) served as Peggy Crosby Center's first director and received the coveted Thomas Jefferson Award for her role in its management, which role Holly Mathiowdis now fulfills.

In 1996 the Highlands Community Foundation, an affiliate of the Community Foundation of Western North Carolina, was created by year-round and seasonal residents to support non-profit organizations in the Highlands area through a permanent charitable fund. Initially chaired by Moyna Kendall Monroe and currently by Dr. Mary "Mo" Wheeler, it has amassed over $100,000 in invested and professionally managed assets to provide grants to local non-profits.

Fire Department

In 1885 the earliest fire inspector of record in Highlands was Joe McGuire, a builder and contractor, who constructed *Gray Cottage* (today's Wolfgangs on Main) and completed the Episcopal Church.[647] Two years later Frank Sheldon, architect and builder of the Davis House (later Lee's Inn), assumed the position of Fire Warden. There was no fire ordinance until Dr. O'Farrell drew up one in 1894, the year Charles Boynton became fire marshal.

The first fire engine arrived on the watch of Fire Marshall Ed Potts, oldest son of Billy Potts, in 1909.[648] Known affectionately as the hose buggy, it consisted merely of two wagon wheels on an axle carrying a hose. This hand-pulled buggy found its first home in 1929 when a $200 "fire station" was built on Oak Street opposite Charlie Brooks' garage. In actuality, the station was a wooden storage box hardly larger than the buggy itself and located at roadside about where the fire station is today.

What we currently know as the Volunteer Fire Department was created by town ordinance in 1939. It was to have a chief, his assistant, a captain, and a lieutenant for each of two companies. The Hose and Chemical Company and the Hook and Ladder Company would be run by six to twelve firemen, ages eighteen to forty-five. The town's intentions were good, but it took two and a half years for the council to elect Tom Potts fire chief and to authorize him at no salary to organize a volunteer fire department.

R to L: Highlands' first "fire station," Community Theatre, and School.
Photo courtesy of Broadie Potts, taken from Potts House ca. 1945.

Twelve more years would pass before Fire Chief Arnold Nelson proposed in August, 1953, as though for the first time, organizing a volunteer fire fighting crew. In the meantime Ed Rogers had served as fire chief; then Tom Harbison, as chief and building inspector. The town bought the old Highlands School property in 1951, with the intention one day of constructing a combination town office, jail, and fire department. Even as construction got underway in late 1953, a new four-wheel-drive rural fire truck arrived from the factory in Clintonville, Wisconsin, at a cost to the town of just over $12,300.

The new truck was promptly dubbed "Ole Betsy," and as the new fire station took shape in conjunction with the new town hall and police station, the old fire shed, which had served the town admirably for a quarter century, bit the dust, its lumber salvaged for public picnic tables and construction of the Jaycee-sponsored Scout Hut.

At first the new truck was parked at the Bryson Gulf Station at Main and 4th because there was no garage large enough to house it. But in 1954, with the completion of the new town hall, it was parked, ready for any emergency, in the center bay where residents today pay their utility bills to the town. Actually two vehicles were squeezed into one bay: the new truck and a Jeepster station wagon with a portable pump.

Town officials standing by the first fire truck are L. to R.: Steve Potts, mayor Wilton Cobb, Ed Potts, Carter Talley, Luther Rice, Sr., Charles Anderson, and Tudor Hall. Walking away from the truck on the left is Tom Harbison. Courtesy of Tammy Lowe.

Arnold Nelson stands between the hose buggy and "Ole Betsy," the first fire truck. Photo 1953, courtesy of Highlands Volunteer Fire Department.

With Carleton Cleaveland heading the newly formed, newly equipped, and newly housed Highlands Volunteer Fire Department, its firemen from the very start were commended by the town for their efficiency in handling fire alerts. In 1961 Highlands purchased its first ambulance, a brand new converted Oldsmobile station wagon. It carried a first aid kit, bottle of oxygen, and volunteer firemen with no formal training but ready to help wherever required. Under Gene Houston the department raised money not only to sustain its operations but also to save for a new station, totally separate from the cramped quarters it shared with town hall and the police station.

Town hall, fire station, police station, completed in 1954. Photo courtesy of Highlands Historic Inventory.

In 1967 a Firemen's Barbeque raised $1,000 toward the purchase of a second ambulance, a converted Ford station wagon. By year's end the ambulance had proved its mettle when a fire started in the kitchen at Skyline Lodge on Flat Mountain Road, and volunteer firemen pumped water from the newly built swimming pool, saving all but the destroyed kitchen and damaged adjacent dining room. As a result, the McClains were able to rebuild the lodge two years hence. The department held its first practice drill when Joseph and Annie Root's forty-one year old home and shop had to be razed to make way for Lewis Reeves' hardware store as it exists today.

In 1968 under Jimmy Talley the department was able to purchase a brand new 750-gallon Ward LaFrance truck which it moved into its newly completed five-bay station on Oak Street. Built by the volunteers and the Nelson Job Training Crew, it was funded in part by the town.

During the summer of this year all the volunteers took part in the massive search for little Cenda Schweers who wandered to her death off the Bowery Road, which will be described later in Chapter Twenty-five. They named their new fire truck the *Cenda*, even as the play area at the Civic Center was also named in her memory. One of the most tragic calls to which this new truck responded on a February night in 1970 was a furnace fire at Dr. Eula Pate's home on the Dillard Road, which broke out while she was on duty at the hospital. Her family of two adults and three children perished in the blazing bedroom surrounded by bitter cold and ice.

During the early seventies the worn out Oldsmobile was replaced by a new GMC Rescue Ambulance, a new 750-gallon Ward LaFrance Chevy Fire Truck, and a third Pontiac ambulance. When state rules and regulations began to apply in 1974, three of the five volunteers attending technical school at Southwestern—Bobby Houston, Sam Zachary, and Romaine Owens—received certification as Highlands' first Emergency Medical Technicians (EMTs); Bobby Creswell and Fred Munger, shortly thereafter.

Within three years the EMTs had an ambulance, meeting all the specifications of the N.C. Emergency Medical Services and paid for by local residents and the county. It was accompanied by a 1550-gallon water-tank truck for use where there were no hydrants, lakes, or creeks. Chief Bobby Houston had a pager system installed to replace the inefficient and time-consuming method of alerts by telephone. As a byproduct of all these improvements the Highlands volunteers received the highest rating a volunteer department could earn—seven—which translated into a great savings in homeowners' insurance premiums within the town.

The department now engaged in the continuous upgrading of equipment and frequent fire and disaster drills, such as the 1978 joint effort with the hospital that staged a rescue of several Boy Scouts supposedly injured from serious falls during a severe thunderstorm at the town's rock quarry. Sufficiently impressed, the county in 1980 gave Highlands' EMS $30,000 and full-time ambulance service.

Before this, the department had operated on a part-time basis, but 1980 put this new full-time service to the test. The estate of Veazey Rainwater burned to the ground during the filming of Alan Alda's *Four Seasons*. The cause of the fire was traced to a space heater used by Universal Studios, which promptly canceled their production and subsequently lost $1.4 million in the resulting damage suit against them.[649]

In 1982 a fire sparked by a faulty fuse gutted the ninety-three-year-old historic Lee's Inn. Bobby Houston was chief at the time, and when John Cleaveland reported the blaze, he told Houston, "Just save the town!" Despite the department's having preplanned for such a misfortune, the enormous responsibility weighed heavily on Houston. He admitted he feared it more than the real dangers faced in fighting the intense heat. The inferno heated the doorknobs at the Rexall drugstore across 4th Street, but by evening the town had been saved.

In 1983 the Highlands rescue system was immensely aided by the purchase of a "Jaws of Life" for emergency extractions from wrecked cars or demolished homes. The following year the county took over the ambulance service, hiring eight fulltime EMTs and then moving the EMS out of the fire station and into shared quarters with the police department constructed by the county next door. Brenda Pierson achieved certification as Highlands' first female EMT.

In 1985 the department burned its second house in a practice drill, the old Charlie Wright home, to make way for Wright Square shopping center. The first home of Charlie and Helen had burned naturally in 1928, this being the fire that scorched Charlie's Carnegie Gold Medal awarded for his heroic rescue on Whiteside Mountain.

Bill Lowe, Chief Mike McCall, and Jimmy Lowe at Fire and Rescue Awards Dinner in 1996. Photo courtesy of Highlands Volunteer Fire Department.

The year that Jimmy Lowe succeeded Olan Vinson as chief, 1987, the Highlands Fire Department recognized ten retiring firemen who had given accumulatively 224 years of their lives to fire, rescue, and ambulance service to the town. The longest serving members among them were former chief Jimmy Talley with twenty-six years and Bobby Creswell and Herb James with twenty-five, the remaining seven having each served at least twenty years: former chiefs Olan Vinson and Bobby Houston, along with firemen Sam and Charles Zachary, Romaine Owens, Fred Munger, and Roy Potts.

It was during Jimmy Lowe's tenure as chief of the department that the great fire consumed the 116-year-old historic King's Inn. The latest major fire that the Highlands volunteers have fought in conjunction with twelve other fire departments and the U.S. and N.C. Forest Services was the Brushy Face Mountain inferno that erupted on May 14, 1997.[650] Starting in Clear Creek and prompted by thirty-five mph winds, it quickly climbed to the top of Brushy Face. During the ten hours that it raged with waves of flames thirty to forty feet high, it burned eighty to 100 acres before Mike McCall's volunteers shortly after midnight succeeded in bringing it under control.

In profound appreciation of the risks and sacrifices these firefighters faced, the restaurants in town—as was customary during similar emergencies of the past—fed them free of charge, and the hardware stores provided all their material needs.

From 1985–97 the fire department serviced a five-mile district on less than $30,000 raised each year from honorary memberships outside of town. Faced with the fact that all other departments in the county had switched to a fire service fee system to cover their increasing costs, the Highlands department now did the same, having just purchased a $108,000 Freightliner Pumper-Tanker, which stood in stark contrast to the hose buggy of eighty years earlier. In 1998 the volunteers responded to 260 fire and rescue calls.

As the century ended, the department adopted a county-wide fire tax system to raise funds for a $200,000 expansion to the rear of the station, in addition to the purchase of a long-overdue rescue boat for the town's several lakes. In contrast to no budget in 1953, the annual operating budget in 1999 stood at $115,000. In 116 years the department had grown from one fire inspector in 1885 to a department of thirty volunteers in 2001, eleven of whom were first responders.

The only complaint, on the part of the department in Bobby Houston's opinion, was that modern regulations imposed so much more paperwork than in the early days when rescuing a man was more important than reporting what you did and how you did it. Inspectors today rarely go into the field, but rather prefer reviewing meticulously detailed reports of fieldwork in the office.

It is almost impossible to single out one or two members of the fire and rescue personnel as community heroes, for, as Bobby Houston claims, their response has always been a group effort. But as a group, their bravery and dedication in emergency situations where life and limb are at risk have earned them the title "heroes" collectively.

High angle rescue training at Pilot Mountain, 2000. Top left: Jeff Munger.
Bottom right: Eric Pierson.

In preparation for their various tasks, six have earned certifications as divers, which proved valuable in fatalities at Dry and Glen Falls as well as Rainbow Falls, where Woodrow Wilson recovered the bodies of two Buncumbe County teenagers, and more recently Windy Falls on the Horsepasture River.

Many of the Highlands volunteers have graduated from the High Angle and Mountain Rescue School, a course spanning five years. Several have passed the sixty-hour course for paramedics, which in the case of Sheriff Carl "Bub" Zachary led to his surviving a code-4 DOA from a heart attack in 1985, for the Highlands EMTs revived him.

During the great blizzard of '93, Chief Jimmy Lowe, rescue captain Jerry Tilson, and their volunteers organized emergency aid and exhausted themselves saving the lives of the elderly and frail, whom they transported through waist- and chest-high drifts of snow from their isolated homes to shelters or hospital care.

Indeed, it was during this snow that Bobby Houston achieved his life's wish, for in the quarter century that he had served with the fire and rescue team, he never had the chance to help deliver a baby. On Monday night after the blizzard he, Lora Speed, and Dr. David Wheeler were plowing through the snow to Sylva with Lila Shearl in the last stages of pregnancy when she went into labor below Lake Thorpe (Lake Glenville). There at the power plant, with little more than a cord clip, receiving tape, a blanket, and scissors, he and Lora helped Wheeler deliver little Michael in the ambulance.[651] Bobby told John Shearl that he should have named his blizzard baby *Thorpe* after the lake where he was born.

Other Service Organizations

Only cursorily discussed in this chapter but vital nonetheless to the welfare of the Highlands community have been the contributions of its churches, the Boy Scouts, Adopt-a-Road cleanups, and recycling centers, as well as fund-raising festivals, tournaments, walks, runs, and auctions.

Volunteers all too often go unthanked in a world of glorified heroes and leaders, perhaps because they are not individuals who prance their fame upon the stage but rather self-effacing foot soldiers who fight the battles that the generals only direct. There are good things in the world that preachers preach about, lawyers plead for, doctors prescribe, and authors write about, but volunteers perform. And in this sense volunteerism, like charity, is the brightest jewel in the crown of humanity. It elevates and ennobles those who practice it by the giving of themselves without thought of reward.

Merely to list all the volunteers who have contributed to the creation and development of Highlands as its exists today would constitute a book in itself, a veritable paean to human acts of kindness and love.

25. Things That Pass Away

Loveliest of lovely things are they
On Earth that soonest pass away.
The rose that lives its little hour
Is prized beyond the sculptured flower.
                    —William Cullen Bryant,
                    "A Scene on the Banks of the Hudson"

The Bible tells us, "Dust thou art, and unto dust shalt thou return."[652] That we all shall die we know; it's but the time that varies, and with it comes the heartache and the natural shocks of sudden loss for those we leave behind. The old go to death in the fullness of time, and we accept it more readily than when death comes to the young, whether by some act of violence or by natural end. Death has visited Highlands on many occasions when the whole community felt its sting and suffered severely from its finality.

On occasion, however, the swing of the scythe would miss its mark, and then death, robbed of its due, would become a subject of ironic humor, depending, of course, on who told the tale. Herman Wilson, for instance, was one of those Clear Creek raconteurs who claimed to be unruly in his youth: "We used to be rough, us Clear Creeks was, no doubt about that, we's rough."

He loved to tell of a time in Highlands when Wiley McCall got shot by his first cousin, escaping an early demise by only a hair's breath. The way Herman told it, he and the Clear Creeks had gathered in the dirt Walhalla road (now Highway 28) a hundred yards or so from where Bryson's Food Store is today. They were laughing and joking, having a good time,

and there's me and Hubert and Wiley McCall and Lyman Picklesimer and Alfred Picklesimer and maybe a few from Satolah, Rabun County down here, and we's laughing and singing some, you know, and this feller Radford McCall was a dating Almetta Picklesimer at the Warren's place up on Satulah. He's a big tall curly headed feller and high tempered, and he come down to us and he said, "Ah, Boys," he said—he talked kinda through his nose—he said, "Cut this out, or we'll be over here and get ever' damn one of yu'uns, you know."

Well, we hadn't done nothing to him, you know. Wasn't none of his business. Well, Wiley McCall down here—he's still living—took it up, and he went to giving him some bad language, you know; I mean the worst kind.

And Radford told him, said, "If you call me that again, I'm a goin' to kill ye." And he did, shore nuf. He whipped his pistol out from under his belt there and shot him six times.

And I said, "Don't shoot him, he's had too much to drink, you know, and don't do it." But he shot Wiley down, and Wiley had on a white shirt and blue pants, like we all wore in the summertime mostly, and when Wiley came up on his feet, his shirt was just as red as my shirt is red, as blood will make it. And I didn't think he'd live but just a little while.

His brother said to me—Emery, the dad of Bill McCall said to me (I's the only one had on a suit in the bunch, don't know why I wore a suit, just to show out, I guess)— he said to me, "Herm, will you take my gun and carry it." He said, "The law will be here and get us," and he said, "Wiley's going to die anyway."

And I said, "Yeah, he's going to die." I said, "You know what's so?" I said, "If a man shoot up my brother like that, I'd follow him to the ends of the earth to kill him."

He said, "Wiley's going to die, and it'd just make bad matters worse," and which he used his head.

We took Wiley up there to where the Satulah and the Walhalla road comes together, and there's a big spreading chestnut tree there, and grass was growing under it, and we laid him there till we could get Charlie Potts there with his Ford and loaded him up, and took him to Durgin's sanatorium, was it? And she's a top nurse, and she put him to bed and done what she could do till they called Dr. Rogers and Dr. Lyle—Dr. Lyle was the first surgeon in Macon County—they came up there, and they probed the bullets, and he just hung between life and death for days, you know. The bullet struck him an inch and a half from the heart.

And he came out of it and got back on his feet, and years later he got hurt out here at the big logging company, known as the Suncrest Lumber Company. Well, he went from there to Dr. Edgar Angel's Hospital for a checkup, and Doc said, "Wiley, you ever been shot?" And Wiley said, "Yeah, I've been shot." And he said, "I see the damn bullet right through the skin on your back. You want me to take it out?"

He said, "What'll it cost me?"

He said, "Five dollars."

Said, "Take her out." It'd been all through him and just barely through the skin in his back there. Yeah, we's rough. We's rough!

Rough—and incredibly fortunate for Wiley McCall. For others, however, fate was not so lenient, like the time in 1938 when two boys drowned in Lake Sequoyah, despite desperate attempts to save them. John Gibson, age eleven, and Andrew Chastain, age fifteen, were on their way with Corbin and David Talley and Clarence Baty to caddy at the Highlands Country Club when they stopped to swim. The water was only three feet deep, but Gibson stepped off into a ten-foot hole about twenty-feet wide. Chastain tried to rescue him but was himself a poor swimmer.

While Clarence and Corbin ran for help, David attempted to rescue both boys. Rear Admiral Newton McCully came by with Jerry Keener, but the hole was too wide and deep for them to locate the boys. It was already half an hour and then fifty minutes before the bodies could be raised, but two hours of trying to resuscitate them found no signs of life.[654]

Some of Highlands' best and brightest were lost to the ravages of war. Garcie Edwards, though of Horse Cove, died in World War I. The town's first casualty of World War II was Albert Rogers, age nineteen, who was reported missing in action in May, 1942, and confirmed dead over a year later on June 29, 1943.[655] By war's end in August, 1945, Highlands servicemen on the Roll of Honor included 200 names, seven of whom were "gold star" fatalities: Albert Rogers, James Baty, George Beal, Thomas Bridgman, Clyde Crisp, Bernice McCall, and Henry Zoellner. Three losses stemmed from the Vietnam War: Robert Meacham, Jr., Lawton Keener, and Thomas McKinney.

About the same time that Highlands was losing all too many of its young men to World War II, it was also in the throes of losing nearly all its ancient trees reportedly to the war effort. In late 1943, three years after the death of Prioleau Ravenel, Jr., his second wife Beatrice, who lived in Charleston and had never been to Highlands, sold her inherited portion of the Ravenel estate, consisting of 1,658 acres of primeval forest, to Powell Lumber Company of Waynesville.[656]

Aware of the unfortunate sale, the local newspaper remarked sardonically, "Many lamentations have been heard over the passing of the forest into the hands of the lumber company—but such is the way of Progress," because for years the primeval forest had been one of the most unique attractions of Highlands, containing among its many giants of nature the largest cherry tree in the world.

Professor Bob Zahner has penned a heartrending lament over this egregious loss to Highlands in his *Mountain at the End of the Trail*. For in 1944 the Powell Lumber Company in conjunction with Champion International Paper and Fiber Company of Canton, N.C., began their logging. Wilford Corbin remembers how he, at age 16, and Furman Houston and Winfred Gregory helped fell trees up to six feet in diameter.

Mature after a thousand years, an ancient hemlock forest was almost totally destroyed in five miserable years, requiring another thousand before its flora and fauna could be restored to their original diversity, integrity, and beauty.[657]

Bob describes this death of "one of the most magnificent forest preserves in all of eastern North America" including the Kelsey Trail in terms of the grisly tractor skid trails, logging haul roads, silt-clogged rivers and lakes, and huge felled hemlock, yellow birch, black cherry, and red maple trees, where hundreds and thousands of interior forest birds and animals, suddenly homeless, once lived their precious lives.

In 1921, when the Highlands Improvement Society was providing stenciled signs to mark twenty-four miles of trails and special sights in the area, Ed Potts had placed a quote from the prelude to Longfellow's *Evangeline* near a group of the finest trees in the primeval forest.

The Primeval Forest, sold for wood pulp products and lumber in 1943. Photo by George Masa, 1929.
"This is the forest primeval. The murmuring pines and the hemlocks,
Bearded with moss, and in garments green, indistinct in the twilight,
Stand like Druids of eld, with voices sad and prophetic."

Herbert Ravenel Sass, in his 1928 romance War Drums, part of which had Whiteside Mountain as its setting, described this same primeval forest as like the "Garden of God."

Truly, it was like God's Garden, that springtime wilderness of Carolina where the white man's axe was yet unknown. It was a garden abloom not only with flowers but with birds more beautiful than golden jessamine or pink Indian rose; a garden not still and silent as most gardens are but astir with abundant life, aquiver with innumerable voices.

There were places where all was silent. Sometimes the trail led through lofty pine woods, carpeted with fern, where the giant trees towered eighty feet without a limb, woods that were vast cathedrals too holy for the little singing birds. [657]

It's ironic that some seventy years prior to the destruction of this Primeval Forest surrounding Whiteside Mountain, the aging Silas McDowell had written its elegy, never imagining, of course, that the forest itself would ever disappear, but lamenting his own inability ever to see it again.

Having visited the white rock and its surrounding green for most of his life but at length growing old and physically as well as mentally feeble, he poured out his grief at having to leave the mountain of his youth in the following lines:

Hail, spirit of the hills
  In thy snow-white shroud!
Doest guard the crystal rills?
  Or, watch the passing cloud?
Say! What do'st thou there,
  On that mountain lone?
Or com'st from where?
  Thou huge ghost of stone!
Did some internal shock
  Upheave thy white dome—
An isolated rock,
  From earth's hot womb?
Or did earth sink in zone,
  Down on a fire-flood,
And thou, as a rib-bone,
  Pierced up through the mud?
How many years hast thou stood
  As a sentinel?
Before or since the flood?
  Or ere Adam fell?
Won't tell thine own history!
  Then tell what of time,
And the dread mystery

Of Life, Death, and Crime.
Still mute! thy counsel keep
Close to thyself.
And hush those echos deep
In thy rocky shelf,
Yet, Ghost, I love thee,
And heave a sigh!
And the thought of leaving thee
Bedims mine eye.
Adieu, adieu, adieu!
One last look, and then
One more fond lingering view
And ne'er see thee again. [658]

Whiteside Mountain barely escaped the fate of the adjacent primeval forests by an act of the U.S. Forest Service in 1974. The Service, which already owned some 66,000 acres in the Highlands District including 831 acres of the Devil's Courthouse tract, acquired Whiteside Mountain through a land exchange and put it into the public domain.[659]

All this resulted after a year of frantic maneuvering, negotiating, and scraping for funding, at the end of which time realtor Andy McDonough struck a deal to buy 144 acres of the mountain and then trade it for a like amount of land which the Forest Service owned along Cowee Ridge on the other side of Highway 64. Completed in March, 1975, the exchange opened for residential development a large tract west of the highway, but it effectively closed off commercial development of the mountain, which at the time was of widespread concern. The old five-acre Indian campground, of course, which lay within a water storage reserve, was never threatened.

All that remains today of the original primeval forest are four patches.[660] One is a stand of ancient hemlocks and yellow birch around the shores of today's Ravenel Lake, originally Osseroga, at the Cullasaja Club. This stand was saved by the wife of one of the loggers, Bayeola Powell, to preserve the beauty of the lake.

A second section is a twenty-two acre tract of Table Mountain pine and Carolina hemlock along Chestnut Ridge, which Henry Wright donated to the N.C. Nature Conservancy in 1964. Known as the "Cat Stairs," it contains stair-like bluffs deep within the woods between Highlands Falls Country Club and Whiteside Mountain.

The National Forest owns a third section of forty-five acres, known as the Kelsey Tract, which it purchased from the Macon County Land Company in 1913. It consists of giant Canadian hemlocks, tulip trees, and yellow poplar.

The fourth part is privately owned by Henry Wright's brother, George, north of Community Bible Church on the Cashiers Road.

Despite the loss of its crowning treasure, the primeval forest, Highlands was surrounded by enough National Forest to ensure much of its remaining beauty against destruction for commercial gain. Even so, as the rose produces thorns, natural beauty harbors perils. Waterfalls have always been a prime attraction in the mountains, despite the annual loss of life that they precipitate.

Dry Falls, viewed from below, inspires awe but little danger, even for those who brave the path under the river to the other side. From above, however, it has on occasion dragged an unwary adventurer over the edge, hurling him to his death in the ravine far below.

John Kilby, a nineteen-year-old youth from Knoxville, Tennessee, plunged over the brink on an early August day in 1952. He was attempting to walk across the top when he lost his footing and nose-dived ninety feet to his death.[661] Two years later a 150-foot railing was installed to insure the safety of subsequent viewers.

Whatever lives it might have saved, it didn't prevent little nine-year-old Janis McGivern from ducking under it while her family was on vacation from Cedar Rapids, Iowa, and disappearing in 1956.[662] Frustrated that her parents wouldn't buy her candy at Luke Rice's concession stand in the parking area, she deserted them in a huff and plunged over the falls. The town shut down the powerhouse and placed sandbags along the top of the dam above the falls just long enough to reduce the flow so that Earl Baty could recover the girl's body from the pool beneath.

Cliffside Lake took the life of eighteen-year-old Charles Crawford in 1959.[663] Twelve-year-old Thomas Monroe Boyer, visiting from Hollywood, Florida, in 1967 lost his life in a 150-foot plunge over Horse Cove Falls.

Glen Falls claimed a victim when a twenty-year-old University of Florida student, Steven Turner, fell fifty feet from the second set of lower falls in 1981, and again when a thirty-eight-year-old Columbus, Georgia, woman, Linda Anne Armas, plunged seventy feet from nearly the same spot in 1984.

William Hood and his daughter Kim were miraculously saved from certain death in 1982 when a pothole about twenty feet from the sheer drop above the third falls caught them both, and the Rescue Squad was able to transport them across the river with ropes and a stretcher and up 700 feet to the parking lot.

Greg Simmons of Atlanta and Highlands was not so fortunate when he lost his life in a headlong fall 150 feet down Picklesimer or Satulah Falls in 1988.

Satulah Falls. Photo by the author, 2001.

Of all the tragedies involving losses in and around Highlands, perhaps the most widely remembered was the fate of little four-year-old Lucinda "Cenda" Schweers from Atlanta who wandered off from her host's home on the Bowery Road in 1968, precipitating the largest search in the history of the town.[664]

For five days 1,000 to 1,500 searchers combed the woods, mountains, streams, and valleys in a bone-chilling deluge of rain. Coming from Highlands, Cashiers, and Franklin, they were joined by the U.S. Forest Service, rescue squads from every town and county of Western N.C., even individuals from other counties of North Carolina, Georgia, and South Carolina.

Among the friends of Mr. Schweer who came from Atlanta to help, Fritz Stone waded out into a creek to peer over a waterfall and plunged fifty feet to his own death on the rocks below.

Volunteers arrived from the Job Corps, recruits from the U.S. Army, 125 Rangers from the Army Mountain School, as well as the N.C. National Guard dispatched by Gov. Dan Moore, the Red Cross Emergency Unit from Asheville, and many policemen from Western N.C. Even a helicopter and crew were assigned from Ft. Bragg some 350 miles away.

On the fifth day, June 10th, Bill Wilson of the Forest Service, R. L. Worley, and Carleton Crane discovered little Cenda in Monroe Lake down in Whiteside Cove. It was never determined when or how she died, whether she was washed over the waterfall above the lake and perished from a severe injury to the head or fell into a stream overflowing with the heavy rain that began on the third day and was washed into the lake, or perhaps from some other accident. An autopsy showed she died, not from drowning, but from the injury to her head.

The whole town felt heartbroken over what had become a community loss. The Fire Department named its new truck the "Cenda," and the town named the play area at the Civic Center in her memory, which name it still bears today.

As if the loss of little Cenda wasn't sad enough, an offshoot two months later added a tragic postscript. Christopher Makle-Hansen, a fifteen-year-old arriving with his grandparents from Charleston for their annual stay in Whiteside Cove, heard Cenda's story and resolved to test the route she was supposed to have taken that ended in Monroe lake. When night came and he wasn't back from his walk, the Jackson County Rescue Squad launched an all-night search. At daybreak a bloodhound refused to approach the waterfall above the lake, and Christopher's body was recovered from the pool below.

For the most part tragedies in Highlands have involved the young. A particularly sad loss in 1967 was ten-year-old William Stephen McCall, whose father Amos Edward McCall worked as night policeman for Highlands, for it was his father's pistol that he accidentally discharged to precipitate his own death.[665]

In addition to the many waterfalls that attract visitors to Highlands with sometimes fatal consequences, there are also the precipitous cliffs that circle the plateau and pose significant risks to the unwary. Fortunately, there have been no reported falls from Satulah, though anyone who has climbed out on its granite face to enjoy the southern Sea of Views has been made keenly aware of the unforgiving nature of a simple misstep.

The Sea of Views from the south face of Satulah. Photo by George Masa, 1929.

Even falls from Whiteside Mountain, though to be expected it would seem, have proven quite rare. Had it not been for Charlie Wright's rescue of Gus Baty, Gus might have been the earliest known casualty of the mountain. In November, 1974, the Highlands Rescue Squad retrieved C. J. Little of Doraville, Georgia, who was hiking with his son under Whiteside and fell a short distance on steep rocks, breaking his shoulder. Alerted by Little's son, Bobby Houston and Bobby Creswell followed the timbered rim of the mountain from Wildcat Cliffs to effect his rescue.

The next year a guard rail was installed on the mountain. But like the railing installed for the safety of visitors at Dry Falls, this rail proved no more effective in preventing a fatality. In 1977 when the car belonging Kerry Brandon, a twenty-two-year-old Western Carolina University student, was left a couple of days in the Whiteside Mountain parking lot, the Rescue Squad was alerted.[666] A search at the base of the cliff on the first day proved fruitless, but the next day Bud Lamb discovered the body a considerable distance out from the base. The boy had plummeted the entire 1,800 feet from the rail-protected top.

Similarly, the year prior, a twenty-year-old Western Carolina University student from Asheboro, Zachary Howard, while camping with two girls on a ledge farther down the face, had stepped off the ledge sometime around midnight and plunged in total darkness to his death 200 to 300 feet below. When the girls couldn't find him the next morning, they summoned the Rescue Squad, and his body was located along the same route as Little's rescue and lowered into Whiteside Cove.

The only person to perish in a fall from Devil's Courthouse was twenty-one-year-old Jeff Bates, who in February, 1978, was trying to photograph its sheer rock face.[667] Two days earlier he had climbed the Courthouse with two companions from Atlanta, but on returning alone to photograph it, he ventured too close to the icy edge of the cliff and slipped off.

Individual falls from the brink of nature's most glorious sights are almost always tragic, but when tragedies come in threes affecting a whole family, they pose a true test of faith in the care and protection of a divine Providence. One family in Highlands that was especially hard hit by such a multiple loss was that of Mack Wilson. Mack had ten children, three of whom suffered violent deaths.

As Mack's brother Herman tells it, Joe Wilson lost his life at a sawmill. He stooped under the blade to clean off the dust. He'd always shut his saw down until that particular time when for some reason he left it in motion, and the blade struck him at the back of the neck. He lived while he was being transported to the hospital in Greenville, S.C., but was dead on arrival.

Gene Wilson, pastor of a church in Statesville, was killed when a little farm tractor turned over on him where he was in charge of a boys' home.

Kurt Wilson ran an electric and gas company in Highlands, and he died in 1976 from an accident at King's Inn. He wasn't aware that so much gas had settled in the basement of the building, but when he flipped on his cigarette lighter to light his way, the gas exploded in a flash fire. He walked to the Community Hospital in the next block, but died from his burns a couple of days later.

Four of Mack's children still live in Highlands: Walter, Tom, Dolly Wilson McCall, and Ellie Wilson Nix. The family's losses were keenly felt by the whole town.

The premature death of a dear friend or cherished relative is almost always grievous, but equally distressing can be the destruction of a tree or house or inn that over long years has earned as much love. The cutting of the altitude oak was just such a loss for the people of Highlands, as were the demolition of the Anderson/Sullivan house, the loss to fire of the Kelsey house, Lee's and King's Inn, the Russell House halfway to Walhalla, and, for individual families, the Rainwater estate, Kenyon Zahner's home on Billy Cabin, and the Rabbit Hole.

For any Highlander who grew up with any of these individuals or buildings or marvels of nature, the loss has been cruel but truly not permanent, for people and treasured things of this quality live in the hearts and minds they leave behind, and in this sense they never die.

26. Yee Haa

That was about the best past-time we had back then. We didn't have any
movies to go to or anything. We had to make our movies.
—Irene James & Almetta Brooks

The children of early Highlands didn't have Nintendo, TV, or a Rec Park
for hanging out with friends. At the turn of the century they didn't even
have Helen's Barn. But that didn't stop Almetta and Irene Picklesimer from
having their share of fun. Their family had a great long stable on a hill that
held about twenty sheep, which they fed regularly. But they also got in the
pen with them, each child climbing on a sheep to ride it as it went bobbing
through the herd.

"It just tickled us to death," said Aunt Mett. "And if we'd fall off, we'd
just hit another sheep, and it was so soft it didn't hurt at all. We kept sheep
for the wool. Mama would spin the wool to make socks and quilts." Irene
agreed, "That was about the best pastime we had back then. We didn't have
any movies to go to or anything." To which Mett added, "We had to *make*
our movies."

Mett said they built a playhouse about eight feet square. They poled it
and hung "dog hobble just right thick around it. And we'd go to Mama's
cows, and we wouldn't milk all of 'em, we'd just get what we wanted, and
we'd put it in bottles and just churn it. We'd just shake it and shake it till
we'd churned it. Then we got to riding the cows. They was way down in the
barn, and the barn and the field would hide us from Dad and Mama. We'd
ride the cows, that was mean, though, to do that. They finally caught up
with us, but they was a long time a-catching us."

One thing they loved to do, straight out of Robert Frost's popular poem,
was go up on the hill and climb birch saplings. They'd swing out and bend
them over, but never hitting the ground. "We'd just go from one sapling to
the other," laughed Mett, "just go right on and on. We rode them so much,
they just turned the way we rode them. You'd see how far you could go and
never touch the ground. When we grew up and got married, you could still
see those trees where we'd ruined them, you know."

Mett and Irene acknowledge there were hazards in their games. Mett said
she wasn't sure what you called it, but they put a stake in the ground,
punched a hole through it, and attached a small sapling to the stake with a
steel pin, like the spoke of a wheel. "And you know we'd just go round, you
could just fly with it." On one occasion when the pinned sapling came
loose, Irene flew about thirty feet and hit a wagon wheel. She said she

landed on her head but wasn't hurt, and laughing added, "It's just the reason I don't know anything now."

The children of early Highlands worked hard, but hard work brought its own rewards, sometimes sooner than later. Irene remembered the bean stringings where they earned permission to go dancing. "Aunt Nan Neely would say, "Whenever you get those beans done, why we'll let ye dance." Sometimes we just hid the beans, Irene confessed, "or we'd a-been there all night. We'd never get any dancing."

For Highlands children who didn't grow up on a farm but shared the same love of nature as those who did, there were trails through the laurel and rhododendron archways dappled with shadows and splashes of sunshine where white Indian pipes bloomed in secret shady spots. If Sarah Hines (later Bailey) wasn't picking blueberries on the Bowery, she was gathering galax leaves for Christmas spending money. Galax leaves weren't edible, but the tiny wintergreen leaves were the bubble gum of her childhood. She'd pick a leaf or two and savor the minty taste as fresh and cheap as any artificial gum available today.

Sarah remembered catching the tiny lively toads that kept hopping across their toes and taking them home in jars to perform in frog circuses. She never took the conventional path up Sunset Rocks, but through mysterious Hoot Owl Glen instead and straight up the rock cliff. Though the trail often disappeared in a dead end of briars and bushes, there were always "rich chunks of mica gleaming like buried treasure from the mossy gray boulders strewn through the forest as if flung down the mountainside by some impetuous giant." Tiny vermilion mushrooms appeared artfully placed as though designed for an effective display.

And occasionally she'd discover "a single wild tiger lily glowing in savage loveliness in a curtain of fern." This memory in particular would haunt Sarah all her life. Years and years later she concluded that the "French have never concocted a perfume as rare as the fragrance of this opulent flower."

What impressed Sarah on her return to Highlands, years after the indelible impressions of childhood had been formed, were the half-forgotten memories of pot holes at the top of Sunset Rocks, which the child in her had believed were made by baby elephants walking across the stone when it was still soft. More memories surfaced of the deep chorus of bullfrogs around Ravenel Lake and the gentle lifting and falling of the water lily pads in response to vagrant breezes. This was "more soul-satisfying than the technical perfection of a symphony and ballet performance in a crowded auditorium."

For Sarah, who had been away from home for too long a spell, it was easy to forget how deep a blue the Highlands sky could be "when one is surrounded by gray buildings, gray smog and the din of airway and highway traffic."[668] It may have been easy for Sarah to forget, but when the lightness and freshness of those childhood sensations washed over her adult emotions, cradled and nourished by an early love of nature, it was all too easy to remember in a flash. How fortunate the child who knew then—or knows now—the real beauty of Highlands!

Fishing in Whiteside Cove. Photo by R. Henry Scadin, 1900, courtesy of Hudson Library archives.

When Virginia Fleming and Bill Crosby were young, they swung through the trees, Tarzan style, from Bill's home at Spruce and 5th to Virginia's home at the end of 5th, four blocks without ever touching the ground!

What Frank Potts recalled from his early childhood were not so much the sensations of nature as the candy pulls at his friends' homes, where you boiled syrup down good and thick, "then got a wad of it in your hand and went to pulling on it—maybe a couple, you know—and it turned white, or almost white, and it made real good candy. 'Course you had to grease your hands or put flour on 'em to keep 'em from sticking, you know." Olive Crane loved the candy pullings too when she wasn't busy with her home-made toys: dolls constructed from corncobs that she'd dress up.

For those who didn't ride sheep, play house, catch hoppy toads, or hand-craft corncob dolls, there were hayrides for the school kids early in the fall, around Halloween, by horse and wagon. And, of course, there was always fishing in the fresh rivers and streams. Joe Reese remembered how he and the boys used to fish down by the Chattooga Iron Bridge on the Bull Pen Road. "We'd fish all day, and the whippoorwills," he complained, "would keep us awake singing all night!"

Herman Wilson and his brother John would fish Overflow Creek, the Chattooga River, and Big Creek, using cane fishing poles that they cut from the banks. Herman credited John with being the better fisher since, as Herman put it, "I just didn't seem to hold my mouth right or didn't use the proper bait." Herman would end up with a bunch of scaly river fish, but between them, they always caught more than they could eat and brought some home for the family.

Deer and coon hunting were other forms of recreation that saw families almost break up in the fall as the men in season abandoned their wives, children, even their jobs for the hunt. As noted previously in Chapter Twenty-three, Uncle Charlie Potts, as soon as he could finally retire as postmaster, plunged fulltime into fox hunting.

But Aunt Mett couldn't wait for retirement before she took up coon hunting. She'd married Charlie Brooks, and they ran the Gulf Station just south of town on the Walhalla Road, where there was a bowling alley and pinball tables before they set up their grocery store. There her unique life-like concrete animals still stand guard over the yard. A huge bear, an eagle, some squirrels and rabbits, and a deer that she created after she was sixty dominated her rock garden, and inside were Ferdinand and a long cement snake, busts of Washington, Lincoln, and Eisenhower, a prairie dog, a sloth, and a monkey holding up lamp shades.

In her seventies she took up painting animal portraits and landscapes, like the Horse Cove and Walhalla roads, many of which were exhibited in

2001 at the Bascom–Louise Gallery. When Aunt Mett wasn't taking care of other people's children, she worked in the station. But she hardly ever missed a coon hunt.

Aunt Mett's cement possums. Photo by the author, 2000.

"I bet I shot at least fifty out," she claimed. "Charlie'd always let me shoot the coon. They's no telling how many miles I've walked a-coon hunting. I know we went three nights on a straight, a-coon hunting 'bout all night. Boy that like to got me. I'd coon hunt all night and run the store during the day. I never failed. We had a bowling alley, and we really had the fun. We'd bowl and we'd dance. I just danced myself to death."

One sport, known to every cub, brownie, girl or boy scout today, played itself out infrequently in Highlands, for seldom was anyone found unfamiliar enough with it to play along. Miss Ruth Oliver, however, couldn't wait, when she took office as the new principal of Highlands School, to embark on a hunt quite different from treeing coons and with far less certain results. The *Franklin Press* reported in 1923 that she, as a new teacher at the school, held open a bag by the roadside in a forlorn gully, patiently awaiting her catch without luck, its being no night for snipes. Miss Margaret McConnell, another new teacher, was placed on a dark night at the foot of Satulah where snipes are more prone to roam. The scream of a "Wild Cat" brought a like yell from Miss McConnell, which caused all snipes in Highlands to migrate to the tropics. Both recruits swallowed hook, line, and sinker such that in each instance only a sucker was caught.

If the Misses Oliver and McConnell came across as naïve, they weren't the only adults to act the fool in Highlands. Wen McKenny's favorite holiday was Halloween which, along with the Fourth of July and Christmas, was celebrated with fireworks made from black powder. The time he remembered best was when he and Henry Baty, themselves too young to participate in the Halloween fun, hid behind a white oak and watched some of their elders load a mail-order cannon, fill it full of powder and half horseshoes, and shoot two holes plumb through Bascom's general store. The cannon blew up, and one of the horseshoes took down a nearby picket fence.[669]

Dancing

Elizabeth Lyon's modern dance class, 1924. Photo compliments of Nancy Lyle.
Far left: Nancy Jussely (now Lyle). Far right: Isabel Jussely (now Robertson).

In tune with the townspeople's love of music, which is discussed as a fine art later in Chapter Twenty-seven, even more popular was their love of dancing. Aside from isolated exceptions, like the Indian dance at Highlands House in 1893, when Wood Bryson imbibed a bit too much and landed in the calaboose, the first public dances were held in the old Emmons School at Shortoff in 1906. Prior to this, dances took place in private homes, some lasting ten days and nights since participants had to travel by horseback from neighboring settlements. It was the custom in those days to scatter corn meal on the floor to make the surface smooth for dancing.

During the late twenties public dances for Highlanders were held in the old Masonic Hall, sponsored by "Miss Harry" and the Red Cross. Private lessons in modern dance were already being conducted by teachers like Elizabeth Lyons, who taught a class on Satulah to the Jussely sisters, Nancy and Isabel, among others. Miss Lyons had taken lessons while in Europe from the renowned Isadora Duncan and had brought back perfectly gorgeous silk pieces, which she draped over the body suits made by the mothers of her students from sleeveless undershirts, dyed in bowls of hot strong tea.[670]

Nancy remembers how her mother, wife of a sea captain who was often away on long voyages from their home in the low country of Georgia and South Carolina, would pack a couple of large trunks and whisk her three young daughters away to spend the summer with their cousins Sarah and Bess Hines in Highlands. It was a long trip in the twenties, first by train with an overnight stop, then by the mail touring motorcar up the long, narrow dirt road. But at the top was a whole summer of hiking, swimming, boating, teas at the lovely Sloan's estate, silent movies at the old schoolhouse on the hill, church activities and bazaars, favorite books to read at the library, and dance classes a short way up Satulah.

Dances were soon scheduled in the school auditorium, where Roy Potts chauffeured Bess and Sarah Hines, and they practiced the foxtrot and waltz between normal sets. The PTA sponsored Valentine's dances to raise money for the playground, and the Hines family entertained with dancing on Mondays, Tuesdays, and Fridays at their home, *Chestnut Burr Cottage*, today's Nick's Restaurant.[671] By the end of the twenties a Highlands Merrimakers Club was meeting at the home of Caroline and Jack Hall for games and masquerades once a week and dances once a month.

Ballroom dancing was generally appreciated in early Highlands, but it was clogging and square dancing that rattled the timbers of the old school building on the hill. The time was ripe for some kind of general recreation hall for the people of the town. In 1931 Rebecca Harris, who had come to Highlands in the early twenties from Florida, originally Cuba, proposed building a Highlands Movie Theatre, Recreation, and Dancing Pavilion on her property at 5th and Main, formerly Kelsey's lot, to meet all the town's recreational needs. It would front Kanonah Lake (now Harris Lake) and feature a 40' x 80' dance pavilion, a miniature golf course, and a 50' x 100' theatre for talking pictures—all on a two-and-a-half acre playground.[672] Rebecca, incidentally, was very hard of hearing, as Frances Miller Wilson remembers, which meant having to talk through a trumpet into her ear.

Nothing came of Rebecca Harris' plan for a recreation hall because the next year Helen Cabe Wright, whose husband Charlie had died in an auto accident leaving her to care for five children, hired Mac Fulton to build her now-famous Barn at the other end of town.

Helen's Barn occupied the southeast corner where an Amoco Station stood in the fifties, Ernest Holland's 66 Station in the early sixties, and now Farmer's Market at 1st and Main. Marshall Reese remembers that the clay there was the thickest and whitest he'd ever seen. The kids would walk in it barefooted.

Helen built her barn on four acres purchased by Charlie with the Carnegie money he had received for his heroic rescue on Whiteside Mountain.

The first Helen's Barn which burned. Helen with two of her children, Barak and Maxie.

The first dance in Helen's Barn was held on May 14, 1932.[673] It was free of charge and a huge success, attended by nearly ninety dance enthusiasts, so that it captured the talk of the town for weeks afterward. Annie Linn Armor remembered how the girls were so excited they wore summer dresses and heels. For the next half century the town would revel in the foot-stomping music of Claude and Jess Keener, Bill Wilson, Doyle Calloway, Bobby Talley, Don and Paul Green, Lester Waldroop, David Potts, and other talented local players and pickers. Stephen Vincent Benét put it best in his "Mountain Whippoorwill" when he wrote, *they could fiddle all the bugs off a sweet-potato-vine*.[674] When none of the regular musicians were available, Jim Elliott and his brother Earl "Sweet Pea" filled in.

Unforgettable characters were born in Helen's Barn. Callie Beale, after a hard day at the laundry, bucked and winged till her wig turned sideways. Callie Beale could buck dance! Helen's twin, Frank Cabe, perfected flat footing. And every girl got asked by Wally Henry to square dance.

It wasn't very long before buck dancing, square dancing, and mountain clogging became such a popular pastime during the Highlands summers that the great rhythm of feet, like jungle drums shaking the ground, could be heard blocks away at the far end of town. People of all sorts skipped to the twang of the banjo and the whine of the fiddle as the caller intoned, "Hands up and circle left! All way round and half way back. Swing your partner and ball the jack!"

Despite the initial popularity of Helen's Barn, it wasn't universally sanctioned. Judith Mackie reported that almost immediately it became the target of pulpit-pounding local preachers. After three months, Mrs. Altstaetter, who ran *Rosemary* boarding house directly across 1st Street, circulated a petition, signed by herself, Mrs. Jim Rogers, Mr. and Mrs. Carl Henderson, and Mrs. Lamb Perry, asking the town council to impose a curfew and shut the barn down at midnight so as not to subject their families and guests to the thundering wump, bump, bump, bump of buck-dancing feet on solid wood and the long, loud, high-pitched, Yee Haas ululating into the wee hours of the morning.

The curfew went on the books, but no one honored it until one night Bennie Rogers, the local law, informed the revelers it was time to go home. "Who's a gonna make us?" was the cantankerous reply. "I am," he fired back and shot out the light.

Two years later in 1934 Anne Altstaetter Rhodes remembers awaking to a bright glow in the wee hours one Sunday morning, September 9th. Helen's barn was aflame, lighting up the whole night sky. The family went outside to watch, but her mother Rebecca, who'd drawn up the petition for the curfew, whispered, "We'd better go back in before they think we did it." Arson was indeed suspected. Harry Wright said a kerosene oil can was found in the ruins, but the culprit was never identified.[675]

Aunt Helen, or "Oopie" as she was best known among her friends, had married Sam Wilson, after Charlie's death, and they hired Fulton to rebuild the barn farther back near the center of the property where it stands today. Helen operated it from 1935 until her death in 1959. Her son Vernon ran it for two years, adding a seating gallery for spectators and ceramic tile restrooms. Daughter Grace Watson ran it after 1961.

Square dances remained so popular during the summer season that they filled four nights a week: Monday, Wednesday, Friday, and Saturday. Initially Lawrence Holt and Sam Baty did the calling, followed by Corbin

Ledford, Harry Brown, Barak Wright, Wally Henry, Johnny Crunkleton, Morris Reed, "Bud" Rucker, Donnie Calloway, and many, many others. When the schedule didn't feature the very popular local bands of Floyd and Steve Lamb, Willard Crisp, or Junior Crowe, frequently accompanied by the equally popular square dance team known as Soco Gap, it offered instead Buddy Lee's Orchestra, a rock-'n-roll African–American band from Anderson, S.C.

Helen's Barn, built in 1932, rebuilt after the fire in 1935. Photo courtesy of Highlands Historic Inventory.

Frances Wright called Helen's Barn the great equalizer, for it amalgamated everyone in town, winter and summer residents alike, into a single class. She recalled how she and her brother Johnny Crunkleton and Charlie Gibson would attend Baptist choir practice, sing a few hymns, dance like crazy at Helen's Barn till ten o'clock, return to church, sing some more, and high tail it home. Many a courtship began at Helen's Barn.

At one point in all the revelry, however, the fun began to degenerate. Mel Keener recalled that people came in drunk, cut up, and tore up things so that Helen was having an awful time. She came out to ask the Keeners if they would play for her.

He and Dixie went with Donald and Shirley and had to put a chain on the door of the fenced-in area so the ruffians couldn't disrupt their playing. Then they got a bouncer: Prat McClure. If folks came in drunk, Prat put 'em out! Soon, with no more drunks harassing folks on the scene, they had the place jammed so tight you could hardly get in, four nights a week. Helen paid Mel $4 a night for the music.

In 1954, despite complaints that the music was still too loud, the tradition was too solidly ingrained in Highlands culture to warrant restraint. Helen's

Barn opened its twenty-third season to Walter Wilson's string band and Cleo McCall calling the figures.

With his big smile and two-tone black-and-white wingtip shoes, Cleo, as Sue Ledford Reese so vividly recalled, "had lightning in his feet and a patter in his voice as he called the set and winged his way through the figures. He kept the set moving and his voice was as clear as a bell".[676] He danced with his head held high and his shoulders laid back like a man in charge.

By 1960 the building was extended 30′ x 30′ feet to include seating for 196 spectators. Added out front were a horseshoe pitching court, a nine-hole Hi-Ho Chip-'n-Putt par-3 golf course, and Shady Lane for miniature golf. Dance times were restricted to Saturday nights, with music by the Top-tuners and a midnight curfew. There being no other large public building in town, the Barn was used, when available, for roller skating, craft shows, plays, auctions, and family reunions.

In 1963 the Chamber of Commerce sponsored an annual square dance at Helen's Barn, attended by 400 people and featuring all three bands—Crowe, Lamb, and Crisp—with Thomas Reese doing the calling. Peanut Henry sang memorable renditions of "On Top of Old Smoky" and the "Ballad of Tom Dooley," Helen and Jerry Green crooned "Down in the Valley," Wymer Bryson accompanied Stephen Foster on the guitar, and Virginia Cleaveland won the clogging contest for best girls.

In 1982 Helen's Barn, managed at the time by Maxie Wright Duke, celebrated its 50th birthday with Atlantans telling her, "People have more pure fun with you on one Saturday night than they do all season long in Atlanta with our theater and professional stars. And that's the truth."[677]

Kate Gillison captured the occasion with a heartfelt "Ballad of Helen's Barn":

> *The insurance came when Charlie was dead*
> *Leaving Helen with six mouths that had to be fed.*
> *She built a barn and painted it red*
> *And the townspeople turned to her and said,*
>
> *"Helen, what you're doing just ain't right—*
> *Building a dance hall in a town this white.*
> *Shoulda' built a church—a roof for your head,*
> *But not a dance hall, and it painted red."*
>
> *Her answer above the jingle of coins firmly clears:*
> *"It takes a lot of cheers*
> *To dam a widow's tears."*

Helen's Barn opened for dancing on Saturday night
Folks came a-cloggin' their feet feeling light
After six days of labor, the red barn's a sight
For throwin' off sweat; and the only sign of a fight

Came from the church who wanted things set right
Down at the barn where the lamps burn bright
Where many a youth first saw the light
Of joy in dancing away fears in the night.

It was Helen's answer to their calls and their jeers:
"It takes a lot of cheers
To dam a widow's tears."

Fifty years of Saturday night digging shins with joy
As many a man danced away there from being a boy.
Helen's young'uns were schooled, fed and kept warm
With money she earned at her old red barn.

As hoe-down music drowned any complaint
To answer those who don't recognize a saint:
"It takes a lot of cheers
To dam a widow's tears."[678]

It was a sad and painful day when Helen's son Harry Wright sold her Barn along with its half-century tradition to Harold Bramer and Ron Allen in May of 1984. The Fire Department disposed of Helen's old dilapidated home place in a controlled burn, the giant pines were felled, and shops commenced to sprout up at Wright Square.

During more than fifty years Helen's Barn had become a mountain tradition that is sorely missed even today as a town remembers it with intense nostalgia. On occasion, attempts have been made to revive its spirit and camaraderie, as when Dennis DeWolf and Paul Schmitt converted the Galax into a movie theater and dance hall in 1987, or when one-night dances were held on Pine Street during the 1990s, but asphalt couldn't compete with hardwood flooring, and dancers who weren't nurtured on callers' figures could scarcely be expected to distinguish square from round dancing. The Bascom-Louise Gallery sponsored a Hoedown dance series at the Recreation Center, which tried recently to tap into the old tradition by featuring Doyle Calloway, who once played at Helen's Barn, and his Uncultured Buttermilk band.

There remain even today *summa cum laude* graduates of Helen's Barn, like Linda Rogers Barker who never lost her love of dancing and, even as a mother of six children, buck danced at the Festival of Champions in Fontana Village and won the 1972 World Champion Female Hoedowner Trophy, appearing the following year on TV's "What's My Line."

Square dancing at Helen's Barn is one of those oldies but goodies that perished in Highlands, perhaps irretrievably, behind the façades of a more lucrative shopping center, but the wish to restore it remains ineradicably strong. The Barn itself became a restaurant, today's Gaslight Café, with the scars of nails and taps still ingrained in its hardwood maple floors.

Carnivals, Pool Rooms, and Sam's Folly

One of the biggest events ever to hit Highlands was the circus in 1923. On October 4, a Thursday, the "Mighty Haag [pronounced Hag' gee] Show" lumbered and rode into town. People in Highlands were astonished to see elephants walking down 5th Street. Dolly Harbison remembered the clowns and how Louis Edwards, whom she claimed was a pest growing up, poked Teeny Rice's balloon and got a good lecture from her mother.

The Mighty Haag Circus, October 4, 1923. Photo courtesy Gene Potts via Earle Young.

Bessie Hines, mother of Sarah, Bess, Jim, and Nancy Elizabeth, remembered the next year when the big tent was raised on the Harris property by Harbison Lake. It cost nearly $4 to experience the spectacle under the big top at night. Marshall Reese remembers the circus of 1930, when he was ten and went with Buzz Baty. There were little ponies, and one little devil hauled off and kicked Marshall on the shin. The circus that year was held near 5th Street in a pavilion used by Hall House for square dances. The circus of 1938 stored its elephants at Lilia Kennard McCall's *Rabbit Hole* on Spring Street.

Elephants on lawn of Rabbit Hole, Summer, 1938. Foreground: Lily McCall Davis.
Photo by Ellsworth Davis.

Apart from the occasional circus, dancing, music, and movies at the Highlands School Theatre, providing recreation in town became the focus of many new commercial ventures, particularly during the thirties. As early as 1911 Porter Pierson had treated the town to a pool room, which by 1913 the town felt compelled to regulate with a 10:00 P.M. curfew. In 1932 Will Edwards introduced his shooting gallery in conjunction with J. E. Loftis' pool tables. Within five years they had become so popular that the town again mandated an 11:00 o'clock curfew to reduce Main Street noise. Helen's Barn, to be sure, added to the growing din before it too was slapped with a curfew.

By the end of the decade Charlie Brooks was running his bowling alley on the Walhalla Road just outside the town limits and next door to Harold Rideout's sandwich shop and soda fountain. Bert Rideout was offering bowling and billiards at his new amusement hall in the Smith building at the east end of Highlands Inn. In 1940 Wilton Cobb constructed a building east of the Smith building (currently the Dry Sink) for his own bowling alley which the town permitted provided he agree to close by midnight or sooner if there were any complaints.

Eventually the town felt it necessary to levy privilege taxes against all new and potential forms of entertainment emerging in Highlands: billiard and pool tables, bowling alleys, chain stores ("chain" meaning at the time more than two shops), auctions, dance halls, slot machines, and itinerant salesmen. With Henry Sloan showing his movies and the tourist trade in full swing, the council added amusement parks, traveling theatrical companies, moving picture or vaudeville shows to the tax list, as well as circuses, carnivals, menageries; wild west, dog or pony shows; real estate auction sales, coal and coke dealers, bicycle dealers, gypsies and fortune tellers, tourist homes and camps, bagatelle tables, merry-go-rounds and other riding devices, soda fountains, dealers in pistols; piano, organ, Victrola, record, or radio sales; and tobacco and cigarettes.

In 1937 the first roadside tavern arrived on the scene. It was the brainchild of Len Appley and Dinty Dennis. For the previous five years Appley had lived at *Hemlock Lawn* on the Walhalla Road and run Highlands Lodge for Boys. Dinty Dennis was sports editor of the *Miami Herald* and had summered in Highlands for four years.

Together they commissioned *The Dugout* on the Franklin Road.[679] Made of oak and hemlock logs, this Joe Webb construction still exists on the east shore of Lake Sequoyah as today's restaurant: On the Verandah. It featured wine and beer on draft over a thirty-foot rustic bar. Outside were a one-stop Amoco filling station, a large boat dock, a swim landing, and bath houses.

Like Helen's Barn the Dugout, named after Appley's well-known dachshund, Dug-Out, offered square dancing Monday, Wednesday, and Saturday nights, but added attractions included visits from national and district star radio musicians and entertainers. Youngsters weren't allowed in, due to high-stake gambling, drinking, and wild dancing, but its appeal to adults who had the necessary card for admission helped it thrive throughout the forties and fifties.

By 1961, however, its star had set. Earle Myers of Fort Lauderdale replaced it with something so sedate and mundane as The Mint, specializing in the auctioning of rare coins, civil war tokens, confederate money, and antique rifles. When On the Verandah moved onto the premises in 1981, something of the old festive atmosphere returned but with a more refined focus on quality dining and dancing.

During the mid fifties Holt's Shooting Gallery provided entertainment on the hill next to Bill's Soda Shop. For five cents a round you could shoot the bear, which is what Button Parham remembers the townspeople called the place: *Shoot the Bear*.

In 1958 a curiosity appeared just up the road from the Dugout, which soon became known as Sam's Folly.[680] Retired Brigadier General Sam Connell of the U.S. Air Force renovated an old fashioned water-powered cornmeal mill on the bank where the Cullasaja River spills into Lake Sequoyah. It was embellished with parts that he collected from three old abandoned mills of Highlands' past. But the central attraction, which could be seen from the Franklin Road, was a two-way cableway that swung down over Naiad Falls to the mill. Jimmy Lowe ran the cable cars, and Butler Jenkins, Jr., the mill.

Sam's Folly, two-way cable car, 1958. Photo by Margaret Rhodes (now Shaffner).

Summer Camps

If the rarefied air of Highlands served to restore health to adults in need of rest and recuperation, as the Sanatorium had proven, it also offered an excellent setting for summer camp for young people. Judge Harvey and Maude Parry came to this realization in 1925 when they bought a hundred-acre grove of white oaks at the crest of Little Scaly mountain on the Dillard Road five miles west of Highlands.[681]

It was originally intended for a summer hotel, but Maude, a graduate of Boston Normal School of Gymnastics and former director of physical education at Agnes Scott College, as well as director of the Girl Scouts of Atlanta, chose instead to create a camp for girls from ages eight to seventeen, which she appropriately named Camp Parry-dise. It offered a summer of swimming, horseback riding, nature lore, arts and crafts, archery, hiking, woodcraft, and dramatics. Since 1920 the only alternative girls' camp in the area had been Camp Merrie-Woode in Sapphire. Maude continued to direct Camp Parry-dise long after Harvey's death in 1931.

In 1937 Mrs. Earl Vance and Mrs. Coyle Moore of Tallahassee, Florida, set up a second summer camp for boys and girls ages eight to twelve.[682] Camp Sequoia opened at Rebecca Harris' former home, *Trillium Lodge* under Sunset Rocks.

Ben and Polly Wax bought Camp Parry-dise in 1956.[683] Having owned and operated Boys Academy in Baton Rouge, Louisiana, for the previous nine years, the Waxes soon converted the once-popular girls camp into Camp Highlander for Boys. They constructed new buildings, up to fifteen cabins, bought the old Highlands School bell for $25.00, and advertised the venture as America's highest summer camp, which thrived for nearly thirty-five years.

The year after Ben died in 1963, Polly sold the camp to Pine Crest Preparatory School of Fort Lauderdale, Florida, which ran it for ten years, nearly tripling its size from 120 campers to 320. It grew too big to manage in Highlands, so it moved with the old school bell to Mills River between Asheville and Brevard, where Gaynell Kinsley runs it today.

The Unitarians bought the Highlands site in 1975, turning it into Mountain Learning Center, their current conference ground. As for the old 360 pound bell which once hung in the first and second Highlands schools, the Highlands Millennium Committee retrieved it from Camp Highlander in 1999, intent on restoring it to its original home where it dwells today in the town clock above town hall, keeping the town apprised of the time of day.

Sports

The *Blue Ridge Enterprise* reported in July, 1883, that "foot-ball was all the rage" in Highlands. It was about the only sport available, to the extent that we find James Rideout complaining in 1892 about the boys playing football at the intersection of Main and 4th and breaking windows in the stores. The town marshal was instructed to stop them.

Eva Wright, Miss Cannon, and Barak Wright. Photo courtesy of the Hudson Library.

From the earliest days horseback riding was a favorite pastime of Highlands residents. By 1901 Potts Livery Stable was renting mounts specifically for this purpose. Not every mount fulfilled his charge, however. One six-year-old, named Ellis Meserve, found the excursion up Satulah embarrassing when his horse showed so little respect for its youthful rider that it kept returning to the stable and wouldn't take the trail. Ellis was offered a mule instead, but his pride hurt terribly, he burst into tears at the insult.

In the early twenties there was a law on the books regulating how fast automobiles but also horsemen could go, which tended to limit a young person's rollicking fun. Anne Altstaetter Rhodes remembers when her brother Raoul and Margaretta Duane (later Wood) galloped through town so fast they were arrested for speeding. It wasn't the first time Miss Ravenel had faced the law on horseback. She was arrested once before for riding on the town's sidewalk. "I didn't even know it had a sidewalk," she objected.

For folks in the thirties who didn't have their own horses, there was Crane's Riding Stables, started in 1932 by Levi Crane and his son Frank. Organized showmanship wasn't as prevalent in Highlands as individual riding for recreation, but the forties opened with the first attempt at an organized exhibition. Six entries competed in the Mirror Lake First Annual Horse Show in 1941, the grand prize going to Lewis Doggett.

Organized sports in Highlands evolved in general during the early twenties. In 1923 Highlands School organized its first "basket ball team," a relatively new game of American origin, intending that it replace the more individualized sport of rope jumping.[684] When T. L. Tolar, a staunch advocate of sports, became principal of the school in 1926, he added wrestling.

But what Cub Rice remembered was basketball. The boys played on a dirt court outside, built by Willie Hays. Willie, who loved sports of all kinds, including wrestling, had heard about basketball, so he mail ordered a ball and hoop and built Highlands' first basketball court. In time every little town around had a team, like Gneiss and Glenville. Highlanders wore maroon and white shorts and played even when it was really cold. The spectators stood up on the bank at the school and often built a fire just to keep warm.

Highlands would travel to Glenville or Cullasaja or Gneiss, but it didn't have enough players, so sometimes, Mary Paul Rice recalled, the girls would fill in. The girls always wore big Blue Sage bloomers with pleats. Bernice Lowe said that when the ball got loose or went out of bounds, it'd bounce clear to the jailhouse, the highway, or Mill Creek before anyone could retrieve it.

When the schools consolidated in 1931, the effect on many small schools, such as Highlands, was to kill sports. Cub Rice was not alone in his disdain of consolidation. He liked sports because they afforded competition with many of the surrounding schools, but Highlands' being so small, it couldn't compete with the bigger schools, so it never had a football team; it only had basketball and baseball. Consolidation unfortunately brought all the schools together to play on one team, which meant there weren't any other teams to play with.

In 1935 the town's conveyance of Highlands Park, situated behind the Community Theatre, to the Satulah Club sparked a ray of hope for basketball players and fans who at last might have an indoor court. In addition to a court, the proposed building would house showers, a kitchenette, and a ladies' club room.

The town's offer of the park was contingent, however, upon the building's being constructed within the next three years, which didn't happen, so basketball suffered a severe setback. Instead, it survived at Highlands School where Prof Newton coached winning teams so long as his brown felt hat stayed on his head. When it came off, they were losing, and there were times when he threw it on the floor and stomped on it.

Highlands baseball team (L to R): 1907–08. Photo courtesy of Gene Potts.
1ˢᵗ Row: Will Cleaveland, Doyle Westmoreland, Ed Potts, Guy Paul
2ⁿᵈ Row: Dick Cobb, Charlie McKinney, Rob & Jim Munger, Mack Jones
Bettie Reese & Bessie Cleaveland made the suits.

Although basketball and baseball were both played at the school, it was baseball that captured the interest of the town. Baseball in Highlands was played wherever an unoccupied field could be found. It wasn't until 1928 that a number of citizens, serving as trustees, located and purchased land between Hickory and Poplar streets for a baseball park with the expectation that the town would reimburse them for it.[685]

This was done five years later, and the deed passed to the town. Fred Hopper hit the first two homeruns on the new Highlands field to climax the 1932 summer season. Managed by Charlie Potts, the team included Willie

Hays, C. J. and Fred Hopper, Bill Potts, Sam Henry, Cub Rice, Dewey Hopper, Kenneth and Elmer McKinney, Sam Baty, and Jack Kinard.

At the end of the 1949 season the Highlands team, despite a good ballpark and an enviable winning record of 21–13, was grumbling that it had little time for practice after work hours. The newly reorganized Highlands Athletic Association concluded that floodlighting would solve the problem, to which end it proposed raising $4,200 to light the field.

Furthermore, during the 1955 season the town voted to borrow $1,500 to build a new grandstand. Spectators sat proudly in their newly completed stand, cheering Highlands' victory over Franklin four to three in a pitching duel that pitted Snook Thompson against a Corbin. Tied in the sixth, it was the sixteenth inning before Jimbo Potts connected for a double. When Houston's Texas Leaguer put Potts on third, he stole home to a deafening chorus of cheers and high-pitched whistles for the crowning score.

It was 1959 before the Lions Club organized the first Little League Ball Team in Highlands. Jamie Keener coached the Braves; H. H. Williamson, the Yankees.[686] In 1969 such teams as the Blue Moon Gift Shop Braves, Highlands P. T. A. Cards, King's Inn Phillies, and Perry Agency Pirates were treating sports fans to baseball cliffhangers, featuring such players of the week as Ben Wax, Timmy Potts, Mike Bryson, Don Keener, James Owens, Skip Keener, and Mike Wood.

For a time, interest waned, but in 1984 the Highlands Jaycees formed another Little League in alignment with the national group. By the end of the eighties the national organization had voted to allow girls to play on Little League teams, a beneficial practice that continues to this day.

Close on the heels of baseball, softball in Highlands increased in popularity with the Men's League playing games twice a week during the eighties. Moreover, in 1990, thanks to organizer David Parrish, soccer was added to the roster of extremely popular Highlands sports for players and spectators alike. In 1998 the Highlands Under–12 boys' team won the Southeastern U.S. regional championship in Greenville, S.C. And in 2001, funded in part by a bequest from Winnie Hertzberg and spearheaded by county commissioner Allan "Ricky" Bryson, a much needed soccer field was created at the old Lyman and Dora Zachary homestead on Buck Creek Road, thus removing the necessity for Highlands to play all its games out of town.

Hillbilly Day, 1952–57

Unique to Highlands over the past half century has been the popularity of an annual undertaking that enjoyed widespread appeal to as many folks outside the town as within it. Hillbilly Day was the brainchild of Isabel Hall Chambers, who dreamed up the idea and fed it to recreational director Bob

DuPree. Bob in turn took it to a skeptical town council, which, against its better judgment proclaimed August 1, 1952, Highlands' first Hillbilly Day.[687] Contrary to all their fears, the notion proved so inspired that for the next five years it blossomed into a proud Highlands tradition.

The decree went out that everyone who came to town on the first day of August had to dress hillbilly style as depicted in the movies. Anyone caught on the streets decked out in less than full regalia was promptly arrested by Cap'm Nelson or Deputy Blakely, fined ten or twelve dough, and carted off to the stockade, there to remain until he could convince someone by phone or courier to come and stand bail. Margaret Shaffner remembers her grandfather Capt. Altstaetter's fury when, like William Tell, he came to town on that day unawares and suffered the humiliation of having to beg his granddaughter to go get her grandmother to pay his release from prison.

The afternoon parade featured a wave of uncouth characters, including Buddy Hall's "car," closely followed by a gal holding his gas tank in place and surrounded by gals dressed in flour sacks and bonnets, some leashed to coon dogs. Floyd Long was dressed in bright red pants and a top hat for his hillbilly wedding. Riley Johnson, sporting a beard and patched at his knees and elbows, was totin' his shootin' ir'n. Peggy Potts wore her Kefauver coon hat, Daisy Mae her skimpy black skirt and red polka dot blouse, and Charlie Anderson his dirty white coveralls and thick black beard.

Jim Hines sauntered onto the scene, his pants hoisted a couple of notches, holes in his hat, and whiskers covering his browned face. Raymond Cleaveland wore a straw hat that preceded him a foot afore and followed a foot b'hind. Bill Holt strutted like a twenty-year-old on his first date. Not to be left in the cold, of course, Clyde Bolt's dog Brownie marched in blue jeans and a polo shirt with matching cap.

The evening square dance took place in the middle of Main Street. Patched, bearded, jug slingin' Dick Rice called the figures, and Bob DuPree, dressed to a T in tight striped pants and bullet-holed hat, served as master of ceremonies. At evening's end in the Municipal Auditorium, appropriately crowned as Hillbilly Queen with a halo of daisies was Hillbilly Day's founder Isa Chambers, garbed as Gravel Gertie and escorted by a shy blond-wigged Louis Edwards. While Mrs. Frank Talbot drug her young'uns, roped and tied, off to bed, Col. Ralph Mowbray following in long flannel nightgown and cap, the stragglers crooned hillbilly songs to the moon before calling it a fully satisfying day.

Total fines collected at the calaboose amounted to $222.22, which filled the till of the recreation center fund. Even the mayor, Wilton Cobb, failed to escape paying a fine to the "depooties" to secure his release from the stockade because he came to town dressed like a "human bean" instead of a self-respecting movie-bred hillbilly.

Hillbilly Day, August 1, 1952. Photo courtesy of Jane Emerson.

The next year added a variety of activities: a hog calling contest, a climb up a greased pole to a $5 bill at the top, logrolling with a go-devil, crosscut sawing, and log hewing. By 1954 the town was cheerfully sponsoring the event, donating $500 to expenses and $250 to the barbecue fund.

Like the eventual situation at Helen's Barn, however, when the amount of drinking became excessive, problems began to dampen the fun. Doc Mitchell had to ask the town board to take measures to reduce the alcoholic consumption. He was joined by the town's ministers, led by Dr. Herbert Koepp-Baker, who asked that advertising promotionals be left to the town to produce and distribute and that no unauthorized floats be permitted in the parade. Some individuals were throwing propriety to the wind in their eagerness to draw laughter.

When the town voted in 1958 not to sponsor Hillbilly Day any longer, Dr. Koepp-Baker proposed that an annual Community Music Festival replace it. Hillbilly Day had seen its day, but the day, while it lasted, had been extraordinarily fun!

Golf

Golf is a game where almost every day, children see men at play. It's the one sport that never grows old. C. D. Jenkins remembers when he and his young buddies couldn't figure what all those men were doing swating at something in the grass with a stick. And where did it go when they hit it?

Highlands first golf links were built long before Bobby Jones appeared on the scene. Edith Inglesby, whose mother managed Islington Inn, said her father, George Inglesby, with help from college boys and mountaineers built a course at the beginning of the Franklin Road across from the Altstaetter house behind today's Citco Station.[688] Tudor Hall remembered it as a three-hole course on property acquired by Memminger, which Memminger purchased in 1902 for a park.

George Inglesby built a second set of links in the Pierson Inn pasture, site of today's Highlands School and known earlier as Muddy Hollow, around 1905, a few years after the Inn opened. Edith remembered a stream dammed to form a lake, by the side of which a boat was docked for retrieving misdirected balls. The links were in use until about 1920.

The Hall House had its nine-hole course soon after the Pierson links with three holes situated between today's Catholic Church and the home of Neville and Edna Bryson and continuing later with seven more holes extending as far as Chestnut Street, east through today's RV Court, and returning to the house. Margaret Hall recalls that the last hole crossed the lake, and a lot of would-be golfers just skipped that one. Marshall Reese says his uncle Robert lost his left eye in 1931 when his club head became detached and, bouncing off a stump, hit his glasses.[689] He was reduced to wearing a patch over that eye.

Golf was smalltime in Highlands until 1927, when Scott Hudson, president of the Atlanta Athletic Club, teamed up with Scotland native Donald Ross, the world-famous golf course architect, to design and build a $200,000 course on 425 acres just south of town. The project, known as Highlands Estates, would include a club house and homes to accompany the course.

The directors for this massive undertaking were Col. Robert Jones, Sr., Samuel Evins, Carleton Smith, and Charles Shepard, all from Atlanta, Robert Smith of Lexington, Ky., and Franklin Pugh of Dallas, aided by attorney Henry Robertson from Franklin. Robertson joined Quincy Pierson and Albertina Staub of Highlands as incorporators by each purchasing one share.[690]

The task facing these directors and incorporators was certainly daunting though not impossible. A vast amount of timber, laurel, and rhododendron had to be uprooted to make way for the long fairways and greens. Streams had to be rerouted through one- to two-foot pipes. In the end, under the direction of construction engineer Joseph Root, it took 125 workers, twenty-five teams of horses, and three tractors to replace all that wilderness with sodded fairways and greens, requiring additionally five tons of grass seed.

Mel Keener claimed that he, Claude Calloway, and Frank Vinson spent seven years of their lives putting in greens and tees on the course. Lyman "Red" Talley mowed the grass. Will Cleaveland moved his big sawmill there to cut the enormouos hemlocks. Guy Paul ran the mill, while Mel fired the boiler.

Red Talley acknowledged it wasn't all work. There were times when Sam Calloway and Walt Houston took breathers to play bear. "Sam would get down on his hands and knees and run through you," Keener explained, "and it'd throw you 'bout forty feet."

When they started building the club house, a forty-two bedroom mansion designed by Atlanta architects Hentz, Adler, and Schutze, five masons worked on what Mel considered the most beautiful chimneys you ever saw. Hanson McCall, Charlie McKinney, Sam Baty, Mack Pierson, and Prince Calloway laid up four native granite fireplaces in the assembly room. When they finished the polished hearths, you could see your face in them. The club house shingles were made from chestnut bark; the rooms were spruce-paneled with oak floors.

In the midst of all the construction, golf writer Glenn Allan of Hearst's *Sunday American* lavished the project with epic praise:

> *The impossible has been done up here. Mountains have been leveled and their proud peaks used to build up valleys. Trees have been felled which flourished in maturity when Ponce de Leon sought his fountain of youth. Roads have been cut where moccasined Cherokees stalked slumbering deer. And far above the same blue sky smiles down on brilliant laurel, on rhododendron and tiny, bright-faced daisies which might have decked the wampum bands of dusky princesses.* [691]

He went on to describe how money was being spent in startling quantities with results obtained that would astonish anyone with any experience at all in building golf courses. Besides being one of the most picturesque courses in all of America, it would also be one of the hardest. No baby holes, he argued. Ross and Hudson had whipped the mountains into submission while employing the natural hazards to a degree unbelievable. And all this just a scant six hours from Atlanta.

Glenn brought his paean to a close with a personal prayer that upon his death he'd hope for nothing more than to be the son of the great chestnut tree guarding the 4th green in this mountain paradise. Just to breathe one lungful of that glorious air would give enough happiness for one departed shade.

Highlands Country Club. Photo by George Masa, 1929.

Hudson claimed he built the course with the idea of challenging golf legend Bobby Jones to try to beat its par 70. Here in the heart of the highest range east of the Rockies was something to stop Jones' fancy shooting with a course record likely to stand well above par 70 for years to come.

Robert T. "Bobby" Jones, Jr. Photo from Sidney L. Matthew's Life and Times of Bobby Jones

Jones, of course, having won both the U.S. Amateur and the U.S. Open tournaments, accepted the challenge. He christened the just-completed first nine holes, played twice, with a triumphant 69, beating Hudson's much ballyhooed par on his first try. He had to admit, however, in praising Ross's design of the course, that every hole had at least one good shot.

Ross's fame rested on his all-important notion, which he had demonstrated here, that the most important shot on any hole is the approach to the green. In the case of the ninth hole, it entailed playing what was then known as the longest tee in the world, over sixty-five yards in length. Bounded on the left by a high, steep bank and on the right by tall trees, the experience of shooting from the back of this continuous tee was, in Bill Marett's estimation, like "hitting out of the Holland tunnel."

During the summer of 1930 the Highlands course became a practice ground for Jones. It so improved his accuracy that by year's end he had accomplished a feat never before equaled: winner of all four amateur and open championships of Great Britain and the U.S. in the same year, the Grand Slam.

In the midst of Jones' fortune, however, disaster struck the Highlands Estates. Mel Keener claimed that workers finishing up the club house left a pile of shavings on the floor, and one night the brand new building burned to the ground. Mel came to work the next morning, and the club house was gone! Not deterred in the least, Scott Hudson had it rebuilt while adding the back nine holes. The reconstructed clubhouse served beautifully for a quarter century before a new one replaced it in 1955, itself lasting thirty years until its replacement by Bill Peacock of Asheville in 1985.

With the completion of the Highlands Estates course in 1930, golf fever spread across Highlands. Little Joe and Willie Hays built their Tom Thumb golf course for the general public in the vacant lot on Main Street, where Phil Tate would latter park cars and Serendipity and Azure Rose exist today.[692] By 1956 Highlands had its first Miniature Golf Course on each side and in back of the old High School Theatre building.

The first of wave of country club courses to settle into what was once Ravenel's primeval forest north of Bear Pen was given the name Sky Lake Golf Course in 1963.[693] It was the only course open to the public. Known today as Highlands Falls Country Club, it was created by Gordon and Lloyd Gibson of Ft. Walton, Florida, who bought Will Edwards' 275-acre tract at the beginning of the primeval forest one mile north on highway 64 and opened a nine-hole par-36 course with two lakes designed by William Amick.

Originally this tract had been developed by Wilton Cobb, who in 1940 opened his Lake Primeval, a twenty-five acre body of water with a 105-foot dam spanning the headwaters of the Cullasaja River. Near the upper end of the development the beautiful Highlands Falls plunged amidst towering hemlocks 5½ to 7½ feet in diameter. In 1966 Lloyd Gibson sold the course to golf pro Bill Meyers of Daytona Beach, Florida. After Myers' death in a 1973 plane crash in Alabama, Sky Lake was converted into Highlands Falls Country Club. No longer public but private, it offered a 300-member equity club featuring single family home sites on 450 acres of a 6,000 yard par-72 course including a Club House.

At the same time that Sky Lake Golf Course was being created, Dr. Bill Matthews, a radiologist who had spearheaded the founding of the Highlands Community Hospital upon his move to Highlands in 1947, began to develop Wildcat Cliffs Golf Course at the base of the north slope of Whiteside Mountain, headwaters of the Cullasaja River at the upper end of Ravenel's former primeval forest.[694]

Incorporated in 1961 by Bill, his wife Beverly, and Joe Jackson, the first nine holes of a George Cobb Championship golf course were completed in 1964 and opened the following year. All eighteen holes were ready by 1969 shortly before the completion of the club house, designed by Atlanta architect Henry Norris and built by Highlands' Alvin Crowe. Highlands architect Jim Fox designed the tennis center, the pavilion by Ravenel Lake, and the fitness center, which were completed in the late eighties and early nineties.

Apart from these two local private golf clubs, the beginning of the sixties served the public's craving for golf on a much smaller scale. Shady Lane Miniature Golf Course opened in front of Helen's Barn in 1959, the year that Helen died. Her son expanded the building and the golf facilities to include a nine-hole Hi-Ho Chip 'n Putt course and horseshoe court. Helen's Barn opened only on Saturday nights during the sixties, but the golf courses opened for play all day.

The early sixties and late seventies saw two golf enthusiasts central to the history of sports in Highlands pass away. Highlands Country Club founder Scott Hudson died at ninety-two in 1962 after thirty years of summer residence in the town. A native of Danville, Kentucky, and son of a famous horseman, he himself had achieved record-breaking feats in horse racing and contributed greatly to the development of golf champion Bobby Jones as well as women's national champion Alexa Sterling. He even founded a fishing club in Florida.[695]

The other sports giant who died in 1971 was Bobby Jones at age sixty-nine. In addition to his having christened the Highlands Country Club course when it opened in 1929, prior to his Grand Slam in 1930, his benefit game for the Hudson Library in 1931, as noted earlier in Chapter Thirteen, actually pulled that organization out of pending bankruptcy. His last exhibition game in 1948 raised money for construction of the Highlands Community Hospital before syringomyelia, a vicious disease of the spinal cord, reduced his extraordinary strength to helpless sensory disturbances, muscle atrophy, and even spasticity. It effectively ended his golf career twenty years before it took his life, by which time it had already confined him to a wheel chair.[696]

For this exceptional sportsman and generous benefactor, it was a particularly heartbreaking ending. He was what Bill Marett called a gentleman in every sense of the word: a combination of grace and goodness, unswerving courtesy, self-deprecation, and consideration of other people.

It was after his sweep of the Grand Slam in 1930 that Bobby Jones bought property on the point of the Highlands Country Club lake intending to build his home in Highlands. However, concerned about the safety of his children so near a lake and the probable lack of privacy due to fans pursuing his autograph, he built instead on Little Yellow Mountain a house designed by Linton Young.

On his abandoned lot by the lake James Floyd built instead the home that stands today. Situated near the 18th hole, Floyd would sit for hours at his boathouse, and whenever a star-crossed golfer dropped his ball into the lake, he'd ring an old ship's bell he'd hooked up to celebrate the occasion.

A fourth private equity golf club was created near Highlands in 1987. Cullasaja Club, an Arvida community, covered 600 acres around Ravenel Lake, itself surrounded by one of the last remaining sections of primeval forest. The 18-hole championship course was designed by Arnold Palmer in the midst of 335 proposed home sites priced from $70,000 to $260,000. The fifth hole fronted a cascading waterfall where the Cullasaja River began and wound through five of the front nine holes before emptying into Ravenel Lake, itself stretching through the back nine. The clubhouse was completed by 1990 in addition to six tennis courts, a heated pool, and private roads for walking, jogging, and cycling.

The newest golf community, which opened recently on 435 acres of forest land beyond Cullasaja Club and across the Jackson County line, was Highlands Cove. Semi-private and designed by Tom Jackson, its 18-hole course combined the Highlands nine with the Cove nine and opened in June, 2000. Joe Bell and Alabama business partners Sid McDonald and Bill Pike planned at the time for 220 home lots and eighty condos ranging in price from $85,000 to over half a million dollars.

Ice Skating, Skiing, and Boating

During the summer seasons boating was popular in the mountains as a relaxing sport. Ideal for this purpose were Lake Sequoyah, Mirror Lake, and—before the establishment of the Biological Station—Lindenwood Lake in Ravenel's park.

Boating on Lindenwood Lake, 1910. Photo from R. H. Scadin Collection, UNC-A.

Two favorite pastimes of old Highlands, which the summer folk never experienced except during winter visits, were snow sledding and ice skating. Cub Rice said that Mill Creek was what he as a child used to call Mill Pond, where John Jay Smith had a big saw and grist mill. Cub and his buddies in wintertime would climb Satulah as far as Mrs. Albert Hill's tea house at Sloan's gate and then slide all the way down to Mill Pond on makeshift sleds. It was much steeper than it is now. Some used store-bought sleds, but more often the sleds were homemade from the metal rims of old wagon wheels bent to make runners.

My wife Margaret remembers during the late seventies how a group of youngsters—including Mike, Jack, and Chuck Crisp, Grey Picklesimer, Jim "Red" Potts, and others—would ride out to the Norton farm near Shortoff and whiz down the lower slope of the mountain into the pasture on inverted car hoods. Volkswagen hoods held one passenger; Ford Falcons, two; 1962 Cadillacs, up to six; and handmade quilts kept the passengers insulated from the freezing metal.

Night runs were popular, lit by a bonfire at the top of the hill, and only occasionally would injuries occur, like when Chuck hit Felix Speed's cow in the pasture and broke its leg. Mike says the Crisp's insurance paid for the cow, Speed cut it up and ate it, and everybody was happy. Red Potts would stand on his Ford Falcon hood, holding a rope attached to the front. Unable to steer it, he would spin down to the bottom of the hill, where a corner would usually catch in a drift and beat him into the snow. Mike vows the incline along one stretch was 80°, and the average speed, as they clocked it, was 45 mph.

During the mid-forties when it didn't snow on Wednesdays in the winter, the children of the town were permitted to roller skate on Main Street. The east lane between town hall (which at the time was housed in the Masonic Hall) and Bill Holt's soda shop at 4th and Main was closed off for the afternoon, and children swarmed to enjoy the fun.

But by far the most fun enjoyed by residents and visitors alike during long cold spells after deep snows was ice skating on the lakes. Steve Potts rented ice skates to those who didn't own their own. A twelve-inch snow in late January, 1940, left Lake Sequoyah in early February frozen to a depth of fifteen inches, attracting skaters in unbelievable droves considering it was off season. This was the year that cars were actually driven out on the lake.

In January, 1957, several thousand visitors, mostly from South Carolina, came to skate on Mirror Lake over the weekend. Parking spaces were impossible to find, bonfires and lights strung along the fringes of the frozen surface kept the sport alive well into Saturday night so that restaurants, drug stores, and shops reported record sales.

Jim Hines skates on Mirror Lake, ca. 1955. Photo courtesy of Tammy Lowe.

A regular showman who never failed to appear, even when the wind whistled bitterly cold, was Jim Hines, Jr. Jim's physical strength and love of the outdoors were legend in Highlands. John Cleaveland tells of the time a circus outfit brought a 400 pound bear, muzzled and gloved, to Highlands and offered $1,000 to anyone who could throw it. No one would take the dare, but Jim made it happen. He wrestled that bear to the ground and pinned him. When the challengers wouldn't pay, it didn't seem to bother Jim, who must have done it just to do it, not for the money.

When Jim undertook his 105-mile hike on the Appalachian Trail in 1949, he completed it alone. He walked from Rainbow Springs to Clingman's Dome in five days, averaging twenty miles a day, slept most of the time out in the open since his fast pace pushed him beyond the shelters, and when the nights grew too cold for sleep, he hiked by moonlight. Powdered malted milk and chocolates gave him all the energy he needed, and when asked why he traveled alone, he would answer typically, "I like solitude."

Jim was eccentric in his love of all things physical. Craig Cranston knew him as a hard worker who helped paint Craig's house in Whiteside Cove and afterwards sat on the porch, drinking every drop of liquor in the house. Then there was the day that Jim stopped Craig on his way to Bill's Soda Shop and invited him on an adventure, saying they might be gone for two or three days so Craig might want to inform anyone concerned not to expect him for a while. They drove as far as Heady Mountain Gap on Hwy 107, where Jim parked the car and announced a hike back to Highlands. No food, no tents, no cooking utensils, just a couple of blankets that Jim had stashed in his car.

They hiked over Heady Mountain and Big Terrapin, surviving during the day on buck berries and camping the first night by the Chattooga. The next day they hiked as far as Black Rock, where they again camped, still on a sparse diet of buck berries.

When they finally reached Highlands, Jim remarked, "Now that's the way to do things!" Craig says it tickled Jim to death, but Craig felt right hungry and relieved to be home.

It was Jim Hines in 1958 who led a party of four on a perilous climb to Whiteside Cave.[697] Six hikers began the ascent at the stairway up the nose end of Whiteside. They took the trail along the base of the cliffs to the edge of the open rock face. Only four brave souls continued up 200 feet to the overhang and inched along the sloping lip of rock to the Crow's Nest. There a two-foot ledge above a 1,000-foot vertical plunge tapered away to nine inches before it entered the cavern reaching back into the heart of the mountain. If Jim was at all frightened during any part of the trip, he never showed it.

The tragedy in Jim's singular life was that during one of his ice skating excursions on the lake, the surface broke and he plunged into the freezing water. On returning to the surface, he missed the hole and actually had to break the ice with his head to breathe again. Those who knew him well claimed he wasn't the same after that, which may have contributed to his tragic end years later in California when he walked into the Pacific. Ironically in retrospect one of his favorite mountain ballads, which he often sang, was "The world is not my home. I'm only passing through. If heaven's not my home, O Lord, what will I do?"

While ice skating and sledding dominated the winter scene in Highlands, skiing also became popular when Gene and Susan Head opened Ski Scaly in 1981. Relying on manmade snow to keep their resort in business throughout the season, they kept the four slopes busy with beginner, intermediate, and advanced skiers seven days a week including week nights. Alternatives to Ski Scaly but at greater distances from Highlands were Sky Valley in Georgia and Fairfield Sapphire Valley east of Cashiers.

The ABC Store

Drink and be merry, for our time on earth is short and death lasts forever. Whether this be an argument for including the Highlands ABC Store in a chapter on entertainment depends entirely on how one views the public attempt to tame the wild anarchy of drink. Shakespeare's Othello voiced the counterargument when he cried out, "O God, that men should put an enemy in their mouths to steal away their brains; that we should, with joy, pleasance, revel, and applause, transform ourselves into beasts."[698] These two opposing views that in turn endorsed and rejected alcohol clashed in 1951 when a petition was circulated, asking the town to introduce legislation authorizing a public vote on the question of a liquor store in Highlands. In times long gone, a war had been fought over the liquor question in Highlands, and a Moccasin youth had perished in the fray on the grounds of Central House.

Proponents of the petition argued the profits from such a store would benefit the hospital, the library, the school, the town, and the county, the very argument that T. Baxter White had deemed the equivalent of saying, "Vote for the Devil and he will assist in the education of your children." Indeed, the Baptist Rev. Paul Nix, who felt exactly that, convinced the town to rescind the request.[699]

Not long after the protests of two more Baptist preachers, the town was requesting in 1955 that Representative Guy Houk introduce a bill authorizing a state controlled liquor store in Highlands on a vote of the people. The profits would be sliced 40% to the town for public purposes, 30% to the hospital, 20% to the county for public use, and 10% for recreational programs. The vote, however, was postponed. Another week passed, and the Methodist Rev. R. T. Houts brought a counter petition opposing a referendum on a liquor store and signed by 43% of all the voters. The issue died in chambers.

Not long after the protests of two more Methodists ministers, the issue again raised its stubborn head when the old schoolhouse was torn down on Knowledge Hill. Again it was nipped in the bud, defeated even before it hit the floor. Not that both sides of the issue weren't adequately represented in Highlands. From the early days of the town's founding, spirits had always been readily available. Indeed, Bill Holt remembers when his mother, Gertrude Cobb Holt, riding into town in a horse and buggy to pick up the mail, and someone was selling corn whiskey right there on Main Street, out in the open where nobody interfered! She saw men sneak up and pay probably a dollar a gallon.

In the forties, if a fellow was averse to "taking kittle benders" straight from the still—as David Moss used to call it at the turn of the century—then he went to the beer joint at the corner of 4th and West Chestnut (now Foreman Road), for upstairs was a speakeasy.[700] A fellow could always ride on out 4th Street beyond the town limits to Homer Potts' Garage near Shortoff where a bit more than grease and oil was available merely for the asking.

Of course, there were times when a fellow took kittle benders and, as Dave Moss would describe it, his head ached plum all over for want of strong coffee. Then Dave would complain that the coffee he drank was so weak "you might tie a grain of it to a rat's tail and swim him up the Potomac river, and the water behind him would be stronger than that coffee."

Dave Moss was no moderate imbiber by any stretch of the imagination. It was Dave who got arrested once on a charge of assault with intent to kill for throwing a plow at two hunters. When he admitted that he was "twelve foot away when I turned the plow loose at 'em," the judge laughed so hard he dismissed the case. Charlie Jenks swore that this actually happened, and knowing Dave Moss, there was little cause to doubt it.[701]

Still, kittle benders could do the ordinary man in. And that's why early Highlands, as noted previously in Chapters Four and Ten, offered a Temperance Union as an alternative, led by Baxter White and meeting on the first Tuesday of every month on or before the full moon.[702]

According to connoisseurs in the know, there were two types of liquor: one bad but the other good. Before his conversion to becoming sheriff, Bub Zachary claimed all he had to do was lose his hat to get in jail. Spent almost every weekend drying out. Bub never touched the wrong kind of liquor, only the right kind. "We didn't do much fighting," he declared. "I drunk that laughing liquor all the time. It's that good kind you have fun with. You don't fight, makes you laugh."

Bert Zachary, who said he didn't believe he was ever in jail but once, remembered how he drank with Luther Johnson, but Luther wasn't the tough character that he made himself out to be. That was just talk, liquor talk. And Bub agreed: "it's 'cording to what kind of liquor he had, the laughin' kind or the fightin' kind."

In 1973 the question of liquor by the drink on the state level was soundly defeated in the general election. Macon County opposed it five to one; Highlands; three-to-two. Four years later, however, the situation reversed. Highlands was asking the N.C. General Assembly to authorize another vote.

In August, 1977, an ABC Store was approved in Highlands two to one in an 85% turnout, the largest ever: 226 to 108.[703] The revenues were to be distributed 15% to the Highlands–Cashiers Hospital, 10% to the recreation park, 2% to the town's scholarship fund, 7% to alcoholic rehabilitation, 5 to 15% to local law enforcement, and the rest to the town's general fund. Within the year, 1978, a new ABC building had replaced the old one on Knowledge Hill, where it remains today.

The Recreation Park

One of the benefactors of the liquor profits was the new Recreation Park on Bug Hill. Back in 1931 Rebecca Harris had proposed a recreation center that never materialized on her own property near today's Harris Lake. Then in 1939 the newly created Cliffside Lake, constructed by the U.S. Forest Service with the help of the young men of the Civilian Conservation Corps (CCC) and the Works Progress Administration (WPA), had given Highlanders a general play area but five miles distant from town.[704]

In 1951 the town bought the old Highlands School Theatre and property to be used in part as a recreational facility, hiring Robert DuPree as Highlands' first recreational director the following year. That was when DuPree supported the first Hillbilly Day, the proceeds from which went toward recreation. Tony Chambers replaced DuPree as recreational director in 1953, followed the next year by Western Carolina University student Richard Thompson.

In 1956 the town set up an advisory board composed of ministers of the Highlands Inter-Church Group. From 9:00 to 5:00 recreation on the play grounds and in the rooms of the old school consisted of tennis, badminton, shuffle board, horse shoes, and hiking, as well as checkers, card games, ping-pong, and dancing on Tuesday and Thursday nights.

In 1957 the town considered tearing down the old school and constructing a one-story recreation center on its foundation with the aim of providing a bowling alley and pool tables, but the idea never gelled. Willard Johnson took over as recreation director, and the school was indeed torn down in 1960 but nothing replaced it.

By 1969 it was small wonder that an irate group of Highlanders went to Franklin to protest what they called "stepchild" treatment by the county board in distributing tax revenues and county resources to a proposed recreation complex for Franklin costing a quarter million dollars.

As late as 1971 the town had no area specifically dedicated for public recreation until in that year it bought the old sanatorium property with money from the Federal Land and Water Conservation Fund. Administered by the state for city and county public recreation, the grant specified that most of the property be preserved in its natural state.

The project began with the clearing of Bug Hill. Proposed were a tennis court, a picnic area, slabs for basketball, ice skating, and shuffleboard, and a playground for small children. Parking at the new Recreation Park would be provided for at least fifty cars. Bud Potts served as chairman of the first phase of development. Phase two included group shelters, hiking trails, etc., when Eric Frazier was director from 1973–78. Jack Cabe took over as the new swimming pool was being constructed in 1979–80.

All this came to pass in preparation for a Civic Center in 1985, the direct result of an extraordinarily generous $2 million gift from coca-cola magnate and philanthropist George Woodruff and his daughter Jane in memory of his late wife, Irene. Ben Wax was in charge of the recreation park when the building was dedicated.

For over half a century the town had dreamed of creating what was now an accomplished fact. The Center today, under Selwyn Chalker's direction, is used for almost every conceivable sport, program, class, lecture, or festival by almost everyone in town, visitor or resident. It was a grateful public that welcomed its completion.

The annual 4th of July festival, which is still celebrated today by an impressive display of aerial fire works, was first fêted in 1969 at the Ball Park, the Community Theatre, and Potts Market, including a street dance and Miss Highlands contest. Recent family games, slow-cooked Rotary barbeque, and daredevil divers from the sky have made it a full-day experience.

Tennis

The sport that rivaled golf for universal popularity in Highlands was tennis. Hall House, the Anderson/Sullivan mansion, all the golf clubs, the Recreation Park, and many private homes had tennis courts. In early Highlands it was not uncommon to see men sporting ties and women long dresses at a Sunday match at the Davis House.

In 1984 a new half-million dollar indoor tennis club opened on the Dillard Road just south of Highlands. Developed by George Schmitt, the Mountain Laurel Tennis Club included an indoor swimming pool and a Nautilus fitness center as well as indoor and outdoor tennis courts and a practice wall for paddleball, racquetball, and handball.

Louise Bascom playing tennis at Davis House. Photo probably by R. Henry Scadin, ca. 1902. Courtesy of Gene Potts via Doris Potts.

On the whole, sports and recreation in Highlands have never suffered for lack of variety and wholehearted participation. As isolated as the town is from life in the flatlands, athletic teams have drawn on their inner resources to create their own entertainment and have not been averse to traveling long distances off the mountain to compete on foreign soil. No giants in sports have sprung from Highlands teams, but sports giants from the world abroad have visited Highlands and benefited from what it had to offer by way of natural challenges in a spectacular setting.

Hunting and Fishing

In the early days of Highlands there was an abundance of all kinds of game. All one needed was a goose quill for making a turkey call, and a flock of up to two or three dozen bronze turkeys would appear, offering the hunter his best choice of targets. Hunting ranged from small game, like rabbit, squirrel, and ruffled grouse, to larger prizes of deer and especially bear, which tasted like tender beef steaks and fed many a family through the winter.

Bear hunting in early Highlands. Satulah House in the background. Photo courtesy of Hudson Library archives.

The thrill of the sport was a vital part of the hunt, but food was the primary need, and families of a dozen or more children survived only on account of plentiful game. Indeed, a family's fondest memories were more often than not, formed at mealtime. A bountiful meal of fresh meat from the hunt or fish from the rivers and streams cooked in a heavy iron kettle hung over a fire on hooks, sour dough cornbread baked under cover of hot coals, white clover honey, homegrown corn or potatoes, roasted chestnuts, and wild strawberries or buckberries or, even better, blackberry or raspberry cobbler or pie—mealtime was a frequent unforgettable experience.

Other Sports

In 1987 Ralph Thomas, Keith Moore, and Barry Ward organized the Highlands Classic, which became an annual event. Sports enthusiasts from throughout the Southeast came to see 100 significant pre-1968 sports and sports racing cars wind for a week through 1,000 kilometers of the Western

North Carolina and Tennessee mountains. The cars were actual Grand Prix high-performance classic cars that raced during the forties and fifties.

By 1994 the event was being held in conjunction with a gathering of local restaurants offering their most popular dishes at a "Taste of Highlands" beneath a large tent at Highlands Plaza. When Ralph's time wasn't consumed by the Highlands Classic, he and his sons Mark and Brooks, were racing his Argo JM 19C at Daytona, Sebring, Atlanta, New York, Savannah, the Virginia International, and even in Italy and the Bahamas.

One form of recreation that doesn't fall within any particular category but which evolved spontaneously on January 24, 1973, and has continued to this very day was the delightful creation of S&B (short for Stitch and Bitch, but known euphemistically as Sew and Blow). A group of eleven women gathered at the home of Betty Parrish and agreed to meet every Wednesday, without officers, without minutes, without dues, just to talk and to knit or sew.

Betty Parrish, Claire Tannahill, Gini Hodgkinson, Pinky Breckinridge, Monabelle Reid, Sally Phillips, Edmonia Haslam, Petey O'Shaughnessy, Janet Baumrucker, Jan Chmar, and Jessie Gilbert were founding members who set their meetings alphabetically from home to home. To celebrate anniversaries, their official dessert was Oreos—no trouble, no work. After almost thirty years the S&Bs still meet without fail, without minutes or dues, but with a great deal of talk and fun.

27. Musicians on the Lake

Our arts are happy hits. We are like the musician on the lake, whose melody is sweeter than he knows; or like a traveler, surprised by a mountain echo, whose trivial word returns to him in romantic thun-ders.

—Ralph Waldo Emerson, *Art*, 1841

Music

Entertainment in early Highlands was by no means restricted to the young. From the outset the people of this isolated gem at the top of the Blue Ridge had to rely on inner resources, creativity, and individual talents to see them through the long winters from September through May.

Highlands String Quartet, ca. 1887. L to R: Frank Sheldon, Prof. Zoellner, S. T. Kelsey, Jr., and Harlan P. Kelsey. Photo courtesy of Hudson Library archives.

As early as 1876 the few people in the new village were enjoying infor-mal sings at Katy Kelsey's home and Mollie Jacobs' boarding house. The arrival of the town's first piano, a Bennett which Aunt Mett's parents would inherit from Baxter White, caused a considerable stir. A debating society invited townspeople and visitors of every age to enjoy or participate in read-ings, recitations, speeches, and a lively exchange of ideas on Friday eve-nings. There were also spirited debates by the Literary Society on such topics as: Resolved, that a neat, cross wife is more to be desired than a slack, good-natured wife, which Sam Kelsey and Dr. George Fritts won in

1883 over Dr. Guy Wheeler and Charlie Boynton. Professor Harbison headed a scientific society that took up the study of mineralogy in 1886.

In 1883 music professor Louis Zoellner, Kelsey's sons Truman and Harlan, and Frank Sheldon formed the Highlands Amateur Orchestra. They became the popular Highlands Quartet, treating audiences to combinations of voice and instrumental music.[705]

In a true sense, this was Highlands' introduction to chamber music, which would prove so popular again when the Hudson Library sponsored a resurgence of baroque chamber music a hundred years later from 1976 through 1983. By then the Highlands–Cashiers Chamber Music Festival, founded in 1982 by Lucas Drew from the University of Miami with a $5,000 grant from Mr. and Mrs. Donald Kahn, would be exposing Highlands and Cashiers audiences to nationally and internationally recognized ensembles. Co-sponsored by the Hudson Library and the Episcopal Church, this annual festival featured initially the Alexander Quartet.

In subsequent years, featured quartets have been the Audubon, Cavani, Ciompi, and Lark in addition to the Sagee Piano Trio. Many individual artists were invited to perform, such as violinists Cecylia Arzewski, Margaret Bashkin-Karp, and Kate Ransom; cellist Benjamin Karp; pianists Judith Burganger and Leonid Treer; harpist Valerie von Pechy Whitcup; flutists Charles and Susan DeLaney; oboists John Dee and Herbert Lashner; clarinetist Brian Moorehead; and soprano Judith Drew. CBS music critic and flutist Eugenia Zukerman was a special guest for the tenth anniversary.

These groups have performed works by Mozart, Beethoven, Schumann, Dvořák, Rachmaninoff, Chopin, Brahms, and Tchaikovsky. Even under the most trying circumstances, performances always occurred on schedule, such as when Eric Pritchard, first violinist with the Alexander String Quartet, played Dvorak's entire *American Quartet* from memory! The audience never realized that the music score on his stand was not the *American Quartet*, which arrived in the mail only after the concert.

Some concerts attracted as many as 140 in the audience who felt a genuine rapport with the musicians. Currently directed by William Ransom of Emory University, the Festival's slogan today would apply just as aptly to that first quartet's intentions a hundred years earlier: "Music to Match the Grandeur of the Mountains."

Although music in Highlands began with informal sings, voice and string quartets, and performances by church choirs, such as those coached by Dr. O'Farrell in 1896, it expanded to include other media, including music boxes which by 1939 had become so popular that an ordinance had to be enacted against disturbances of the public between 11:00 at night and 9:00 in the morning.

One very popular series that opened in 1952 was the annual Pops Concert. Conducted by Dr. James Christian Pfohl, this Brevard-based Transylvania Music Camp Faculty Orchestra played at the High School Auditorium to benefit the Highlands Community Hospital. It was still performing in Highlands eleven years later when in 1964 it became the Brevard Music Center Symphony.

Another popular program that even outlasted the Pops Concert in Highlands began with a very stirring song service in 1939 at the School Theatre.[706] This first performance of the African–American servants of Highlands was so well received that beginning in 1948 it continued annually for the next twelve years. It featured spirituals, anthems, and gospel songs, all sung straight from the heart. Offerings collected at the performances were distributed to the hospital but also to the Methodist Church building fund in exchange for that church's hosting separate Sunday afternoon religious services for the town's servants.

Directed by Miss Carrie Smith, Mrs. Emma Mathis assisting, and Mr. Pem Steele on the piano, the musicals soon expanded to include Spanish hymns. The presentations raised annually between $400 and $600 for both causes, with door receipts surpassing $1,000 in 1960.

In appreciation of such generosity the Hospital and Church requested in 1953, the year before integration was made the law of the land, that W. S. Davis speak to the town council about providing some form of recreation for Highlands servants during the summer months. In 1955 an area back of the old theatre building on Oak Street was designated as a place for meetings; and the right section of the Galax Theatre, for viewing shows. A dance hall was provided on Hickory Hill Road near the Big Creek bridge, but it burned.

During the early fifties Mary Morrow from Polk County, Florida, who lived in the first Margaret Young house at the end of Many Drive, had a Highlands Social Club built across the road for her servants and other African-Americans in the area. She willed it to the town in 1961 for use by African-Americans to socialize.

In recent years, with the focus in Highlands on chamber music, Bel Canto found a ready audience among its devotees. Inaugurated in 1993 by Richard Joel to raise money for the permanent art collection, this popular annual recital featured familiar arias, duets, and piano solos by leading American artists, such as sopranos Katherine Luna, Brenda Harris, Mary Paul, and Shelley Jameson; baritones Lawrence Alexander, Braden Harris, and Jeff Mattsey; bass Joel Jameson; and virtuoso pianist Stephen Dubberly.

In a less formal atmosphere Highlands' own Sylvia Sammons has been heard each season since 1982 performing her free concerts from the balcony of her Woodcraft Shop on 4th Street hill. A professional folk singer and composer who accompanies herself on guitar, harmonica, recorder, French horn, piano autoharp, and lute, Sylvia is also an accomplished craftsman who creates in her shop, canes, candle holders, towel racks, knife holders, lighters, and lamps, which she cuts and shapes herself with an electric saw, drill press, and electric sander and a special vise clamp, much to the astonishment of her customers, for it was in her sixth year that she lost her sight.

The Highlands Pipes and Drum Band, organized by Michael Waters, has performed its hearty music at parades, weddings, funerals, and sports events. Its performances of classical bagpipe music ranging beyond but including *Amazing Grace* and *Scotland the Brave* have received national recognition and been recorded on cassette and compact disk.

Perhaps music in Highlands has come full circle. It began with intimate chamber performances of classical favorites and individual recitals at the end of the nineteenth century. It evolved into traditional foot-stomping, banjo picking, and fiddling to the delight of large crowds at Helen's barn during the early part and middle of the twentieth century. And it climaxed with a return to classical entertainment at century's end. Highlanders have shown a wide-ranging appreciation and love of music whatever the type!

Art

Art like music has always found a natural home in Highlands. Whether attracted by the natural beauty of the area or its relative isolation from the hustle and bustle of the flatlands, many practitioners of the visual and literary arts have come and stayed for a while or settled permanently. Some were famous; some, not so famous but gifted nonetheless, and some even now await recognition in years to come.

In 1931 an early master of the visual arts visited his friend Dr. Percy Thompson in Highlands. At the time he was completing several historic paintings in the dome of the U.S. Capitol, which had remained unfinished for years.[707] Having studied with John Singer Sargent under Carolus Duran of Paris, George B. Matthews was well known for his paintings in the State Library in Richmond, Virginia, and the Christ at Mount Clemens Cathedral in Michigan. He had also painted several portraits of Highlanders, including Dr. Thompson's wife, Helen McKinney Cleaveland Thompson, when she was only seventeen, and Charlie Wright, still famous four years after his death for his heroism at Whiteside. He planned to paint Carl Zoellner's little daughter Barbara during his stay at the Thompsons'.

During the same year that George Matthews visited Highlands, another well-known painter and resident donated her paintings of Southern flowers to the University at Chapel Hill.[708] Miss Marie Huger's portfolio consisted of seventy-four drawings including trilliums, orchids, azaleas, yellow jessamine, gentians, wild violets, blue bells, columbine, anemone, *Shortia*, wild lilies, and rhododendron. Her niece, Charlotte Elliott, was the great-granddaughter of Stephen Elliott, whose two-volume *Sketch of the Botany of South Carolina and Georgia,* published fifteen years earlier, was one of the first major botanical works to treat the American South.

Mountain Clogging, by Polly Knipp Hill. Hudson Library permanent art collection.

George and Polly Knipp Hill, both of whom were internationally recognized artists, were summer residents from St. Petersburg.[709] They painted at Hill Studio on Hicks Road during the fifties. George exhibited his paintings and murals regularly in Europe and the U.S. His stained glass masterpieces, revealing a keen eye for meticulous detail, careful research, and high craftsmanship, graced many churches in the Country, including the Episcopal Church in Highlands. Polly exhibited her mountain etchings and prints during the fifties at the Library of Congress in Washington, D.C., and during the sixties at the Smithsonian National Gallery. Among her hand-tinted etchings that captured Highlands scenes were *Bean Stringing*, *Chestnutting on Little Bear Pen Mountain*, *Granny Woman*, *Old Timey Mountain Music*, and *Old Home Place*, owned today by the permanent art collection of the Hudson Library. *Mountain Clogging*, *Apple Cutting*, *Hillbilly Day*, and *Leather Britchering* are displayed on library loan at town hall.

Tatham Eskrigge of Highlands, by Hubert Shuptrine, 1971. Released by permission from Jericho, Oxmoor House.

During the summer of 1971 famed artist Hubert Shuptrine, a native of Chattanooga, Tennessee, who had served as visual communications special-ist for NASA during the Saturn 5 project, moved into the Elliott house on Satulah.[710] He embarked on a series of numbered prints called "Highlands

Home." For the next three years, in collaboration with the poet James Dickey, author of the novel *Deliverance*, he painted people and places that he visited in his travels across the South. The result was an astonishing achievement of traditional realism, published in coffee-table format by *Southern Living* on October 15, 1974, entitled, *Jericho: The South Beheld*.

A girl of Clear Creek and her new puppy, by Hubert Shuptrine, 1971. Released by permission from Jericho, Oxmoor House.

Disavowing the magnolia-and-moonlight view of the South, he and Dickey focused on the landscapes, seascapes, mountains, rivers, and human life of the actual South as experienced through the sense of sight and sound of words, seeking in a memorable way to reduce the romanticized myth to a real sense of place.

A number of his paintings depicted still-life scenes in and around High-lands, all crafted in watercolor: an orchard barn, winter onions, September red apples, a high oak on Satulah, the first bloom of spring, and Jabe's bell in front of the Phelps House.

Others were portraits, such as Shuptrine's neighbor Tatham Eskrigge, who posed for the *Mountain Gentleman*. A man of Southern upbringing, fresh after a morning hike in pursuit of gem stones, Indian artifacts, and mushrooms, Tatham is seated on the open-beamed veranda of his home, *World's End*. Wearing the hat he acquired in Spain, he grasps his cane with strong hands while lost in fond memories, his face conveying the personal warmth that springs from genuine fulfillment.

For the bearded, red-haired, husky Shuptrine, a character study was the height of artistic expression and posed the greatest challenge. His portrait of the *New Puppy* at Clear Creek seeks to portray a little girl's love of her dogs. Caught between the careless freedom of childhood and the heavy re-sponsibilities of adulthood, she mirrors in her eyes the hidden shadows of the soul, the longings that inevitably break the calm surface with sinister hints of human remorse and pain.

Shuptrine's *Patient Turn* depicts Tommy Barnes of Buck Creek Commu-nity, who at eighty-one betrays neither his age nor his lifelong struggles that have endured hard times. His attitude or "turn" is one of patient acceptance and heartfelt gratitude.

Shuptrine left Highlands soon after the publication of *Jericho* but in 1987 published its sequel, *Home to Jericho*, covering fifteen states from Texas to Vermont, including North Carolina. This book, more people-oriented than its prequel, featured an array of residents in and around Highlands. He de-picted Alma Henderson Keener's process of bleaching or what she called "sulphuring" apples at her farm at the end of Flat Mountain Road. Two paintings resulted: *Alma's Apples* and *Alma's Cellar*.

His *Study of John* depicted the enchanting personality of John Lebus at his home, the former "House of David" Watson above Bridal Veil Falls. He captured the essence of the last *Wild Apples* that the late Tatham Eskrigge had left in his kitchen windowsill at *World's End*. He drew Marty Wilson when she was only five or six years of age doing house chores, including a portrait of the Wilson home.

Having majored in veterinary science before earning a degree in fine arts painting from the University of Tennessee, Shuptrine loved portraying ani-mals and painted one of Carl Neely and his black coon dog, *Janie of Clear Creek*. Also included was *The McKinney House*. His Jericho paintings, which sold initially for $2,000, topping $8,000 by 1973, currently sell for $25,000 to $50,000.

Tommy Barnes of Buck Creek, by Hubert Shuptrine, 1972. Released by permission from Jericho, Oxmoor House.

In 1976 the first "High Country Crafters" fair was organized to celebrate and promote mountain arts and crafts. A non-profit enterprise, it was held at Helen's Barn to help beginning and established artists and craftsmen improve their skills and widen their markets.

But there were also those who already enjoyed established markets. From 1975–80 Henry La Cagnina summered in Highlands, bringing with him his extraordinary talents in painting, building and designing furniture, and creating colorful enamels.[711] He came from a long and distinguished career extending back to the Depression, when President Roosevelt commissioned him as an artist to revitalize Key West, Florida. He taught at various universities and exhibited in galleries from Puerto Rico to Mississippi to New Hampshire.

His contribution to Highlands was in the form of hand-painted enamels depicting scenes from the life of Christ on the chapel doors of the Episcopal Church. Now a permanent resident of the town, at 92 he still draws and paints, his murals, decorative furniture, and carved doors adorning private homes and public buildings across the nation.

The works of some of Highlands' major artists, such as Polly Knipp Hill but also those outside Highlands who have painted Highlands scenes, have earned admission into the Hudson Library's Permanent Art Collection, established by the late Watson Barratt. Elsa Dodd of Atlanta and Highlands, whose husband created the syndicated Mark Trail cartoon, was herself the creator of two conte drawings of the *Old Dry Cleaner's Building* on North 4th Street.

Old Dry Cleaner's Building, Elsa Dodd, 1980. Hudson Library permanent collection.

Julia Daugette, also of Atlanta and Highlands, depicted *Winter in Highlands* and *4:30 on Satulah* in oil. Her son Walter Hunt mastered the art of pointillism in his nature scenes and depictions of Highlands buildings, including *Old Edwards Inn*, the *Episcopal Church*, and the *Presbyterian Church*. Elsie Dresch of Atlanta, who teaches workshops in Highlands, did a pastel of *Ravenel Lake* at the Biological Station; William Whiteside from Cashiers, a traditional, figurative acrylic of *Winter on the Upper Cullasaja*; and William Thomas Shaddick from Gainesville, Florida, watercolor scenes of Highlands landscapes, including *Queen Anne's Lace*.

Amelia James from Atlanta and Highlands is a nationally known portrait artist, whose life-like oil portraitures have captured the personalities of her subjects in artistic ways that photography cannot achieve, such as her portrayal of a young golfer. Depicting individuality through gestures, expressions and color, she invests her paintings with the personality and energy of her particular subjects. She also paints art in bloom from her garden, such as *Sun Worshippers* in the Library's Collection and zinnias in *My Garden*.

Rosemary Stiefel's detailed watercolors of the environment include her river meditations on *Dry Falls* and the *Cullasaja River*, which represent her technique of interpreting a poem, a piece of music, a philosophical premise, a feeling, or a scene from nature in abstract forms that intend to evoke strong emotional responses from the viewer.

Lucien Harris' specialty was birds and flowers of the South, especially his acrylic *Hummingbirds in Rhododendron*, as well as exotic birds and butterflies of Trinidad's rain forests. A resident of Highlands and Winter Garden, Florida, he was a great grandson of Joel Chandler Harris of *Uncle Remus* fame. He changed careers late in life from banker to artist and, through his attention to detail, achieved a luminous richness and jewel-like authenticity worthy of Audubon art.

Susan Robert's oils start with a realistic idea of a plant or a figure or a fruit and explore all its possibilities through a series of abstract expressionist works, such as her *Politically Incorrect Series: Figure Study*. Linda Anderson, a well-known folk artist from Clarksville, Georgia, had her oil painting *Winter Scene* chosen by the International Habitat for Humanity as its Christmas card.

Other Highlands artists, not represented in the library's collection but of high quality, include Julyan Davis from England and Alabama, who paints his waterfalls and vistas of the mountains while on the scene, such as his oil renderings of *Middlecreek Falls* and *Dry Falls* and his Whiteside Mountain panorama. John Collette Fine Arts carries his masterworks today. Philip Read, a New York native living in West Palm Beach and the south of France, summered in Highlands and created large-scale murals and impressionistic and surrealistic paintings that grace the walls of Tiffany's, Car-

550

tier's, the presidential dining room of the Mayflower Hotel, and the Montreal Expo stadium.

Dry Falls, by Julyan Davis, 1998.

Marsha Montoya of Palm Beach, Florida, recently moved to Highlands as an internationally recognized sculptor of figures in bronze and stone. Jackie Meena, Edwina Goodman, and Sudie Manning, are residents of Highlands and Jackson, Mississippi. Jackie concentrates on design, as in her *Falcon Ridge* and *Pick of the Chicks*; Edwina, on abstractions; and Sudie, on flora in watercolor and oil. Madeleine Watt of Highlands and Atlanta recreates landscapes in watercolor and pastel.

Among today's galleries that sell regional paintings, photographs, and handcrafted art in Highlands is Ann Jacob's of Atlanta, the oldest gallery in the Southeast, in Highlands since the late eighties. Others include Harllee Gallery/CK Swan, the Summer House, Robert A. Tino Gallery, Southern Hands, Master Works, Thomas Kinkade At Highlands, I'm Precious Too, and Oak Street Gallery.

The Bascom–Louise Gallery, located since its founding in 1985 as a non-profit organization in the Hudson Library building, has focused on promoting public awareness of the arts and crafts in Highlands through exhibits, workshops and classes for adults and children, as well as art auctions to assure its own continued existence as a popular forum for the visual arts. It initiated its Affaires d'Arts dinners at various homes in 1998.

Dane Morgan, an architect and artist from Naples, Florida, was the originator of Studio Alive, which for almost two decades has supported the arts and artists in Highlands with weekly meetings. Similarly, the Art League of Highlands, founded in 1980 as an association of practicing amateur and professional artists, is another promoter of art in town, particularly through its monthly meetings, newsletters, member art shows, field trips, and sponsorship of scholarships for outstanding students in the arts.[712] Even the Chamber of Commerce has sponsored since 1997 an annual Art Walk featuring artists and their work on the sidewalks of town.

One of the most recent boosts to the craft of art, established in Highlands in 1996 by George and Bonnie Siek of Belleair, Florida, has been the Museum of American Cut and Engraved Glass, a non-profit, dazzling display of American-made antique cut and engraved glass from the Brilliant Period, 1876 to 1916.

George Keener from Walnut Creek, a descendant of the Keeners of Highlands and Goldmine, was a "shade tree mechanic" for forty years, rebuilding automatic transmissions, but his first love was painting. He took his first art course in his late thirties. Prior to that, he claims he did pin-ups. Not from models, he says; "I just made 'em up. You can make 'em up like you want 'em. After I got married [to Dottie Owens], I had to do horses."

Since his retirement in 1988 he has devoted full time to painting the hills, mountains, streams, and countryside of the southern Appalachians. His realistic oil and acrylic paintings are consistently among the top 100 selected by the Academy of Arts for National Parks in its annual contests for artists. His landscapes hang in Highlands homes, North Carolina and Georgia galleries, and the Smithsonian Institution in Washington. He considers each scene that he paints a religious or spiritual experience that springs straight from the heart before it reaches the brush. "Art," he claims, "is like putting grease on a wagon wheel. If you know what you're doing, it goes on easy. God gives you the talent, and if you use it, you can go as high as you want to."

Among his masterworks are *Spring on the Cullasaja*, *Whiteside*, *Winter Solitude*, *October Sunlight*, *Shades of Autumn*, and *Pastel Colors of Spring*, depicting a scene near the old quarry on the Franklin Road.

George Keener's *Whiteside Valley*. Photo by the author, 2001.

With organizations like these flourishing in Highlands the visual arts and crafts remain very much alive on the plateau.

Cinema

Five years after D. W. Griffith's *Birth of a Nation* established motion pictures as an art form of tremendous power, Henry Sloan brought the first movie to Highlands.[i] Shown in May, 1920, in the Masonic Hall, it was a western, presumably *The Virginian*, appearing in black and white, over captions instead of voices. Some of the young people were so anxious for it to come to Highlands that they met the projector eight miles down the road in Scaly.

By July movies were being shown in the school auditorium. The projector rested on a tripod set up in the middle of the aisle toward the back of the room, but not as far back as the "buzzard roost." It broke down and had to be rewound many times during each showing, always just when the hero was clutching the heroine to his manly bosom or the villain was about to get his just deserts. Jim Hicks would try to correct the problem, while Henry Sloan, in his beautifully tailored plus-fours, made announcements.

Though the movies were silent, Bessie Hines or Gertrude Holt provided music on the old piano to the left of the screen. They would crane their necks around the piano to watch the screen and match the tempo of the action. "If it was horses, why they'd run the piano keys," remembered Cub Rice. Fatty Arbuckle movies called for allegretto, Lillian Gish for hearts-and-flowers music, and Rudolph Valentino for something sultry.

Henry W. Sloan. Photo courtesy of Hudson Library archives.

Later Mr. Sloan had two pot-bellied stoves installed for warmth and a little projection booth built up in the bleachers. It was covered with asbestos sheeting, as film in those days was highly flammable. Whenever a movie failed to arrive, he would show *The Virginian*, so that Highlanders became fairly familiar with this ancestor of the Western, especially that macho line: "When you call me that, smile." The kids of Highlands hardly missed a movie; indeed no one missed a movie because this was about the only entertainment there was on Saturdays.

The old schoolhouse auditorium, while ideal for movies, was a convenient setting for other civic events as well: the annual community Christmas tree lighting, box suppers, cake walks, PTA meetings, even the tonsilpulling clinic on its stage. The movies that were shown to residents ranged from bright comedy reels to clean Westerns and included educational pictures. Admission to *When a Man's a Miner*, a story of romance, love, and adventure, in 1930 ranged from 10¢ to 25¢, depending on where you sat.

In 1932, when "talking pictures" had outpaced Mr. Sloan's silent equipment, the Boylan Brothers from Bryson City showed talkies in Highlands. The next year, 1933, Otto Summer, principal of the school, ran the movies from one portable projector, which he had to shut down every ten minutes to change reels. During the break, local merchants showed slides on the roll-up screen, and there were games. Once a week some forty-five adults and twenty-two children enjoyed *Little Orphan Annie*, *King Kong*, Joe E. Brown in *Elmer the Great*, and George Arlis in *Working Man*. Adults paid 25¢; children, 15¢.

When a new High School Auditorium, now the Highlands Playhouse, was built in the summer of 1934, movies were shown four to six days a week, even through the winter.[714] Planned by an Asheville architect for $50, the building was contracted to Guy Paul, Sr., who created a wood-shingled building to match the school beside it. Even to this day the acoustics are nearly perfect.

Except for one silent movie *Saratoga*, starring Jean Harlow and Clark Gable, which was shown for the benefit of Highlands School, all the films now were talkies: Loretta Young and Tyrone Power in *Café Metropole*, Shirley Temple in *Wee Willie Winkie*, Errol Flynn and Anita Louise in *Green Light*, Spanky McFarland in *General Spanky*, and Constance Bennett and Cary Grant in *Topper*.

In 1945 Mr. Summer bought out the school movie interest and for the next three years ran the shows himself. Then in 1948 he, Will Edwards, and Doc Mitchell built the Galax Theatre on Main Street. Emblazoned across the marquee, which today announces "Annawear," was the *Daughter of Rosie O'Grady* "in the miracle of Technicolor."

The Galax Theatre brought to Highlands such classics as *Gone with the Wind*, *Hound Dog Man*, and Disney's *Parent Trap*, *Pillow Talk*, and *Pollyanna* with Haley Mills. *Magnificent Obsession* opened in 1954 with Jane Wyman, Rock Hudson, and Barbara Rush. Two years later *The Wedding in Monaco* brought together Grace Kelly and Prince Rainier as a short. Sure hits featured Shirley Temple, Fred Astaire and Ginger Rogers, Judy Garland, or Will Rogers, but the greatest favorites were *The Guns of Navarone* and *Lawrence of Arabia*, along with two movies set at Tallulah Falls, Georgia: *I Climb the Highest Mountain* and *The Great Locomotive Chase*.

When Cinemascope and wide-screen movies enlarged and curved the stage in 1954, the projectors and sound system had to be constantly upgraded, and a soundproof "cry room" was added for mothers with babies to separate them from the 400 spectators.[715]

A new form of visual entertainment was just beginning to offer the people of Highlands an alternative to movies at the Galax. Called television, it was available only to those fortunate enough to have access to an enormous floor set capable of receiving WFBC-TV on Channel 4.

Throughout the early years of the Galax Theatre, the locally mimeographed *Mountain Trail*, which had preceded the Theatre by ten years, and the *Galax News*, which appeared every summer from 1952 through 1971, announced upcoming movies in enticing detail. This was a prime reason why these publications were so well received by folks in Highlands.

The Highlands Community Theatre, now Highlands Playhouse, built in 1934. Photo courtesy of Highlands Historic Inventory.

The Stage

At the same time that movies were capturing the attention of the Highlands populace, local actors and actresses were being introduced to the stage. In 1937 a group of Funmakers, headed by Virginia "Ted" Wilcox, began sponsoring an annual Highlands Playday in August, a kind of precursor of the Highlands Little Theatre, organized two years later in 1939. The Little Theatre presented its first play in this year, George Kauffman and Marc Connelly's *Dulcy*, to a full house in the old School Auditorium.[716] Reserved seats sold for 50¢; general admission in the bleachers, 35¢.

Billed as a hilarious comedy, *Dulcy* portrayed a young wife whose well-meaning but flighty attempts to help her husband in his business proved disastrous. It starred Anne Altstaetter, recent graduate of the Royal Academy of Dramatic Arts in London, with a supporting cast of Frank Lowman, Tony Moore, Jack Wilcox, Polly Raoul, Margaret Rankin, Edgar Neely, Jr., Herbert Milkey, Sarah Bridges Thompson, and Henry Zoellner. Clemson professor of architecture Tom Fitz Patrick directed it with help from theatre director and head of the Department of Drama at Earlham College Arthur Little and his wife Sarah.

Virginia "Ted" and Jack Wilcox. Photos by Charles J. Wick.

By the following year the Little Theatre was officially incorporated as the Highlands Community Theatre. It immediately assumed the ambitious task of raising some $3,000 to erect a building for its performances at the northwest corner of the ballpark. Though the stated aim was to produce five shows a year, they had to content themselves with only one, at first in the High School Auditorium, then at the Nature Center amphitheatre, then Helen's Barn, and during one year as far away as the court house in Franklin. Rehearsals took place in Jack and Virginia "Ted" Wilcox's barn.

Soon the theatre began taking on a few professional actors who shared the stage with summer and winter thespians. Old and young alike, practically the whole town grew addicted to the magic of theatre. But when America entered the Second World War, acting on stage in Highlands ceased, the last production starring Harriet Zahner in Frank Davis' *Gold in the Hills*, directed by Tom Fitz Patrick, and staged in the amphitheatre of the Museum.

L to R: Skip Foley, Arthur Little, Arnold Keener, Jack Wilcox, Vic Smith, Frances Deere, Peggy Potts, Barbara "Bobbie" Curry (Jungmeir) in Mary Roberts Rinehart's "The Bat." Photo by Charles Wick, 1949.

Within a month after V.E. Day in 1945, the Theatre group was displaying in the town office a model of its proposed new building. Productions recommenced in 1946 to widespread enthusiasm, beginning with Hugh Herbert's *Kiss And Tell*, staged at the Museum, and the following year Ayn Rand's *The Night of January 26th*, a courtroom trial performed appropriately at the Franklin Courthouse. In 1948 the Theatre featured four plays, including Emlyn Williams' popular *Corn Is Green*, involving practically the whole community. Church choirs introduced the set, singing beautifully "Work for the Night Is Coming."

The following year featured many local actors and actresses in Mary Roberts Rinehart's *The Bat*. Thornton Wilder's *Our Town* featured Arthur Little's cousin Fred Allen directing at Helen's Barn, where Maxie Wright (now Duke) played the lovely, dead Emily Webb, and Helen's dog, Joe, bayed when the train whistle blew.

| *Arthur Little* | *Col. Mowbray* | *Maxie Wright* | *Arnold Keener* |

Collin Wilcox and Richard Melvin in John Van Druten's Bell, Book and Candle

Fred directed two more plays in 1950: Patterson Greene's *Papa Is All* and Molière's *The Doctor in Spite of Himself*. Ionesco's *Marriage Proposal* had to be performed at Helen's Barn, because when Highlands School moved to Muddy Hollow in 1951, the town bought the schoolhouse property, including the Highlands School Theatre. Robert DuPree tried to secure the Theatre for seasonal productions, offering $2,000 in advance rent if the town would permit its use by the Little Theatre group during the following summer.

Although the town board accepted his offer, it heard the next year an amended deal from Jack Wilcox, president of the group. He asked for four rent-free nights a week until the Theatre Group could repay the costs of installing new curtains and enlarging the stage, figured at 12% of gross receipts. Despite these ambitious pleas and proposals, nothing materialized, and the once lively now defunct Highlands School Theatre remained dark and empty.

By 1953 Chuck Chalker was proposing that a stock company of professional talent from New York be invited to present plays during the summer months, for the people of Highlands sorely missed their theatre experience. Not until 1957, however, at the town's request, did the Highlands Community Theatre reopen with renewed energy and enthusiastic interest, presenting four or five productions a year, almost all directed by Fred Allen.

Anne Sullivan Doggett described Fred Allen as having educated a Highlands generation in theatre. "He gave us all the gift of theatre as a resource to enjoy all our lives," she said, "taught us how to enjoy work, and made our summers magical. Added to that he was brilliant!" Carol Futch described the Community Playhouse as just that: "our Playhouse." She remarked that the audience came to enjoy the plays but also to see their family and friends perform. For the young folks, being involved with the theatre gave them feelings of importance as well as self-confidence, self-reliance, and incentive.

Starring new additions alongside old standbys, popular casts included Tom and Beverly Fitz Patrick and their son Kevin, Bob DuPree and his son Bobby and daughter Peggy, Jack and Ted Wilcox and their daughters Collin and Jeremy, Martha Cobb and her daughter Marna, Col. Ralph Mowbray, Edward Fernow, Edna Faxon, Ellison Magruder, Nick Koepp-Baker, Peggy Potts, Arnold Keener, James Bridges, Lucille Pierson, Clarence Mitchell, and Richard Melvin, even whole families like the Altstaetters, Raouls, Saussys, Zahners, Halls, and Wrights. Many of these could be found after each last performance socializing at Bill Raoul's Hobo Stew parties. Larry Gates from Atlanta and Jimmy Reese would eventually become well-known names in New York Theatre.

In 1959–60 the old school building next to the theatre was offered for sale to the highest bidder with the request that it be dismantled and removed from the premises.[717] The following year the school hill was leveled off to provide more parking spaces and the drive resurfaced to accommodate large audiences that were now enjoying a resurgence of plays including New York actors, such as William Inge's *Picnic* and George Bernard Shaw's *Androcles and the Lion*.

Director Fred Allen, ca. 1950. Photo by Charles J. Wick

One of the great legacies of the Highlands Community Theatre was its creation of accomplished professionals from raw amateurs. It prepared Collin Wilcox to act in the hit movie of 1963: Harper Lee's Academy

Award winning *To Kill a Mockingbird*. Collin played Mayella, the farm girl whose false accusations stuck so vividly in her throat in the courtroom scene. This movie was shown at the Galax Theatre in July to a highly appreciative hometown audience.

Collin's career began with her first role at the age of ten as one of the dead in *Our Town*. Soon she was performing in Chicago, on and off Broadway in New York, and in London, where the *London Times* called her "the funniest American export since Judy Holliday." She acted in the extremely popular *Period of Adjustment* by Tennessee Williams in 1963.

Her career on stage and in films and television led her eventually to return to Highlands and give back some of what it had given her. She founded the Studio of the Arts to teach a new generation the magic she herself had experienced on the stage. Ted Shaffner, Carrie Mayer, and Christine Perkins in New York are three protégés who still carry that dramatic torch.

In 1967 the directorship of the Theatre passed to Sam Sanfilippo, and the golden age of Arthur Little and Fred Allen was over. Much had been accomplished under these two talented directors by the casts and volunteers, from twelve-year-old Buddy Hall, Bob Foreman, and Jim Painter in charge of lighting; to Winnie Eskrigge managing the stage, the props, prompting, ticket sales, and advertisement; to Fred himself, who took on sets and costumes, props, sound, even publicity outside his role as director.

All the local talent gave way now to imported actors and directors. With the older standbys gone and the young ones departing for distant colleges and universities, the enthusiastic fun of amateur theatre had reached its end.

In 1969 Michael "Mike" Hall from Ocala, Florida, became managing director, assisted by designer Frank Bennett. The Highlands Community Theatre by 1973 was almost entirely professional. This was the year that the name was changed to Highlands Playhouse. Jere Hodgin and Ernie Zulia took over as artistic directors and producers in 1983 and brought in actors from Atlanta.

In 1989 the Playhouse signed a deal with the University of Georgia Drama Department, and Dr. Gus Staub served as its producer, sponsoring three plays and a musical each season until 2000. During his tenure, attendance grew from six or seven thousand a season to nine or ten thousand with national recognition extended by the *New York Times*, *National Geographic*, and the *Wall Street Journal*. In 2001 the artistic directorship passed to Harold Leaver of Atlanta; with Stacey Shaw of Charleston, managing director.

Drama has by no means died in Highlands. Indeed, there has even been a recent renewal of local interest in amateur acting, which gave birth to the Highlands Community Players, the long lost child of the Highlands Community Theatre. Their hope has been to recapture the magical appeal that once bonded the Highlands community as a unit, and if it's any indication of their success in this regard, they play to standing room only. Their most recent achievement was the role they played in staging the very popular first Walk in the Park, created in 2000 by the newly reactivated Highlands Historical Society, Inc. to introduce Highlanders to early characters in the town's history as portrayed in its cemetery.

Literature

If, as Buckminster Fuller once claimed, the poet is the one who puts things together, then literature helped unite Highlands when the town was still in its infancy. If certain poets of the area were unknown outside their private circle, indeed outside their family and immediate friends, they were no less poets by the quality of their impassioned songs.

Laura Hawkins, for instance, a rather lonely but inspired member of Dr. Alfred Hawkins' family at Rock House Farm southeast of Highlands, was composing heartfelt lyrics as early as the 1880s. She sang of her lovely world of mountain trails over plateaus and ridges and along the cliff's bare edge, of woodland fruits and forest flowers laden with delight, and of lizards like lightning flashes on the cool wet pebbles in crystal streams.[718] She basked in the joys of nature: rosebuds folded tight, the songs of birds, the first gleam of morning, and the beauty of the stars. She also wrote of loss in nature: trees that once stood round like comrades in a merry forest, reduced in her time to a single wayside trunk and canopy. One of her most poignant poems, "Songs of the Captives," laments civilization's invasion of the forests:

> The native legions of the woods are conquered
> But fragments of their hosts are now retained
> And these by walls enclosed and fields surrounded
> Are but like captives in a triumph chained.

> But when at any time I walk among them
> In shade of summer or in bloom of spring
> They sing at once in glad and eager welcome
> The sweetest songs that captives sad can sing.

> The cradle songs and stirring strains of battle
> The store of wondrous legends weird and wild
> All songs that they have known from Earth's creation
> The captives sing to me, the conqueror's child.

She also sang of personal loss, of her brother's baby with all his laughter and glee stolen away to his new home in the valley, leaving all sounds sad behind, nothing glad, no warmth left in the sun.

Since little in the way of poetry or prose was actually published in early Highlands, lovely works like Laura's might never have found their way into print. Similarly, the poetry of Christina Anderson Rice, daughter of Dr. Will Anderson and wife of the butcher Luke Rice, showed considerable literary talent, but it exists today solely in a booklet bound by her descendants.[719] Her poems described with deep insight and feeling the crags and glens, dark with the shade of the rhododendrons and laurels up to the summit of the very loftiest peak, such as her lyric "Clouds":

There is a crag on Blue Ridge Crest,
I dearly love to climb.
There on the soft green moss I rest
In solitude sublime.

I look across to Highlands Falls
And hear the water roar,
It seems to me a voice that calls
From all time gone before.

And just beyond there rises high
Old Whiteside's hoary head,
It reaches almost to the sky
Above the laurel bed.

And all around there seems to be
No living thing at all,
Just mountains, clouds, and me,
And God, up over all.

Christina had her father's sense of humor, which she displayed in this delightful poem on the pangs of "Love":

Once, I judged love from the books that I read.
I thought Cupid the spirit of song.
Then, I judged life from what people said,
I now know my judgment was wrong.

For I've had some experience with love myself,
And I've passed thru great struggle and strife,
I now know that Cupid is a mean, sneaking elf,
And the way to judge love is from life.

Christina composed poems under her own name but also under a pseudonym, Eugene Lee Hamilton. Frederick Koch, drama professor at the University of North Carolina at Chapel Hill and regarded as the father of American folk drama, asked to use a number of her poems in his classes and convinced her to publish a few in the *Southern Ruralist*.

Another early poet in Highlands who composed poems for newspapers and magazines and collected them in book form was Mary Chapin Smith.[720] Her *Earth Songs*, published in Boston in 1910, is still held by the Hudson Library. More intellectual than emotional, her poems are strong, finely honed, and filled with colorful similes and metaphors, such as this one about snow:

> *The white-winged snow falls down most silently*
> *And softly in large flakes, like many small*
> *White birds that fly to earth; the snowbirds come*
> *With fluttering wings, alighting on the tree,*
> *The little tree that is their resting place,*
> *Their fluffy feathers white like heaps of snow*
> *Upon the limbs; they come in endless flight,*
> *Blown through the air and dropping down to earth,*
> *As swift and silent as the falling snow.*

Or this verse about love of life from "Sweet Mother Earth":

> *Death paused awhile without my door;*
> *I did not bid him enter in,*
> *For joys of Paradise can nevermore*
> *Seem sweeter than they seem, in spite of sin*
> *And wo, the joys of this dear earth.*

One of the earliest books to feature Highlands as its chief setting was a detective story written by summer resident Dorothy Ogburn, entitled *Death on the Mountain*, and published by Little Brown in 1931, the same year that Horace Kephart, the "Golden Voice of the Highlands" and author of the still highly respected *Our Southern Highlanders*, died in a tragic automobile wreck near Bryson City.[721]

A popular Highlands author, who rarely, if ever, published under her own name, was Dorothy McPherson Farnsworth, an Athens, Georgia, native and wife of Patrick Farnsworth who lived in the old Hutchinson/Frost home. Her writing career began with a poem that she published when she was only thirteen. Over the years she adopted twenty-one different pen names, with a specific reason for each one. For her verse published in *Scribner's* magazine, she called herself Robert Emmet Ward; for her songs, Ann F. Barr, both in the United States and in England.

In the May, 1930, issue of *St. Nicholas* her poem "Consider the Llama," by Robert E. Ward, was illustrated by Reginald Birch, the artist for *Little Lord Fauntleroy* and other works by Frances Hodgson Burnett. Mrs. Farnsworth claimed a preference for writing humorous verse, as she would rather see laughter than tears.

Louise Bascom and Helen Hill Norris in their teens. Photo courtesy of the Hudson Library archives.

Another popular and prolific writer, a Wellesley graduate and resident of Highlands, was Louise Bascom Barratt, daughter of H. M. Bascom and wife of Broadway scene designer and producer Watson Barratt.[722] She published many stories and articles under her maiden name, Louise Rand Bascom, in over forty magazines, beginning with *Harper's Weekly* and including *Good Housekeeping, Housewife, Ladies' Home Journal, Youth's Companion, American Boy, New York Dramatic Mirror*, and many others.

Her subjects ranged from the practical advice of "Adventure in High Finance" and "Modern Fairy Godmother" to the romance of "Aunt Sarah and the Policeman: How He Helped Her to Have Her Fling." Her romantic serial "Story Time in Prose and Rhyme" in *Today's Housewife* proved particularly popular, running from April, 1919, to October, 1920, as did "Peacock Robe: A Story of Mystery and Love," which *Today's Housewife* carried from May till October in 1921.

She wrote dialect mountain stories, set in Western North Carolina, which *Harper's Magazine* published as "White Shoes" in 1914 and "The Better Man" in 1916, the year that *McBride's* featured "Corilla's Corn." "Uncle Sam in Appalachia" appeared in 1915 in *Outlook*. She contributed household articles to *Table Talk*, *Good Housekeeping*, *Delineator*, *Designer*, and *Housekeeper* and wrote columns on how to write, which appeared in *Editor* magazine from from 1910–16. Topics included how to build a logical plot, examples of effective writing, economy in writing, how to bolster the memory, and point of view, with warnings against strained figures and the pitfalls of vivid verbs. In the April issue of 1911 she unveiled "The Three Secrets of Literary Success" and in a November issue, 1915, she advised how to handle manuscript rejections.

Her one book for children was *Bugaboo Men*, but she wrote seven plays and several dozen children's stories and dialogues for use in the public schools. *Today's Housewife* carried twenty-seven of her original stories for children, twenty-seven original poems, and many of her drawings. There were also children's stories in *American Motherhood*, such as "The Nicest Part of Christmas" and "How Dicky Lost His Fear of the Wind" and "How Dicky Learned to Listen."

Under her married name, she co-authored a guide book to entertainment and theatre in New York. She edited *New York in Seven Days* during the twenties; and in 1937, the *New York Visitor* for the Central Railroad. All these works are archived at the Hudson Library and Bascom-Louise Gallery.

A native of Highlands and Horse Cove who ran a column in the *Highlander* from its founding in 1958 until her death ten years hence was Helen Hill Norris, granddaughter of Dr. Charles Frost and of Highlands' first mayor, Stanhope Hill. These articles about early days in Highlands she published in 1961 and 1963 as two volumes bearing the name of her newspaper column: *Looking Backward*. With a great deal of authority and personality they recorded the stories that she had been told as a child about the region's past history, as evidenced by their titles: "She Had to Boil Her Clothes," "The Lost Gold Miner," "The Tooth Dentist Comes to Town," "The Time the Lightning-Rod Man Came," and "Lace Curtains and Bull Calves."

When a reader of the *Highlander* complained that she should shift her focus to present-day Highlands or to the future rather than dwell so intently upon the past, she defended herself as writing about what she knew best, and her ardent fans agreed.

During the early thirties Sarah Hicks "Hixy" Hines, the oldest of Judge Jim Hines' daughters, wrote fascinating articles for the *Franklin Press* about Highlands past and present. Some of them were collected into book form but published posthumously in 1999 under the title *Shaking Down the Chestnuts*.

Sarah's sister, Bess Hines Harkins wrote both prose and poetry, the latter of which won numerous bicoastal awards for its beauty and literary power. On the local level she wrote a series of very popular articles for the *Highlander*, called "Our Mountains," depicting Highlands during the late twenties and early thirties.[723]

Bess' first book of poetry, *Singing of the Heart*, appeared in 1943 under her maiden name Bess Hinson Hines. It was followed in 1958 by *Unknown Seas* with its love of the beauty of the mountains of Highlands and in 1964 by *Songs Out of Silence* with its setting by the sea in California. The editor of *American Bard* said of Bess: "The melody of her poetry lingers on, long after the singing has ceased—that intangible music of wind and sky and sea—the irresistible rhythms of the Universe . . . Hers are the poems that keep singing in one's soul."[724] *Earth Songs* appeared in 1975, *Sequoia Bound*, which she co-authored with her husband Butler Harkins, in 1978; and *Dream Blue Altitudes*, before she died, in 1986.

Variously known as "the Emily Dickinson of the Blue Ridge Mountains" or, as she called herself, "Bess the Woods Wanderer," she was also regarded as the Poet Laureate of Highlands for her portrayal of the beauty and majesty of the mountains and waterfalls tinged with reverent awe for all beauty in nature and the spirit. Bess spent each winter in California, but her heart remained always in Highlands, her steps turning homeward every spring:

> *I never sail the high sea*
> *Or view its endless rills*
> *But O, beyond the hue of it,*
> *I'm looking for the hills . . .*
>
> *The blue hills, the rolling hills,*
> *The grey hills wrapped in rain . . .*
> *But O, to take the trails of them,*
> *To know the heights and vales of them—*
> *Day and night I long for them*
> *As the homeless long for home.*
>
> *I never dream at night-time*
> *Or close my eyes by day*
> *But there I have the might of them,*

The windswept, cloud-kissed sight of them
That calls my soul away . . .

O deep dreams, and happy dreams—
It's dreaming still I'd be—
For though the sea I'm waking on,
That my heart is breaking on,
And it's far where I'd be sleeping
With the blue hills over me. [725]

Bess' poem "To Be in Highlands"—used as the epigraph for this book—distilled the essence of what it meant to her from birth until her final year when Butler brought her back to wander through her beloved woods and die at home.

The freshness and the fragrance
Glint of a woodsy stream
Blue misty lift of the mountains
Green eternal dream

Bright wonder of the morning
After a sweet night rain:
It is not earth but Heaven—
The birds are making it plain

And the pines are reaffirming.
Where else would you go
But to Highlands, heart of the Blue Ridge
Above the world below!

Butler Harkins shared his wife's love of nature, but from an Oriental slant. His poetry sprang from his admiration of the classic Eastern poets. A dedicated teacher for fifty years, he inspired his classes in creative writing to such an extent that the California legislature cited him for outstanding service to the field of education. A Pied Piper of sorts, he was ever leading his students, indeed children of all ages, to the magical mountain, not to lose themselves *in* nature and poetry but *to* nature and poetry. His favorite form was the haiku, which he perfected by steeping himself in the Japanese master, Matsuo Bashō, among others, and encouraging his students to free themselves from their restraints by delving into this elusive form and its cousin the harquain.

Dividing his time with Bess between California and Highlands, he composed poems of humor and pathos in his book, *Booted Thru Boot Camp*. His remaining titles attest to the combined poet–naturalist in him: *Leaves of the*

Ginkgo; *Leaves Triumphant*; *Leaves of Autumn, of Elation, of Aloneness,* and *of Amber*; and *Maple Leaf Moments*. His haikus sparkle with wit and sensitivity, like his claim that haikus are hard to write.[726]

> *Writing a haiku*
> *Is more difficult than*
> *Threading smoke ringlets*

Or his love of nature:

> *The rose vine trembles*
> *With the weight of the moon, how*
> *Heavy the fragrance.*

> *One cannot be sad*
> *With butterfly happiness*
> *On every flower*

And his philosophy of life[727]:

> *Let us dance for we have only such*
> *a little while to play, such meager*
> *moments to address our fate*
> *Solemnity can wait!*
> *Let us rejoice, the music stirs us*
> *to our feet, the melody of strings,*
> *the pulse of drums, a harmony pre-*
> *vails, romance entreats . . .*
> *Whatever will . . . will come*
> *We pause in unbelief to learn*
> *that joy shared, fulfills!*

Highlands' first historian was Thurlow Weed Reynolds, a prose writer who was actually a retired engineer from Amsterdam, New York. He attended Columbia School of Journalism and wrote for technical magazines in New York City, Europe, Canada, and across the U.S. before settling in Highlands. In 1964 he published a collection of stories of the Carolina mountains that centered around *High Lands*. He followed it almost immediately with *Born of the Mountains*; and in 1966, with two volumes of the *Southern Appalachian Region*.

High Lands gave a detailed coverage of the Highlands plateau from Sylvia, N.C., through Georgia to Walhalla, S.C., where the mountain slopes finally died out. At age seventy-four, having spent seven years interviewing and traveling "some thousands of miles back and forth and over and over again" along secondary roads that "warn't fitten to travel," Reynolds said he wrote the book because "the mountains always fascinated me."[728]

While acknowledging that he himself wasn't a native of Highlands, that he hadn't lived here for eighty or ninety years, nor had his grandpappy before him, Reynolds defended his book as something no native before him had taken the time or shown the interest to write. And though all natives might not agree in every detail with all the stories he related, it might be that they couldn't agree with one another either, so that what he told, as near as he could assure its accuracy, was "as told to me," and that had the value of his having recorded what surely would have otherwise been lost.

Reynolds' subjects included the Whiteside Mountain rescue, the naming of Cashiers and Horse Cove, the Hawkins family, a brief history of the founding of Highlands, the Blue Ridge Railroad and Stumphouse Mountain Tunnel, the naming of Satulah, and many more, as he laid out six detailed tours of the area within a forty-five mile radius. His other three books extended the coverage to much of Western Carolina, as far as the mountains of Georgia, South Carolina, and Virginia and into Eastern Tennessee.

Behind all four books lay extensive research into the etymology of place names, detailed maps of all the roads, trails, and points of interest discussed, and Reynolds' own talent and experience in telling a good story. His books constituted—and still do—a fascinating read.

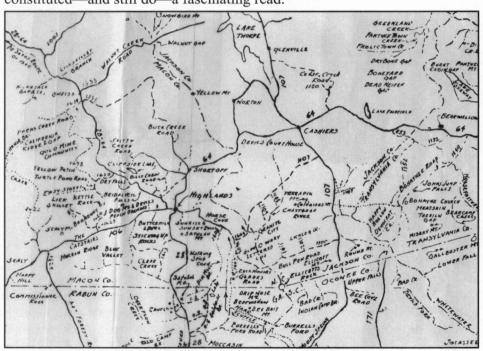

T. W. Reynolds' 1966 map of Highlands area

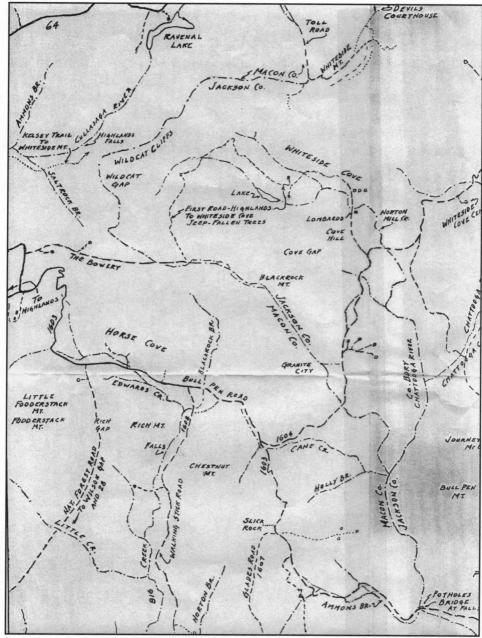

T. W. Reynolds' 1966 map of Horse and Whiteside coves

Highlands' second historian was the librarian at the Hudson Library, Gert McIntosh, who published her *Highlands, North Carolina . . . a walk into the past* in 1983, revised and updated with a chronological history and index in 1990. Her history was inspired by numerous requests at the library for information about Highlands, which was available at the time only in newspaper clippings, pamphlets, and brochures. Her book supplied a real need for all those interested in the origin and development of the town.

Dee McCollum, a poet/painter from Franklin, owned The Paintin' Place on Main Street (formerly Sara Gilder's grocery, Buck's Coffee Shop today) from the late 1960s to the early 1990s. While she painted and sold art work, she also wrote award-winning poetry, producing two collections of her works: *Summer Mountain: Poems of the Hills* in 1986 and *Poems for Women* in 1993. In almost every poem, her wit and wisdom reigned, as in the clever "Apparent Situation."[729]

> *If a parent spanks a child*
> *Whether angrily or mild,*
> *We all know the parent is at fault.*
> *If the child is a terror*
> *And the parent's 'no' is never,*
> *It's vowed that the folks aren't worth their salt.*
>
> *When the child is in his teens*
> *And his jeans are full of beans,*
> *Mom and Pop are looked on with a frown.*
> *But if the youth stays under thumb*
> *Till he's accused of being dumb,*
> *His parents are bad-mouthed all over town.*
>
> *The strain is very taxing*
> *Because the world is so exacting,*
> *There isn't any way they can win.*
> *I've done some long reflection*
> *And till children reach perfection,*
> *The parents will have to take it on the chin.*

The Highlands author who best filled the void left by the late Bess Hines Harkins was Virginia Edwards Fleming, whose *So Tender the Spirit* in 1985 and *Wellspring* in 1986 established her as heir to the woods wanderer. Though most of her poetry is written for or about children, its primary focus is on the natural beauty she knew so well as a child growing up in Highlands. A published poet at the age of nine, she later wrote for magazines, newspapers, and books while teaching nursery school in New Jersey and summering at the old family home in Highlands. She has been active in poetry societies in North Carolina, New Jersey, and Pennsylvania, winning numerous prizes, assisting children with creative writing, and entertaining audiences through public readings of her poetry. Her latest book, *Be Good to Eddie Lee* in 1993, was a plea for understanding and compassion of the Down's syndrome child.

Her lyrics sing of the sun sinking into a sea of coral and amber, of coon dogs tearing through the timber; kittens dozing, tail curled to nose in a tiny ball; fragrant wisteria, purple phlox, red Service leaves signaling the coming of fall, and the leaving of home, too painful to feel the loss. Like her friend Bess, she too wrote a loving tribute to Highlands.[730]

> *I would return to the mountains again*
> *In the spring and know once more*
> *The freshness of the falling rain,*
> *The woodland, sweet with trillium to explore.*
>
> *I would return to the mountains soon*
> *In summer and, climbing to great height,*
> *Would grasp the closeness of the moon,*
> *Rising above the treetops, beckoning the night.*
>
> *I would return to the mountains when*
> *The fall appears and I would gaze*
> *Into Blue Valley once again*
> *At variegated trees ablaze*
> *And, should the winter come around*
> *So quickly, as it oft can do,*
> *My feet would up and homeward bound*
> *To snow-topped mountains, skies clear blue.*

Ironically, of all the poets of Highlands, perhaps the one least honored in his own village was a former biographee of *Who's Who in the World*. Poet, publisher, and man of letters, he was revered by the American poet, critic, and editor Ezra Pound as one of the few men of his generation "whose business it is to define culture and make civilization." The dean of American poets, Dr. William Carlos Williams, said of his poetry and the poetry of those he chose to publish, "It is because of the quality of your poems and those of your peers that I feel my generation counted for something. The democratic idiom is all there."

Jonathan Williams, an Asheville native and distant cousin of novelist Thomas Wolfe, has lived in Highlands part of every year since 1941.[731] In 1951 he founded the Jargon Society at Black Mountain College to publish and support unknown, obscure, or "difficult" writers and poets. Jargon published authors who might otherwise be ignored by large publishing houses because they lacked the large public appeal needed to make the bestseller lists. It operated, as Jonathan described it, "in the back of the beyond," trying to publish "the strays, the mavericks, the generous, the non-adventitious, that is, those afflicted with both vision and craft."

Modern authors like Robert Creeley, Robert Duncan, Charles Olson, Denise Levertov, Louis Zukofsky, Irving Layton, Michael McClure, and many more owe their current reputation to a large extent to their birth in a *Jargon* publication. Counting from its first issue, the Jargon Society had published by the end of the twentieth century 118 titles.

When Jonathan wasn't wintering at *Skywinding*, his Scaly Mountain home, he was summering in a nineteenth-century hiding at Corn Close, his cottage in Dentdale, Sedbergh, Cumbria, England. By 1965 he had published eleven collections of his own poems and given more than three hundred readings at universities. American novelist, critic, and poet Edward Dahlberg called him "the most lyrical of the young poets—and you can throw in most of the older, decayed ones too. The most cultivated of the whole brood."

In 1969 he became the first poet in North Carolina history to be published by the University of North Carolina Press with his *Ear in Bartram's Tree: Selected Poems 1957–1967*. James Dickey praised him as "a man, a poet, and a joyous laborer in the literary world, my generation has not the equal of Jonathan Williams or anything like it."

The fact that few in Highlands know Jonathan Williams is quite understandable to Jonathan himself. Poetry for him has always been something not made just to be sold. "When I write a poem about my neighbor Uncle Iv Owens," he explains, "it's a celebration of Uncle Iv and what he was, not something I make to sell."

There have been times, of course, when he despaired that anything he ever achieved would be recognized west of the Yadkin River, for even Uncle Iven, his kindly mountain neighbor, would skirt the difficult issue of the poet and tell people that Jonathan was in the "poultry business." And Jonathan would agree that if a poet made the mistake of counting heads, he'd do better getting a "real job" and becoming "a statistic." Poets, he felt,

are an endangered species. They are in the same position as the morel, the pileated woodpecker, and the rattlesnake, all of which are endangered. Still I would personally feel a loss at living in a locale without those creatures, and I think that poets are the same way . . . . Poetry is an enhancement to existence, and there would be something missing without it just like the world would be a little worse off without the pileated woodpecker or the morel.

Jonathan, by his own admission, is first a poet, and then a designer, editor, photographer, publisher, polemicist, champion correspondent, evangelist, idiot, world-class hiker, and sorehead. He appreciates the great outdoors, having hiked almost 2,000 miles of the Appalachian Trail and almost as many in the British Isles and on the European continent. He favors country living and banjo pickers like Earl Scruggs, yet has a cultured taste for gourmet food, fine wines, and classical music. He is a man of imposing physical size with a soft yet deep, authoritative voice.

At first glance his works might appear obscure, if not iconoclastic. William Carlos Williams described the affect of his poetry: "At first it shocks, even repels, such a man as myself, but in a few days, or a month, or a year, we rush to it drooling at the mouth, as if it were a fruit, an apple in winter."

With titles like *Elite/Elate Poems* published in 1979, *Get Hot or Get Out* and *Magpie's Bagpipe: Selected Essays* in 1982, *In the Azure Over the Squalor: Ransackings and Shorings* in 1985, and *Blues & Roots/Rue & Bluets: A Garland for the Southern Appalachians* also in 1985, it's little wonder that the average Joe would show no interest in his publications. Indeed, the only title published by his Jargon Society that truly captured the public's fancy was Ernest Mickler's *White Trash Cooking*, which Jonathan gave to Ten Speed Press because it "sold."

But to hear him speak on "Aunt Mnemosyne's Punktatum Conserve, or How to Make Poems out of Macon County, North Carolina," as Highlanders did at the Hudson Library in 1975, was to revel in the man's finely honed sense of humor and his keen appreciation of all the various facets of life.

His definition of a writer was that of a man who listened to talk, heard with sharp ears, and took the trouble to write it down. Poems were not supposed to be understood so much as heard. His favorite word was "common," for it was the common words of the common people that had the earthiness, the tang of the language.

And for his audience that evening in 1975, the examples he read from his own poetry opened ears and hearts to the genuine essence of poetry.[732] Consider his lyric about Highlands' own Butler Jenkins:

> *you live until you die—*
> *if the limb don't fall*

And Sam Creswell, Auto Mechanic:

> *your points is blue*
> *and your timing's*
> *a week off*

Aunt Creasy on work:

> *Shucks*
> *I make the livin*

576

Uncle
just make the livin
worthwhile.

Creasy Webb Jenkins and her husband John

About Doris Talley, as housewife and gardener:

but pretty though as
roses is
you can put up with
the thorns

Or Ben Hensley's lyrical thoughts on nature from his home foundry near Spruce Pine:

up on Smoky
you ease up at daybust
and see the first
light in the tops of the tulip trees

now boys that just naturally
grinds and polishes
the soul

Jonathan was born in Asheville in 1929, educated at Black Mountain College, the Illinois Institute of Technology, and spent a year at Princeton University. But it was not so much his formal education as his innate soul that produced in 1969 such works as *Six Rusticated, Wall-eyed Poems* with graphics by Dana Atchley and *The Apocryphal, Oracular Yeah-Sayings of Mae West* with lithographs by Raoul Middleman.

With the publication of his latest work, *Blackbird Dust*, in 2000, Jonathan has established himself, from Buckminster Fuller's perspective, as America's Johnny Appleseed; in Hugh Kenner's estimation, as America's truffle-hound of poetry. Ray Olson calls him the "Buster Keaton of aesthetes," whose poems and essays "modulate from fustian to foolery, from compassion to outrage, so virtuosically that all you can do is bark, like you do when a house wall falls on Buster, who stands precisely where the paneless window lands." Williams, he claims, "also knows where to stand, and what for."

In Williams' view of himself he is a Southern-Fried Bourgeoisophobe who prefers mountains to humanoid ant heaps and finds value only on the margins, discovering people and places that no one knew they needed to know or look at or listen to or visit.

Jonathan's assistant at directing the Jargon Society is Thomas Meyer, a graduate of Bard College who also lives at Scaly Mountain and in Cumbria, England, and has published poetry since the late sixties. His first collection, *The Bang Book*, appeared in 1971. Among his subsequent books, pamphlets, and portfolios were *Poikilos, Umbrella of Æsculapius* in 1975, *Uranian Roses* in 1977, *Staves Calends Legends* in 1979, and *Sappho's Raft* in 1982, the last of which Guy Davenport reviewed as "sharply original" in that it showed poetry to be "an art rather than a letter scrawled to the world or mumbled at random."

Tom collaborated with Sandra Fisher over a period of twelve years on three occasions involving paintings, pastels, monotypes, sonnets, inventions, and translations. His latest book, *At Dusk Iridescent*, appeared in 2000, a collection of twenty-five years of his poems. In it he defines the art of poetry as something that begins in the moment before silence is broken, existing first as an actual presence in the mouth and lungs that moves outward into time, the mind, and the body, capturing the imagination with abstractions and then concretizing them for the ear. In a holistic view, poetry for Tom is as much abstract as it is concrete, achieving an astonishing union of both through magic.

Sydney King Russell was a poet and musician who lived part-time in Highlands for over thirty years, achieving national recognition before his death in 1976.[733] A native of New York City, he began writing poetry at age seven, selling his first poem for publication at fourteen. His work appeared extensively in the *New Yorker, American Mercury, Good Housekeeping*, etc., and was anthologized in Thomas Moult's *Best Poems*, the *New Yorker Book of Verse*, and the very popular *Best Loved Poems of the American*

People. The founder and editor of *Poetry-Chap Book*, Russell was also co-editor of *Voices* magazine.

One of his poems, "Midsummer," sings from nostalgia about unrequited love.

> *You loved me for a little,*
> *Who could not love me long;*
> *You gave me wings of gladness*
> *And lent my spirit song.*
>
> *You loved me for an hour*
> *But only with your eyes;*
> *Your lips I could not capture*
> *By storm or by surprise.*
>
> *Your mouth that I remember*
> *With rush of sudden pain*
> *As one remembers starlight*
> *Or roses after rain . . .*
>
> *Out of a world of laughter*
> *Suddenly I am sad. . . .*
> *Day and night it haunts me,*
> *The kiss I never had.*

Bil Dwyer, the nationally syndicated comic strip artist, was a writer, artist, publisher, social commentator, philosopher, inventor, and farmer, who lived in Highlands.[734] Bil sold his first cartoon to a national magazine when only a farm boy of twelve. From then until his graduation from Yale, he published regularly in *Colliers*, *Judge*, *Life*, *Saturday Evening Post*, *Cosmopolitan*, and the *New Yorker*. He created the comic strip "When Mother Was a Girl" in the early thirties and followed it with "Dumb Dora" and the farm strip "Sandy Hill," which ran during the fifties in over 400 newspapers.

For three years he worked with Walt Disney studios helping to direct *Bambi*, *Pinocchio*, and *Fantasia*. Paramount Pictures hired him to interview actors and actresses in New York and write their personality profiles. He drew personal portraits for Will Rogers, James J. Corbett, Rudy Vallee, John Ringling, Sinclair Lewis, Norman Thomas, Leopold Stokowski, Babe Ruth, Dizzy Dean, and many others.

Even in retirement at the mountain cove of Horse Shoe, N.C., where he hoped to find a well-earned measure of peace and quiet while raising cattle and hogs, he discovered he couldn't relinquish his enormously productive way of life. He taught a correspondence course in Oriental art to over 5,000 students worldwide and imported Oriental artwork from the Far East to sell by mail order. He invented and patented the "Moist-Pal," a plastic artist's palette, and the "Cholly Chop," a kitchen appliance, both of which he marketed across the U.S.

His coming to Highlands in 1970 was a second attempt at retirement that in the end also failed. The year after his arrival he and his wife Louise established the Merry Mountaineers, a complete commercial printing and graphic service, in the old Baxter Wilson home adjacent to Central House. The first book off the press was a self-illustrated *Dictionary for Yankees and Other Uneducated People*. Based on his twenty-year study of Southern English, it purported to correct definitions "for words most often misused by Northern friends," but it also defined 900 authentic usages of Southern dialect, such as "She's gettin' too ageable to marry," and "cat-a-gogling" for walking sideways, and keeping your "daubers" up for showing courage.

In 1974 Louise helped him produce *Southern Appalachian Mountain Cookin'*, a collection of old recipes gathered from mountain women who rarely bothered to write them down, including chitterlin's, hoot n' holler biscuits, fried green tomatoes, roast stuffed coon, and 'simmon cake. The book contained excellent recipes, including adjustments for high altitude baking, and ended with a chapter on "Moonshine Makin'" and a diagram for brewing one's own.

Over the next ten years there followed a stream of successful books. *Thangs Yankees Don' Know* and *Southern Sayin's for Yankees and Other Immigrants* were published at the Main Street shop before the Merry Mountaineer moved in 1977 to the Cashiers Road.

2001 Southern Superstitions and *How Tuh Live in the Kooky South* appeared the next year, followed shortly by *Cookin' Yankees Ain't Et*, *Sexy Birds of the South*, and *Ol' Mountain an' Southland Songs*. All together these nine titles sold hundreds of thousands of copies across the U.S., particularly in the South.

Even while producing his books, Bil continued to paint. He held one-man shows of his watercolors from Tampa and St. Petersburg to the National Gallery in Washington, selling over four hundred to eager buyers. At the time of his death in the nineties he was discovering and developing a new style of art that incorporated primitive symbols of the American Indian and hieroglyphics of ancient Egypt and Indian Sanskrit into works of child-like simplicity. He once confided to me his conviction that the child of art is all too often destroyed by training, indeed that greatness in art begins with the child.

Highlands summer resident and author Lloyd Wendt was a journalist who was hired by the *Chicago Tribune* in 1934 and eventually became its Sunday editor. He covered the Selma, Ala., scene during one of Martin Luther King's civil rights marches and was one of the first American newsmen to report from behind the Berlin Wall in East Germany, Poland, and Russia. He covered the war in Vietnam and the Six-Day conflict between Israel and Egypt and was a frequently interviewer of President Nixon. Opposed to adversarial journalism, he believed in investigative journalism that treated its subjects with respect without harassing them.

Among the books he authored were histories of two famous newspapers, the *Chicago Tribune* and the *Wall Street Journal*, and a famous department store, Marshall Field and Company, along with several investigations of Chicago machine politics. He wrote a story of the American Indians and, most recently, a world history of the evolving relationship between men and dogs. He divided his retirement between Highlands and Sarasota.

Sandra Mackey is another journalist from Highlands and Atlanta whose books on Saudi Arabia, Lebanon, Iraq, and Iran gave fresh personal insights into the history, religion, and politics of the Middle East, including the status of women in strict Islamic societies. Internationally recognized as an expert on the rich and complex Arabic culture, she has sought to create a climate of American understanding and empathy with its people.

Sometimes authors owe much of their authenticity to their editors, such as the debt owed to Max Perkins by Thomas Wolfe, Ernest Hemingway, Marjorie Rawlings, and F. Scott Fitzgerald. Dr. Barbara "Bobbie" Reitt of Highlands has served in this capacity as editor of publications in the life sciences, as well as history, philosophy, and religion.

Having established Reitt Editing Services, she has clarified and polished complex and technical works for the American Geriatric Society, Family Medicine Review, Southern Regional Education Board, Southern Council on Collegiate Education for Nursing, N.C. Medical Society, Spina Bifida Association of America, and Centers for Disease Control and Prevention. In addition she has authored publications about the history and role of the professional editor and published articles on Southern writers, especially women.

Near the end of the twentieth century the little town of Highlands was recognized for its potential in the world of literature when the spring edition of Highlands School's literary magazine, *Crossroads*, won first place in the 1998 Senior High School Division of the N.C. Literary and Historical Association's statewide competition. Sponsored by English teacher Beverly VanHook, it was only in its third year of publication, having won second prize the previous year.

In 2000 VanHook herself became the first teacher at Highlands School to earn certification by the National Board for Professional Teaching Standards.

Photography

If the man who paints a tree, or flower, or person exactly as it appears before him is an artist, then the king of the imitative artists is the photographer. But when the photographer sees through the surface of his model to its core, then he transcends imitation to become the creator, the true artist.

The earliest of the true artists of photography to discover Highlands was John Bundy, who arrived from Indiana in August, 1883, to live with Joshua Hadley in the recently vacated Dimick house on East Main.[735] For the next two months, beginning with a photograph of Highlands House, he took views of the new village and its surroundings, including street scenes, the mountains Satulah, Fodderstack, and Whiteside and Glen and Cullasaja (Dry) Falls. These he put on exhibition for the public at Bascom's store.

Photo of Cullasaja (Dry) Falls taken by John Bundy in 1883.

Bundy's successor in Western North Carolina was R. Henry Scadin, a twenty-five-year-old photographer and fruit grower who came to North Carolina with his wife Kate in 1886 after living in Michigan and Vermont.[736] Scadin kept meticulous diaries of his life from 1886 to 1921, which Kate and his son Dewey continued until five years after his death in Vermont in 1923.

With the eye of a genuine artist, Scadin photographed the local scenery and people near the present towns of Brevard, Tryon, Saluda, Sapphire, and

Asheville, extending as far west as Highlands. Since 1989, the University of North Carolina at Asheville has collected 1,200 of his glass plate negatives, covering 1889–1920, in its D. H. Ramsey Special Collection, including forty-three manuscripts of his own diaries and five of his wife and son.

Cullasagee (Dry) Falls, 1898. Photo from R. H. Scadin Collection, UNC-A.

Granite City, 1901. Photo from R. H. Scadin Collection, UNC-A.

Over fifty of these photographs focus on Highlands and vicinity, including mountains and waterfalls; overviews of the town from Sunset Rocks,
Bear Pen, Satulah, and Dog Mountain; and the various Inns: Highlands
House, Satulah House, Hall House, Davis House (later Lee's Inn), and Islington (later King's Inn). His shots of these and other scenes, such as the

584

sanatorium, *Castle Far-a-way*, *Kalalanta*, the primeval forest, the Episcopal and Presbyterian churches, and several roads approaching Highlands are the views we still have today.

On occasion he felt inspired to compose a poem and illustrate it, such as this lyric about Highlands.[737]

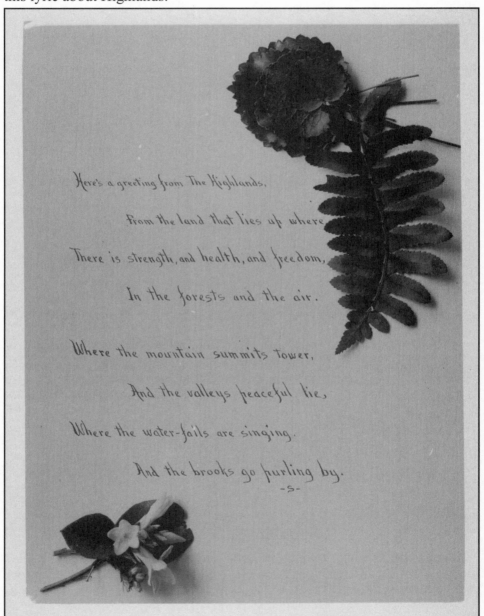

Here's a greeting from The Highlands,

From the land that lies up where

There is strength, and health, and freedom,

In the forests and the air.

Where the mountain summits tower,

And the valleys peaceful lie,

Where the water-falls are singing,

And the brooks go purling by.

-5-

Photo from R. H. Scadin Collection, UNC-A, 1897.

Here's a greeting from the Highlands,
From the land that lies up where
There is strength, and health, and freedom,
In the forests and the air.

Where the mountain summits tower,
And the valleys peaceful lie,
Where the water-falls are singing,
And the brooks go purling by.

R. Henry Scadin. Photo by Hiram Glover, 1903. Photo from R. H. Scadin Collection, UNC-A.

He captured sights of Whiteside Cove and Mountain, Shortoff, Satulah, Horse Cove, Glen and Dry Falls, and Lower Cullasaja Falls that few photographers since have been able to surpass for their perspective and composition as well as graphic detail.

In 1897 he put together some "combination views" for a booklet of Highlands, and Mrs. Baxter White sold them for him at her country store. His photos were also available through H. M. Bascom, Alex Anderson, Frank Walden, and Capt. Ravenel.

Many of his subsequent Highlands scenes he photographed during 1897 and 1898, despite frequent colds and periods of homesickness that left him physically debilitated and mentally depressed. Beginning in 1907 he converted a number of his photos into hand-colored postcards, which Miss Albertina Staub sold for him in Highlands. He added street scenes and panoramic views in 1910.

But by 1913 poor health had begun to take its toll. Accustomed to walking between Highlands and Whiteside Cove, Horse Cove, Franklin, and Sapphire, he complained at age fifty-two that the treks had become very tiring. "I will have to give up such tramps before long as I find them very hard for me to do now," he lamented in his diary.

In 1913 he wrote to Alex Anderson that he had moved for his health from Amherst, Massachusetts, to Dana, N.C. And having received from Anderson no further orders for Highlands cards, he had destroyed the glass negatives rather than transport them with him.

By 1915 he was asking Miss Staub to put up all his pictures and postcards "for sale at half price, as I want to close them out." No further mention is made of photos taken at Highlands. His most productive period on the plateau had spanned sixteen years from 1896 to 1912, and many of his masterpieces are still circulated today as copies of those originals that once sold as individual pictures, postcards, booklets, and calendars.

The next photographer of note to pass through Highlands was a Japanese immigrant living in Asheville whom Frank Cook hired to photograph several Highlands scenes. George Masa, born as Masahara Izuka in 1881, was pursuing a career in engineering at Meige University when a Methodist missionary converted him to Christianity and introduced him to the United States.[738] The twenty-year-old youth stole passage on a ship and registered as George Masa at the University of Califomia, where he majored in mining engineering. He worked in Colorado as an engineer and in 1915 came to Asheville as an employee of Grove Park Inn. There he fell in love with the mountains and developed a passionate interest in photography.

George Masa (Masahara Izuka), 1881–1933

An avid hiker, he was also a perfectionist who would hike for twenty miles to remote spots and wait for hours for the perfect photo. Consummate engineer that he was, he mapped hundreds of uncleared trails in the Southern Appalachian Mountains with a contraption he'd built to measure distance. Removing the seat and back wheel from a bicycle, he attached an odometer to the front wheel which he pushed ahead as he walked, a bandana around his head to catch the perspiration, for he walked at a swift gait. One tourist, who was hiking with Tom Alexander in 1972 and felt faint from exhaustion, stopped only long enough to glimpse Masa whiz by and promptly implored Alexander, "Take me home! I just saw an Indian chasing us on a bicycle!"

Masa was taking pictures for an article by Horace Kephart in National Geographic when Frank Cook invited him to Highlands in 1929. It cost Cook more than he had anticipated, for Masa stayed two weeks, refusing to take a picture unless the light was exactly right. He photographed Satulah; the views from Robert Eskrigge's *World's End*, Sunset Rocks, and Sunrise Rocks; *Kalalanta*, which belonged at the time to the Salinases; Whiteside Mountain from Bearpen, the new Highlands Estates Golf Course, Camp Parry-dise, and several falls, including Glen Falls and Cullasaja (Dry) Falls. Some of these he incorporated into *Land of the Sky*, a promotional booklet published in 1930. In 1933 he and newspaperman George McCoy published a *Guide to the Smoky Mountains National Park* based on Masa's measurements and maps. In the eighteen years that he practiced his craft, he earned the unrivaled honor of being called "the greatest photographer of the Great Smoky Mountains."

Masa's ending was pitiable, for with all his talent and fame, including his role as founder of the Carolina Appalachian Trail Club, he died of influenza at age fifty-one on June 21, 1933, penniless.

L to R: Billy McCoy, Albie McCall, Minnie Edwards, Harvey Talley

L to R: Ed Picklesimer, Alma Keener, Wen McKinney, Callie Beale
Photos by Burton Talbott, 1970–73

Burton Talbott, a Missourian who lived in the old Rogers house in Buck Creek, was a portrait photographer who came to Highlands from Atlanta during the 1940s and spent the seventies and eighties recording some 200 of the area's well-known pioneers until arthritis spoiled his aim.[739] His subjects, which he displayed in black-and-white and color at his Church Street shop, Burdick Galleries, came from Highlands, Buck Creek, Gold Mine, and Ellijay.

He captured striking facial expressions of Uncle Billy McCoy, Aunt Albie McCall, Aunt Minnie Edwards of Central House, Harvey Talley, Gene Potts, Ed Picklesimer, Mack Wilson, Ketmit Rogers, Alma Keener, Uncle Wen McKinney, and Callie Beale and published them in the *Highlander* to accompany Lawrence Wood's genealogies. He preferred the faces of children and old-timers because they had two things in common: "First of all, they don't lie; and second, they can spot a phony a mile away."

In 1973 James "Jimmy" Valentine, son of Manson Valentine, who researched Charles Berlitz's book on the Bermuda Triangle, held his first exhibit of truly beautiful coastal photographs at the Memorial Art Center in Atlanta. They were published in 1977 in book form as *Guale, The Golden*

Coast of Georgia. With his interest in preservation and conservation of our natural resources, he established Quest Foundation in Highlands, a conservation educational center for the advancement of the environmental study of art, photography, and sound.

Bridal Veil Falls, Winter, 1977. Photo by James Valentine.

In 1979 his extraordinary perspectives on *North Carolina* appeared with text by Marguerite Schumann, containing 130 color reproductions of natural scenes from across all 500 miles of the state. Several were taken near Highlands, such as Bridal Veil Falls crystallized during the freeze in 1977, molded gneiss rock at Glen Falls, and the swirling mists of Dry Falls after a flooding rain.

In conjunction with the University of North Carolina, Valentine founded the Center for Environmental Art, Photography and Sound in Highlands, which evolved in 1982 into the Environmental Arts Center of the Highlands Biological Station. Two years later Gil Leebrick, a photographer living in

Durham, N.C., whose own photographic images focused on the quiet wonders of the land and landscape, became its director. His black and white works relied on light for their dramatic impact and effect on the emotions.

Dick Dillon was a teacher of photography at Highlands School who specialized in three-dimensional views. He could often be seen during the mid seventies flying his Cessna 150 over the Highlands area in order to take perfectly spaced aerial photos for a hand-held stereoscope. His 3-D scenes of the surrounding mountains were impressive, especially his view of Highlands crowned by Whiteside in the background, which appears as the frontispiece of this book.

The Cullasaja River in Summer, 1996, and Ravenel Lake (formerly Lindenwood Lake) in Winter, 1990. Photos by Kevin Fitz Patrick.

Kevin Fitz Patrick, who held a master's degree in media arts, and Howard Hill created Media Divide in 1984, which produced a program on the scenery, flora, fauna, climate, and history of Highlands and some of its institutions. The name of their business expressed the fact that the Eastern Continental Divide passed through Highlands.

Kevin's multi-imaging talents produced *Passage*, set to Aaron Copeland's "Appalachian Spring" and featuring the natural beauty of Highlands through the four seasons, which was presented at the 1982 World's Fair in Knoxville. He was the recording engineer for National Public Radio's broadcasts of selections from the Highlands Chamber Music Festival beginning in 1994. And he recorded a number of local interviews, conducted mostly by Anne Chastain but also Sylvia Thomas between 1979–89, which helped preserve the history of Highlands through the thoughts, beliefs, and voices of its old-timers before they passed away. Listed later in the Appendix, several of these interviews served as the basis for personalities portrayed in this book.

Mark Hutchinson of Kennesaw, Georgia, does not live in Highlands, but he has been photographing Highlands scenes for over eighteen years, having produced a booklet, *Highlands: Pictures in Serenity*, in 1993 that focused, not on the town and its growth, but on scenes of nature surrounding it. A student of landscape photographer Eliot Porter, Hutchinson's close-ups feature mountains, waterfalls, and rivers but also rocks, trees, shrubs, flowers, and living creatures in extraordinary color and detail. Almost none of his subjects are man-made since his stated intent is to unfold the wonders of the land that is not yet civilized; in other words, untamed.

Lake Sequoyah. Photo by Mark W. Hutchinson, 2001

Public Lectures and Seminars

Highlanders have always enjoyed lectures, debates, and seminars, beginning with the Highlands Debating, Literary, and Scientific societies in the 1880s. Lectures have flourished at the Highlands Museum since its founding in the 1930s and at the Hudson Library throughout its history.

In 1989 the library sponsored a lecture series organized by Curtis Meltzer and Ran Shaffner of Highlands and Cliff Lovin and Max Williams of Cullowhee, which soon expanded into the Highlands–Western Carolina University Lecture Series. By 1992 it had joined Southwestern Community, Piedmont, and Brevard colleges as sponsors of a series of summer seminars, lectures, and cabarets, known today as the Center for Life Enrichment.

The center began conducting seminars in continuing education in 1993, including classes in nature study, architecture, financial planning, music appreciation, computer instruction, Civil War history, literature, creative writing, beginning and duplicate bridge, psychology, Bible study, health and nutrition, cooking, and memory improvement. During the 2000 season as many as 1,500 interested adults participated in the program series, led today by Walter Kalaf of Highlands and St. Petersburg, Florida.

A parallel to the Center for Life Enrichment was the Mountain Retreat and Learning Center, popularly known as The Mountain, which arose in 1979 on the abandoned site of Camp Highlander, where Camp Parry-dise once thrived. An independent affiliate of the Unitarians, it serves today as a youth and intergenerational facility with classes celebrating the indigenous Appalachian heritage and students drawn from all across the Country.

With liberal intentions, it holds spiritual retreats and workshops for all ages on such topics as spirituality, ecology and the environment, a caring community, and the diversity of life. Directed since 1990 by Tom Worth, it was listed in *USA Today* as one of ten great places in the U.S. to renew the soul.

In 1987 Dr. Creighton Peden, along with twenty-five nationally recognized religious scholars, founded what would eventually become the Highlands Institute for American Religious and Philosophical Thought (HIARPT), a scholarly community intent on reconciling the ancient antagonism between religion and philosophy.

Ever since its founding, it has treated the public to free lectures, seminars, and workshops on topics of religion and philosophy in America, especially liberalism and naturalism.[740] It has also held international conferences on philosophical theology at St. Andrews University in Scotland and in conjunction with the American Academy of Religion in Washington, D.C.

By the last eighties Highlands was hosting a wide variety of visual and performing arts scattered among the Playhouse, Civic Center, Community Building, Nature Center, Hudson Library, Bascom–Louise Gallery, and local churches. Indeed, some of the arts lived like nomads with no home at all. A group of devotees of the arts inspired by Elizabeth Griffin considered creating a Cultural Arts Center to house all these various arts under one roof.

But the time was not right. The idea had to wait twelve years before another group succeeded in purchasing the vacated Community Bible Church building on Chestnut Street and, supported by the town, renovated it as a new Performing Arts Center, designed by architect Peter Jefferson. In 2000 this Center brought together the Highlands-Cashiers Chamber Music Festival, the Highlands Community Players, the Bascom–Louise Gallery film Series, the Highlands Institute for American Religious and Philosophical Thought, the Center for Life Enrichment Lecture and Cabaret series, and music groups such as Kathy Teem's popular Highlands School Band and Highlands Community Band. If it's true that a culture is in full flower where the fine arts flourish, then Highlands today is in full bloom.

28. For Years to Come

To preserve the quality of life in our mountain communities, the land on which it lies, and the animal/plant life that inhabit this area. Our goals are not to stop expansion altogether, but to promote environmentally safe, low-density development that will enhance our townships in years to come.

—Highlands/Cashiers Conservation League, 1999

The ancestor of the present-day Highlands Land Trust was the Highlands Improvement Association, which existed as early as 1883. It was formed to monitor the town's growth eight years into its existence.[741] In that year a Ladies Floral and Industrial Society created a "permanent" two-acre Highlands Park on the site of the current Playhouse and Fire Station. The intent of both organizations was to protect and preserve as well as promote the natural beauty of Highlands while the business district was growing.

Catawba Rhododendron (rhododendron catawbiense) and Kalmia or Mountainlaurel of the Southern Appalachians. Latin names are useful here since native Highlanders call rhododendron laurel *and laurel* ivy.

The president of the unofficial Highlands Improvement Association in 1887, when it was known as the Highlands Advertising and Improvement Association, was the physician Dr. Henry O'Farrell. By the turn of the century, with the introduction to Appalachia of tradesmen, land speculators, and lumber men preaching "modern improvements," the Highlands Improvement Society officially incorporated under the presidency of Dr. Emma Billstein, wife of Baltimore printer Nathan Billstein.

The intent of the new corporation in 1905 was first and foremost to preserve the natural beauty and rural aspect of the Highlands region as stated in its purpose: "to promote the prosperity and progress of Highlands by systematic effort; to guard its natural beauties and as far as possible to restore those that have perished; to guard and maintain its healthful climate; to initiate and aid public measures that tend directly or indirectly to further these aims; to create by word and deed an enlightened public opinion that shall cherish and safeguard its unique scenic and sanitary possessions."[742]

To this end the society formed a trail committee to erect signs and keep the trails cleared to places of scenic interest. In 1908 it planted maple trees along Main and 4th streets. It helped improve the road to the top of Sunset Rocks and the spring near the rocks.

In 1909, under the leadership of Miss Marguerite Ravenel, the society made its first purchase. It bought the summit of Satulah Mountain, which Miss Ravenel's father, Capt. Prioleau Ravenel, Sr., had made accessible in 1890 by building a road to the top. The organizer of the purchase, who herself was subsequently president, was Louise Hill of Charleston, S.C., and Washington, D.C. At a meeting on September 1, 1909, a subscription list was begun with over $250, and by October 6 the entire purchase price of $500 was subscribed. The 32-acre park was dedicated to public use in perpetuity.

Looking back as late as 1930, Professor Harbison wrote about the significance of this gift of the summit of Satulah Mountain in terms of genuine pride. The top of Satulah, he exclaimed, "is OURS, ours to keep forever. No money grubbing skinflint without any soul can ever acquire this top and then put up a toll gate to charge admission to what he the same as stole from God. I mean just what I say. No man has a right or can acquire a right to charge his fellow man toll to visit the tops of God's mountains."

As a start, the society built at the top of Satulah a stone shelter house "for the benefit and protection of those who desire to spend the night on the summit for the purpose of beholding the beauties of the sunset, of the starlit heavens, and the glories of the sunrise." It improved Ravenel's access road, opened and cleared trails to otherwise inaccessible areas, and marked them by signs.

Miss Albertina Staub and Mrs. Luther Rice contributed tirelessly to these projects until property had changed hands enough to restrict further access. In the early 1920s the Kelsey Trail, overgrown with low branches and shrubbery, was reopened to Whiteside Mountain. The Improvement Society gave $100 toward that end and helped work on the trail and the mountain.

Meanwhile, the original motives for founding the Improvement Society had found their rebirth in another permanent dedication of land for public use. Just as the society had preserved the summit of Satulah from future development, a new organization arose to save Sunset Rocks as well. After the death of Capt. Ravenel in 1902, a Ravenel Park Association was formed in 1914 and Ravenel's heirs donated Sunset Rocks to the town of Highlands.[743] Eventually the two public parks would enjoy the joint protection of the combined Satulah Summit and Ravenel Park Association.

While the Improvement Society still shared the new association's concern for preserving Highlands' natural beauty, it was also interested in a variety of projects promoting the town's general welfare. For instance, Florence Perry, an English resident of Highlands, led its efforts to raise $400 to construct a town clock, which sat atop the two-story school on the site of the present ABC store. She wrote a witty play, filled with local color and well attended, to supplement moneys raised by public subscription.

The society also used on occasion the considerable influence of its members to influence its legislators in Raleigh and congressmen in Washington to favor conservation causes, protect the National Parks, and pass laws beneficial to the region. For example, its members lobbied Senator Overman and Representative Weaver to protect all national reservations, especially the beautiful Bechler Meadows in the Yellowstone National Park, which was being threatened by the state of Idaho on behalf of its sugar-beet growers.[744]

On many occasions the society planted and cared for trees to improve the Highlands environment. In 1929 it created a small triangular park at the intersection of Church and 5th, having rerouted 5th around to the east, and erected a granite memorial to Samuel Kelsey, Sr., honoring him as one of the founders of Highlands. It raised well over $200 to construct a drinking fountain in the little park, which was located within sight of Kelsey's old home.

Soon the activities of the society diminished, and membership dwindled to the point that it almost disbanded. Before expiring entirely, however, it merged in 1934 with a very active Highlands Community Club, intent on raising money for recreational programs for the young people of the town. This club, founded in 1925 by Stella Marett and a number of civic-minded women including Isabel Gilbert, was hoping to erect a recreational building. While it planned box suppers, benefit dances, etc. to raise the necessary funds, its members also held sewing bees to make clothes for needy school children and infants.

The merger of the Highlands Improvement Society and the Highlands Community Club on September 25, 1934, produced under a new name the Satulah Club, an active independent social civic organization.[745] Although the hope for a recreational building was not fulfilled, a meeting room was added to the Hudson Library in 1939. With $825 and a bond that the women had received as a gift, their husbands constructed the Satulah Room to the rear.

Over the years, meeting from September to June, the Satulah Club held bake sales and rummage sales to raise money for such causes as a monthly contribution to the lunch fund at Highlands School, as well as support of the Highlands Cemetery Association and Head Start. Through its Bazaar it supported the hospital with substantial annual donations, while storing its white elephants in the Satulah Room. When the Hudson Library sold its building to the Episcopal Church and moved into its present quarters in 1985, the Satulah Club met in the community room of the First Presbyterian Church or at members' homes.

In 1987 the still active Satulah Summit and Ravenel Park Association chose to incorporate. In 1990 it voted to change its name to the Highlands Land Trust, Inc., the name it bears today, and began to acquire property through donations, purchases, and easements. The intent was to preserve the property in its natural state, which included protecting native plants and animals for the perpetual enjoyment of the public.

Highlands from Bear Pen, 1919. Photo from the R. H. Scadin Collection, UNC-A.

In addition to Ravenel Park and Sunset Rocks, properties placed in trust to date have included the South Satulah Summit and John Hobson parks, Ravenel Park and Sunset Rocks, Gertrude Harbison's Spring on the Walhalla Road, the Bridgers property at the northwest corner of 4th and Foreman Road, the Sargent conservation easement near the Biological Station, and various nature trails.

Most recently the Trust raised over half a million dollars to purchase the north summit of Satulah, thus ensuring that the entire top of the mountain would be a public park forever, as intended by the original purchase of the south summit by the Improvement Society ninety years earlier.[746] It also acquired the Kelsey Trail Preserve from the Edwards family at the north end of 5th Street, so as to safeguard the last remnant of Highlands' most famous trail in its natural state. And in 2001 it bought the 7.8-acre Betty Lindsey tract to protect the rest of the trail to the top of Little Bearpen Mountain. In 2000 Christine Simmons gave the Trust a conservation easement on the eighty-six acres of her Clear Creek property in order to preserve the pristine condition of its wooded hillsides, open pastures, streams, and ponds.

With purchases and gifts like these, history had come full circle, for such attention to preserving the natural beauty and rural heritage of the area had been the stated purpose for the founding of the original Highlands Improvement Society way back in the town's infancy.

In early 1999 a group of environmentally conscious individuals, facing the very real threat of overdevelopment of the Highlands plateau, formed the Highlands/Cashiers Conservation League. It sought to preserve the quality of life in the surrounding mountain communities, by protecting the land on which they thrived and the animal and plant life. The League's stated goal was "not to stop expansion altogether, but to promote environmentally safe, low density development that will enhance our townships in years to come."[747]

President Pat Boyd, vice president Edna Foster, and treasurer Ed Harless led thirty-five dedicated conservationists, who felt that a conservancy league of individuals and organizations might help assure quality development in an environmentally fragile rainforest such as the Highlands plateau. They set as top priorities the identification and strict monitoring of new developments for environmental safety.

Working hand in hand with the Highlands Land Trust, this new organization addressed immediately two perceived threats to the environment. One was a proposed U.S. Forest Service exchange of forty-nine acres near Franklin for thirty acres near Shortoff Mountain. Mark Murrah intended to develop Shortoff, which the Conservation League felt would eliminate popular hiking trails, a vital wildlife habitat, and essential watershed protection in the Cullasaja River drainage. The exchange was averted.

The other involved Highlands Cove, a new multi-million dollar golfing community proposing to develop over 225 homes, a restaurant, golf course, clubhouse, townhouses, condominiums, and retail shops in an environmentally sensitive area in Jackson County between Highlands and Cashiers.[748] The impact such a development might have on the watershed, including its wetlands, bogs, creeks, lakes, and wells, and on traffic along U.S. 64 was considered sufficient cause for concern. At century's end the League was engaged in an intense campaign for redesign and reissued permits for the Cove project.

"Save the Planet" has been the general cry of a growing number of groups, like the Land Trust and the Conservation League, intent on protecting the natural beauty of Highlands and the quality of its environs. The recently formed Upper Cullasaja Watershed, Little Tennessee Watershed, and Chattooga River Watershed associations along with the Western Carolina Alliance, Highlands Biological Station, and Nature Conservancy are all functioning according to long-term goals that regard short-term motives as suicidal.

The Devil's Courthouse tract of land north of Whiteside Mountain, guarded by the shadow of the Bear. Photo by the author, 5:30 P.M., October, 1988.

The premise for their concerns was perhaps best expressed by Chief Seattle's now-famous response to President George Washington's request to buy what Washington presumed to be Seattle's land. Seattle, responding on behalf of his Suquamish tribe, argued,

> *This we know: the earth does not belong to man, man belongs to the earth. All things are connected like the blood that unites us all. Man did not weave the web of life, he is merely a strand in it. Whatever he does to the web, he does to himself.*

The wise Chief, like his tribe, felt that any decision affecting land should be governed by how it would affect those living on it to the seventh generation. The distinction between short-sighted and far-reaching decisions was for him crucial: a matter of life or death. He told General Washington,

Your destiny is a mystery to us. What will happen when the buffalo are all slaughtered? The wild horses tamed? What will happen when the secret corners are heavy with the scent of many men and the view of the ripe hills is blotted by talking wires? Where will the thicket be? Gone! And what is it to say goodbye to the swift pony and the hunt? The end of living and the beginning of survival.

Highlands from Biscuit Rock, early 1896. Photo probably by R. Henry Scadin, courtesy of Hudson Library archives. Construction on the Episcopal church would not begin until August of 1896.

29. A Lament and a Prayer

*This time, like all other times, is a very good one, if we but know wh at
to do with it.*

—Ralph Waldo Emerson

Wouldn't the old gentleman who thought Highlands looked "plum like a
city" in 1884 be amazed today? Highlands is huge! On the other hand, in the
opinion of an Atlantan or a visitor from Miami, Washington, or New York,
our "city" will never ever be more than a village. With 1,047 residents, it
can hardly be considered the great population center that Kelsey envisioned,
even inclusive of the 20,000 that reportedly swell the summer season.

Such a comparison, however, doesn't detract in the least from the basic
truth:

In the big world things happen that are important;
in the little world, even more so.

The threat of urban growth looms ever more destructive in a village or
small town than in a metropolis where it is far less noticed. The argument
that has propelled Highlands into its present stage of urban development has
claimed that if a town doesn't grow, it dies. Indeed, proponents of the "bigger is better" argument state that growth is inevitable. They give little or no
consideration to an optimum population, which the town must not exceed,
lest in doing so it lose its essential bloom and die from overgrowth.

Russell England, who was asked by the Macon County League of
Women Voters and the Little Tennessee Wattershed Association in 1999 to
speak on the desirability of growth and progress, pointed out that as long as
planning was driven by population projections, it would certainly benefit
banks, developers, and the media, but at what cost to the populace in loss of
quality of life?[749]

It is true that Highlands, like other popular American towns in the throes
of development, has already begun to suffer higher taxes, more crime, air
and water pollution, congestion, noise, proliferation of debt, depletion of
stored energy, and loss of individual freedoms with more laws and more
rules—all problems that Russell regarded as accompanying growth.

He argued that without impact fees to make developers rather than the
public financially responsible for increased infrastructural needs, growth in
the long term becomes no longer sustainable. Open spaces and farm lands,
gobbled up by speculators at little cost to themselves, are converted to high
density housing developments and shopping centers at great profit.

The big question involves equating growth with progress. When small
business supports growth to the point that big stores and chains arrive and

dominate the market, then small businesses crumple and fail where they once struggled but survived.

There's a strong argument for the fact that if Highlands were to bring growth to a screeching stop and consolidate what it has currently achieved, it would not die at all but live like any adult that no longer needs the quantity of nourishment demanded by the famished child or insatiable adolescent. Undoubtedly the stakes are higher for a village like Highlands than for larger cities whose residents visit the town for love of what makes it different rather than what duplicates what they already have at home.

The old adage, you pay a price for what you get, usually means that the high cost of progress is not so much financial as human. Weimar Jones, owner of the *Franklin Press* from the late forties to late fifties, singled out two paradoxes of growth and development in our modern age. First, the more time-saving devices we have, the less time. And second, ironically, the more free time, the less time we devote to such things as reading, visiting, and neighborliness.[750] For those who still find the occasion and opportunity to live out these values in Highlands, the town has not grown too much to have lost its humanity.

Highlands from Sunset Rocks. Photo by the author, 1985.

The hope for Highlands' future lies in preserving many of the natural and human qualities that it still has. This, in part, is the current task faced by mayor Buck Trott and town council members Amy Patterson, Herb James,

Ron Sanders, Creighton "Zeke" Sossomon, and Mike Cavender. But in a real and larger sense the town is in the hands of its people.

Lamentations over what is forever lost are painful but futile if loss is only illusory. Bob Zoellner, great grandson of pioneer Louis Zoellner who came to Highlands in 1884, himself graduated from Highlands School as valedictorian in 1966 amidst the turmoil of America at war. Yet he expressed in his commencement address one of the best perspectives on the past, present, and future that I have encountered, especially as it applies to the little town of Highlands confronting its own intense crises on the eve of its 126th year.[751]

Bob opened with a word of advice from Ralph Waldo Emerson:

"This time, like all other times, is a very good one, if we but know what to do with it."—Ralph Waldo Emerson

There never has been an age that did not applaud the past and la-ment the present. "The illusion that times that were are better than those that are, has probably pervaded all ages," said Horace Greeley.

The Precepts Papyrus, dating back six thousand years or more—the oldest bit of known writing in existence—starts off with these star-tlingly familiar words: "Alas, times are not what they used to be!"[752] And in one way or another people have been saying that same thing in all the centuries since.

In the long panorama of man's progress, the trend has since been smooth or straight; it has been broken periodically by failures and mistakes, by crushing setbacks, and by dark periods of war and de-pression. But always, irresistibly, the element of progress has been at work. Always, out of great struggles or disasters has come a new dawn, a rebirth of life and spirit, and a powerful surge of progress carrying man onward and upward again.

Nevertheless, in times of crises people tend to lose faith in the fu-ture. Today, too, there are many who feel we have reached the end of progress, perhaps the end of civilization. There are many who feel the future holds only darkness and despair. It is true that we are faced to-day with some of the most difficult and trying problems the nation has known. It is true that the recent past does not encourage confidence or peace of mind.

But we have come through serious crises before—and America has grown stronger with each succeeding one. The times may be "piled high with difficulty," as Lincoln said in another, earlier period of cri-sis, but "we must rise with the occasion. We cannot escape history!"

No, we cannot escape history. But we can learn much from the les-sons of history. We can gain strength and courage and understanding from the past to help us meet the challenge of our modern times. The ever-recurring evidence of history is that no time is as bad as it seems. This time, like all other times, is a very good one, if we but know what to do with it.

Emerson's inspiring words are as true today as they ever were. The frontiers are never closed; the limits of progress are never reached. The future will be what we ourselves make it.

For many folks, just living in the mountains has been a struggle, even after these many years since Kelsey first founded the town on its isolated plateau. For others, it has been a vacation resort where restoration of the soul is the lure. In either case, the benefit is often a full life. Whether Highlands in the end will sell its soul or save itself is not for this book to predict. But in looking over its past, one truth emerges as paramount: there are many folks who have fallen in love with Highlands and won't forsake it.

Home of Barney and Melvina "Meb" Rose Hicks Wilson, built by Billy Webb, which they rented from Eléonore Raoul near the foot of Brushy Face on the Walhalla Rd. L. to R.: Frances (Nix), Louise, Meb, L. B., Corinne, Louis "Dud" (Louise's twin), and Patsy the donkey. Not shown: Woodrow (named after the President[753]), Bill, Tolliver, and the family's coon dog, Drum. Photo by George Masa, 1929.

Frances Wilson tells of Barney Wilson when he was young and had to leave Highlands for a short spell to install heating and plumbing for a family in Seneca.[754] He would often stand facing the mountains which he said were calling him home. Perhaps, like Barney Wilson, there are many who hear in the call of Highlands the call home.

Frances looks back on Grandpa Barney's days in the mountains as gone. Yet even now, just like then, it's still true—many children, grandchildren, great-grandchildren, and great-great-grandchildren later—whenever any Wilsons leave, the mountains call them home. It's a love that Frances claims never goes away.

Highlands from Little Yellow Mountain. Flat Mountain to the left, Billy Cabin ridge and Shortoff to the right. Photo by the author, 2000.

30. Appendices
Appendix 1
Mayors of the Town of Highlands

1879-83	George A. Jacobs	1927-29	William S. Davis
1883	Stanhope W. Hill	1929-30	George W. Marett
	(1st elected mayor)	1930-31	William S. Davis
1884-85	H. M. Bascom	1931-33	James A. Hines
1885	Stanhope W. Hill	1933-35	S. Porter Pierson
1885-86	H. M. Bascom	1935-36	S. E. "Gene" Potts
1886-87	Ebenezer Selleck	1936-37	Will W. Edwards
1887-88	Dr. H. T. O'Farrell		(acting mayor)
1888-89	John Jay Smith	1937-39	William S. Davis
1889-90	Charles L. Boynton	1939-41	Will W. Edwards
1890-91	Dr. H. T. O'Farrell	1941-47	Wilton H. Cobb
1891-92	Ebenezer Selleck	1947-49	J. O. "Buck" Beale
1892-93	Prof. T. G. Harbison	1949-55	Wilton H. Cobb
1893-94	Theron D. Walden	1955-59	V. W. "Bill" McCall
1894-1900	Dr. H. T. O'Farrell	1959-61	Charles C. Potts
1900-	H. M. Bascom	1961-62	Wilton H. Cobb
Records are missing		1962-65	A.C. "Pat" Patterson
for the years 1901–08.		1965-66	Ted Crunkleton
-1909	Prof. T. G. Harbison	1966-68	Otto F. Summer
1909-11	H. M. Bascom	1968-75	A.C. "Pat" Patterson
	(acting mayor)	1975-81	Harry R. Wright
1911-13	Charles N. Wright	1981-83	J. Steve Potts
1913-25	H. M. Bascom	1983-97	John W. Cleaveland
1925-27	John Jay Smith	1997-	A. L. "Buck" Trott

Appendix 2
Police Chiefs of Highlands

1885-	Seven-man police force: William Duncan, Wilbur Trowbridge, H. M. Bascom, John Jay Smith, Charles A. Boynton, Frank Sheldon, and William B. Cleaveland
1887-	William L. Pool (1st town marshal, Billy Potts' brother-in-law)
-1891	I. Cloer
1891-	N. C. Nicollson
1909-	W. P. Wilson
1912/13-	Ed "Bennie" Rogers
1921-22	Ike Crunkleton (town marshal)
1922-	Joseph C. Richert (1st police chief)
-1934	Ed "Bennie" Rogers
1935-36	Harold R. Rideout
1936	C. F. McKinney (reg. Policeman)
1937	Paul Seay
1937	Sam Reese
1937-45	Ed "Bennie" Rogers
1945-49	Olin Dryman
1952-53	M. Arnold Nelson
1953	Bert Wilkey
1954	P. Russell Paxton
1955-58	Henry Chastain
1958-62	Olin Dryman
1962-67	Joe Baty
1968-73	Olin Dryman
1974	Joe Baty
1974	Olin Dryman
1975-77	Wm. "Bill" Wheeler
1977	Joe Neal
1978-79	Frank Leach
1980	Cliff Saunders
1980	Ken Signor
1981	Allan Bryson
1982	Jerry Dalton
1983-88	John Fay
1988-	Jerry Cook

Appendix 3
Fire Chiefs of Highlands

1885	Joseph A. McGuire (Fire Inspector)
1887	Frank Sheldon (Fire Warden)
1894	Charles L. Boynton
1909	J. E. "Ed" Potts
1925-	Ed M. Rogers
1939	Vol. Dept. organized
1941-	Thomas Potts
1946-	Ed "Bennie" Rogers
1947-	Tom C. Harbison
1952-53	M. Arnold Nelson
1954-61	Carleton Cleaveland
1962-66	Gene Houston
1967-74	Jimmy Talley
1975-83	Bobby Houston
1984-86	Olan Vinson
1987-95	Jimmy Lowe
1996-	Mike McCall

Appendix 4
Ministers of Highlands
Methodist Church (S.=South)

1882-83	John H. Moore (S.)
1883	M. C. Smith
1883-84	David McCrackin
1884	J. D. Roberson
1884-86	J. H. Brendle (S.)
1886	J. H. Gillespie
1886-87	T. F. Marr
1887	W. S. Spencer
1887-88	A. H. Moore (S.)
1888-89	A. W. Jacobs
1889-90	J. C. Logan
1890-91	Henry Renno
1891-92	C. H. Curtis
1893-95	J. E. Abernathy
1895	George Mann
1895-96	T. B. Johnson
1896-98	W. O. Owens
1899	J. C. Campbell
1900-03	J. J. Edwards
1903-05	A. G. Loftin
1906-07	Joseph Fry
1907-08	A. N. Lewis
1908-10	R. L. Andrews
1910-12	A. P. Foster
1912-13	F. O. Dryman
1913-14	A. C. Gibbs
1914-15	W. C. Bowden
1915-16	E. B. Bell
1916-18	D. V. Howell
1918	Maldon
1918-19	Warner P. Davis
1919-20	J. C. Umberger
1920-21	S. H. Hilliard
1921-23	C. S. Plyler
1923-24	Huyler
1924	V. Howell (summer)
1924	J. G. Holloway
1925-26	R. C. Kale
1927	C. E. Williams
1928	J. L. Tigue
1929-31	L. E. Crowson
1932-33	G. A. Hovis
1934	H. D. Jessup
1935-38	W. F. Beadle
1939-43	J. Silvester Higgins
1943	W. R. Ormond
1943-44	Leonard Smith
1944-45	W. T. Medlin, Jr.
1946	Robert M. Hardee
1947-48	W. T. Medlin, Jr.
1948-53	Robert E. Early
1954-56	R. Tom Houts, Jr.
1957	Gene H. Little
1958-61	John C. Vernon
1962-63	James M. Thurman
1964-65	Vance Davis
1966-67	William B. Penny
1968-71	Julian M. Aldridge
1972-76	Conrad C. Washam
1976-79	D. Mike Jordan
1980-86	R. B. "Ben" Bullard
1986	Horwood P. Myers
1986	Lee F. Tuttle
1986-88	John M. Rufty
1988-93	Thomas R. Steagald
1993-	Carl W. Lindquist

First Presbyterian Church

1879-81	A. Melvin Cooper	1957-58	C. Ray McCain
1882-86	James E. Fogartie	1961-65	G. Dan McCall
1886-99	Joel T. Wade	1965-68	Grover C. Sewell
1900-10	Supply clergy,	1968-70	Henry J. Mueller
incl. Dr. Tolliver Thompson, Sr.		1971-75	Ray D. Barfield
1910-29	Church closed	1976-81	W. Woody Johnson
1929-36	Raymond McCarty	1982-84	Michael G. Wingard
1936-41	R. B. "Bob" DuPree	1985-95	Ronald A. Botsford
1941-43	Harold T. Bridgman	1995-97	Leslie Tucker
1943-48	Jack B. Davidson		(interim)
1948-51	R. B. "Bob" DuPree	1997-	J. Hunter Coleman
1952-55	Robert M. Hart		

Community Bible Church

1984-88	Robert Bryan
1989-93	Jerry Robinson
1994-	Steve Kerhoulas

Episcopal Church of the Incarnation

1896-1907	J. Archibald Deal, priest-in-charge, circuit rider in 1879
1907-09	Alfred S. Lawrence
1910-11	Various supply or visiting clergy
1912-13	John H. Crosby
1913-24	John H. Griffith, Archdeacon
1924	Oscar S. Michael
1931-33	Norvin C. Duncan
1934-40	Frank Bloxham
1940-55	A. Rufus Morgan, 1st Rector
1955-60	Herbert Koepp-Baker
1960-71	Gale D. Webbe
1972-79	Frederick "Fred" Hovey, Jr.
1979-94	Charles "Charlie" A. Bryan
1994-95	Robert "Bob" Reuss (interim)
1995-	R. Michael "Mike" Jones

612

First Baptist Church of Highlands

1884-87	S. H. Harrington	1942-43	Herman M. Alley
1888-92	D. L. Miller		(Judge Alley's son)
1896	A. T. Hord	1944-47	Dr. Thom N. Carter
1897	C. A. Bartlett	1948-51	Paul C. Nix
1898	A. T. Hord	1951-53	John C. Corbitt
1899	A. B. Thomas	1953-55	John Buell
1900	W. R. Rickman	1955-58	L. Eugene Walter
1901-02	J. W. Briggs	1958-61	J. Henry Propst, Jr.
1903-05	J. W. Kesterton	1962-63	R. Clinton Bailey
1906	L. M. Lyla	1963-67	L. C. Pinnix
1908	W. T. Potts	1968-75	Harvey L. Stewart
1909-12	J. J. Vinson	1975-85	Lewis W. Gibson
1914-15	W. T. Potts	1986-88	William C. Carpenter
1918	J. B. Stallcup	1989-92	Herbert L. Gibson
1919-21	Jose A. Bryson	1993	Robert Clegg
1923-25	V. W. Thompson		(interim)
1926	A. S. Solesbee	1993-96	Tim C. Worthington
1928-33	W. T. Potts	1996-97	Clyde N. Kerley
1933-37	J. E. Brown		(interim)
1938-41	J. B. Benfield	1997-	Dan D. Robinson

Westside Baptist Church

1993-97	Tom Harris (Terry Dixon in 1996)
1998-	John Cannon (interim)

Our Lady of the Mountains Catholic Church

[In serving a mission, the Catholic priests in Highlands had overlapping terms]

1950-54	Charles J. O'Connor
1954-60	Vincent Erb
1958-60	John G. O'Brien
1960-63	Henry Becker
1963-65	Charles Mulholland
1966-71	Edward Sheridan
1972	George M. Kloster
1972-83	Mike Langell of St. Francis in Franklin
1983-85	Myles Quail
1985-86	Henry Becker, 1st and only full-time priest
1986-89	Carl del Guidice of St. Francis in Franklin
1986-92	John Hoover of St. Jude in Sapphire Valley
1992	Joe Ayathupadam of India
1989-94	Frank Connolly of St. Francis in Franklin
1994-98	Richard T. McCue
1995-96	Ray Berg
1998-	William "Bill" Evans

Highlands Assembly of God

1970-75	Claude and Barbara Head
1975-77	Dennis and Martha Preston
1977-79	Gary L. Fisher
1980-94	Fred Sorrells
1995-97	Ray Conner
1997-98	Kenneth Howell
1998-	Scott Holland

Lutheran Church of the Holy Family

1993-99	Frank J. Meleschnig
1999-00	Michael Weaver
2000-	Pam Mitcham

Appendix 5

Postmasters of the Highlands Post Office

1875-89	T. Baxter White
1889-93	William A. "Bill" Coe
1893-97	David Norton
1897-1901	Gran W. Matney
1901-07	James E. Rideout, Sr.
1907-14	John Jay Smith
1914-17	James A. Hines
1917	W. T. Potts
1918-23	James A. Hines
1923-35	"Nellie" Cleaveland
1935	Charles C. Potts (acting postmaster)
1936-39	S. E. "Gene" Potts
1939	James R. "Jim" Wright (acting postmaster)
1940-56	Charles C. Potts
1956-58	Jean Rice (acting)
1958-61	Carl Talley (acting)
1961-85	Louis "Bud" Potts
1985-92	Keith Barnard
1992	Norman O'Kelly (acting postmaster)
1993	Charlie Moore (acting)
1994-	Elizabeth Kelley

Appendix 6
Librarians of the Hudson Library

1883	Laura Kibbee
1884-85	Mary L. Sheldon
1885	Miss Ellison
1887	Thomas G. Harbison
1889-95	Jessie E. White
1895-1912	Albertina Staub
1912-13	Mary Chapin Smith (acting librarian)
1913-18	Lucy P. Elliott
1918-19	Rebecca Nall
1919-23	Christina A. Rice
1923	Charlotte B. Elliott
1923-24	Rebecca Nall
1925-26	Leila Lewis Marett
1926-74	Gertrude Harbison
1974-75	Dolly" Harbison (acting librarian)
1975-77	Anne Ham
1977	Melinda Russell
1977-78	Martha H. Keener
1978-87	"Gert" McIntosh
1987	Tracy E. Strain
1987-88	Andrea Rudisill (acting librarian)
1988-90	Karen Herchen
1990-94	Carolyn Strader
1994-98	Henley Haslam
1998-	Mary Lou Worley

Appendix 7
Principals of Highlands School

1878	Edward H. Baxter
1878	Mr. Holway
1878	Rev. J. C. Lukens
1878-84	Orpha E. Rose
1884-85	Rev. James E. Fogartie
1885	Miss Mary E. Brown
1885-86	Sumner Clark
1886	Mrs. S. C. Davis
1886	H. S. Duncan
1886-93	Thomas G. Harbison
1893-95	
1895-96	Thomas B. Harbison
1896-97	Mollie Carpenter
1897-	
1915-16	Miss Annie A. Vaughn
1916	Mr. Waddell
	Miss Caroline Robinson
1920	Rebecca C. Nall
1925	Miss Barber
1925	Mrs. Ruth Oliver
1926-29	T. L. Tolar
1929-42	Otto F. Summer
1942-44	Prof. W. C. Newton
1944-51	Otto F. Summer
1951-55	F. N. Shearouse
1955-56	Joseph E. Bowles
1956-57	Otto F. Summer
1957-58	W. C. Newton
1958-59	Frank I. "Frog I" Watson
1959-61	Guy Sutton
1961-65	Charles F. Hendrix
1965-69	W. C. Newton
1969-73	Stoney G. Hinkle
1973-76	James M. "Jim" Shepherd
1976-77	Larry Brooks
1977-79	Larry Allison
1979-99	Larry Brooks
1999-	Jack Brooks

Appendix 8
Newspapers of Highlands

There follows a list of local newspapers listed chronologically, many of which are accessible on microfilm at the Macon County Library in Franklin, N.C. Original issues held by the Hudson Library in Highlands are starred.

(1) *Blue Ridge Enterprise.** January 3, 1883–Jan. 22, 1885. First newspaper in Highlands, a four-page format devoted to village chatter and politics, editorials, and advertisements; appeared weekly on Thursdays. Edited by E. E. Ewing, former publisher of the *Topeka Daily Capital* and *Kansas Farmer*, located for three months in Rideout's store next to Highlands House before Albert F. Clark took over and moved it to his new printing office at 4th and Mill Creek.

(2) *Highlander.** August 7, 1885–February 25, 1887. Ed. Richard Goldie in 1885, then Mrs. Albert F. "Minnie" Clark of Highlands Publishing Co., a group of leading citizens of the Town.

(3) *Star*. May 1, 1890–June 3, 1891. Ed. Charles H. Coe, printer William A. Coe.

(4) *Number Four*. June 4–July, 1891. Pub. weekly by No. 4 Pub. Co. Ed. T. G. Harbison.

(5) *Mountain Eagle*. September 9, 1891–1892, 1893. Ed. T. G. Harbison, then the Rideout Brothers, Herman and James E., Jr.

For 37 years (1893–1930) Highlands was without its own newspaper.

Franklin Press (1889–1932) July 11, 1889–Dec. 24, 1902, T. Baxter White contributed the "Highlands" column. [1903–1919, copies of issues for these years were destroyed in the great fire that swept the Franklin Press on Dec. 20, 1922.] Jan. 23, 1920–1928, "News of Week of Highlands: Brief Items of Interest from Macon's Pretty Mountain City as Told by Correspondent of The Press." 1929–Feb., 1931, Sarah Hicks Hines, "Highlands Flings," in "Highlands—The Roof Garden of the Southeast." 1931–April 28, 1932, "Social and Personal News from Highlands."

(6) *Highlands Maconian.** Sept. 3, 1930–April 27, 1932. Ed. J. J. "Joe" Moore.

Franklin Press and Highlands Maconian (*Franklin Press* folded, merged with *Highlands Maconian*, May 5, 1932) May 5, 1932–July, 1937, Mrs. Thomas C. Harbison, "Highlands Highlights." [1936. Issues missing, never microfilmed.] July, 1937–June, 1938, Mrs. Frank Bloxham, "Highlands Highlights," quite detailed, including school news. June 1938–Sept., 1938, Mrs. E. A. "Stella Marett" Burt, Jr., "Highlands Highlights." September, 1938–1953, Mrs. H. G. Story, "Highlands Highlights." 1954,

618

James Blakley, "Highlands People." 1955, Jan Burnette, "Highlands People." December, 1955, Mrs. Wayne E. Crowe, columnist. [1956–Dec. 24, 1968. No Highlands column.]

Franklin Press. January 1, 1969–.

(7) *Highlander*.* Aug. 6–Sept. 4, 1937. Ed. S. J. Fullwood, a local newspaper that ran for only five issues.

(8) *Mountain Trail*.* Nov. 24, 1938–May 25, 1952, a mimeographed weekly published by the Highlands School Theatre; Prof. Otto F. Summer, general manager, Mrs. H. G. Story, news editor, & Ronald Baty, business manager. 1940, ed. Eugene Paul; Herbert M. Paul, in 1943; Barbara Zoellner, in 1944; Doris Hedden, in 1945; Lois Potts, in 1952; Otto F. Summer, advisor.

(9) *Galax News*.* July 16, 1952–Sept. 2, 1971, a mimeographed weekly published during the summer season by the Galax Theatre, ed. Miss Mary Summer et al., up to thirty pages in 1956.

(10) *Highlander*.* May 23, 1958–, founded by Jim & Martha Goode, editor. 1970–79, ed. Helen Hopper; 1979–81, Skip Taylor; 1981–84, Howard Patterson; 1984–89, Skip Taylor; 1989–, Ralph Morris. Currently published twice a week in season and once a week during the off-season.

Appendix 9
Population Figures of Highlands

1880 Jun 1: Population of Highlands village, 82; of Blue Ridge Township incl. Highlands, 436; of Franklin Township, 1,840 [*Compendium of The Tenth Census* (June 1, 1880), Part 1, Washington: 1883, p. 240]. Macon County Indian population, 13 in 1880, 39 in 1870, and 55 in 1860 [p. 365.]

1883 Sept.: Population of Highlands 300 (*Blue Ridge Enterprise*, 9/27/1883), number at Highlands House 409, vs. 181 the previous year (*Blue Ridge Enterprise*, 10/4/1883).

1884: Kelsey's real estate column claims Highlands has a permanent population of ca. 300 [*Blue Ridge Enterprise*, 1/3/1884].

1886: Highlands is advertised in the [Baltimore] *Sun* as a little village with a population of 300, mostly northern people, containing two churches, a Presbyterian and a Methodist, a schoolhouse, a circulating library, and no saloons (*Highlander*, 9/17/86).

1900 census: population of Highlands is 249 (*Highlands Maconian*, 9/3/30).

1910: population 268

1920: population of Highlands is 313 (*Franklin Press & Highlands Maconian*, 4/24/30, p. 1).

1921: town population is 267 (*FP&HM*, 1/7/21).

1926 Dec 27: population of Highlands is 524, according to census by Willie Hays (Board of Commissioners Minutes, 12/27/26, Bk. E, p. 113).

1928: town population is 547; summer, 2,500 (*Franklin Press*, 7/5/28, p. 5).

1928 July: population of Highlands: 547, summer 2,500, more than 100 summer homes (*Franklin Press*, 7/5/28)

1930 census: 447 residents in corporate limits, summer population more than 2,500 (*Highlands Maconian*, 9/3/30), 447 and 3,000 according to *Highlands Maconian*, 7/29/31. Population in 1900 was 249, 1910 was 268 (increase of 18 or 7%), 1920 was 313 (increase of 45 or 17%), and 1930 was 447 (increase of 134 or 43%). Predicted for 1940 was 930 (increase of 483 or 108%). Town was growing approximately 2½ times every ten years. (*HM*, 9/3/30, p. 6).

1940: population of Highlands is 547 (*N.C. Dept. of Conservation & Development*, "Community Data," 3/20/56).

1950: population of Highlands is 514 (*N. C. Dept. of Conservation & Development*, "Community Data," 3/20/56).

1960: population of Highlands is 592; township, 1,418.

1970: population of Highlands is 583, township, 1,450 (*N. C. Almanac*)

1980: population of town is 653 (U.S. Census Bureau, Washington, D.C.) *Highlander*, 6/24/80, says 637 people (up 54 or 9.3%), 657 houses (up 33 or 5.3% from 624 in 1970).

1984: population of town is 971 [48% increase in four years, but annexation took place in July, 1980. Town doubled in area and added 100–150 full-time residents (*Highlander*, 1/7/86)].

1986: population of town is 1,032.

1990: preliminary census figures show 944 (up 44.6% from 1980 when adjusted for 1980 annexation).

1993: population of town is 970; township, 1,700.

1994: population of town is 1,035 (increase of 9.6% over 1990).

1997: population of town is 1,047.

2000 census: not in yet.

Comparisons

Date   Population

1880, 82

1883, 300 (266%)→tripled in 3 years

1890, 350 (17%)

1900, 249 (-29%)→fell 1/3 at century's end

1910, 268 (7%)

1920, 313 (17%)→same as 1883

1930, 447 (43%)→summer, 2,500–3,000

1940, 547 (22%)→up 3/4 in 20 years

1950, 514 (-6%)

1960, 592 (15%)

1970, 583 (-2%)→unchanged from mid 40s–mid 70s

1980, 653 (12%), summer, 20,000 (annexation in July, 1980)

1986, 1032 (58%)

1993, 970 (49%)

1994, 1035

1997, 1047; 643 registered voters

summary of three growth periods:

    (1) 1880–83→population tripled in three years.

    next 40 years→basically stable, except for 1/3 decrease at century's end.

    (2) 1925–45→up 2/3 in twenty years, summer growth significant.

    next 30 years→stable.

    (3) 1975-present→up 2/3 in 25 years, incl. annexation of 1980.

Overall growth:

    1885–2000→population tripled in 125 years, summer pop. up 700% in 70 yrs. (from 2,500–20,000).

Appendix 10
Recipients of the Robert B. DuPree Award

1980	Robert B. "Bob" DuPree
1983	Anne Chastain
1984	Louis A. "Bud" Potts
1986	Glenn Magner
1987	Norma T. "Boots" Pierson
1988	John W. Cleaveland
1989	Herb James
1990	Carlyle T. "Mike" Mangum
1991	Robert L. "Bob" Rhodes
1992	Ernest O. "Ernie" Wood
1993	James L. "Jimmy" Lowe
1994	Patricia M. "Pat" Benton
1995	Selwyn Chalker
1996	J. Steve Potts
1997	V. W. "Bill" McCall
1998	George Schmitt
1999	Florence and John Lupoli
2000	M. Wister Gary

Appendix 11: Weather Data

1962-2000 Annual Temperature Averages in Highlands				
Year	Av. High	Av. Low	Combined Av.	Difference from 38-yr. Av.
1962	61.50	38.71	50.10	(0.18)
1963	60.83	38.63	49.73	(0.55)
1964	61.02	39.72	50.37	0.09
1965	61.27	38.90	50.08	(0.20)
1966	58.93	39.21	49.07	(1.21) *
1967	61.64	40.69	51.17	0.89
1968	59.46	38.25	48.85	(1.43) *
1969	58.98	38.98	48.98	(1.30) *
1970	60.73	40.40	50.57	0.29
1971	59.95	40.64	50.30	0.02
1972	60.73	39.78	50.26	(0.02)
1973	60.50	39.56	50.03	(0.25)
1974	61.75	41.01	51.38	1.10 *
1975	61.81	40.46	51.13	0.85
1976	60.41	38.43	49.42	(0.86)
1977	60.88	40.69	50.78	0.50
1978	60.45	38.32	49.38	(0.90)
1979	59.77	39.50	49.63	(0.65)
1980	61.46	39.41	50.43	0.15
1981	60.93	39.55	50.24	(0.04)
1982	61.85	41.42	51.63	1.35 *
1983	61.00	40.19	50.60	0.32
1984	61.78	40.63	51.20	0.92
1985	61.05	40.69	50.87	0.59
1986	62.13	41.15	51.64	1.36 *
1987	60.98	39.64	50.31	0.03
1988	59.71	37.63	48.67	(1.61) *
1989	59.91	40.43	50.17	(0.11)
1990	62.51	41.66	52.08	1.80 *
1991	60.55	41.48	51.01	0.73
1992	59.36	39.66	49.51	(0.77)
1993	60.49	39.68	50.09	(0.19)
1994	60.84	39.88	50.36	0.08
1995	60.08	39.62	49.85	(0.43)
1996	59.43	38.89	49.16	(1.12) *
1997	60.09	38.92	49.50	(0.78)
1998	62.83	42.21	52.52	2.24 *
1999	57.66	39.95	48.80	(1.48) *
2000	62.21	40.15	51.18	0.90

15, 22, and 38 Year Averages

1962-77	60.64	39.55	50.09	(0.19)
1978-2000	60.75	40.11	50.43	0.15
1962-2000	**60.70**	**39.86**	**50.28**	

1962-2000 Annual Precipitation in Highlands			
Year	Inches	Difference from 38-yr. Av.	
1962	77.12	(10.78)	
1963	75.80	(12.10)	
1964	112.46	24.56	*
1965	74.95	(12.95)	
1966	79.98	(7.92)	
1967	99.57	11.67	
1968	77.72	(10.18)	
1969	94.55	6.65	
1970	78.84	(9.06)	
1971	85.72	(2.18)	
1972	92.40	4.50	
1973	102.45	14.55	
1974	90.19	2.29	
1975	99.65	11.75	
1976	96.31	8.41	
1977	93.44	5.54	
1978	67.99	(19.91)	*
1979	115.62	27.72	*
1980	70.21	(17.69)	
1981	64.15	(23.75)	*
1982	96.70	8.80	
1983	96.45	8.55	
1984	84.74	(3.16)	
1985	74.26	(13.64)	
1986	68.76	(19.14)	
1987	74.97	(12.93)	
1988	67.27	(20.63)	*
1989	108.50	20.60	*
1990	97.09	9.19	
1991	102.25	14.35	
1992	106.23	18.33	
1993	71.27	(16.63)	
1994	101.12	13.22	
1995	97.58	9.68	
1996	92.03	4.13	
1997	86.75	(1.15)	
1998	91.32	3.42	
1999	101.61	13.71	
2000	60.10	(27.80)	*

15, 22, and 38 Year Averages

1962-78	**88.18**	0.28
1979-2000	**87.68**	(0.22)
1962-2000	**87.90**	

Appendix 12
Historical Charts of Main Street and 4th Street

The following charts of buildings and their occupants, which have existed on Main Street and 4th Street during the period 1876–2001, are incomplete, and they still contain errors. But they are accurate enough to help identify the history of the town's physical development and the location of a quite a number of businesses and homes mentioned in the text.

The following key may facilitate the use of these charts:

(1) <u>Kelsey lot numbers</u>: at the top and bottom of each chart are references to lot numbers as they appear on the town map of 1895, which subdivided the original Kelsey map of 1881 into individual lots by number. These are the numbers that often appear on deeds of sale.

(2) <u>911 street addresses</u>: On each side of Main and 4th streets are references to street addresses for each building, as recently assigned by the emergency 911 system of identification.

(3) <u>Chronology</u>: The history of each building proceeds from the current occupant on the street back through earlier occupants and ultimately to the date of the building's construction.

(4) <u>Coverage</u>: Charts 1–8 cover Main Street from just west of 1st Street eastward to the Bowery Road. Charts 9–13 cover 4th Street from just south of South Street and the Walhalla Road northward as far as the Recreation Park.

(5) <u>5th Street</u>: Chart 7 includes at the top two important buildings on north 5th Street plus Highlands Manor.

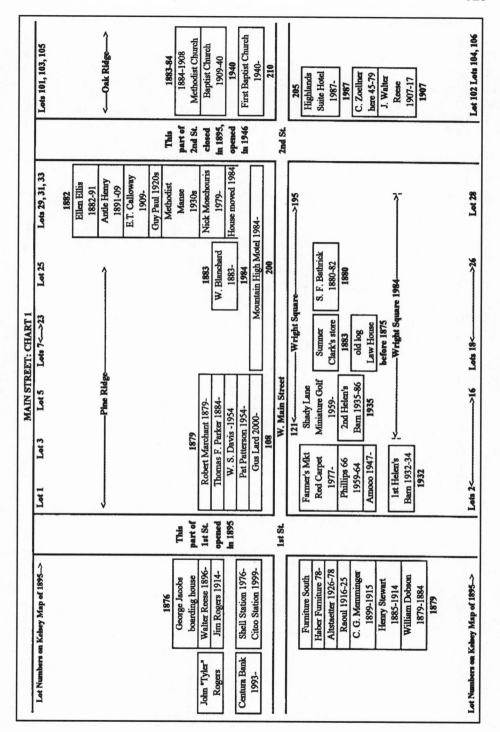

MAIN STREET: CHART 1

MAIN STREET: CHART 2

Lot 107 | Lot 109 | Lot 111 | Lots 113, 115 | Lot 117 | Lot 119 | Lot 121 | Lot 123 | Lot 125

Lot 201 | Lot 203 | Lot 205

‹———Oak Ridge———›

1935 — 302-314
- Hill's Sinclair Service Station
- Prealeau Hedden 1935-
- W. S. Beardon 1939-
- Potts' Sinclaire 1960-
- 1984
- ‹——————Oak Square——————›

W. Main Street

3rd St.

1881 — 270
- Boynton home, 1881-1905
- David Norton home, 1905-16
- Crisp House 1924-36
- Potts House, 1936-57
- Paxton House, 1952-54
- Tate House, 1957-64
- Phelps House, 1964-73
- Eduardo's, 1974-75
- Phelps House 1975-98
- Main Street Inn 1998-

305
- Parker 1883
- Whisker's 1991-
- Keener Real Estate 1973-91
- Alice Inman 1962-72
- Tar Heel Restaurant late 1940s
- Town Hall 1933-50
- Dr. Gilbert 1924-26
- Masonic Hall 1892

Lot 202 | Lot 204

1883 — 260
- William Partridge 1883-09
- a Mr. Madison?
- Luke Rice 1909-68
- James A. Hines 1912-74
- Howard Bond?
- Executive Gifts

1882 — 240
- Judge Dana Hunt 1883-85
- Aaron Esty 1886-96
- Jim Hines 1912-24
- Darthula Rice 1924-41
- Clark Witherall 1941-
- Jesse & Daisy Pierce 1973-
- White Oak Antiques 1985-2000

1882
- Judge Dana Hunt 1882
- Granville Willey 1883
- Jesse Hadley 1883-
- 1939
- Baptist parsonage 1939-

W. Main Street

275 — 1970
- Reeves Hardware 1970-

1970
- Root's Gift Shop 1931-67
- & Alice Inman's 1940-61
- 1926
- Ed Cunningham 1887

225 — 1979
- Highlands Pharmacy 1981-
- Perry Agency 1979-81

Lot 108 | Lot 110 | Lot 112 | Lots 114‹ | ›124 | Lot 126

MAIN STREET: CHART 3

Lot 207	Lot 209	Lot 211	Lot 213	Lot 215	Lot 217	Lot 219	Lot 221

Lot 221
- W. T. Pott's residence ca. 1914?
- Nellie Cleaveland West's Residence in 1945
- empty lot Frank Scudder's Galleries 1976-
- 352

Lot 219
- Nellie's Post Off. early 1930s
- Real Est. Office
- **1956 Tate Bldg.**
- Reeves Hardware 1956-70
- Tate's Supermarket 1970-74
- Village Smithy Restaurant 1974-76
- **1930**

Lot 217
- Little Joe and Tom Thumb Golf Course (J. & W. Hays) **1970**
- A L L E Y — Tate's Mkt Parking Lot 1970-82
- Brush Creek & Co. **1982**
- Serendipity 1992- | Azure Rose 1996-
- 342 | 344

Lot 213
- Baxter Wilson store **1884**
- Ernest Brown Clothing 1929- (torn down 1950) **1929-50**
- Martha Reese's Klip 'N Kurl ?62- **1963**
- Esther's Beauty Shop 1963-
- Wilson/Bryson Barber Shop 1963-
- Cracked Pot 1971-
- Mtn Tops Gifts-2000
- Scent-sations 2001-
- 338

Lot 211
- Albert Brown pool room in 1945 date? **1941**
- People's Dept. Store **1965**
- McCampbell Gem 1962-69
- C. Billingsley Dry Goods
- Pink Dogwood 1969-70
- Highlands Book Store 1971-
- Le Pavillon Native Sport 1970-82
- Mr. & Mrs. T's 1982-90
- Highlands Sportswear 1990-
- Village Boutique 1994-
- 326 | 330

Lot 209
- Frazier Redden building **1933**
- Jam Pot Gifts 1938-
- Maynard's Colonial Shop 1961-70
- Town & Country 1971-80
- Brush Strokes 1981-94
- Nancy's Fancies 1994-
- 322

Lot 207
- **1935**
- Talley/Burnett Grocery 1935-50
- Wash Pot -1963
- Mary Norton Dress Shop 1968-
- Royal Scott 1981-94
- 318

W. Main Street

Lots 206, 208	Lot 210	Lot 212	Lot 214	Lot 216	Lot 218	Lot 220	Lot 222

Lot 210
- Methodist Church 1909-
- 315

Lot 212
- Rosenthal Furs 1993-
- Pink Dogwood 1970-
- 341

Lot 214
- Moreland home 1937-62 (torn down)
- New Paul home 1921-37
- Guy Paul home 1919-21 (torn down)
- White's Post Office 1875-1911
- **1875**

Lot 216
- Town Square 1984-
- **1984**
- Town House Motel 1956-1984
- Dr. W. P. Hedden 1962-67
- **1956**

Lot 218 / Lot 220
- Lindy's Gifts 1989-
- Little Luke's
- Tar Heel Restaurant 1964-68
- Town House Restaurant -1963
- Annawear 1991-
- Galax Theatre 1948-88
- S. T. Marett 1945-56
- G. W. Marett Residence 1940-
- 349
- 357

628

MAIN STREET: CHART 4

Lot 223 — Lot 225 — Lot 227 — Lot 229 — Lot 231 (upper tier)
Lot 224 — Lot 226 — Lot 228 — Lot 230 — Lot 232 (lower tier)

Lot 223

1883

360
- Henry Skinner Printing Press 1883-89
- Charles Coe, Post Off. 1890-91
- Mountain Eagle' 1891-93
- Hiram Paul Store 1897-1905
- Vacant in 1945
- Clyde & Charlotte Mehder in 1971
- 2000

366
- <--Kent Lt Juliana's--> 1980-

Lot 225

Open Space (Pond in 1912)

1927 Hicks building

370
- The Cut In barber shop 1927-47
- Town Hall 1938-39
- Highlander Restaurant 1948-56
- Tate's Restaurant 1957-78
- Mountaineer Restaurant 1978-99
- Kilwin's 2000-
- 2000

- Highlands Grille 1927-47
- E. Cleaveland, D. Speed/J. Hays, Prileau Hedden

Lot 227

Sinle Hood's quarters
Pilings installed over a spring. 1940

374
- Post Office 1940-66
- Byers Style 1946-69
- McCampbell Gem 1970-
- Village Boutique 1989-1994
- Village Kids 1995-

376
- Esther's 1961-63
- Yrene's 1964-
- Nancy's Fancies 1983-94
- Suzette's

[big hole here]

Lot 229

1928 Rice & Thompson bldg.
Luke Rice's Market & Grocery

382
- F. Thompson Tea Room 1930-35
- Bert Rideout's Satulah Café 1935-37
- Harold Rideout's Drug Store 1939-40
- Wit's End 1940-

384
- Lillie Pierson 1930-36
- Sara Gilder 1937-65
- Paintin' Place 1968-94
- Kilwin's 1995-99
- Buck's Coffee Café 2001-

Lot 231

1902

388
- Potts Livery Stable 1902-10
- H. Dillard & Sons 1910-1926
- **1926**
- Potts Brothers 1926-56
- Highlander Restaurant 1957-99
- Highlands Fine Art
- Dutchman's Designs
- Apple Trout 1999-

Lower tier

363
- Country Club Properties
- Andy McDonough Real Estate 1976-91
- Cyrano's Bookshop 1978

365
- Pizza Place 1992-
- My Place Pizza 1978-91

369
- Toy Store 1992-

371
- Mountain Heritage 1990-
- <------Highlands Art Gallery 1954-92------->
- Boy Scout Cabin in 1939
- John Arthur's home 1879-1925?
- 1879

375
- Highlands Emporium 2001-
- Goodwin Weavers 1992-2000
- <-----Highlands Art Gallery 1954-92-------->
- built 1954

381
- Robert Tino Gallery 2000-
- Mtn Weavery -2000
- <-----Gallery------>

383
- Suzette's Boutique 2000-
- Fireside Books 1987-

387
- Lt1 Flower Shoppe 1980s
- Jim Fox & Jeff Cox architects
- Mrs. E. Heards Antique Nook 1968-
- Chamber of Commerce & Western Union 1948-68

MAIN STREET: CHART 5

Lot 301 (1882)
- Rideout & Company 1882-89
- Blue Ridge Enterprise here 1883
- Dr. O'Farrell's Highlands Drugs 1887-90
- Capers Drugs 1890-
- Bascom Real Estate in 1930
- Frank Cook Real Estate -1980
- Country Inn Antiques -2000
- Upper Crust Pastry 2001-410

Lot 302
- Art/Andrea Williams
- Rip & Pat Benton 1982-87
- 18 yrs. empty
- Will W. Edwards 1934-early 1950s
- Edwards Inn 1934-35
- W. S. Davis 1920-34
- P. Pierson 1911-20
- W. T. Potts 1905-11
- Rideout Granite Store 1889-1905
- Rock House 1889

caution light 1935
stop light 1947

4th St.

Lot 237 (1883)
- Bascom's Hardware 1883-1924
- Highlands Hardware 1925-38
- Bert Rideout Café 1938-40
- Texaco Gas Pumps 1986-

Lot 235 (1885)
- Bascom's Barn & Livery Stable 1885
- S. T. Kelsey, Jr., in 1896
- small Candy Store 1880s
- (1925) G. Marett's Grocery 1925-40
- Highlands Tea Room 1926-32, upstairs
- W. S. Davis 1932-34
- Stribling & Holt Restaurant upstairs
- (1941) Gulf Station 1941-85
- Trader Joe's 1986- 398

Lot 233 (1885)
- W. B. Cleaveland's Grocery 1885
- W. T. Potts 1902-14
- Bud Clark, mgr. 1902-08
- Charlie Wright 1914-20
- (1920) Fred Edwards Store 1920-52
- Steve's Country Store 1952-60
- Yrene's 1960- here 71
- Alice Inman Shop 1981
- Ann Jacob Gallery 1986- 394

Lot 234 (1945)
- F. A. Edwards extension 1945-52
- Tudor Hall Real Estate 1952-78
- Cyrano's Bookshop 1979- 390

W. Main Street

Lot 234 (1888)
- Ralph DeVille 1977-
- Etta J. DeVille 1968-76
- Harvey Talley home 1945-68
- Stell Cleaveland 1893-
- W. B. Cleaveland home 1888-93

W. Main Street

Lot 238 (399) (1883)
- House of Wong 1990-
- Cleveland 1981-90
- Real Estate, Long 1974-81
- Bill's Soda Shop 1939-72
- Rideout & Rice Drugs 1936-39
- Town Hall 1930-32
- Gus Holt's Store 1913-36
- Phone Company 1920ff.
- Post Office 1907-14
- Walden Drugs 1884-87
- Frank Walden jeweler
- Martin Meat Mkt 1883

398
- House of Wong 1970-90
- Antiques by Lee 1968-69
- McGruder/Obrien Real Estate 1950s & 60s
- J. Collins 1945-
- Harry's Café/Taxi 1937-45
- Post Office 1936-39
- Sara Gilder mid 1930s

395
- Stone Lantern 1976-
- Ed Purdom Furniture
- Crawford/Wilson Barber Shop
- Norton & Hicks 1950s
- Mitchell bldg.
- A. Dimick's Cheap Cash Store 1882

Lot 236
- Stone Lantern 1960-
- Mitchell bldg.
- A. Dimick's Cheap Cash Store 1882

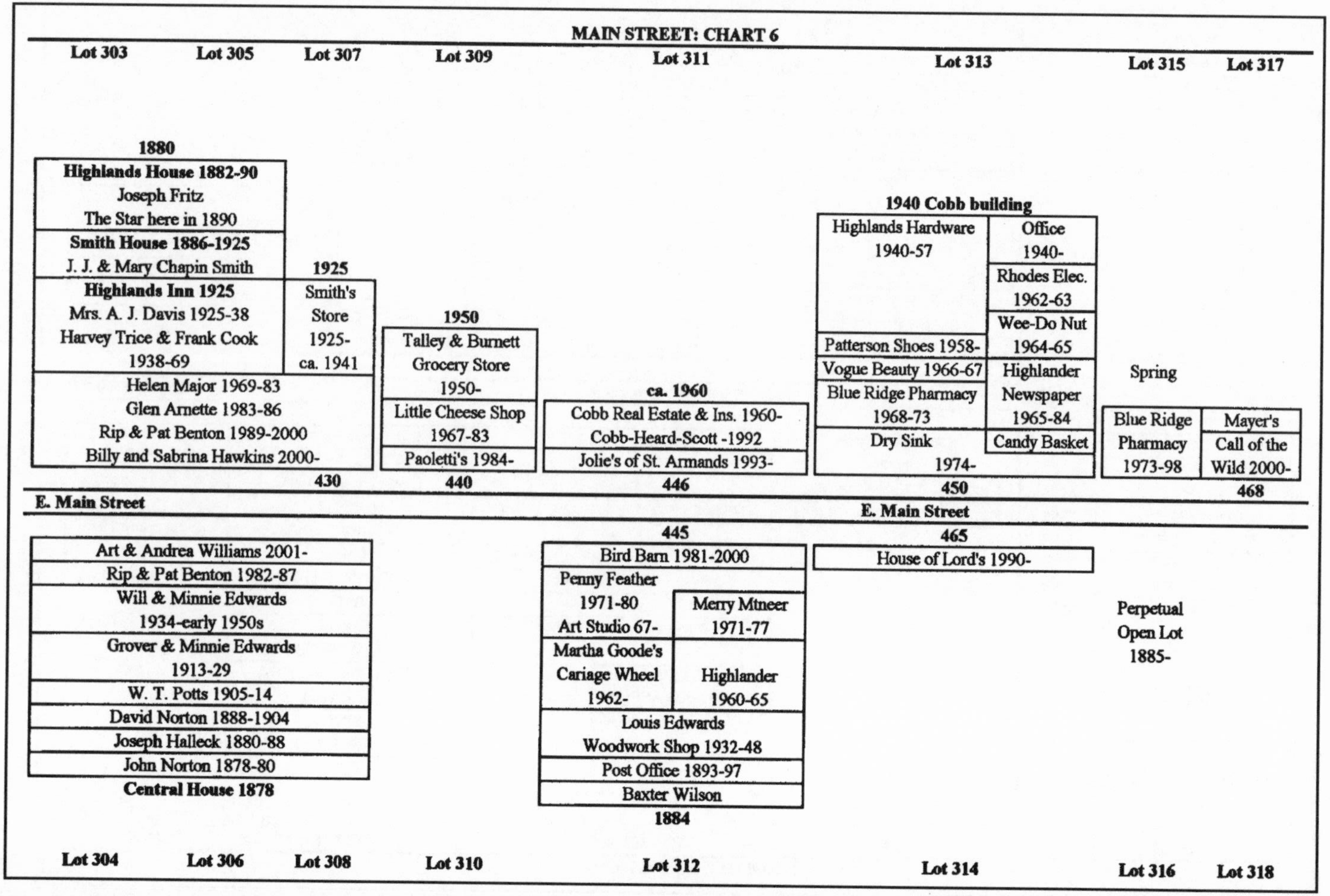

MAIN STREET: CHART 6

| Lot 303 | Lot 305 | Lot 307 | Lot 309 | Lot 311 | Lot 313 | Lot 315 | Lot 317 |

1880

Highlands House 1882-90
Joseph Fritz
The Star here in 1890
Smith House 1886-1925
J. J. & Mary Chapin Smith

1925
Smith's Store 1925-ca. 1941

Highlands Inn 1925
Mrs. A. J. Davis 1925-38
Harvey Trice & Frank Cook 1938-69

1950
Talley & Burnett Grocery Store 1950-
Little Cheese Shop 1967-83
Paoletti's 1984-

Helen Major 1969-83
Glen Arnette 1983-86
Rip & Pat Benton 1989-2000
Billy and Sabrina Hawkins 2000-

430

ca. 1960
Cobb Real Estate & Ins. 1960-
Cobb-Heard-Scott -1992
Jolie's of St. Armands 1993-

446

440

1940 Cobb building

Highlands Hardware 1940-57

| Office 1940- |
| Rhodes Elec. 1962-63 |
| Wee-Do Nut 1964-65 |

Patterson Shoes 1958-
Vogue Beauty 1966-67
Blue Ridge Pharmacy 1968-73
Dry Sink 1974-

Highlander Newspaper 1965-84
Candy Basket 1974-

450

Spring

Blue Ridge Pharmacy 1973-98

Mayer's
Call of the Wild 2000-

468

E. Main Street

House of Lord's 1990-

465

Bird Barn 1981-2000

Penny Feather 1971-80
Art Studio 67-
Martha Goode's Carriage Wheel 1962-

Merry Mineer 1971-77

Highlander 1960-65

Louis Edwards Woodwork Shop 1932-48
Post Office 1893-97
Baxter Wilson

1884

445

| Lot 304 | Lot 306 | Lot 308 | Lot 310 | Lot 312 | Lot 314 | Lot 316 | Lot 318 |

E. Main Street

Art & Andrea Williams 2001-
Rip & Pat Benton 1982-87
Will & Minnie Edwards 1934-early 1950s
Grover & Minnie Edwards 1913-29
W. T. Potts 1905-14
David Norton 1888-1904
Joseph Halleck 1880-88
John Norton 1878-80
Central House 1878

Perpetual Open Lot 1885-

631

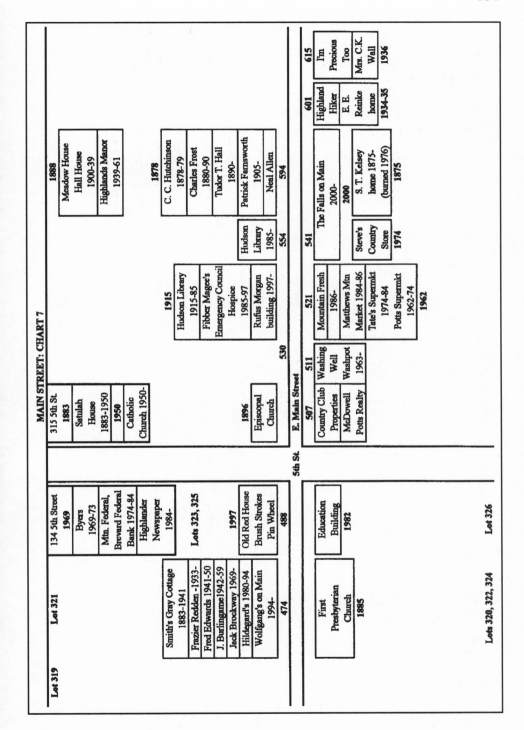

MAIN STREET: CHART 7

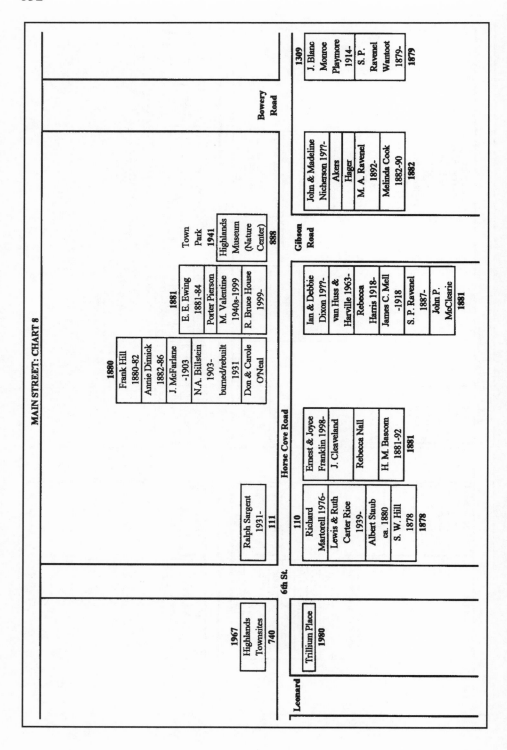

MAIN STREET: CHART 8

1309
J. Blanc
Monroe
Playmore
1914-
S. P.
Ravenel
Wantoot
1879-
1879

Bowery
Road

John & Madeline
Nicherson 19??-
Akers
Hager
M. A. Ravenel
1892-
Melinda Cook
1882-90
1882

Gibson
Road

Town
Park
1941

Highlands
Museum
(Nature
Center)
888

1881
E. E. Ewing
1881-84
Porter Pierson
M. Valentine
1940s-1999
R. Bruce House
1999-

1880
Frank Hill
1880-82
Annie Dimick
1882-86
J. McFarlane
-1903
N.A. Billstein
1903-
burned/rebuilt
1931
Don & Carole
O'Neal

Ian & Debbie
Dixon 19??-
van Huss &
Harville 1963-
Rebecca
Harris 1918-
James C. Mell
-1918
S. P. Ravenel
1887-
John P.
McClearie
1881

Horse Cove Road

Ralph Sargent
1931-
111

Ernest & Joyce
Franklin 1998-
J. Cleaveland
Rebecca Nall
H. M. Bascom
1881-92
1881

110
Richard
Martorell 1976-
Lewis & Ruth
Carter Rice
1939-
Albert Staub
ca. 1880
S. W. Hill
1878
1878

6th St.

1967
Highlands
Townsites
740

Trillium Place
1980

Leonard

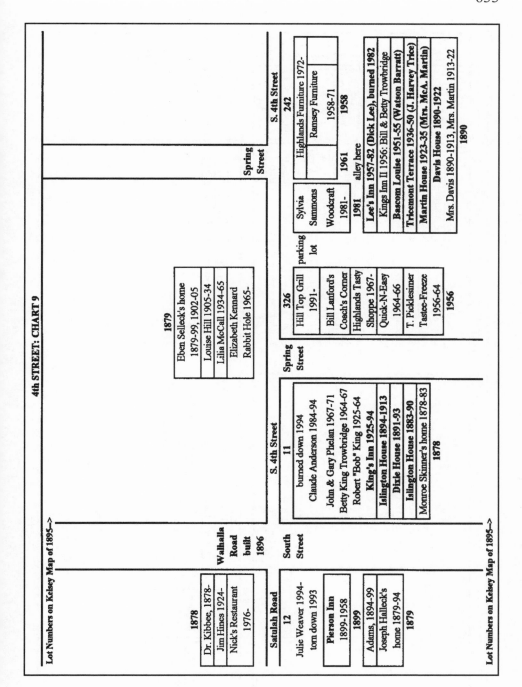

4th STREET: CHART 9

Lot Numbers on Kelsey Map of 1895–>

S. 4th Street

242

Highlands Furniture 1972-

Ramsey Furniture

1958-71

1961   1958

alley here

Sylvia
Sammons

parking
lot

Woodcraft
1981-
1981

Lee's Inn 1957-82 (Dick Lee), burned 1982

Kings Inn II 1956: Bill & Betty Trowbridge

Bascom Louise 1951-55 (Watson Barratt)

Tricemont Terrace 1936-50 (J. Harvey Trice)

Martin House 1923-35 (Mrs. McA. Martin)

Davis House 1890-1922

Mrs. Davis 1890-1913, Mrs. Martin 1913-22

1890

Spring
Street

1879

Eben Selleck's home
1879-99, 1902-05

Louise Hill 1905-34

Lilia McCall 1934-65

Elizabeth Kennard
Rabbit Hole 1965-

326

Hill Top Grill
1991-

Bill Lanford's
Coach's Corner

Highlands Tasty
Shoppe 1967-

Quick-N-Easy
1964-66

T. Picklesimer
Tastee-Freeze
1956-64

1956

Spring
Street

S. 4th Street

11

burned down 1994

Claude Anderson 1984-94

John & Gary Phelan 1967-71

Betty King Trowbridge 1964-67

Robert "Bob" King 1925-64

King's Inn 1925-94

Islington House 1894-1913

Dixie House 1891-93

Islington House 1883-90

Monroe Skinner's home 1878-83

1878

Walhalla
Road
built
1896

South
Street

1878

Dr. Kibbee, 1878-

Jim Hines 1924-

Nick's Restaurant
1976-

Satulah Road

12

Julie Weaver 1994-
torn down 1993

Pierson Inn
1899-1958

1899

Adams, 1894-99

Joseph Halleck's
home 1879-94

1879

Lot Numbers on Kelsey Map of 1895–>

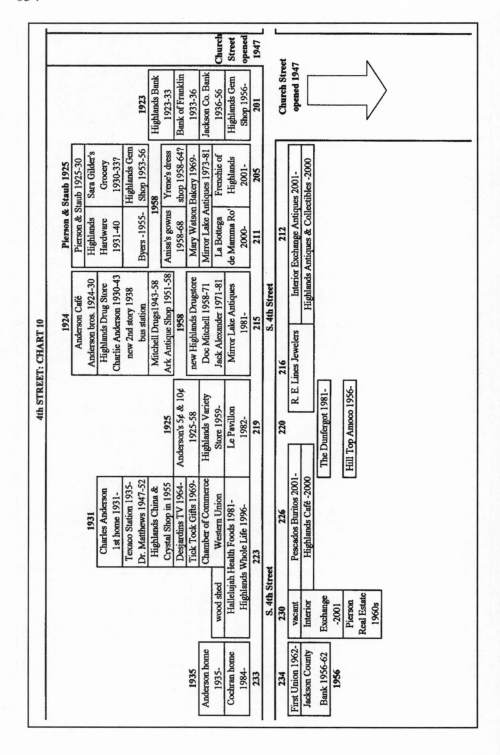

4th STREET: CHART 10

Church Street opened 1947

1923

Highlands Bank 1923-33
Bank of Franklin 1933-36
Jackson Co. Bank 1936-56
Highlands Gem Shop 1956-
201

Pierson & Staub 1925

Pierson & Staub 1925-30
Sara Gilder's Grocery 1930-33?
Highlands Gem Shop 1953-56
205

1958

Yrene's dress shop 1958-64?
Mary Watson Bakery 1969-
Mirror Lake Antiques 1973-81
Frenchie of Highlands 2001-
211

Highlands Hardware 1931-40
Byers -1955-
Anisa's gowns 1958-68
La Bottega de Mamma Ro' 2000-
211

1924

Anderson Café
Anderson bros. 1924-30
Highlands Drug Store
Charlie Anderson 1930-43
new 2nd story 1938
bus station

1958

Mitchell Drugs 1943-58
Ark Antique Shop 1951-58
new Highlands Drugstore
Doc Mitchell 1958-71
Jack Alexander 1971-81
Mirror Lake Antiques 1981-
215

S. 4th Street

Interior Exchange Antiques 2001-
Highlands Antiques & Collectibles -2000
212

R. E. Lines Jewelers
216

1925

Anderson's 5¢ & 10¢ 1925-58
Highlands Variety Store 1959-
Le Pavillon 1982-
219

The Dunfergot 1981-
220

Hill Top Amoco 1956-

1931

Charles Anderson 1st home 1931-
Texaco Station 1935-
Dr. Matthews 1947-52
Highlands China & Crystal Shop in 1955
Desjardins TV 1964-
Tick Tock Gifts 1969-
Chamber of Commerce Western Union

wood shed

Hallelujah Health Foods 1981-
Highlands Whole Life 1996-
223

S. 4th Street

Pescados Buritos 2001-
Highlands Café -2000
226

1935

Anderson home 1935-
Cochran home 1984-
233

vacant
Interior Exchange -2001
Pierson Real Estate 1960s
230

First Union 1962-
Jackson County Bank 1956-62
1956
234

Church Street opened 1947

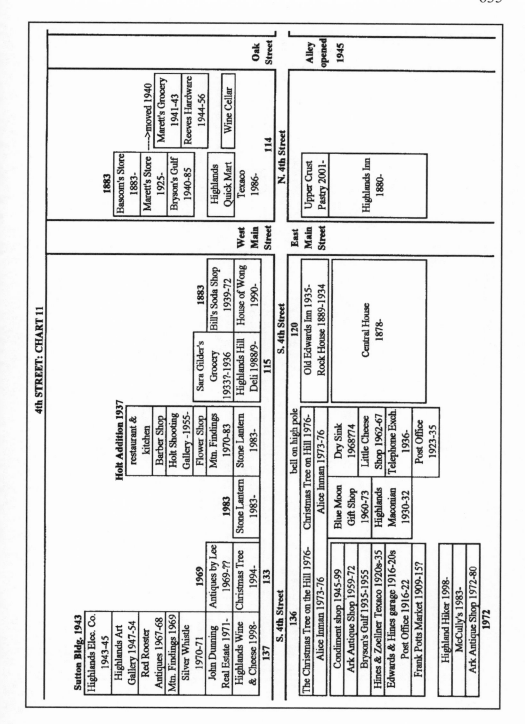

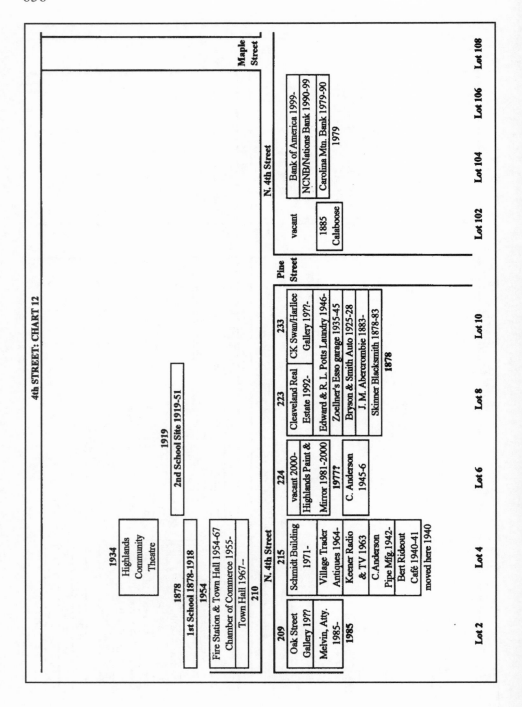

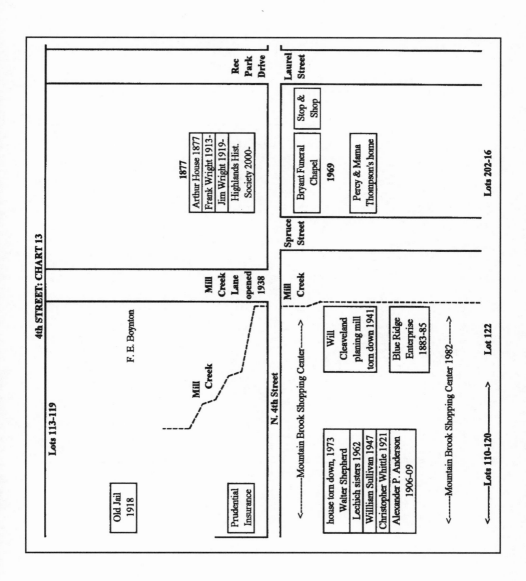

4th STREET: CHART 13

Lots 113-119

Old Jail 1918

F. E. Boynton

Mill Creek

Prudential Insurance

Mill Creek Lane opened 1938

1877

Arthur House 1877
Frank Wright 1913-
Jim Wright 1919-
Highlands Hist.
Society 2000-

Rec Park Drive

Laurel Street

Stop & Shop

Bryant Funeral Chapel 1969

Percy & Mama Thompson's home

Spruce Street

Lots 202-16

N. 4th Street

Mill Creek

<----Mountain Brook Shopping Center---->

Will Cleaveland planing mill torn down 1941

Blue Ridge Enterprise 1883-85

house torn down, 1973
Walter Shepherd
Lechich sisters 1962
William Sullivan 1947
Christopher Whittle 1921
Alexander P. Anderson 1906-09

<----Mountain Brook Shopping Center 1982---->

Lot 122

<----Lots 110-120---->

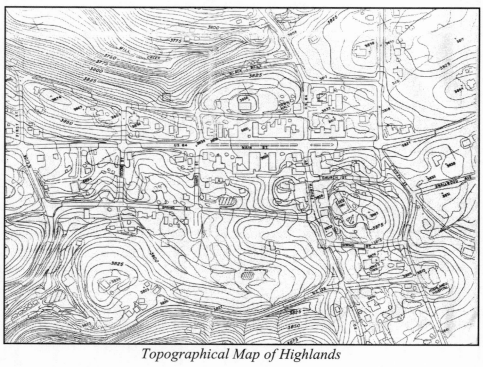

Topographical Map of Highlands

31. Bibliography

The following are fairly reliable articles on early Highlands history in general: E. E. Ewing, "Site of Highlands Was Carved from the Wilderness," *Highlands Maconian*, June 24, 1931, pp. 2 and 4, continued in July 29, 1931, pp. 2 and 4, and "Eight Years old To-day," March 29, 1883; "Charm of Highlands Mountains Lured Prof. Harbison, Botanist," *Franklin Press*, July 5, 1928, pp. 1, 2, and "Brief History of Highlands, Highest Town East of the Rockies," p. 4; J. J. Moore, "Site of Highlands Was Carved From Mountain Wilderness," *Highlands Maconian*, June 24 and July 29, 1931; Mrs. H. G. Story, "Highlands Goes Forward in Ten Years of Progress," *Franklin Press*, June 5, 1941; Elias D. White, "Early Highlands Days, An Historical Sketch," *Franklin Press and Highlands Maconian*, June 6, 1941; and Mrs. Gertrude C. Holt, "Highlands As It Used to Be," *Galax News*, July 22, 1953, pp. 1, 3, 7.

Articles

"Brief History of Highlands, Highest Town East of Rockies," *Franklin Press*, July 5, 1928, p. 4.

Copple, Lee. "Rideout Was Part-Time Expert on Fleas," *Highlander*, Oct. 19, 1978, Sec. B. Feature article on James Elbert Rideout.

Davis, Richard, and Rebecca Harding. "By-Paths in the Mountains," *Harper's New Monthly Magazine*, Vol. 61(Sept., 1880), pp. 532–47, esp. pp. 541–45. A view of Highlands in 1876 during its first year.

Dibble, E. T. "Our Lady of the Mountains: Jubilee—50 Years of Thanksgiving," July 15, 2000. A brief history of the Catholic Church in Highlands.

"Elderly Group Gathers for Unusual Cashiers Birthday Celebration," *Asheville Citizen-Times*, Sept. 7, 1941. Article on Nathan H. and Zebulon Vance McKinney, Mrs. Martha Norton Gottwals, Mrs. Carolina McKinney Cabe, and Frank H. Hill.

Ewing, E. E. "History of the Settlement of Highlands." *Blue Ridge Enterprise*, Vol. 1, No. 1, Jan. 25, 1883. One of the best and most accurate accounts of the early founding of Highlands, printed in the first issue of Highlands' first newspaper.

Harbison, Gertrude. "Satulah Club History," *Galax News*, Aug. 1, 1963, rpt. *Highlander*, July 26, 1979.

Hines, Sara-Hicks. "Highlands Has Unique History: Two Interesting Stories Related of Town's Establishment," *Franklin Press and Highlands Maconian*, June 30, 1932; rpt. July 20, 1939, in *Franklin Press* and March 24, 1966, in *Highlander*.

Hines, Sara-Hicks. "Noted Explorer Helped Survey Site of Highlands with Pocket Compass," *Highlands Maconian*, March 18, 1931, p. 1.

Holt, Gertrude C. "Highlands As It Used to Be," *Galax News*, July 22, 1953, pp. 1, 3, 7.

"Hubert Shuptrine," *American Artist*, July, 1973.

"Inscription Explanation Questioned by Citizens." *Highlander*, Dec. 8, 1966. Discussion of Spanish inscription at Devil's Courthouse.

Johnson, Melvin. "An Artist Who Went North to Paint the South," *Boston Globe*, Oct. 21, 1973, pp. 7–8.

Keener, George, in Rachel Rubin Wolf, ed. *Art from the Parks* (Cincinnati, Ohio, 2000), p. 42. A brief account of Keener's painting.

King, Edward. "The Great South: Among the Mountains of Western North Carolina," *Scribner's Monthly*, vol. 7 (March, 1874), pp. 513–44. Available also on microform in *American Periodical Series III: Civil War Reconstruction*, reel 346. Pages 530–36 describe the Highlands plateau in 1872, three years before the founding of the town.

Moore, J. J. "Stirring the Dust of 37 Years," *Highlands Maconian*, Sept. 3, 1930, p. 2. A comprehensive article on the early newspapers of Highlands.

Paul, Guy. "The Assets of Highlands," *Highlander*, Sept. 4, 1937. A speech made at the graduation exercises of Highlands High School and subsequently printed in the newspaper.

Reinke, E. E. "The Highlands Museum of Natural History: Report on the Necessity of a Mountain Biological Research Station in the South." Highlands, 1930.

"Site of Highlands Was Carved From Mountain Wilderness," *Highlands Maconian*, in two parts: June 24, 1931, p. 2, 4, and July 29, 1931, pp. 2, 4. Except for a few significant errors, a good general history of early Highlands based primarily on the recollections of pioneer John Jay Smith.

Story, Mrs. H. G. "Highlands, The Place and Its People," *Franklin Press and Highlands Maconian*, Summer Souvenir Ed., July 20, 1939, Sec. C, p. 1. A very general description.

Smith, J. Jay. "Highlands, N.C., Founded 1875," *Franklin Press*, Jan. 29, 1926. An account of the rapid progress made from 1875–1926. Includes Smith's version of the origin of the name "Highlands."

Smith, Mary Chapin. "Highlands, North Carolina," *Highlands Maconian*, 1931, rpt. *Highlander*, Nov. 18, 1971.

Taylor, Melinda. "Highlands Fire and Rescue: Past and Present Day." A paper for English 11, May 21, 1981, rpt. in part in *Franklin Press*, Oct. 7, 1987.

Totten, H. R., W. C. Coker, and H. J. Oosting. "Dr. Thomas Grant Harbison," *Journal of the Elisha Mitchell Scientific Society*, vol. 52 (1936), pp. 140–45. A detailed account of Professor Harbison's life.

"Town board Oks planting of trees down Main Street," *Highlander*, Oct. 4, 1985.

"Visitor recalls 1901 Highlands," *Highlander*, July 13, 1978. Recollections of Ellis Meserve.

Elias D. White, "Another Chapter Added to Early Highland Days," *Franklin Press and Highlands Maconian*, Aug. 20, 1942, pp. 5, 8. White's recollection of Richard Harding Davis' visit to Highlands in 1876.

———. "Early Highlands Days, An Historical Sketch," *Franklin Press and Highlands Maconian*, June 5, 1941, pp. 4–5. A thorough coverage of education in early Highlands.

Books

Alley, Felix E. *Random Thoughts and the Musings of a Mountaineer*. Salisbury, N.C., 1941.

Arthur, John Preston. *Western North Carolina: A History (1730–1913)*, Asheville, N.C., 1914, rpt. Johnson City, Tenn., 1996.

Bahnson, Charles F. *North Carolina Lodge Manual for the Degrees of Entered Apprentice, Fellow Craft, and Master Mason*. Raleigh, 1957.

Benét, Stephen Vincent. *John Brown's Body*. New York, 1928.

Beverley, Robert. *Western North Carolina Almanac, 2nd ed*. Franklin, N.C., 1993. An extremely well-researched production from an encyclopedic mind.

Bolgiano, Chris. *Appalachian Forest*. Mechanicsburg, Pa., 1998. An excellent plea for the preservation of our natural heritage.

Bryson, Mrs. Vernon. *Macon County, North Carolina*. Franklin, N.C., 1972.

Davis, Donald Edward. *Where There Are Mountains: An Environmental History of the Southern Appalachians*. Athens, Ga., 2000.

Davis, Evangeline M. *Lure of Highlands*. Highlands, N.C., 1981.

Dykeman, Wilma. *French Broad*. Newport, Tenn., 1992.

Fleming, Virginia. *Be Good to Eddie Lee*. New York, 1993.

———. *So Tender the Spirit*. Highlands, 1985.

———. *Wellspring*. Highlands, 1986.

Gallegos, Eloy J. *Melungeons: The Pioneers of the Interior Southeastern United States: 1526–1997*. Knoxville, 1997. In Gallegos' series of books about *Spanish Pioneers in United States History*.

Gibson, Lewis W. *History of First Baptist Church, Highlands, N.C.: 1884–1984*. Highlands, 1985.

Hamilton, Alice McGuire. *Blue Ridge Mountain Memories: The True Story of a Mountain Girl at the Turn of the Century.* Atlanta, 1977. A thinly disguised and charming account of the Norton community and Jackson County.

Harkins, Bess Hines. *Dream Blue Altitudes.* Highlands, n.d.

———. *Earth Songs.* San Benito, Texas, 1975.

———. "Our Mountains" (a series of fifteen prose reflections on life in Highlands during 1920s and 1930s), *Highlander*, Feb. 10–June 23, Oct. 29, and Dec. 8, 1966.

——— and Butler S. Harkins. *Sequoia Bound.* N.p., 1978.

———. *Songs Out of Silence.* Oxnard, Calif., 1964.

———. *Unknown Seas.* Los Angeles, 1958.

Hedin, Lydia E., Jean M. Chesley, John P. Anderson, and Louise A. Sargent. *Alexander P. Anderson: 1862–1943.* Red Wing, Minn., 1997.

Hines, Bess Hinson. *Singing of the Heart.* Atlanta, 1943.

Hines, Sarah Hicks. *Shaking Down the Chestnuts.* Santa Barbara, Ca., 1999.

Holt, Betty. *History of the First Presbyterian Church: Highlands, North Carolina, 1885–1985.* Highlands, N.C., 1985.

Hoppin, Dorothee Ann. *The Episcopal Church of the Incarnation: First 100 Years, Highlands, N.C.* Highlands, N.C., 1996.

Hudson, Charles. *Knights of Spain, Warriors of the Sun: Hernando de Soto and the South's Ancient Chiefdoms.* Athens, Ga., 1997. A blend of archeology, history, and geography that definitively establishes De Soto's path across the Southeast.

Inglesby, Edith. *Happy Highways.* Charleston, 1981. Charming recollections of Highlands prior to the first World War.

Jordan, Elaine. *Indian Trail Trees.* Ellijay, Ga., 1997.

Jordan, Francis Marion. *Life and Labors of Elder F. M. Jordan.* Raleigh, N.C., 1899.

Kelsey, Harlan P. *Kelsey-Highlands Nursery: Rhododendrons and Azaleas, Specimen Evergreens, Rare Plants.* Salem, Mass., 1925.

Kephart, Horace. *Our Southern Highlanders.* New York, 1913.

Kelsey Kindred. *Kelsey Genealogy.* A history of the descendants of William Kelsey the Puritan in seven vols. and a supplement, covering generations 1 through 15.

Laderoute, Linda. *Harlan P. Kelsey: Landscape Architect, Horticulturist, Conservationist.* Boxford, Ma., 1999.

Law, S. [Soyrieta] Van Epp. *Status Quo.* Stuart, Fla., 1971. A book of short stories about the Law's life and olden times in Cashiers Valley.

Lombard, Frances Baumgarner. *From the Hills of Home in Western North Carolina.* Whiteside Cove, N.C., 1972, rpt. 1993. A charming collection of childhood memories of a way of life reaching back to the early 1800s and fast disappearing.

Macon County Historical Society. *Heritage of Macon County, Vols. 1 and 2*. Franklin, N.C., 1987 and 1998.

Matthew, Sidney L. *Life and Times of Bobby Jones*. Chelsea, Mich., 1995.

McCollum, Dee. *Poems for Women*. N.p., 1993.

———. *Summer Mountain: Poems of the Hills*. N.p., 1986.

McRae, Barbara, and Rebekah Leverette. *Macon County NC in the 1850 Census: A Snapshot in Time*. Franklin, N.C., 1997.

———. *Records of Macon County N.C. 1849–1858*. Franklin, N.C., 1999.

McRorie, Johnson Davis. *"Knowing Jackson County . . ." People, Places, and Earlier Days*. Sylva, N.C., 2000.

McIntosh, Gert. *Highlands, North Carolina . . . a walk into the past*. Rev. ed. Birmingham, Ala., 1990.

Mooney, James. *Myths of the Cherokee and Sacred Formulas of the Cherokees, from the 19th and 7th Annual Reports of the Bureau of American Ethnology*. 1891, 1897–98, rpt. Nashville, Tenn., 1982.

N.C. Municipal Population. Office of State Planning, Raleigh, N.C., Fall, 1997.

Norris, Helen Hill. *Looking Backward*. Highlands, vols. 1 and 2, 1961 and 1963.

Ogburn, Charlton. *Southern Appalachians: A Wilderness Quest*. New York, 1975.

Perdue, Theda. *Native Carolinians: The Indians of North Carolina*. Raleigh: Division of Archives and History, 1985.

Perrin, Carol Carré. *Highlands Historic Inventory: Project Completion Report*. Greenville, S.C., 1982. A carefully researched survey of 173 significant properties within the town limits of Highlands, conducted in the fall of 1980.

Reynolds, T. W. *High Lands*, Highlands, N.C., 1964.

———. *Born of the Mountains*, Highlands, 1964.

———. *Southern Appalachian Region, Vols. 1 and 2*, Highlands, 1966.

Rice, Christina Anderson. In. Bette Rice, ed., *When the Laurels Bloom and Other Poems*. Highlands, 1999.

Rossman, Douglas A. *Where Legends Live: A Pictorial Guide to Cherokee Mythic Places*. Cherokee, N.C., 1988.

Sargent, Ralph M. *Biology in the Blue Ridge: Fifty Years of the Highlands Biological Station, 1927–1977*. Highlands, N.C., 1977.

Shaffner, Randolph P. *Good Reading Material, Mostly Bound and New: The Hudson Library, 1884–1994*. Highlands, N.C., 1994.

Sloan, Dave U. [Jr.]. *Fogy Days, and Now; or, the World Has Changed, The Innovations of the 19ᵗʰ Century.* Atlanta, 1891. A nostalgic look at scenes and customs of the days of fogyism through poetry and prose by an Atlantan professor of Telegraphy.

Smith, Mary Chapin. *Earth Songs.* Boston, 1910.

Stained Glass Windows of the Highlands United Methodist Church. Highlands, N.C., 1993.

Sullivan, Claude Townsend. *A Tale of Highlands.* Greenville, S.C., 1970.

Talley, Ed T.. *Shortoff Missionary Baptist Church.* Highlands, N.C., 1985.

Torrey, Bradford. *World of Green Hills: Observations of Nature and Human Nature in the Blue Ridge.* Boston, 1898.

Towles, Louis P., ed. *A World Turned Upside Down: The Palmers of South Santee, 1818–1881.* Columbia, S.C., 1996.

Van Noppen, Ina W. and John J. *Western North Carolina Since the Civil War.* Boone, N.C., 1973.

Watson, Peggy S. *Webbmont.* Highlands, N.C., 1995. An excellent history of Joe Webb's log homes.

Weeks, Charles J., Jr. *An American Naval Diplomat in Revolutionary Russia: The Life and Times of Vice Admiral Newton A. McCully.* Annapolis, 1993.

Williams, Jonathan. *Blackbird Dust.* Chappaqua, N.Y., 2000.

———. *Blues and Roots/Rue and Bluets: A Garland for the Southern Appalachians.* Durham, N.C. 1985.

———. *Ear in Bartram's Tree: Selected Poems 1957–1967.* Chapel Hill, N.C., 1969.

———. *Elite/Elate Poems.* Highlands, N.C., 1979.

———. *Get Hot or Get Out.* Metuchen, N.J., 1982.

———. *In the Azure Over the Squalor: Ransackings and Shorings.* Frankfort, Ky., 1985.

———. *Magpie's Bagpipe: Selected Essays.* San Francisco, 1982.

Wood, Lawrence E. *Mountain Memories.* Highlands, N.C., 1972.

———. *Young and Montgomery Families of the South.* Franklin, 1978.

Zahner, Robert. *Mountain at the End of the Trail.* Highlands, N.C., 1994. An eminently readable memorial to Whiteside Mountain.

Zeigler, Wilbur G., and Ben S. Grosscup. *Heart of the Alleghanies or Western North Carolina; comprising its topography, history, resources, people, narratives, incidents, and pictures of travel, adventures in hunting and fishing and legends of its wildernesses.* Raleigh, N.C., 1883.

Diaries

Barker, Daisy Hill. "Morning of My Life." Unpub. reminiscences, 1964. A beautiful recollection of growing up in Horse Cove from 1881–87.

Hines, Bessie Hinson. Unpub. diary, Jan. 1–Dec. 31, 1924.

Jenkins, Butler, Jr. Unpub. memoirs, written shortly after 1977.

Kelsey, S. T. Unpub. diary, "Record of Weather and Work," in 2 vols. Vol. 1: Ottawa University Farm, March 19, 1866 to July 4, 1869, and Highlands, North Carolina, Sept. 10th 1875 to July 17th 1878. Vol. 2: Highlands, N.C., July 17, 1878 to May 24, 1882. A daily report of the weather and Kelsey's horticultural work in Kansas and Highlands, with occasional but vital references to early settlers and events in Highlands.

Kelsey, S. T. *Time Book*, 2 vols. April 3, 1875–Oct. 18, 1879, and Dec. 6, 1879–May 29, 1886. Log books of days worked on Highlands roads.

Phillips, R. Julius "Jule." Work ledger, 1883–97.

Reese, Joseph Walter. Unpub. diary covering the years 1885–1957, begun Sept. 1, 1947 and finished Jan., 1957. An excellent eye-witness account of early Highlands.

Sargent, Louise Anderson. *Reminiscences of Highlands Summers*. Highlands, 1894. Prepared in 1989 by daughter Lydia Sargent Macaulay.

Scadin, R. Henry. Unpub. diaries covering the years 1886–1921 in 43 vols., but missing vols. for 1888–91 and 1895–96. Further vols. by Kate Scadin, 1916, and Dewey Scadin, 1917–20. Available in manuscript cartons and in Melissa Baldwin, trans., digital format. Accompanied by 1,200 glass plate negatives. Asheville, N.C., R. H. Scadin Photographic Collection, Ramsey Library Special Collections, University of North Carolina at Asheville.

Interviews

Arnold, Marion Day. Telephone interviews by the author, Oct. 29, Nov. 5, and Dec. 9, 1993.

Billingsley, W. F. "Dub." Telephone interview by the author, April 11, 2001.

Bolick, Terry. Interview at his home in Buck Creek by the author, June 2, 1999.

Brooks, Almetta, and Irene James. Cassette interview by Anne Chastain at Mett's place on Hwy 107, March 2, 1989. Highlands, Kevin Fitz Patrick, Media Divide.

Bronk, Erin, Highlands Forest Ranger. Interview by the author, June 9, 1999.

Calloway, Ethel. Interview by the author, Nov. 8, 1993.

Chalker, Marna Cobb. Interview by the author, Nov. 17, 1993.

Chmar, Jan Chambers. Interview by the author, Sept. 24, 1993, Feb. 23, 1994.

Cleaveland, John. Interview by the author, May 18, 2001.

Cook, Jerry. Interview by the author, May 16, 2001.

Crane, Olive. Cassette interview by Anne Chastain at residence on Hicks Road, Jan. 23, 1986. Highlands, Media Divide.

Cranston, Craig. Interview by the author, Oct. 18, 1993.

Dedication, Highlands Civic Center, May 21, 1985 on cassette. Highlands, Media Divide.

Dedication, Hudson Library, June 9, 1985 on cassette. Highlands, Media Divide.

Dryman, Olin and Edna. Cassette interview by Anne Chastain and Sylvia Thomas at residence in Scaly Mountain, Oct. 19, 1986. Highlands, Media Divide.

Hall, Margaret Gilbert. Interview by the author, Nov. 11, 1993.

Harbison, Dorothea "Dolly." Interview by the author, Sept. 22, 1993.

Hertzberg, Mrs. Rudolf "Winnie." Interview by the author, Sept. 30, 1993.

Holt, Richard C. "Bill." Interview by the author, Oct. 14, 1993.

Houston, Bobby. Interview by the author, April 3, 2001.

James, Irene. Interview with the author, April 8, 1998.

Keener, George. Interview by the author, April 17, 2001.

Keener, Joe. Cassette interview at Wilson cabin on Fork Mountain Road, ca. 1979. Highlands, Media Divide.

Keener, Mel and Dixie. Cassette interview by Anne Chastain at residence on Flat Mountain Road, March 16, 1989. Highlands, Media Divide.

Lowe, Bernice Rice, and Herbert and Mary Paul Rice. Cassette interview by Anne Chastain at Rice house on Buck Creek Road, March 8, 1986. Highlands, Media Divide.

Lowe, Tammy. Interview by the author, March 31, 1999.

Lyle, Nancy Jussely. Interview by the author, Nov. 4, 1993.

McDowell, Charlie. Interview by the author, Oct. 30, 1993.

McNamee, Sarah Thompson. Interview by the author, Oct. 27, 1993.

Medlin, June Thompson. Interview by the author, Nov. 9, 1993.

Meisel, Louise Edwards. Interview by the author, Sept. 29, 1993.

Miller, Bessie. Cassette interview by Anne Chastain and Sylvia Thomas at residence in Scaly Mountain, Sept. 19, 1986. Highlands, Media Divide.

Mitchell, Clarence E. "Doc" and Peggy. Cassette interview by Anne Chastain at residence in town, March 9, 1989. Highlands, Media Divide.

Norton, Frank. Cassette interview by Anne Chastain at residence on Buck Creek Road, Jan. 25, 1986. Highlands Media Divide. 2nd interview at 98th birthday party at Rice House on Buck Creek Road, June 25, 1986. Highlands, Media Divide.

Nix, Edith Bolton. Interview by the author, April 7 and 8, 2001.

Potts, Arthur and Pearl. Cassette interview by Anne Chastain at residence on Spruce Street, Jan. 16, 1986. Highlands, Media Divide.

Potts, Louis A. "Bud." Interview by the author, Oct. 17, 1993.

Reese, Coleman Marshall "PeeWee." Interview by the author at residence off Dillard Road, Oct. 21, 1998.

Reese, Joe and Lucille. Interview by the author, Dec. 1, 1993.

Reese, Wayne. Interview by the author, March 31, 2001.

Rhodes, Anne Altstaetter. Interview by the author, Oct. 31, 1993.

Rice, W. Herbert "Cub." Interview by the author, Jan. 10, 1994.

Shay, Esther Huger Elliott Cunningham. Telephone interview by the author, Dec. 7, 1993

Smith, Victor. Interview by the author, Nov. 1, 1993.

Stelling, Elizabeth Russell. Interview by the author, March 20, 2001.

Sullivan, Lamira Henley. Interview by the author, Oct. 6, 1999.

Talley, Bernice. Interview by the author, April 2, 1999.

Talley, Lyman "Red" and Leora Carver. Cassette interview by Sylvia Thomas and Anne Chastain at residence on Walhalla Road, Sept. 12, 1986. Highlands, Media Divide.

Taylor, Walter. Interview by the author, May 11, 1994.

Van Houten, Harriet Zahner. Interview by the author, Sept. 30, 1993.

Vinson, Furman. Interview by the author, March 30, 2001.

Wax, Polly. Interview by the author, April 13, 1998.

Weaver, Julie. Interview by the author, March 2, 2001.

Williams, Georgette. Interview by the author at residence on Dillard Road, July 28, 1999.

Wilson, Everett. Interview by the author, Sept. 28, 1993.

Wilson, Herman. Cassette interview by Anne Chastain at Wilson Gap residence, March 23, 1989. Highlands, Media Divide.

Wilson, Louis and Frances. Interview by the author, January 29, 2001.

Wilson, Wade. Interview by the author, Oct. 10, 1998.

Wright, Henry Wright. Cassette interview by Ralph Sargent and Kevin Fitz Patrick, ca. 1982. Highlands, Media Divide.

Wright, Harry. Interview by the author Oct. 29, 1993, and at residence on West Main, April 1, 1998.

Zachary, Bert and Carl "Bub." Cassette interview by Anne Chastain at residence on Buck Creek Road, March 8, 1986. Highlands, Media Divide.

Letters

Inglesby, Edith. Letter to Tom Crumpler about the history of Highlands, Nov. 1, 1974.

Jennings, Minerva P. Letter to Miss Margarite Ravenel, Aug. 19, 1939.

Kelsey, Samuel T. Letter to the citizens of Pomoma, Kansas, *Pomona Republican*, Aug. 10, 1916. Includes a personal account of Kelsey's early life.

White, T. Baxter. Letter to Barak Wright in Short Off, mailed from La Verne, Calif., Oct. 2, 1920.

Winstead, Nathaniel S. Letter to Randolph Shaffner, Feb. 5, 2001, concerning weather trends in Highlands from 1962–99.

Manuscripts

Anon. "Memoir of Mr. S. T. Kelsey." An undated, unsigned sketch of Kelsey's life by "the first person to whom Mr. Kelsey revealed his plans at Linville, North Carolina."

Crowe, Bobby. "Family Tree." Unpub. genealogy, early 1990s.

Crumpler, Thomas B. "History of Highlands." Unpub. MS, ca. 1975.

Smith, Mary Chapin. "A Sketch of the Highlands Improvement Society," June, 1928. Unpub. article.

Thornton, Helen Hill. "Historical Sketch of the Episcopal Church of the Incarnation, Highlands, N.C." Unpub. MS given to *Franklin Press*, ca. 1958–60.

Wright, Harry. "History of the Methodist Church." Unpub. MS, n.d.

Maps

Accurate Maps. *Western North Carolina*. Spartanburg, S.C., 1995.

Cumming, William P. *North Carolina in Maps*. Raleigh, 1966.

Denman, James, R. E. Norton, and J. E. Root. *Map of a Portion of Highlands, N. C.: Main Street and Vicinity*. Highlands, N. C., Nov. 28, 1945, and April 1, 1946.

Fisher, Richard Swainson, M. D. *Johnson's New Illustrated Family Atlas*. New York: Johnson and Ward, 1864, esp. pp. 39–40 (North Carolina).

Franklin, James. *District 13 (Scaly area) of the 18 Original Districts of Old Macon County*, 1820.

Greville, Thomas. *Map of Highlands and Vicinity*. Highlands, N.C., Sept. 13, 1931.

Gudger, James. *District 16 (Franklin area) of the 18 Original Districts of Old Macon County*, 1820.

Haake, A. von. *Post Route Map of the States of North Carolina and South Carolina showing Post Offices with the intermediate distances and mail routes in operation on the 1ˢᵗ of June, 1896*. Chapel Hill, N.C., North Carolina Collection.

Hutchinson, Arthur H. *Tracing of Kelsey's Map of Highlands*. New York, Jan. 7, 1881.

Kelsey, Samuel T. *Original Map of Highlands*. Highlands, Jan. 1, 1881.

Kerr, W. C., and Wm. Cain. *Map of North Carolina, 1882*. Washington, D.C., Library of Congress.

Lindenkohl, A. *Map of Virginia, North Carolina, and South Carolina, 1865*. Raleigh, State Department of Archives and History.

McDowell, Charlie W. *Map of Two Separate Tracts of Land Annexed by the Town of Highlands*. Highlands, N. C., July 11, 1977.

McDowell, Daniel. *District 12 (Upper Cullasaja River area) of the 18 Original Districts of Old Macon County*, 1820.

Miller, John. *District 18 (Horse Cove area) of the 18 Original Districts of Old Macon County*, 1820.

N.C. Bartram Trail Society. *Bartram Trail*, 6 sections. Scaly Mtn., N.C., 1993.

N.C. Dept. of Transportation. *Macon County, North Carolina*. Franklin Area Chamber of Commerce, 1986.

N.C. State Highway and Public Works. *Road Map of Highlands–Franklin Area*. 1944 and 1956.

Norton, R. E. *Map of Highlands Cemetery*, delineated by Pope H. Fuller. Highlands, N.C., Feb. 8, 1978.

Ranger Office. Highlands Hiking Trail Maps. Highlands, N.C., n.d.

Reynolds, T. W. *Area Map of Horse and Whiteside Coves*. Highlands, N.C., 1966.

———. *Map of Highlands Area*. Highlands, N.C., 1966.

Seaborn, Margaret Mills. *Cherokee Indian Towns of Oconee County, South Carolina, from 1730 through 1776 with Principal Paths*. Oconee Co., S.C., 1974. Compiled for the 1976 Bicentennial American Revolutionary Celebration.

State Land Grants in Macon County, N.C. Franklin, Macon County Register of Deeds, n.d.

Town of Highlands. *Kelsey's Map, Enlarged and Expanded*. Highlands, N.C., 1895.

U.S. Forest Service. *Nantahala National Forest, North Carolina*. U.S. Dept. of Agriculture, 1991.

———. *Paved, Dirt, and Primitive Roads of Macon and Jackson Counties, N.C.* 1965.

U.S. Forest Service. *Southern Nantahala Wilderness and Standing Indian Basin: Nantahala National Forest and Chattahoochee National Forest*. U.S. Dept. of Agriculture, 1997.

U.S. Geological Survey. *Fontana Lake, N.C.–Tenn.–S.C.–Ga*. Tennessee Valley Authority, 1983.

————. *Highlands, N.C., Quadrangle*. 1927.

————. *Topographic Quadrangle Maps* of Cashiers, Corbin Knob, Franklin, Glenville, Highlands, and Scaly Mountain, N.C., and Rabun Bald, Satolah, and Tamassee, Ga. U.S. Dept. of the Interior, 1946–61, photorevised 1979–91.

Newspapers

Blue Ridge Enterprise (Highlands). Jan. 1, 1883–Jan. 22, 1885, now on microfilm.

Highlander (Highlands). August 7, 1885–February 25, 1887. Feb. 19, July 16, 23, and 30, 1886, now on microfilm.

Star (Highlands). May 1, 1890–June 3, 1891.

Number Four (Highlands). June–July, 1891, four issues.

Mountain Eagle (Highlands). September 9, 1891–1892, 1893.

Carolina Mountains. June, 1893. Asheville, N.C.

Franklin Press, on microfilm:

> Sept. 20, 1888–December 24, 1902. T. Baxter White, "Highlands," always on p. 3.
>
> 1903–1919. destroyed in the great fire.
>
> January 23, 1920–1928. "News of Week of Highlands." See especially the July 5, 1928 Highlands ed.
>
> 1929–February, 1931. Sarah Hicks Hines, "Highlands Flings," in "Highlands—The Roof Garden of the Southeast."
>
> 1931–April 28, 1932. "Social and Personal News from Highlands."

Highlands Maconian (Highlands). September 3, 1930–April 27, 1932, now on microfilm.

Franklin Press and Highlands Maconian

> May 5, 1932–1953: "Highlands Highlights," except for 1936 issues, which were never microfilmed. See special eds. of July 20, 1939, and July 5, 1947.
>
> 1954–55: "Highlands People."
>
> 1956–December 24, 1968. No Highlands column.

Highlander (Highlands). August 6–September 4, 1937. Edited by S. J. Fullwood. A local newspaper that ran for only five issues.

Franklin Press. January 1, 1969–.

Galax News. July 16, 1952–Sept. 2, 1971. Summers only.

1952–56 [began with a tiny 7-page issue, grew in 20 years to 30 pages, ed. Miss Mary Summer (later Mrs. Jimmy W. Norman)]

1957–60

1961-63 [61 ed. Ella Jayne Cabe and Tina Harbison, 62-3 ed. Mrs. James "Tina" Newton, assist. Jessie Harbison]

1964-66 [64-65 ed. Jessie Harbison, assist. Frieda McCall, 66 co-ed. Betty Holt and Elizabeth Worley]

1967-69 [67 co-ed. Betty Holt and Jessie Harbison, 68-9 co-ed. Dotty Dendy, Susan Whitmire, and Dotty Dendy]

1970–71 [co-ed. Dotty Dendy, Sarah Summer, and Susan Whitmire]

Mountain Trail. July 7, 1939-Sept. 12, 1941, Jan. 23, 1943, May 23, 1952. Pub. by Highlands School Theatre

Highlander (Highlands). May, 1958–, on microfilm.

Booklets and Pamphlets

Brigham, Sue. *History of Wildcat Cliffs Country Club*. Highlands, N.C., 1995. A well-researched, articulate account.

Beyond Satulah Lies Highlands. Plates and printing by Jacobs and Co., Clinton, S.C., 1923. A pamphlet promoting both Highlands "Heart of the Hills" and Walhalla, S.C. "The Gate-Way."

Deal, Rev. John A. *The American Mountaineer*. N.d. An assessment of the Southern Appalachian mountaineer at the end of the 19th century by the itinerant Episcopal priest of Franklin, Highlands, and Cashiers.

Highlands Land Trust, Inc. Highlands, 1998.

Highlands Industrial Committee. *Highlands, North Carolina—Facts & Figures for Industry*. Highlands Chamber of Commerce, 1956. A survey prepared to attract industry to Highlands.

"In the Heart of the Mountains" Lies Highlands Western North Carolina. Plates and Printing by Jacobs and Co., Clinton, S.C., 1890. A pamphlet prepared by the Coe Brothers of Highlands. Rev. ed., 1929, alternate title *Beyond Satulah Lies Highlands*, includes panoramic foldout, Monroe estate, sylvan view on a by-road, and view of Satulah Mountain from five miles south.

Kelsey, S. T. *Blue Ridge Highlands in Western North Carolina*. Greenville, S.C., 1876. Kelsey's 1st promotional pamphlet.

Kelsey, S. T. *Highlands, North Carolina: The Most Perfect Climatic Sanitarium in the World*. Rising Sun, Md., 1887. Kelsey's 2nd promotional pamphlet.

Morris, Ralph, ed. *Stained Glass Windows of the Highlands United Methodist Church*. Highlands, N.C., 1993.

Owens, Jessie Potts, and Nancy Potts Coward. *The Story of the John Palmer and Jane Gribble McKinney Family*. 1997.

Smith, Rev. C. D., *Brief History of Macon County, North Carolina*, and W. A. Curtis, *The Topography of Macon County*. Franklin, N.C., 1905.

Smith, Mary Chapin. *History of the Hudson Library Association*. Highlands, 1931.

Souvenir Guide Book to Highlands, N.C. Franklin, N.C., 1934.

Totten, H. R., W. C. Coker, and H. J. Oosting. "Dr. Thomas Grant Harbison," *Journal of the Elisha Mitchell Scientific Society*, vol. 52 (1936), pp. 140–45.

Public Documents

Highlands Biological Station. Computer-generated spreadsheet of the mean, maximum, and minimum temperatures; greatest precipitation; and greatest snowfall for each day of the year during fifty-year period of record: Jan., 1948–Nov., 1998.

Highlands Biological Station. Record of monthly precipitation and average temperature highs and lows during forty-nine-year period from June, 1961–Dec., 2000.

Land Use Plan of the Town of Highlands, State of North Carolina, as adopted by the Board of Commissioners, Sept. 20, 1989.

Land Use Plan: Results of the Citizen Survey, Appendix I (Asheville, 1988).

Land Use Plan Update. Report of the Planning Board, July 28, 1993.

Minutes of the Hudson Library Association, Secretary's Book, 7 vols.: April 26, 1884–present. Missing Jan., 1955–July, 1970.

Record of First Sunday school, Highlands, N.C., March 12, 1876. Original document.

Minutes of the Floral and Industrial Society of Highlands, 2 vols.: Secretary's Book (July 17, 1883–Sept. 7, 1899) and Accountant's Book.

Minutes of the Southern Blue Ridge Horticultural Society of Highlands, Secretary's Book: Jan. 3, 1891–Nov. 2, 1895.

Minutes of the Board of Supervisors for Blue Ridge Township (Road Work), 2 vols.: May 1, 1879–Apr. 5, 1905, June 13, 1913–Nov. 26, 1919.

Minutes of the Highlands Rail Road Company, Secretary's Book, Feb. 4, 1882–Nov. 16, 1887.

Minutes of the Board of Commissioners of Highlands, N.C., Bks. A–G and 1–3, covering May 28, 1883–Nov. 16, 1959. 1960–present. Missing Bk. B (Jan., 1899–May, 1908) and Bk. D (Aug. 9, 1920–March 23, 1925 except for loose minutes from Sept. 3, 1921–March 14, 1923).

Minutes of the Mount Hope Cemetery Association, Highlands, N.C., Record
Book, 2 vols. Bk. 1 (Nov. 15, 1880–April 8, 1968), Bk. 2 (April 8, 1969–
Feb. 23, 1998). Name changed to Highlands Cemetery Co. on Jul. 25,
1887, pursuant to Deed of Oct. 11, 1881.

32. Index

668

Thomas, A. B., 612
Thomas, Mark & Brooks, 538
Thomas, Ralph, 333, 537
Thomas, Sylvia, 590
Thomas, William H. "Will", 13
Thompson, A. W., 150, 265
Thompson, Florence, 394
Thompson, H. P. Percy, 304, **305**, 542
Thompson, Helen McKinney
    Cleaveland "Mama", 305, 406, 470,
    542
Thompson, Hugh Miller, xxiii, 90, 154
Thompson, John R., xxiii, 150, 154
Thompson, Mary, 410
Thompson, Meriwether M. S. "Bud",
    367
Thompson, Mike, 388
Thompson, Richard, 534
Thompson, Snook, 519
Thompson, Tolliver, Sr., 611
Thompson, V. W., 612
Thompson, W. T., 325
Thornton, Nancy, xxvi
Thorpe Lake. See Lake Glenville
Thurman, James M., 610
Thurman, Milida P., 337
Tichenor, David, 341
Tick Tock Gifts, 395, 418
Tigue, J. L., 610
Tilson, Jerry, 485
Tin Can Tourists, 424
Tippett, David, 204
Toby West Antiques, 118, 452
Todd, Dave, 417
Todd, Lee, 417
Tolar, T. L., 224, 517, 616
Toll house, Cashiers, 158
Toll road, Cashiers, 92, 166
Toll road, Whiteside, 181
Tomita, Mutsuo, 413
Topography, W.N.C., 3
Topside, 452
Torrence, Larry, 421
Torrey, Bradford, 153, 157
Tour of Homes, 250
Town and Country, 396
Town hall, 167, 197, 409, 530
Town House Motel, 305, 410, 423, 441

Town Square, 410, 423, 441
Townsend, C. T., 307
Trail Committee, 594
Trail of Tears in 1838, 9
Trailer parks, 462
Trapier, Alicia, 247
Trapier, William, 247
Treaty of 1819, 9
Treaty of 1835, 9
Treer, Leonid, 540
Trees
    altitude oak, **xxiv**, 392, **397**, 424,
        498
    Carolina hemlock, 409
    chestnut, 347
    clear-cutting, 425
    dogwoods, 409
    Fraser fir, 348
    hawthorne, 121
    ideal street, 343
    linden, 121, 346
    maples, 409
    tree board, 424
    tree committee, 424
    trees on Main Street, 182, 399, 424,
        474
    tulip poplar, 2, 345
    willow, 121
Trice, Angelyn, 321, 331, 413
Trice, J. Harvey, 321, 331, 401, 406
Tricemont Terrace. See Davis House
Trillium, 218
Trillium Lodge, 69, 448, 515
Trillium Place, 461
Trock, Arthur, 405
Trott, Allen L. "Buck", 435, 602, 607
Trowbridge, Betty K., 327, 328, 332
Trowbridge, Marietta, 299
Trowbridge, Wilbur C., 81, 187, 608
Trowbridge, William J., 327
Trussell, Malvina, 353, 425
Tucker & Laxton, Inc., 383
Tucker, Leslie, 611
Tudor Hall Real Estate, 290, 402
Turner, Walter, 372
Turtle Pond, 389
Tuten, Joe, 406
Tuttle, Lee F., 610

33. Notes

[1] The book that coined the phrase, "Land of the Sky," in 1875, the same year that Highlands was founded, was the tenth novel of Christian Reid (pseudonym for Frances Christine Fisher Tiernan) of Salisbury, N.C. *"The Land of the Sky:" or, Adventures in Mountain By-ways* (New York, 1876) immortalized the mountains of Western North Carolina, where the great Appalachian system reached its loftiest altitude, as the most beautiful mountains she had ever seen, indeed, the most beautiful, she thought, which could be seen anywhere.

[2] For Weimar Jones' imitation of mountain English, see *My Affair with a Weekly* (Winston-Salem, N.C., 1960), p. 116.

[3] For the alleged naming of Walking Stick Road after the Cherokee chief by that name, see Helen Hill Norris, *Looking Backward*, vol. 1 (1961), pp. 48–49.

[4] For Woodrow Wilson's reference to Jno. R. Thompson's Lane, see his letter of July 30, 1879, to Robert Bridges, as quoted in the *Franklin Press and Highlands Maconian*, Sept. 6, 1956, p. 1. For the reference to John R. Thompson's Lane in minutes of Board of Supervisors of Roads in Highlands Township, 1879–1905, see District No. 1, pp. 1ff.

[5] For the suggestion of *Sau-gwil-lah* as a better name for Horse Cove eleven years before its being actually adopted, see "Indian Words," *Blue Ridge Enterprise*, March 8, 1883, p. 1.

[6] For the actual paving in front of Highlands Inn the next year, see "Street Improvement Being Planned in Highlands," *Franklin Press and Highlands Maconian*, April 22, 1948.

[7] For Sidney McCarty's view on the altitude oak, see *Highlander*, Dec. 24, 1991. For commissioners elected to the town board in May, 1947, see minutes of Board of Commissioners, Bk. 2, p. 144, May 6, 1947: James O. Beale elected mayor, commissioners J. E. Potts, J. D. Burnett, W. A. Hays, Joe Reese, and Sidney McCarty.

[8] Butler Jenkins, Sr., married Jennie Webb; Allen Jenkins married Sarah Webb; John Jenkins married Creasy Webb; and Thomas Jenkins married Betsy Webb. See Lawrence E. Wood, *Young and Montgomery Families of the South* (Franklin, N.C., 1978), p. 316.

[9] Actually the world's oldest mountains no longer exist, so the Caledonians and Appalachians are the oldest, if only by default.

[10] For naturalist Donald Culross Peattie's list of southeastern species closely akin to those found only in East Asia, see Robert Beverley's *Western North Carolina Almanac*, 2nd ed. (Franklin, N.C., 1993), pp. 41-2.

[11] For Margaret W. Morley's description of the wild azaleas, see her *Carolina Mountains* (Boston, 1913), p. 52.

[12] The last great ice age, from which we are just emerging, reached its climax about 20,000 years ago. According to present calculations, the earth's climate will grow increasingly warmer until 20,000 A. D., and the next ice age will begin around 50,000 A. D. Current melting will eventually raise sea level by more than 100 feet, enough to

submerge New York, London, Paris, and most of the great seaports and coastal areas of the earth.

[13] Theda Perdue, a leading authority on Indian history, remarks in his *Native Carolinians: The Indians of North Carolina* (Raleigh, 1985), p. 1: "For a long time, scholars believed that man came to the Americas only during the latter period [28,000 to 10,000], but the discovery of new sites and the more precise dating of others indicate that people very likely crossed the land bridge during the earlier period [50,000 to 40,000]."

[14] For the etymology of the word *Cherokee*, see Charles Hudson, *Knights of Spain, Warriors of the Sun: Hernando de Soto and the South's Ancient Chiefdoms* (Athens, Ga., 1997), p. 186. See also Hudson's *The Juan Pardo Expeditions: Exploration of the Carolinas and Tennessee, 1566–1568* (Washington, D.C., 1990), pp. 84-5.

[15] For the Cherokee name for themselves, see James Mooney, *Myths of the Cherokee and Sacred Formulas of the Cherokees*, from the 19th and 7th Annual Reports of the Bureau of American Ethnology (Nashville, rpt. 1982), p. 15.

[16] For de Soto's alleged camping in Highlands, see *Highlander*, March 13, 1975.

[17] For the Smithsonian claim, see the 1930s federal commission report chaired by Dr. John R. Swanton.

[18] For Hudson's revision of the Smithsonian claim, see his *Knights of Spain, Warriors of the Sun*, pp. 186–214 and 480. See also the map on p. 148.

[19] For Cherokee name of Devil's Courthouse, see Silas McDowell's article in *The News and Farmer*, 1877, rpt. *Highlander*, Sept. 14, 1972.

[20] For T. W. Reynolds' first account of the Spanish inscription, see his *High Lands* (Highlands, N.C., 1964), pp. 14–16. For his subsequent explanation, see his *Southern Appalachian Region* (Highlands, 1966), vol. 1, pp. 6–11 and 136.

[21] For Henry Wright's perspective on the Spanish inscription, see "Inscription Explanation Questioned by Citizens," *Highlander*, Dec. 8, 1966.

[22] For Bob Zahner's account, see his *Mountain at the End of the Trail* (Highlands, 1994), pp. 106, 110–11, and 116–19. For Bob Padgett's conclusions, see *Highlander*, Nov. 20, 1990.

[23] For Eloy Gallegos' translation of the Spanish inscription, see his Spanish Pioneers in the United States History series, particularly *The Melungeons: The Pioneers of the Interior Southeastern United States: 1526–1997*, pp. 137–38.

[24] For Will Cleaveland's collection of Indian relics, begun by his father, see "Move on Foot to Build Museum at Highlands," *Franklin Press*, Sept. 22, 1927.

[25] Wilbur Zeigler and Ben Grosscup mentioned Indian ladders in the vicinity of Whiteside and Devil's Courthouse before 1880. See *Heart of the Alleghanies; or, Western North Carolina* (Raleigh, N.C., 1883), p. 21. For an interesting account and photographs of these ladders as Cherokee sign posts or trees permanently bent to mark trails, see Elaine Jordan, *Indian Trail Trees* (Ellijay, Ga., 1977).

[26] For the Cherokee burial ground on Ledford's land, see *Franklin Press*, May 6, 1990. For Ledford's purchase of his property from Felix Kilpatrick, see *Bk. of Deeds* F, p. 334 (Aug. 7, 1851), for 50 acres of Section 47 south of Sugartown River in District 12, costing $35.

[27] For the drawing of Whiteside Mountain in 1877, see Wilbur Zeigler and Ben Grosscup, *Heart of the Alleghanies; or, Western North Carolina*, p. 13.

[28] For Barak Norton's arrival in Whiteside Cove, see Mary Norton's obituary, *Blue Ridge Enterprise*, April 5, 1883. He was born May 10, 1777, and died in Sept. 1, 1869, at age 92. Mary was born Jan. 31, 1788, and died March 26, 1883, at age 95. See also Arthur, *Western North Carolina, A History from 1730 to 1913* (Asheville, N.C., 1914; rpt. Johnson City, Tenn., 1996), pp. 498–99. Barak Norton took out State land grants in Whiteside Cove as early as May, 1836.

[29] For John H. Alley's arrival in Whiteside Cove, see Judge Felix Alley's *Random Thoughts and the Musings of a Mountaineer*, p. 2.

[30] S. W. Hill took out State land grants in Horse Cove as early as May, 1843, but moved there from Cherokee, S.C., in 1847. See *Blue Ridge Enterprise*, May 10, 1883, p. 3.

[31] For Judge Felix Alley's account of Kirk's Raiders, see *Random Thoughts and the Musings of a Mountaineer* (Salisbury, N.C., 1941), pp. 3–4. See also Helen Hill Norris "When the Raiders Came," *Looking Backward*, vol. 1, pp. 37–38.

[32] For George and William Barnes as the first to settle Horse Cove, see Arthur, *Western North Carolina*, p. 499. See also the detailed history of Horse Cove by Mary Jane Edwards in *Heritage of Macon County*, vol. 1 (Franklin, N.C., 1987), pp. 53–55.

[33] For the arrival of James McKinney (born 1795, died 1872 or 1875) and naming of Cashiers, see Dave U. Sloan [Jr.], *Fogy Days, and Now; or, the World Has Changed, The Innovations of the 19th Century* (Atlanta, 1891), p. 22. See also *Franklin Press and Highlands Maconian*, Aug. 7, 1941, p. 5, and "Elderly Group Gathers for Unusual Cashiers Birthday Celebration," *Asheville Citizen-Times*, Sept. 7, 1941.

For the naming of the valley after Wade Hampton's bull, see Jonathan Daniels, *Tar Heels: A Portrait of North Carolina* (New York, 1941), p. 238. For its being named after an Indian trader, among other explanations, see T. W. Reynolds, *High Lands*, pp. 29–36. Mrs. Melbourne Smith includes this account in a definitive article she wrote in 1950 for the *Asheville Citizen* entitled, "Cashiers Valley People Disagree on How It Received Its Name," rpt. in S. Van Epp Law's *Status Quo*, pp. 112–14. Wilbur Zeigler and Ben Grosscup in their 1883 edition of *Heart of the Alleghanies; or, Western North Carolina* appear content with the unvarnished claim that the charming valley got its name "for no other reason than a man's horse was once lost in it" (p. 324).

[34] For the name change from Cashiers Valley to Cashiers, see Max Williams, ed., *History of Jackson County* (Sylva, 1987), p. 131.

[35] For the date of the Winding Stairs Turnpike, see letter from John S. Palmer to his daughter Harriet on Aug. 14, 1857, in Louis P. Towles, ed., *A World Turned Upside Down: The Palmers of South Santee, 1818–1881* (Columbia, S.C., 1996), pp. 211–12: "We are now promised a fine turnpike to commence at Tunnel Hill and come out to meet a road being constructed from Webster's by [Allison D.] McKinney's [house]. . . . Clearly it will be made as the states of North and South Carolina have given aid to the understanding." Col. William Sloan was the engineer in charge of building the Old Blue Ridge Tunnel at Stumphouse Mountain, S.C.

[36] William Holland Thomas, or Wil Usdi as he was known by the Cherokee Indians, was elected in 1836 the first white chief of the Eastern Band of Cherokees. In addition to lobbying congress successfully on their behalf, he bought land, in his own name as a white man, for many of the approximately one thousand Cherokee Indians who had escaped the Trail of Tears to remain in their traditional homeland.

[37] For the gubernatorial debate over the Winding Stairs Turnpike extension, see "Elderly Group Gathers," *Asheville Citizen-Times*, Sept. 7, 1941.

[38] For Millsaps as the first white settler of Cashiers Valley, see Arthur's *Western North Carolina*, p. 497. See also S. Van Epp Law's *Status Quo*, p. 125. Haywood County was formed from Buncombe County in 1808 and included today's Macon and Jackson counties, which weren't formed until 1828 and 1851, respectively.

[39] Col. Zachary took out State Land Grant No. 124 in Cashiers Valley in 1835. For an account of the Zachary arrival, see S. Van Epp Law, *Status Quo* (Stuart, Fla., 1971), pp. 114–16.

[40] James Wright was born July 4, 1811, and died April 19, 1886. His wife Jemina Norton Wright was born Dec. 3, 1816, and died July 22, 1897. Both are buried in the Highlands Cemetery.

[41] Marion Wright was born in 1846 and died in 1923. Barak was born in 1847 and died in 1926. Both are buried in the Highlands Cemetery.

[42] Isaac Peter Rice took out State land grants in Whiteside Cove as early as Aug., 1859. He was born June 16, 1836, and died in 1914, reportedly in Texas. Vinetta Rice, whom he married in 1862, was born Sept. 22, 1842 in Whiteside Cove and died in Sept. 21, 1928, at age 86 in Highlands.

[43] Elias Norton was born in 1812 in Pickens District, S.C., and died Oct. 28, 1854. His grandson Frank Norton claimed he was killed in Whiteside Cove. He is buried in the Norton Cemetery.

[44] For Polly Norton's home, see "Elderly Group Gathers," *Asheville Citizen-Times*, Sept. 7, 1941.

[45] Silas McDowell was born May 16, 1795, and died July 14, 1879. See Gary S. Dunbar's biography: "Silas McDowell and the Early Botanical Exploration of Western North Carolina," *N.C. Historical Review*, vol. 41 (1964), pp. 425–35. See also Macon County Historical Society, *Heritage of Macon County*, vol. 1, pp. 352–3, and vol. 2, pp. 329–30.

[46] There were other Sugartowns of the Cherokee, such as the Sugartown on the Toxaway River between Toxaway and Keowee. See Margaret Mills Seaborn's map of *Cherokee Indian Towns from 1730 through 1776 with Principal Paths* (Oconee Co., S.C., 1974).

[47] For Wilma Dykeman's assessment of Rutherford's raids on the Indians, see *The French Broad* (Newport, Tenn., 1992), p. 35.

[48] The Cherokee surrender of May 20, 1777, resulted in the first treaty of the newly formed United States.

[49] For the meanings and origins of Cullasaja, Sugartown, and Sugar Fork as names of the river between Highlands and Franklin, see James Mooney, *Myths of the Cherokee and Sacred Formulas of the Cherokees* (Nashville, Tenn., 1882), p. 525.

For supporting explanations of the term, see *Galax News*, Aug. 26, 1965, p. 15; T. W. Reynolds, *Cherokee and Creek* (Highlands, 1966), pp. 58–59; Nancy Turner's *Summer Times* (Tampa, Fla., 1994), p. 115; and Bob Zahner's "Cullasaja's Tree" in *Leaf Season in the Mountains, Fall 1999* (*Highlander* and *Crossroads Chronicle* newspapers), pp. 89-93, and "River of the Honey Locust Place," in *Highlander*, Oct. 24, 1995.

[50] For a short biography of McDowell, see Theodore F. Davidson's "Carolina Mountaineer—The Highest Type of American Character," *First Annual Transactions of the Pen and Plate Club* (Asheville, N.C., 1906), pp. 87–92, and his *Reminiscences and*

Traditions of Western North Carolina (Asheville, 1928), pp. 19–21. See also J. W. Davidson, *Living Writers of the South* (New York, 1869), pp. 357–59.

[51] For McDowell's articles on the thermal belt, see *North-Carolina Planter*, vol. 1 (June, 1858), pp. 261–63; vol. 3 (1860), pp. 328–29; and esp. his "Belt of No Frost, or Thermal Belt," *U.S. Agricultural Report of the Commissioner of Patents for the Year 1861*, Smithsonian Institute, Washington, D.C.: 1862, pp. 146–47. For more information on the thermal belt, see "The Thermal Belts of the Blue Ridge," as quoted from *Germantown Telegraph* in *Blue Ridge Enterprise*, Feb. 8, 1883. For Wilbur Zeigler's and Ben Grosscup's tribute to Silas McDowell for his discovery of the thermal or "no frost" zone, see their *Heart of the Alleghanies*, pp. 191–92.

[52] For McDowell's poem, see one-page MS, undated but probably 1858, in Silas McDowell Papers, Southern Historical Collection, University of North Carolina, Chapel Hill.

[53] For McDowell's promotion of Highlands, see *North Carolina Citizen*, vol. 4, no. 24 (June 26, 1873), p. 2; vol. 5, no. 27 (July 23, 1874), p. 1; vol. 6, no. 6 (March 4, 1875), p. 2; esp. vol. 6, no. 18 (April 22, 1875), p. 2.

[54] For Kelsey's and Hutchinson's arrival in N.C., see Kelsey's *Record of Weather and Work*, vol. 1, Sept., 1875.

[55] For Silas McDowell's naming of Highlands, see his "Sugartown Highlands in Macon Co., as a Health Center," *North Carolina Citizen*, April 22, 1875, p. 2. For an excellent article on how Highlands got its name, see Robert Zahner, "Silas McDowell and his 'Sugartown Highlands,'" *Highlander*, Aug. 20, 1996.

[56] *Cartoogechaye*, or *Cartoo-ge-cha-che-yah* in Cherokee, meant "the village beyond," so named because the little creek by that name emptied into the Little Tennessee river just beyond the old Cherokee village of Naquessa. For an interesting article on the Cherokee language as taught by Albert Siler, who learned it as a child playing with Cherokee children, see Margaret R. Siler, "Cherokee Lore," *Franklin Press and Highlands Maconian*, Feb. 15, 1934, pp. 1–2.

[57] Dobson's relevant land grants were as follows: State Grants 1084 and 1085 of May 28, 1844, or 640 acres each, totaling 1,280 acres at 10¢ per acre [*Bk. of Deeds* G, pp. 405-6]; Grant 1444 of Aug. 30, 1854, totaling 50 acres at 10¢ per acre [*Bk.* G, p. 470]; Grant 3112 of Oct. 13, 1858, totaling 100 acres at 12½¢ per acre [*Bk.* N, p. 277]; and Grant 3106 of Feb. 7, 1860, totaling 150 acres at 10¾¢ per acre [*Bk.* L, p. 435]. All of these were located on the Sugar Fork or Sugartown River.

[58] For Hugh Gibson's land purchase, see State Grant 861 in *Bk. of Deeds* F, p. 146 (entered Feb. 21, 1848).

[59] For Jackson Johnston's purchase of Dobson's Highlands tracts along with William M. Addington, see *Bk. of Deeds* L, p. 2 (April 5, 1869), and *Bk.* L, p. 352 (Dec. 7, 1869).

[60] For James D. Russell's land purchase, see State Grant 2062 of 100 acres at five cents per acre, *Bk. of Deeds* I, p. 34 (entered Oct. 4, 1853).

[61] For Felix Kilpatrick's land purchase, see State Grants 3464 (entered Sep. 23, 1859) and 3470 (entered Dec. 2, 1859) in *Bk. of Deeds* J-3, pp. 186 and 188. Robert Rogers bought Kilpatrick's land Oct. 26, 1881; see *Bk. of Deeds* S, p. 582.

[62] For Billy Webb's arrival on the Highlands plateau, see the memoirs of Butler Jenkins, Jr., p. 19. For a description of Billy Cabin and the Webb family, see Lawrence

Wood, Aug. 18, 1977, p. 3. For Billy Webb's Indian Hills home, see *Bk. of Deeds* P, p. 633 (Jan. 31, 1875).

[63] For Joe Webb's death, see *Blue Ridge Enterprise*, Feb. 15, 1883. See also Butler Jenkins' memoirs, p. 20.

[64] For an account of the lay of the land before the founding of Highlands, see "Eight Years Old To-day," *Blue Ridge Enterprise*, March 29, 1883.

[65] For Edward King's trek up the Cullasaja River in 1873, see his "Great South: Among the Mountains of Western North Carolina," *Scribner's Monthly*, vol. 7 (March, 1874), pp. 513–44. Available also on microform in *American Periodical Series III: Civil War Reconstruction*, reel 346. Pages 530–36 describe the Highlands plateau in 1873, two years before the founding of the town. See also King's reprint in book form: *The Great South* (rpt. Baton Rouge, 1972), ch. 61 ("The 'Sugar Fork' and Dry Falls— Whiteside Mountain,"), pp. 490–502.

[66] Jackson Hole Trading Post and Gem Mine was established on the Franklin Road in 1948.

[67] For the drawing of Lower Sugar Fork Fall in 1873, see King, "The Great South," in *Scribner's Monthly*, vol. 7 (March , 1874), p. 513, or his *Great South*, p. 495.

[68] For the sketch of Dry Falls in 1873, see King, "The Great South," in *Scribner's Monthly* (March, 1874), p. 520, or his *Great South*, p. 490.

[69] For the sketch of Dry Falls in 1876, called Cullasaja Falls, see Richard and Rebecca Harding Davis, "By-Paths of the Mountains," *Harper's New Monthly Magazine*, vol. 61 (Sept., 1880), p. 542.

[70] Two useful articles on Charles N. Jenks are "Impressions of an Old Timer," *Highlands Maconian*, Sept. 16, 1931, p. 4, and "Noted Explorer and Miner in Highlands for Summer," *Franklin Press and Highlands Maconian*, June 30, 1932, p. 3.

[71] For the story of Hiram Crisp's life and discovery, see Silas McDowell's "Hiram Crisp: The Unlettered Scientist of the South," written April 15, 1879, and quoted by Lawrence Wood, *Highlander*, Sept. 26, 1974, p. 6.

[72] For King's comparison of Whiteside Mountain to a high waterfall, see his "Great South," in *Scribner's Monthly* (March, 1874), p. 534, or his *Great South*, p. 500. For Silas McDowell's comparisons of Whiteside to a great monster or a huge hog, see his article, "Whiteside Rock," in *The News and Farmer,* 1877., rpt. *Highlander*, Sept. 14, 1972.

[73] For the sketch of Whiteside cave in 1873, see King, "The Great South," in *Scribner's Monthly* (March, 1874), p. 524, or his *Great South*, p. 501.

[74] For Charles Jenks' description of the narrow path to Whiteside cave, see *Highlands Maconian*, Sept. 29, 1931. See also Sarah Hines Bailey, "Whiteside Cave," *Mountain Trail*, Sept. 1, 1939.

[75] For the Spear-finger legend and its association with Whiteside cave, see James Mooney, *Myths of the Cherokee,* pp. 316–19. See also *Harper's Magazine*, Vol. 61 (Sept., 1880), p. 544; Frank Jarrett's "Oconneechee," as retold by Mrs. Tom Harbison, Mountain Trail, Aug. 25, 1939; and Douglas A. Rossman, "Spearfinger," *Where Legends Live: A Pictorial Guide to Cherokee Mythic Places* (Cherokee, N.C., 1988), p. 9.

[76] The jeep road at the base of Whiteside begins at the end of Twin Lakes Road in Whiteside Cove.

[77] *Sa-too-lah* in Cherokee means "a sudden puff of wind," according to a correspondent in *Blue Ridge Enterprise*, March 8, 1883, p. 1.

[78] For the Cherokee name of Fodderstack Mountain, see Mooney, *Myths of the Cherokee*, pp. 473 and 519. See also Douglas A. Rossman, *Where Legends Live,* p. 18. Rossman reports that Fodderstack was one of four mountains under which the bears held council and danced before denning for the winter.

[79] For John Jay Smith's speculation about the naming of Highlands, see his recollection, "Highlands, N.C. Founded 1875," *Franklin Press,* Jan. 29, 1926.

[80] *Chattooga*, or *chatawga* in Cherokee, means "chicken."

[81] *Tuckasegee*, or *tsiksitsi* in Cherokee, means a "place of the terrapin" or, when applied to water, "sluggish."

[82] *Nantahala*, or *Nan-toi-yar-la* in Cherokee, means "sun middle" or "middle sun," often translated "river of the noon-day sun," because the river bearing that name flowed through such deep gorges in some places that the sun's rays reached its waters only in the middle of the day.

[83] For Kelsey's mention of this town site survey that took just over a week in 1878, see his *Record of Weather and Work*, vol. 1, June 18–25, 1878.

[84] For Richard and Rebecca Harding Davis' visit to Highlands in 1876, the year after its founding, see "By-Paths in the Mountains," *Harper's New Monthly Magazine*, Vol. 61 (Sept., 1880), pp. 532–47, esp. pp. 541–45.

[85] For one possible location of Hugh and Ann Gibson's cabin, see Elias D. White, "Another Chapter Added to Early Highlands Days, *Highlands Maconian*, Aug. 20, 1920, p. 5. Baxter White's son Elias remembered the Gibsons' log cabin as located "across a meadow to the east of the S. T. Kelsey home," the land sloping downward to a creek. A hundred yards or more farther on stood the cabin, presumably at today's site of Trillium Place. On the other hand, Helen Hill Norris and Lawrence Wood claim it was located to the north of Kelsey's home, across Mill Creek about where Hall House would stand in the 1900s, today's Mill Creek Manor. See Helen Hill Norris' reference in her story of the dismantling of Highlands Manor (formerly Hall House) in *Looking Backward*, vol. 1, p. 31, and Lawrence Wood's article on the Gibsons, *Highlander*, Nov. 9, 1972.

[86] For Davis' recollection of the Gibsons and his gift to them of the alarm clock, see Elias D. White, "Another Chapter Added to Early Highland Days," *Franklin Press and Highlands Maconian*, Aug. 20, 1942, p. 5.

[87] For the lithograph of the Gibsons, see Richard Harding Davis, *Harper's New Monthly Magazine*, Sept. 1880, vol. 61, p. 543, and pp. 541–44 for the section relating to Highlands.

[88] William Dobson sold to Hutchinson 839 acres of five of his father William's state grants (part of S.G. 1084 from Satulah to Mill Creek and including today's town proper, part of S.G. 1085 north of Mill Creek to Little and Big Bear Pen mountains, part of S.G. 1444 containing the beginning of today's Horse Cove Road, part of S.G. 3112 surrounding today's Bowery Road, and part of S.G. 3106 including Little and Big Bear Pen). All of Hutchinson's land lay north of Satulah for a total cost of $1,678; see *Bk. of Deeds* N, p. 497.

[89] For Kelsey's choice of the name "Highlands," see his *Record of Weather and Work*, vol. 1, Sept. and Dec. 20, 1875.

[90] For Richard Harding Davis' assessment of Highlands' future, see *Harper's New Monthly Magazine*, Sept. 1880, vol. 61, p. 543. For Wilbur Zeigler's and Ben Grosscup's agreement, see *Heart of the Alleghanies; or, Western North Carolina*, pp. 326–27.

[91] For Highlands as a convenience center, see S. T. Kelsey's first promotional pamphlet, *The Blue Ridge Highlands in Western North Carolina* (Greenville, S.C., 1876), p. 9. Kelsey distributed this pamphlet the year after his arrival on the Highlands plateau.

[92] For a history of the descendants of William Kelsey the Puritan, see *Kelsey Genealogy*, published by the Kelsey Kindred in seven volumes and a supplement, covering generations one through fifteen.

[93] For an account of Samuel T. Kelsey's early life, see his letter to the citizens of Pomona, Kansas, *Pomona Republican*, Aug. 10, 1916.

[94] For the account of Kelsey's decision to become a nurseryman, see his letter to the Kansas State Horticultural Society, Dec. 4, 1905.

[95] Kelsey's first child, Laura Olin, was born Aug. 3, 1867, in Ottawa, Kansas. See *Kelsey Genealogy*. Laura married twice: Augustus C. Barr in 1885 in Highlands, two children, and Ansel R. Odgen in 1905 in Knoxville, Tenn., one child.

[96] For Kelsey's search for a town site, see his *Record of Weather and Work*, vol. 1, Sept. 1875.

[97] For the destruction of Kelsey's "Kanonah" house by fire, see *Highlander*, Oct. 28, 1976.

[98] For the creation of Harbison/Kanonah/Harris Lake, see *Blue Ridge Enterprise*, Dec. 20, 1883.

[99] For the protection of trees from rabbits, see Kelsey's *Record of Weather and Work*, vol. 2, Feb. 8, 1882.

[100] For Harlan Kelsey's role as nurseryman, see "The Highlands Nursery," in *National Nurseryman* (Rochester, N.Y., Feb., 1910). See also Linda Laderoute, *Harlan P. Kelsey: Landscape Architect, Horticulturist, Conservationist* (Boxford, Ma., 1999), p. 4. For publication of the catalog see *Highlander*, Jan. 29 and Feb. 12, 1886.

[101] For Kelsey's, Stewart's, and Ravenel's roles in the founding of Linville, see John Preston Arthur, *Western North Carolina,* pp. 410–12. See also Ina W. and John J. Van Noppen, *Western North Carolina Since the Civil War* (Boone, N.C., 1973), pp. 325–6.

[102] For mention of Kelsey's death, see T. Baxter White's obituary, "Macon Pioneer Passes Away," *Franklin Press*, Aug. 4, 1922. For a biography of "Samuel Truman Kelsey," see *Highlander*, "Centennial Issue," July 19, 1975, Sec. B, p. 6.

[103] For Harlan Kelsey as conservationist, see Linda Laderoute, *Harlan P. Kelsey*, p. 16. For a brief biography of Harlan Kelsey, see *Who's Who in America: 1950–51.*

[104] Hutchinson's deed calls his home "Corrymela." See *Bk. of Deeds* P, p. 317 (May 9, 1879). For a history of the Hutchinson/Frost house, see Helen Hill Norris, "Looking Backward," *Highlander*, July 10, 1964. For description of Farnsworth's Connemara, see *Franklin Press*, May 15, 1930, pp. 1 and 5.

[105] For a description of pre-Highlands inhabitants, see Kelsey's first promotional pamphlet of 1776, *Blue Ridge Highlands*, pp. 7 and 8.

[106] Walhalla, pronounced Valhalla in German, was the pre-Christian Norse equivalent of heaven, literally the banquet hall of their chief god, Odin. For the Sesquicentennial Committee's history of this town, see *Walhalla: 150 Years in the Garden of the Gods.*

[107] For a listing of all twenty-seven states, see "Eight Years Old Today," *Blue Ridge Enterprise*, March 29, 1883, p. 2. They were Maine, New Hampshire, Vermont, Massachusetts, Connecticut, New York, New Jersey, Pennsylvania, Ohio, Indiana, Illinois, Wisconsin, Michigan, Minnesota, Nebraska, Kansas, Virginia, Tennessee, North Carolina, South Carolina, Georgia, Arkansas, Texas, Florida, Louisiana, Delaware, and Oregon.

[108] For T. Baxter White's obituary, see La Verne's local newspaper, July 20, 1922. He was born Oct. 9, 1834, in Marblehead, Mass., but moved to Lynn at age nine. He died July 14, 1922, at age 87 in La Verne, California.

[109] For Baxter White's home, post office, and country store, see Elias D. White, "Early Highlands Days, An Historical Sketch," *Franklin Press and Highlands Maconian*, June 5, 1941. Dr. Jessie Zachary Moreland lived about fifteen feet back of this site in the 1950s. Baxter White built his home/post office in early summer, 1975, but he didn't officially own the land until July 17, 1878 [See *Bk. of Deeds* P, p. 83]. It was not uncommon at the time for the sale of property to precede its recording by many months. In 1879, for instance, the land that the Anderson/Whittle/Sullivan mansion would later occupy was sold by Kelsey to Henry Maxwell and John Anderson in July, 1878, but wasn't recorded until six months had passed, in January, 1879. See Kelsey's *Record of Weather and Work*, vol. 2, July 22, 1878, for the sale and *Bk. of Deeds* P, p. 260 (Jan. 25, 1879), for the deed of sale.

[110] J. P. "Dock" McKinney was born Jan. 13, 1854, and died May 17, 1938. His grandfather James McKinney was born in 1795 and died in 1872 or 1875.

[111] For Allison D. McKinney's date of birth, Nov. 18, 1876, see Jessie Owens and Nancy Coward, *The Story of the John Palmer and Jane Gribble McKinney Family* (1997), p. 22. At his death on July 7, 1943, Allison's obituary claims he was the "first" white child born in Highlands; see *Franklin Press and Highlands Maconian*, July 15, 1943. See also his mother's obituary, *Franklin Press and Highlands Maconian*, Dec. 26, 1935. Allison's sister Miss Montie Louise McKinney was credited with being the second child born in the town of Highlands on Aug. 18, 1878, but Samuel Kelsey's daughter Edith was born May 23, 1878, making her the second after Al and before Montie. And yet, according to Walter Reese, William McHenry Jackson, son of John E. Jackson, was first, even before Al McKinney; see "Diary of Joseph Walter Reese, 1885–1957" (unpub. MS, 1957), p. 9. No record of William Jackson's actual date of birth has been found yet to confirm Reese's claim.

[112] For George A. Jacobs' appointment as mayor, see *Blue Ridge Enterprise*, April 5, 1883.

[113] For first incorporation, see Act of the General Assembly of the State of NC, Chapter 43 of the laws of 1879. For second incorporation, see *Blue Ridge Enterprise*, Feb. 27 and April 5, 1883. See also "Original Act of Incorporation," *Highlander*, "Centennial Edition," July 19, 1975, p. 9-C. On March 7, 1889, the second act of incorporation was amended to exclude certain lands owned by Henry Stewart and others west of the east boundary line of State Grant No. 1085.

[114] For the petition to change Blue Ridge township to Highlands township, see *Blue Ridge Enterprise*, Feb. 22, 1883, p. 3.

[115] For James Soper's land purchase, see *Bk. of Deeds* O, p. 192 (Feb. 29, 1875).

[116] For dim hopes in early Highlands, see E. E. Ewing's "History of the Settlement of Highlands," *Blue Ridge Enterprise*, Jan. 25, 1883.

[117] For David Keener's determination to travel to Highlands, see his testimonial in Kelsey's second promotional pamphlet, *Highlands, North Carolina, The Most Perfect Climatic Sanitarium in the World* (Rising Sun, Md., 1887); for the Minnesotans who were turned away, see *Highlander*, Feb. 19, 1886. For John Houston's scorn of Kelsey's proposed town, see *Franklin Press and Highlands Maconian*, Oct. 19, 1939.

[118] For A. T. House's building of his mill and residence, see E. E. Ewing's "History of the Settlement of Highlands," *Blue Ridge Enterprise*, Jan. 25, 1883. See also Kelsey's *Record of Weather and Work*, vol. 1, May 5 and Sept. 11, 1877, and *Bk. of Deeds* P, p. 154 (July 17,1878). House's was the first sawmill built within the town limits of Highlands.

[119] Stanhope W. Hill was born in Rutherford County, N.C., in 1815 and died Dec. 11, 1894, at age 79. His wife Celia was born May 31, 1819, and died June 21, 1888, at age 69. Both are buried in the Little Church in the Wildwood cemetery in Horse Cove.

[120] For Stanhope Hill's election as mayor, see "The First Municipal Election in Highlands," *Blue Ridge Enterprise*, May 10, 1883, p. 3.

[121] For Laura Kibbee's life and death, see Helen Hill Norris, "Looking Backward," *Highlander*, July 13, 1962; "News of Week of Highlands," *Franklin Press*, April 14, 1922; and "Mrs. Kibbee, Ex-Highlands Resident, Dies," *Franklin Press and Highlands Maconian*, Feb. 20, 1947. She died Jan. 31, 1947, near Los Angeles at age 83.

[122] For Horace Kibbee's obituary, see *Franklin Press and Highlands Maconian* Apr. 27, 1950. He died March 23, 1950, in Los Angeles at age 83.

[123] For Monroe Skinner's purchase of his first home lot, see *Bk. of Deeds* P, p. 188 (Nov. 13, 1878). For his purchase of his second home lot, a fifty-acre tract, see Kelsey's *Record of Weather and Work*, vol. 2, March 3, 1879. For his blacksmith shop, see *Bk. of Deeds* R, p. 340 (March 1, 1883).

[124] For Henry Skinner's house and store, see *Blue Ridge Enterprise*, July 19 and Nov. 15, 1883. See also land purchases for his house in *Bk. of Deeds* DD, p. 532 (March 1, 1883); and his print shop, *Bk. of Deeds* X, p. 578 (Sept. 3, 1888).

[125] For the Maxwell and Anderson purchase of land, see Kelsey's *Record of Weather and Work*, vol. 2, Jul. 22, 1878.

[126] William Partridge was born Dec. 25, 1823, and died Jan. 17, 1908. He is buried in the Highlands Cemetery.

[127] For Partridge's mill, see *Bk. of Deeds* S, p. 413 (March 2, 1880). For his involvement with the Ruskin Community, see Walter Reese's diary, p. 2. See also article by T. Baxter White, *Franklin Press*, Dec. 20, 1899.

[128] For Charles L. Frost's obituary, see *Franklin Press*, Dec. 7, 1892, and June 28, 1893. See also Luther Turner Jr.'s article in *Heritage of Macon County, Vol. 2*, p. 240. For Frost's arrival in Highlands, see Kelsey's *Record of Weather and Work*, vol. 2, April 21 and Sept. 14, 1880. For the secret room in the Frost home, see Helen Hill Norris, "A Short History of Connemara," *Highlander*, July 10, 1964. For his building of Meadow House, see *Highlander*, Sept. 29, 1892. Frost was born on June 16, 1821, and died June 9, 1893, at age 72. He is buried in the Highlands Cemetery.

[129] Jonathan Heacock was born Dec. 9, 1842, and died Jan. 26, 1929, at age 86. He is buried in the Highlands Cemetery.

[130] For Heacock's naming of Glen Falls, see Sarah Summer's article in *Galax News*, July 2, 1970, p. 3. For the alternative name, see "West Highlands" in *Blue Ridge Enterprise*, June 7, 1883. For the alternative pronunciation, see Zeigler and Grosscup,

terprise, June 7, 1883. For the alternative pronunciation, see Zeigler and Grosscup, *Heart of the Alleghanies; or, Western North Carolina* (1883), p. 328, where they are called "Omakaluka Falls"; and *Highlander*, Jan. 8, 1886, "Oumekeloke Falls."

[131] For T. Baxter White's obituary, see "Macon Pioneer Passes Away: T. Baxter White, for Many Years a Resident of Highlands, Died on July 14, at La Verne, California," *Franklin Press*, August 4, 1922. He was born Oct. 9, 1835, and died July 14, 1922, at age 87. For his opposition to strong drink, see *Franklin Press*, Oct. 22 and 29, 1902. For his politics, see *Franklin Press*, Feb. 13, 1895.

[132] For Baxter White's reluctance to leave Highlands, see his letter to Barak Wright in Short Off, mailed from La Verne, Calif., on Oct. 2, 1920.

[133] For Olive Sheldon's obituary, see "Death of Mrs. Olive M. Sheldon," *Franklin Press*, May 31, 1928. She was born Olive White on Oct. 14, 1868, and died on April 24, 1928. For Walter Reese's memories of her, see his diary, p. 1.

[134] For Jessie White's obituary, see "Miss White, Daughter of Highlands Founder, Succumbs In California," *Franklin Press and Highlands Maconian*, April 12, 1956.

[135] For migration west and the return, see *Franklin Press*, June 18, 1902. See also Frances Lombard's account in her *From the Hills of Home in Western North Carolina* (Whiteside Cove, N.C., 1972, rpt. 1993), pp. 103–25.

[136] For Baxter White's account of Thomas Houston's return home, see *Franklin Press*, Nov. 21, 1894.

[137] For the Crowe family reunion, see *Franklin Press and Highlands Maconian,* Sept. 15, 1938. See also Bobby Crowe, "Family Tree" (an unpub. genealogy, early 1990s), pp. 5–8. The spelling of the family name was changed by Alvin Crow(e).

[138] For John Jay Smith's background, see his obituary, "John Jay Smith's Life Sketched, Served Town as Mayor, Road Builder; Artist And Craftsman," *Franklin Press and Highlands Maconian*, Sept. 11, 1941. He was born in 1863 and died on Sept. 2, 1941, at age 78. See *Blue Ridge Enterprise,* July 19, 1883, for the arrival of his steam saw-mill; July 24, 1883, for his sash and blind shop; Aug. 24, 1884 and Sept. 20, 1884, for the burning and rebuilding of his mill; and Nov. 20, 1885, for the start-up of his new mill. For his renovation of Highlands House in 1887, see *Highlander*, Jan. 28, 1887.

[139] For Walter Reese's memories of John Jay and Mary Chapin Smith, see his diary, p. 2.

[140] Gray Cottage was built for Miss Chapin by Joseph A. McGuire. See *Blue Ridge Enterprise*, Feb. 15, 1883, and July 12,1883, and *Highlander*, May 26, 1886. For the land purchased from John Norton by Mary Chapin's mother, Cynthia Loomis Chapin, see *Bk. of Deeds* Q, p. 478 (Feb. 11, 1882). The *Highlander* ran a story, "The Gray Cottage Has Interesting History," on May 26, 1966.

[141] Many of the poems in Mary Chapin Smith's *Earth Songs* were published originally in *Watson's Jeffersonian Magazine*, *Journal of Outdoor Life*, *Taylor-Trotwood Magazine*, and *Book News*. For her history of the Improvement Society, see "Women Do Much for Highlands: The Highlands Improvement Society Sponsors Many Things Benefiting the Town and Vicinity," *Franklin Press*, July 5, 1928

[142] For Mary Chapin Smith's obituary, see "Mrs. John Jay Smith Dies Tuesday: Highlands Pioneer Was Poet, Artist and Botanist," *Franklin Press and Highlands Maconian*, April 4, 1940. She was born March 3, 1855, and died April 1, 1940, at age 85.

[143] For Margaretta Duane Wood's reminiscences about her grandfather S. Prioleau Ravenel, Sr., see "Railroaded to Highlands?" *Highlander*, Nov. 1, 1985.

[144] For S. P. Ravenel, Sr.'s real estate holdings, see his son's obituary, "S. P. Ravenel [Jr.] Dies Wednesday," *Franklin Press and Highlands Maconian*, Aug. 22, 1940.

[145] For construction in progress of the Ravenel house, see *Western Reporter* (Franklin, N.C.), April 2, 1880. See also Stanhope Hill's sale of his farm to S. P. Ravenel for $2,200, *Blue Ridge Enterprise*, Nov. 15, 1883.

[146] For Margaretta Ravenel's purchase of M. I. Skinner's home, see *Blue Ridge Enterprise*, Nov. 15, 1883. See also *Bk. of Deeds* R, p. 396 (May 22, 1883).

[147] King's Inn burned on Feb. 20, 1994. See *Highlander*, Feb. 22, 1994, and March 1. 1994, also *Asheville Citizen-Times*, Feb. 21, 1994.

[148] For Tony Richardson's rescue of his wife Emma, see *Highlander*, Dec. 11, 1885.

[149] For the building and naming of *Kalalanta*, see *Blue Ridge Enterprise*, Oct. 10 and 18 and Nov. 22, 1883. For the haunting, Walter Reese's diary, p. 7. For subsequent ownership of *Kalalanta* by Salinas, see *Highlands Maconian*, Sept. 30, 1931; and by Fleming, *Highlander*, July 6, 1967. The Fleming reference misrepresents the term *Kalalanta* as Hawaiian rather than Cherokee. See also "X Marks the Spot" in *Galax News*, July 2, 1970, pp. 23–24.

[150] For Gene Howerdd's building of Fairfield Sapphire Valley Country Club, see *Cashiers Chronicle Journal*, Sept. 22, 1983.

[151] For the building of the Locust Pin Factory, see *Franklin Press,* February 13, 1901. For the fire that destroyed Bishop Thompson's Inn, see *Franklin Press*, Nov. 20, 1901.

[152] For Ravenel, Sr.'s, telephone line into Highlands, see *Franklin Press*, May 8, 1901. For his having one of the first telephones, see Daniel Ravenel's letter to Frank B. Cook, Nov. 16, 1970.

[153] For news of the attempted assassination of Pres. McKinley, see *Franklin Press*, Sept. 18, 1901.

[154] For Ravenel, Sr.'s role in the founding of Linville, see Arthur, *Western North Carolina*, pp. 411.

[155] For tributes to S. P. Ravenel, Sr., including recognition of the Ravenel contribution of Sunset Rock to the town, see "Highlands' Fitting Tribute to Samuel Prioleau Ravenel," *Franklin Press and Highlands Maconian*, Aug. 29, 1940. See also his obituary: "Highlands," *Franklin Press*, May 28, 1902. He was born in 1822 and died on May 14, 1902, at age 80.

[156] For Ravenel, Jr.'s opening of Lindenwood Park, see *Franklin Press*, Oct. 9, 1895.

[157] For Mrs. S. P. Ravenel, Jr.'s obituary, see *Franklin Press*, May 18, 1923. She died at her home in Biltmore, Asheville, N.C., on May 12, 1923. For her husband S. P. Ravenel, Jr.'s obituary, see "S. P. Ravenel [Jr.] Dies Wednesday," Franklin Press and Highlands Maconian, Aug. 22, 1940. He was born Jan. 12, 1868, in Paris, and died Aug. 21, 1940.

[158] For Ravenel, Jr.'s sale of land to the government for National Forest, see letters from J. Q. Pierson to S. P. Ravenel, Jr., Oct. 27 and Nov. 4, 1913. He sold 2,302 acres, some for only $5 and $6 per acre. For a general account of land purchased under the Weeks Law, see "Nantahala National Forest" in "History of Macon County," *Franklin Press,* June 26, 1924, pp. 4-5, and Chris Bolgiano's *Appalachian Forest* (Mechanicsburg, Pa., 1998).

[159] For Margaret W. Morley's appreciation of the Ravenels' philanthropy, see her *Carolina Mountains* (Boston, 1913), p. 252. For Walter Reese's praise of the Ravenels, see his diary, p. 6.

[160] For Kelsey's first reference to his preparing a map of Highlands, see his diary, vol. 1, March 21, 1877. For his actually drawing one, see vol. 2, Jan. 1, 1881. For the Hudson Library's receipt of this map in 1949, see "Old Map of Highlands Presented Museum By Former Local Resident," *Franklin Press and Highlands Maconian*, January 27, 1949.

[161] For 1895 retraced and corrected map of Highlands, see minutes of Board of Commissioners, Bk. A, p. 213, Nov. 8, 1895.

[162] For Thomas Greville's making of his map, see *Franklin Press and Highlands Maconian,* June 23, 1932, p. 5.

[163] T. W. Reynolds' mountain area maps, printed by Westminster News, S.C., covered Blue Valley and vicinity, Bull Pen-Whiteside Cove vicinity, and local regions in N.C., S.C., and Ga. See *Galax News*, June 9, 1966, p. 16.

[164] For the description of Highlands in 1883, see "Eight Years Old To-day," *Blue Ridge Enterprise*, March 29, 1883. Population figures are taken from the *Compendium of the Tenth Census* (June 1, 1880), Part 1, Washington: 1883, p. 240, and *Blue Ridge Enterprise*, Sept. 27, 1883.

[165] For Henry Martin Bascom's obituary, see "H. M. Bascom Final Rites, Prominent Highlands Resident Dies At Home of Daughter in N.Y.," *Franklin Press*, March 5, 1942. He was born on July 13, 1853, and died on Feb. 24, 1942, at age 88. For the building of his store, see *Blue Ridge Enterprise,* March 29 and Aug. 2, 1883.

[166] For Florence Bascom's background, see her obituary in *Franklin Press and Highlands Maconian*, Feb. 4, 1943, p. 3. She was born in Coffin's Station (now Dunreith, Indiana, in 1858 and died in Highlands on Jan. 30, 1943. For her marriage to H. M. Bascom, see *Highlander*, Feb. 25, 1887.

[167] For the *Tribune*'s recognition of H. M. Bascom, see "Bascom—Town Builder and Merchant Prince of Highlands, Retires," *New York Tribune*, October 21, 1920. For Walter Reese's memories of H. M. Bascom, see his diary, p. 3.

[168] For William B. Cleaveland's obituary, see "Highlands," *Franklin Press*, Dec. 20, 1893. He was born in 1849 and died on Dec. 14, 1893. He is buried in the Highlands Cemetery.

[169] For Will N. Cleaveland's obituary, see "Highlands Man Taken By Death, W. M. Cleaveland Dies At Home Saturday Morning," *Franklin Press*, Nov. 17, 1932. He died Nov. 12, 1932.

[170] For Walter Reese's memories of Ida Estelle "Stell" Cleaveland, see his diary, p. 5. Walter was born Jan. 5, 1881, and died Aug. 2, 1960, at age 79. He is buried in the Highlands Cemetery.

[171] For an account of Jule Phillips' family, see Edna Phillips Bryson's article in *Heritage of Macon County, Vol. 2*, pp. 368–9, and Walter Reese's diary, p. 4. For Jule Phillips' land purchase, see State Grant 3735 in *Bk. of Deeds* S, p. 524 (Feb. 21, 1882). For his construction projects, see his work ledger, 1883–97. Jule Phillips was born Oct. 21, 1857, and died May 15, 1915. His wife Mary Wright Phillips was born April 2, 1853, and died Oct. 19, 1929. Both are buried in the Highlands Cemetery.

[172] For Sargent's and Boynton's finding of *Shortia galacifolia*, see *Highlander*, Nov. 12, 1886. See also A. Rufus Morgan, *From Cabin to Cabin* (Franklin, N.C., 1977), pp. 24–25

[173] For Sumner Clark's home, see *Bk. of Deeds* R, p. 180 (Dec. 2, 1882). For his store, see *Blue Ridge Enterprise,* Nov. 29, 1883. For his Farmers' Alliance, see *Franklin Press,* May 6, 1890. His wife, Ann Mason Clark, is buried in lot 63 of block 6 of the Highlands cemetery.

[174] Jeremiah Pierson was born April 10, 1850, and died May 22, 1912, at age 61. His wife, Emma Adams Pierson, was born July 5, 1853, and died Oct. 3, 1925. For their arrival in Highlands in 1882, see Thomas B. Crumpler, "History of Highlands" (unpub. MS, written ca. 1975), p. 18. Their children were Lake (born Oct. 7, 1877), John Quincy (born 1879, died 1935), and S. Porter (born July 10, 1881, died July 26, 1956). All are buried in the Highlands Cemetery. For Porter Pierson's courtship of Marjorie Marden, see Crumpler, "History of Highlands," p. 19.

[175] For a detailed account of Rideout's life, see Ralph L. Rideout, Sr., "James and Margaret Smith Rideout Family," *Heritage of Macon County* (Franklin, N.C., 1987), pp. 436–7. See also Lee Copple's "Rideout Family Contributed to Early History of Highlands," *Highlander*, July 1, 1976, pp. 14–15. For Rideout's first home, see *Book of Deeds*, Bk. R, p. 234 (Jan. 15, 1883); his temporary home, *Highlander*, April 16 and 23, 1886; and his final home, see *Highlander*, Aug. 20 and Sept. 24, 1886. For the move of his store into Main Street, see minutes of Board of Commissioners, Bk. A, p. 82, Feb. 5, 1889. See also his purchase of Rock Store lot in *Book of Deeds*, Bk. Y, p. 264 (Apr. 8, 1889). For his damage complaint, see minutes of Board of Commissioners, Bk. A, p. 142, May 9, 1892.

[176] For Rideout's naming of Bufo vulgaris, see "Visitor recalls 1901 Highlands," *Highlander*, July 13, 1978. For his lecture to the Literary Society, see Lee Copple, "Rideout Was Part-Time Expert on Fleas," *Highlander*, Oct. 19, 1978, Sec. B. For his Washington trip, see "Highlands Items," *Franklin Press*, Sept. 28, 1892. For the Sunset Rock incident, see *Franklin Press*, July 22, 1896.

[177] James Rideout, as his gravestone indicates, was at one time a first lieutenant, but he was later promoted to a breveted captain. See genealogical records in possession of Ralph L. Rideout, Jr.

[178] For Rideout's interest in astronomy, see *Franklin Press,* May 16, 1900. For Walter Reese's description of Rideout's telescope, see his diary, p. 3, which includes Rideout's prophesies about Highlands.

[179] For Henry Scadin's viewing of the moon through Rideout's telescope, see Scadin's diaries, May 7, 1897.

[180] For Anna G. Dimick's obituary, see *Highlander*, Jan. 29, 1886. She was born in 1848 and died Jan. 21, 1886, at age 39. Her husband Frank was born in 1843 and died in 1882, also at age 39. They are both buried in Highlands Cemetery. For Bascom's purchase of Annie's inventory, see *Blue Ridge Enterprise*, Jan. 3, 1883. For Baxter Wilson's purchase of her inventory, see *Blue Ridge Enterprise*, Oct. 23, 1884.

[181] For John H. Durgin's arrival in Highlands, see *Blue Ridge Enterprise,* May 24, 1883. See also "Highlands Man, 95, Has Had Dangerous, Colorful Career," *Franklin Press and Highlands Maconian*, Sept. 22, 1938. See also obituary, *Franklin Press and Highlands Maconian*, Feb. 23, 1939. He was born in Sept., 1843, and died Feb. 21, 1939, at age 95.

[182] For Dr. W. H. Anderson's arrival in Highlands, see *Blue Ridge Enterprise*, Oct. 23, 1883. See also his obituary in *Franklin Press*, April 24, 1912. He was born May 24, 1840, and died April 11, 1912. For Dr. Anderson's paean to Highlands, see *Girard (Kansas) Press*, Nov. 25, 1883, rpt. in *Blue Ridge Enterprise*, Dec. 27, 1883. For the Ohio man's letter to Dr. Anderson, see *Highlander*, Jan. 22, 1886.

[183] For Satulah as allegedly volcanic, see James Mooney, *Myths of the Cherokee and Sacred Formulas of the Cherokees* (1891, 1897–98, rpt. Nashville, Tenn., 1982), p. 471; T. W. Reynolds, *High Lands*, p. 101; and S. Van Epp Law, *Status Quo*, pp. 131. For Helen Hill Norris' account, see *Looking Backward*, vol. 1 (1961), pp. 9–10.

[184] For Henry Stewart's life, see *Highlander*, March 8, 1892. For Walter Reese's memories of Henry Stewart, see his diary, p. 1.

[185] For Louis Zoellner's obituary, see *Franklin Press and Highlands Maconian*, April 14, 1938. He was born in Herborn, Germany, May 7, 1859, and died in Highlands, April 8, 1938, at age 78.

[186] For T. D. Walden's arrival in Highlands, see *Highlander*, Oct. 23, 1885; for his organizing the Free Mason lodge, *Franklin Press*, Apr. 10, 1890; his membership on the school board, minutes of Board of Commissioners, Bk. A, p. 124, July 11, 1891; and his election as mayor, *Franklin Press,* Dec. 7, 1892. For his collection of cacti, see *Franklin Press*, May 6, 1890. Walden was born Jan. 13, 1858, and died Sept. 12, 1906. He is buried in the Highlands Cemetery.

[187] For J. Frank Walden's role as timekeeper, see minutes of Board of Commissioners, Bk. A, p. 179, July 4, 1894.

[188] For Highlands' population of 200 in 1886, see H. B.'s (probably H. M. Bascom's) "Mountain Lands of North Carolina: Written for the New England Farmer, April 29, 1886," *Highlander*, June 25, 1886; but *Highlander*, Sept. 17, 1886, sets its population at 300. For altitude corrections, see *Highlander*, Aug. 6, 1886. For population of surrounding cities, see *Highlander* Oct. 1, 1886.

[189] For Baltimore *Sun*'s appraisal of Highlands in 1886, see *Highlander*, Sept. 17, 1886.

[190] For commercial advertisers in Highlands in 1886, see *Highlander*, June 25, 1886.

[191] For Thomas G. Harbison's arrival in Highlands, see "Charm of Highlands Mountains Lured Prof. Harbison, Botanist," *Franklin Press*, July 5, 1928, pp. 1, 2. T. G. Harbison was born in Forest Hills, Pa., on April 23, 1862, and died in Chapel Hill, N.C., Jan. 12, 1936.

[192] For R. J. Reynolds' arrival in Highlands, see Helen Hill Norris, *Looking Backward*, vol. 1, p. 22.

[193] For Dr. O'Farrell's advertisement, see *No. 4*, June 20, 1891.

[194] For reminiscences of the Cobbs, see Gertrude Cobb Holt, *Galax News,* July 22, 1953. See also Gertrude Cobb's obituary in *Franklin Press and Highlands Maconian,* Nov. 29, 1934. For her first impression of Highlands, see interview with Richard C. "Bill" Holt, grandson of Judson M. Cobb and son of Gertrude, who married A. C. "Gus" Holt.

[195] For the late spring freeze in early May, 1891, see *Franklin Press*, June 3, 1891.

[196] For Hiram Paul, see Jessie Potts Owens, *The Family of William Thomas and Martha Ammons Potts* (Raleigh, N.C., 1987), p. 72. See also "The Paul Family" in *Heritage of Macon County, Vol. 2*, p. 362-3.

[197] For Betty Speed Wood's memories of Calvin Speed, Jr., see *Heritage of Macon County*, Vol. 2, p. 432.

[198] For information on W. T. and Mattie Potts, see W. Arthur Hays Jr.'s articles in *Heritage of Macon County, Vol. 2*, pp. 406–08. See also obituary for W. T. Potts, *Franklin Press and Highlands Maconian*, Nov. 21, 1935. He was born Aug. 16, 1857, and died Nov. 18, 1935. For the first reference to the Potts livery and mail service, see *Franklin Press*, June 11, 1894. An excellent source for information on the Potts family's origins and history is Jessie Potts Owens, *The Family of William Thomas and Martha Ammons Potts* (Raleigh, N.C., 1987).

[199] For an account of the Crunkletons, see Walter J. Taylor's article in *Heritage of Macon County, Vol. 1*, pp. 200–01.

[200] For C. G. Memminger's obituary, see *Asheville Citizen*, Aug. 14, 1930, pp. 1–2. He was born in Charleston, Aug. 10, 1865, and died in Asheville, N.C., Aug. 13, 1930.

[201] For George Saussy's obituary, see *Highlander*, Oct. 2, 1964. He died Sept. 27, 1964, at age 66. For his wife's obituary, see *Highlander*, May 27, 1976, p. 5.

[202] In the century and a half since their publication between 1836 and 1857 more than 120 million copies of McGuffey's *Eclectic Readers* in original and revised editions have been sold. They combined moral lessons with selections from literature and helped shape the tastes of generations of Americans even into the twentieth century.

[203] For W. S. Davis' obituary, see *Franklin Press and Highlands Maconian*, June 16, 1955, p. 5-A. William Smith Davis, known as "Smith" in Hampton, Ga., was born July 15, 1864, and died June 12, 1955, at age 90. His wife, Lake Pierson Davis, was born in 1878 in Norton Community and died May 21, 1960.

[204] For Col. John S. Sewell's obituary, see *Franklin Press and Highlands Maconian*, April 25 and June 13, 1940. He was born Jan. 16, 1869, at Butler's Landing, Tenn., and died in Highlands, April 20, 1940.

[205] For Sara Gilder, see "Miss Sara Gilder Withdraws from Grocery Business," *Galax News*, June 28, 1956, and her obituary in *Highlander*, Oct. 29, 1966. She died Oct. 23, 1966, at age 86.

[206] See Frank Potts obituary in *Highlander*, Jan. 6, 1961. He was born in Aug. 1, 1888, and died on Dec. 24, 1960 at age 72.

[207] Tudie Rice left Thomas Wolfe's suite to the Archie Jellen family when she died.

[208] For Luke Rice's obituary, see *Highlander*, Oct. 3, 1968. See also Helen Hopper, "Luther Rice, Sr., Public Servant," *Highlander*, July 19, 1975, Sec. B, p. 3. He was born in 1879 and died on Sept. 24, 1968 at almost 89 years of age.

[209] For Luther Rice, Jr.'s obituary, see *Galax News*, July 25, 1968. He was born in July, 17, 1915, and died on his 53rd birthday, July 17, 1968.

[210] For Charles J. Weeks, Jr.'s biography of McCully, see *An American Naval Diplomat in Revolutionary Russia: The Life and Times of Vice Admiral Newton A. McCully* (Annapolis, 1993).

[211] For Dr. George Sandor, see *Highlander*, Aug. 22, 1986.

[212] For Burt Reynolds' concerns about overdevelopment, see his letter in *Highlander*, Sept. 10, 1981, p. 2.

[213] Nathaniel Macon lived from 1758–1837.

[214] The town of Franklin, unlike the state of Franklin, was not named after Benjamin Franklin but rather Jesse Franklin, who served from 1820–21 as governor of North Carolina.

[215] For Richard and Rebecca Davis' description of the Cullasaja River trail in 1876, see *Harper's New Monthly Magazine*, Sept. 1880, vol. 61, pp. 541–42 with accompanying lithograph of Cullasaja [Dry] Falls, p. 542.

[216] For Zeigler's and Grosscup's description of the Glade Road in 1877, see their *Heart of the Alleghanies; or, Western North Carolina*, pp. 324–25.

[217] For Woodrow Wilson's visit to Horse Cove, see his letter to Robert Bridges, July 30, 1879, as quoted in the *Franklin Press and Highlands Maconian*, Sept. 6, 1956, p. 1, and discussed by Mrs. Vernon Bryson's history, *Macon County, North Carolina* (Franklin, N.C., 1972), pp. 73–77.

[218] For Kelsey's welcome of good citizens nationwide, see his promotional pamphlet, *Blue Ridge Highlands*, p. 10.

[219] For Russell House, see historic plaque erected on site by the Andrew Pickens Rangers of Sumter National Forest. See also Lawrence Wood's "Memories of the Old Russell Home," *Highlander*, Aug. 19, 1976, and "History Buffs, Family Mourn Loss of Russell House," *Highlander*, May 20, 1988. For Mr. Russell's death, see Louise Sargent, "Reminiscences of Highlands Summers," p. 3, and Edith Inglesby, *Happy Highways* (Charleston, 1981), p. 3. William G. Russell was born July 2, 1835, and died Oct. 16, 1921.

[220] For Kelsey's view of Highlands as the hub of a wheel, see "Site of Highlands Was Carved From Mountain Wilderness," *Highlands Maconian*, June 24, 1931, p. 2.

[221] For roadwork statistics, see Minutes of Board of Supervisors of Roads in Highlands Township, May 1879, pp. 1–3, 12–13.

[222] For the choice of roadwork or tax payment, see minutes of Board of Supervisors of Highlands Township, May 22, 1891, pp. 25 and 27.

[223] For Bradford Torres's description of road work, see *A World of Green Hills: Observations of Nature and Human Nature in the Blue Ridge* (Boston, 1898), pp. 113–14.

[224] For Albert Staub's characterization of the road law as unfair, see "Our Roads," *No. 4*, June 20, 1891, p. 1.

[225] Stooley, also Stooly, is an early name for Satulah Mountain. These two forms of the name are used in minutes of Board of Supervisors; see District No. 7 in 1880 and following. By 1886 the mountain is called Satooly, District No. 9; and by 1891, Satula, District No. 4. In an article entitled "In the Mountains," published by the *Franklin Western Reporter* on April 2, 1880, the mountain is called Stooley. For the road's rocky condition in the early 1890s, see *Franklin Press*, March 8, 1892.

[226] For the creation of the Walhalla Road around Satulah, see Franklin Press, Aug. 24, 1892; minutes of Board of Commissioners, Bk. A, p. 200, April 23, 1895; pp. 204–5, May 27, 1895; and p. 221, May 25, 1896.

[227] For public joy over the 1896 Walhalla Road, see *Franklin Press*, June 17, 1896.

[228] For Highlands Traction Company, see Claude Townsend Sullivan, "A Tale of Highlands" (Greenville, S.C., 1970), p. 4.

[229] For the condition of the Gnat Ridge Road into Georgia, see Notice to the Board of Commissioners of Macon County, in minutes of Board of Supervisors, p. 48, Nov. 27, 1894.

[230] For the creation of today's Dillard Road as far as the Flats, see *Blue Ridge Enterprise*, Sept. 27, 1883. For its proposed extension to the Tennessee River, see surveyor's record, Experimental Line from Highlands to Tennessee River, begun June 12 and completed June 27, 1883.

[231] For John Jay Smith's building of the Dillard Road, see "Site of Highlands Was Carved From Mountain Wilderness," *Highlands Maconian*, June 24, 1931, continued July 29, 1931. For today's route, see *Franklin Press and Highlands Maconian*, March 18, 1937.

[232] For first mention of Turtle Pond Road, see minutes of Board of Supervisors, p. 24, May 22, 1891.

[233] First mention of Stewart's pond as completed (today's Mirror Lake) occurs in minutes of Supervisors of Roads, p. 26, Sept. 5, 1891. For Bradford Torrey's account of its creation, see his *World of Green Hills*, p. 72.

[234] For the road from Cowee Gap to Hamburg, see Kelsey's *Record of Weather and Work*, vol. 2, Jan. 5, 1880. For description of early Hamburg, see *Blue Ridge Enterprise*, Aug. 9, 1883. For creation of Lake Glenville in 1940–41, see *Highlander*, July 30, 1981.

[235] For a description of Ravenel's turnpike, see *Franklin Press*, June 26, 1901. For completion of the turnpike road, see *Franklin* Press, Sept. 17, 1902.

[236] For the new road to within a quarter mile of the top of Whiteside Mountain, see *Blue Ridge Enterprise,* May 10, 1883. For its completion see *Blue Ridge Enterprise*, July 12, 1883.

[237] For Herbert Ravenel Sass description of Whiteside, see his *War Drums* (New York, 1928), pp. 240–41. For a translation of Sanigilagi as "the place where they took it out," see Douglas A. Rossman's *Where Legends Live*, p. 24. Rossman claims the name "refers to the destruction by the Thunders of the western summit of the mountain, which formed the eastern end of Spearfinger's great rock bridge."

[238] For Whiteside Road controversy, see *Blue Ridge Enterprise*, Feb. 15 and 22, 1883. For first use of the Kelsey Trail, see *Blue Ridge Enterprise*, July 12, 1883

[239] For the 1886 shortcut to Whiteside, see *Highlander*, Aug. 20, 1886. For 4th Street extension from cemetery to Shortoff in 1891, see minutes of Board of Supervisors, p. 23, May 22, 1891. For Whiteside Mountain toll road, see *Galax News*, Aug. 12, 1953.

[240] For first mention of a Franklin Road, see minutes of Board of Supervisors p. 21, March 1, 1889.

[241] Terry Bolick believed it emerged at today's Chuckberry Road, and it probably did when he was doing roadwork in the 1930s.

[242] For the 1896 Franklin Road through Laurel Heights, see minutes of Board of Supervisors, p. 52, May 2, 1896. For the Laurel Heights–Flat Mountain connection at today's Hammond Road, see "Changes" at end of Peggy Watkins, *Webbmont* (Highlands, 1994). Laurel Heights was changed to Webbmont in 1931 in honor of Joe Webb; see *Highlands Maconian*, Sept. 16, 1931.

[243] For the construction of the Big Creek bridge, see minutes of Board of Supervisors, p. 99, May 5, 1903.

[244] For the construction of the Shookville Road from Buck Creek, see *Blue Ridge Enterprise*, Oct. 11, 1883.

[245] For a summary of roadwork in early Highlands, including Kelsey's hours, see his *Time Book* (Kansas/Highlands, N.C.), Sept. 12, 1885.

[246] For the decision not to build a town hall in 1884, see minutes of Board of Commissioners, Bk. A, p. 25, Sept. 8, 1884. It was 1954 before Highlands had a combination

town office, jail, and fire house at the corner of 4th and Oak, the current town hall; see minutes, Bk. 3, p. 99, May 18, 1953.

[247] For Kelsey's deeding of lot 102 on north 4th Street to town for a town hall, see *Bk. of Deeds* S, p. 449 (August 21, 1883). For sale of this lot at auction by Mayor Harbison to S. P. Anderson, see *Bk. of Deeds* D-3, p. 463 (May 11, 1909).

[248] For the *Franklin Press* lament over Highlands' muddy roads, see Feb. 13, 1895.

[249] For Rideout's remark about constructing the Chattooga iron bridge, see *Franklin Press*, March 11, 1891; for the bridge's completion, see Dec. 13, 1893.

[250] For the filling of the Main Street swag, see minutes of Board of Commissioners, Bk. A, p. 195, April 1, 1895.

[251] For the grading of 4th Street hill and construction of Mill Creek bridge and pond, see *Highlander*, Aug. 13, 1886. See also minutes of Board of Commissioners, Bk. A, p. 49, Aug. 10, 1886.8/10/86.

[252] For Joel Teague's account of the building of the 4th Street bridge, see his letter to the editor from Portland, Ore., about "Old-Time Georgia Tonic," *Highlands Maconian*, July 22, 1931.

[253] For the formation of the railroad company, see Highlands Rail Road Company, Secretary's Book, Feb. 11, 1882, p. 12. For ratification of its charter by State Legislature, see *Blue Ridge Enterprise*, April 4, 1883. For Kelsey's work on a Highlands Railroad, see his diary, vol. 2, March 2–April 4, 1882. For railroad delays and rumors, see *Highlander*, Oct. 30, 1885, and Dec. 3, 1886.

[254] For the *Star*'s position on railroad bond vote, see *Star* "Extra," Sept. 20, 1890.

[255] For the Three-States Road from Walhalla to Highlands, see *Franklin Press*, Oct. 29, 1920, and Dec. 15 and Feb. 23, 1922.

[256] For the Highlands/Franklin road via Georgia, see *Franklin Press*, Oct. 21, 1926.

[257] For proposed gorge Highway 28 to Highlands, see *Franklin Press,* Oct. 27, 1927, quote from *Asheville Times*. The *Press* article mistook Bridal Veil Falls for Dry Falls, presumably because of the name *Dry*. It claimed the proposed route would pass under Dry Falls. See also May 26, 1927.

[258] For the glowing paean to the Cullasaja Gorge project, see *Franklin Press*, April 5, 1928.

[259] For the town's maintenance of its own roads, see minutes of Board of Commissioners, Bk. D, p. 219, July 1, 1929.

[260] For the fountain at 4th and Main, see minutes of Board of Commissioners, Bk. E, p. 38, July 5, 1925, and Bk. E., p. 173, April 6, 1928. For its removal see *Highlands Maconian*, Sept. 23, 1931.

[261] For center parking on Main Street, see minutes of Board of Commissioners, Bk. D, p. 251, May 5, 1939.

[262] For Bess Hines Harkins' memories of the Dillard Road, see "Our Mountains," *Highlander*, Feb. 10, 1966.

[263] For Franklin controversy over new road to Highlands, see *Franklin Press and Highlands Maconian*, Aug. 18 and Sept. 8, 1932.

[264] For the Three-States Road delays, see *Franklin Press and Highlands Maconian,* Dec. 14, 1933; Sept. 27, 1934; April 1 and July 8, 1937; and Aug. 25, 1938.

[265] For Horse Cove CCC camp, see *Franklin Press and Highlands Maconian,* Sept. 20, 1934, and March 25, 1937.

[266] For the paving of the Dillard road, see *Franklin Press and Highlands Maconian*, March 18, 1937.

[267] For the Highlands airport, see minutes of Board of Commissioners, Bk. G, p. 159, May 6, 1935.

[268] For the paving many town roads, see *Franklin Press and Highlands Maconian*, Sept. 17, 1942.

[269] For the beginning of diagonal parking on Main Street, see minutes of Board of Commissioners, Bk. 3, p. 71, July 7, 1952, and Bk. 3, p. 149, June 20, 1955.

[270] For a discussion of time limits and parking meters, see Bk. 3, p. 190, July 17, 1957, and Bk. 3, p. 194, Oct. 7, 1957. For planting of the side trees, see minutes of Board of Commissioners, June 3, 1957; and consideration of the center trees, see April 1, 1957.

[271] For the paving of Flat Mountain Road in 1955, see *Highlander*, Jan. 20, 1959.

[272] For the construction of the Wilson Gap Road in 1958, see *Highlander*, Nov. 20, 1958.

[273] For the quarry controversy, see minutes of Board of Commissioners, Bk. 3, pp. 35, 48, 173, 177, 180, and 189, and *Highlander,* Aug. 4, 1961.

[274] For Hunnicutt's accident, see *Galax News,* July 15, 1954.

[275] For the Bridal Veil bypass, see minutes of Board of Commissioners, Bk. 3, p. 206, May 19, 1958.

[276] For street work in front of the Presbyterian Church, see minutes of Board of Commissioners, Bk. 3, p. 215, Dec. 3, 1958, and *Galax News*, June 19, 1962.

[277] For the N.C.–Ga. dispute over the State line, see *Highlander*, July 29, 1971, and *Galax News* Aug. 12, 1971, pp. 7 and 14, and Aug. 19, 1971, p. 14. For W. A. Curtis' discovery of the discrepancy, see *Topography of Macon County* (Franklin, N.C., 1905), p. 23. See also Arthur, *Western North Carolina*, pp. 28–36, esp. 36.

[278] For Sloan's and Greenwood's view of the N.C.–Ga. Dispute, see John Parris, "Surveyor Tells Where They Drew the Line," *Asheville Citizen*, rpt. in *Highlander*, Sept. 2, 1971, p. 8.

[279] For Nicholson's arrest, see minutes of Board of Commissioners, Bk. A, p. 144, July 11, 1892.

[280] For Helen Hill Norris' account of the calaboose break, see *Looking Backward*, vol. 1, pp. 5–6.

[281] For the butcher's law, see minutes of Board of Commissioners, Bk. A, p. 23, June 16, 1884; p. 66, July 28, 1887; p. 75, May 22, 1888; p. 89, May 18, 1889; p. 105, May 10, 1890; p. 125, July 18, 1891; p. 147, Aug. 10, 1892; and p. 223, July 29, 1896.

[282] For the ordinance forbidding whiskey, see minutes of Board of Commissioners, Bk. A, p. 105, May 10, 1890. For arrest of Rideout, see *Highlander*, Dec. 18, 1885; for arrests of Norton, Edwards, and McGuire, see Bk. A, p. 98, Sept. 24, 1889.

[283] For the dog law, see Ordinances of 1888–90, Article IX.

[284] For the Literary Society's debate over the Highlands hog and the newspaper's opinion, see *Blue Ridge Enterprise*, Feb. 22, 1883, p. 3. For the hog law, see *Blue Ridge Enterprise*, Sept. 13 and Dec. 27, 1883. For destruction of the hog pound, see minutes of Board of Commissioners, Bk. A, p. 101, March 5, 1890. For town marshal's complaints, see p. 116, Sept. 17, 1890.

[285] For the hogs' hindrance of mail delivery, see T. Baxter White, "Highlands," *Franklin Press*, Dec. 7, 1898.

[286] For public concern over smells, see *Highlander*, Jan. 8, 1886, and minutes of Board of Commissioners, Bk. A, p. 96, Sept. 5, 1889.

[287] For penalties, opportunities to work them off, and the need to secure the jail, see Ordinance of 1883, Sec. 17; Ordinance of 1888; and minutes of Board of Commissioners, Bk. A, p. 100, Dec. 23, 1889.

[288] For Chastain's stint in jail, see *Highlands Maconian*, Aug. 19, 1931.

[289] For the following laws, see Town Ordinances of Highlands, N.C.,1922.

[290] For interviews with J. D. Head, Bub Zachary, Radford Talley, and Furman Vinson, see *Highlander*, Aug. 26, 1986; Sept. 30, 1986; Nov. 25, 1986; July 21, 1987, respectively.

[291] For the hiring and firing and hiring of Olin Dryman, see minutes of Board of Commissioners, Nov. 21, 1946; March 1, 1949; March 6, 1950; and July 17, 1956.

[292] For the rocking of blacks, see minutes of Board of Commissioners, Bk. G, p. 42, Sept. 7, 1932.

[293] For telephone rates in 1956, see Highlands Industrial Committee, *Highlands, North Carolina—Facts and Figures for Industry* (Highlands Chamber of Commerce), p. 8.

[294] For news reports of the Keener incident, see *Franklin Press*, June 24 and Sept. 2, 1921.

[295] For the high attrition within the Highlands police force between 1975–81, see *Highlander*, July 23, 1981.

[296] For Ron Elliott's indictment and sentencing, see *Highlander*, Oct. 6, 1983, and Dec. 2, 1986.

[297] For Terry Chastain's murder, see *Highlander*, May 2 and Oct. 10, 2000.

[298] For the official date of the Moccasin War, see minutes of Board of Commissioners, Bk. A, p. 27, April 14, 1885. Joseph Fritts owned and managed Highlands House, known after 1886 as Smith House, which is what Judge Felix E. Alley mistakenly calls it in his account. For Judge Alley's account, see *Random Thoughts and the Musings of a Mountaineer*, pp. 284–86. For a first-hand account of the event, see Elias White, "Early Highlands Days," *Franklin Press and Highlands Maconian*, June 5, 1941, p. 5. See also Sarah Summer's "Moccasin Massacre or the Great Moonshine Feud, *Galax News*, Aug. 20, 1970, pp. 7, 17, 19, and 24.

[299] For Mayor H. M. Bascom's election by a single vote, see minutes of Board of Commissioners, Bk. A, p. 19, May 5, 1884.

[300] For Stephen Vincent Benét's praise of Georgia booze, see "The Mountain Whippoorwill," Stanza 48.

[301] For Frank Hill's account of the Moccasin War, see the article by his daughter, Helen Hill Norris, "Oak Trees and the Whiskey War," *Looking Backward*, vol. 1, pp. 54–56.

[302] For Walter Reese's version of the Battle of Highlands, see p. 9 of his diary, composed on Dec. 15, 1956.

[303] For a thoroughly entertaining account of schooling in early Highlands by the son of its first resident and postmaster, T. Baxter White, see Elias White, "Early Highlands Days," *Franklin Press and Highlands Maconian*, June 5, 1941.

[304] For John Arnold's land purchase, see State Grant 3694 in *Bk. of Deeds* T, p. 67 (entered Oct. 6, 1879). For a brief biography, see "Civil War Service of J. N. Arnold," in Mrs. Vernon Bryson, *Macon County, North Carolina* (Franklin, N.C., 1972), pp. 7–8. John Arnold was born in 1840 and died on Jan. 15, 1936.

[305] For Emma White's schooling at "Billy Cabin" in 1875, see her obituary in *Franklin Press and Highlands Maconian*, Aug. 1, 1946. She died July 13, 1946, in Los Angeles at age 84.

[306] For Fremont's death, see Elias White, "Early Highlands Days," *Franklin Press and Highlands Maconian*, June 5, 1941. See also Baxter White's letter to Barak Wright at Short Off, mailed from La Verne, Calif., Oct. 2, 1920.

[307] For the formation of the Mount Hope Cemetery Association, see Mount Hope Cemetery Record Bk. 1, Nov. 15, 1880, p. 3. For land donation by Kelsey, see Feb. 26, 1881, p. 4, and *Bk. of Deeds* R, p. 77 (Oct. 11, 1881). For name change to Highlands Cemetery, see Record Bk. 1, July 25, 1887, p. 7; and to Highlands Memorial Park, see Record Bk. 2, April 5, 1966, p. 111. On Dec. 18, 1997, the Highlands Cemetery Co. was dissolved and conveyed to the Town of Highlands; see minutes of Board of Commissioners, Bk. I-22, p. 1717.

[308] The school property, extending to the east line of lot 22 on Oak Street, was given by Kelsey to School Trustees District # 3 on December 23, 1878. See *Bk. of Deeds* P, p. 280.

[309] For Mrs. S. C. Davis as principal of the four grades of Highlands High School, see *Highlander*, Jan. 15, 1886.

[310] For Kelsey's intent to establish a quality school, *Blue Ridge Highlands*, p. 9.

[311] For a detailed summary of her father's life, see Dolly Harbison's talk to the Highlands Garden Club, "T. G. Harbison, Botanist," *Highlander*, Jan. 25, 1973, p. 3. See also a biographical tribute after his death by H. R. Totten, W. C. Coker, and H. J. Oosting, "Dr. Thomas Grant Harbison," *Journal of The Elisha Mitchell Scientific Society*, vol. 52, (1936), pp. 140–45.

[312] For Prof. Harbison's establishment of Highlands Academy, see *Highlander*, Oct. 1 and Nov. 19, 1886. For Kelsey's hiring of Harbison to run the Academy, see "Romance of Highlands," *Greenwood (S.C.) Index-Journal*, August 24, 1929. For additional accounts of the Academy, see "Charm of Highlands Mountains Lured Prof. Harbison, Botanist," *Franklin Press*, July 5, 1928, p. 2, and article against "Loafing" in *No. 4*, June 20, 1891, p. 3.

[313] For Gertrude Holt's memory of the first schoolhouse, see "Highlands As It Used to Be," *Galax News*, July 22, 1953, p. 7.

[314] For the first Highlands School board of trustees, see *Highlander*, Jan. 21, 1887.

[315] In 1896 the Town bought Harbison's school desks for $30. See minutes of Board of Commissioners, Bk. A, p. 226, Nov. 2, 1896. Dolly Harbison effectively described her father's life in a detailed talk to the Highlands Garden Club: "T. G. Harbison, Botanist," *Highlander*, Jan. 25, 1973. For course offerings at the Highlands Academy, see advertisement in *Highlands Star*, May 8, 1890.

[316] For Highlands School as a public graded school and as a free school, see minutes of Board of Commissioners, Bk. A, p. 99, Nov. 6, 1889 and Bk. A. p. 103, April 21, 1890. See also *Franklin Press*, July 22, 1891. For first Highlands School Board, see minutes of Board of Commissioners, Bk. A, p. 124, July 11, 1891.

[317] For Harbison's donation of the school annex to the Hudson Library, see Elias White, "Early Highlands Days," *Franklin Press and Highlands Maconian*, June 5, 1941. For an assessment of his own library, see "Carolina Mountain Towns: Highlands," *Asheville Carolina Mountains*, June, 1893. See also "Dr. Thomas Grant Harbison," *Journal of Elisha Mitchell Scientific Society*, vol. 52 (1936), p. 141

[318] For Arthur B. "Shine" Potts' assessment of Prof. Harbison, see author's interview of Bill Holt, October 14, 1993.

[319] For Annie Pierson's and Harbison's tenure at Shortoff School, see *Heritage of Macon County, Vol. 2* (Franklin, N.C., 1998), p. 58.

[320] For Miss Carpenter as principal, see, *Franklin* Press, Oct. 23, 1895.

[321] For the creation of the Highlands School District in 1897, see Macon Co. League of Women Voters, *Know Your Public Schools* (Franklin, 1992), p. 6.

[322] For Annie Whipp Pierson's obituary, see *Highlander*, Dec. 19, 1968. She was born in 1884 and died on Dec. 16, 1968, at age 84.

[323] For the first N. C. compulsory attendance law, see "Know Your Public Schools," p. 5.

[324] For the ghost at the Wells place, see Sarah Summer's "Ghosts of Highlands," *Galax News*, Aug. 27, 1970, p. 6A.

[325] For the Town Clock Tower, see minutes of Board of Commissioners, Sept. 4, 1916.

[326] For the completion of the new school, see minutes of Board of Commissioners, May 13 and Oct 3, 1919. For a description of the second Highlands School, see *Franklin Press*, Jan. 7, 1921.

[327] For T. L. Tolar's becoming principal of Highlands School, see *Franklin Press*, Sept. 16, 1926.

[328] For Tolar's two articles on school consolidation, see *Franklin Press*, particularly April 12, 1928, p. 1, but also May 3, 1928, p. 8. For the vote on school consolidation, see *Franklin Press*, June 14, 1928.

[329] For the creation of the 4-H clubs, see *Franklin Press,* Feb. 16, 1928. For the Boy and Girl Scouts, see *Franklin Press*, Oct. 3, 10, and 17, 1929.

[330] For quotes of Ethel Calloway, see *Highlander*, Oct. 22, 1985, and interview with the author, Nov. 8, 1993.

[331] For Prof. Summer's accomplishments, see *Franklin Press and Highlands Maconian,* Aug. 6, 1942, p. 3. See also *Galax News*, June 18, 1964, p. 7. Otto Summer actually retired twice, once in May, 1964, and again when replacing Charles Hendrix in July, 1965. He resigned for the last time Aug. 5, 1965 for health reasons. See *Highlander*, May 23, 1968, and *Galax News*, July 29, 1965, p. 1.

[332] For the proposal and completion of new high school auditorium, see *Franklin Press and Highlands Maconian*, Nov. 23, 1933, and Aug. 29, 1935.

[333] Contraction of the flu usually starts with sneezing as its first symptom, which is how the custom of saying "Bless you" originated in 591 A. D. to wish protection from influenza by God's blessing on anyone heard sneezing. The 1893 flu epidemic was the one that took W. B. Cleaveland's life in Highlands through pneumonia. For tonsillectomies in Highlands, see *Franklin Press,* Nov. 17, 1922.

[334] For Highlands School statistics in 1938, see the first issue of *Mountain Trail*, Nov. 24, 1938, and *Franklin Press and Highlands Maconian*, Nov. 17, 1938.

[335] For the town's purchase of the old Highlands School, see minutes of Board of Commissioners, Bk. 3, p. 50, Nov. 5, 1951.

[336] For the ad concerning tearing down the old schoolhouse, see minutes of Board of Commissioners, Bk. 3, p. 231. Oct. 19, 1959.

[337] For playground problems at the new school, see *Galax News*, Dec. 18, 1954.

[338] For the creation of the Highlands School band, see *Galax News*, Dec. 18, 1954.

[339] For the creation of Head Start, see *Galax News*, June 17, 1965, p. 7.

[340] For the first Sunday School, see "Record of First Sunday School, Highlands, N.C., March 12, 1876."

[341] For a well-written centennial history of the church, see Betty Holt, *History of the Presbyterian Church: Highlands, North Carolina 1885–1985* (Highlands, N.C., 1985).

[342] For the date of Robert W. Reese's arrival in Highlands, see his son Walter Reese's diary, p. 1, where Walter claims to have been the second Southern boy in Highlands. If Walter was the second Southern boy in Highlands, then the first was Dock McKinney's son, Allison "Al," unless, of course, it was William McHenry Jackson, as Reese noted on p. 9.

[343] For a summary of the earliest Methodist Church buildings, see Elias White's "Early Highlands Days," *Franklin Press and Highlands Maconian*, June 5, 1941, p. 5, and Mrs. Gertrude C. Cobb's "Highlands As It Used to Be," *Galax News*, July 22, 1953, p. 7. For records of Northern Methodist's loan and mortgage, see *Deeds of Trust* 1, pp. 22 and 25 (June 21, 1882). For Northern Methodist's receipt of land from Kelsey, see *Bk. of Deeds* R, p. 27 (July 3, 1882). For dedication of the new church, see *Blue Ridge Enterprise*, Feb. 15, 1883. For partial completion of the church, see March 29 and April 12, 1883. For Rev. Moore's departure from Highlands, see Sept. 13, 1883.

[344] For the Northern Methodist's receipt of land from Kelsey, see *Bk. of Deeds* R, p. 27 (July 3, 1882). For dedication of the new church, see *Blue Ridge Enterprise*, Feb. 15, 1883. For partial completion of the church, see March 29 and April 12, 1883. For Rev. Moore's departure from Highlands, see Sept. 13, 1883.

[345] For the Southern Methodists' proposal to buy the unfinished church, see *Blue Ridge Enterprise*, Nov. 22, 1883. For completion of the church, see *Blue Ridge Enterprise*, Aug. 28, 1884. For arrival of the church bell, see *Highlander*, Oct. 23, 1885, and for dedication of the church, see *Highlander*, Aug. 7, 1885, p. 4.

[346] The July 16, 1886, edition of the *Highlander* lists the various pastors and the days of their services in its Directory.

[347] For the Southern Methodists' deed to their property, see *Bk. of Deeds* BB, p. 574 (Dec. 25, 1888). For incident of the high wind and the debt repayment for repairs, see *Franklin Press*, April 10, 1890, and Aug. 24, 1892.

[348] For an early history of Christian Endeavor, see *Franklin Press and Highlands Maconian*, Feb. 17, 1938.

[349] For the Northern Methodists' mortgage and bond repayments, see *Bk. of Deeds* RR, p. 174 (Aug. 4, 1904). For sale of Methodist Church building to the Baptists, see *Bk. of Deeds* RR, p. 218 (Sept. 3, 1094). For purchase of the current Methodist Church property by the Highlands Methodist Episcopal Church South for $200, see *Bk. of Deeds* C-3, p. 227 (Sept. 25, 1908). For Southern Methodist donation of their building and land to Rev. W. T. Potts, see *Bk. of Deeds* D-3, p. 307 (April 30, 1909). Rev. Potts became Baptist minister in 1908 for one year, again in 1914–15, and finally in 1929–32.

[350] For the Afro-American concerts, see *Galax News*, Sept. 1, 1960, p. 4. For Methodist renovation as a consequence, see *Galax News*, July 14 and Aug. 25, 1955.

[351] For Dr. Upton C. Ewing's life, see his obituary in *Highlander*, Feb. 1, 1968.

[352] The history of *The Episcopal Church of the Incarnation: First 100 Years*, p. 21, claims that the first service of record was held on Oct. 30, 1879. John Archibald Deal was born near Fayetteville, N.C., Nov. 26, 1844, and died May 6, 1928, at his home

in Gainesville, Ga. His wife Cornelia Ann Fitch was born June 17, 1854, and died Sept. 18, 1937. Both are buried in Woodlawn Cemetery in Franklin, N.C.

[353] For Rev. Deal's description of his circuit, see *The American Mountaineer* (n.d.), p. 27.

[354] For praise of Deal by Rev. Frank Siler of Lake Junaluska, see Rev. Deal's obituary in "Brief History of Rev. John A. Deal, *Franklin Press*, May 17, 1928.

[355] See *Bk. of Deeds* DD, p. 347 (Oct. 22, 1895), for purchase of 100 square feet for $100 by the Protestant Episcopal Church Trustees from James Rideout. For other facts of the Church, see Clyde Beale, "Episcopal Church at Highlands Will Note Its 55th Anniversary," *Asheville Citizens*, May 31, 1951. For the original name of the Highlands church, consecrated on Aug. 19, 1896, see A. Rufus Morgan, *History of St. John's Episcopal Church* (Franklin, N.C., 1974), p. 2. For the bell and chandeliers, see Helen Hill Thornton, "Historical Sketch of the Episcopal Church of the Incamation, Highlands, N.C.," written ca. 1958–60.

[356] For Rufus Morgan's autobiography, see his *From Cabin to Cabin* (Franklin, N.C., 1980). See also Rev. Howard W. Lull's interview, "The Life and Times of A. Rufus Morgan, Priest," in *The Living Church* (April 9, 1978). Rufus Morgan was born in 1885 and died Feb. 14, 1983. For Jonathan Williams' poem to Rufus Morgan, see his *Blues and Roots, Rue and Bluets* (Durham, 1985).

[357] For growth of the Episcopal Church, see "The Church of the Incarnation," *Galax News*, July 2, 1970, pp. 7 and 21. See also "Episcopalians Start Land Purchase Fund" in *Highlander*, Dec. 1, 1961.

[358] The old library was deeded to the Episcopal Church for $65,000. See Hudson Library minutes, Sept. 19, 1985.

[359] For the establishment of the Baptist Church in Highlands, see *Life and Labors of Elder F. M. Jordan* (Raleigh, N.C., 1899), p. 245. For the flea episode, see p. 246. For Baptist baptism locations, see Butler Jenkins' diary, March 13, 1949. For Harrington's fund raising for a Baptist church, see *Blue Ridge Enterprise*, Dec. 11, 1884. For Baptist land purchases, see *Bk. of Deeds* C-3, p. 225 (Sept. 16, 1890), and CC, p. 357 (Sept. 5, 1891).

[360] For the Baptist purchase of the Methodist Church from trustees T. Baxter White, Walter Talley, and T. Newton Rogers, see *Bk. of Deeds* RR, p. 218 (Sept. 4, 1904). For permit to construct a new church on the site of the old Methodist Church, see minutes of Board of Commissioners, Aug. 5, 1940.

[361] For Rev. Gibson's account of the lessons he learned in the mountains, see Lewis W. Gibson, *Meeting God in the Mountains* (Walhalla, S.C., 1996).

[362] For Rev. and Mrs. Henry Emmons' obituaries, see *Franklin Press*, November 29, 1899.

[363] Bess Hines Harkins, "Definition," *Earth Songs* (San Benito, Texas, 1975), p. 14.

[364] For the first listing of a Unitarian meeting, see *Highlander*, Dec. 10, 1886. For early meeting places, see Harry Wright's unpub. MS, "History of the Methodist Church."

[365] For the Unitarian references to Highlands, see annual reports of the *Anniversary of the American Unitarian Association* issued on April 30th of each year, particularly 63rd (1888), pp. 24–25; 64th (1889), p. 11; 65th (1890), p. 20; 67th (1892), pp. 34 and 69; 68th (1893), pp. 33 and 66; and 69th (1894), p. 65.

[366] For Kelsey's depiction of Highlands as a health resort, see his promotional pamphlet, *Blue Ridge Highlands*, pp. 2–3.

[367] For the founding of the Hudson Library, see Mary Chapin Smith, *History of the Hudson Library Association* (Highlands, 1931), p. 1. See also minutes of the Hudson Library Association, Secretary's Book, vol. 1, p. 1.

[368] Bess Hines Harkins, "Deep Certainty," *Earth Songs*, p. 24.

[369] Dr. Edward Everett Hale expressed this rule of the Lend-a-Hand Society in "Ten Times One Is Ten," a poem published in 1870, ten years before the Society's offer of a helping hand to Mrs. Hudson's friends.

[370] For the Book Committee's selection of books for the library, see Mary Chapin Smith, *History of the Hudson Library Association*, p. 3.

[371] *St. Nicholas: An Illustrated Magazine for Young Folks* (New York) was published monthly from 1873 to 1940. Joel Chandler Harris, whose fame rests on his creation of Uncle Remus, contributed his *Daddy Jake, the Runaway* (1889) and *Chronicles of Aunt Minervy* (1899) as installments to *St. Nicholas* before they were published in book form, so the *St. Nicholas* versions of these works, rather than the books themselves, are valued as authentic first editions.

[372] For Stephen Vincent Benét, see Tom Crumpler, "History of Highlands," p. 31. See also the Stephen Vincent Benét Centennial Committee publications, Bethlehem, Pa., 1998.

[373] For Mary Chapin Smith and Benét, see her *History of the Hudson Library Association*, p. 8.

[374] Several popular titles in the Elsie Dinsmore series by Martha Farquharson Finley were *Elsie at Home, Elsie in the South, Elsie's Young Folks, Elsie and Her Loved Ones,* and *Elsie on the Hudson.*

[375] Concerning Miss Charlie Elliott, see Smith, *History of Hudson Library Association*, p. 10.

[376] For the organization of the League of Woman Voters, see *Franklin Press*, March 9, 1923, p. 2, and March 22, 1928.

[377] The quote comes from Charles Reade's *The Cloister and the Hearth*, chapter 24: "Courage, mon ami, le diable est mort!"

[378] For the Bobby Jones benefit, see "Library Fund Increased $500," *Highlands Maconian*, Aug. 19, 1931, and Mary Chapin Smith, *History of the Hudson Library Association*, p. 12.

[379] Marna is the daughter of Wilton H. Cobb, former mayor of Highlands.

[380] For Albertina Staub's obituary, see "Miss Staub Passes," *Franklin Press and Highlands Maconian*, July 2, 1942. She was born in Netstal, Switzerland, in 1866 and died June 27, 1942, at age 76.

[381] Although Miss Gertrude didn't become librarian until 1926, she began work as an aid in the library in 1924, thus the fifty year celebration in 1974. She was born Nov. 8, 1903, and died April 17, 1980.

[382] For Louise Bascom Barratt's obituary, see "Mrs. Barratt's Funeral Held in Highlands," *Franklin Press and Highlands Maconian*, Sept. 8, 1949. She was born in Highlands in 1885 and died Sept. 3, 1949, at age 64.

[383] For Watson Barratt's obituary, see "Watson Barratt Dies in New York Hospital: Highlands Summer Resident Was Famous Theatrical Designer," *Highlander*, July 13, 1962. See also "Watson Barratt, Designer, 78, Dies," *New York Times*, July 8, 1962, for his full name at birth: George Watson Barratt. He was born in 1884 and died July 6, 1962, at age 78.

384 For the location of *Blue Ridge Enterprise* office in 1883, see *Blue Ridge Enterprise*, Feb. 8, 1883, p. 3. A good summary of early newspapers in Highlands is J. J. Moore's "Stirring the Dust of 37 Years," *Highlands Maconian*, Sept. 3, 1930, p. 2. For E. E. Ewing's arrival in Highlands, see letter from his son, Cecil E. Ewing, in *Highlands Maconian*, Dec. 17, 1930. For Ewing's proposals for Highlands first newspaper, see "Prospectus of the Blue Ridge Enterprise," signed by thirty-two supporters from Highlands, Cashiers Valley, Franklin, Whiteside Cove, etc. For Clark's printing office on lot 122, see *Bk. of Deeds* S, p. 87 (Nov. 5, 1883).

385 For Jackson County's first newspaper, see Johnson Davis McRorie, *"Knowing Jackson County . . ." People, Places, and Earlier Days* (Sylva, N.C., 2000), p. 138.

386 For Goldie's epistle, "To Our Brethren of the Press," see *Highlander*, Aug. 7, 1885.

387 For the annual price of the *Highlander,* see Jan. 15, 1886.

388 For harassment of a black youth, see *Highlander*, July 30, 1886.

389 For Minnie Clark's closing of the Highlander newspaper, see *Highlander*, Feb. 25, 1887.

390 For the anonymous letter attacking the *Star*, see *Highlands Star*, Sept. 16, 1890. For Henry Stewart's attack on Charles Coe, see *Franklin Press*, Sept. 9, 1890. For *Franklin Press* attack on *Highlands Star*, see Allison D. McKinney's letter to *Highlands Maconian*, October 15, 1930.

391 For the Coe brothers' printing of *In the Heart of Highlands*, see *Highlander*, March 10 and 27, 1890.

392 For Allison McKinney's memories of early newspapers, see his letter, *Highlands Maconian*, October 15, 1930.

393 For a recollection of Harbison's prediction of the 1892 presidential election, see *Highlands Maconian*, Oct. 22, 1930.

394 For Joe Moore's newspaper standards, see *Highlands Maconian*, Sept. 3, 1930.

395 For a retrospective on Martha Goode, see "Woman of the Week," *Asheville Citizen*, July 12, 1965.

396 For Helen Hopper's reminiscences about the newspaper, see *Highlander*, Oct. 4, 1991. See also her retirement in *Highlander*, May 5, 1983.

397 For Ralph Morris' policies as editor, see *Highlander*, May 18 and 21, 1993.

398 For the "Always a Newsman" poem, see *Highlander*, Oct. 7, 1971, rpt. from the *Arizona Publisher.*

399 Dr. Kibbee's death is reported by C. C. Hutchinson's son, Arthur, in "Pioneer's Son Visits Macon," *Franklin Press and Highlands Maconian*, Aug. 31, 1939, and by Elias White, "Early Highlands Days," *Franklin Press and Highlands Maconian*, June 5, 1941, p. 5.

400 For the doctor's plight in Highlands, see *Highlander*, Feb. 25, 1887.

401 For Alfred Hawkins' life, see obituary by T. G. Harbison, in *Franklin Press,* Sept. 17, 1920, p. 4. See also T. W. Reynolds' chapter on "The Hawkins Family," *High Lands*, pp. 46–58.

402 For detailed accounts of these two miracles performed by Herman Rideout, see article by Ralph L. Rideout, Sr., in *Heritage of Macon County*, vol. 1, p. 436.

403 For the rabies incident, see *Franklin Press*, Jan. 23 & 30, 1901. For Dr. G. W. Hays' background, see article by W. Arthur Hays, Jr., in *Heritage of Macon County*, vol. 1, pp. 267–68. Dr. Hays was born Oct. 7, 1873, in Knox County, Ky., and died in Highlands April 6, 1905, at age 31.

[404] For a brief biography of Dr. Mary Lapham, see unpub. MS, "History of Highlands" (ca. 1975) by Dr. Tom Crumpler, who from 1971 until 2000 lived in her home at Faraway. See also her obituary in *Detroit Herald*, Jan. 27, 1936, p. 1: "Woman Leader in Conquest of Tuberculosis Dies at 75." She was born in 1861 and died Jan. 26, 1936. For a description of Faraway, see *Highlander*, July 1, 1976, p. 9, and July 10, 1980, Sec. B, p. 1. See *Franklin Press*, April 27, 1898, for the original name of the house.

[405] For the property given to Mary Lapham by Marietta Trowbridge, see *Bk. of Deeds*, E-3, p. 225 (Nov. 19, 1908). For descriptions of the sanatorium, see *Galax News*, June 18, 1970, pp. 13 and 17, and *Highlander*, Jan. 21, 1971.

[406] For Judge Hines as mayor, see *Highlands Maconian*, March 8, 1931.

[407] For the report of the fire at Bug Hill, see Helen Hopper, *Highlander*, Jan. 21, 1971.

[408] For Margaret Harry, see *Highlander*, March 14, 1974, and Aug. 25 and Sept. 8, 1977.

[409] For an account of Dr. E. R. Gilbert, see article by Margaret Hall and Isabel Chambers in *Heritage of Macon County, Vol. 2*, pp. 244–45.

[410] For the flu epidemic of 1937, see *Franklin Press and Highlands Maconian*, March 18, 1937.

[411] For Dr. Dabney's attempt at a hospital in Highlands, see minutes of Board of Commissioners, Bk. G, pp. 128–29, April 2, 1934 .

[412] For Dr. Matthews' success at establishing a hospital, see *Franklin Press and Highlands Maconian*, April 17, 1947; minutes of Board of Commissioners, Bk. 2, p. 155, Dec. 1, 1947; and *Galax News,* June 22, 1967, p. 11. For the opening of the Highlands Community Hospital, see "Hospital Continues Tradition of Expert Medical Care," *Highlander*, Centennial Edition, July 19, 1975.

[413] For the hospital controversy, see *Highlander*, Feb. 3, 1966, p. 4.

[414] For Highlands–Cashiers Hospital expansion, see *Galax News*, Aug. 5, 1965, p. 7, and Aug. 11, 1966, p. 1.

[415] For an article on Mike Mangum, see *Highlander*, Nov. 15, 1985.

[416] For the hospital's accreditation, see *Highlander*, June 9, 1977.

[417] For the proposal and opening of Chestnut Hill retirement community, see *Highlander*, April 17, 1990, and July 23, 1993.

[418] For Joseph Halleck's picket fence fronting Central House, see *Blue Ridge Enterprise*, Sept. 4, 1884.

[419] For the five boarding houses open in Highlands in 1898—Davis, Highlands, Stuly, Central, and Islington—see *Franklin Press*, June 22, 1898.

[420] For the Rideout and Norton exchange of Central House on Oct. 24, 1888, see *Bk. of Deeds* Y, pp. 7 and 11.

[421] For David Norton's obituary, see *Franklin Press,* July 5, 1912. He was born Aug. 28, 1834, in Jackson County and died July 1, 1912, in Highlands at age 77. Mattie was born Jan. 8, 1848, and died Dec. 12, 1909, at age 61. Both are buried in the Highlands Cemetery.

[422] For Arthur B. Potts' description of the inn when his family ran it, see pamphlet, *Old Edwards Inn and Central House* (Highlands, 1984), p. 13.

[423] For Billy Potts' sale of the Stone Store to Porter Pierson for $1,000, see *Bk. of Deeds* K-3, p. 389 (May 11, 1911). For his sale of Central House to Grover Edwards for

$100, see *Bk. of Deeds* U-3, p. 462 (July 24, 1914). For Pearl Potts' memories of Central House, see *Old Edwards Inn and Central House*, p. 15.

[424] For Porter Pierson's sale of Stone Store to W. S. Davis for $2,500, see *Bk. of Deeds* E-4, p. 506 (July 23, 1920).

[425] For the additions to Central House, see minutes of Board of Commissioners, Nov. 30, 1925 (Bk. E, p. 61).

[426] For W. W. Edwards' purchase of Rock Store from W. S. Davis for $3,500, see *Bk. of Deeds* U-4, p. 190 (Jan. 29, 1932). For the building of Hotel Edwards, see *Highlands Maconian*, Jan. 27, 1932, and *Franklin Press and Highlands Maconian*, May 16, 1935: "New Inn Opens at Highlands: Hotel Edwards Is Handsome Modern Three-Story Building." For Bernice Hedden's memories of Central House, see *Old Edwards Inn and Central House*, pp. 16-18. For Bob DuPree's and Steve Potts' leasing of Old Edwards Inn, see *Franklin Press and Highlands Maconian*, Jan. 5, 1950.

[427] For Old Edwards Inn's closing in 1964 and reopening in 1982, see *Highlander*, April 29, 1982, Sec. B, p. 1. For its sale by the Edwards to the Bentons, see *Bk. of Deeds* B-14, p. 91 (Sept. 10, 1981), and O-15, p. 15 (Jan. 11, 1984).

[428] For John Norton's trade of Central House to Joseph Halleck for Highlands House, see *Bk. of Deeds* Q, pp. 10 and 357 (Sept. 15, 1880).

[429] For the town population and number of guests at Highlands House in 1883, see *Blue Ridge Enterprise*, Sept. 27 and Oct. 4, 1883.

[430] For Eliza Wheaton's purchase of Highlands House, see *Bk. of Deeds* V, p. 363 (Sept. 24, 1886). For Highlands House statistics, see John Jay Smith, Proprietor, "Highlands House, Highlands, Macon County, N. Carolina," Franklin, N.C., 1898. For the Smiths' sale to Davis and Allen for $12,500, see *Bk. of Deeds* M-4, p. 142 (Oct. 20, 1925).

[431] For Miss Crowinshield's account of the azalea and the rattlesnake at Highlands House, see her "Visit to 'Highlands House' in 1888."

[432] For the Trices' lease of Highlands Inn for $700/year, see *Bk. of Deeds* W-4, p. 410 (April 2, 1934). For their purchase of Highlands Inn from the widow Davis for $250,000, see *Bk. of Deeds* C-5, p. 231 (April 12, 1938), and *Deeds of Trust* 35, p. 472. For half interest and shared indebtedness of $13,250 with Cook, see *Bk. of Deeds* B-5, p. 473 (June 17, 1938). For the Trices' sale to the Cooks, see *Bk. of Deeds* B-6, p. 257 (April 1, 1952), and for Cook's sale to Helen Major with a $70,000 mortgage, see *Bk. of Deeds* I-8, p. 146 (Feb. 8, 1969).

[433] For Glenn Arnette's sale to Walter Hood, see *Bk. of Deeds* B-17, p. 402 (Oct. 15, 1986). For the Bentons' $400,000 mortgage, see *Bk. of Deeds* X-16, p. 257 (July 11, 1986).

[434] Billy Hawkins is son of Corbin Hawkins, whose father Huber Hawkins was Dr. Alfred Hawkins' son.

[435] For Ralph Rideout, Sr.'s article on the Rideout family, see *Heritage of Macon County*, vol. 1, pp. 436–37. For Rideout's exchange of land with Charles Frost, see *Bk. of Deeds* Y, p. 9 (May 1, 1888).

[436] For Skinner's sale of his home to Margaretta Ravenel for $1,500, see *Bk. of Deeds* R, p. 296 (May 22, 1883). See also *Blue Ridge Enterprise*, Nov. 15, 1883. For Islington House renovations, see *Highlander* Nov. 12, 1886.

[437] For reports of the earthquake and its aftershocks, see *Highlander*, Sept. 3 and Oct. 29, 1886.

[438] For Mary Dixie's obituary, see *Franklin Press*, Jan. 30, 1895. The name is variously spelled "Dixey" and "Dixie" in this article, but a deed between Joseph Halleck and McD. Adams dated Jan. 25, 1894, refers to "Mrs. Dixie's Hotel" [See *Bk. of Deeds* EE, p. 262.]

[439] For Margaretta Ravenel's decision to sell Islington House, see letter to Mr. F. A. Schuyler from J. Quincy Pierson, Feb. 20, 1913. For Bob King's purchase of Islington House in 1925 for $6,000, including a pipe line to the spring on J. Blanc Monroe's (formerly Ravenel's) property, see *Bk. of Deeds* J-4, p. 510 (May 6, 1925).

[440] For Trowbridge's purchase of the Bascom–Louise from Watson Barratt, see *Bk. of Deeds* G-6, p. 675 (Nov. 5, 1955). See also ads in the *Galax News*, August 18, 1955, and June 21, 1956. For King's Inn improvements see *Galax News*, June 21 and June 28, 1956. For the Trowbridge sale of the Tastee-Freez property to T. B. and Margaret Picklesimer, see *Bk. of Deeds* I-6, p. 265 (May 16, 1956), and *Deeds of Trust* 57, p. 5. For Betty Trowbridge's purchase of King's Inn, see *Bk. of Deeds* C-7, p. 198 (Feb. 18, 1964). For her sale of it to the Phelans with an $83,607.45 mortgage, see *Bk. of Deeds* S-7, p. 416 (June 23, 1967).

[441] For John Phelan's poem, see *Highlander*, "Centennial Edition," July 19, 1975, Sec. C, p. 8.

[442] For the Dunnings' purchase of King's Inn with a mortgage balance of $67,318.08, see *Bk. of Deeds* X-8, p. 257 (Aug. 31, 1971). For sale to Real Dynamics Properties, see *Bk. of Deeds* A-10, p. 164 (Nov. 2, 1973); and to Mountain Inns, Ltd., of Highlands and Cruze and Garcia of Tampa, Fla., see *Bk. of Deeds* K-14, p. 31 (March 23, 1982).

[443] For accounts of the King's Inn fire, see *Asheville Citizen-Times*, Feb. 21, 1994, and *Highlander*, Feb. 22 and March 1, 1994.

[444] For the sale of the land by the Kelseys to Mrs. Mary A. Davis for $800, see *Bk. of Deeds* Y, 303 (Feb. 7, 1889).

[445] Frank Sheldon built his home in the fall of 1886; see *Highlander*, Oct. 8, 1886. It was subsequently owned by Rev. Joel T. Wade, second minister of the Presbyterian Church, Claudian B. Northrop of Washington, D.C., and Roy "Nick" Potts of Potts Brothers in town. Currently it is the home of the Randolph Shaffners. For Sheldon's obituary, see "Frank S. Sheldon, Former Highlander Passes In California," *Franklin Press and Highlands Maconian*, February 3, 1944. He died on Jan. 5, 1944. For construction of Davis House, see *Franklin Press,* March 27 and May 27, 1890.

[446] For Mrs. Martin's leaving Islington House to take over Bascom's Davis House, see letter to Mr. F. A. Schuyler from J. Quincy Pierson, Feb. 20, 1913. Martin bought the inn on April 21, 1923 [*Bk. of Deeds* K-4, p. 98] and sold it to Louise Bascom Barratt on March 30, 1930 [*Bk. of Deeds* Q-4, p. 388].

[447] For Watson Barratt's Bascom–Louise, see *Franklin Press and Highlands Maconian*, Dec. 7, 1950.

[448] For Dick Lee's purchase from William and Betty Trowbridge, see *Bk. of Deeds* N-6, p. 122 (June 12, 1957). See also *Galax News*, June 18, 1956, and "Lee's Inn Celebrates 10th Anniversary," *Highlander*, May 5, 1966. For construction of the cottages, see minutes of Board of Commissioners, April 6, 1959, Bk. 3, p. 221. For Jean Lee's sale to Dick Lee, who assumed a $125,400 mortgage on Aug. 18, 1969, see *Bk. of Deeds* H-8, p. 43, and *Deeds of Trust* 75, p. 149.

[449] For the Lee's Inn fire, see "Lee's Inn Destroyed: Fire Sweeps Through 90-year-old Landmark," *Highlander*, Dec. 9, 1982.

[450] For T. T. Hall, see Margaret Gilbert Hall's article in *Heritage of Macon County, Vol. 2*, pp. 261–62. Tudor T. Hall was born Dec. 6, 1844, and died Aug. 28, 1918, at age 73. His second wife, Meta Norton Frost Hall, was born Apri. 16, 1864, and died Jan. 28, 1942, at age 78. Both are buried in the Highlands cemetery.

[451] For the Halls' practical jokes, see S. Van Epp Law, *Status Quo* (Stuart, Fla., 1971), pp. 104–08. For the story of the Crane family, see *Heritage of Macon County, Vol. 2*, p. 197.

[452] For the renaming of Hall House, the Highlands Manor, see *Mountain Trail*, Aug. 14, 1939. For the end of Hall House as Highlands Manor, see *Highlander*, Oct. 20, 1961.

[453] For the Piersons' purchase of the inn, see *Bk. of Deeds* II, p. 447 (Dec. 27, 1899). For background on the Pierson Inn, see *Franklin Press and Highlands Maconian*, May 2, 1935; May 26 and Nov. 25, 1943; April 22, 1948; and *Galax News*, July 3, 1958, p. 12. In 1935 D. A. Cunningham of Parrott, Ga., leased the inn, and in 1943 Mrs. Fred M. Moll of Jacksonville, Fla., held the lease.

[454] For Natalie Hammond and her cottage, see her obituary in *Franklin Press and Highlands Maconian*, Dec. 6, 1937.

[455] For Kalmia Court's opening, see *Franklin Press and Highlands Maconian*, July 16, 1947.

[456] For the opening of Skyline Lodge, see *Galax News*, June 17, 1965. For the fire, see *Highlander*, Nov. 30,1967. Frank and Pauline Davis bought the lodge in 1971. When Frank died in 1974, Paul Roberge succeeded him.

[457] For the Scientific Society's statement of purpose, see *Highlander*, Dec. 31, 1886. For its founding, see *Highlander*, Nov. 12, 1886.

[458] For anyone interested in horticulture, including the selection, care, and placement of plants, the Minutes of the Southern Blue Ridge Horticultural Society of Highlands from Jan. 3, 1891, through Nov. 2, 1895, make a fascinating read.

[459] For James Smith's article on "The Ideal Tree," see Secretary's Book, Southern Blue Ridge Horticultural Society of Highlands, pp. 75–79 and 35–38.

[460] For Bob Padgett's article on the Horse Cove Poplar, see *Highlander*, May 6, 1982, Sec. B, p. 1, rpt. from *The State* magazine. For naming the Horse Cove poplar after him, see *Highlander*, Aug 29, 1997.

[461] For Clark Foreman's proposal for a Highlands Museum, see minutes of the Hudson Library Association, August 10, 1927. For his argument concerning the need for a Highlands museum, see "Move On Foot To Build Museum At Highlands," *Franklin Press*, Sept. 22, 1927.

[462] For the naming of Ravenel Lake, see "Lindenwood Lake Changed to Ravenel Lake," *Highlands Maconian*, Sept. 9, 1931, p. 2.

[463] For the Caucasian use of Cherokee names, see T. W. Reynolds, *Cherokee and Creek* (Highlands, 1966), p. 3.

[464] For the chestnut blight in N.C., see *Franklin Press*, Oct. 5, 1923, and Elsie Quarterman, *Highlands Museum and Biological Laboratory*, 1947, p. 5.

[465] For the arrival of the Japanese Beetle, see *Franklin Press and Highlands Maconian*, August 12, 1932.

[466] For Bob Zahner's article on the Champion Fraser fir and Champion clammy locust in Highlands, see *Highlander*, April 21, 1998.

[467] Henry Wright was born on Jan. 22, 1893, and died June 2, 1983. He is buried in Highlands Cemetery.

[468] For Henry Wright's discovery of the orchid subsequently named in his honor, see Ralph Sargent, *Biology in the Blue Ridge*, p. 39.

[469] For E. E. Reinke's prophecy, see *The Highlands Museum of Natural History: Report on the Necessity of a Mountain Biological Research Station in the South* (Highlands, 1930), p. 6. See also "Biology Post Opens in July," *Highlands Maconian*, April, 29, 1931, pp. 1, 4–5, the quote's appearing on p. 5.

[470] For Bill Marett's account, see his *Courage at Fool's Rock* (Highlands, 1975).

[471] For a reprint of Rev. G. W. Belk's article, see "Recall Heroic Rescue Done In North Carolina Mountains: Death of Charlie Wright Revives Story of Thrilling Heroism on Cliff on Whiteside Mountain," *Franklin Press*, March 1, 1928, p. 1. This reprint claims that the original article appeared in the *Charlotte Observer* in October, 1911. A reprint did in early November, 1911, in the *Wilson Daily Times* of Wilson, N.C. See also the report of the *Carnegie Hero Fund Commission* (Pittsburgh, Pa., 1914) and "Heroic Rescue of Gus Baty from Whiteside Mountain Precipice Retold," *Highlander*, Jan. 25, 1963, pp. 1, 4. For other accounts of the rescue, see Felix Alley, *Random Thoughts and the Musings of a Mountaineer*, pp. 490–492; T. W. Reynolds, High Lands, p. 7, and Gert McIntosh, *Highlands . . . a walk into the past*, p. 63.

[472] The Carnegie Foundation did not bestow gold medals lightly. By the time Charlie Wright received his medallion, the Foundation's 840th award, it was only the 16th gold medal awarded since the Foundation's establishment in 1904. In a section entitled "Acts of Heroism Which Have Been Recognized Since the Establishment of the Fund to and including January 31st, 1914 and the Award Made in Each Case," the first gold medal was bestowed on Capt. Mark Casto, age 31, for a 1906 rescue of a steamer's passengers and crew in New Jersey. Three more gold medals were given in that same year, eight more in 1907, and three in 1911 before that of Charles N. Wright, aged thirty-eight, merchant, who helped to save R. Augustus Baty, aged twenty-six, carpenter, from an impending fall, Highlands, N.C., May 14, 1911. See Carnegie Hero Fund Commission (Pittsburgh, Pa., 1914), p. 195. Will Dillard's Silver medal is now in the possession of his niece and nephew, the Morris Browns of Dillard.

[473] Charlie Wright died Dec. 4,1927.

[474] For the average temperature and rainfall from 1883–97, see letter of Oct. 11, 1897, from U.S. Dept. of Agriculture Weather Bureau in Raleigh, N.C., to Albertina Staub.

[475] For Elias White's report of early air pollution, see his "Early Highlands Days," *Franklin Press and Highlands Maconian*, June 4, 1941, p. 4.

[476] For the drought of 1883, see *Blue Ridge Enterprise*, Sept. 20, 1883.

[477] For the 1886 temperature low, see *Highlander*, Jan. 15, 1886.

[478] For the proposal of a new county, see *Highlander*, Dec. 31, 1886. For subsequent efforts to form a new county, see *Blue Ridge Enterprise*, Nov. 20, 1884, and *Highlander,* Jan. 28 and Feb. 25, 1887.

[479] For Mary Chapin Smith's poem about snow, see her *Earth Songs* (Boston, 1910), p. 16.

[480] For various reports of the "deep snow" of 1886, see "This Winter At Highlands Mild, Old Paper Suggests," *Franklin Press & Highlands Maconian*, February 7, 1946; "Site of Highlands Was Carved from Mountain Wilderness," *Highlands Maco-*

nian, July 29, 1931; "Romance of Highlands," *Greenwood (S.C.) Index-Journal,* August 24, 1929; "Highlands Site of Beautiful Estates," *Franklin Press,* Teacher Training ed., April 10, 1930; and "Charm of Highlands Mountains Lured Professor Harbison, Botanist," *Franklin Press,* Highlands ed., July 5, 1928.

[481] For the snow of 1942, see *Franklin Press and Highlands Maconian,* March 12, 1942. See also Gertrude Harbison, as quoted in *Highlander,* Sept. 27, 1973.

[482] Snow depth of sixteen and a half inches provided by the Highlands Biological Station, December 8, 1993.

[483] For Gertrude Harbison's weather report, see *Franklin Press and Highlands Maconian,* Jan. 7, 1937.

[484] For Biological Station records during the fifty years from Jan., 1948–Nov., 1998, see computer-generated spreadsheet of mean, maximum, and minimum temperatures; greatest precipitation, and greatest snowfall for each day of the year.

[485] For the coldest day, according to Highlands Biological Station, see *Highlander,* Feb. 3, 1966: "Worst Winter on Record Hits Highlands Area."

[486] For the weather in 1895, see *Franklin Press,* Feb. 13, 1895.

[487] For Barry C. Hawkins' 1930 report, see "Weather Observations Near Highlands Reveal Great Contrasts and Variations," *Highlands Maconian,* Dec. 10, 1930, p. 1.

[488] For the 1966 record low temperature, see *Highlander,* Feb. 3, 1966.

[489] For the average annual rainfall, see records of the Highlands Biological Station, including the extremes of 115.62 inches in 1979 and 53.44 inches in 1925. See also "Miss Harbison Recognized," *Highlander,* Sept. 27, 1973. For a list of statistics before 1955, see *Franklin Press and Highlands Maconian,* Apr. 28, 1955. See also letter of Oct. 11, 1897, from U.S. Dept. of Agriculture Weather Bureau in Raleigh, N.C., to Albertina Staub for average precipitation during the 14 years from 1883 to 1897, namely, 72.3 inches per year. In 1956 the Highlands Industrial Committee reported the annual average rainfall at 82 inches.

[490] For the 1876 flood, see Kelsey's *Record of Weather and Work,* vol. 1, June 15, 1876.

[491] Gertrude Harbison made these observations in an interview with John Parris, as reported in *Highlander,* Sept. 27, 1973.

[492] For the flood of 1940, see "Heavy Rains Wreak Havoc at Highlands," *Franklin Press and Highlands Maconian,* Sept. 5, 1940. The actual measurements were 9.69 inches on Aug. 13, 1940, and 11.65 inches on Aug. 29; total for the month, 25.57 inches.

[493] For an entertaining eye-witness reminiscence of the great flood, see Bud Thompson's "The Night I Was Saved," *Highlander,* Sept. 4, 1969, p. 3.

[494] For the collapse of Mirror Lake dam in 1962, see *Galax News,* Aug. 2, 1962. For the flood of 1964, see *Highlander,* Oct. 2, 1964.

[495] For the record rainfall in a single 24-hour period—11.87 inches on Sept. 29, 1964—see the Highlands Biological Station's records for 1961–2000. Cf. 11.65 inches on Aug. 29, 1940.

[496] Weather data for average high temperatures is taken from U.S. Weather Bureau Information for 1915–55, as published by the Highlands Industrial Committee, *Highlands, North Carolina—Facts & Figures for Industry* (Highlands Chamber of Commerce, 1956), p. 5, and from the Highlands Biological Station's records for 1961–2000.

497 The annual average Highlands temperature of 50.43° for the period 1979–2000 and 50.28° for the 1962–2000 period are based on the Biological Station's records, including before and after the move of its instruments in 1978. See Appendix 12: Weather Data, Annual Temperature Averages in Highlands.

498 For the highest temperature in 1913, see letter to S. P. Ravenel from J. Quincy Pierson, July 28, 1913.

499 For the drought of 1883, see *Blue Ridge Enterprise*, Aug. 30, 1883.

500 For the town board's hiring of a dowser, see minutes of Board of Commissioners, Bk. 3, p. 143, April 21, 1955.

501 For Hurricane Opal, see *Highlander*, Oct. 6, 1995.

502 For lightning accounts, see *Highlander*, Aug. 14, 1885. For the Emmons School strike, see letter to S. P. Ravenel, Jr., from J. Quincy Pierson, July 28, 1913, and interview with Henry Wright by Ralph Sargent and Kevin Fitz Patrick of Media Divide, ca. 1982.

503 For Edward King's account of lightning, see his "Great South," *Scribner's Monthly*, vol. 7 (March, 1874), 535.

504 For Gertrude Harbison's Jefferson Award, see *Asheville Citizen*, September 3, 1978.

505 For the list of stores in 1884, see *Blue Ridge Enterprise*, Jan. 3, 1884.

506 For Tanner Cobb's arrival in Highlands, see *Highlander*, Sept. 11 and Nov. 20, 1885, and his first advertisement in July, 1886.

507 For the number of stores in Highlands in 1890 and 1891, see Charlie Coe's *Highlands Star*, as quoted in Walter Reese's diary, p. 8.

508 For W. T. Potts' livery stable, see *Franklin Press*, June 18, 1902.

509 For Shine Potts' recollection of Highlands in 1911, see *Highlander*, Nov. 8, 1985.

510 For Highlands' first building code, see minutes of Board of Commissioners, Dec. 1, 1919, and June 16, 1922.

511 For growth in Highlands in 1925, see John Jay Smith, "Highlands, N.C., Founded in 1875," *Franklin Press*, Jan. 29, 1926.

512 For 1927 population figures, see *Franklin Press*, "Highlands Edition," July 5, 1928, p. 5. For construction of Lake Sequoyah, see minutes of Board of Commissioners, Bk. E, pp. 5, 17, 24, 25, and 82, and *Franklin Press*, Feb. 6 and Dec. 11, 1925, and May 7, 1926.

513 For the Shockley affair, see minutes of Board of Commissioners, Aug. 7, Sept. 6, and Oct. 1, 1926.

514 For the electric system cost overruns, see minutes of Board of Commissioners, Bk. E, Feb. 25,1927

515 For Duke Power's installation of power lines to Highlands, see *Galax News*, Aug. 4, 1966, p. 9.

516 For the completion of the water and electric project, see "Highlands Is Enjoying New Power Supply," *Asheville Times*, April 17, 1927. See also *Highlands Maconian*, July 29, 1931, p. 4.

517 For the naming of Lake Sequoyah, see minutes of Board of Commissioners, Bk. E, p. 183, July 2, 1928, and Sarah-Hicks Hines' article in *Franklin Press*, June 26, 1930, p. 6.

518 For the construction of Potts Brothers store, see *Franklin Press,* June 23, 1926.

519 For the construction of Jim Hick's barber shop and Elinor Cleaveland's grill, see minutes of Board of Commissioners, Bk. E, May 24, 1927, p. 147.

[520] For the construction of Irvin Rice's building, see *Franklin Press*, Feb. 23 and April 5, 1928.

[521] For telephone service by the Hall family, see Douglas Peach, "Town of Highlands," *Highlander,* Sept. 6, 1984.

[522] For the installation of today's Loafer's Bench, see *Highlander*, May 23, 1974.

[523] For Turtle Pond news, see *Franklin Press*, March 12, 1920.

[524] For Harbison's view of the Great Depression, see "Professor Harbison Gives Reason for Hard Times," *Franklin Press*, Sept. 18, 1930, pp. 3, 6.

[525] For 1930 population figures and predictions, see *Highlands Maconian*, Sept. 3, 1930.

[526] For revitalization of the Chamber of Commerce, including its earlier formation, see *Highlands Maconian*, Feb. 25, 1931, pp. 1 and 4, and March 4 and 11, 1931. For the earlier organization specifically, see Bessie Hinson Hines' mention of a Chamber meeting in her *Diary of Bessie Hinson Hines, Sr.*, July 28, 1924.

[527] For background on Sidney McCarty, see *Highlander*, Dec. 24,1991.

[528] For the town board's first discussion of the altitude oak in 1928, see minutes of Board of Commissioners, Bk. E, p. 171, April 2, 1928. For the decision to cut it, see Bk. 1, p. 67, April 4, 1938: "Moved by Commissioner G. W. Marett, seconded by D. W. Wiley that the three trees on Main Street between fourth and fifth streets be removed. Motion carried." Mayor pro-tem was W. H. Cobb, since mayor W. S. Davis was ill and unable to attend the meeting

[529] Highlands' average altitude of 4,118 included much of Satulah mountain within its corporate limits. The actual altitude on Main Street was 3,834; the top of Satulah just outside the corporate limits measured 4,560 feet.

[530] From Stephen Vincent Benét, *John Brown's Body* (New York, 1928), Book 4. Benét summered in Highlands prior to and during the early years of World War I.

[531] Stanza 1 of George Pope Morris' "Woodman, Spare That Tree," composed in 1830.

[532] For the legislative bill to extend the town limits in 1949, see minutes of Board of Commissioners, Bk. 2, p. 179, Feb. 7, 1947, and *Franklin Press and Highlands Maconian*, Feb. 27, 1947.

[533] For areas annexed, see *Highlander*, July 14, 1977, and Charlie McDowell's map of Highlands, dated July 26, 1977, Plat Bk. 5, p. 13. For actual annexation, see *Highlander*, July 3, 1980.

[534] For Harlan Kelsey's suggestion for Main Street improvement, see *Mountain Trail*, June 27, 1941.

[535] For the Highlands Inn porch controversy, see minutes of Board of Commissioners, Bk. 1, p. 233, April 3, 1940, and p. 238; continuing in Bk. 2, pp. 107, 110, 131, 137, and 185; and ending in Bk. 3, p. 53, on Dec. 17, 1953.

[536] For Highlands' first stoplight, see minutes of Board of Commissioners, Bk. 2, p. 136, Jan. 10, 1947.

[537] For the eulogy to the Mountaineer Restaurant, see Ran Shaffner, "Biscuits in Sausage Gravy."

[538] For R. E. Norton's 1951 map of Highlands, see minutes of Board of Commissioners, Bk. 3, p. 44, July 24, 1951.

[539] For parking regulations, see minutes of Board of Commissioners, Bk. 3, p. 101, June 1, 1953. See also *Galax News*, June 20, 1963, p. 8, and June 25, 1970, p. 1.

[540] For the TV film shown throughout Eastern America, the article in *The State*, and the new brochure about Highlands, see minutes of Board of Commissioners, Aug. 2, 1954, and Aug. 3, 1959, and *Galax News*, June 18, 1964.

[541] For the community planning program, see minutes of Board of Commissioners, Bk. 3, p. 217, Jan. 19, 1959.

[542] For John Parris on Highlands as a flower-box town, see *Highlander*, June 25, 1970.

[543] For the creation of the Highlands Township Taxpayers Association, see *Highlander*, July 11 and Aug. 15, 1974, and Aug. 28 and Sept. 11, 1975.

[544] For voter approval of a Highlands district in Macon County, see *Highlander*, Nov. 4, 1976. For legislative approval of a Highlands representative on the County Board of Education, see *Highlander*, April 21, 1977.

[545] For the letter found at Faraway by Tom Crumpler, see *Highlander*, Sept. 4, 1975, p. 9.

[546] For the arrival of cable TV in Highlands, see *Highlander*, Nov. 16, 1978; Oct. 11, 1979; and July 8, 1982.

[547] For Carolina Mountain Shops, see *Highlander*, April 8, 1982.

[548] For Mountain Federal Savings and Loan Association, see *Highlander*, March 14, 1974.

[549] For Carolina Mountain Bank, see *Highlander*, Nov. 1, 1979.

[550] For Carol Perrin (Cobb)'s depiction of Highlands' two personalities, see *Highlands Historic Inventory: Project Completion Report* (Greenville, S.C., 1982).

[551] For Highlands Village Square, see *Highlander*, Aug. 21, 1975.

[552] For Sarah-Hicks Hines' view of Highlands' future, including the tin can tourist, see *Franklin Press*, Oct. 13, 1932.

[553] For the creation of the Highlands Merchants Association, see *Highlander*, Oct. 25, 1984. For its merger with the Chamber of Commerce in 1989, see *Highlander*, April 25, 1989.

[554] For the red maple planting on Main Street, see *Highlander*, October 4, 1985.

[555] For the final tree laws, see Highlander, Feb. 28 and March 21, 1989.

[556] For tree cutting on Philip deVille's property, see *Highlander*, March 18, 1997; for the zoning amendment protecting trees over eight inches, see *Highlander*, July 17, 1998.

[557] For the German introduction of clear-cutting as a method of land clearance, see Donald Edward Davis, *Where There Are Mountains: An Environmental History of the Southern Appalachians* (Athens, Ga., 2000), p. 104. For the Forest Service policy set by William L. Hall, Southern Appalachia's first forester, who considered "selection" preferable to "clear cutting," see p. 172.

[558] For Dr. Trussell's opposition to clear-cutting, see *Galax News*, Aug. 19 and 26, 1971.

[559] For the growing public opposition to clear-cutting in the National Forests, see *Highlander*, March 7, 1989; April 29 and May 15, 1990; and July 4, 1994 (Zahner's letter).

[560] For the architectural drawing of Oak Square, see *Highlander*, Sept. 6, 1985, p. 11. For Norma Pierson's and the zoning board's concerns about construction in town, see *Highlander*, Sept. 13, 1985.

[561] For proposed zoning changes, see *Highlander*, Nov. 10, 1987.

[562] For the distribution of the 1987 Land Use Survey and its results, see *Highlander*, Oct. 9, 1987, and Aug. 5, 1988. See also Appendix I of the *1989 Land Use Plan: Results of the Citizen Survey* (Asheville, 1988).

[563] For construction costs from 1983 through 1993, see *Highlander*, Jan. 4, 1994.

[564] For the Main Street parking crisis in 1988, see *Highlander*, Feb. 23 and March 22, 1988.

[565] For the paving issue, see *Highlander*, June 23, 1989.

[566] For the 1989 land use plan, see *Land Use Plan of the Town of Highlands, State of North Carolina*, as adopted by the Board of Commissioners, Sept. 20, 1989. See also *Highlander*, June 30, 1989.

[567] For DOT's recommendations concerning parking problem in Highlands, see summary in my letter to the editor in *Highlander*, Sept. 1, 1989. For the land use plan's recommended parking requirement and the town board's decision not to implement it, see *Highlander*, Aug. 25 and Sept. 8, 1989.

[568] For the 1989 tree protest and town board election, see *Highlander*, Nov. 10 and 21 and Dec. 5, 1989.

[569] For statistics on business turnover in Highlands, see Howard Patterson's editorial in *Highlander*, May 6, 1982.

[570] For the town board's decision against extraterritorial zoning, see *Highlander*, Oct. 12, 1990.

[571] For the creation of an appearance commission, see *Highlander*, Feb. 26, 1991.

[572] For the appearance commission's recommended "design guidelines," see *Highlander*, June 12, 1992.

[573] For the resurrection of the League of Women Voters in Highlands, see *Highlander*, March 6, 1990. For the League's five articles on "Planning for Our Future: Notes on Growth Management," see *Highlander*, Jan. 25–March 1, 1994.

[574] Herb James was town clerk from 1961–89.

[575] For the planning board's recommendations, see *Land Use Plan Update*, Report of the Planning Board, July 28, 1993.

[576] Olive Crane was born at Turtle Pond on Sept. 21, 1891.

[577] For Kelsey's reference to his first map of Highlands, see his *Record of Weather and Work*, vol. 2, Jan. 1, 1881.

[578] At the end of 1876 there were only three occupied houses in Highlands: Baxter White's, Kelsey's, and James Soper's, according to E. E. Ewing, "History of the Settlement of Highlands," *Blue Ridge Enterprise*, Jan. 25, 1883. Dobson's home appears on the map of 1881.

[579] For land purchases by J. E. and S. F. Bathrick, see Kelsey's *Record of Weather and Work*, vol. 1, April 15, 1878, and vol. 2, Nov. 27, 1878. See also *Bk. of Deeds* Q, p. 14 (March 12, 1880).

[580] For Ed Cunningham's and John Morton's home and store, see *Blue Ridge Enterprise*, Jan. 25, 1883, p. 1.

[581] For Baxter White's claim to the oldest house in Highlands, see *Highlander*, Aug. 7, 1885.

[582] For John P. Arthur's land purchase, see *Bk. of Deeds* P, p. 453 (Sept. 18, 1879).

[583] For Martin's store, see *Blue Ridge Enterprise*, Aug. 2, Oct. 10 and 25, and Nov. 15, 1883. For his departure from Highlands, see Jan. 3, 1884.

[584] For Baxter Wilson's home, see Walter Reese's diary, p. 9.

[585] For Kelsey's house, see his diary, vol. 1, June 17, 1875.

[586] For Orpha E. Rose's cottage, see *Blue Ridge Enterprise*, Nov. 22, 1883.

[587] For S. W. Hill's home, see Kelsey's *Record of Weather and Work*, vol. 1, April, 11, 1878; for H. M. Bascom's and J. M. McClearie's homes, see vol. 2, June 2, 1881.

[588] For the home of E. E. Ewing, see Kelsey's *Record of Weather and Work*, vol. 2, Aug. 10, 1881.

[589] For Frank H. Hill's house, see *Bk. of Deeds* Q, p. 291 (Aug. 18, 1881).

[590] For C. C. Hutchinson's house, see Kelsey's *Record of Weather and Work*, vol. 2, Sept. 16, 1878.

[591] For Mary Chapin's house, see *Blue Ridge Enterprise,* Feb. 15 and July 12, 1883.

[592] For J. E. Rideout's store next to Highlands Inn, see *Bk. of Deeds* R, p. 232 (Oct. 18, 1882).

[593] For C. A. Boynton's house, see Kelsey's *Record of Weather and Work*, vol. 2, Aug. 3, 1881.

[594] For William Partridge's home, see *Blue Ridge Enterprise*, March 8, 1883.

[595] For Judge Hunt's second home, see *Blue Ridge Enterprise*, Dec. 6, 1883.

[596] For Robert Marchant's house, see Kelsey's *Record of Weather and Work*, vol. 2, Feb. 22, 1879, and *Bk. of Deeds* S, p. 512 (Sept. 13, 1882).

[597] For Ellen N. Ellis' house, see *Bk. of Deeds* R, p. 221 (Nov. 23, 1882).

[598] For William Blanchard's house, see *Bk. of Deeds* S, p. 436 (Aug. 20, 1883), and *Blue Ridge Enterprise*, July 12, 1883.

[599] For George Jacobs' home, see *Bk. of Deeds* O, p. 107 (Jan. 1, 1876). See also *Blue Ridge Enterprise*, Jan. 25, 1883, p. 1.

[600] For Charles Allen's home, see Kelsey's *Record of Weather and Work*, vol. 1, Feb. 26, 1878, and vol. 2, April 28, 1879; for Halleck's purchase, see April 28, 1879.

[601] For Dr. G. W. Kibbee's house, see Kelsey's *Record of Weather and Work*, vol. 1, April 8, 1878.

[602] For M. I. Skinner's house, see Kelsey's *Record of Weather and Work*, vol. 2, March 3, 1879.

[603] For Joseph Halleck's house, see Kelsey's *Record of Weather and Work*, vol. 2, Nov. 13, 1879.

[604] For E. Selleck's house, see Kelsey's *Record of Weather and Work*, vol. 2, June 5, 1879.

[605] For Sumner Clark's land purchase, see *Bk. of Deeds* R, p. 180 (Dec. 2, 1882).

[606] For O. W. Ricketson's house, see Kelsey's *Record of Weather and Work*, vol. 1, June 12, 1878, and *Bk. of Deeds* P, p. 71 (July 2, 1878).

[607] For Abercrombie's home and shop replacing Monroe Skinner's, see *Blue Ridge Enterprise*, March 22 and April 12, 1883.

[608] For A. T. House's home, see *Blue Ridge Enterprise*, Jan. 25, 1883, p. 1.

[609] For J. A. McGuire's house, see Kelsey's *Record of Weather and Work*, vol. 2, March 8, 1879, and *Bk. of Deeds* T, p. 306 (Feb. 17, 1880).

[610] For William Duncan's land purchase, see *Bk. of Deeds* T, p. 477 (July 28, 1884). For the description of Duncan, see Walter Reese's diary, p. 11.

[611] For W. S. Clingon's house, see Kelsey's *Record of Weather and Work*, vol. 1, Jan. 26, 1877.

[612] For Benson Wells' land purchase, see Kelsey's *Record of Weather and Work*, vol. 1, May 20, 1878.

[613] For C. B. Edwards' house, see Kelsey's *Record of Weather and Work*, vol. 2, Nov. 22, 1878.

[614] John Z. Gottwals was born Sept. 7, 1830, and died Jan. 9, 1913. He is buried in the Highlands Cemetery.

[615] For Henry Downing's land purchase, see *Bk. of Deeds* Y, p. 428 (Sept. 13, 1889).

[616] Connemara was also the name of Carl Sandburg's home in Flat Rock, N.C., after the mountainous region of Galway, Ireland.

[617] For a detailed description of Henry W. Sloan's "Cheeononda" when it was offered at auction, see *Highlander*, July 15, 1976, p. 14.

[618] For an excellent history of Webbmont with a focus on Joe Webb's log cabins, see Peggy S. Watkins, *Webbmont* (Highlands, N.C., 1995).

[619] For population figures and home count in 1928, see *Franklin Press*, July 5, 1928.

[620] For new homes and highest temperature in 1932, see *Franklin Press and Highlands Maconian*, Oct. 13, 1932, pp. 1 and 6.

[621] For the survey of Highlands for industrial development, see Highlands Industrial Committee, *Highlands, North Carolina—Facts and Figures for Industry* (Highlands Chamber of Commerce, 1956).

[622] For a loving account of the Anderson home and family, see Louise Anderson Sargent, "Reminiscences of Highlands Summers" (Highlands, 1894).

[623] For W. W. Sullivan's obituary, see *Franklin Press and Highlands Maconian,* April 1, 1937. See also Anne Doggett's article in *Heritage of Macon County, Vol. 2*, pp. 442–43.

[624] For the tearing down of the Anderson house, including photograph, see *Highlander*, March 29, 1973.

[625] For Highlands Townsite Condominiums, see *Highlander*, July 7, 1967.

[626] For Pinebrook Condominiums, see *Highlander*, July 5, 1973.

[627] For the names and dates of early postmasters of Highlands, see *Franklin Press and Highlands Maconian*, Nov. 1, 1956, p. 12.

[628] For an account of Grimshawe's post office, see Frances Lombard, *From the Hills of Home*, pp. 69–78. See also "Post Office At Grimshawes, Nation's Smallest, Closed," *Asheville Citizen*, Aug. 20, 1953.

[629] For the Grimshawes' tragedy, see the plaque posted at the gravesite in Cashiers. For Henry Scadin's report, see his diary entry for Oct. 3, 1899.

[630] For the "Passmore trail," see Lombard, *From the Hills of Home*, p. 76.

[631] For Helen Hill Norris' depiction of Gene Mays, see "Looking Backwards," *Highlander*, Feb. 5, 1960, p. 2.

[632] Post office statistics for fiscal year 2000, ending September 30, are from Postmaster Elizabeth Kelley, Nov. 16, 2000.

[633] The quotation about acts of kindness has been ascribed to many, including Stephen Grellet (1773–1855), but its source remains undetermined, perhaps appropriately so.

[634] For a centennial history of the Masonic Lodge in Highlands, see *Highlander*, March 20, 1990.

[635] For the definition of freemasonry, see Charles F. Bahnson, *North Carolina Lodge Manual for the Degrees of Entered Apprentice, Fellow Craft, and Master Mason* (Raleigh, 1957), p. 17.

[636] For the organization of the Highlands Lions Club, see *Franklin Press and Highlands Maconian*, Feb. 24, 1938. For reorganization, see *Galax News*, Dec. 18, 1954.

[637] For the organization of the Highlands Rotary Club, see *Franklin Press and Highlands Maconian*, April 19, 1945.

[638] For a brief history of the Inner Wheel Club, see *Highlander*, June 16, 1989.

[639] For the founding of the Order of the Eastern Star, see *Franklin Press and Highlands Maconian*, May 5, 1949.

[640] For a short history of the Highlands Garden Club in its twenty-fifth year, see *Highlander*, June 9, 1977.

[641] For the establishment of the Humane Society, see *Galax News*, Aug. 29, 1963, p. 4. For the shelter, see *Highlander*, Nov. 13, 1980.

[642] For a succinct history of the Woman's Club, see *Highlander*, Nov. 7, 1989.

[643] For the establishment of Fibber Magee's, see *Highlander*, March 16, 1978.

[644] For the organization of the Highlands Jaycees, see *Highlander*, March 15, 1973; for their first Monte Carlo benefit, see *Highlander*, Sept. 13, 1973.

[645] For the formation of the Jaycettes, see *Highlander*, April 25, 1974.

[646] For articles on the Red Cross shelter, see *Highlander*, May 7, 1996, and July 7, 1998. For the Emergency Council, see *Highlander*, Nov. 23, 1983.

[647] For J. A. McGuire's appointment as fire inspector, see *Highlander*, Nov. 6, 1885. For Frank Sheldon as fire warden, see minutes of Board of Commissioners, Bk. A, p. 71, Nov. 8, 1887. For first fire ordinance, see minutes of Board of Commissioners, Bk. A, p. 178, June 18, 1894.

[648] For the first fire engine, or hose buggy, see minutes of Board of Commissioners, June 6, 1909, and first fire station, Bk. E, p. 195, Jan. 14, 1929. For the first volunteer fire department, see minutes of Board of Commissioners, Bk. 1, p. 150, Jan. 31, 1939. For Arnold Nelson's proposal of a volunteer fire crew, see minutes of Board of Commissioners, Bk. 3, p. 108, Aug. 31, 1953. For the first fire truck, see minutes of Board of Commissioners, Bk. 3, p. 85, Feb. 2, 1953. A well-organized, well-researched, and well-written history of the Highlands Fire and Rescue Squad was written by Melinda Taylor for her high school English class on May 21, 1981, rpt. *Franklin Press*, Oct. 7, 1987, p. 4.

[649] For the fire at the Rainwater Estate, see *Highlander*, March 13, 1980. For the resultant suit, see Dec. 30, 1982, p. 2.

[650] For the Brushy Mountain fire, see *Highlander*, May 16, 1997.

[651] For the birth of Michael Andrew Shearl on Tuesday, March 16, 1993, see *Highlander*, April 6, 1993.

[652] *Genesis* 3: 19.

[653] For the Gibson and Chastain drownings, see *Franklin Press and Highlands Maconian*, Sept. 1, 1938.

[654] For Albert Rogers' death, see *Franklin Press and Highlands Maconian*, July 8, 1943. For the remaining WWII fatalities, see Nov. 15, 1945. For those killed in Vietnam, see *Highlander*, Jan. 16, 1969, and April 30, 1970.

[655] For the sale of the primeval forest, see *Franklin Press and Highlands Maconian*, Dec. 16, 1943.

[656] For Bob Zahner's heartfelt lament over loss of the primeval forest, see *Mountain at the End of the Trail*, pp. 51, 69–77.

[657] For the quote from Herbert Ravenel Sass, see his *War Drums* (New York, 1928), pp. 156–57.

[658] For Silas McDowell's poem about Whiteside Mountain, see *The News and Farmer,* 1877, rpt. in part in *Highlander,* Sept. 14, 1972, p. 7.

[659] For the Forest Service purchase of Whiteside Mountain, see *Highlander,* Feb. 21, 1974.

[660] For the remnants of the primeval forest, see Bob Zahner, *Mountain at the End of the Trail,* pp. 74–75.

[661] For the deaths at Dry Falls, see *Galax News,* Aug. 6, 1952; July 8, 1954; and June 28, 1956.

[662] For Janis McGivern's fall, see *Galax News,* July 5, 1956.

[663] For the fatality at Cliffside Lake, see *Galax News,* July 15, 1959. For fatalities at the various waterfalls, see *Galax News,* July 6, 1967, for Horse Cove Falls; *Highlander,* June 25, 1981 (also *Asheville Citizen,* June 22, 1981), and Sept. 27, 1984, for the two Glen Falls accidents. The Glen Falls rescue occurred on June 21, 1982. See *Highlander,* June 14, 1988, for the plunge over Picklesimer Falls.

[664] For the fate of Cenda Schweers, see *Highlander,* June 13, 1968, and *Galax News,* June 13, 1968, pp. 1, 11, 12.

[665] For William Stephen McCall's accident, see *Galax News,* June 15, 1967.

[666] For Kerry Brandon's fall from Whiteside, see Oct. 20, 1977, in Bobby Houston's journal. For Zachary Howard's fall, see *Highlander,* Feb. 19, 1976.

[667] For Jeff Bates' fall, see *Highlander,* Feb. 9, 1978.

[668] For Sarah Hicks Hines (Bailey)'s love of Highlands, see "Highlands Revisited," *Galax News,* Aug. 16, 1956.

[669] For Wen McKinney's recollections of Halloween, see *Highlander,* Nov. 22, 1973.

[670] For Elizabeth Lyons' dance class, see letter to the author from Mrs. David (Nancy Jussely) Lyle of Rock Hill, S. C., November 4, 1993.

[671] For Highlands life in 1924, see *Diary of Bessie Hinson Hines,* Jan. 1–Dec. 31, 1924. For the Merrimakers Club, see *Franklin Press,* Nov. 11, 1929.

[672] For Rebecca Harris' proposed pavilion, see *Highlands Maconian,* July 22, 1931.

[673] For two entertaining articles on Helen's Barn, see A. J. Baty (now Mackie), "Helen's Gamble," *North Carolina State* (September, 1982), pp. 12–14, and Frances Crunkleton Wright and Maxie Wright Duke, *Heritage of Macon County, Vol. 2,* pp. 50–51.

[674] Stephen Vincent Benét, "The Mountain Whippoorwill" (1923), stanza 22.

[675] For the destruction of Helen's barn by fire, see *Franklin Press and Highlands Maconian,* Sept. 13, 1934. For claim of arson, see Harry Wright's deposition against opening Poplar Street, Oct. 26, 1998.

[676] For Sue Reese's memories of Cleo McCall, see *Highlander,* Nov. 19, 1996.

[677] For Atlantan Glenn Manos' appreciation of Helen's Barn, see *Highlander,* June 3, 1982, Sec. B.

[678] For Kate Gillison's "Ballad of Helen's Barn," see *Highlander,* June 3, 1982, Sec. B, p. 1.

[679] For the building of the Dugout, see *Franklin Press and Highlands Maconian,* May 20, 1937.

[680] For Sam's Folly, see *Galax News,* June 19, 1958, and June 25, 1959.

[681] For Camp Parry-dise, see *Franklin Press,* July 5, 1928, and *Highlands Maconian,* Aug. 5, 1931.

[682] For Camp Sequoia, see *Franklin Press and Highlands Maconian*, April 29, 1937, and *Highlander*, Sept. 4, 1937.

[683] For Camp Highlander, see *Galax News*, June 12, 1958, pp. 1 and 15.

[684] For the beginning of basketball in Highlands, see *Franklin Press*, Sept. 14, 1923. For Highlands basketball in the late twenties, see interview with Bernice Rice Lowe and the Luther Rice family on Buck Creek Road, March 8, 1986, Media Divide. For an entertaining description of Willie Hays, including his love of basketball, see W. Arthur Hays, Jr.'s article in *Heritage of Macon County*, vol. 1, pp. 268–69.

[685] For the purchase of the ballpark, see minutes of Board of Commissioners, Bk. E, p. 192, Dec. 8, 1928, and Bk. G, p. 112, Sept. 5, 1933.

[686] For the beginning of Little League Baseball in Highlands, see *Galax News*, Aug. 29, 1957.

[687] For detailed accounts of the first Highlands Hillbilly Day, see *Galax News*, July 23 and Aug. 6, 1952.

[688] For the earliest golf courses, see Edith Inglesby's letter about the history of Highlands, written to Tom Crumpler, Nov. 1, 1974. See also her *Happy Highways*, p. 4. Edith was born in 1895 and died in 1981 at age 86. For Tudor Hall's recollection of Memminger's golf course as quite possibly "the first golf club in North Carolina," see Douglas Peach, "Town of Highlands," *Highlander*, Sept. 6, 1984.

[689] For the news account of Reese's accident, see *Highlands Maconian*, Feb. 4, 1931.

[690] For articles on the founding of the Highlands Estate Country Club, see *Franklin Press*, June 23, 1927, and July 5, 1928, pp. 1–2. Evangeline M. Davis wrote a tribute to the club's creation in her *Lure of Highlands* (Highlands, N.C., 1981).

[691] For Glenn Allan's praise of the club, see the reprint in *Franklin Press*, July 5, 1928.

[692] For the construction of the Tom Thumb golf course, see *Franklin Press*, June 19, 1930, p. 2.

[693] For the creation of the Highlands Falls Golf Course, see *Galax News*, July 3, 1958, Aug. 9, 1962, and June 13, 1963. For Wilton Cobb's Lake Primeval development, see *Franklin Press and Highlands Maconian*, July 11, 1940. For its conversion to Highlands Falls Country Club, see *Highlander*, Oct. 25, 1973.

[694] For the creation of the Wildcat Cliffs Country Club, see *Galax News*, Aug. 9, 1962, p. 7; July 23, 1964, p. 11; and July 1, 1965; p. 6. See also Sue Brigham's excellent *History of Wildcat Cliffs Country Club 1995.*

[695] For Scott Hudson's obituary, see *Highlander*, July 13, 1962.

[696] For Bobby Jones' obituary, see *Highlander*, Dec. 23, 1971. For Bill Marett's assessment of Jones, see *Highlander*, July 21, 1983, p. 4.

[697] For Jim Hines' hike to Whiteside Cave, see *Highlander*, Aug. 15, 1958, p. 6.

[698] Shakespeare's *Othello*, Act. 2, Scene 3, lines 293 ff.

[699] For the controversy surrounding the proposal to have an ABC store, see minutes of Board of Commissioners, Bk. 3., p. 26, April 2, 1951, and Bk. 3, p. 140, March 10, 1955. See also *Franklin Press and Highlands Maconian,* March, 17, 1955.

[700] Ben and Georgette Williams' Highlands Fling opened in 1951 and closed in 1986.

[701] For Charles Jenks' obituary of David Moss, see *Highlands Maconian*, Aug. 19, 1931, p. 2.

[702] For the Temperance Union, see *Blue Ridge Enterprise*, January 22, 1885.

[703] For the final vote on the ABC Store, see *Highlander*, Aug. 18, 1977.

[704] For the creation of Cliffside Lake Recreation Area, see *Mountain Trail*, July 21 and Aug. 28, 1939.

[705] For the quartet and orchestra, see *Blue Ridge Enterprise*, April 26 and June 14, 1883.

[706] For the African-American musicals, see *Mountain Trail*, Aug. 18, 1939, and *Galax News*, Aug. 12, 1954; Aug. 25, 1955; and Sept. 1, 1960.

[707] For George B. Matthews, see *Highlands Maconian*, June 3, 1931.

[708] For Marie Huger's paintings, see *Highlands Maconian*, Aug. 12, 1931.

[709] For the works of George and Polly Knipp Hill, see *Galax News*, Aug. 31, 1967, p. 7, and *Highlander*, Feb. 13, 1969.

[710] For Hubert Shuptrine, see *Highlander*, July 22, 1971; Aug. 3, 1972; March 7, 1974; and Dec. 1, 1987. See also "Hubert Shuptrine," *American Artist*, July, 1973, and Melvin Johnson, "An Artist Who Went North to Paint the South," *Boston Globe*, Oct. 21, 1973, pp. 7–8.

[711] For Henry La Cagnina, see article by Jann Tuten in *Highlander*, Oct. 6, 2000.

[712] For a clear distinction between the Bascom-Louise Gallery and the Art League of Highlands, see Ann Baird's "Gallery, Art League separate organizations," *Highlander*, June 23, 2000.

[713] For the first movie shown in Highlands, see minutes of Board of Commissioners, May 21, 1920.

[714] For the proposal and completion of the School Auditorium in the summer of 1934, see *Franklin Press and Highlands Maconian*, Nov. 23, 1933, and Aug. 29, 1935.

[715] For an account of motion pictures in Highlands, see *Galax News*, Sept. 13, 1970, pp. 9, 13, and 17. For the arrival of TV in Highlands, see *Galax News*, June 24, 1954.

[716] Concerning the Highlands Little Theatre's first play, see *Franklin Press and Highlands Maconian*, Aug. 24, 1939, and *Mountain Trail*, Aug. 25, 1939. See also Anne Doggett's excellent history of the Highlands Community Theatre in *Heritage of Macon County, Vol. 2*, pp. 48–49, and Virginia "Ted" Wilcox's account in *Galax News,* June 20, 1957, p. 8.

[717] For the dismantling of the second school, see minutes of Board of Commissioners, Bk. 3, p. 231, Oct. 19, 1959.

[718] For Laura Hawkins and her poetry, see T. W. Reynolds, *Born of the Mountains* (Highlands, 1958), pp. 34–35, 78; *High Lands,* pp. 23–25, 51–55; and *Southern Appalachian Region* (Highlands, 1966)*,* vol. 1, pp. 30–33, 37. See also Frances Lombard, *From the Hills of Home*, pp. 20–24.

[719] For Christina Anderson Rice's poetry, see Bette Rice, ed., *When the Laurels Bloom and Other Poems* (Highlands, 1999), which includes "Clouds" and "Love." For Mary Chapin Smith's praise of Rice as a poet, see her *History of Hudson Library Association*, p. 9.

[720] Many of the poems in Mary Chapin Smith's *Earth Songs* were published originally in *Watson's Jeffersonian Magazine, Journal of Outdoor Life, Taylor-Trotwood Magazine*, and *Book News*. For her poem on snow, see *Earth Songs* (Boston, 1910), p. 16, and p. 7 for "Sweet Mother Earth."

[721] For Horace Kephart's death, see *Franklin Press*, April 9, 1931, p. 2.

[722] For Louise Bascom Barratt's obituary, see *Franklin Press and Highlands Maconian*, Sept. 8, 1949.

[723] For Bess Hines Harkins' fifteen articles on "Our Mountains," see *Highlander*, Feb. 10 through June 23, Oct. 29, and Dec. 8, 1966.

[724] For Enid Daniel Jones' appreciation of Bess Hines Harkins, see *Highlander*, July 4, 1958.

[725] Bess Hines Harkins, "The Highlander," *Singing of the Heart* (Atlanta, 1943), p. 31.

[726] Butler Harkins, *Leaves of Aloneness*, pp. 1 and 2.

[727] Butler Harkins, *The Harkins Clan*, p. 1.

[728] For T. W. Reynolds' writing of *High Lands*, see *Galax News*, June 18, 1964, p. 2. See also his book's introduction, pp. 3–6.

[729] Dee McCollum, *Poems for Women* (N.p., 1993), p. 19.

[730] Virginia Edwards Fleming, "Homeward," *So Tender the Spirit* (Highlands, 1985), p. 35.

[731] For local articles on Jonathan Williams, see *Galax News*, July 29, 1965, pp. 2, 11, 22, and June 26, 1969, p. 5, and *Highlander*, Aug. 28, 1975, and May 18, 1978, pp. 6–7.

[732] Samples of Jonathan Williams' poetry come from *Blues and Roots/Rue and Bluets* (Durham: Duke University Press, 1985).

[733] For Sydney King Russell, see *Highlander*, Dec. 2, 1976. For Russell's poem, "Midsummer," see *Best Loved Poems of the American People* (New York, 1936), p. 28.

[734] For articles on Bil and Louise Dwyer, see *Highlander*, May 20, 1971, and April 22, 1976. See also Lewis Green's feature on Dwyer in the *Asheville Citizen Times*, rpt. on the flyleaf of Dwyer's *Dictionary for Yankees*.

[735] For John Bundy, see *Blue Ridge Enterprise*, Aug. 16 and 30 and Oct. 18, 1883.

[736] R. Henry Scadin was born Sept. 18, 1861, and died in 1923.

[737] Scadin's poem about Highlands is photo number 277 of the collection.

[738] For articles on George Masa, see *Franklin Press*, Sept. 19 and 26, 1929, and April 24, 1930, p. 2; *Highlander*, May 5, 1977, p. 3; and *Asheville-Citizen Times*, Jan. 10, 2000, Sec. B2.

[739] For Burton Talbott, see Sylvia Thomas' article in *Highlander*, June 16, 1987. For forty-seven of his photo portraits, see *Highlander*, Oct. 30, 1969; then almost weekly between Oct. 8, 1970, and Sept. 30, 1971; March 9 and June 1, 1972; and Jan. 4, Oct. 4, Nov. 15 and 22, 1973.

[740] For the founding of HIARPT, see *Highlander*, June 30, 1987.

[741] For the earliest reference to Highlands Improvement Association, see *Blue Ridge Enterprise*, Feb. 8, 1883. For the creation of Highlands Park, see Floral and Industrial Society minutes, p. 17, Feb. 20, 1883.

[742] For the stated aim of the Highlands Improvement Society, see Gertrude Harbison, "Satulah Club History," *Galax News*, Aug. 1, 1963, rpt. *Highlander*, July 26, 1979. For Mary Chapin Smith's history of the Highlands Improvement Society, see "Women Do Much for Highlands: The Highlands Improvement Society Sponsors Many Things Benefiting the Town and Vicinity," *Franklin Press*, July 5, 1928.

[743] For the creation of Ravenel Park, see *Bk. of Deeds* V-3, p. 56 (Aug. 16, 1914).

[744] For the Improvement Society's lobbying of the legislature and congress, see Mary Chapin Smith's "Women Do Much for Highlands," *Franklin Press*, July 5, 1928.

[745] For an account of the Satulah Club, see Gertrude Harbison, "Satulah Club History," *Galax News* Aug. 1, 1963, rpt. *Highlander*, July 26, 1979.

[746] For Land Trust purchases and gifts, see *Highlander*, Jan. 20, 1998, the Satulah purchase; Sept. 4, 1998, for the Edwards purchase; March 20, 2001, for the Lindsey tract purchase; and June 6, 2000, for the Simmons home purchase.

[747] For the Highlands/Cashiers Conservation League's statement of purpose, see *Newsletter for the 1ˢᵗ Quarter, 1999*, Vol. 1, Edition 1, p. 1.

[748] For Highlands Cove, see *Highlander*, Sept. 4, 1998.

[749] For the views of Russell England, Georgia Department of Natural Resources, about growth, see *Macon County News and Shopping Guide*, Nov. 18, 1999.

[750] For Weimar Jones' paradoxes of progress, see *My Affair with a Weekly* (Winston-Salem, N.C., 1960), pp. 34–35.

[751] For Bob Zoellner's commencement address, see *Highlander*, June 9, 1966.

[752] This quote comes from the Precepts of Ptahhotep, called "the world's oldest book" and preserved on papyrus roll ca. 2,500 **B.C**. It's usually translated, "O Ptah, the progress of age changes into senility."

[753] Barney Wilson's father, Peary Wilson, named Barney's second son Warren Woodrow after President Wilson because he was a democrat and liked Woodrow Wilson, according to Woodrow's sister Frances Wilson Nix, who still lives in Highlands.

[754] For Frances M. Wilson's article on the family of Barney Wilson, see *Heritage of Macon County, Vol. 2*, pp. 470–71.